THE WORLD ATLAS OF
GOLF
The great courses and how they are played

THE WORLD ATLAS OF
GOLF

Contributing editor: Pat Ward-Thomas

**Mitchell
Beazley**

The World Atlas of Golf
was edited and designed by
Mitchell Beazley Publishers Limited,
14-15 Manette Street, London W1V 5LB

Editor	Iain Parsons
Art Editor	Mel Petersen
Assistant Editor	Nicholas Bevan
Editorial Assistants	Victor Stevenson
	Richard Widdows
	Janet Wilson
Designers	Javed Badar
	Michael Rose
	Celia Welcomme
Picture Researcher	Jackie Webber
Production	Hugh Stancliffe
Executive Editor	Paul Bradwell

Additional text contributions by:
Peter Dobereiner, Michael Gedye, Peter Hildyard,
Keith Mackie, Marvern Moss, Arvid Olson, Donald Steel,
Larry Wood, the late Alfred Wright.

© Mitchell Beazley Publishers Limited 1976
First edition published 1976
Reprinted 1979, 1981, 1983, 1984, 1986
Reproduction of any kind in part or in whole
in any country throughout the world is reserved
by Mitchell Beazley Publishers Ltd.

ISBN 0 85533 088 0 (Hardbound Edition)
ISBN 0 85533 184 4 (Paperback Edition)
Mitchell Beazley Publishers Limited.
14-15 Manette Street, London W1V 5LB

Photoset in Great Britain by Tradespools Limited, Frome,
and Key Film (Trendbourne Limited), London.
Colour separations in Great Britain by Gilchrist Brothers
Limited, Leeds
Printed in Portugal
by Printer Portuguesa Lda.

"The fine flower of many landscapes"

On the opening day of a recent Masters tournament, *The Times* (of London, as we say in these parts) carried a dispatch from a correspondent in Augusta, Georgia, sketching out the memorable history of the course. Among the many splendid, even original, things in that perceptive article was the information that in transforming a tree nursery and former plantation into what is surely the most beautiful inland course in America, Robert Tyre Jones Jr. was assisted at every turn "by Dr Alister Cooke".

This is not strictly accurate, as Mr Jones and a couple of generations of nurserymen and greenkeepers will testify. For some psychological reason not too hard to fathom, I have never bothered to write to *The Times* and refute this clanger. But at the time I was agreeably pestered night and day with invitations to—oh, I don't know—redesign Sunningdale, convert Hyde Park into a pitch and putt, abolish Pine Valley. The most embarrassing of these bids came from Pat Ward-Thomas in the present instance: namely, to write a preface to this formidable work. I must say I should have thought that Ward-Thomas knew as well as anyone that Jones's co-worker in the creation of Augusta National was none other than Dr Alister Mackenzie, the Scottish doctor who put his indelible imprint also on Cypress Point and Royal Melbourne.

The scabrous truth had better be revealed here for the first time. I have never designed anything, not even a Christmas card. While I'm at it, I had better make what they rather rudely used to call a clean breast of it: until a dozen years ago, I thought of Bermuda as an island, and fescue I should have guessed to be a Shakespearean clown. Nevertheless, I accepted the invitation of Pat Ward-Thomas with alacrity and a large dollop of vanity. For it offered a duffer the opportunity to write about golf architecture, something that I believe has not been done before in the history of the game. Indeed, few duffers have ever thought much about golf architecture, but every duffer willingly carries on about the wonders of his own course. Ask the average golfer to explain the principles of strategic design and he will humbly disavow all such knowledge; tell him that he doesn't know the difference between a good course and a bad one, and he will knock your block off. In other words, in a variation on the duffer's platitude about art, we don't know much about "architecture" but we know what's good.

It was quite by luck that I became wary of this cliché soon after I took up the game. Being a journalist, I naturally fell in with golf writers, and it was soon my good fortune to make lasting friendships with two distinguished writers, and one fine amateur golfer, who wrote or talked better, and seemed to know more, about the mysteries of golf architecture than anyone else I met. Playing some great course in England with Pat Ward-Thomas, or with Herbert Warren Wind in the eastern states, or in California with Frank Tatum Jr. I had the feeling that I was being taken over a Handel score by the late Sir Thomas Beecham. (Often, of course, and especially with the eloquent Tatum, I had the feeling that I was simply being taken.) I discovered to my enjoyable relief that a great golf course, like a supreme piece of music, does not reveal its splendours at a first or second reading; nor, for most of us, ever. Its subtleties will always be beyond us. I don't mean beyond our performance but beyond our recognition.

That is where Pat Ward-Thomas, Peter Thomson, Charles Price and Herbert Warren Wind come in. If you are willing to follow them closely, and to forget for the moment your resentment that your own club course has been carelessly omitted from this selection, you can begin to see the differences between the good,

the better, and the best. This coaching will not only enhance your pleasure if you have the luck to play any of these famous battlegrounds, but it will, I do believe, sharpen your feel for the alternative shots offered by a good hole anywhere. To the common objection that "taking things apart" spoils one's pleasure in the assembled object, I can only retort that the most enlightened criticism of poetry has been written by the best poets, and that it takes a watchmaker to be truly moved by the best Swiss watches.

This book is, of course, meant for consumption in every country that plays golf, most of all in Britain and the United States. This reminder exposes a famous bone of contention that is gnawed on periodically on both sides of the Atlantic. It has to do with the rooted prejudice, which the duffer retreats into more than anybody, about the two different orders of golf course. At the latest count, there are roughly fourteen million golfers in the United States and something like two million in the British Isles.

Most Britons, of whatever skill, have been brought up to regard a links course as the ideal

playground, on which the standard hazards of the game are the wind, bumpy treeless fairways, deep bunkers and knee-high rough. Most Americans think of a golf course as a park with well-cropped fairways marching, like parade grounds, between groves of trees down to velvety greens. Along the way there will be vistas of other woods, a decorative pond or two, some token fairway bunkers and a ring of shallow bunkers guarding greens so predictably well watered that they will receive a full pitch from any angle like a horseshoe thrown into a marsh.

There is a marked element of national character in these opposing preferences: the British taking strength through joy in the belief that discomfort is good for the character, the Americans believing that games are meant for pleasure and should not be played out in moral gymnasiums (unless you are going to make money at them, in which case they become the whole of life).

The Scots say that Nature itself dictated that golf should be played by the seashore. Rather, the Scots saw in the eroded seacoasts a cheap battleground on which they could whip their fellow-men in a game based on the Calvinist doctrine that man is meant to suffer here below and never more than when he goes out to enjoy himself. The Scots, indeed, ascribe the origins of golf to nothing less than the divine purpose working through geology. Sir Guy Campbell's classic account of the formation of the links, beginning with Genesis and moving step by step to the thrilling arrival of "tilth" on the fingers of coastal land, suggests that such notable features of our planet as dinosaurs, the prairies, the Himalayas, the seagull, the female of the species herself were accidental by-products of the Almighty's preoccupation with the creation of the Old course at St Andrews.

Americans are less mystical about what produced their inland or meadow courses: they are the product of the bulldozer, rotary ploughs, mowers, sprinkler systems and alarmingly generous wads of folding money. And often very splendid, too. It seems to me that only a British puritan on one side of the Atlantic, and an American Sybarite on the other, will deny the separate beauties and challenges of the links and the inland course.

Pasture, meadowland, links, oceanside, whatever its type, a fine golf course will obey certain elementary rules best stated forty years ago by Bobby Jones: "The first purpose of any golf course should be to give pleasure, and that to the greatest number of players ... because it will offer problems a man may attempt according to his ability. It will never become hopeless for the duffer nor fail to concern and interest the expert; and it will be found, like Old St Andrews, to become more delightful the more it is studied and played." In a word, the fine golf course offers rewards for the duffer's limited skill; the moderate player senses exciting possibilities; the good player a constant challenge; and the great player knows that only when he is consistently at his best can he hope to conquer it.

Begging the pardon of our authors, I must say that this famous prescription is not exactly filled by all of these awesome seventy. Among the experts there will be furious debates—as, for instance, why should Medinah, a claustrophobia of woods, be in, and the lovely, cunning Inverness of Ohio be out? The members of Maidstone will no doubt mount a civic protest against their exclusion from what the late Al Wright has called "the three best unplayed courses in America", meaning the three old cheek-by-jowl links courses at the end of Long Island: National, Shinnecock and Maidstone. (My own private conviction is that Shinnecock was designed by Lady Macbeth.)

But all such doctors' disagreements aside, it is probable that a committee of international golfers of the first chop would agree with 75 per cent of these choices. For the rest of us, this colossal book comes along, none too soon, to review the history of great golf architecture from its invention by Willie Park Jr. just before the turn of one century to its likely demise just before the end of the next. For in the United States at any rate, an amendment to the federal tax law, allowing the states to reassess land taxes according to the doctrine of "best possible use", could soon tax golf courses at either the real-estate or public rate and doom once and for all the private playground. In the interim period—between God's rude links and Mammon's foreclosure—there is the consolation for us duffers that the population explosion and public housing campaigns together will drastically arrest the movement of the 1960s towards 7,000-yard courses and holes made only for Nicklaus. Even so astute a team of architects as that of Robert Trent Jones & Sons foresees only a shaky future for the traditional layout; rather, there will be appendages to housing estates having short holes and a par of 60. This should usher in the golden age of the senior golfer with the arthritic pivot but the cagey short game.

While there is yet time, then, let us turn these pages and read and weep. Here are the power and the glory, the fine flower of many landscapes preserved in the microcosm of the golf course. Here are the masterpieces carved out in the eighty years that saw the dawn, the high noon and possibly the twilight of golf architecture. This book may well be, whether the authors knew it or not, a memorial tribute to the game before Nader's Raiders, followed by the Supreme Court, decide that the private ownership of land for the diversion of the few is a monstrous denial of the Constitution under the Fourteenth ("the equal protection of the laws") Amendment.

When that happens, old men will furtively beckon to their sons and, like fugitives from the guillotine recalling the elegant orgies at the court of Louis XV, will recite the glories of Portmarnock and Merion, of the Road Hole at St Andrews, the 6th at Seminole, the 18th at Pebble Beach. They will take out this volume from its secret hiding place and they will say: "There is no question, son, that these were unholy places in an evil age. Unfortunately, I had a whale of a time."

Alistair Cooke

Golf's grand design

The game of golf has a lasting hold on mankind. In the United States it has become a pastime involving millions of people and billions of dollars; in Japan, a fanatical cult. Wherever the quest for sunshine has been exploited, golf has become the centrepiece of development. Less than a century ago it was almost unknown anywhere outside Scotland. In India, Scottish merchants had started clubs in Calcutta (1829) and Bombay (1842), and there were only two courses in England when the club at Pau, in southern France, was formed in 1856. The Scots were the great prophets of golf, spreading its gospel from Perth (where the six-hole links on the city's North Inch was the first recognizable course), St Andrews, Prestwick and Dornoch to every corner of the earth where Empire held sway—and beyond. England was the first conquest; Blackheath, Old Manchester and Westward Ho! the earliest outposts. By the turn of the century the tide had swept across Britain, on to the continent of Europe and even to Japan, where an ardent pioneer designed four holes on a mountain. In 1888 John Reid inspired the first permanent club in the United States, St Andrews GC at Yonkers, NY. The appeal of golf is infinite; it tempts and destroys, seduces and rejects. It is a game of eternal hope; beyond every horizon is a promised land, even though it proves to be elusive. The golfer is blessed, like no other player of games, in the settings for his pleasure. The seventy courses which are featured in detail in this book come from thirty-one countries, but they have one thing in common—the quality of their design marks them apart from all other courses. The foundations of their greatness were laid in one of the four eras into which the development of golf architecture can be naturally divided. Some of them later underwent significant change but, whether much or little altered, the dates of their emergence closely parallel the growth of the game around the world.

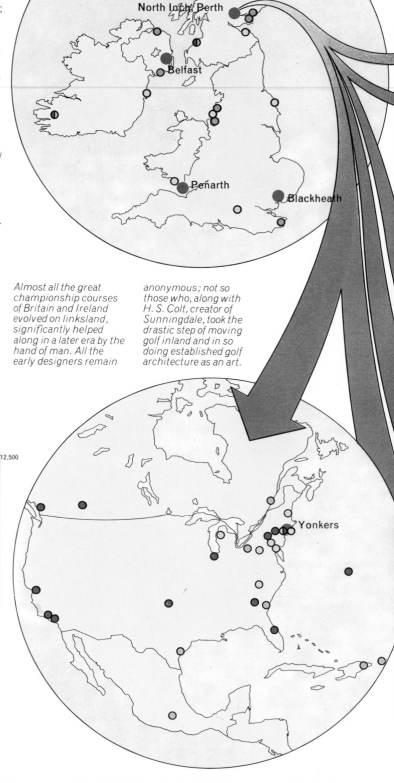

Almost all the great championship courses of Britain and Ireland evolved on linksland, significantly helped along in a later era by the hand of man. All the early designers remain anonymous; not so those who, along with H. S. Colt, creator of Sunningdale, took the drastic step of moving golf inland and in so doing established golf architecture as an art.

The first of four eras in the history of golf architecture saw the evolution of courses on natural linksland. In the second, beginning about 1890, foundations were laid to be built upon in the Golden Age between the wars. The modern era followed World War II.

- ● Natural links
- ○ Early architecture
- ● Golden Age
- ○ Modern era
- ● Golf takes root

Unlike Britain, where over half of today's golf courses were in existence—sometimes in rudimentary form— before 1900, golf in the United States is very much a 20th century sport. There have been two real boom periods, the 1920s and 1960s.

Golf courses in Great Britain (blue) and USA (red)
12,500

1895   1975

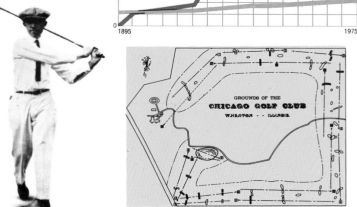

Chicago Golf Club was the first American club to build an eighteen-hole course, right; 5,877 yards long, it was designed by Charles Blair Macdonald and opened in 1894. That same year the club became one of the five founding members of the United States Golf Association and in 1911 the course was the site of the Open won by Johnny McDermott, left, the first native-born American to win.

The building of North America's finest courses follows very closely the pattern of settlement on the mainland. They appeared first on the East Coast, Charles Blair Macdonald being responsible for the two most influential early courses, Shinnecock Hills and National Golf Links on Long Island. During the Golden Age, nowhere more glittering than in the United States, the marvellous West Coast courses were created, together with those of the South and Mid-West. Bermuda apart, courses of quality came to the offshore islands much later.

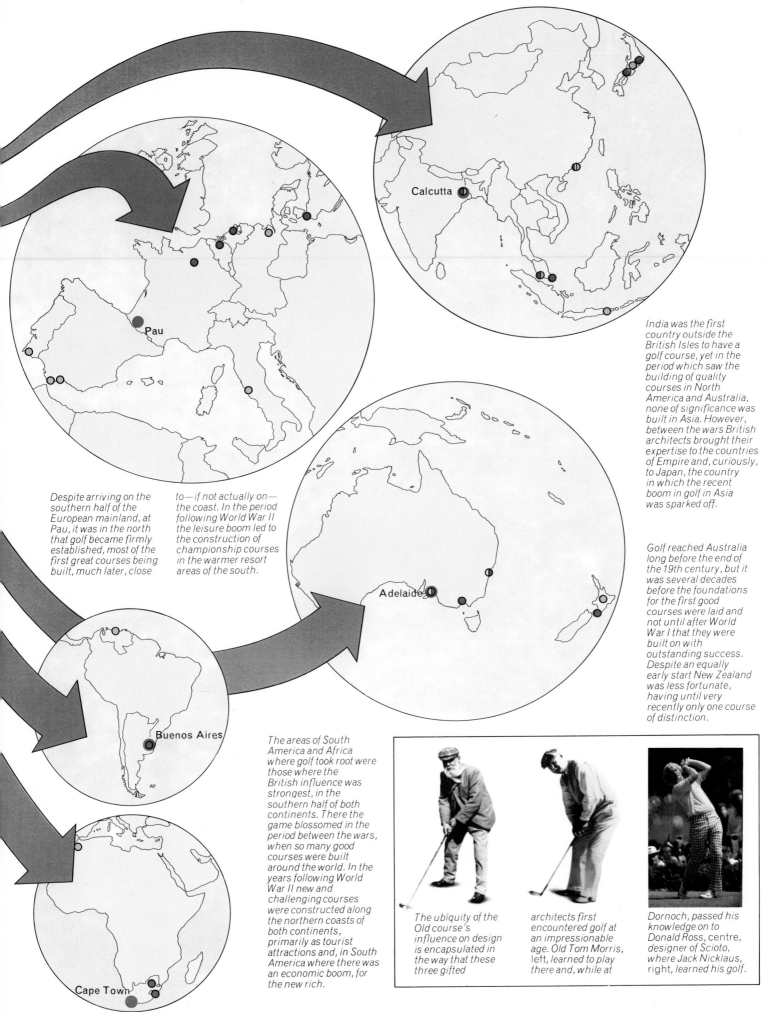

India was the first country outside the British Isles to have a golf course, yet in the period which saw the building of quality courses in North America and Australia, none of significance was built in Asia. However, between the wars British architects brought their expertise to the countries of Empire and, curiously, to Japan, the country in which the recent boom in golf in Asia was sparked off.

Golf reached Australia long before the end of the 19th century, but it was several decades before the foundations for the first good courses were laid and not until after World War I that they were built on with outstanding success. Despite an equally early start New Zealand was less fortunate, having until very recently only one course of distinction.

Despite arriving on the southern half of the European mainland, at Pau, it was in the north that golf became firmly established, most of the first great courses being built, much later, close to—if not actually on—the coast. In the period following World War II the leisure boom led to the construction of championship courses in the warmer resort areas of the south.

The areas of South America and Africa where golf took root were those where the British influence was strongest, in the southern half of both continents. There the game blossomed in the period between the wars, when so many good courses were built around the world. In the years following World War II new and challenging courses were constructed along the northern coasts of both continents, primarily as tourist attractions and, in South America where there was an economic boom, for the new rich.

The ubiquity of the Old course's influence on design is encapsulated in the way that these three gifted

architects first encountered golf at an impressionable age. Old Tom Morris, left, learned to play there and, while at

Dornoch, passed his knowledge on to Donald Ross, centre, designer of Scioto, where Jack Nicklaus, right, learned his golf.

The evolution of clubs and balls

Comparisons in scoring at golf down the ages have always been difficult to measure, but there can be no doubt that the game is now very much easier than once it was, primarily because of the advances in the manufacture of clubs and balls. Few changes in sport compare with that wrought by the rubber-core ball. There have been minor revolutions, notably the advent of steel shafts, but improvements in the ball have made the greater difference. Three types of ball dominate the history of golf: the feather ball, or feathery, which reigned supreme for about 400 years; the gutta-percha ball, or gutty, first made in 1845; and finally the rubber-core ball, invented by Coburn Haskell. Sandy Herd used a Haskell in winning the 1902 Open championship at Hoylake and, because of its promise of length, a new and lasting era was launched. As Bernard Darwin once wrote, "Men will do anything in reason to add a cubit to their stature as drivers," and Old Tom Morris obviously felt the same when the gutty replaced the feathery. He maintained that it was a more reliable ball which could be hit farther. He was even prepared to put his job at St Andrews in jeopardy on account of his views. The impression that the weak player was helped far more than the good one by the introduction in the 1920s of steel shafts is supported by the fact that Bobby Jones remained faithful to hickory throughout his competitive life. However, the new clubs made it easier to hit the ball straight and, sadly, required less artistry and improvisation in the fashioning of shots. But whatever the advances in equipment design, golf architecture has always kept in step. The siting of tees and bunkers, and the size, angling, shaping and bunkering of greens, form the most frequent counters. The battle to combat increasing length is best summed up by the American architect A. W. Tillinghast: "A controlled shot to a closely guarded green is the surest test of any man's golf."

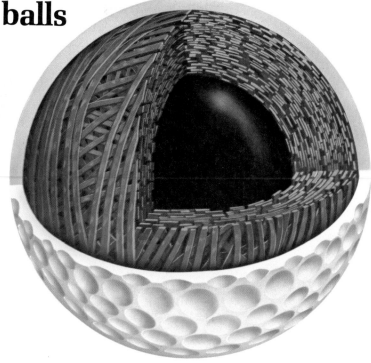

The modern ball, above, has changed very little since the expiry in 1915 of the patents of Coburn Haskell, who invented the rubber-core ball in 1898. The modern ball may have a core of rubber, as did Haskell's, liquid (the water core was introduced in 1902), steel or even glass encased in rubber, and it will usually be wound with rubber thread, just as Haskell's was. Most balls still have balata covers, first used in 1903. All balls are dimpled, a feature first introduced in 1908.

The feather ball was made by stuffing a top-hatful of boiled feathers into a casing of two pieces of leather sewn together with twine. The tools used were steel awls, long wrought-iron stuffing-irons, with wooden handles shaped on the top to fit the chest, and wooden stuffing-wedges. The ball was pounded round and given three coats of paint. It was a laborious task; in a day a craftsman could make only four good balls, which sold at around £1 for a dozen.

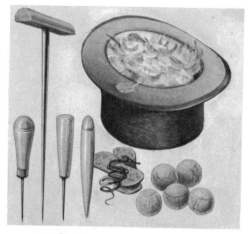

The feather ball, left, the first made specially for golf, was seldom round and was prone to sogginess, which led to rapid disintegration. However, it remained virtually unchanged for four centuries until 1848, when the gutta-percha ball, right, was introduced. Cheaper and more durable, it was made from the sap of trees found in India.

The first gutta-percha balls were rolled by hand and scored to simulate the feather ball seam. Following the discovery that after being nicked and cut they no longer ducked quickly in flight, a hammer was used to give them indentations. Later a variety of regular surface patterns was made possible by the introduction of moulds (top). To return a gutty to its original shape after a round it was warmed in boiling water, then placed in a hand-press (below), where it was left overnight.

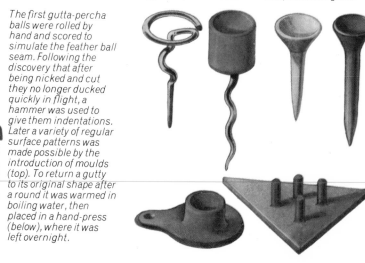

The first tees were no more than a pinch of convenient sand. Sand boxes and water were then provided, and later moulds to standardize tee height. Rubber tees (below) came into use in the 1890s and they were followed by the tees (left) of Dr William Lowell, a New Jersey dentist. His first tees were made of wire or wire and wood, but, because they were so easily lost and inhibited mowing, he developed the wooden tee, the shape of which remains standard, though plastic has since replaced wood.

In the days of the feather ball, golfers carried two putters—a driving putter, which was used for approach shots from as far away as a hundred yards, and a green putter, **1**, for use nearer the hole, particularly on the hard, bare fairways of links courses in the summer. In the gutta-percha era the putter became a specialist club, its use being restricted to the greens, and changed from wood, **2**, to a blade of iron or brass, **3**. Mallet putters followed, the Marston, **4**, dating from 1923, making use of aluminium with a hard-wearing brass sole plate, but retaining the traditional hickory shaft.

The two-handed grip and the slender, tapering shafts of the clubs used in the feather ball period required bulky grips of leather strips wound over layers of wool (top). Towards the end of the 19th century the overlapping grip was popularized by Harry Vardon and the smaller diameter it required was achieved simply by eliminating the wool padding (centre). With the introduction of steel shafts the addition of the grip became a complicated process involving eleven operations and six materials—layers of fabric, tape, felt, rag, and leather finished with a coating of lacquer, left. Wooden plugs were inserted in the tops of the hollow shafts. The whole operation was greatly simplified by the use of moulded rubber composition and, finally, rubber and

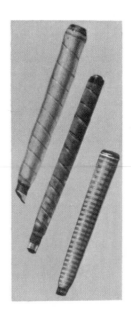

cork with an indented and textured surface (bottom) to ensure a firm grip in wet weather, something that had never been possible with leather.

The heavy bunker iron, **1**, was one of only four types of iron used with the feather ball. Irons became more refined and more specialized in the gutta-percha period, when wood faces, **2**, were used to cushion the shock of hitting the hard gutty ball. Later, scoring patterns, sometimes of rubber, **3**, were applied to club-faces in attempts to achieve control. The continuing search for a lofted club to get under the ball produced the L.A. Young sand wedge, **4**, in the 1920s.

Feather ball woods, **1** (driver) and **2** (middle spoon), had whippy shafts of ash and heads of hedgethorn. A piece of bone was fixed to the sole to prevent wear, and mass given by hollowing out the back of the clubhead and adding lead.

With the introduction of the harder gutty ball, softer fruitwoods were used for clubheads and hickory for shafts. The slender driver, **3**, gave way to the more robust bulger driver, **4**, and some aerodynamic control was achieved by scoring clubfaces. With the Haskell ball came laminated persimmon heads with hard inserts in the face, left.

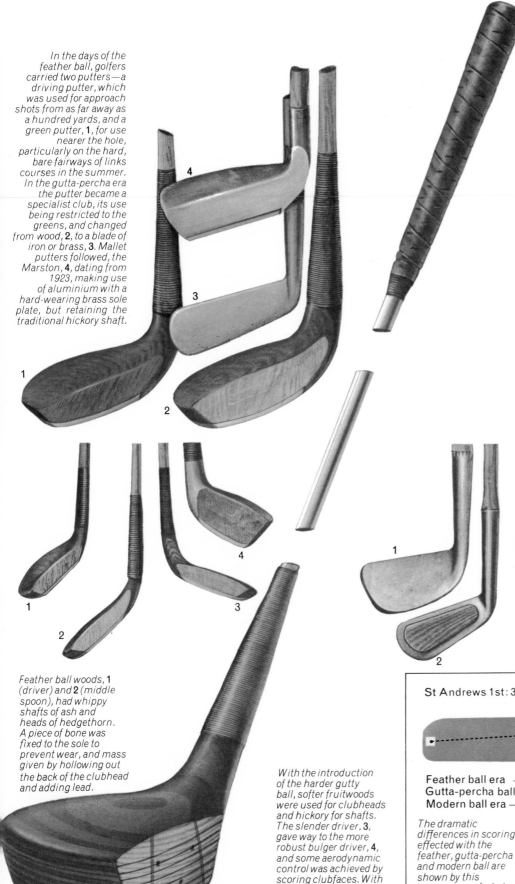

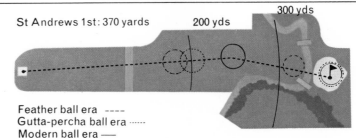

St Andrews 1st: 370 yards   200 yds   300 yds

Feather ball era ----
Gutta-percha ball era ......
Modern ball era ——

The dramatic differences in scoring effected with the feather, gutta-percha and modern ball are shown by this comparison of what a good player could hope to achieve with each on the 1st at St Andrews. With a feather ball it would be a par-five, a mashie being used to lay-up short of the Swilcan Burn and a niblick to chip on. With a gutta-percha ball it would be a very hard par-four, a baffy, the equivalent of today's 4- or 5-wood, being used to reach the green. With the modern ball the hole is an undemanding par-four, no more than an 8-iron to the green.

Links courses: nature's gift to golf

Golf architecture is now recognized as a distinct art, the creation of a great golf course being achieved with a subtle alchemy of skill, imagination and technology upon which another dimension of greatness can be conferred by the staging of a championship. But not every championship setting owes its quality to the hand of man. St Andrews, Prestwick and Carnoustie are relics of the old, natural links on which the game first became popular. To this day nobody knows who laid them out, but even they are refinements of the earliest golfing arenas used when the game was played across country. There were no fairways, no tees and no greens, simply agreed starting and finishing points. The game had reached St Andrews, Carnoustie, Leith, Dornoch, Montrose, North Berwick and Musselburgh by the beginning of the sixteenth century. Golf thus became established on linksland. These strips of coastal land, left when the seas receded after the last ice age, were once a wilderness of sand. Slowly, sparse vegetation grew up and something akin to a fairway with fine-bladed grass threaded its way amongst the gorse. St Andrews became—and still is—one long fairway, with nine holes out to a distant point and nine holes back. Those unfamiliar with links courses expect it to have more definition and more colour. Yet the Old course's influence on generations of golf architects has been immense—so pervasive that every golf course is essentially built in imitation. The Old course served as a model for the early architects, Old Tom Morris, Willie Park Jr and the Dunns, who in their early days did little more than site eighteen teeing grounds and greens on the splendid golfing ground that was put at their disposal. Unfortunately, for a period the blessings of nature were often overlooked and some courses took on a stiff and unnatural appearance. Designs incorporated stone walls, blind shots, hedges, regularly shaped mounds and greens in geometric shapes.

The hidden bunkers that riddle the Old course's 12th fairway, right, started out as natural sandy depressions and were probably enlarged by sheep sheltering from the wind. These, along with dune bunkers as shown left, crucially sited some 230 yards from the tee in the centre of Royal St George's 4th fairway, are common on links courses where the first bunkers were not designed but evolved through use.

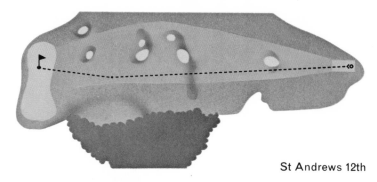

St Andrews 12th

Situated between the 250- and 350-yard marks, the Cardinal bunker, right, dominates Prestwick's 482-yard 3rd. The Cardinal, the fine sand of its face shored up by railway sleepers, is a double cross-bunker, a type of hazard that the more predictable behaviour of the gutta-percha ball made easier to site. Prestwick was opened in 1851, three years after the gutty was introduced, and since its extension in 1883 from twelve to eighteen holes it has changed very little. Rather, having been the home of the first British Open in 1860 and the succeeding eleven, it has become something of a golfing shrine.

Lahinch, left, was laid out in 1893 over terrain so perfect that Old Tom Morris had only to sketch out the holes that made best use of it.

Its fairways undulate over old dunes shaped by tide and wind and then grassed with springy seaside turf, cropped and fertilized by sheep.

Prestwick 17th

The par-four 17th (Alps) at Prestwick, left, is typical of the many blind holes that once existed on the old links courses. It used to be considered a sporting hole, but its emphasis on the vagaries of fortune—their cruellest twist epitomized by the deep bunker, below—to the almost total exclusion of skill, makes the Alps an anachronism.

The Swilcan Burn, around which the 1st at St Andrews, above, has evolved, is the essence of the simple but alarming natural hazard, confirming that the approach shot is the greatest test of a golfer's ingenuity, judgement and nerve.

The famous Postage Stamp at Troon, left, acknowledged as one of the classic short holes of golf, is deceptively simple. Its construction was effected merely by levelling off a teeing ground and flattening out a dune to form a green, the sand being left for bunkers.

The primitive condition of early links courses called for some unusual clubs, amongst them the track iron (left),

used for hitting out of cart tracks, and the baffing spoon (right), the most lofted of the numerous wooden clubs carried.

13

The birth of golf architecture: man takes a hand

Towards the end of the last century came a welcome return to simplicity and naturalness. Great courses continued to be built on traditional linksland (Muirfield and Portmarnock, built in the 1890s, were routed in refreshingly new ways), but due to a radical decision to build on the sandy heathland west of London, they were for the first time created inland. Courses had previously been built away from the sea—but on non-porous soil, soggy in winter and rock hard in summer; this new land was superbly drained and easy to contour, and on it the genius of Willie Park Jr, Herbert Fowler, Tom Simpson, H. S. Colt and Charles Alison flourished. In America, Charles Blair Macdonald created the National Golf Links, the first course of real quality built beyond the shores of Britain and Ireland, and in the years until the end of World War I some exceptional courses were carefully nursed into existence by truly gifted men—George Crump (Pine Valley), the Fownes family (Oakmont), A. W. Tillinghast (San Francisco GC) and Hugh Wilson (Merion). All of these men, British and American, made careful studies of the fine old linksland courses and incorporated the best features into their designs, but they also introduced new ideas of their own and formulated two divergent schools of thought on golf architecture—the strategic and the penal. A penal hole dictates the line of play and punishes a player who strays from it out of all proportion to the degree of his error. The strategic hole offers a number of routes of varying difficulty and, while hampering the poor shot in subsequent play, rewards the good one. These men also understood the value of good drainage, the virtues of suitable grasses, the subtleties of green size in relation to the approach shot, and they did away with the lottery of blind holes, building instead holes that made no secret of their hazards. In their knowledge and its application golf architecture, part intuition, part science, was born.

The good drainage of the heather-strewn, sandy ground that has to be carried at the short 13th on Sunningdale's Old course, right, is what attracted architect Willie Park Jr to the site in the 1890s. His course, a wilderness of heather and scrub, was transformed by the planting of trees to enclose the holes when H. S. Colt modified the course, making it the first heathland course of championship calibre. Britain's first successful inland course was Royal Wimbledon, built on the common near London in 1865 (only a year after Westward Ho!, the first course built in England), but it was Sunningdale that really inspired golf's movement inland.

Because natural hazards did not occur on inland courses with the same frequency as they did on links courses, they had to be created. One of the first and most obvious departures involved the utilization of water, which had hitherto occurred only naturally. Amongst the earliest constructed water hazards was the pond at the 5th at Sunningdale, left. Later, at Pine Valley, one of the earliest heroic holes was created, the short 14th, right, with water all the way to the green.

Pine Valley 1st and 2nd

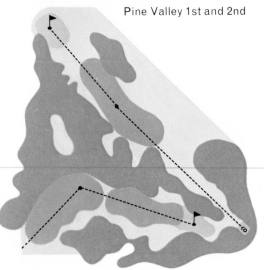

The 2nd at Pine Valley, right, is one of the most dramatic and fearsome holes on a course which, apart from being considered the most difficult in the world, introduced the concept of island fairways, left. These fairways dictate not only line but also length and are isolated amongst vast areas of sandy scrubland which, along with the more formal bunkers set around the greens, are never raked.

The very size of the American continent meant that golf had to move inland—indeed, the first eighteen-hole course in the United States was built at Chicago. But the first parkland course of lasting worth, which was to have a powerful and controversial influence, was Oakmont, left, laid out in 1903 by H. C. Fownes. Because it was built on pure parkland, Oakmont lacked naturally penal features and to compensate for this it was given almost 300 bunkers, those engulfing the 8th green, below, being typical. Although its terrors have since been moderated, Oakmont gave birth to a new style of architecture —the penal, whereby the golfer departing from the prescribed lines is heavily penalized, regardless of how far he has strayed. Its influence was to be felt until the 1930s.

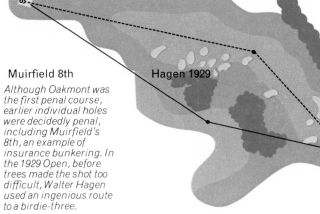

Muirfield 8th

Although Oakmont was the first penal course, earlier individual holes were decidedly penal, including Muirfield's 8th, an example of insurance bunkering. In the 1929 Open, before trees made the shot too difficult, Walter Hagen used an ingenious route to a birdie-three.

Hagen 1929

Muirfield   Portmarnock

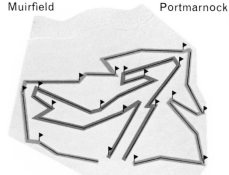

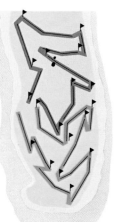

Muirfield, left, and Portmarnock, right, were among the earliest courses to depart from the then accepted principle of nine holes out to a distant point

and nine holes back. On both courses only once do three successive holes pursue the same direction, forcing the golfer to play the wind from all quarters.

The revolutionary Haskell ball gained acceptance in the USA through its successful use by Walter J. Travis, above, in the 1901 US National Amateur.

The Haskell ball brought changes in club construction, hard inserts, at first made from leather, being added to the faces of wooden clubs (left) to act as shock absorbers and to prevent the heads from splitting. The putter was given a centre-shaft for the first time in 1904, the famous Schenectady putter (bottom) of Walter J. Travis being banned in Britain— though not in America—on the grounds that it made putting too easy.

The Golden Age: a universal quest for perfection

Golf's popularity soared in the period between the wars, particularly in the United States, where the feats of Bobby Jones caught the public imagination. Thus, when he retired and built his ideal course, it was bound to be influential. Fortunately, Augusta National, which Jones designed with Alister Mackenzie, proved to be a worthy model. Its wide fairways, sparing but telling use of bunkers, subtle mounding, huge greens and its capacity to test golfers of all abilities, demonstrated irrefutably that strategic design was superior to penal design, which had enjoyed an inexplicable vogue in the 1920s. Other design features emerged as, with a sounder knowledge of the technical problems of building and maintenance and with increasing subtlety, architects pitted their wits against players whose consistency was considerably enhanced by the switch from hickory to steel-shafted clubs. They patiently sculpted their greens, angled them and tilted them; they held out baits, forced decisions, encouraged boldness, indulged the growing taste for spectacular drop-shots and popularized the heroic, all-or-nothing type of hole. Their growing preoccupation with balance was best summed up by Donald Ross, creator of Seminole and Pinehurst Number 2: "The championship course ... should call for long and accurate tee shots, accurate iron play, precise handling of the short game and, finally, consistent putting. These abilities should be called for in a proportion that will not permit excellence in any one department of the game to too largely offset deficiencies in another." In those years many other architects were given marvellous land on which to build, and on it they created some unforgettable courses: Jack Neville at Pebble Beach, A. W. Tillinghast at Baltusrol, Stanley Thompson at Banff, Charles Alison at Hirono, Mackenzie at Royal Melbourne. They made the period between the wars into golf architecture's Golden Age.

In the period between the wars shallow traps became popular in America. The bunkering on the 10th at Augusta (the most influential course built in those years), right, allows the golfer to find the sand and still make a par without too much difficulty. The more traditional deep bunkers favoured in Britain, typified by the cross-bunkers on the 14th at Gleneagles, below, are much more likely to inflict penalty.

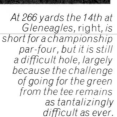

When the 10th hole at Augusta National, above, was built in 1931 very few players were able to get home in two with ease. Now it is a drive and a medium iron for the pros. despite its 485 yards, over the usual par-four limit in America.

At 266 yards the 14th at Gleneagles, right, is short for a championship par-four, but it is still a difficult hole, largely because the challenge of going for the green from the tee remains as tantalizingly difficult as ever.

Pebble Beach The 8th: 425yards par 4

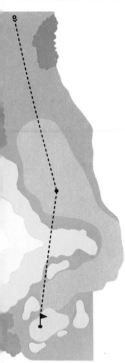

The 8th at Pebble Beach, left, is a magnificent example of the heroic hole which came into its own in the years between the wars. Unlike so many other death-or-glory holes, the 8th does offer a less adventurous alternative to the player who has hit a bad drive: he can play to the left and get home in three. However, for those who dare to go for it, the second shot, seen from the small, heavily bunkered green, far left, is a thrilling experience, requiring a carry of some 150 yards to clear the sea and the cliff-edge bunker short of the green. Pebble Beach, on which work was begun in 1918, has eight holes set along the rockbound coast of Carmel Bay and it was the forerunner of a host of imitative, and usually inferior, spectacular seaside courses.

The wide, open fairway of Augusta National's 15th, above, is deceptive. The trees on the left can interfere and nothing less than an accurate tee shot will give completely uncluttered access to the green. The course is hard to attack but, in keeping with Bobby Jones's aim, it is not too demanding for the average player. In contrast, the trees that crowd Olympic's 12th fairway, left, are penal, demanding too much of the ordinary player.

In the 1920s and the 1930s the differences between American and British courses became more marked, not least in the approach to rough. The neatly trimmed rough alongside Baltusrol's 5th fairway, above, looks innocuous, but the ball does not sit up and it is tenacious enough to prevent any clear hit of the ball, making it difficult to stop pitch shots to the green. The uncut rough at Turnberry's 7th looks (and, because of its unpredictability, can be) fearsome, but it is very often possible to get the clubface near the ball and impart some backspin.

Between the wars came the transition from hickory (left) to steel shafts. The change was dramatic because steel eliminated the torsion present in hickory, which had made the shaft twist as well as bend when swung. The changeover took time, the first perforated steel shaft (right), devised by Allan Lard of Massachusetts in 1903, proving inadequate. The breakthrough came with the development of the seamless steel shaft, legalized in Britain in 1929, which led to matched sets of clubs with consistent feel and characteristics.

The modern era: the land yields to the machine

Few courses were built in the years immediately following World War II, the prime concern being the reinstatement of courses that had been neglected or partially destroyed. Then in the late 1950s more money, more leisure time and the magnetism of Arnold Palmer again made golf into a boom sport. Increased mobility led to a demand for courses in exotic vacation areas where golf had barely been heard of, and a championship golf course became an essential for every chic resort, just as it did for the proliferation of expensive real estate developments. Elaborate water systems, new construction techniques and better machinery made them possible, just as these were instrumental in the transformation of desert, mountain and marsh into land that was fit for golf. Some of the results have been predictably disastrous, but one welcome by-product has been the creation of a plethora of heroic holes in glorious settings around the world. Water has become a dominant feature of design, particularly around the green. Fairway bunkers are now commonly staggered, though all too often flat and far too easy to escape from. Small greens are again finding favour, ensuring the survival of the art of chipping. Golfers of all abilities are catered for by long tees or, more imaginatively, by numerous smaller tees scattered to provide variations not only in length but also in the line of attack. A period of undue emphasis on length seems to be drawing to a close, but throughout the modern era the contribution of the architects who have built courses of real worth has been to stay with the classic verities of the masters who preceded them while adding their own individual signatures. Among the most successful are Dick Wilson (Royal Montreal), the ubiquitous Robert Trent Jones, Pete Dye (Harbour Town), Ralph Plummer (Cypress Creek), Joe Lee (Lagunita), Jack Nicklaus (Muirfield Village) and Peter Thomson and Michael Wolveridge (Bali).

Prompted in part by the prodigious distances that so many of the modern professionals hit the ball, and in part by the awe with which less informed sections of the golfing public treated holes of enormous lengths, the 1950s and 1960s saw an increasing emphasis on sheer length. At 625 yards, the 16th hole at Firestone, left, is one of the longest holes in golf. Only two players, Bobby Nichols and Arnold Palmer, have reached the green in two, though others have been pin-high. The essence of the par-five is a tightly protected green to make a birdie possible only with an exceptional shot, while ensuring that those playing conservatively do not have an open target. The inordinate length of the 16th means that these elements come into play only for the very longest of hitters.

One of the benefits of the increased mobility which has been such a feature of life since World War II has been the way in which it has led to the building of golf courses in some of the more remote countries of the world, where full advantage has been taken of some spectacular sites. The most striking of these courses have made attractive and challenging use of water, which in its fresh form is vital for the upkeep of courses in excessively sunny climates. The 8th hole at Cajuiles in the Dominican Republic, left, is one of six holes calling for shots across the ocean. Architect *Pete Dye's design has some unusual features, not the least of which are the alternate fairways and the peninsula tee built out into the sea. At the short 3rd, above, on Princeville's Ocean nine in Hawaii, Robert Trent Jones set a wide green by a still lake beneath an elevated tee.*

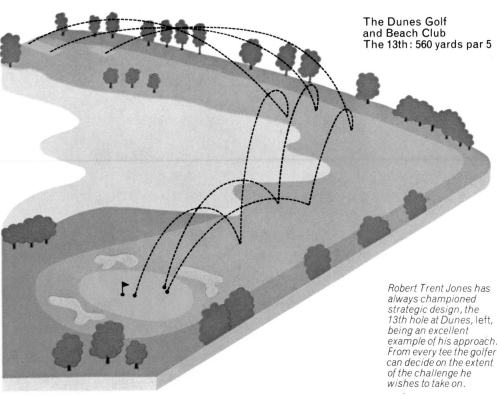

The Dunes Golf
and Beach Club
The 13th : 560 yards par 5

Robert Trent Jones has always championed strategic design, the 13th hole at Dunes, left, being an excellent example of his approach. From every tee the golfer can decide on the extent of the challenge he wishes to take on.

The extremes of the modern approach to bunkering are shown by the retention during the rebuilding of Turnberry after World War II of the traditionally deep and genuinely punishing bunker, right, and the decorative but largely ineffective trap used at Fiji's Pacific Harbour, below. The explanation lies in Turnberry's role as a championship course and Pacific Harbour's prime function as a resort course for golfers of varying abilities.

Harbour Town 13th

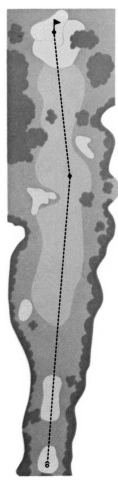

The modern practice of staggering flanking fairway bunkers is perfectly illustrated by Pete Dye's 1969 design for the 13th at Harbour Town, left. The ideal tee shot must be threaded between the left-hand bunker and a lone oak tree but kept out of the right-hand bunker. Dye also made interesting use of trees, a device which is becoming increasingly popular, by using two oaks to guard the entrance to the green. In 1966 Robert Trent Jones built the 600-yard 1st hole at Spyglass Hill, above, around a lone pine, the hazards of which became apparent when the tree died.

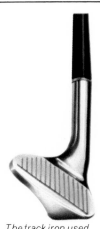

The track iron used in the feather ball era was the first in a long line of well-lofted clubs designed to get under the ball in hazards. None was really effective in sand until Gene Sarazen (right) developed the straight-faced sand wedge with a heavy sole to allow it to move through the sand. He first used it in 1932, but its full impact was not felt until after World War II when, in its modern form (left), it revolutionized the art of bunker play.

The science that transforms design into reality

Since World War II it has been possible to build a golf course almost anywhere—given the two major requirements, money and the technical knowledge. Swamps can be reclaimed, jungles cleared, deserts irrigated and mountains moved. However, only in the last twenty years or so has it been necessary to even contemplate such radical action to bring a golf course into being. It was finally forced by soaring demand, combined with the rapid escalation in the cost of land and the scarcity of suitable sites. Previously, architects had, with comparative ease, found land that without too much effort could be made fit for golf. With the limited means at their disposal, usually hand labour and horses hauling drag pans, they were able to create courses with the naturalness they so coveted. Occasionally the very earliest designers were unable to route their courses around unwanted sandhills and blind holes resulted, but they were almost the only insurmountable problem. Today the challenge is altogether different. The architect is given a piece of land, often highly unsuitable, upon which he must construct a course; occasionally, as Pete Dye was able to do at Cajuiles, he is able to search out less uncompromising ground, although even then it is likely to require considerable effort to make it into a golf course. To further complicate his problems the harsher environments of the more remote sites now frequently chosen have called for new grass strains, specially bred and selected to give the best playing qualities in extremes of climate. Thus a knowledge of agronomy, geology, drainage, engineering, forestry, machinery and heavy construction has become an essential part of the architect's armoury. But golf architecture is an art as much as a science and the aims remain the same as they have always been—to blend sand, water, fairways and greens, course and surroundings as naturally as possible into a combination pleasing to the senses and thrilling for golf.

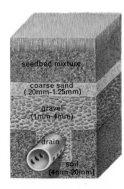

The consistency and distribution of materials in a modern green, right, are tailored to climatic conditions, but the aim is to ensure controlled growth through use of a balanced seedbed mixture—so important that it is often imported —and good drainage. The sand absorbs excess water, which filters through gravel to be drained off through perforated piping.

seedbed mixture

coarse sand (.20mm-1.25mm)

gravel (1mm-4mm)

drain

soil (4mm-20mm)

Like all the early courses actually built to a design, Muirfield was constructed by hand with the help of horses pulling shallow scoops, or drag-pans, right. The architecture benefited from the limitations of this slow but controlled method because it was easier to give earthworks constructed in this way a pleasing natural contour.

This series of photographs shows the emergence of the course at Calabasas Golf Club in California. To the practised eye of the architect the rolling terrain, left, is obviously suitable for golf, but only after extensive clearing and levelling operations have been carried out does it become

recognizable to the untrained eye as good golfing land. The deposits of sand for use in the bunkers give a clear indication of the designer's aims, centre, and the finished result, right, fits naturally into the surroundings. When land is less ideal, construction may involve the moving of some

2,000,000 cubic yards of earth as it did at Korakuen Country Club in Japan, where cuts of up to sixty feet and fills of fifty feet were carried out. At the other extreme, the earthmoving at the Cajuiles and Bali Handara courses, both completed in the 1970s, was limited enough to be done almost entirely by hand.

The construction of the 5th hole at Fairview Country Club, left, illustrates the way in which modern techniques have made the building of water hazards a comparatively simple task. In its finished form, below, the lake not only makes a more adventurous hole while adding to the beauty of the course, but also stores the water so vital for its upkeep. Construction methods have always shaped architectural thinking in subtle ways. In the days when courses were built by horse and scoop, heroic holes were rare because their sites had to occur naturally. However, blind holes, such as the old 3rd at Royal St George's, below, offered sporting alternatives. A new green —wholly visible—has since been built on a rise.

Royal St George's 3rd

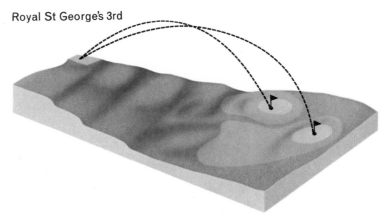

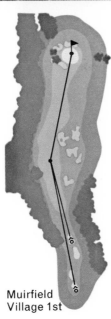

Muirfield Village 1st

The 1st hole at Muirfield Village, right, with its numerous bunkers, rolling fairways, thoughtfully contoured green and carefully shaped multiple tees, above, is typical of the course—and of what can be achieved when

$2,000,000 are spent on construction. The annual upkeep of the course costs some $300,000—almost half what it cost in 1975 to build a course with a full irrigation system and the moving of 100,000 cubic yards of earth.

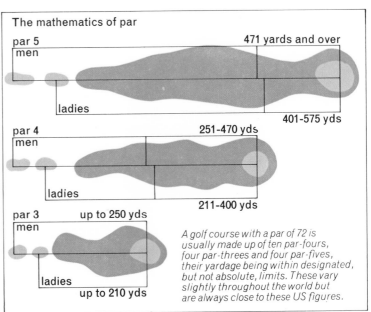

The mathematics of par

par 5   471 yards and over
men

ladies   401-575 yds

par 4   251-470 yds
men

ladies   211-400 yds

par 3   up to 250 yds
men

ladies   up to 210 yds

A golf course with a par of 72 is usually made up of ten par-fours, four par-threes and four par-fives, their yardage being within designated, but not absolute, limits. These vary slightly throughout the world but are always close to these US figures.

Greens: the ultimate target

No part of the golf course can have as much influence on a golfer's score as the greens—the ultimate target. They form the most important part of the construction work and often are the most costly item. No two are alike, but their nature has had an obvious bearing on the difficulty of a course ever since the principles of golf architecture became accepted. Greens influence scoring in two ways: in the target they present for shots hit into them, and in the effect which they have on putting—that controversial game within a game. At first greens were little more than cut extensions of the fairway, though sometimes they were sited in hollows or on plateaus; some were flat, others eccentrically undulating, but all were natural. It was unreasonable to expect a golfer to flight a mashie shot with a feathery or gutty over greenside bunkers and stop his ball on a rough, unprepared surface. Thus in the early days greens were relatively unguarded, but later were given protection, as a means of calling for more control and as a counter to the ever improving clubs and balls. First sand and later water, sometimes both, were used, often completely encircling the putting surface, their severity depending on the type and length of approach to be played. Greens were angled, raised or lowered to favour those who had hit their previous shot to the ideal place. With the advent of watering and improved strains of grass, it was not so much a question of hitting the green as one of hitting it in the right place. Pin placement became an art in itself, practised, with weather conditions in mind, to vary the severity of the test. It came to be universally accepted that if a player aimed for the fat of the green he might face difficulty in getting down in two putts, whereas should he be bold enough to play for the pin the margin for error was slight but the potential rewards great. The putting surface itself should be receptive to the well-struck shot and, ideally, be firm, fast and true.

The fast, undulating 18th green, right, is typical of those at Oakmont, which are generally acknowledged to be the most terrifying in America, not simply because of the premium they place on putting but because they call for such perfect placement of approach shots. In spite of their fearsome contours, Oakmont's greens are fair because they contain no grain, which affects not only the distance a putt will roll but also in which direction it will bend.

The 15th hole at Pebble Beach is 406 yards long from the championship tee, and the effect that pin placement can have on scoring can be gauged from the difficulty engendered by the siting of the flag at the right rear, close to a big curving trap, right. Because the winds make the Pebble Beach greens faster and harder than on most American courses, even professionals would find this pin position extreme enough to settle for the safe approach and aim for the centre of the green. For those under pressure to attack, the margin for error is slight.

Winged Foot 11th

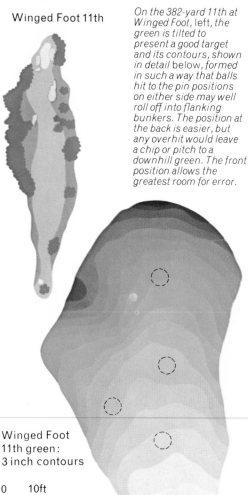

On the 382-yard 11th at Winged Foot, left, the green is tilted to present a good target and its contours, shown in detail below, formed in such a way that balls hit to the pin positions on either side may well roll off into flanking bunkers. The position at the back is easier, but any overhit would leave a chip or pitch to a downhill green. The front position allows the greatest room for error.

Winged Foot 11th green: 3 inch contours

0   10ft

The short 7th hole at Pebble Beach, left, is famous for its beauty. Despite its length of only 120 yards, it is a great golf hole, its challenge lying in the size of the green—eight yards wide and twenty-four yards long—its siting along the line of approach and the tight ring of bunkers which enclose it.

The entrance to the 14th green at Augusta National, right, replaces the usual bunkers with beautifully contoured protective mounds, which deflect any mishit approach away from the putting surface. When it was opened in 1933, Augusta had only about thirty bunkers and its huge greens, so in keeping with the heroic scale of the course, were the first of such size in North America.

Island greens, like that of the 16th at Golden Horseshoe GC in Williamsburg, Virginia, right, were made possible by construction techniques introduced after World War II and by watering, which softens greens to allow target golf.

In extreme climates, such as that encountered 4,700 feet up at the Garhwal Himalaya course, below, oil greens —levelled sand compacted with oil— make the only practical putting surface.

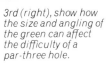

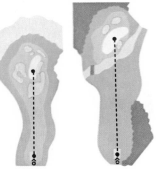

These three very short holes, Pebble Beach 7th (left), Augusta 12th (centre) and Country Club of North Carolina 3rd (right), show how the size and angling of the green can affect the difficulty of a par-three hole.

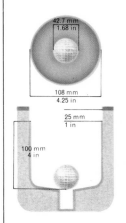

42.7 mm
1.68 in

108 mm
4.25 in

25 mm
1 in

100 mm
4 in

The delicate operation of cutting a hole and sinking the cup is now carried out with an intricate gadget (left) that ensures that the hole is of the regulation size, shown in relation to that of the American ball (far left). Tests have shown that the larger American ball is less susceptible to slight inequalities in the putting surface than its British counterpart, which is 1.62 inches in diameter. The two sizes were first regulated in 1921.

Elements of greatness – a classic course

No 1	Royal St George's	415 yards	par 4
No 2	Scioto	436 yards	par 4
No 3	Durban Country Club	506 yards	par 5
No 4	Baltusrol	194 yards	par 3
No 5	Mid Ocean	433 yards	par 4
No 6	Royal Melbourne	428 yards	par 4
No 7	Cajuiles	195 yards	par 3
No 8	Pine Valley	327 yards	par 4
No 9	Muirfield	495 yards	par 5
	Out	3,429 yards	par 36
No 10	Muirfield Village	441 yards	par 4
No 11	The Country Club	445 yards	par 4
No 12	Augusta National	155 yards	par 3
No 13	Harbour Town	358 yards	par 4
No 14	St Andrews	567 yards	par 5
No 15	Oakmont	453 yards	par 4
No 16	Carnoustie	235 yards	par 3
No 17	Cypress Point	375 yards	par 4
No 18	Pebble Beach	540 yards	par 5
	In	3,569 yards	par 36
	Total	6,998 yards	par 72

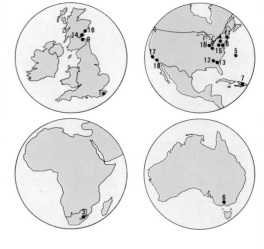

A great hole may be an architect's dream fashioned in a setting of rare beauty; it can have acquired greatness by constant usage and exposure; it may be a creation from the drawing board; or, like many of the old Scottish links, it may simply have evolved from use down the centuries. Whatever its origins or its claims to greatness, to support them it must be a challenge and an enjoyment to every golfer, no matter how meagre or mighty his talents. It must pose problems that can be strict for the masters and yet readily leavened for the humble; it must require thought and reward those who think; its playing values must be high but not unfair. In the words of architect Robert Trent Jones, it should be a demanding par and a comfortable bogey.

No two holes anywhere in the world are precisely similar in any respect but length. The

Beauty alone does not make a golf hole great, but it considerably enhances the pleasures of playing the tricky 12th at Augusta National, with its angled green protected by Rae's Creek.

contours of the land, the setting and the architect's ideas are bound to differ, and so the manifestations of his skill are infinite. His creation may inspire admiration from one golfer, dislike from another. Golfers are highly egocentric where their own game is concerned and their judgement of a hole frequently is conditioned by personal experience alone.

With all the world to choose from, selecting the eighteen holes which will best combine to create a golf course, with all the considerations of balance and variety that the word implies, can be an endless challenge to memory, research and imagination. Some will inevitably find fault, claiming that this 7th, 15th or whatever is not the finest in the world, but who could claim without fear of contradiction that any particular hole was? Far too many imponderables are involved, but all will stand fair com-

parison and all embrace uncommon qualities of design and natural beauty—and surely few would disagree that together they make a classic course.

In creating this classic test of golf, faith has been kept with the number of each hole; thus the 9th is the 9th at Muirfield, and the 18th is the tremendous climax to Pebble Beach. To devise a course otherwise would be false to the concept, since the quality of a hole may be indisputable, but its lasting greatness in the minds of golfers owes something to its position in the round and the imprint of history upon it. Would the 12th at Augusta have been as famous, or infamous according to experience, had it been the 7th and not the Machiavellian centre-piece of Amen Corner? Would the 14th at St Andrews have influenced the course of so many events had it been earlier in the round? Obviously not.

The features that make a great hole depend to some extent on their play on courage and fear. A golfer will take risks early in the round which he would not take towards the end. In creating closing holes the architect usually tries to present challenges that will strike fear into the hearts of the frail, inspire the accomplished player, and possibly cause indecision for those protecting a favourable position.

The eighteen holes come from courses as far apart as California and Carnoustie, Melbourne and Muirfield, Durban and the Dominican Republic. Their settings range from the timeless linksland of Britain, where the influence of man and machine on their creation was minimal and nature was the original architect, to verdant countryside where artifice and nature, tranquil or savage, have been gloriously combined, and to rock-bound ocean coasts where, as Jack Neville and Douglas Grant could not fail to perceive, the great holes of Pebble Beach, now

famous the world over, were begging to be made.

The preservation of natural beauty, or an imitation of it, is crucial to the fashioning of a great hole. The impact of a formidable task is leavened if its background is appealing. Whose heart would not quicken, however apprehensive he may be of making the stroke, on the tee of the 5th at Mid Ocean, with Mangrove Lake gleaming far below him, or on the 17th tee at Cypress Point with that enticing sweep of fairway across the curve of a bay, where the ocean forever pounds and the gnarled old cypress trees writhe in the distance?

More often than not architects have pleasing landscape for their work, but the great expansion of golf has made it necessary to build courses where space is available, even though, as in Florida or the western deserts of America, there may be a lack of agreeable features. Then the machine and the imagination of the architect come into their own and miracles are wrought. But on this course the setting of every hole, and many of its basic features, are natural.

All the holes fulfil Robert Trent Jones's philosophy that a par must be hard-won but a bogey easily scored, it even being possible to skirt the lake at Baltusrol's short 4th. The other tee shots are not uncompromising. Demands on straightness may be fairly severe on holes like the 9th, 10th, 14th, 15th and 18th if there is to be lively hope of a par, but the handicap golfer has no fearsome task to keep the ball in play.

Increasingly on modern courses water is being used for penal and strategic purposes, and in differing degrees the golfer could not fail to be aware of it on seven of the holes. At the 5th and 17th it serves to lure him into attempting overmuch; at the short 4th and 7th holes those in hope of a par must carry it; and on the 18th the Pacific acts as a fairly substantial lateral

water hazard. Rae's Creek, protecting the 12th green, is an insidious, mind-torturing menace, even for the greatest players, but the quiet pool on the 11th serves both to please and to threaten. Such can be the variety of water's uses.

Every great course should be balanced in its demands on the player's skill. Ideally, it should have two par-fives and two par-threes in each half, and the par-fours should be varied in length and difficulty. Some holes should be straight, like the 1st at St George's, and others curve left or right without overly favouring one shape of shot. The pronounced movement to the right of the 6th is balanced at the 11th where, after driving to a rising crest of fairway, the hole swings left and flows across a gentle valley. The lake at the 5th destroys the hook; the ocean at the 17th punishes the slice.

The growing number of golfers who power their drives away has diminished the effect of numerous long holes. Many, like the beautiful 13th at Augusta, have become par $4\frac{1}{2}$ or less to the masters. Even for lesser mortals, unable to make the carry over the creek to the green, the demands on the second shot are far from severe. A famous old player once said, somewhat irreverently, that he could make pars on all the long holes at Augusta using a putter for his second shot. This may be true of many other par-fives, but not of these; they have stood the test of time.

Few golfing aspects are more discouraging than a long toil up from the tee, and the best architects avoid them wherever possible. Aside from the gentle rise of the 11th and 15th fairways the one uphill drive is the 10th at Muirfield Village, the only one on Jack Nicklaus's superb course, and it is not forbidding because the shot is over a valley.

The course is not overly long but it provides the perfect rebuttal to those who would argue that no course of less than 7,000 yards is of championship calibre. Balance and variety are maintained within the par-fours. Whereas, for example, long, accurate driving is essential to evade fairway bunkers and set up a good position for an attacking approach on the 2nd, 10th and 15th, restraint of length from the tee can be crucial playing the 13th at Harbour Town, one of Pete Dye's gems of creation. Again on the 8th at Pine Valley the cruel beauty of the hole lies in the taxing nature of the pitch.

Many may disagree with the composition of the course, but nobody could fairly dispute that it would call upon a golfer to demonstrate skill in every department of the game; that it embraces the qualities of exceptional design, and much of the beauty with which golf is blessed; that it would command respect from the mighty and be a great deal of fun for anyone to play.

▷

No. 1

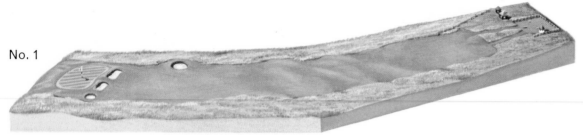

No. 2

No. 3

The 3rd fairway at Durban Country Club switchbacks around bunkers (deep enough to preclude all but the most conservative escape shots) to an elevated green, which favours the precisely hit pitch shot.

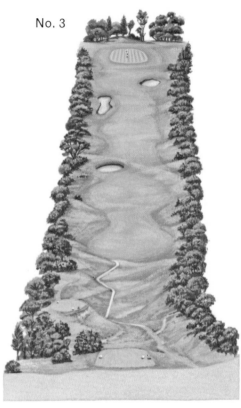

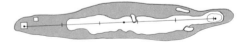

1st Royal St George's: 415 yards, par 4

The paramount requirement for an opening hole is that it should enable play to flow from the outset—that golfers should not be delayed waiting for a green to clear, as on a par-five within range of two shots. It should also whet the golfer's appetite for the test ahead, a mission more easily accomplished should its prospect be instantly appealing. To stand on the tee on a summer morning, with the breeze fresh from the sea and the larks in full voice—as they always seem to be at Sandwich—and look down the crumpled spread of fairway, would make any golfer rejoice. The drive is not demanding, but the stance for the second shot, usually a medium iron, may be uneven in the classic links fashion. A cross-bunker, steeply faced and cut deep into a gentle upslope, protects the approaches to a green that falls away from the striker, although the bold shot is not unduly punished. Any golfer still in need of encouragement will delight in the trueness of the green.

2nd Scioto: 436 yards, par 4

At Scioto's 2nd hole the golfer is immediately brought face to face with stern reality. In anybody's language the hole is the severest par on the course, and it reflects something of the beauty of Donald Ross's design. It might have been created for Jack Nicklaus, who learned his golf there, because of the demand on the tee shot: unless it carries to the crest of a fairway rising out of a valley there is no clear sight of the green. If the drive is smothered or hit with a diving hook it can vanish in a stream hidden behind a screen of sycamore and fir trees, and those who press for distance risk two large fairway bunkers, trees, or the out-of-bounds that pursues the hole throughout its length. The entrance to the green is narrowed between spreading bunkers; trees stand sentinel on either hand and, as usual with Ross, the green is slightly elevated and subtly contoured. In the 1928 PGA, then a matchplay event, three matches went to extra holes; all were decided at the 2nd.

3rd Durban Country Club: 506 yards, par 5

The prospect from a tee poised high above the fairway is at once dramatic and, to a handicap golfer, disturbing. The valley unfolds below, rising through a series of mounds and undulations to a green in the shadow of a tree-covered dune. Off to the right the Indian Ocean tumbles silver on a shining beach, but it is of no concern to the golfer, whose line is narrowed by dense shrubs. Contrary to expectation the drive will not be deflected off the valley walls, where the spongy grass tends to smother the bounce. But the drive is not the most difficult shot and the degree of difficulty encountered thereafter relates directly to the ambition of the golfer. A second which is intended merely to open the green is fairly straightforward, but for the man trying to get home in two a mass of bush on the left will devour the hook. The approach itself must be precise, for the dead ground in front and the pronounced shoulders of a raised green do not favour the run-up shot.

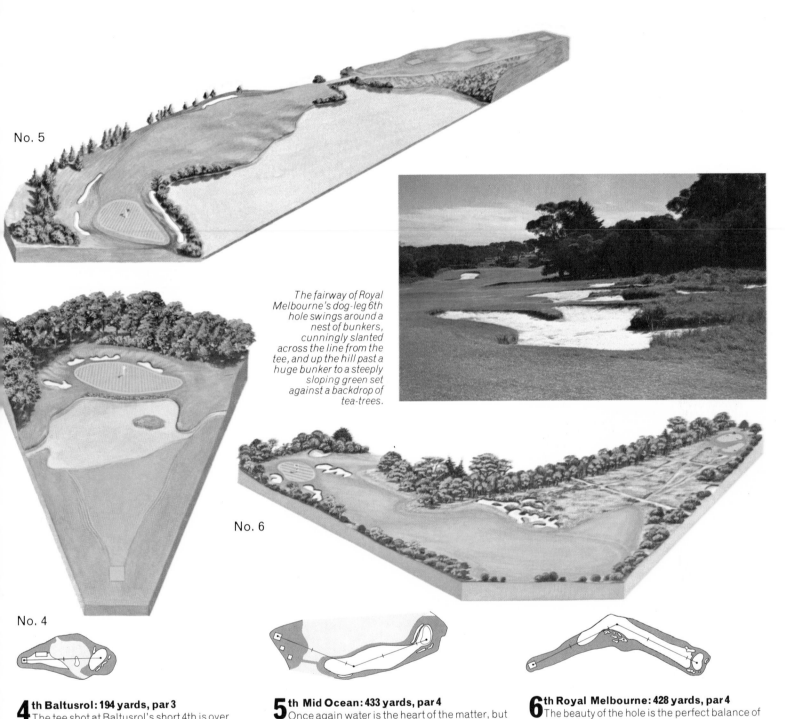

No. 5

No. 4

No. 6

The fairway of Royal Melbourne's dog-leg 6th hole swings around a nest of bunkers, cunningly slanted across the line from the tee, and up the hill past a huge bunker to a steeply sloping green set against a backdrop of tea-trees.

4th Baltusrol: 194 yards, par 3

The tee shot at Baltusrol's short 4th is over water to a green that begins abruptly atop the stone retaining wall of a lake. The green is large but well trapped to the left and the rear. The problems of this hole are really psychological. The easiest way to threaten the peace of mind of most golfers is to confront them with a stretch of water that must be carried. The handicap golfer may mishit into the water simply because he has a faulty swing and therefore frequently mishits, but more often failure to make the carry is bred in fear. The expert is concerned only with the pin placing, choosing the right club and deciding which part of the tilted green he should aim for to give him the most favourable putting position. The joy of seeing the ball fly safely across water and nestle near the flag is instantaneous, the satisfaction total. Every course should have one hole where the basic challenge is uncompromising—the thrill of being equal to it is unsurpassed in golf.

5th Mid Ocean: 433 yards, par 4

Once again water is the heart of the matter, but not as threateningly as at Baltusrol. The shining expanse of Mangrove Lake lies between tee and green, but no golfer could make the carry even with a hurricane behind him and so the hole is a nice exercise in bravery or caution. Experience tells how much of the lake can be carried to reach the fairway; the longer the better, for then the second shot between guardian bunkers to the green is shorter. The flanking bunkers are long and narrow, that on the left side snaking the entire length of the green. The hole is classic in the simplicity of its challenge; there is nothing devious or subtle about it. Either you make the carry or you do not, but the frail of heart or swing do have an alternative: the green then is out of range in two, but at least the bogey is not difficult to make. In this Charles Blair Macdonald, who designed the course in 1924, observed one of the basic principles of good golf course architecture.

6th Royal Melbourne: 428 yards, par 4

The beauty of the hole is the perfect balance of its challenge, a quality of which its creator, Alister Mackenzie, was always deeply aware. However the hole is approached it is never mastered until the final putt is down, and yet it is beautiful rather than alarming to contemplate. From a tee amid the tea-trees, the fairway swoops downhill then swings to the right, mounting to a green set on a hillside against a backdrop of trees. A huge bunker is cut in its left flank, and an abundance of sand awaits the over-corrected shot to the right. Within the curve of the hole lies dense rough and a clustered nest of bunkers; if these can be carried the next shot is appreciably shortened, but the ball will need to fly some 220 yards. A commercial shot straight down the fairway leaves a demanding stroke, usually from a downhill stance. Unless the distance is judged perfectly the danger of three putts is acute because the fast green slopes steeply up from front to back.

No. 7

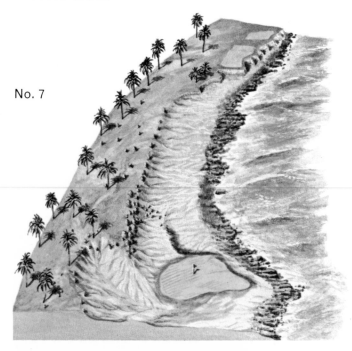

No. 8

The 7th at Cajuiles, a fine natural hole, curves along a magnificent crescent of rocky coastline. Even from the forward tees the golfer must steel himself for an all-or-nothing shot across sea and sand.

No. 9

7th Cajuiles: 195 yards, par 3

Occasionally an architect comes across a situation in the land which clearly begs the making of a golf hole, especially if he is as devoted to making the finest use of natural settings as Pete Dye. A rock-bound curve of the southeastern coast of the Dominican Republic must have jumped to his mind as the setting for a glorious short hole that is less forbidding than it looks and, because of the prevailing trade winds, usually plays some two clubs shorter than its length suggests. The mishit can leap to perdition from the rocks or be trapped in acres of sand, but forward tees help diminish the perils of a shot to a green more receptive to the iron shot that is feathered rather than driven. Any apprehension felt by the golfer standing on the tee above the frothing surf of the azure Caribbean is considerably assuaged by the sheer beauty of the setting. This aspect of golf architecture can be overemphasized, but it is always present to some degree in the great holes.

8th Pine Valley: 327 yards, par 4

No great course would be complete without at least one hole where length is of no account but accuracy is all. The 8th at Pine Valley is just such a hole. Although the fairway slopes gently down and a good drive will finish within a hundred yards of the green, the approach must be one of the most taxing pitch shots in the world. The green is shaped like a slender pear and is protected on all sides by deep bunkers, unraked as is traditional for all bunkers at Pine Valley. A pitch is the only shot, its margin of error is minimal and, more often than not, it is played from a downslope with the striker standing above the ball. It is therefore the shanker's nightmare. Legion are the tales of disaster, not least that of the Walker Cup player who took sixteen despite a good drive. The virtue of the short par-four cannot be exaggerated, and all good architects are aware of it. A player's skill and nerve can be as thoroughly examined on a hole of 320 yards as on one of the full length of 470 yards.

9th Muirfield: 495 yards, par 5

A true five must be a continuing test of control and thought. Many examine the tee shot and the final approach, but often the second shot is simply a matter of making forward progress. Not so at Muirfield's 9th, where into a prevailing wind there is no question of relaxing after hitting a safe shot. This in itself can be demanding, for the fairway becomes a narrow waist between bunkers and uncommonly tenacious rough. Whether going for the green or not, according to the strength and direction of the wind, the rippling lawn of the approaches may look inviting and not too difficult to find. But pull, and out-of-bounds lurks over the grey stone wall; fade or block the shot overmuch, and a whole series of bunkers is waiting. Quite apart from testing to the very last shot the player intent on a good score over the front nine, the hole comes as a timely reminder to the golfer who, having reached the turn, cannot now be in any doubt as to the sternness of his task.

No. 10

The slight incline of the 10th fairway at Muirfield Village stretches away from the delightfully contoured tees that are such a pleasant feature of the Ohio course. The fairway is wide, but the trouble on either side severe.

No. 11

No. 12

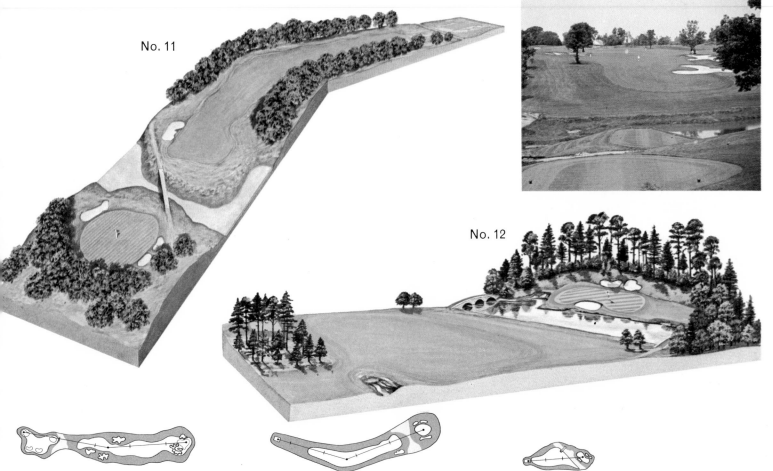

10th Muirfield Village: 441 yards, par 4

The second nine begins on a sterner note than the first. Although the immediate prospect of the 10th at Muirfield Village is appealing rather than formidable, it is a hole demanding of excellence and comparable with the splendid 10th holes common to most of the great championship courses. The first essential is a well-placed tee shot where water lurks but hardly threatens. The drive that drifts to the right will be fortunate to escape bunkers, and if it is pulled while striving for undue length, a gathering of trees and more sand await. The green, which is comparatively small, is protected on the right by a multi-fingered bunker, while another will snare the shot held up overmuch. The hole reveals an admirable aspect of design common to the whole Muirfield Village course, in that Jack Nicklaus uses separate tees of varying shapes and does not rely on the single long strip, which can make the golfer playing from forward markers feel inferior.

11th The Country Club: 445 yards, par 4

There has been no undue insistence on length on the par-fours on the back nine, but it is none the less demanding for that. Indeed, the most challenging part of The Country Club course at Brookline, as used on its recent great occasions, is the outset of the homeward journey, the heart of which is the beautiful rise and sweep of the 11th fairway and the lovely shot that follows. The hole tempts—and dangerously so, because of deep woods—a pull from the tee in order to shorten the second shot, which is usually a long iron over a lake in a valley to the inviting green, a small target tightly ringed by trouble. Water protects the front, sand the right side and trees enclose the whole in a stately but potent embrace. Conceivably, the hole cost Arnold Palmer the 1963 Open. In spite of dropping several strokes there to par, including a seven when a hooked drive finished against a tree stump, he tied with Jacky Cupit and Julius Boros; Boros won the play-off.

12th Augusta National: 155 yards, par 3

As Masters follows Masters, the fame of the 12th at Augusta grows apace. No short hole (and rarely is it more than a 6-iron) has caused greater uncertainty as to choice of club, and more apprehension as to the fate of the shot. At the peak of its flight the ball is at the whim of the breeze that ever stirs amid the tall trees. The slightest change can mean the difference between a putt for a two or a desperate struggle for a four. Every golfer who ever challenged for the Masters has known tribulation there. Every golfer, regardless of handicap, is greatly relieved to have made the green at the first attempt. It is not deep and the tee shot, slightly overhit for fear of falling short in Rae's Creek, can leave a frighteningly delicate sand or chip shot back. Judgement and finesse are qualities more important to the making of fine golf shots than the ability to power the ball a long way, so a hole of this length is essential to any great course.

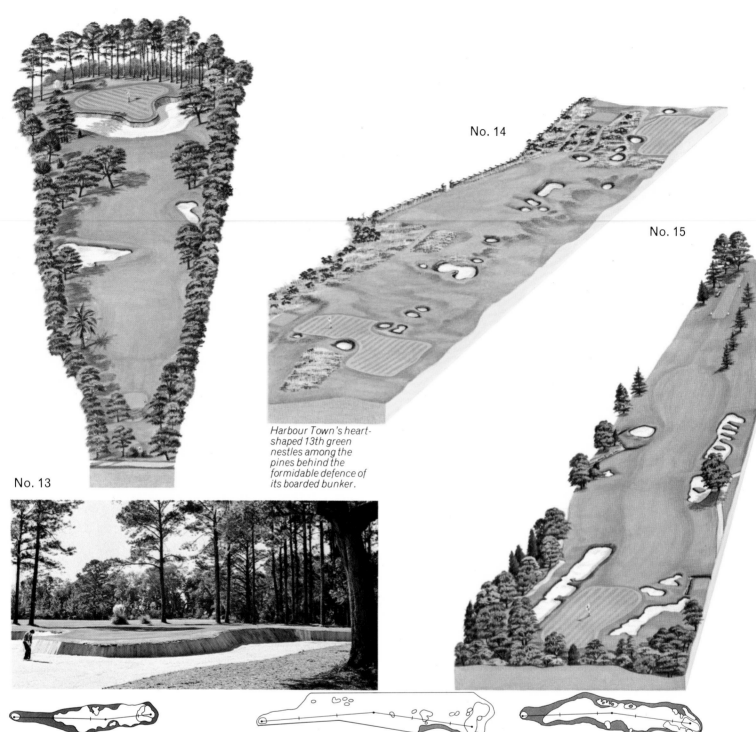

No. 13

No. 14

No. 15

Harbour Town's heart-shaped 13th green nestles among the pines behind the formidable defence of its boarded bunker.

13th Harbour Town: 358 yards, par 4

For the short par-four to be effective it must have well-nigh unassailable defences, such as the 13th at Harbour Town, where precision rather than power is the essence. Many will refrain from using a driver in order to avoid the bunker on the left of the fairway and to finish in a good position for the pitch to the heart-shaped green—guarded by a huge bunker, at some points as deep as a man is tall and faced with boards in the manner of many of the famous old links courses. Tall, stately pines, clothed in Spanish moss, line the fairway, creating a delightful feeling of calm seclusion without in any way inhibiting the play. However, two large oak trees stand sentinel some seventy yards before the green, which is only opened up by the truly accurate tee shot, frequently made with a 3-wood. Together with the massive bunker that encircles the front half of the green, the shape of which makes for some tough pin positions, this matches any trial posed by sheer length.

14th St Andrews: 567 yards, par 5

The greatness of the Long Hole at St Andrews lies in the almost boundless extent of its problems. They can vary from hour to hour according to the wind and the state of a golfer's game and nerve, and can swiftly damn the unknowing or unthinking stoke. After the drive has survived the perils of out-of-bounds and the Beardies bunkers, and found brief sanctuary in the Elysian Fields, comes the time of trial when a decision must be made. Aside from the obvious danger of Hell straight ahead—can it be carried or not?—there is the invisible menace beyond of the Grave and Ginger Beer bunkers. Those who take too cautious a line to left or right are assured of a testing third, frequently from an uneven stance, to the shelf of green tilting away from a steep bank. Surmounting this can demand a shot of fine touch, whether putting, chipping or pitching. In a helpful breeze the strong will hope for a birdie; but rare is the man who is unhappy to settle for a five.

15th Oakmont: 453 yards, par 4

If the comparative failure of Ben Hogan to master a hole is a fair indication of its quality then the 15th at Oakmont must stand high in the company of long par-fours. In the 1953 Open he had a six and a five there in his last two rounds, but won the championship by six strokes. The drive must mount the long rise of fairway to a narrow landing area between church pew bunkers on the left and bunkers and ditches on the right. The fairway then falls gently towards an enormous long green slightly offset to the right and embraced by bunkers; the longest stretches ninety-five yards. The essence of the second shot is in judgement of length, since the greens are normally slippery as ice and those who misjudge the approach can be in lively danger of three putts or more. In 1973 Johnny Miller, soaring to the peak of his incomparable 63, played the hole to perfection: a vast drive, a 4-iron to ten feet and one putt. But rarely does the hole yield so lightly.

No. 17

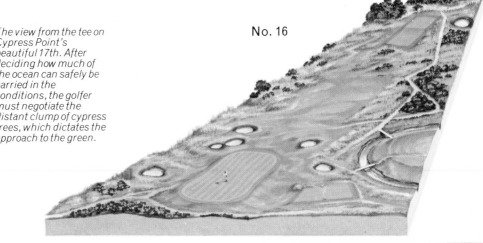

The view from the tee on Cypress Point's beautiful 17th. After deciding how much of the ocean can safely be carried in the conditions, the golfer must negotiate the distant clump of cypress trees, which dictates the approach to the green.

No. 16

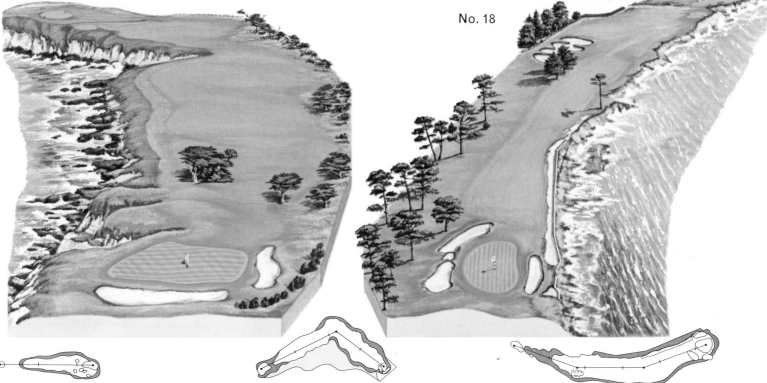

No. 18

16th Carnoustie: 235 yards, par 3

In any finish on a championship course the more accomplished player should be given the opportunity for his greater skill to take effect. At this point in a round the pressure is at its greatest and this stiffens the already formidable challenge of the 16th at Carnoustie. Few short holes anywhere demand a long shot of more exacting straightness. The green, beyond a narrow gap between bunkers, is a plateau, and the shot that leaks a little either way has faint chance of remaining on the putting surface. Tom Watson must have set some sort of record, at least in modern times, by winning the 1975 Open without making a single three there in five attempts (including the play-off with Jack Newton). The importance of thoughtful setting of the tee-markers on a hole of this type was evident in the 1968 Open, when in one round only the supremely powerful Nicklaus, using a driver, was able to hit his ball beyond the flag. However, not even he managed a single birdie in four attempts.

17th Cypress Point: 375 yards, par 4

No golf architect was more richly endowed with natural features for his work than Alister Mackenzie at Cypress Point. Majestic woodland, a hint of links and heathland here and there and the savage nobility of the coast made for unforgettable holes. The 17th is not as fierce or famous as its immediate predecessor, but in less demanding fashion it asks the golfer how brave he is. The drive from a tee high on a rocky peninsula above the ocean at once is tempting and disturbing according to how much of the bay's curve he tries to carry. The beauty of the hole is the extent to which a great cluster of black cypresses come into play for the second shot. According to where the drive has finished, the second may be played over or to either side, but gallant or foolhardy is the man who takes the right-hand route over the ocean. Even without a strong hole to follow, as is the case at Cypress Point, this is a great 17th. With the 18th at Pebble Beach it makes for a heroic finish.

18th Pebble Beach: 540 yards, par 5

The glory of the 18th at Pebble Beach is that its supreme challenge and beauty are entirely natural. The long curve of the coast from tee to green brings the ocean into play as on no other par-five in the world, and in so doing emphasizes the essential virtues of a great finishing hole. The man who is down or needs a birdie-four has a chance, while the golfer over-anxious to protect his lead may be confounded. Forever the golfer is aware that to pull is to die, so the tendency to block the shot is great, although bunkers and trees harass the conservative approach. The farther to the right it is played the longer the hole becomes, and eventually the golfer must turn towards the ocean. The green is so close to it that even the shortest approach cannot be treated lightly; it can so easily scuttle across the green and down on to the rocks beyond. In contrast, meeting the challenge of going for the green needs courage and control of a very high order.

The imperishable genius of the master architects

Not the least of golf's attractions is the fact that it is the one game that is played on natural terrain, or, failing that, on terrain that has been diligently moulded so that it has the aspect and the feel of natural terrain. Nearly every other game is played on a court or field especially prepared for it, and whose dimensions must adhere to certain prescribed measurements. It is generally agreed that the best land for golf resembles the gently rolling terrain of the British linksland on which the game slowly developed and reached its first stage of maturity. Today, when a golfer plays the Old course at St Andrews and many other British or Irish links, the land, with only occasional slight alterations, twists and turns and slides and heaves very much the way it did centuries ago when uncivilized man walked it without a lofter, a baffy, a brassie, a 5-iron, or a bull's-eye putter in his hand. In the United States and other countries where there is a paucity of true linksland and where, in building a golf course, trees and underbrush have to be ripped out and the bulldozer has to be called in again to move the earth and shape the tees, fairways and greens, the desideratum, to a considerable degree—even on inland courses hundreds of miles from the nearest salt water—has been, and continues to be, to create holes which, with certain necessary variations, possess the character of the best linksland courses.

In this connection all genuinely first-rate golf courses have many traits in common, and at one and the same time each genuinely first-rate golf course is astonishingly singular. Take the first great American course, the National Golf Links at Southampton, on Long Island, which was opened in 1911, ten years after the idea for the course first came to its designer, Charles Blair Macdonald, and four years after the actual construction began. It probably would not have been a great course had Macdonald not been steeped in British golf—he met the game during the period he was attending St Andrews University—and had gotten to know the best one-shot, two-shot and three-shot holes on the island so well that he frankly set out to reproduce them on his stretch of bramble-covered duneland off Sebonac Bay. It would not have been a great golf course either had Macdonald not had the excellent common sense not to try to reproduce the famous Scottish and English holes yard for yard and slope for slope, but, instead, modified his models as the land he was working with suggested. The point is not that most golf critics think that Macdonald's Redan is a much better golf hole than the original Redan at North Berwick, or that they consider that Macdonald's Road Hole at the National is not at all in the same class as the original at St Andrews. Rather, the point is that by understanding what made great holes great, and by intelligently adapting this knowledge to his own acreage, Macdonald reached his goal, which was to have the National Golf Links "serve as an incentive to the elevation of the game in America". Until the National was built, all but a few American courses were hack jobs laid out by golfing illiterates. After the unveiling of the National, the pilgrims who came from every part of the country to study it began to gain a clear idea of what golf course architecture was all about.

So much has been written about the history of golf architecture that I think it would be wise not to inflict on the reader yet another detailed chronicle stretching from the first rudimentary Scottish courses to those recently designed by Ben Hogan (The Trophy Club, in Texas) and Jack Nicklaus (Muirfield Village, in Ohio). At the same time, I would feel remiss in a way if I did not excerpt one of the key passages from Sir Guy Campbell's account of the birth of the linksland courses—which first appeared in *A History of Golf in Britain*, published by Cassell & Co Ltd in 1952—since, firstly, the subject matter is fascinating, secondly, the author's awesome learning and his descriptive powers make it one of the most exciting pieces ever written about golf, and, thirdly, so comparatively few golfers have had the treat of reading it.

British golf was first played over links or "green fields".... Nature was their architect, and beast and man her contractors.

In the formation and over-all stabilization of our island coastlines, the sea at intervals of time and distance gradually receded from the higher ground of cliff, bluff, and escarpment to and from which the tides once flowed and ebbed. And as during the ages, by stages, the sea withdrew, it left a series of sandy wastes in bold ridge and significant furrow, broken and divided by numerous channels up and down which the tides advanced and retired, and down certain of which the burns, streams, and rivers found their way to the sea.

As time went on, these channels, other than those down which the burns, streams, and rivers ran, dried out and by the action of the winds were formed into dunes, ridges, and knolls, and denes, gullies, and hollows, of varying height, width, and depth.

In the course of nature these channel-threaded wastes became the resting, nesting, and breeding places for birds. This meant bird droppings and so guano or manure, which, with the silt brought down by the birds, streams, and rivers, formed tilth in which the seeds blown from inland and regurgitated from the crops of the birds germinated and established vegetation. Thus eventually the whole of these areas became grass-covered, from the coarse marram on the exposed dunes, ridges, and hillocks and the finer bents and fescues in the sheltered dunes, gullies, and hollows, to the meadow grasses round and about the river estuaries and the mouths of the streams and burns. Out of the spreading and intermingling of all these grasses which followed was

established the thick, close-growing, hard-wearing sward that is such a feature of true links turf wherever it is found.

After getting the grass started, Sir Guy goes on to relate how, successively, heather and whins and broom took root on the linksland; rabbits were attracted to start warrens there; foxes came down the runs to hunt the rabbits; man came down to hunt the foxes; and, later, when golf was just starting up and man was looking for the most suitable place to play it, the links was the obvious solution. Incidentally, a rough version of the Old course at St Andrews had been established by 1414, the year that St Andrews University, the oldest in Scotland, came into existence.

I was thinking about this extended essay by Sir Guy one day in the spring of 1958, I think it was, when I was en route to a resort in northern Virginia, called the Tides Inn, where Sir Guy was in the process of building a nine-hole course. By that time he was well into his seventies. Behind him lay a colourful career: Eton (where he had captained the cricket team); golf (he was a semi-finalist in the British Amateur in 1907); the military (I think I remember his having served as a colonel with the British Army in India in the Khyber Pass country); golf writing and other journalism; golf course architecture (he was best known for his work on Deal, Killarney, Rye, West Sussex, and the new Prince's, which he restored in collaboration with John Morrison); and soldiering again (though close to fifty-five when World War II broke out, he managed to rejoin the King's Royal Rifle Corps as a second-lieutenant). On the flight to Richmond that day, as I say, I found myself thinking about Sir Guy's piece on the birth of linksland golf, and, proceeding from

Beyond the beautiful contours of its lush fairway, the green at Augusta National's 11th hole nestles hard by Rae's Creek. "When the course was formally opened in January, 1933, there were only about thirty bunkers . . . and no rough to speak of. Its challenge lay in the imaginative use made of its wonderful rolling terrain and the creeks that crossed its lower stretches."

that I began to muse about the slow, curious, often muddled stages by which golf architecture had developed down through the centuries to the then present day when Sir Guy, a man whose permanent residence had long been St Andrews, was trying to come up with nine acceptable holes on a not too promising tract of land in Virginia that resembled linksland about as closely as you and I resemble Cary Grant at his peak. Those musings, among other things, touched on the following phases of golf course architecture during the past century and a quarter:

O How, shortly after the gutta-percha ball replaced the feather ball in the middle of the nineteenth century, blind golf holes were thought to be the last word in golf architecture. As a result, Prestwick, the proud possessor of the Himalayas (the short 5th) and the Alps (the long two-shot 17th)—on both of them the green is hidden behind a Brobdingnagian sand-dune—was regarded in the golf world as the *crème de la crème.*

O How, as the game spread throughout Britain and around the globe towards the end of the century, the top professionals became the busiest golf course architects. There followed a deplorable period of geometric, non-natural design which featured square tees, bunkers that ran the width of a fairway in a straight line, and "gun platform greens" guarded by mounds shaped like chocolate drops. (Many golf champions have proved to have a true talent for golf architecture, but it ain't necessarily so.)

O How the happy discovery was made near the turn of the century that the copious unused stretches of sand and heather and fir outside London could be transformed into splendid courses, such as Walton Heath and Sunningdale. The porosity of the soil was a key factor. On many of the earlier inland courses built in England, the loamy earth tended to compact tightly in cold weather, and pools of water regularly collected in the fairways.

O How, shortly after the turn of the century, thanks to the tardy recognition that artificial design had no merit at all, golf course architecture came to be regarded as a respectable and useful profession. There followed in Britain a return to courses that emphasized the natural and the simple. Concomitantly, this led to a much better understanding of the principles of "strategic" architecture. In a word, the essence of a strategically designed hole is that the more accurately a golfer places his tee shot, the better his position for his approach shot to the green. Or conversely, the greater a golfer's degree of error on any shot, the more difficult the ensuing shot. A strategically designed hole encourages a golfer to take chances—to cut corners, fly hazards, go for the pin—rewarding him if he accepts a dangerous challenge and pulls it off, and punishing him when he doesn't, in a fair ratio.

O How, when the rubber-cored ball replaced the gutta-percha ball early in this century, holes had to be lengthened. In the view of H. N. Wethered and Tom Simpson, just as the gutta-percha ball had shortened the "feather holes" 20 per cent, the rubber-cored ball shortened the "gutty holes" 20 per cent.

O How in the United States, even after Macdonald's National had dramatized the virtues of strategic design so memorably, a strange vogue set in for "penal" design. Briefly, the essence of penal golf architecture is its insistence that a golfer follow the narrow route ordained for him to travel from tee to green. He is penalized severely if he makes only a mild error—his ball will end up in one of the plethora of deep bunkers that punctuate the fairway and protect the green. The pasha of penal courses, Oakmont, outside Pittsburgh, at one time found room for over 200 bunkers and twenty-one traversing ditches. Penal architecture violates that cardinal rule of enlightened design: a first-class hole should present the player with an alternate route—or alternate routes—to the green. One man who preached this gospel, and who practised what he preached, was Donald Ross, a transplanted Scot from Dornoch who became the resident professional and architect at Pinehurst, the famous spa in the Sandhills country of North Carolina. During his distinguished career, Ross designed, or helped to design, over six hundred courses in the United States, stretching from the Northland Country Club in Duluth to the Seminole Golf Club in North Palm Beach.

O How the most important contribution, perhaps, of the renowned course at the Augusta National Golf Club, which Bobby Jones designed in collaboration with Dr Alister Mackenzie, the noted Scottish architect, was that, as the home of the Masters, it demonstrated forcibly and handsomely the superiority of strategic design to penal design. For instance, when the course was formally opened in January 1933, there were only about thirty bunkers on the eighteen holes, and no rough to speak of. Its challenge lay in the imaginative use made of its wonderful rolling terrain and the creeks that crossed its lower stretches. Like every great course, the Augusta National could be set up so that, from the back tees, it was a formidable test for the leading professionals and, from the regular tees, a layout which the average golfer could handle and enjoy. Through no fault of its own, the Augusta National—the most influential course built in the United States since Macdonald's National—had one unfortunate effect on American golf. It started a trend towards mammoth-sized greens which, in the years following World War II, became epidemic. At the Augusta National the very large greens looked right and played right since they fitted in with the overall heroic scale of the course, but it is hard to think of another American course where they seem natural and improve the playing qualities of the holes. (It is pleasant to report that a swing back to the small green is now under way.)

O How, during the affluent post-war period, when a good number of American architects were given the financial backing, time, land, and support (not to mention vastly improved grass strains, better irrigational methods, and all the rest of the advances in knowledge and technique) to build courses of championship standard, more often than not they funked it, chiefly because of their preoccupation with making as much money as possible, which meant becoming involved in as many as twenty ▷

▷ projects simultaneously. Consequently, what should have been a Golden Age of Golf Architecture yielded little beyond that rhinestone jewel of a thought: the mistaken concept that a course over 7,000 yards in length is automatically a championship course—and that the first tour tournament played over it is automatically entitled to call itself a Classic.

○ How, today, we still have our problems—two in the main. The first is that here in the United States, anyway, it now takes almost five and a half hours to play a round of golf, and heaven knows the panacea for this. The second is that the inordinate distance the ranking pros hit their shots, due to more powerful clubs and livelier balls, has now reached the point where many of the celebrated championship courses no longer provide a bona fide test. In the 1970 British Open, at St Andrews, for example, the opening round was played on a windless day, and, as a result, just about half the field broke or equalled par. On the next three days, fortuitously, a brisk wind blew in from the west, and the Old course again became a sturdy test of a player's shot-making ability. Today, unless a good wind is roaming the countryside, none of the courses on the British Open rota provides a fitting examination for the best players, and in the United States, unless steps are taken to specifically tighten up a course for the Open (and provided it doesn't rain), the same situation obtains. However, with the adoption of the ODS—the Overall Distance Standard for Golf Balls—help is on the way.

Well, back to Sir Guy Campbell standing in the alien corn in northern Virginia. He was looking well, I thought. His white hair glistened in the sun, and his blue eyes gleamed with vitality. He was wearing a sort of bush jacket, a multi-pocket affair made of khaki cloth, which brought to mind such folk heroes as Sir Guy Standing and C. Aubrey Smith, who had flourished so unforgettably on the Northwest Frontier. Without much ado, Sir Guy whisked me out to see his nine holes. They had reached a stage of sufficient advancement—the fairways were cleared, the hazards roughed out, the greens outlined—where a golf-architecture buff like myself had no trouble reading Sir Guy's intentions clearly.

For some odd reason, though I thought that Sir Guy had certainly gotten the most that was possible out of his limiting tract of land, only three holes remain fixed in my memory, one of them—the 1st—principally because it was an enigma. The terrain dictated that it be a short par-four of about 340 yards. That's fair enough: nothing wrong with starting out with a short four to give a golfer a chance to get himself unwound before he faces the stern stuff. After all, the starting hole on the Old course is only 370 yards long. However, whereas the 1st on the Old course presents some pawky problems—there is out-of-bounds along the right, and the Swilcan Burn separates the fairway from the green—the terrain on Sir Guy's first hole was pretty banal, and he was dissatisfied with all of the ideas for turning it into an interesting hole which he had tossed around. For example, he didn't want a golfer to be able to swat away freely off the tee—that would leave him only a little flip for his second; on the other hand, he didn't want to toughen up the hole by introducing some strident fairway bunkering about 230 yards out—one doesn't like to make a golfer lay up short of a hazard off any tee or to call on him to hit a powerful enough opening drive to carry a major hazard.

We must have sketched out and rejected more than fifteen plans for dealing with that first hole during the two days we walked and studied Sir Guy's nine holes. It was heartening to see him in such a happy mood, for he was positively intrigued by his problems and was looking forward eagerly to the next day's work. I mention this because there is something magical about working with earth, especially when you are shaping it into holes for a stimulating, many-sided game like golf.

My two-day visit with Sir Guy, in which he fussed with one small detail after another, also served to clarify for me why so many of the acknowledgedly great American courses have been built by amateur architects—Oakmont (love it or leave it) by Henry C. and W. C. Fownes, steel magnates; Merion by Hugh Wilson, an insurance broker; Pine Valley by George Crump, a hotelier; and Pebble Beach (which may be the best course in the world) by Jack Neville, a real-estate salesman who never built another course on his own. As amateur architects they were able to lavish on their projects the countless hours, the perfectionistic fervour and the plain love that distinguishes the fine arts from lesser efforts.

This does not mean that professional architects do not occasionally give as much of themselves to their courses, but all too frequently, because of the crush of their schedules, the success or failure of their designs depends on how well they are executed by the construction superintendent. (One hears it was an inspired local superintendent who made Mackenzie's Royal Melbourne such a magnificent layout, and one suspects that a similarly superior superintendent followed through on Mackenzie's Cypress Point.) There really is no substitute, though, for the architect's staying with the job himself and employing the most effective and not the quickest means to achieve the tiny touches that make exceptional holes exceptional. When Donald Ross was remodelling Pinehurst Number 2 in the mid-1930s and making it, among other things, into the finest chipping course on the continent by the fastidiousness with which he fashioned the little knolls and valleys in the green areas, he eschewed tractors and other such machinery—they couldn't have done the job. He used "drag pans" drawn by mules. I once asked Dick Tufts, of the old Pinehurst family, to explain how this operation worked, and his description went as follows:

Those drag pans were sort of like the blade of a broad, flat sugar scoop with two handles attached to the back. When these handles were raised a little by the operator, the front edge of the pan picked up a thin slice of soil or a deeper slice, depending on how high the handles were raised. When the pan was full, the handles were lowered and the scoop full of earth could be dragged to where it was to be dumped. The handles were then lifted almost straight up, and the dirt could be dumped all in one place or spilled gradually over a wider area. Donald used to use five or ten mules, usually moving in a rough circle, scooping up the soil here and dumping it there, as he directed them. You will see that this enabled him to model the surface of the green into exactly the slopes, hollows and ridges that he wanted. I do not know how this can be accomplished as exactly with modern equipment.

This is probably the point at which to collect ourselves and ask, "Why all this concern about what makes for good golf architecture? What

does good golf architecture accomplish?" The answer, I think, might well begin with the statement that the average golfer, no different from a Sam Snead or a Mickey Wright or a Gary Player, feels in his bones whether or not a hole is laid out correctly and possesses true shot values, just as a child of, say, four, knows instinctively who is a handsome man and who is a beautiful woman and who isn't. Both the average golfer and the champion golfer enjoy playing a sound, enticing, well-conditioned hole much more than a bland one, because a good hole makes it absolutely clear to golfers of all degrees of skill what shots he should play from tee to green and how he should handle the green. Consequently, when a golfer is able to execute the shots that are called for, the pleasure he experiences is far greater than when he merely manages to hit a fine shot on an indifferent hole—though, I hasten to add, any time a golfer hits a fine shot, the satisfaction is considerable. In golf, because of the nature of the game, a beautiful hole is not one that has a lovely stream flowing across it. It is a hole that has a lovely stream flowing across it at the right place. It would be wrong to deny that a golf course benefits from a charming setting, but a beautiful golf course is one whose beauty is as functional as L'Enfant's Washington and Haussmann's Paris.

As goes without saying, a good course is one where the fundamentals are right: where the implicit strategy of each individual hole is apparent to the golfer as he stands on the tee; where, as John Low put it long ago, "the ground determines the play"; where the hazards are frankly visible (always allowing for the exception to every rule that is the Old course); where there is a judicious variety of fairway lies; where the holes do not present the wrong sort of difficulty—the kind that skill cannot cope with —but, rather, possess a beckoning spirit of adventure, like the cliffside holes at Ballybunion in County Limerick or at Turnberry in Strathclyde; where the routeing of the holes is both thoughtful and appealing, like at Muirfield, where the first nine moves in a clockwise arc outside the counter-clockwise pattern of the second nine, and like at the Augusta National, where one does not encounter two holes with

"A good course is one where the fundamentals are right ... where the hazards are frankly visible ... where the holes do not present the wrong sort of difficulty —the kind that skill cannot cope with—but, rather, possess a beckoning spirit of adventure." The quality of the 8th at Muirfield Village, its green an emerald island in the sand, is readily apparent from the tees.

the same par back to back until the 9th and the 10th, two par-fours; where the greens offer plenty of diversity in the way they are positioned, shaped, and contoured; and where, when all is said and done, the raison d'être of the course is the suitableness of the land for golf—Kasumigaseki, in Japan, is an outstanding example— and not the necessity of winding nine or eighteen pseudo-golf holes through a grove of new, high-rise condominiums whose management has advertised, "A championship golf course lies literally at your door."

Just as the delight of playing golf depends so critically on the quality of the course, so, too, as we have touched on briefly, does the pleasure and excitement of watching the game's virtuosos in action in the big international events. We all know they can "hit the ball a ton" and play it high, low, left-to-right, right-to-left, straight, soft, hard—the works. What we don't know is whether they can come through with the shot that is called for when they are confronted with an arresting challenge when the pressure is on. The top courses present these challenges hole after hole, and this is why for just about a century now people who appreciate golf have turned out in large numbers to watch the championships.

For example, let's say the year is 1896 and we are at Muirfield following a young man named Harry Vardon, who has never done anything much, play the 72nd hole of the British Open. It is a long two-shotter, over four hundred yards to a raised green, on which the crucial hazard is a bunker with an intimidatingly steep front wall that lies in wait just before the green. J. H. Taylor, the defending champion, is in with a total of 316. Vardon has driven well. If he can get his four, that will give him a total of 315, but the trouble is that this means he will have to carry the bunker, almost two hundred yards away, with his second, and that might mean ending up with a buried lie in the face of the bunker and, eventually, with a total of 317. What a moment! Vardon, after much cogitation, elects to lay up short of the beast, make certain of his five, and take his chances on beating Taylor in a play-off. The next day he went out and won the first of his six British Opens.

As the old saying goes, behind each successful champion stands a provocative, soundly strategic course which imposes difficult decisions and sometimes elicits historic shots. Let me describe three other such dramatic moments that come quickly to mind.

The Inwood Country Club on Long Island, the 1923 United States Open. Bobby Jones, who had thrown the Open away the day before by taking a double-bogey six on the 72nd and therewith allowing Bobby Cruickshank to tie him, stands all even in their eighteen-hole play-off as they come to the home hole: 425 yards long, trees hemming in the fairway, the green set beyond a lagoon. The door opens for Jones— Cruickshank has hooked his drive and must lay up short of the water hazard. Jones's drive has finished on loose, pebbly dirt at the right-hand edge of the fairway. Now he faces a problem. Should he lay up safely short of the water, or should he risk it all, touchy lie or not, and go for it? He reaches for his mid iron (or 2-iron) and sets up carefully. Then he moves into that deceptively easy swing with its full body turn, makes clean contact with the ball, and sends it flying in a high parabola towards the flag 190 yards away. He watches it carry the lagoon, come down on the green, and roll to within six feet of the hole. The Age of Jones has begun.

Merion, outside Philadelphia, the sun beginning to haze out late on the last day of the 1950 US Open. Wonder of wonders: sixteen months after the automobile accident that almost cost him his life, Ben Hogan is back. Not only is he back, but if he can play the last seven holes in two over par, he will win the Open. The strain begins to tell, however. Bogeys on the 66th and the 69th. Another on the 71st. Now, in order to tie George Fazio and Lloyd Mangrum and qualify for the play-off, he must make his par-four on the 72nd, a rough 458-yarder on which the drive must be rifled down a fairly narrow chute and the long second shot hit so that the ball will have the proper rotation and not scoot on over the mildly elevated green. An easy hole to play rather well and still miss one's par. Hogan's drive is perfect, but it does leave him with a somewhat downhill lie. No, a fairway wood is out of the question. Too hard to stop it. What is the right club to play in order to reach and hold that elusive green? Hogan ponders his choice a bit longer than is customary for him and then settles on a 2-iron. Ready to go now. Into the shot, so perfectly on balance that he could have been making a practice swing on the practice tee. The ball streaks in a low trajectory for the left side of the green and deviates not an inch in its flight. It lands on the green and, having been struck so correctly, sits down nicely. Ben holes out in two putts for his four. The next day he defeats Fazio and Mangrum in their play-off. He is back, to say the least.

Muirfield, the 1966 British Open, seventy years after Vardon's break-through victory. Final round. Jack Nicklaus, who has never won the championship, may have lost another wonderful chance. Leading the field by three strokes with only nine holes to go, he has tossed them away by missing his pars on the 65th, the 67th, and the 68th. Pars on the next two. To win, he now needs a birdie and a par—probably in that order, since the 528-yard 71st offers a golfer with Jack's tremendous length a good crack at a four. It's an odd hole, the 17th or 71st. The tee shot is a blind one, up and over a rising fairway which breaks to the left—bunkers in the elbow. Far away in the distance, as you walk to your ball after your drive, you take in the small, old-fashioned green, half-hidden by a rugged ridge which thrusts itself out into the fairway from the right a hundred yards or so from the green. Today, the wind is out of the west, directly behind Nicklaus off the tee. Accordingly, he decides to go with a 3-iron instead of the 1-iron he used on the first three rounds. He whacks his tee shot—following wind, small British ball, remember—a full 290 yards down the right side of the fairway. All right, where do we go from here? Wind— from off the left and a little behind. Lie—all that one could ask for. Jack decides on a 5-iron and takes aim on the left side of the green. If he flies the ball all the way to the green, it won't hold the resilient surface. He wants to bounce it on—hence the 5-iron. His swing is very smoothly executed. Yes, he's played an extremely good-looking, high-arcing shot. The ball lands in the narrow channel of fairway about six yards short of the green, gets a nice slow bounce, and finishes about twenty feet from the pin. It is the winning shot, in effect. Nicklaus cozies the ball up close to the cup and gets that all-important birdie. On the tough 72nd, two more superlative irons—a 1-iron and a 3-iron banked into the wind coming off the right—and the par-four that wraps up his first victory in the British Open.

On the great courses, it is a great game— quite possibly, as several million golfers claim, the best game that has ever been invented.

The yardages quoted throughout this book for courses and for individual holes are from the championship tees unless otherwise specified. Within the descriptive text they have on occasion, for reasons of clarity, been rounded up or down.

Europe

Born, cradled and nurtured on the wild coasts of Scotland, golf is native to the British Isles and an exotic plant everywhere else—although, like many exotics it has often found conditions even more to its liking where it has been imported. Scotland's pride are the natural links where time and the seasons were the principal architects of courses like Royal Dornoch, that noble links of the north, and the austere, patriarchal St Andrews, the shrine to which the greatest still return to pay homage. Golf began its travels when it was taken south to England by the Stuarts and then to the four corners of the earth by the men of both nations in the Empire-building days of the nineteenth century. Progress was tardy on the European mainland, where even now clubs number only a third of the 2,000 or so that thrive in Britain. Among the earliest of courses on the Continent of Europe were those built during Queen Victoria's reign at watering places to which the wealthy British migrated annually to take the cure: spas like Baden-Baden in Germany, Karlovy Vary and Marienbad in Czechoslovakia (then a realm of the Hapsburgs), and Pau, in the foothills of the Pyrenees, the earliest of them all (1856). Most progress, outside Britain, has been made in northern Europe—the Low Countries (where there are echoes of Scottish linksland), Sweden and Germany, which each have more than a hundred courses. Changing patterns of wealth and tourism have seen the emergence recently of new seaside courses like Vilamoura and Sotogrande at Europe's other extreme, the Mediterranean and Atlantic coastlines of the Iberian Peninsula. Similar in appearance and atmosphere to the resort courses of North America, they have been built as commercial developments by entrepreneurs and have had the benefit of some of the best architects that money can buy. Their sunlit, Sybaritic ambience seems a world away from the windswept linksland of the Scottish coast where the game took root, almost organically, as part of the life of small, tightly knit communities.

1 St Andrews
2 Carnoustie
3 Royal Dornoch
4 Muirfield
5 Turnberry
6 Royal Liverpool
7 Royal Lytham & St Annes
8 Sunningdale
9 Royal Birkdale
10 Ganton
11 Royal St George's
12 Royal Porthcawl
13 Royal County Down
14 Royal Portrush
15 Portmarnock
16 Killarney
17 Kennemer
18 Royal Antwerp
19 Falsterbo
20 Club Zur Vahr
21 Olgiata
22 Chantilly
23 Nueva Andalucia
24 Sotogrande
25 Vilamoura

Nature fashions an ageless masterpiece

For centuries, the eyes and thoughts of golfers everywhere have turned towards St Andrews: in all their world there is nothing to compare with the ancient university city and the Old course spreading away from its doors. Here is the very heart of golf, the very breath of its history on links that, for countless ages, have known so little change. Every golfer there ever was has wanted to play at St Andrews, and down the years it has attracted more pilgrims than any other course in the world.

At first sight, the Old course may not seem remarkable. One will have been charmed by the intimacy of its approaches from within the city and the beauty of the spacious rectangle of green, sweeping down from the Royal and Ancient clubhouse, grey, four-square and slightly forbidding. On one side are the smaller clubs, Old Tom Morris's shop, hotels and houses; on the other a rolling sward of putting green and, beyond, the superb bay, leagues and leagues of golden sand curving away towards the distant estuary of the Tay. The Old links has

The 1st tee and the 18th green of the Old course at St Andrews are overlooked by the headquarters of the Royal and Ancient Golf Club, which came into existence in 1754. Ten years later it decreed that the number of holes on the Old course should be reduced from twenty-two to eighteen, an arrangement that became standard when the club later emerged as the arbiter of all that was correct in golf.

Royal and Ancient Golf Club of St Andrews, Fife

Old course

Out	3,528 yards	36
In	3,432 yards	36
Total	6,960 yards	par 72

Record: 65, Neil Coles, The Open 1970

been condemned as an anachronism and cursed as being unfair, but no course has commanded greater affection and respect from those who have learned to appreciate its subtleties and charms. It can be as tantalizing as a beautiful woman, whose smile at once is a temptation and a snare, concealing heartbreak and frustration for some, joy and fulfilment for others, but possession only for the very fortunate few. It does not yield its ancient secrets lightly or take kindly to contempt and impatience, but it does reward those who give their best in thought, temper and technique.

Furthermore, St Andrews is the setting for the Royal and Ancient Club. It was founded on May 14, 1754, when twenty-two "Noblemen and Gentlemen, being admirers of the ancient and healthful exercise of the Golf", met to subscribe for a silver club, to be the trophy of an annual competition. Since then its sphere of influence has become almost universal, except in the United States, which has its own governing body in the USGA.

There is no telling when golf began at St Andrews, but the earliest written evidence was a licence, issued in 1552, which permitted the

Card of the course

No 1	Burn	370 yards	par 4	No 10	Bobby Jones	342 yards	par 4
No 2	Dyke	411 yards	par 4	No 11	High (in)	172 yards	par 3
No 3	Cartgate (out)	398 yards	par 4	No 12	Heathery (in)	316 yards	par 4
No 4	Ginger Beer	463 yards	par 4	No 13	Hole o'Cross (in)	425 yards	par 4
No 5	Hole o'Cross (out)	564 yards	par 5	No 14	Long	567 yards	par 5
No 6	Heathery (out)	416 yards	par 4	No 15	Cartgate (in)	413 yards	par 4
No 7	High (out)	372 yards	par 4	No 16	Corner of the Dyke	382 yards	par 4
No 8	Short	178 yards	par 3	No 17	Road	461 yards	par 4
No 9	End	356 yards	par 4	No 18	Tom Morris	354 yards	par 4

The Old course at St Andrews, shaped like a shepherd's crook, is nothing less than the golfing shrine for the entire world. Golfers who have never seen Britain's shores know St Andrews' bunkers by name—Students and College between the 3rd and the 4th, or the more emotive Coffin, Cat's Trap and Lion's Mouth between the 12th and 13th. But St Andrews is not unrelenting; the tempting green expanse of fairway at the 14th is known as the Elysian Fields.

Among these golfers on the 1st tee at St Andrews are two of the greatest players of their age. The boy is Jamie Anderson, three times winner of the Open in the 1870s; on his left is Allan Robertson, whose death in 1859 is said to have brought the Open into being as others sought an official version of the crown that had been indisputably his.

The memorial to Young Tom Morris at St Andrew's Cathedral. The inscription reads: "Deeply regretted by numerous friends and all golfers, he thrice in succession won the championship belt and held it without rivalry and yet without envy, his many amiable qualities being no less admired than his golfing achievements."

community to rear rabbits on the links, and "play at golf, futball, schuteing . . . with all other manner of pastimes". The proprietor was bound "not to plough up any part of said golf links in all time coming" but to reserve them for the comfort and amusement of the inhabitants. So, for more than 400 years, every golfer has enjoyed a right to play over the course, and only within the present century has a modest green fee been imposed. The Old course remains a monument to the origins of golf as a game played on links by the sea. In the beginning it knew no architect but nature; it came into being by evolution rather than design; and on no other course is the hand of man less evident.

In all the years since the Royal and Ancient Club was formed, the outline of the course has never changed. It was then no more than 40 yards wide, a rolling strip of linksland between the gorse bushes in the shape of a huge billhook. There was not room for separate holes going out and home, so the golfers played eleven (later nine), out to a distant turn by the shining waters of the Eden estuary, and returned using the same fairways and greens.

St Andrews must have had its perilous

moments in those days—and it still can, for seven of the double greens remain—but nowadays there is more delay than danger on a crowded day. The double greens are so huge that only an extremely wayward shot will find its way on to another man's province. If so, the player can face a length of putt undreamed of on any other course in the world. Nowhere does the old excuse for an indifferent score of taking three putts hold less water. The man in search of sympathy for such failings is an optimist; he is saying, in effect, that his golf through the green was prodigal in its length and direction.

The greens are further evidence of nature's bounty; most of them are on plateaus, sometimes only slightly raised above the level of their surrounds but plateaus none the less. When the wind stands firm and the turf is hard and swift, the man who pitches to the hole can be lost; the pitch and run or the plain running approach must be used, though such conditions nowadays are the exception rather than the rule at St Andrews. In common with many other links it has lost something of its seaside character; the grass on the fairways is richer, the greens more holding than of old. Often enough, it is

possible to pitch to them and low scoring is easier in consequence. When the Open was there in 1964, Nicklaus played the course twice on the final day in 134 strokes yet still gained only four on Tony Lema, who won the contest with commanding ease.

Another remarkable feature of the course is the multitude of bunkers, most of which are named, ranging from vast sandy caverns to little holes of varying depth often allowing room only for an "angry man and his niblick". All are natural, many are relics of the days when people dug for shells deposited by the sea before the links were formed, while others were made by sheep sheltering from the wind. Over the years great numbers were filled, but enough remain to test and infuriate the mightiest, because they are not always visible and seem to lurk in the most unexpected places.

Lying within the curve of a bay on the northeastern shores of Fife, the course is vulnerable to every caprice of the wind. Many are those who have played to the turn against it and then, hoping for assistance on the homeward journey, had to face it all the way back. The strategy of play can change within the ▷

The 17th: 461 yards par 4

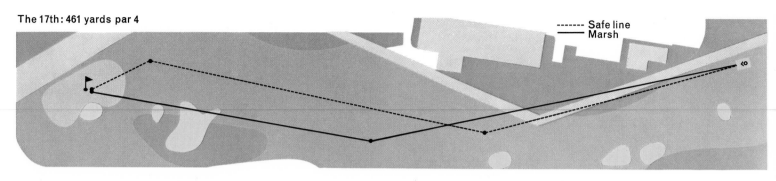

- - - - - Safe line
——— Marsh

The 17th: The winning of the Walker Cup

When England's David Marsh stood on the 17th fairway on a May evening in 1971, he was one up on Bill Hyndman of the United States and knew that if he could halve the hole and become dormy the Walker Cup was won. His drive was slightly to the left of centre of the fairway; he had some 220 yards to go to the flag. The light breeze, from right to left, was helping slightly so he took a 3-iron, aiming to pitch the ball short and hoping it would run up the bank of the green on to the top level.

In spite of the awesome pressure, and the clamorous excitement mounting all around him, Marsh played the shot exactly as he intended. The ball pitched about fifteen yards short of the green and came to rest twenty-five feet short of the flag, a comfortable distance of two putts for his team's victory. The stroke was the greater because he had to wait before playing and faced a frighteningly narrow margin of error. A fractional pull might finish in the Road bunker or, possibly, leave it between him and the hole; a slice, push or overhit could mean death on the Road, and any kind of mishit could open the door for Hyndman—whose shot, in fact, just failed to mount the bank of the slightly raised green.

At such moments, once having decided the shape and type of shot, the golfer can but trust his swing, making it as smooth as possible and his concentration absolute. Unless the shot is clearly visualized the odds are that it will not succeed. Obviously both Hyndman and Marsh knew what they were about and had faith in their swings.

*The Road bunker cut
into the 17th green.*

The 17th: A splash shot of the utmost delicacy

The Road bunker on the 17th has probably ruined more cards than any other in the world. It has also seen many heroic strokes, none more so, in the cruelly ironic fashion of the fates, than that played by Doug Sanders in the fourth round of the Open in 1970. The ball lay well in the sand, but the bunker is small, its face steep and the hole only a few yards beyond it. A splash shot of the utmost delicacy, one that would feather the ball over the lip and make it land softly, was demanded of him. A fraction too much sand or too little could be fatal. For such strokes it is essential to complete the backswing, when the instinct of most golfers is to make it short and hurried. Sanders played it beautifully and his four was safe.

▷ hour. Such are the whereabouts of the hazards that the slightest variations in the wind can mean the difference between being trapped in an infuriating little bunker and having a straightforward shot to the green. There is no standard way of playing the holes, except for the first and the last. Everything depends on the wind; an approach may be a brassie one day, a short pitch the next. Because of this no distances are given on the tees, a fact that visitors, particularly Americans, may find disturbing. But the information anyway would be of little use to them.

The Old course makes a wonderful play on courage and fear but, above all, it is an examination of a golfer's thinking: he can never relax. In view of this it is not surprising that nearly all the great golfers throughout the ages have grown to respect the place, and some, like Bobby Jones, to love it. With Jones it was not love at first sight. In the third round of the 1921

Open he was a dozen or more strokes over par and, after taking six on the short 11th, tore up his card. The world knows how he redeemed that failure with a famous victory six years later, and another in the Amateur championship, the first stage of the "Grand Slam" in his imperishable summer of 1930.

When, almost thirty years later, Jones was given the freedom of St Andrews and made an Honorary Burgess of the city—a distinction not conferred upon an American since Benjamin Franklin—he said: "The more I studied the Old course, the more I loved it and the more I loved it, the more I studied it, so that I came to feel that it was for me the most favourable meeting ground possible for an important contest. I felt that my knowledge of the course enabled me to play it with patience and restraint until she might exact her toll from my adversary, who might treat her with less respect and understanding."

The beginning of the course seems innocence itself. The widest fairway in existence—shared by the first and last holes—looks inviting, but at its limit winds the Swilcan Burn, an immediate menace to peace of mind for it must be carried by the shot to the 1st green, and this invariably is longer than it looks. From the 2nd tee the long trail outwards begins down the narrow ribbon, perhaps a hundred yards across, of crumpled, saffron links, broken only by the emerald pools of the double greens and the countless folds, falls and hummocks of the ageless land. This second hole is a perfect example of the course at its best, especially when the flag is towards the left of the green. The only reasonable approach is from the right, so either the drive risks bunkers and gorse or the second shot must be played to the right-hand part of the green, leaving a long and formidable putt.

The problem at the 3rd is the same—a

The 18th: To pitch or run?

Many, wise in the ways of the Old course, must have wondered why Doug Sanders chose to pitch to the 18th green in the final round of the 1970 Open instead of using the classic method of the pitch and run. Unless the ground is heavy and slow this is usually the safer shot. The overwhelming concern in this situation is not to fall short in the insidious grassy hollow of the Valley of Sin, from where it is simplicity itself to take three putts, as Jack Nicklaus had done only a few moments earlier.

Although Sanders was more accomplished than most Americans in shaping the kind of shots needed on a links course he decided to pitch. He later said: "The ball jumped off my sand wedge a bit." It finished some thirty feet above the hole, from where the putt looks more downhill than it is, and he left himself short to be finally deceived by the well-nigh invisible left-to-right break on his second putt. As irony would have it, in the play-off next day Sanders, then one behind Nicklaus, approached in the traditional fashion, hitting a perfect running shot with a 4-iron. But it was too late, for Nicklaus was able to match his birdie three to win by one stroke.

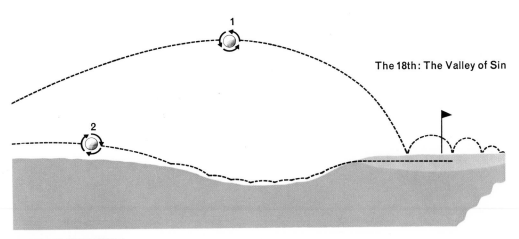

The 18th: The Valley of Sin

Doug Sanders settles himself before making a perfect pitch and run to the 18th green in his playoff against Jack Nicklaus for the 1970 British Open.

Doug Sanders's approach shots at the 18th in the 1970 Open, *above.* In the final round Sanders chose to pitch over the grassy hollow of the Valley of Sin, which can be seen, *below,* at the front left hand corner of the 18th green. His pitch shot (1) was hit with loft and landed, as he intended, close to the pin, but, despite the backspin, the ball failed to stop. The following day, from a similar position, Sanders hit a classic pitch-and-run shot with top-spin (2) through the Valley of Sin and up to the pin.

measure of risk must be taken from the tee for a clear pitch to the pin; likewise at the 4th, with its drive along a valley between a plateau and the inevitable gorse and bunkers on the right. A host of bunkers awaits the drive to the 5th which is aimed too straight at the distant pin; this is the Hole o'Cross, the longest of all, which forces a decision whether to attempt to carry a hill with two large bunkers in its face or play short, leaving a longish third to the green. In the 1933 Open, with the ground bone-hard and a gale behind him, Craig Wood drove into one of these bunkers, almost a quarter of a mile from the tee. A slight ridge protects the sixth green and makes the approach seem shorter than it is, a common feature of the Old course. The stranger is forever underclubbing.

The next six holes form what is commonly known as the Loop, where the foundation of low scores invariably is made; on occasion they have been played in eighteen strokes or less.

The drive to the 7th is one of the most testing—practically blind, with a sea of gorse to punish the slice—but the 8th is not a severe short hole. Good drives make threes readily possible at the next two holes, but the little approach to the 9th is dead flat. It has caught many a player in two minds as to whether to pitch or run it, and has often resulted in a scuffle.

Of all the great short holes, the 11th stands high. The green is on a considerable slope, with the waters of Eden beyond; to the left is the deep Hill bunker. The essence of the shot is to avoid these and yet not to have a fiendishly difficult putt. To finish above the hole with the wind off the estuary is to invite three putts; men have been known to putt off the green. Gene Sarazen once took six there, with three shots in the Hill bunker, and eventually lost the championship by one stroke.

There never was a hole more obviously the work of the Devil than the 12th, where seeming innocence conceals all manner of evil. However well one knows the hole, it is hard to realize that so much danger exists between tee and green, only some 300 yards away. None of it is visible, but the fairway, a gentle green slope, is infested with bunkers.

After the 13th, with its second over broken, heathery hills, the task is stern indeed. No single hole in golf has brought more championship competitors to grief than the 14th; the number of great golfers who have taken sevens and worse there is legion. In any kind of wind, save a helping one, the prospect from the back tee is fearsome indeed, with the five Beardies bunkers clustered together to trap the slightest pull and a low greystone wall jutting into the line from the right. Only the bold or the very strong attempt to carry the great Hell bunker and its attendants, and then remains the problem of judging the third shot over a sleek, steep bank. The 15th presents no great difficulty ▷

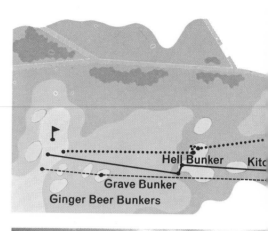

Doug Sanders ducks for cover as Jack Nicklaus's putter lands behind him. Nicklaus, a man not normally given to public displays of emotion, had thrown his putter aloft in elation, not so much at winning the 1970 British Open as at having done so over the famous Old course.

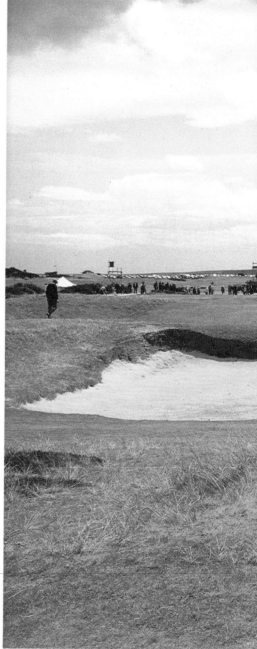

▷ apart from the wretched little Sutherland bunker, precisely on the cautious line from the tee. Long ago, one Green Committee ordered its removal, but rebels went in the night, opened it again and there it remains.

The confident or the unthinking will drive between the railway and the Principal's Nose bunker, a threateningly narrow approach to the 16th. The railway, whose fences remain, is nowadays out-of-bounds. But in olden days, when it was a cart track, golfers carried a track iron, one of which can be seen in the Royal and Ancient Museum. The prudent line from the tee is to the left, but the Wig bunker by the green must be avoided. Then at last the golfer stands on the tee of the most famous hole in the world.

The drive over the corner of the hotel grounds, where black railway sheds once stood, is not as alarming as it looks, but the green on a little plateau is an awesome sight. On the left, "eating its way into its very vitals" as Bernard Darwin once wrote, is the Road bunker, while beyond the narrow green is the road itself, at the foot of a sharp little shelf with nothing to prevent the ball rolling down. The second may be anything from wood to mid iron, but only the brave go for the top level of the green. The majority play short, but even the little approach is fraught with danger. The ground draws into the bunker, from where there is no more terrifying recovery, with the road awaiting any overhit.

Whatever may have befallen the golfer on the 17th the broad, guileless swoop of the last fairway is infinitely appealing. The drive can be aimed anywhere to the left; to slice out-of-bounds at this point would be lunacy indeed. Only the Valley of Sin, a smooth bowl which gathers the timid approach, remains to be avoided and so on to Tom Morris's green.

Always it seems there are people leaning from the windows and over the fences. Behind them rises the cloistered little city, grey, peaceful and so very old.

This was the setting for the most dramatic last hole the Open has known in modern times. When Doug Sanders, at the end of a torturous day of wind in 1970, hit a long drive up the last fairway, victory was there for the taking; he needed a four to beat Nicklaus. The task seemed only a formality but, as all the world knows, he took three putts, finally missing from a yard—and Nicklaus had enjoyed the escape of his lifetime.

In the play-off the following day Sanders bravely fought back from four behind to one as they stood on the last tee. Nicklaus, with an unconsciously masterful gesture, took off a sweater for greater freedom and unleashed a thunderous drive that almost hit the pin. It ran through the green into thick rough, from where he chipped to six feet. As the putt just curled in he flung his putter high in the air, a rare show of emotion for Nicklaus and a heartbreaking moment for Sanders.

Less than a year later the old green saw another triumph, closest of all to British and Irish hearts—victory in the Walker Cup for the first time since 1938. On the last afternoon they needed to win five and halve one of the singles. Michael Bonallack, whose captaincy had been a decisive factor, lost to Lanny Wadkins; but in the next six matches it was the Americans who proved vulnerable and the British who produced the telling strokes, playing with a confidence and control under pressure that few had believed possible. Four years afterwards there were no such heroics, and one of the strongest of all American teams was never in danger of losing command of the match.

The 14th: 567 yards par 5

····· Sarazen
—— Locke
----- Thomson

Fields

escent Bunker

Beardies

Hummocks, clad in typically tough, tussocky rough, hide the four bunkers of the dreaded Beardies which, together with an out-of-bounds area to the right, create a narrow opening to the uncharacteristically level fairway of the 14th. This tempting, trouble-free area, the Elysian Fields, is brought to an abrupt end about 440 yards from the tee by Hell bunker.

Hell bunker, which yawns so menacingly at the end of the Elysian Fields, forces the player to choose a right- or a left-hand line to the green and thereby court trouble of a different sort. The left side of the green is well protected by the Ginger Beer bunkers.

The 14th: An impressive list of victims

In Open after Open the 14th is the Old course's sternest line of defence. Because it can be so hard to play safe, it is invariably a hole to survive rather than to conquer. In 1939 Bobby Locke was five under par in the first round when his drive in a strong wind was pulled into one of the deadly Beardies, a cluster of four bunkers from where, unwisely using a 7-iron, he failed to emerge at the first attempt. He then hit his fourth shot with wood into Hell bunker and took an eight.

Locke had been severely punished for neglecting a fundamental rule. The ancient maxim of making sure of getting out of a bunker and forgetting about length is never more true than on the Old course.

The lesson also was forced home on Gene Sarazen in 1933. He was at the height of his powers and in good shape to retain the title he had won at Prince's the previous year but, in going for a birdie after a long drive into the Elysian Fields, he hit his brassie shot out of the heel. It swung in the left-hand wind and thudded into Hell. In striving to reach the green, a shot of a hundred yards or more, he caught his sand shot a shade thin and buried it in the wall of sand. An eight was completed with three putts and he finished only one stroke behind the tie between Craig Wood and Densmore Shute.

In 1955 Peter Thomson joined the 14th's mightily impressive list of victims but, unlike most, he survived disaster and triumphed. He was cruising to victory when his drive found the Beardies and his third the Grave which, with the Ginger Beer bunkers, awaits those who attempt the safe line to the left of Hell. He took a seven and his insurance strokes had gone but, in keeping with his remarkable poise, he hit a perfect shot to the 15th, made his birdie, and all was well again.

Character to test a champion's judgement

In common with most of the links courses of Scotland, the beginnings of golf at Carnoustie are a matter of legend and vague historical references. Early in the sixteenth century Sir Robert Maule, one of the first known golfers, delighted in exercising the "gowf" on the Barry links, adjoining Carnoustie on the northern shores of the Firth of Tay. The club was formed in 1842, in the early years of Victoria's reign, a prolific age for the birth of Scottish clubs; in 1867 the genius of Young Tom Morris first came to light there when, aged 16, he played against and defeated all comers. Almost ninety years later a golfer named Ben Hogan came to Carnoustie and confirmed, in a masterful act of supremacy, that he was the greatest player of the age.

Rarely can it be said of any course that it has no weakness, but this is true of Carnoustie. Every hole is different in character. Only three are short, and at no point during the round do more than two follow exactly the same direction. The problems set by the wind, therefore, are ever-changing—and furthermore Carnoustie lies on the flatlands between the estuary and the low, distant hills, so that judgement of distance is critical. In every way it is a big course, and even from the ordinary competition tees it is a test of golf for good players. Most of the hazards, which include the sinuous menace of the Barry Burn at several holes, are placed to threaten the stroke that is slightly less than perfect, rather than one that is slightly better than awful.

The evolution from the ten-hole course made by Allan Robertson in the middle of the nineteenth century was a long one. Even after the extension to eighteen holes under the guidance of Tom Morris it knew many changes, until in 1926 James Braid made some new greens, tees and bunkers. The result was a superb course. Within its general confines is another, smaller, eighteen-hole course—the Burnside—and both are held in trust by the town council, which provides members for a joint management committee with the four clubs that share the courses with one another.

Since the last years of the nineteenth century, almost 300 young men of Carnoustie have become professionals. A great number went to the United States and three of the most notable were the Smith brothers. The eldest, Willie, won the American Open in 1899; Alex was twice champion thereafter, but poor Macdonald always failed. In twelve years from 1923 he was second, third and fourth twice each in the British Open, and was runner-up to Bobby Jones in both his victories in 1930. No more distinguished golfer ever failed to win an Open.

The early development of American golf owes much of its strength to the men of Carnoustie. It is written that, at various times, every State title had been held by one of them. Stuart Maiden, famous mentor of Jones, Archie Simpson and many another, sought fame and fortune far from the great links that had brought forth their skills.

There is no gentle introduction to the course. From the long rise of the first fairway a considerable stroke is needed to reach a hidden basin of green. In his first round in the 1953 Open, Hogan used a 2-iron, searing into the fresh westerly wind. The next day he was home with a pitching club; each time the ball finished in the same place on the green. Controversy—particularly among professionals, many of

Carnoustie Golf Club, Tayside

Championship course
Out   3,546 yards   36
In   3,555 yards   36
Total 7,101 yards   par 72

Record: 65, Jack Newton, The Open 1975

Card of the course			
No 1	Cup	406 yards	par 4
No 2	Gulley	464 yards	par 4
No 3	Jockie's Burn	384 yards	par 4
No 4	Hillocks	379 yards	par 4
No 5	Brae	397 yards	par 4
No 6	Long	524 yards	par 5
No 7	Plantation	397 yards	par 4
No 8	Short	174 yards	par 3
No 9	Railway	421 yards	par 4

No 10	South America	453 yards	par 4
No 11	Dyke	372 yards	par 4
No 12	Southward Ho!	478 yards	par 5
No 13	Whins	166 yards	par 3
No 14	Spectacles	488 yards	par 5
No 15	Luckyslap	461 yards	par 4
No 16	Barry Burn	235 yards	par 3
No 17	Island	454 yards	par 4
No 18	Home	448 yards	par 4

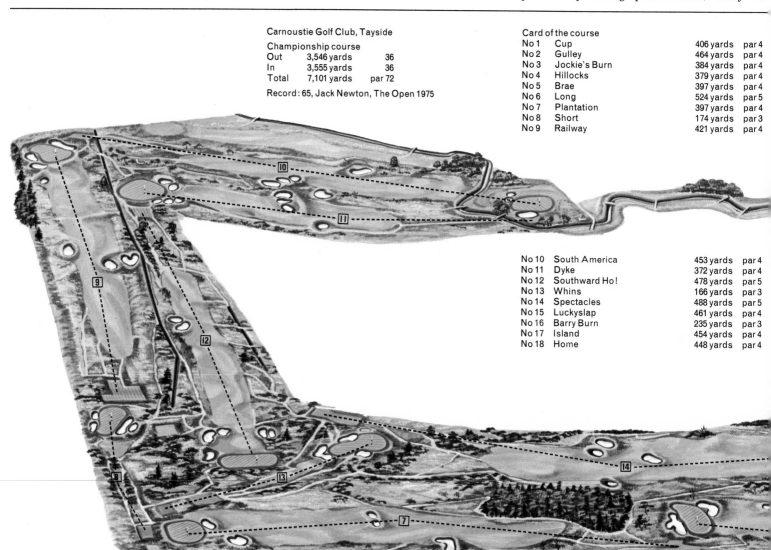

whom seem to think that driving should be an unthinking process—has long centred upon Braid's bunker in the middle of the second fairway, where a good straight drive may finish. There is sufficient room to either side and why, occasionally, should the drive not have to be exactly lined?

The 3rd is a beautiful little hole, with its pitch over a stream to an awkward green, and then one turns again towards the prevailing wind for a finely shaped par-four with a long second over dead level ground. On the left-hand side is a thick, dark wood of firs, a pleasing break in the bleak severity of the scene, and the 5th, again angled to the right, with its approach to a raised green, runs along the wood's farther side.

By any reckoning the 6th is one of the great long holes in golf. Far down the fairway, which has a boundary fence the full length on the hooking side, are two bunkers which a good drive can reach. Again hard thought is called for on the tee: to play short or to either side? The right is the safer, and from there a long second must be placed on to the left of the fair-

way to avoid the mean little Jockie's Burn, which cuts in from the right. Then, and only then, is the 3rd to the green fairly straightforward.

The 7th, a good straight hole, moves to the farthest corner of the course and then, at last, is the first short hole. The shot to a slightly raised plateau green is never easy to judge and here again a little spinney leavens the setting. The 9th is downhill—the only perceptible change in level on the whole course apart from the 12th, which ascends a parallel course with equal gentleness. Carnoustie, mercifully, does not hasten coronaries.

Many have wondered why, in this Scottish fastness, the 10th should be called South America. Seemingly, a young citizen of Carnoustie, in the days when it produced more emigrant golfers than anywhere else on earth, had hopes of reaching that continent but, presumably, celebrated his departure too freely and got no farther than the spinney by the 10th before succumbing to after-effects. The green here is within a loop on the Barry Burn, which cruelly snares the underhit shot as well as the one that is sliced. One drives across it from the

next tee, but at no substantial range. The real menace of the water is yet to come.

The short 13th, tightly trapped though it is, brings some breathing space before what is probably the most exacting finish in Britain. The second shot from the long, curving 14th fairway must carry a hill in which have been carved the "Spectacle" bunkers. This shot deceived Hogan into underclubbing more than once and cost him the only five in his final round of 68, but it brought lasting fame to Gary Player when he held off the challenge of Nicklaus fifteen years later. The 15th swings along a hog's-back fairway into duneland and—except in a helping wind—is a demanding four.

By modern par standards the 16th is a short hole, but only by a yard or so from the back tee; by any standards it is ferociously difficult, with its tiny entrance between bunkers to a narrow shelf of green. And then the ghoulish fun of the finish begins in earnest. A solid drive in the right direction from the 17th tee will carry the Barry Burn twice, but against a strong wind the tee shot must be placed on what is virtually an island amidst its wicked curves. ▷

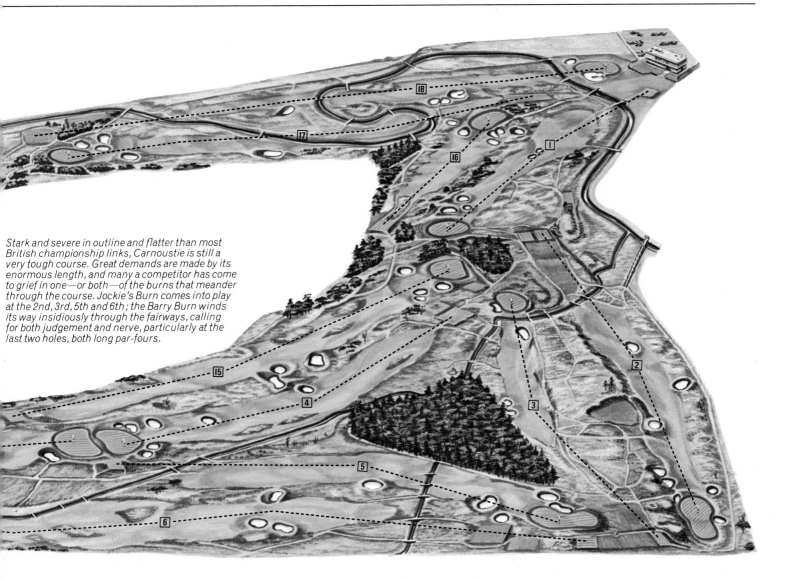

Stark and severe in outline and flatter than most British championship links, Carnoustie is still a very tough course. Great demands are made by its enormous length, and many a competitor has come to grief in one—or both—of the burns that meander through the course. Jockie's Burn comes into play at the 2nd, 3rd, 5th and 6th; the Barry Burn winds its way insidiously through the fairways, calling for both judgement and nerve, particularly at the last two holes, both long par-fours.

▷ The drive to the last, haunted by the burn and out-of-bounds, is formidable enough except with the help of a prevailing wind. Then comes the last challenge, the carry over the burn, which is no mere stream but twenty feet or more across. Gene Sarazen tells of how, one evening during a championship, bets were made on the possibility of jumping it. A famous amateur wagered quite heavily that he could, but finished, dinner jacket and all, in the water.

The history of the Open is as much one of tragedy as of triumph and few would wish to match the fate of José Jurado of the Argentine in 1931. Tommy Armour had set the pace with a closing 71, but Jurado could beat him by playing the last two holes in nine strokes. After a smothered drive had cost him six at the 17th, Jurado (unaware of Armour's total, for scoreboards did not exist in those days) played short of the burn, took five and then learned that he could have tied with a four when he had been within range to risk the carry. Macdonald Smith also might have won if he had finished with three pars, but the 16th cost him a six.

There was no talk of tragedy in 1937, when Henry Cotton achieved his finest hour. The whole American Ryder Cup team was competing and the weather was appalling. Cotton began his last round in a deluge and there was a danger that play might be abandoned, but he was round in 71, a tremendous performance. Al Laney, one of the finest and most perceptive of all American writers, was there and later described Cotton perfectly: "A strange, forbidding man in those days, but he could handle a golf club with his three-quarter swing more expertly than anyone I have seen since except Ben Hogan. When Cotton hit an iron to the green with chilling, humourless concentration it seemed magic. Like Hogan again, he gave the impression of coldness, but there was also the same feeling as with Hogan that the ball had been given no option, that there was nothing he could not achieve."

When Hogan won, the greens (as he said) were like putty and he had great difficulty in getting the ball up to the hole. His winning 282 was an overstatement of the quality of his golf. From tee to green he mastered the course as nobody else has ever done and his victory was the climax of an achievement that may never be equalled. In that summer of 1953 he won the Masters and both the great Opens, all by commanding margins. It was fitting that the last act should be at Carnoustie. An enduring memory of the place will always be the sight of Hogan, after he had holed his final putt, bowing impassively to the multitudes. He seemed alone, humble rather than exultant, and alone he was on a supreme peak of greatness.

Jockie's Burn winds along the right side of Carnoustie's long 6th. On a windless day, like the one Hogan encountered on the last day of the 1953 Open, it presents few problems. But against a headwind the second shot requires careful judgement and the shallow green is hard to hold with a long third shot. This could lead to trouble in the big, deep bunker at the back. Falling short means a nasty little chip with no guarantee of a par.

The 6th: The weakness of links golf

Memories of Hogan's conquest of Carnoustie in 1953 are indelible for the purity of his striking and the ruthless precision of his golf. He twice destroyed the 6th hole on the final day. Morning and afternoon his drives screamed through the still, grey air, perfectly lined past the right hand of the fairway bunkers and finishing in almost exactly the same spot. From there brassie shots boomed straight for the green, easily clearing Jockie's Burn and stopping some thirty yards from the hole. Each time he made his birdie.

This was an instance of modern technique and equipment rendering course design almost meaningless. For Hogan that day the hole offered little challenge beyond the hitting of two fairly straight, full shots, never a great problem to him. He played it as if the bunkers and Jockie's Burn did not exist. They came even less into the reckoning on the first three days of the 1975 Open, when the fairways were faster and a light breeze was helping. Scores of people were home with irons for their second shots. Such is the way of seaside golf in Britain, where par-fives often are defenceless against the experts because there are few features to restrain the length of the first two shots and little or no penal element around the greens, the majority of which are invitingly open.

The 6th: 524 yards par 5

——— Hogan
-------- Safe line

Ben Hogan, whose technique rendered Carnoustie impotent in the 1953 Open.

One of the great championship finishes

The 1968 Open was in destiny's melting pot when Gary Player and Jack Nicklaus came to the 14th in the last round. Player was two ahead and had to wait on the fairway while Nicklaus, lucky to have a wooden club lie, extricated himself from the trees on the right. He smashed a 4-wood which finished just off the green and then, even before the excitement for Nicklaus had subsided, Player hit the shot of a lifetime. The 1975 Open was also decided by a great shot, by Tom Watson at the 18th.

Gary Player, left, and Jack Nicklaus, right, fought a memorable duel over Carnoustie's

tough finishing holes to decide the 1968 Open. Player, with a 289 total, won by two strokes.

Jack Nicklaus and Gary Player stride up the 17th fairway at the close of the 1968 Open. Despite a mammoth drive beyond the farthest crossing of the burn, Nicklaus was unable to collect a birdie-three and increase the pressure on Player, who remained two strokes ahead.

The 14th to the 18th: Sorting out the winners

In the 1968 Open, Gary Player made a perfectly timed thrust at the 14th. Concentrating wonderfully, he struck a magnificent spoon over the Spectacle bunkers to within two feet of the hole. Down went the putt for an eagle.

The look of a champion was about Player that year; he was less tense, more relaxed and philosophical than usual, and his courage was beyond dispute. He had need of it all, because from that point Nicklaus outgunned him from the last four tees with a sequence of thunderous strokes with a driver, the like of which few will ever see. The one that lingers most in people's minds, although he was the only player that day past the flag at the 16th, was at the 17th. Everyone had been playing short of the final crossing of the Burn, but Nicklaus was still two behind and the light breeze was helping. His massive hit, all of 340 yards, soared over the Burn and left him only a wedge to the green. But he did not make a three and Player was almost safe. A point worth noticing about Nicklaus when he is intent on a particularly big drive is that he takes the club away from the ball even more deliberately than usual, and he never hurries this first crucial movement. It helps to ensure that no suspicion of undue haste shall mar the rhythm of the swing.

In 1975 the 18th was reduced to 448 yards, whereas for previous Opens it had been a par-five. This was done to emphasize the challenge of the carry over the burn for the second shot instead of forcing the majority to lay up short, as the longer hole often did. It also intensified the drama for the watching thousands in the amphitheatre around the green. The decision certainly was justified as Tom Watson, for one, would agree.

The 14th to the 18th ——— Player
-------- Nicklaus

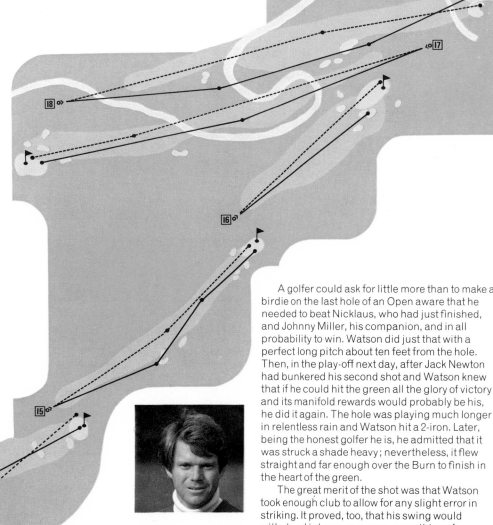

A golfer could ask for little more than to make a birdie on the last hole of an Open aware that he needed to beat Nicklaus, who had just finished, and Johnny Miller, his companion, and in all probability to win. Watson did just that with a perfect long pitch about ten feet from the hole. Then, in the play-off next day, after Jack Newton had bunkered his second shot and Watson knew that if he could hit the green all the glory of victory and its manifold rewards would probably be his, he did it again. The hole was playing much longer in relentless rain and Watson hit a 2-iron. Later, being the honest golfer he is, he admitted that it was struck a shade heavy; nevertheless, it flew straight and far enough over the Burn to finish in the heart of the green.

The great merit of the shot was that Watson took enough club to allow for any slight error in striking. It proved, too, that his swing would withstand intense pressure, something of enormous importance to one who had failed under it in the two previous United States Opens.

Tom Watson, winner in 1975 of the fifth Open played at Carnoustie.

Historic links and noble traditions

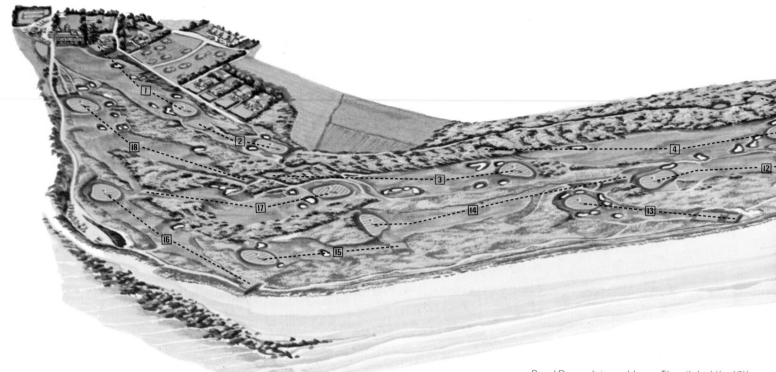

Royal Dornoch is world famous for its wild beauty and the natural feel of its links.

The pitch at the 17th, below, must clear the awkward bunkers and hold the plateau green.

Northernmost of the world's great golf courses, Dornoch shares its latitude with the Bering Sea and Hudson Bay and its antecedents with those other places on the North Sea coast of Scotland, where golf had its beginnings. Among the early evidence of the antiquity of its links is a book, *The Earldom of Sutherland*, by Sir Robert Gordon, who was tutor to the family in the seventeenth century. Writing of Dornoch, he said: "About this town are the fairest and largest links of any part of Scotland, fitt for Archery, Goffing, Ryding, and all other exercises; they doe surpasse the fields of Montrose and St Andrews." It is possible, therefore, that a form of golf as it is now recognized was played at Dornoch over 300 years ago, although there is no definite record of this until the autumn of 1876. The club was formed in the following spring by Alexander McHardy, pioneer of golf in the north of Scotland, and Dr Gunn, who learned the game at St Andrews.

For the first ten years of its life the course had only nine holes, but gradually more people were making the long pilgrimage beyond the Highlands and it was decided that old Tom Morris should be called upon to add another nine. He was charmed with the place from the outset, particularly with the presence of many natural plateaus which could serve for greens. From time to time alterations were made—notably by John Sutherland, a famous secretary—but for the most part the golf is wonderfully natural. The beautiful seaside turf, the dunes, hummocks, and undulating fairways owe little to the hand of man.

Because of its remoteness, many golfers may not be aware of Dornoch's existence; others, aware of its fame, have never ventured so far in search of their game, for it is some sixty miles north of Inverness. Those who have speak of its glory with one voice. Dornoch stands comparison with all the finest in Britain.

It curves along the shores of Embo Bay at the mouth of Dornoch Firth, a setting of wondrous isolation from the foulness of the cities—London is over 600 miles away—and a place of madly contrasting moods. The wind may be firm, bringing forth the golf at its splendid best; it can be a roaring gale, thundering down the valleys through the old western mountains, making the course a fearsome test of all the strength, purpose and technique that a man can muster; or its voice may be stilled and the day alive with sunshine.

On such a day the golfer is reminded of the words of a man who visited Dornoch long ago and wrote: "Looking westward and, indeed, bounding the view from the Ord of Caithness on the north-east to the far away hills of Aberdeenshire, in the south, there is a grand circle of highlands before us, embracing all the finest 'Bens' in Sutherland, Ross and Inverness. On fine summer days the play of cloud shadows and sunlight gleam on these distant mountains is a very remarkable feature of the scenery."

Let it not be thought that Dornoch is normally afflicted with tempest and extremes of climate. It can often be more temperate the farther north one travels—but how swiftly it can change, as the golfer discovers when enduring the challenge of the ferocious wind. This can be fun for the average golfer, except perhaps in competition, for rare pleasure can be had in improvising the strokes necessary to combat a wind.

The 1st, along a shallow rippling valley, and the 2nd, a pitch to a table green, are tricky rather than severe, especially if the turf is keen. From the 3rd tee the course falls away to the great curving basin of the links itself. Now follow two lovely holes of medium length, then a pitch to a long, narrow green high above the fairway and a beautiful short 6th, with its green a shelf hard against the flank of a heathery hillside. This must be climbed to the 7th tee, and for a moment the golf is that of open heathland. But the drive to the 8th plunges towards a green in a secret hollow.

To the golfer at one with his game, and helped perhaps by a prevailing breeze, the course thus

Royal Dornoch is a links of splendid isolation rather than the bustle of championships, but two great golf architects, Pete Dye and Donald Ross, have bestowed on it the accolade of imitation. Dye's short par-four 5th at the Columbus Golf Club, Ohio, is patterned after Dornoch's 15th, while the basic character of Ross's famous Number 2 course at Pinehurst, North Carolina, also derived from Dornoch—where Ross was born and learned his golf under Old Tom Morris, four times British Open champion, in the 1890s.

Card of the course

No 1	333 yards	par 4	No 10	148 yards	par 3
No 2	180 yards	par 3	No 11	444 yards	par 4
No 3	415 yards	par 4	No 12	501 yards	par 5
No 4	417 yards	par 4	No 13	170 yards	par 3
No 5	359 yards	par 4	No 14	459 yards	par 4
No 6	165 yards	par 3	No 15	325 yards	par 4
No 7	465 yards	par 4	No 16	403 yards	par 4
No 8	387 yards	par 4	No 17	407 yards	par 4
No 9	498 yards	par 5	No 18	457 yards	par 4

Royal Dornoch Golf Club, Dornoch, Highland

Out	3,219 yards	35
In	3,314 yards	35
Total	6,533 yards	par 70

Record: 65, Jim Miller (Am), Freser Shield 1971
66, Bernard Gallacher (Pro), Northern Open 1973

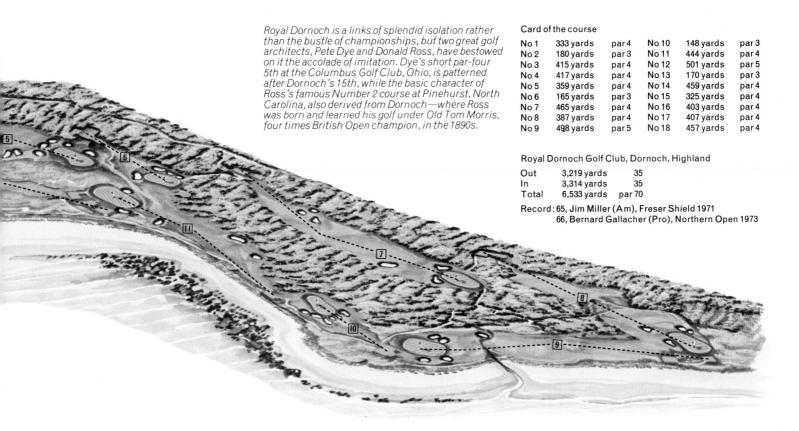

far may not seem unduly difficult; but thenceforth his task begins in earnest with one of the most glorious stretches of seaside golf to be found anywhere in the world. From the 9th tee one turns for distant home and the next seven holes follow the gentle left-handed curve of the bay—a great scimitar of blue and silver and grey. This is true linksland golf, compelling not only strong, accurate driving but fine judgement of long approaches if par is to be achieved. Should the wind be against the golfer, or from either hand, control of flight and length will be examined to the utmost. There is respite of a kind at the short 10th and 13th, but their greens are far from generous targets and true strokes alone will prevail.

The one hole that does not instantly appeal is the 16th, with its steep, mounting fairway and no sight of the green unless the drive is very long; but the 17th is dangerously attractive with its drive to an unseen valley, whence the pitch must be truly struck or it will not reach the tableland of green. Two good shots will see one home at the last. The length of the second can be deceptive but the green stands free and open, inviting a good bold stroke.

Analyse and examine the course as you will, the conclusion is inescapable that it is sufficient to test the most accomplished golfers in the world. There is little hope that it will, because of its remoteness. Dornoch will always attract its pilgrims and many distinguished golfers have come to love it, not least Sir Ernest Holderness and the Wethereds. Perhaps it is fitting that it remains in such splendid solitude, far removed from the turmoil and the excitement of championships.

The 14th: Character for export

The 14th is the greatest of all Dornoch's beautiful seaside holes and the most demanding for those hopeful of a par. Long known as Foxy (and with good reason), it measures 459 yards and nothing short of two outstanding shots will suffice. The fairway swings to the left at about the range of a solid drive, then pursues its original direction before moving to the right again and rising to the plateau green. The beauty of the hole is its simplicity of design and the way in which the natural feature of a formidable hummock of dune on the right has made possible the two changes of direction. It has no need of artificial hazards and there is not a single bunker. Ideally, the drive should draw slightly with the tilt of fairway into a position from where a wood or long iron can be faded over the corner of the hill to the green.

For those (and there are many) whose approaches fall short of the green there is the alternative of pitching their third shot or nursing

it up the slope with a running shot. Although few modern links play as fast as they once did, the pitch and run, or the pure run shot played with a fairly straight-faced club, is still essential to the successful golfer's armoury.

Undoubtedly the natural character and subtlety of Dornoch had a great influence on Donald Ross, who was professional and head greenkeeper there before going to America at the turn of the century and becoming one of the greatest of all architects. Numerous examples of his work there remain today.

One of Ross's basic principles in designing a green was to raise its surface slightly—three or four feet—above the level of the fairway and then fashion subtle undulations. This meant that the slightly erring shot would tend to roll off the greens rather than hold on the fringe, thus creating a delicate chipping situation. It is likely that many a green in the United States was inspired by the character of the 14th at Dornoch.

Many an American green was inspired by the character of the 14th at Dornoch, and Pinehurst Number 2 is regarded as one of the most exacting tests of chipping in America because of its Dornoch-style crown greens. Harry Vardon, in his prime when the fame of Dornoch spread at the turn of the century, described the 14th as "the finest natural hole I've ever played".

A punishing kind of perfection

To define the perfect golf course is well nigh impossible; so many factors of design, situation and personal taste are involved. Nevertheless, no course in the British Isles embraces more of the qualities one seeks in a great and fair challenge of skill than Muirfield, home of the Honourable Company of Edinburgh Golfers, generally recognized as the oldest club in the world. Its records are continuous since 1744, when "several Gentlemen of Honour skilful in the ancient and healthful exercise of Golf" petitioned the City of Edinburgh to provide a silver club for annual competition on the links at Leith.

For almost half a century the Company played over the five holes there, but eventually encroachment caused difficulties and they went to Musselburgh. In time this links also became disagreeably crowded, and in 1891 the Company again moved east, down the Firth of Forth to Muirfield. At first the new course met with much

abuse, partly because the club had taken the Open championship with them. This championship had been started by the Prestwick club, and was played there for the first time on October 17, 1860. Willie Park of Musselburgh won the handsome red morocco challenge belt.

Ten years later Young Tom Morris, a supreme golfer, annexed it for himself by winning for the third successive year. There was no Open in 1871, and thereafter the Honourable Company and the Royal and Ancient joined with Prestwick in subscribing for the present trophy and in managing the championship. For the next twenty years it was played on each of their courses in turn. The disappointment of Musselburgh in losing the championship may have prompted unkind comment about its successor, for apparently it was neither long nor testing enough, albeit surrounded by a grey stone wall and with water about. Andrew Kirkaldy, a

famous professional of the time, notorious for his sharp tongue, was moved to dismiss Muirfield as an old water meadow. In spite of this the first championship to be played there in 1892 has a place in history. For the first time it was over 72 holes instead of 36, and was won by Harold Hilton, one of the great Hoylake amateurs. His score of 305 with the gutty ball was considered to be remarkably low; he won again five years later and since then no amateur, except Jones, has been Open champion.

Thereafter the stature of Muirfield grew apace. Every few years down the generations it has been the setting for one or other of the great occasions. Harry Vardon won the first of his six Open titles there in 1896, after a play-off with J. H. Taylor. The third member of the great triumvirate, James Braid, also won his first victory at Muirfield and, just before World War I, the vast figure of Ted Ray bestrode the links and a

The Honourable Company of Edinburgh Golfers, Muirfield, Lothian.

Out	3,479 yards	36
In	3,415 yards	35
Total	6,894 yards	par 71

Record: 65, Peter Butler, The Open 1966

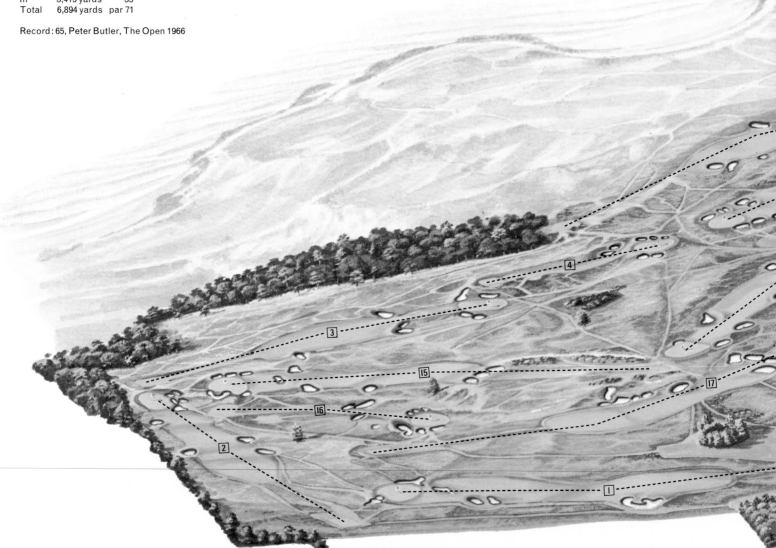

championship. It is unlikely that he was afraid of the thick, clinging rough which, long before his time, had struck fear and fury into the hearts of golfers.

The first post-war champion to arise at Muirfield became one of the greatest amateurs of the period. Although the American challenge was not regarded by the British in the apprehensive light of nowadays, there must have been acute anxiety abroad the afternoon Cyril Tolley beat R. A. Gardner in the final. Tolley was three up and four to play, but the American squared the match on the last green. In 1920 the 1st was a short hole: Tolley followed Gardner's fine shot to the green with a better one, and eventually holed for a two and the championship.

After his first pilgrimage to Britain in 1921 Jones was only beaten once in three subsequent visits and five championships. This was in the quarter-finals of the Amateur in 1926. His con-

Muirfield clubhouse, the headquarters of the Honourable Company of Edinburgh Golfers, which was founded in 1744 and is the club with the longest continuous existence. The intriguing bunker guards the right side of the 18th green.

queror was a young Scottish golfer, Andrew Jamieson, who, it is said, practised his putting for three hours on the eve of the match. Jones previously had beaten Robert Harris, the defending champion, an occasion in itself because never before had the champions of Britain and the United States met in either event. O. B. Keeler, who for so long played Boswell to Jones's Johnson, was certain that his hero would win this championship and his agony must have been considerable, for he wrote later, "In all my life I have never heard anything as lonely as the cry of the peewit in that twilight on the rolling Muirfield course, nor was I ever so lonesome." The peewits and the curlews still cry over the links; it is a place that haunts the memory.

Walter Hagen's victory in the 1929 Open championship was a classic instance of a champion playing with great skill. While others, including most of the American Ryder Cup team, ▷

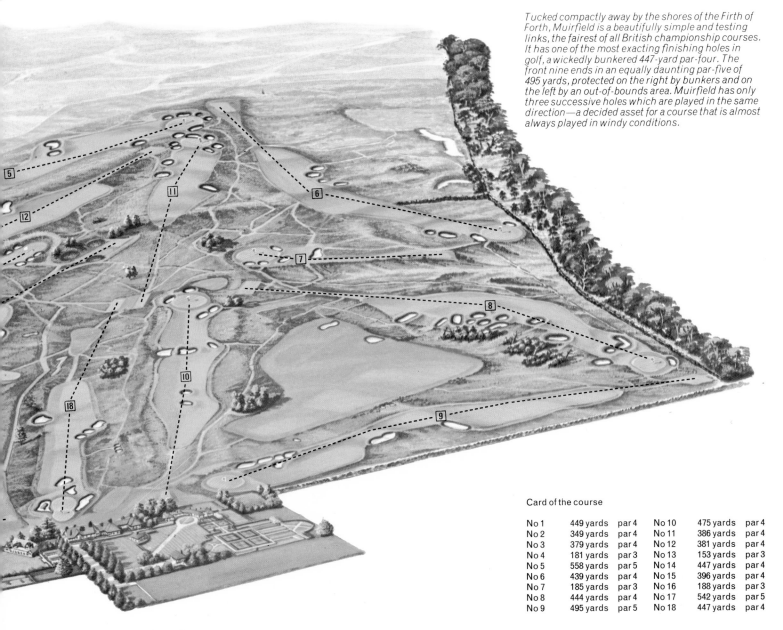

Tucked compactly away by the shores of the Firth of Forth, Muirfield is a beautifully simple and testing links, the fairest of all British championship courses. It has one of the most exacting finishing holes in golf, a wickedly bunkered 447-yard par-four. The front nine ends in an equally daunting par-five of 495 yards, protected on the right by bunkers and on the left by an out-of-bounds area. Muirfield has only three successive holes which are played in the same direction—a decided asset for a course that is almost always played in windy conditions.

Card of the course

No 1	449 yards	par 4	No 10	475 yards	par 4
No 2	349 yards	par 4	No 11	386 yards	par 4
No 3	379 yards	par 4	No 12	381 yards	par 4
No 4	181 yards	par 3	No 13	153 yards	par 3
No 5	558 yards	par 5	No 14	447 yards	par 4
No 6	439 yards	par 4	No 15	396 yards	par 4
No 7	185 yards	par 3	No 16	188 yards	par 3
No 8	444 yards	par 4	No 17	542 yards	par 5
No 9	495 yards	par 5	No 18	447 yards	par 4

▷ were blown to oblivion by a gale, Hagen shrewdly used less lofted clubs than previously, improvised all manner of shots under the wind and won by a street. The 8th hole at Muirfield is a big dog-leg to the right, and within its curve there is an alarming cluster of gathering bunkers. On the last day Hagen, instead of playing down the fairway and having a long second over a great cross-bunker to the green, drove far out into the rough on the right, scorning the architect's purpose and considerably shortening the hole. He was rewarded with two threes, but soon afterwards a spinney was planted to defeat such liberties.

Much of the greatness of Muirfield is in its test of driving. The fairways need not be menacingly narrow, but the rough (unlike the normal links grass) is consistently lush and tenacious. To be in it invariably means the loss of half a stroke or more. This is as it should be, for many British links do not penalize the erring stroke enough. However strong a man may be, he cannot score low without accurate driving. When Henry Cotton won his third Open at Muirfield in 1948 he missed only four fairways in 72 holes. His second round of 66 was played in the presence of King George VI, which was a rare gesture to majesty.

The rough caused much speculation before the 1966 Open. It had been allowed to grow exceptionally thick, and Sanders was moved to say after finishing second that he wished he had the hay concession. Never was rough more punishing; but Jack Nicklaus approached the course with a finely preserved balance between attack and defence, frequently used an iron

Harold Hilton, twice winner of the Open and the only Briton to win the US Amateur. His earliest Open victory came in 1892, the first year the event was played over 72 holes and the first time the Open was played at Muirfield. His winning total then was 305.

from the tees and was rewarded, one stroke ahead of Sanders and Thomas, with a total of 282. Their closest pursuers included the most accomplished golfers in the field, proof that the course was a fair, if severe, examination. In one round P. J. Butler returned a 65, which set the record. This victory was a climax in Nicklaus's career. At the age of twenty-six he had won the four major titles of the world: so another illustrious name was added to the roll of Muirfield's champions.

Rough is not the only problem, for the bunkering reveals an imagination of design that would be cruel if it were not so fair. Rarely at Muirfield does a ball jump a bunker; if the shot is fading or drawing towards one then in it will go, for the bunkers have been fashioned, with sleek, beautifully preserved surrounds, to gather the slightly erring stroke. This can be maddening, but always in one's heart there is the know-

The 5th: A round transformed

Occasionally a single stroke transforms a round, as it did for Johnny Miller when he stood on the 5th fairway, five over par on the second day of the 1972 Open championship.

His long drive was perfect, lined some 280 yards and safely past the hidden dangers on the right. He had about the same distance to go and hit a spoon shot, faded slightly to hold the right-to-left fall of the approach to the green. It did precisely that, ran on to the green as if intent on one destination alone and fell into the hole for an albatross (double eagle). At his finest Johnny Miller provides a perfect example of the virtue of being in the classically relaxed, long position at the top of the swing, from which, as Miller himself says, "Coming down, you will react much quicker and get more clubhead speed."

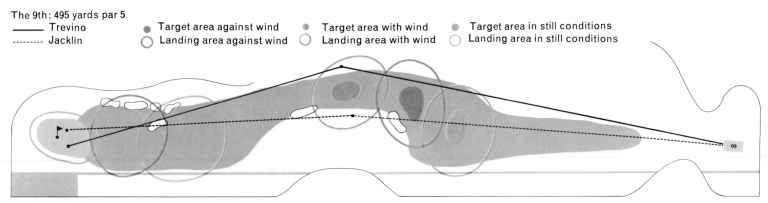

The 9th: 495 yards par 5

——— Trevino
------- Jacklin

● Target area against wind   ● Target area with wind   ● Target area in still conditions
○ Landing area against wind   ○ Landing area with wind   ○ Landing area in still conditions

The 9th: A fierce test of control

Of all the demanding holes at Muirfield none can have caused greater havoc than the 9th. The tee shot is of the essence; if it fails to hold the fairway, which narrows sharply in the landing area between a bunker on the left and the rough, there is little prospect of getting near the green with the second shot. Sometimes, in a difficult wind, it pays stronger players to take a club from the tee which will not reach the bunker—anything to have a good lie from which to carry the hummocks of thick, clinging rough which sweep in from the left.

Given a solid drive into the neck of the fairway, the next shot is played to an open plain running unbroken into the green—though it must be aimed away from a diagonal line of bunkers on the right, an awkward distance from the putting surface, and somewhat towards the grey stone wall with out-of-bounds beyond.

When the wind is contrary, as it normally is, the hole can be a fierce test of control. Even though the

wall is almost five feet high it is all too easy to pull either the second or third shot out-of-bounds, as Peter Thomson can testify: when his wooden club shot began its lethal curve, his cause in the 1959 Open was arrested.

The hole can be a test of patience as well as technique; it does not take kindly to being forced. In 1966, when well placed in the Open, Palmer took six there because he used a driver from the tee when discretion plainly called for a safe "lay-up" shot with an iron.

At other times, as in 1972 when an easterly breeze was helping and the ground was firm, the hole's teeth are drawn and the penalty for finding the rough from the tee greatly minimized. In the last round, when Jacklin and Trevino were locked in their desperate contest with Nicklaus, both drove into it but remained comfortably within iron range of the green. Their shots, perfectly judged, pitched some twenty yards short and ran on to the green. Both holed for eagles.

Peter Thomson, whose chances of winning his fifth British Open went awry in 1959 when his second shot curved over the wall and out-of-bounds at Muirfield's 9th hole.

Arnold Palmer, who came to grief at the 9th in 1966 when he elected to go for length from the tee and failed to find the narrow neck of the fairway.

ledge that the stroke was imperfectly struck or aimed. The man playing good golf, or the man who knows his course and his limitations, need have no fear of Muirfield. It is a far-from-fearsome place: there are no trees, no water, no unduly strenuous carries, and only one blind stroke to play.

The greens are not enormous (in fact some tend to be small), but this is another strength, for the influence of putting is kept within reasonable proportion. Those of the short holes, in particular, are sharply defined within their embracing bunkers. Always the golfer can see what is expected of him in the approach to the green: in this respect Muirfield is unique among the championship courses of the British Isles and for that reason likely to commend itself more readily than any other to American eyes, used to golf on the target principle. A man gets what he hits and, what is more, can see it happen; no

golfer could justly claim that the course took unfair advantage of ignorance.

All this is contrary to the common conception of a seaside course and, in appearance, Muirfield resembles none of them. There is nothing of a long desolate sprawl of dunes and linksland, with holes that are subtle in their identity and not easily memorable for the casual visitor; there is nothing, either, of the sense of limitless freedom that one feels at Sandwich, Carnoustie or Westward Ho!

It lies on the southern shores of the Forth and its boundaries are precise, for the grey wall patrols three sides. To the north are the dunes, protected by great banks of buckthorn, and beyond is the great estuary—a magic stretch of water, whether dancing silver in sunshine and a brave wind, tranquil in the haze of summer or eerily haunted as ships, booming in the mist, steal upstream to Leith and Rosyth. Across the

Forth spreads the graceful coast of Fife, ever-changing in its patterned hues as the cloud shadows glide by. Along the eastern side of the course the dark gnarled trees of Archerfield heel forever from the winds—the woods of Archerfield are called Graden Sea Wood in Robert Louis Stevenson's *Pavilion on the Links*. Away to the west stands Gullane Hill, commanding not only the two splendid courses on its flanks but also a view of rare majesty, from Bass Rock, sentinel of North Berwick, to "Auld Reekie" itself, smokily enchanted in the distance.

The immediate impression of Muirfield is of a place beautifully contained and private, but spacious in its policies. The eye can roam the course in a glance, and therein is one of its greatest charms. It was laid out in two approximate loops: the first nine holes form an outer ring in a clockwise path, the homeward half runs within but is less constant in its counter ▷

▷ arc. The result is that no hole is more than a few minutes' walk from the clubhouse, and only once, from the 3rd to the 5th holes, do as many as three consecutive holes follow the same direction. The golfer thus is never bored by having the wind against or behind him for long spells as on many links of an older fashion, but always he must take heed of its changing angle of approach.

Straightaway the golfer at Muirfield is made aware that he is setting forth on a considerable exercise of his powers. The opening drive must be exact to find a narrowing waist of fairway between subtly placed bunkers on the left and rough on the right; as often as not the wind will be against it, and the second, a lovely, straight long shot, may not get home. If the greens are fast the next hole demands the greatest care; the fairway leans from right to left and the drive must hold its lower side or the pitch to a

wickedly sloping green will be uncommonly difficult. A well-placed drive to the 3rd leaves a tempting view of the green through a vale between the dunes, otherwise the distance of the approach is hard to judge.

The first of the short holes is at once disturbing and beautiful, for the green is a plateau, closely protected at the front and on either hand by deep bunkers, and if in fear of them the tee shot is too bold, it will leave a long downhill putt. This can easily happen in the prevailing westerly wind; and there is some slight criticism of the course in that the short 13th and 16th are similarly helped and tend to play too short. Their comparative simplicity to an accomplished golfer was emphasized in 1959 when Gary Player, four strokes behind the leaders at lunch on the final day, won the Open with a memorable round of 68. He used only a short iron to these holes, pitched close at the 13th and 16th and

holed for twos. This is not to say that they are all that easy, and in a cross-wind the 13th can be the very devil to hit and hold. It lies in a cleft between dunes, with bunkers eating into the long narrow green; as at the 4th, the stroke finishing at the back of the green can mean a fearsome putt.

The story goes that Hagen deliberately played into one of the bunkers short of the green, preferring an uphill shot from sand to a long slippery downhill putt, but this was on a severe day. For the most part the holes offer absolutely fair targets. The remaining short hole, the 7th, faces west and also has a high plateau green exposed to all the moods of the wind. It was lengthened in preparation for the 1966 Open, and against any wind at all demands a stroke of unerring accuracy and power.

As already noted, Muirfield is a great test of driving. The long 5th curves from left to right

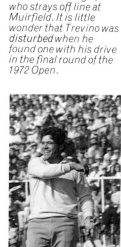

These fairway bunkers at the 17th are typical of the fearsome hazards which await the golfer who strays off line at Muirfield. It is little wonder that Trevino was disturbed when he found one with his drive in the final round of the 1972 Open.

The 17th: A crushing blow for Jacklin

In the last round of the 1972 Open, Muirfield's 17th hole was the setting for one of the most dramatic turns of fortune in modern championship golf. Tony Jacklin and Lee Trevino were level on the tee, needing, as events proved, two pars to beat Jack Nicklaus. Trevino pulled into the nearest bunker, exploded out, slashed a wood into the rough short and to the left of the green and walked after it looking a dejected and defeated man. Jacklin meanwhile had followed a fine, solid drive with

another good shot into a perfect position for a chip.

When Trevino's fourth shot raced over the green into the fringe rough it seemed certain that he would fall at least one, if not two, behind. But, even before Jacklin had time to mark his ball on the green after chipping rather short, Trevino hurriedly played his chip as if heedless of the outcome. It was not an easy one against the grain of the grass on to the fast green, but all the gods were with him. It vanished into the hole, dealing a crushing blow to Jacklin, who then took three putts to fall behind.

Lee Trevino, left, looks delighted and Tony Jacklin, right, smiles ruefully after Trevino retained his Open title at Muirfield in 1972. Trevino's unnerving chip into the cup and Jacklin's three putts at the 17th made this hole the turning point.

The 17th: 542 yards par 5

—— Trevino
----- Jacklin

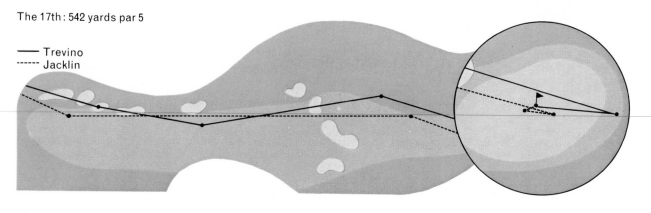

with an obvious temptation to carry a shoulder of ground on the right and shorten the hole. Unless this tactic is resisted the drive almost certainly will vanish into one of a nest of bunkers designed to punish those who try to cheat the hole of its glory. A pull at the 6th can likewise be disastrous; the problems of the 8th have already been mentioned, and then comes one of the finest par-five holes in existence.

From the far southeastern corner of the course, where Archerfield Wood comes to an end, one drives to an ever-narrowing fairway with a large bunker defying those who try to play the hole absolutely straight; it was not designed for this. To have a clear third to an unusually open green, the second must be played to a broad expanse of rolling fairway, but this Elysian field ends abruptly against the wall that runs the length of the hole.

Now one is by the clubhouse, and the long ribbon on the 10th, a superb two-shot hole, stretches away in the distance. Here again cross-bunkers challenge the second shot, yet somehow at Muirfield they do not seem old-fashioned but entirely fitting; and there are more to come. The drive to the 11th is blind but not unduly alarming; the 12th, with its falling fairway and long, narrow green, is a charming hole; the 14th needs a drive that must not be pulled, and keen judgement of distance for the second; the 15th fairway is invitingly wider than most, but the measure of these last three holes is a prevailing wind. If there is a wind, substantial second shots are needed. Even then the 14th may be out of range, but toil hereabouts will find recompense on the mighty 17th, which then can be reached with two good shots. With a helping breeze behind him Nicklaus was home, using a 3-iron and a 5-iron, in the last round of his Open. Here again temptation to cut a corner must be sternly resisted. Innocent though the prospect may seem, a horrid wasteland of humps and bunkers awaits the pull. The round offers few more satisfying moments than the sight of a long second soaring over the great range of bunkers that traverse the fairway, but anyone unsure of his capacity to carry the bunkers is well advised to play short; rare is the third shot that reaches the green from their depths. The 18th has few peers as a finishing hole. The slightly angled tee shot must be held away from bunkers on the left and rough on the other side. Then a wonderfully challenging stroke remains to a green tightly embraced by bunkers, but with no trouble beyond.

This is a feature common to Muirfield: the straight bold stoke rarely, if ever, is seriously punished, but the timid and the wayward as rarely will escape retribution. This surely is the mark of a great golf course.

The 18th: Trevino realizes a famous victory

Lee Trevino's playing of the 18th in the final round of the 1972 Open is an excellent example of a great player making the most of good luck, one of the marks of a fine competitor. The outrageous turn of fortune on the previous hole, when he went one shot ahead of Tony Jacklin by holing a chip from behind the green, could have unsettled many another competitor. Within moments of seemingly casting away the championship Trevino realized that victory again was possible.

The hole was playing short that day, but its problems still existed in the drive to a fairway with bunkers staggered on either side. If he were trapped or in the rough his gains could be surrendered. To ensure that he could play without the slightest delay, as is his custom, he took his time going to the tee. He placed his drive far down the fairway. After Jacklin, now a sadly forlorn figure, had driven into the rough and bunkered his second shot, Trevino hit a superb 8-iron a few feet past the flag. His four to win was a formality.

It looked easy and in a sense probably was, although the green is not that wide and its embracing bunkers can be very penal. Trevino would be high on anyone's list of players who could be trusted to hit a true shot under pressure, because his highly individual method has the great virtue of keeping the club on line longer probably than any other golfer. He is a notable example of the left wrist leading the club at impact, whereas the reverse is true of most players.

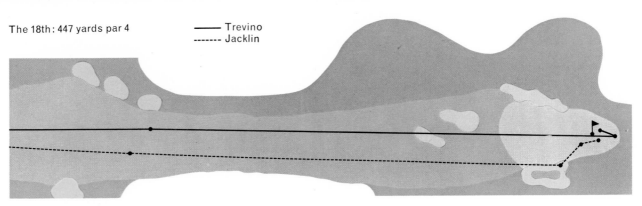

The scene at the 18th green on the last day of the 1972 Open. Trevino and Jacklin, still out on the course, head the leader board. Jacklin's second shot into the bunker in the foreground cost him a vital stroke, allowing Jack Nicklaus to finish in second place.

The 18th: 447 yards par 4

——— Trevino
------- Jacklin

Vision and faith resurrect a compelling course

No small part of the pleasure of golf is that the game is so often played in beautiful surroundings—which can soothe anger, console frustration and enhance joy. Such a place is Turnberry and, travel the world as he will, the golfer would be hard-pressed to find its like. As a course it stands high in any championship company and was endowed by nature with a background that none of the others can surpass. It lies on a curve of rock-bound coast, far from the anxious turmoil of everyday, in the southern reaches of Strathclyde where the river estuary spreads forth to the sea.

Across the waters the great mass of Arran's mountains, the long curves of the Mull of Kintyre and the lonely rock of Ailsa, rising like some primeval beast from their depths, make a scene of compelling majesty. Other courses may have sea and mountains for their setting, but none compare with those at Turnberry, which are forever changing with the whimsical

moods of the weather. It can be transformed within the hour from a place haunted by mist, or savage in wind and rain, to one of entrancing beauty. On a fresh day, with the sea tranquil and deepening in its blueness as the sun rises higher, or at evening when the mountains turn black in the fading light and the sky is livid with colour, Turnberry is incomparable.

There are two courses, the gentle Arran and the nobler Ailsa—scene of many championship events, but to stage its first British Open only in 1977. Both courses date from the early twentieth century and both have survived mutilation through their transformation into an airfield in two world wars. The extensive wartime levelling operations, laying of runways and building destroyed not only the courses themselves but also many natural features. Anyone seeing Turnberry in 1945 would have found it hard to imagine that a first-class course had once existed there, and

In the still of a summer evening the bulk of the Ailsa Craig can be clearly seen from every hole on the course to which it lends its name. Such perfect golfing conditions are rare at Turnberry, where wind is a big influence.

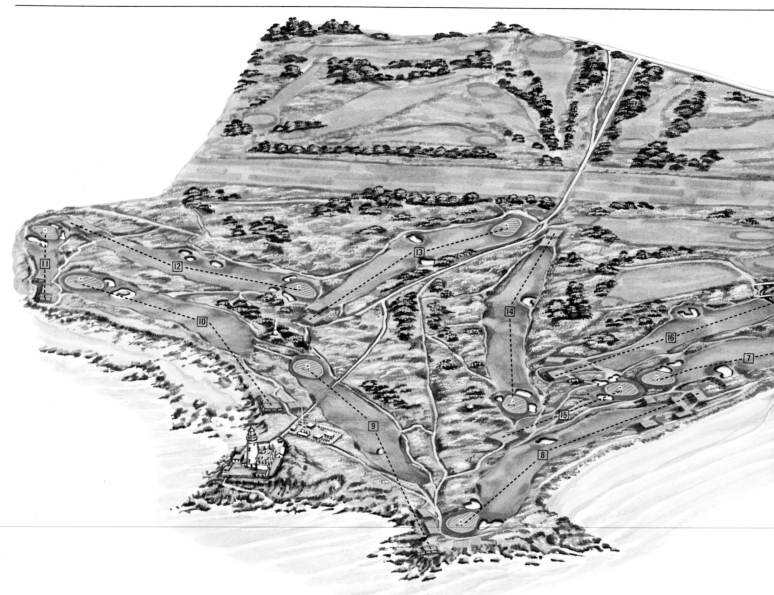

harder still to believe that it ever would again. Within a few years it had been restored, involving vast movements of concrete and sand —to all intents, the creation of a new course. It remains a tribute to Mackenzie Ross, the architect, and to the vision of men like Frank Hole, who had faith in the future of its golf.

After a comparatively quiet beginning the course gathers momentum, so to speak. The 2nd and 3rd holes can be formidable, depending on the wind, and even if there is none they are still considerable. By then the coast is reached. The tee of the short 4th is hard by the lapping waves, the line is over the edge of a sandy bay, and the slightest pull to a green cradled in the dunes will find its way on to the beach. The hole, not inaptly, is called Woe-be-Tide. A long valley contains the great curve of the 5th and, whatever the weather conditions, the stroke to the 6th—one of the longest of short holes—is always a substantial hit, often with a driver.

As on all really fine courses accurate driving is essential and never more so than on the next three holes. The carry to the narrow 7th fairway, sharply angled across the line of flight, needs a powerful stroke and then follows a long second over rolling ground to a far green. The 8th fairway leans from left to right, and unless the drive is true it will fall towards bunkers; the green is a plateau, the shelf of rock behind it a hint of glories to come.

There are few more spectacular or beautifully sited tees than the 9th on its pinnacle high above the rocks, and few more forbidding prospects to the frail in heart and swing. The carry is not enormous, but the sight of the cliffs, the abyss below and the knowledge that a mishit will be lethal, is disturbing. The hog's-back fairway is by no means easy to hold nor, once one has arrived there, is the second shot easy to judge. This is a superb golf hole, marked for the viewer from afar by the slender white

pencil of the Turnberry lighthouse. To stand on the 10th tee at the height of a summer morning is to know the full beauty of Turnberry. Past the remains of a castle, a base for some of Robert the Bruce's stirring deeds, the hole plunges down beside the rocky shore; there are few more satisfying moments than the sight of a drive arching away to the broad, crested fairway. Small wonder the golf hereabouts has stirred memories for many Americans of the great courses of Monterey.

Again on the 11th there is the feeling of being at one with the sea and the rocks, for here is another pulpit tee, though the hole is short and not overly taxing. As the course swings for home along the 12th traces can be seen of the airfield that Turnberry became on two occasions. The monument placed on the hill high above the green commemorates those who died in World War I.

The 13th, with an elusive plateau green, and ▷

With eight of its first eleven holes played alongside—and often over—the ocean's edge, the championship Ailsa course is no place for the golfer suffering from a hook. The outward half culminates in the spectacular Bruce's Castle, where the drive is from a spit of rock above the sea, with, for the brave, a carry of 200 yards over the sea and rocks towards a cairn on the horizon. Further inland, the shorter Arran course—unmarked here—is gentler, but still a stiff test of golfing skills.

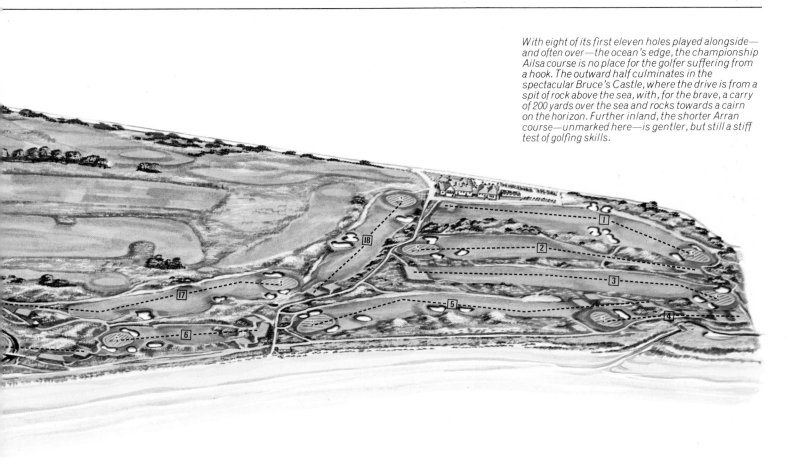

Card of the course

No 1	Ailsa Craig	365 yards	par 4
No 2	Mak Siccar	440 yards	par 4
No 3	Blaw Wearie	475 yards	par 4
No 4	Woe-be-Tide	170 yards	par 3
No 5	Fin' me oot	490 yards	par 5
No 6	Tappie Toorie	245 yards	par 3
No 7	Roon the Ben	520 yards	par 5
No 8	Goat Fell	440 yards	par 4
No 9	Bruce's Castle	475 yards	par 4
No 10	Dinna Fouter	460 yards	par 4
No 11	Maidens	180 yards	par 3
No 12	Monument	395 yards	par 4
No 13	Tickly Tap	385 yards	par 4
No 14	Risk-an-Hope	440 yards	par 4
No 15	Ca Canny	220 yards	par 3
No 16	Wee Burn	415 yards	par 4
No 17	Lang Whang	515 yards	par 5
No 18	Ailsa Hame	430 yards	par 4

Turnberry Hotel courses, Turnberry, Strathclyde

Ailsa course

Out	3,620 yards	36
In	3,440 yards	35
Total	7,060 yards	par 71

Record: 64, Brian Huggett, John Player Classic 1972

The 7th: Weiskopf's mastery of the wind

Golf offers few finer sights than wooden club shots flawlessly and powerfully struck in a strong wind, and when the striker is Tom Weiskopf the experience is sublime. For most of the outward holes in the opening round of the John Player Classic in 1973 the wind was hard from the cloud-crested mountains of Arran, from ten o'clock as it were, perhaps the hardest angle of all to combat. Weiskopf, consistently the straightest long hitter in the game, just reached the crest of the 7th

fairway from the tee. From there he hit a spoon with a purity and power that few golfers in history could have matched. It flew as if the wind did not exist, piercingly straight, never wavering from a perfect line.

His drives from the next three tees were the same, proof that the American-size ball, truly struck, will hold its line in any wind. In these conditions it is essential to preserve balance, to complete the backswing making a full turn of the shoulders, and to keep the rhythm smooth.

Tom Weiskopf, who needed all his skill and power with woods to tame Turnberry's 7th.

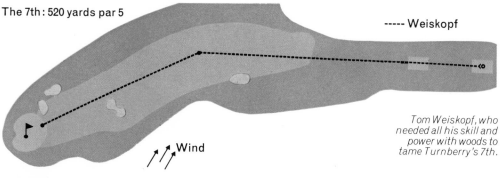

The 7th: 520 yards par 5

----- Weiskopf

↗↗ Wind

The 16th: Failure for the faint-hearted

The very nature of British courses, where allowance for run after pitching often has to be made, encourages underclubbing. Usually the penalty for doing so is not severe because fairways flow into greens, but there are holes where the aerial route is essential. Just such a hole is the 16th at Turnberry, where a deep, steep-sided cleft in the land, containing a little stream known as Wee Burn, winds across the fairway immediately in front of the putting surface. There is nothing subtle about the hole; in most obvious terms it warns: Take enough club for the second shot.

In the 1963 Walker Cup match several experienced British golfers signally failed to do so when an uphill green with banks behind and the wind against begged for a bold shot. Many of them stood on the 16th fairway dithering between a 3- and a 5-iron, usually choosing the more lofted club, often with dire results.

The Wee Burn, which makes the 16th so tricky.

▷ the 14th, which can be reached only with two splendid shots, usually into wind, form a prong towards the hills and bring a welcome variety of direction to the long homeward trail. The 15th is a classic short hole, normally a long iron to a green with bunkers on its left to trap those who steer too safely away from a steep hollow on the right. At the 16th comes a hole decisive to the outcome of the Walker Cup match in 1963, when there might have been a British victory—but for the stream in front of the green.

After the long valley of the 17th, with its second to a green on the uplands, the last hole is not severe. The drive is testing enough with bunkers on the inside curve and great banks of gorse on the right, but the pitch to the broad green is inviting and a memorable round is done. It will have tested the golfer to the limit of his skill—and beyond, if the wind was firm:

its direction is of no consequence, because the holes are angled with subtlety and imagination. There is nothing of monotony. Every one is a challenge and every prospect a joy. The golfer, whether talented or humble—or simply in search of exercise and beauty—will find fulfilment in rich measure.

Over the years Turnberry has had many great moments. The women golfers were the first to avail themselves of its beauty in 1912, and nine years later Cecil (Cecilia) Leitch, the strongest golfer of the period either side of World War I, beat Joyce Wethered (as she was then) in the final of the British championship. In a sense this was a historic occasion; Miss Leitch avenged her defeat of the previous year in the English championship in which Miss Wethered achieved the remarkable performance of winning at the first time of entering.

But the old order was changing. Miss Wethered had ascended her throne, there to remain supreme until her abdication in 1929.

Long ago J. H. Taylor said that the best way to win a championship was to win easily—a dictum that he himself observed on many occasions. But, in the history of the game, few have proved their right to the title in more emphatic fashion than Michael Bonallack in the 1961 Amateur championship. He won eight matches and only on the morning of the thirty-six-hole final against J. Walker was he called upon to play the last two holes. This was a triumph of many qualities: rare devotion to the game, boundless perseverance and determination and a charming, natural, modest manner at all times. After that Bonallack won many championships, but this was the start and there could have been no more perfect setting for it.

An exercise in fear

Hoylake is older than all but one of the English seaside golf courses (Westward Ho!, founded in 1864, is its senior by five years) and is considered foremost of all the links of northern England because of its traditions and infinite merits. It was responsible in 1885 for starting the Amateur championship, the oldest event of its kind in the world. The first international of all, between England and Scotland, was played there in 1902. In the same year Alex Herd won the Open with a rubber-cored ball and the gutty was dead for evermore. In 1921 the first men's match between the United States and Britain was played at Hoylake, inspiring George H. Walker to inaugurate his contest—the Walker Cup—the following year.

Long before golfers came, Hoylake was a sig-

nificant place. Late in the seventeenth century the broad Dee estuary, at the mouth of which Hoylake stands, sheltered a fleet which transported the army of William of Orange to Ireland for the battle of the Boyne. In time the estuary filled with silt and at low tide it looks as if one could walk across to Wales. The importance of Hoylake diminished with the gathering sands and Robert Browning, in his scholarly *History of Golf*, wrote that the waste of dunes and links, on which the course now lies, would not then have fetched £10. In 1911 the Royal Liverpool Club bought it for £30,000.

Until 1876 the golfers shared the links with a racecourse and it cannot have been amusing, even in those days when courses were not sleek and manicured, to find one's ball in a hoof mark.

Now only faint traces of racing remain; a post or so, an old saddling bell and the names of the first and last holes, the Course and the Stand.

The club soon became a lively spirit in English golf. In 1884 the honorary secretary, Thomas Owen Potter, suggested that an open amateur tournament be held the following year. At once the club was faced with the problem of what was an amateur; status was not defined in those days. An entry was received from Douglas Rolland, a Scottish stonemason who had won second prize in the previous Open championship. Rolland was ruled out—but what of Hoylake's greatest son, John Ball, who, as a boy of fifteen, had played in the Open some years before and had accepted a half-sovereign for finishing sixth? The decision in favour of him ▷

The long second shot over the out-of-bounds practice ground, left, that faced Roberto de Vicenzo of Argentina, right, in the last round of the 1967 British

Open. Challenged by Jack Nicklaus, who had already birdied the hole, Vicenzo was almost too long off the tee, but he was able to get home with a spoon and maintain his slim lead.

The 16th: Success or sudden death

Although no modern architect would consider creating a hole exactly like Royal Liverpool's 16th, the merit of its design is undeniable. Basically its challenge is simple. The protrusion into the fairway of one corner of the out-of-bounds field tends to make the player drive to the left, otherwise his second shot must be played across as much of the danger as he dares to attempt.

Aiming for the green involves a considerable carry and brooks no sort of mishit. If too cautious a line is taken the drive will finish in bunkers or rough from where substantial progression is unlikely; then a long third shot remains to be taken. Also the angle to the open entrance of the green will be narrowed.

When Roberto de Vicenzo came to the tee in the last round of the 1967 Open he was leading by three strokes and knew he had only to beat Nicklaus, who was playing immediately ahead. For a horrible moment it seemed that Vicenzo had

driven too far on a straighter line than he intended. His ball was heading towards the shallow bank separating fairway from field, but fortunately for him it stopped a few yards short. From his angle the green was open and welcoming and it was in range, but the line was clean over the field.

Hitting spoon shots from a good lie normally would come as second nature to Vicenzo, but a lifetime's ambition could rest upon this one. If he struck it a fraction thin it might hit the bank in front of him and finish in the field, a fraction heavy and it might not clear the far boundary.

As it was he swung easily into the ball and hit as noble a shot, considering what was at stake, as imagination could conceive. It soared straight and true to the heart of the green and soon he was walking like an emperor down the last fairway to a reception which for sustained warmth and affection has rarely been approached, a rightful tribute to a magnificent golfer—the finest South America has produced—and a rare human being.

16th: 533 yards par 5

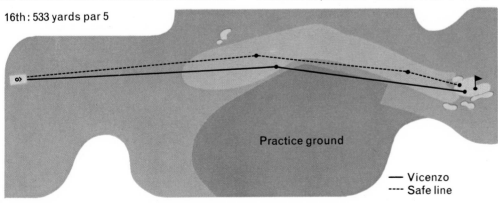

Practice ground

—— Vicenzo
---- Safe line

J. H. Taylor was the only one of the "triumvirate" —himself, James Braid and Harry Vardon—to win an Open at Hoylake. He mastered a gale in 1913 to finish eight shots ahead of Ted Ray.

John Ball, the first Englishman to win the Open. Son of the owner of the Royal Hotel in Hoylake, he and Harold Hilton became famous early members of the Royal Liverpool.

▷ doubtless was delicate and possibly tinged with nepotism. In the long years to come Ball was amateur champion eight times, a tally that probably will never be approached.

Comparison between the ages is fruitless, but Ball was supreme in his own time. Apparently his grip was unorthodox and his stance a little stiff, but the swing was described as the "true poetry of motion, the most perfectly smooth and rhythmical imaginable". He was a formidable competitor with an austere approach to the game but was, withal, a modest man. After he had retired to a home in the Welsh hills someone asked to see his medals; he had given them all away. In 1890 he was the first amateur and the first Englishman to win the Open; he was amateur champion the same year, a feat equalled only by Bobby Jones in 1930. A measure of his enduring skill was that he competed in the Amateur championship of 1927, forty-nine years after his first appearance in the Open.

Remarkably, Ball's greatest amateur rival also was a Hoylake member. Not only did Harold Hilton win the Amateur four times and in 1911 the American championship at Apawamis, but he was Open champion twice again, an achievement that only Jones among amateurs has surpassed. Hilton was said to be the most accurate wooden club player of his day, with a swing of great vigour. He also had a lively intelligence and love of experiment. He and Ball were great masters; another, Jack Graham, was almost so and it was small wonder that Hoylake worshipped these men.

Hoylake is unique among British championship links because it is possible to be out-of-bounds within the confines of the course, and innumerable golfers have condemned it on this count. Until 1920 the penalty for out-of-bounds was loss of distance only and thus the golfers of old were not so harshly punished. Now, Hoylake can inflict the tortures of the damned. There is always an alternative to flirting with danger, but what an exercise in fear some of those holes can be.

The right angle of the 1st makes a forbidding opening hole. On the left from the tee is the clubhouse with its silken putting green; on the right, for the full length of the hole, is the sinister "cop", a bank no more than three feet high which encloses the practice ground. A good drive will finish past the corner, but a long shot remains with the haunting thought that a slice will be fatal if one aims for the green, which is hard against the cop. Many a player has been out-of-bounds with his drive and approach; many have run out of hope of ammunition before completing the hole. It is a fiendish 19th.

Before the 3rd was changed, and a fine new short 4th created in readiness for the 1967 Open, the slightest pull would sail out-of-bounds over another cop. But now the golfer is free until the 6th. This is the famous Briars, where a high-fenced orchard is in line for the drive; against a strong prevailing wind the carry from the back tee is terrible to behold.

No hole in Britain has caused more argument than the 7th, named Dowie after Hoylake's founder. The narrow ellipse of green is protected on the left by yet another cop, and it is possible to hit a perfect long iron to the heart of the green and see the ball hop over the bank out-of-bounds within a few yards of the flag. Unless the green is soft, to aim at the flag is either heroic or stupid, depending on the state of the game. To play safely out to the right leaves a tricky chip through a little swale. In the last round of the Open in 1930 Jones needed two fours to be out in 35. After two long shots over the crumpled 8th fairway he was no more than fifteen yards from the green but, as he wrote later, he took seven for the hole "in the most reasonable manner possible". His torment of mind is only too easy to imagine; so too is the enormous effort of will and control that enabled him to finish just safe from pursuit. This was the second leg of the "quadrilateral".

From the 8th the golf is of the old, true seaside character, dipping and curving along the sandhills, with estuary at hand, silver and grey, or golden when the tide is down; Hilbre Island and its myriad birds and the quiet hills of Wales are in the distance. The 9th with its bowl of a green, the superb short 11th, the Alps, its green an oblong oasis in the dunes, the lovely sweep of the 12th, and the tightest of pitches to the 13th, with its necklace of bunkers, make a splendid prelude to the long, long finish on the plain below.

Now the field comes into play again. It is possible to slice into it from the 15th tee, and its corner cuts clean across the direct line to the

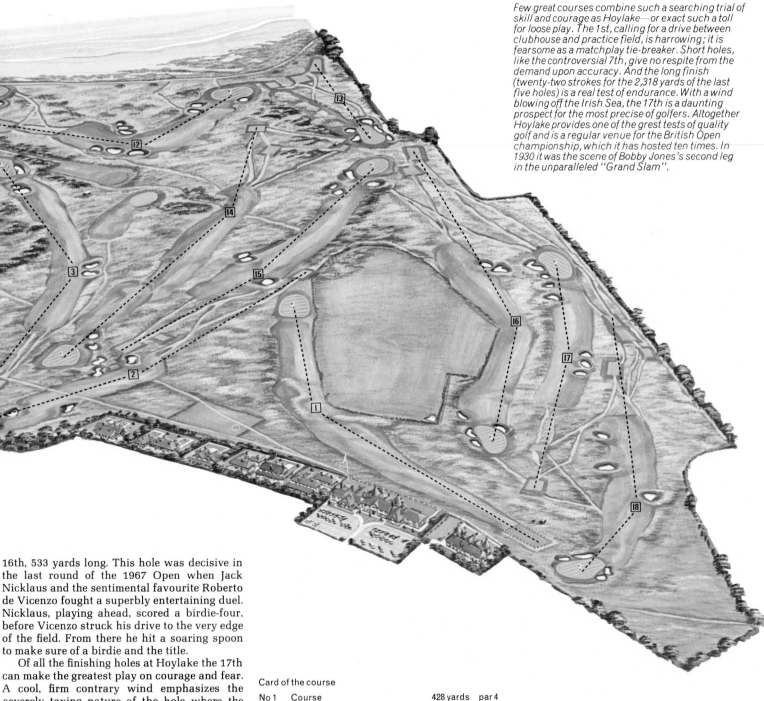

Few great courses combine such a searching trial of skill and courage as Hoylake—or exact such a toll for loose play. The 1st, calling for a drive between clubhouse and practice field, is harrowing; it is fearsome as a matchplay tie-breaker. Short holes, like the controversial 7th, give no respite from the demand upon accuracy. And the long finish (twenty-two strokes for the 2,318 yards of the last five holes) is a real test of endurance. With a wind blowing off the Irish Sea, the 17th is a daunting prospect for the most precise of golfers. Altogether Hoylake provides one of the grest tests of quality golf and is a regular venue for the British Open championship, which it has hosted ten times. In 1930 it was the scene of Bobby Jones's second leg in the unparalleled "Grand Slam".

16th, 533 yards long. This hole was decisive in the last round of the 1967 Open when Jack Nicklaus and the sentimental favourite Roberto de Vicenzo fought a superbly entertaining duel. Nicklaus, playing ahead, scored a birdie-four, before Vicenzo struck his drive to the very edge of the field. From there he hit a soaring spoon to make sure of a birdie and the title.

Of all the finishing holes at Hoylake the 17th can make the greatest play on courage and fear. A cool, firm contrary wind emphasizes the severely taxing nature of the hole where the green is angled across the line of flight, with a road flanking its far side and approaches. The slightest overhit, cut or pushed second shot can easily trickle out-of-bounds under the fence, while the cautious, playing to the left, risk deep bunkers from where the recovery must be played towards the road, a disagreeable prospect. To have a reasonable shot for the flag the drive must hold the right side of the fairway and escape the bunkers that lurk there for the shot that leaks, as shots are inclined to leak in times of stress. Although the last hole is not overly demanding, the man who has played the last five in fours is no mean golfer.

Card of the course

No 1	Course	428 yards	par 4
No 2	Road	369 yards	par 4
No 3	Long	505 yards	par 5
No 4	Cop	195 yards	par 3
No 5	Telegraph	449 yards	par 4
No 6	Briars	423 yards	par 4
No 7	Dowie	200 yards	par 3
No 8	Far	479 yards	par 5
No 9	Punchbowl	393 yards	par 4
No 10	Dee	409 yards	par 4
No 11	Alps	200 yards	par 3
No 12	Hilbre	454 yards	par 4
No 13	Rushes	157 yards	par 3
No 14	Field	512 yards	par 5
No 15	Lake	460 yards	par 4
No 16	Dun	533 yards	par 5
No 17	Royal	418 yards	par 4
No 18	Stand	395 yards	par 4

Royal Liverpool Golf Club, Hoylake, Merseyside

Out	3,441 yards	36
In	3,538 yards	36
Total	6,979 yards	par 72

Record: 67, Robert de Vicenzo, Gary Player, 1967 Open

Soft to the eye, steel to the touch

After unobtrusively running the length of the course the railway cuts in closer at the 8th, forcing many players to play safe and take an iron from the tee.

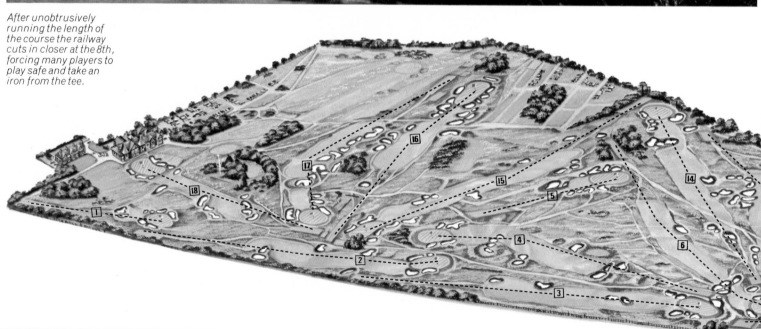

Though it lays no claim to be the most attractive course in Britain, Lytham St Annes is certainly one of the most difficult, demanding both nerve and subtlety. It has become less of a links and more of a seaside course over the decades—softer and lusher—but none the less it remains essentially a testing layout and a premier championship venue.

Unlike some of its peers among British links, the Lytham and St Anne's course, founded in 1886, has no visual splendour. It has an urban setting, hedged about for much of the time by houses and with a railway forming one boundary. No noble sandhills mark its horizons, the ground does not move in dramatic fashion and the sea might be miles away. But let nobody be deceived by this apparent tranquillity and smoothness. The course is a test of golf many times proven to be among the finest in Britain.

The clubhouse is serene, substantial and Victorian, similar to others in the northwest of England; it is at one with the links, which touches its very walls. There is, too, a dormy house—a rare facility at British clubs nowadays and about its grounds a garden atmosphere that makes a soothing background to the earnest pursuit of golf.

The club has a proud place in the championships of the past half-century. It was there in 1926 that Bobby Jones won the first of his three Opens in Britain. Soon afterwards he won the United States Open as well, becoming the first man to hold both titles in the same summer. In 1935 Lawson Little, the most formidable force in amateur golf of the post-Jones era, successfully defended the Amateur championship against a gallant William Tweddell. After World War II an international parade of champions, Bobby Locke, Peter Thomson and Bob Charles, had their hours before Tony Jacklin arrested the tide of overseas domination. And in 1974 Gary Player won one of the most emphatic victories of his generation.

Twice in the 1950s, Opens were memorable for the imperishable presence of Gene Sarazen,

one of the last enduring links with an earlier golden age of golf. On both occasions he played through the championship finishing well up the lists and giving a remarkable exhibition of varied shots with the more lofted fairway woods. In 1958 he recalled how on the same links thirty-five years earlier he had won a tournament and Harry Vardon had been one of his partners. Vardon played his first Open in 1893, Sarazen his last eighty years later at Troon, an incomparable span.

Lytham's tally of champions is an impressive tribute to the quality of the course, of which Bernard Darwin, the first golf writer of real distinction, wrote long ago: "If the day is calm and we are hitting fairly straight the golf seems rather easy than otherwise; and yet we must never allow ourselves to think so too pronouncedly or we shall straightaway find it becoming unpleasantly difficult." Many great golfers of today would agree with him.

The short first hole, with its tee in a pleasing arbour, is comparatively placid, but the shots to the next two are haunted by the adjoining railway and in a flanking wind it is all too easy to slice or push out-of-bounds. Bunkers, too, are nicely set up to harass those who take an overly cautious line to the left. If a breeze helps on the opening holes it certainly does not on the 4th. It is a timely reminder of what may lie in wait on the homeward journey. Often the island of fairway between dunes and rough can seem disconcertingly remote and the green is angled to the left. An early birdie can easily be countered here, and anything but a straight and truly judged shot to the short 5th is more likely than not to be punished.

In normal summer conditions the next two holes quicken thoughts of birdie fours, given a fair stance on the crumpled 6th fairway from which to carry cross-bunkers and hold an exposed crown of green and a drive threaded down the long ribbon of the 7th. The green here is concealed by a bank between sentinel dunes, but in a helping breeze Nicklaus—and his like in power from the tees—have been home with medium irons.

Hereabouts the course has more the expected character of a links; the dunes are wild and owe nothing to the hand of man. High on a plateau among them is the 8th green, an exposed and deceptive target for the approach from the valley below. Many players take irons from the high tee because—with the railway taking its last look at the course—straightness is all. The 9th is a pure target shot down to a green nestling amid bunkers and is rather more taxing than it looks, though numerous golfers have made light of the outward half. In 1963 Thomson and Tom Haliburton turned in 29 on the first day of the Open, a record for the championship, but few such starts have not been retarded by the demands of the closing holes.

The 10th, a relic of other days with its drive blind to a tumbling fairway and its tilted little green, and the long dull plain of the 11th, where huge bunkers challenge the drive, may not be too severe. The 12th is quite another matter: it is the only short hole on the inward half, and presents the most difficult and uncompromising shot to a green of the whole round. A wood shelters the tee from the prevailing left-hand wind and the shot—long iron or even wood—must be held against it if the ▷

Card of the course

No 1	206 yards	par 3	No 10	334 yards	par 4
No 2	420 yards	par 4	No 11	485 yards	par 5
No 3	458 yards	par 4	No 12	189 yards	par 3
No 4	393 yards	par 4	No 13	339 yards	par 4
No 5	188 yards	par 3	No 14	445 yards	par 4
No 6	486 yards	par 5	No 15	468 yards	par 4
No 7	551 yards	par 5	No 16	356 yards	par 4
No 8	394 yards	par 4	No 17	413 yards	par 4
No 9	162 yards	par 3	No 18	386 yards	par 4

The Royal Lytham and St Annes Golf Club

St Annes-on-Sea, Lancashire

Out	3,258 yards	35
In	3,415 yards	36
Total	6,673 yards	par 71

Record: 65, Christy O'Connor, The Open 1969

Deep bunkers with steep faces are a feature of Lytham St Annes, and are particularly prominent on three of the four closing holes. Although no hole stands out as a classic, the course has few weaknesses.

▷ raised green, with bunkers to the left and front right, is to be reached.

If the shot slides away or is overhit, like Johnny Miller's in the second round in 1974, out-of-bounds is perilously close. Miller was hard in pursuit of Player until his shot finished close to the fence. He took three more to reach the green and the six eroded his challenge. The hole is as finely designed as any of its length on a British links and is the introduction, after a breather at the 13th, to a finish that rarely fails to influence the outcome of any event.

To say that a championship course is a good test of driving is to belabour the obvious, but even without aggressively penal hazards, some are stronger in this respect than others. Writing before the 1969 Open, Thomson remarked that straight pin-point driving was the key to victory; it certainly had been for him in 1958. He was referring mainly to the inward half, which changes direction more often than the outward and involves frequent readjustment, particularly if there is a wind.

The 14th is straight enough, but even in a light cross-wind the fairway is hard to hit and hold and so, from the rough, is the green, which falls gently away from the striker. Unless the drive to the 15th cuts off a substantial slice of the curving, rising fairway there is little hope of reaching or even getting a sight of the green. The line for the approach is between dunes, with cross-bunkers just beyond, devilish rough to the left of the green and bunkers the other side. "God, it's a hard hole," said Nicklaus in 1974, and the facts supported him. The hole, at 468 yards, played overlong into wind and for the first three days the stroke average of the whole Open field was more than one over par, the highest the Open had seen for many a year.

Dramatic, emotive and unorthodox finishes

The Open has had few more exciting finishes than those played at Lytham, where the strength of the last two holes has heightened the drama. Bobby Locke, Peter Thomson and Bob Charles won there after some tense moments on the 17th and 18th, but it is the manner in which Lytham's three other Open winners have finished that is best remembered. Bobby Jones demonstrated his supreme control under pressure, Tony Jacklin's win was an emotional moment in British golf and Gary Player struck the most unorthodox final approach of any Open.

Bobby Jones's magnificent recovery shot at the 17th in the 1926 Open is marked by this plaque.

The 17th: The supreme pressure stroke

Going into the last round of the 1926 Open championship, only three men, Bobby Jones, Walter Hagen and Al Watrous, were thought to have a chance. In the event Hagen could not match the other two, who came to the 17th on level terms. There, after Watrous had reached the green in two, Jones found himself faced with a desperate situation. His drive had found a bunker to the left of the fairway some 175 yards from the green and it seemed he must lose a stroke—if not the Open. But Jones thought otherwise. He took his mashie iron, the hickory-shafted equivalent of today's 4-iron, and struck a flawless shot which finished "inside" Watrous. An infinitesimal margin of error either way would have been disastrous. He picked the ball cleanly, ensuring that no sand prevented him from making perfect contact with the ball. Jones thus was able to get his par, but Watrous took three putts. With all to play for, Jones had produced one of the supreme pressure strokes of all time.

Jones's view of the 17th for his historic second. "There goes a hundred thousand bucks," said close rival Al Watrous when it hit the green.

With his second landing right by the wall of Lytham's Victorian clubhouse, above, on the last hole of the 1974 Open, Gary Player played left-handed with his putter, below. He missed his par but still won his third Open.

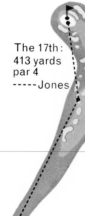

The 17th: 413 yards par 4 ----- Jones

The 18th: Player wins left-handed

In the last round of the 1974 Open, Gary Player's approach to the 18th ran through the green and lodged against the side wall of the Lytham clubhouse, leaving him without room for his swing. He avoided taking an extra stroke by electing not to hit away from the green but to play the shot left-handed. He used his putter and stroked the ball to the centre of the green. Player said later that he had been careful to take a short backswing and to play the shot with a long follow-through.

In his amateur days, Jack Nicklaus, faced with a similar situation, but lying considerably farther from the green, swung left-handed with a 5-iron and produced a shot of about 150 yards. He favoured the 5-iron because he could turn it over and, using the orthodox left-handed grip, hit the ball with the club face.

When the 15th is tough the 16th offers relief and likely birdies, but the blind tee shot must be placed to avoid bunkers, and to take advantage of the opening to the guarded green, to which the strength of the short approach must be perfectly judged. Then the course attacks once more. The driving area from the 17th tee narrows between, on the left, a nest of shallow bunkers and real wilderness and, on the right, rough to an appendix of fairway which ends abruptly against a bank of sandhills. The hole then swings to the left with an inviting shot to an open green with bunkers on either hand—

but it is inviting only to the man who has driven far enough on the right line. Ideally, the shot should be as far as possible down the right side of the fairway. If short or to the left the green is invisible.

It most certainly was for Jones in 1926, as he faced the shot which, down the ages, was to become a legend. Rarely has the destiny of a championship depended on one stroke and the balance between disaster and triumph been so sharply defined. Jones had come from behind in the last round and he and Al Watrous were level after 70 holes. Watrous hit a good drive into

position for a clear shot to the green, but Jones pulled into one of the little bunkers just off the fairway. Between his ball and the flag, some 170 yards away, were all kinds of perdition—sandhills, thick scrub and rough. Watrous played to the edge of the green and his feelings can be imagined as he waited for Jones to play. He must have thought that he would lead by at least a stroke going to the last tee.

Jones must have been angry with himself for what seemed likely to be a fatal drive, but when he saw the ball lying clean, hope must have stirred anew. He had to go for the green; a safe ▷

The 18th: A supreme moment for Jacklin

In all British golf there has never been a moment to compare with that when Tony Jacklin walked on to the 18th tee in the last round of the Open at Lytham in 1969. He was two strokes ahead of Bob Charles, his partner and closest challenger, and the championship was his for the taking. It was to be the first British victory since Max Faulkner had won at Portrush in 1951, and the end of the longest span of overseas domination since Henry Cotton had arrested American supremacy at Sandwich in 1934. The vast amphitheatre of stands embracing the last green was packed with thousands and the flanks of the fairways were solid with people, tense, expectant and longing to explode with pride and

acclaim for the young and popular champion.

It was a classic situation, one that every young golfer, not least Jacklin, has dreamed upon, and now those dreams were about to become reality. It was no time to think of the wealth and fame that victory would bring, nor of the joy it would give to British followers of sport everywhere, but to concentrate only on making one last true swing. Situations such as these are the ultimate test of technique and temperament.

The greatness of the hole, only 386 yards, is in the tee shot. Across the fairway in the driving area are two diagonal lines of bunkers, seven in all. The farthest of these from the tee are on the left, threatening the drive pulled away from the

wilderness of bushes on the right. Except in a following wind the safe landing area is very small for a driver shot. It is the most demanding final tee shot on any British links; no other has been of greater significance in recent Opens. It destroyed the hopes of Eric Brown, Christy O'Connor and Leopoldo Ruiz in 1958, and of Nicklaus five years later, but not of Jacklin.

Watching his swing for the drive was sufficient to know whether the shot was good because the pace of the takeaway was so smooth and deliberate. It proved to be a superb stroke, absolutely straight, far clear of any danger, and leaving him only a quiet 7-iron from the green.

Tempo or rhythm had always been the key to Jacklin's best golf. In his younger years he would whip the club away from the ball too quickly, but as he progressed towards the heights he concentrated on making his backswing much slower and thereby smoother. Throughout that Open he preserved his finest tempo, concentrating his practice each day, mostly with a 7-iron, towards the point where he felt that the slow tempo was natural to him.

Rare is the golfer who would not profit greatly from striving to find the rhythm best suited to him. It can vary considerably according to individual temperaments, but once discovered it is worth preserving, so that in moments of pressure the swing is less likely to become a nervous snatch.

Playing with supreme control and authority, Tony Jacklin ended eighteen years of foreign domination of the Open with his fine win at Lytham in 1969, when he led in three previous holders—Bob Charles, Peter Thomson and Roberto de Vicenzo. His walk down the 18th fairway, below, *was one of the supremely emotional moments in the not unstirring history of British golf.*

▷ recovery to the fairway would probably cost a stroke and leave Watrous with the psychological advantage and the lead. It was all or nothing. He took his mashie iron (which remains a precious reminder in the clubhouse) and struck the deathless stroke. It finished on the green inside Watrous.

The wonder of the stroke, now marked by a plaque on the side of the bunker, was that Jones had the control of nerve, rhythm and swing to strike the ball perfectly at such a moment; the margin of error was so slight. As later he wrote of this moment: "An eighth of an inch too deep with your blade, off dry sand, and the shot expires right in front of your eyes. And if your blade is a thought too high. . . . I will dismiss this harrowing reflection."

The effect on Watrous must have been fearful. Suddenly all the pressure was upon him and who would condemn him for taking three putts? He was bunkered by the last green and Jones was safe except from Walter Hagen, who eventually had to hole his second shot to tie. Hagen, with his love of the dramatic, had the flag removed. His ball very nearly pitched into the hole but it went over the green. Jones moved nearer to Olympus.

Crisis and the 17th seem almost inseparable. In 1958 David Thomas, who for many years was as accurate with a driver as most men are with

a medium iron, and uncommonly long at that, hit a huge drive into precisely the right place. Although he had a good sight of the green, his 6-iron shot was a shade heavy; he took five, and lost to Peter Thomson in a play-off the following day.

Five years later Nicklaus stood on the 17th fairway in the last round, knowing that two fours would probably be good enough to win. They would have been, but a 2-iron was a club too much for the second shot. It ran through the green into heavy rough, from where he took three more. His last drive was pulled into the left hand of the seven bunkers that make the hole so testing from the tee and he took another five. This was one of the rare occasions when Nicklaus could be said to have cast away a major championship. A few minutes later Bob Charles and Phil Rodgers made their fours on the last hole to beat him. The next day Charles became the first—and maybe for generations to come the last—left-hander to win one of the world's major championships.

There was no crisis for Jacklin in 1969. He could afford to take five at the 17th and still remain two ahead of Charles. With all the confidence in the world he played the last hole superbly and strode down the fairway towards a moment the like of which even Lytham, in all its long history, had never seen before. He had

become the first champion Britain had produced in eighteen years.

In 1974 the large 1.68-in ball was made compulsory for the Open and the elements combined to make the golf a severe test of control and patience. It confirmed the greatness of Gary Player. After 36 holes he was five clear of the field, the largest halfway margin since Henry Cotton, forty years earlier, had led by nine at Sandwich.

Although the course was not playing short, Player frequently used a 1-iron instead of a driver to ensure hitting the fairways, thus observing the first and most fundamental principle of mastering Lytham. Of his eight major championship victories it was unarguably the most commanding, and his winning margin of four was less than he deserved.

The last two holes were responsible. Player was leading Peter Oosterhuis by six shots when he pulled his second into the menacingly deep rough to the left of the bunkers guarding the green. Several minutes' frantic search followed before the ball was found; he could hardly move it at his first attempt, but chipped dead for his five. His second to the 18th was too strong and overran the green to settle close to the wall beneath the clubhouse windows. From there, the Open champion played his last, dramatic approach—left-handed, with a putter.

A putting stroke that destroyed Phil Rodgers

Ask any number of tournament professionals the name of the finest putter since Bobby Locke at his best and almost with one voice they will pick Bob Charles, the only world-class golfer who played left-handed. It would be hard to make a stronger case for anyone else, in spite of the fame on the greens of men like Bob Rosburg, Billy Casper and others. Year in and year out Charles has been wonderfully consistent, and it is doubtful if any other golfer has holed more long putts.

The Open he won at Lytham in 1963 was a good example, especially in the play-off, when his putting tortured and destroyed Phil Rodgers with a merciless finality that was almost inhuman. In the morning round he had single putts on no fewer than eleven greens, having played to them less accurately than Rodgers. If ever putting was the name of the game it was for Charles that day.

His putting method is wonderfully simple. He eliminates his wrists from the stroke, using his arms and club exactly like a pendulum. The movement of the clubhead originates from the shoulders but he has said that he likes to feel that a point at the centre of the back of his neck is the true pivotal point. If this swing is true, the blade of the putter will always be square to the line at the moment of impact, and that simply is the heart of the matter.

Although the pendulum style might not suit every golfer—putting is always an individual business—two points about Charles are worthy of note. He has used the same type of centre-shafted putter and basically the same method throughout his career. Not for him the desperate and usually futile switching of clubs and styles indulged in by so many golfers. His guiding principle has been to develop a sound method, practice enough to gain confidence in it and then—to leave it well alone.

It is beyond doubt that Bob Charles is the best left-hander in the history of the game and the finest player ever produced by New Zealand. He is almost certainly the supreme putter of his era, rivalled only by Billy Casper. His smooth pendulum style was never more effective than at Lytham in 1963, when he demoralized American Phil Rodgers in the Open play-off with devastating effect, taking only one putt on eleven holes in the morning round. He might well have repeated his victory on the same course six years later, when he opened with a blistering 66 and led for two days, but he lost control for a short spell in the third round and finished second, two shots behind Tony Jacklin.

The supreme heathland course

Early golf in Britain was confined to links beside the sea. Apart from a few courses in Scotland it was not until the late nineteenth century that it was played to any extent elsewhere. As the game increased in popularity, the eyes of golfers turned inland; courses were laid out on public commons and in private parks and a new conception of the game was in being. The most significant development was the discovery that even rough heathland could swiftly be converted into ideal golfing ground. The outcome was a wealth of splendid courses which, in their fashion, have become almost as distinctive an expression of British golf as the ancient links themselves.

The finest examples of heath courses lie on a stretch of country west of London. All have common features of pine, birch, heather and wonderfully firm, smooth turf that, on account of the sandy subsoil, absorbs moisture with rare speed. Of all these courses Sunningdale is supreme.

The Old course owed its foundation to the enterprise of two brothers, who conceived the idea of golf on the wild heathland spreading away to Chobham Common. It was owned by St John's College, Cambridge, which granted leaseholds for a course and the building of houses near by. This was one of the earliest instances in England, if not the first, of property development in harness with the creation of a golf course. Willie Park, son of the first Open champion, was commissioned to lay it out for £3,800—a sum that would hardly suffice for one hole today.

The club was fortunate—or inspired—in its choice of Park, for he was one of the pioneers of modern course architecture. He had the experience from being a great player, having won the Open twice, and was educated and ambitious to a degree rare in professionals of those days. In his appreciation of the classic features of the old courses, and his awareness of the changing needs of the time, he set unusual standards that, doubtless, influenced many of his successors.

Seeds were sown in the late summer of 1900 and a year later the course was ready. The soil on the heath was poor and sour and, apparently, ▷

The prospect of Sunningdale is one of great charm rather than severity, and the Old course's best sequence of holes probably begins with the drive downhill from the 5th tee, left. The second must carry the pond which, though small, restricts the entry to the green. The 6th is another downhill drive in the same direction, but with the pine woods closing in on either side. The green sits up on a shelf-like plateau with a formidable trio of bunkers awaiting the underhit approach shot. Play becomes tighter at the "Switchback" 7th, where the blind drive must carry a ridge before the tee and the second shot to another plateau green is menaced by a fairway narrowing to a few yards in width.

Sunningdale Golf Club, Berkshire
Old course

Out	3,101 yards	36
In	3,432 yards	36
Total	6,533 yards	par 72

Record: 63, Norman Von Nida

Much of Sunningdale's air of open innocence disappears when the golfer off the tee arrives to play his second shot, with tricky pitches to raised greens and well-placed bunkers to catch anything that rolls. The course starts off in unusual fashion with a very long hole, just short of 500 yards. The boundary is to the right, but the fairway is comfortably wide. However, playing to the left and too much safety can leave an awkward chip up the banked side of the plateau green and, with bunkers set into it, there is little room for error. With half the greens placed on hills, Sunningdale rewards good chipping and pitching.

▷ some decried the project as folly. Not long afterwards they were claiming that anyone could make a course in such splendid, natural golf country.

The course is one of enchantment, rarely of menace; its challenge is one of subtlety rather than length. When the fairways are running in summer the longest holes, the 1st and 14th, can be reached in two shots. At no time is the Old overpowering and it offers an appealing variety of shots, not least at the short par-fours. The 3rd green can be driven, but the normal tee shot leaves an approach of rare delicacy to an away-sloping green. The 11th is a gem; the blind drive to a falling fairway must avoid a bunker on the left and a copse of pines on the right, but the greatness of the hole is in deciding how to play

the little approach to the raised table of green.

Several tees command superb views and offer the exhilaration of driving from high places: from the 5th with its green beyond a shining pond, and the 6th mounting into the wooded distance from an island fairway; from the 10th where the driver looks down upon a promised land with, far beyond over the woods, a glimpse of the russet and white of the club-house; and the short 13th, with its deceptive shot from a pinnacle tee to a green part-embraced by an insidious little grassy trench.

The 15th, a taxing shot across the prevailing wind, is a noble short hole which begins a sternly beautiful finish. Unless the drive is long the approach to the 16th green must be flighted from a downhill lie over cross-bunkers on the far side of a shallow valley. Again, at the 17th— unless the drive flirts with a spinney lurking on the left—the approach must be played from a hanging stance.

The gentle incline towards the home green, with a great spreading oak just beyond, makes for a fine drive and an approach that was im-proved by German bombs in 1940. One bomb made a crater to the right of the green which prompted the idea of converting it into bunkers. The shot can be demanding, the more so because a path marks out-of-bounds beyond bunkers

flanking the left of the green and is more in play than the striker from the fairway might imagine.

There never was a course that someone did not murder on occasion. In kindly weather, when the beautiful greens are at their best, the expert can readily enjoy himself. Shortly after World War II, Australian Norman Von Nida burned his way to victory with a 63 in the last round of the Dunlop Masters. Gary Player, in winning the first important event of his life in 1956, played the Old in 64; but the most famous of all rounds were those of Bobby Jones when qualifying for the Open in 1926. The first, a 66, was often quoted as the perfect round; 33 putts, 33 other shots, every hole in three or four. The next day he did have one five and one two in a 68 and it was no wonder that he said later, "I wish I could take this golf course home with me." Other golfers must have thought likewise after playing one of the loveliest of all courses.

The New course, designed by Colt in 1922, is quite different from its elegant sister. Where the Old might be feminine in its grace and wiles the New is sterner, more masculine. It is more ex-posed to the winds and bleaker in prospect but it has beauty in the emerald fairways curving through the heather, the broadness of the scene and the downs rolling away in the distance. And the challenge of the golf is undeniable.

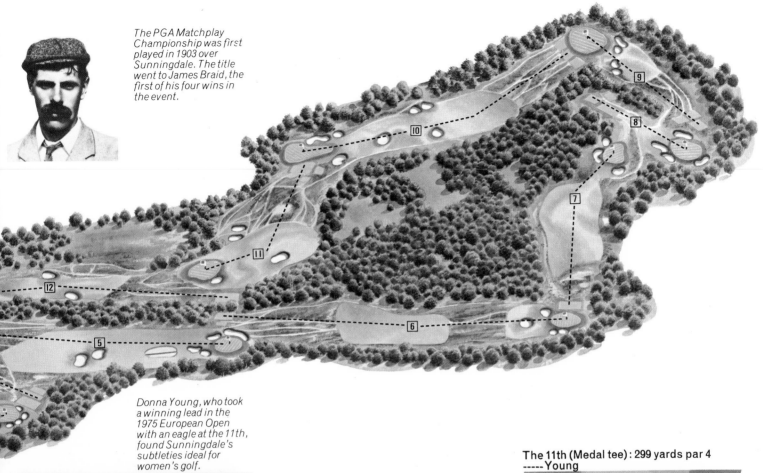

The PGA Matchplay Championship was first played in 1903 over Sunningdale. The title went to James Braid, the first of his four wins in the event.

Donna Young, who took a winning lead in the 1975 European Open with an eagle at the 11th, found Sunningdale's subtleties ideal for women's golf.

The 11th: Donna Young's cool decisiveness

Indecision is a ruthless wrecker of strokes. Every player should try to visualize the type and shape of stroke intended; if doubt exists, any stroke has little chance of succeeding. The 11th on the Old course at Sunningdale offers a classic play on a golfer's ability to make up his mind. Although the fairway cannot be seen from the tee, a spinney of pines indicates the line. However, they snare the slightest fade and can effectively stymie recovery from a shot that is wider. A pulled drive may escape a large bunker but another one, shrewdly placed by the left corner of the green, guards the approach to the flag.

The hole, only 325 yards, has often been driven, although most golfers are content to find the sloping fairway. Then comes the essence of the hole, the need to decide whether to pitch or run the little shot to the plateau green. Either needs delicate judgement if the ball is not to finish short or trickle maddeningly down the steep bank at the back of the green. The problem is intensified when the pin is beyond a slight crown on the green which can halt the hesitant shot or accelerate the one that is slightly too strong.

The type of shot is determined by the state of the golfer's mind. Donna Young must have been confident when she chose to pitch in the last round of the Colgate European Open in 1975. She struck it perfectly with her beautiful slow rhythm and saw it roll into the hole for a two. The eagle she scored here gave her the lead from Sandra Palmer and soon afterwards command of the championship was hers.

The 11th (Medal tee): 299 yards par 4
----- Young

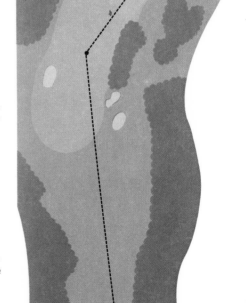

A young course worthy of the hundredth Open

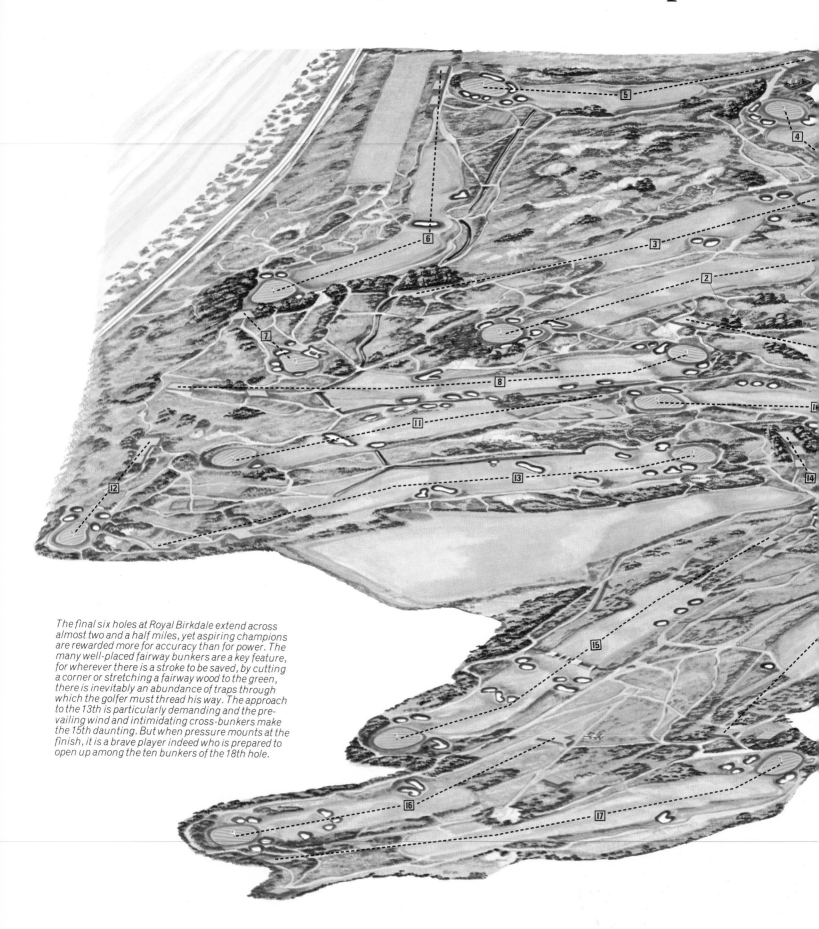

The final six holes at Royal Birkdale extend across almost two and a half miles, yet aspiring champions are rewarded more for accuracy than for power. The many well-placed fairway bunkers are a key feature, for wherever there is a stroke to be saved, by cutting a corner or stretching a fairway wood to the green, there is inevitably an abundance of traps through which the golfer must thread his way. The approach to the 13th is particularly demanding and the prevailing wind and intimidating cross-bunkers make the 15th daunting. But when pressure mounts at the finish, it is a brave player indeed who is prepared to open up among the ten bunkers of the 18th hole.

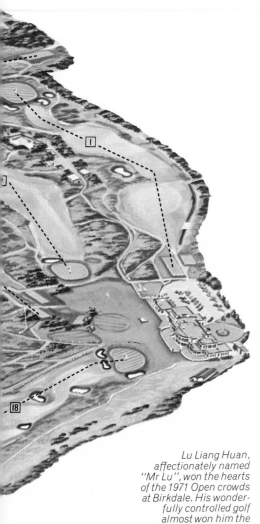

Lu Liang Huan, affectionately named "Mr Lu", won the hearts of the 1971 Open crowds at Birkdale. His wonderfully controlled golf almost won him the title, too, and for many provided the first proof of the ability of Oriental golfers to hold their own amongst the very best of the West.

Card of the course

No 1	450 yards	par 4	No 10	384 yards	par 4
No 2	423 yards	par 4	No 11	415 yards	par 4
No 3	410 yards	par 4	No 12	184 yards	par 3
No 4	206 yards	par 3	No 13	505 yards	par 5
No 5	343 yards	par 4	No 14	198 yards	par 3
No 6	468 yards	par 4	No 15	542 yards	par 5
No 7	150 yards	par 3	No 16	404 yards	par 4
No 8	470 yards	par 4	No 17	526 yards	par 5
No 9	410 yards	par 4	No 18	513 yards	par 5

Standing within a glorious expanse of dunes on the Lancashire coast, Royal Birkdale has been the setting for more championships and international matches than any other British course since the end of World War II—not even St Andrews has been as richly endowed. Without the variety of Muirfield or Newcastle, the charm of St George's or the subtleties of St Andrews, Birkdale has none the less tested the mighty and produced champions of enduring stature.

Birkdale arose from the inspiration of a handful of visionaries who rented for a mere £5 a plot of land, so plentiful on the Lancashire coast where dunes tumble in wild profusion; the first clubhouse was a five-shillings-a-week room in a private house, and the first professional discharged his duties for only three times that sum. The club has been extremely fortunate in its professionals. The present incumbent, Robert Halsall, has been there since 1928 and his predecessor, David McEwan, had served a long term since the last century.

The course, mainly designed by George Low, did not follow the principle, beloved by architects of old, that blind shots were essential. Instead, the holes were laid out in valleys between the towering sandhills and were not the adventurous exercise they might have been. A new clubhouse was built and pulled down again when it was found to be on someone else's land. The foundation of present eminence did not really begin until 1931, when Southport Corporation bought the land and gave the club a ninety-nine-year lease. Thenceforth all was progress. Fred Hawtree and J. H. Taylor redesigned the course and the clubhouse was built.

Even then Birkdale was not a seaside course in the traditional sense. Many of the fairways are flat and pose no problems of stance; the greens mostly are outlined against the dunes, often in clefts between them, giving a perspective of distance to help the golfer and also some protection from the wind when putting. There is nothing of the typical old seaside green with its flag shimmering on some distant horizon, and all manner of folding ground to make the hole look shorter than it is.

More than any other British championship course Birkdale offers golf of a target nature. But if problems of judging distance are not so acute, others are emphasized—notably the cardinal virtue of straightness. It is well enough to say that a green is a sharply defined target, like the 2nd, 10th or 17th, but it still has to be hit. To miss the greens at Birkdale, even narrowly, can leave an infernally difficult stroke from the clinging willow scrub, which abounds on the course, and often from a hanging lie at that. When the fairways are narrowed for a championship they make a fine test of driving, and should they happen to be fast as well, accuracy is crucial and power of little significance. The Open championship in 1965 was a fine example; it brought victory to Peter Thomson, simply by virtue of his unerring straightness, and precious little reward to Arnold Palmer and Jack Nicklaus.

In preparation for this memorable year in Birkdale's history—the Ryder Cup followed a few months after the Open—further alterations were made in the course. These involved a new 12th, a short hole cradled in the dunes, the elimination of the short 17th and the lengthening of the finish. Birkdale became possibly the only course in the world with four of the last six holes measuring over 500 yards.

In the 1954 Open, Birkdale's first, Peter Thomson's winning score of 284 was about strict par for the event; seven years later Arnold Palmer won with the same total but in dreadful conditions. The days were never free of wind, with a gale for the second round. Not since 1938, when wind almost wrecked an Open at Sandwich, had the golfers been as violently assaulted as that day at Birkdale. Before play began many tents were flat and the fairways were heavy with casual water but Palmer, loving the challenge of it all, was inspired to attack.

Few had ever seen iron play such as his that fearful morning; his massive hands rifling the ball under the wind made the senses reel. He was three under par for the first five holes. A magnificent round was in the making, but it was not to be. The 7th tee is high, yet protected from a sea wind, and Palmer should have forced a low shot. Instead he used a 9-iron; the ball was swept away and when he pulled from the next tee the spell was broken.

The 9th is one of the more testing drives because the angled fairway is not quite visible from the tee. Birkdale tends to punish the hook rather than its opposite. The 10th and 11th certainly do so, but offer no great problem if the drive is straight. Then, after a brief excursion into the lonely sandhills for the 12th, the homeward task begins in considerable earnest. The 13th has a long diagonal carry from the tee to a fairway fringed with bunkers, and the last short hole, again from a high, sheltered tee, is over a valley to a closely trapped green. The design of the short holes is not a distinctive feature of a splendid course.

The 15th is a superb hole, compelling a drive in the fairway if a great gathering of bunkers is to be carried with the second shot. These are ▷

Two champions show their powers of recovery

Both Peter Thomson and Arnold Palmer won their first British Open victories at Royal Birkdale and in doing so showed to the full their skill and composure in recovering from awkward situations, a talent vital for success at the highest level and often the hallmark of a champion.

The 15th: Palmer explodes in a shower of scrub

In his great years crisis was in the very nature of Arnold Palmer's golf; the capacity to resist and overcome the bad break or the erring shot was no small part of his extraordinary magnetism. One such instance befell him in the last round of the 1961 Open. When he came to the 15th (now the 16th) all seemed serene; Dai Rees, his closest challenger, was playing behind him and had not begun the brilliant spell that was to bring him within a stroke of Palmer at the finish. Palmer's drive, aimed a fraction overmuch to the right, the shortest distance to the green, socked deep in heavy scrub only a foot from the fairway.

The green, on its plateau, is heavily protected by bunkers. To reach it Palmer had to carry 140 yards or more. Where most golfers would have had to hack the ball out with a wedge and settle for a

five, Palmer used a 6-iron and swung it with all his might. The ball exploded out in a shower of scrub and reached the green. It was a phenomenal stroke, evidence of his fearsome strength and confidence. He made his four, the crisis had passed and he moved masterfully towards his first triumph in Britain.

The big danger in playing such strokes is that the club will catch in the rough before it can make contact with the ball, so that the shot will be smothered. Talking later about this, Palmer said: "The rough was very deep. My only thought was to get the club through as hard as I could and maybe the ball would run on to the green. I closed the face slightly to get it through as fast as possible and I was amazed that I was able to get it through as fast as I did. The ball finished up about fifteen feet from the flag."

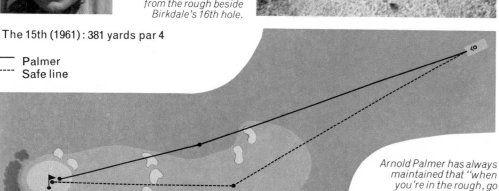

Dai Rees, left, pursued Arnold Palmer all the way in the 1961 Open only to lose by a stroke.

A plaque, right, marks the spot from which Palmer hit his now legendary recovery shot from the rough beside Birkdale's 16th hole.

The 15th (1961): 381 yards par 4

— Palmer
---- Safe line

Arnold Palmer has always maintained that "when you're in the rough, go for the green". His shot at Birkdale's 15th took both courage and power.

▷ angled so that the player going for the green must attempt the longest carry. The 16th green, poised on a table of rising land, has only sky for background, so the approach can be difficult to judge. From the 17th tee—a platform in an ocean of willow scrub—the line is guarded by huge dunes, Scylla and Charybdis, on either side of the fairway's entrance; it is a forbidding shot under pressure. In 1971 Lee Trevino pulled into one of these in the last round and his struggling seven enabled Lu Liang Huan (Mr Lu) of Taiwan to challenge to the end. Trevino, however, joined Jones, Sarazen and Hogan as the only players to have won the British and American Opens in the same summer.

Palmer, too, survived a savage break on this

hole in 1961. Down the hard wind his second whistled through the green into a small bunker. Normally recovery would have been easy, but the wind moved the ball as he struck. He skimmed it into bushes beyond the green and holed out in six. On reporting to officials that he had hit a moving ball he was automatically penalized another stroke.

Many were saddened by the disappearance of the old 17th, setting for the climax of two of the finest matches of the age. In the 1951 Walker Cup match Charles Coe, then a thin, grey ghost of a man and one of the most accomplished of modern amateurs, lost a classic encounter to Ronnie White, whose solid, true striking has had few peers. Throughout a long summer day

Coe's beautiful golf had the edge, but when he faltered—only slightly—the implacable White struck. His final stroke, a long iron, thumped to within a few feet of the flag. Two years later White himself was undone by Gerald Micklem in the final of the English championship—a remarkable triumph of character, for White then was deemed invincible.

As on other great links—such as Lytham, Turnberry and Westward Ho!—women were the pioneers in holding a championship at Birkdale. In 1909 Dorothy Campbell (later Mrs Hurd) won the trophy with "beautiful and deadly cleek play". She remains the only woman to have won the British and American titles more than once.

Some fifty years passed before Birkdale was

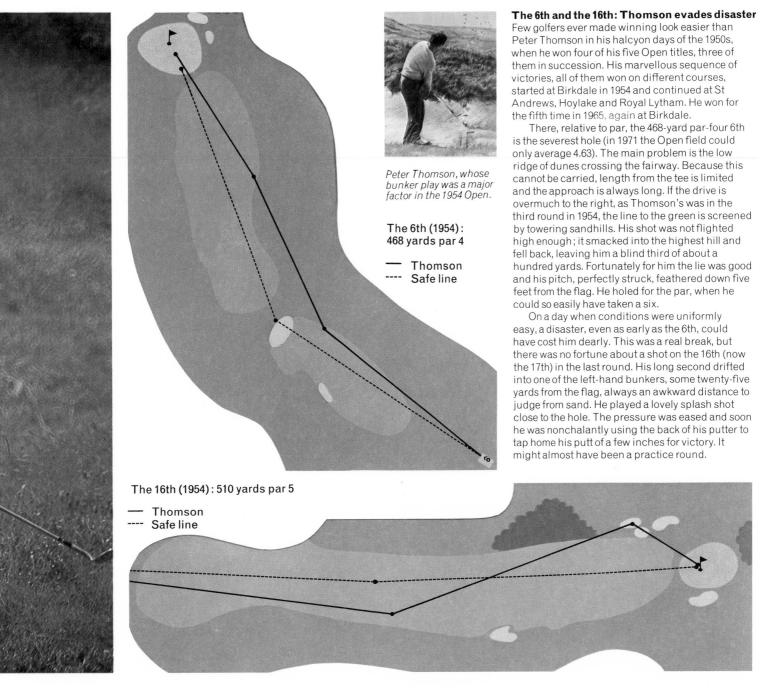

The 6th and the 16th: Thomson evades disaster

Few golfers ever made winning look easier than Peter Thomson in his halcyon days of the 1950s, when he won four of his five Open titles, three of them in succession. His marvellous sequence of victories, all of them won on different courses, started at Birkdale in 1954 and continued at St Andrews, Hoylake and Royal Lytham. He won for the fifth time in 1965, again at Birkdale.

There, relative to par, the 468-yard par-four 6th is the severest hole (in 1971 the Open field could only average 4.63). The main problem is the low ridge of dunes crossing the fairway. Because this cannot be carried, length from the tee is limited and the approach is always long. If the drive is overmuch to the right, as Thomson's was in the third round in 1954, the line to the green is screened by towering sandhills. His shot was not flighted high enough; it smacked into the highest hill and fell back, leaving him a blind third of about a hundred yards. Fortunately for him the lie was good and his pitch, perfectly struck, feathered down five feet from the flag. He holed for the par, when he could so easily have taken a six.

On a day when conditions were uniformly easy, a disaster, even as early as the 6th, could have cost him dearly. This was a real break, but there was no fortune about a shot on the 16th (now the 17th) in the last round. His long second drifted into one of the left-hand bunkers, some twenty-five yards from the flag, always an awkward distance to judge from sand. He played a lovely splash shot close to the hole. The pressure was eased and soon he was nonchalantly using the back of his putter to tap home his putt of a few inches for victory. It might almost have been a practice round.

Peter Thomson, whose bunker play was a major factor in the 1954 Open.

The 6th (1954): 468 yards par 4

— Thomson
---- Safe line

The 16th (1954): 510 yards par 5

— Thomson
---- Safe line

---

host to an important men's championship. Then, in 1946, the prodigious recovery power of James Bruen was too much for Robert Sweeny's graceful golf in the final of the Amateur championship. Bruen made light of the willow scrub, a feature of Birkdale and a fearsome hazard for ordinary mortals. He was the first of Birkdale's famous champions.

Since then a host of great events have been held at Royal Birkdale, not least the 1969 Ryder Cup match, when the home side held the Americans to a tie. Remarkably, of the thirty-two games played, foursomes, four-ball and singles, no fewer than sixteen were decided on the last green, and the last of all made an unforgettable climax. The countries were even

when Jacklin, who had holed a monstrous putt on the 17th to square his game, and Nicklaus stood on the last tee in the final match—all to play for between the two finest golfers of the generation from their respective countries. The hole was halved, Nicklaus holing from four feet and immediately conceding Jacklin's short putt, which was by no means dead. It was a gesture totally in keeping with the man and it ensured that a proud day for Britain and Birkdale would pass into history.

The story of Birkdale came full circle in 1971 with the 100th Open championship in which Lee Trevino, ultimate extrovert of golfers, impressed his name in the record books by becoming the fourth player to win the British and

American Opens in the same summer. This was the peak of a sustained spell of success that had rarely been matched in the game's history. Trevino played with formidable confidence, skill and attack; his command of the championship was absolute on the last day until he took a seven on the 71st hole, which enabled Lu Liang Huan to challenge until the last putt. Lu's beautiful straight golf over the fast-running fairways, his effortless rhythm and courtly manners endeared him to the huge crowds, which were a record for the Open in England. His was the only lasting threat to Trevino, although Jacklin summoned all his reserves of courage, after a disappointing season in America, and finished in third place.

An inland course of seaside character

Apart from scattered jewels on the coasts of Kent and Norfolk, the eastern flanks of England are not richly endowed with golfing places. But at Ganton, in Yorkshire, there is one which stands in the finest company of inland courses. It lies a few miles from Scarborough on the high road to York in the peaceful vale of Pickering, with wooded hills and patterned meadowland rising gently on either side. As one turns down the lane to the club there is a sense of remoteness from the workaday world.

The course is in open heathland, quietly undulating on turf that seems unusually restful to the tread. The grass is in fact of true seaside type with sandy subsoil; on occasions, ground staff have even turned up seashells in the bunkers. Ganton has been likened to the courses of Surrey and Berkshire, though in reality the resemblance is slight because only on four holes do trees normally come into play. There are no avenues or confinement by woods and only occasionally, where great banks of gorse can threaten, is there not an awareness of space.

In all England, Woodhall Spa, Lincolnshire, is probably Ganton's only peer for depth and expanse of bunkers; a player who is bunkered quite often vanishes from view, but not unfairly. It is a welcome feature in an age when the trend in design is towards the easing of hazards.

Trees serve mainly for strategic purposes, such as the one at the 14th, a short par-four that strong men can drive in a helping wind. The tree menaces the drive aimed away from the deep cross-bunkers guarding the approaches to the green. At the 16th a handsome group on the left of the beautiful falling fairway forms a hazard for those who, fearful of letting their shot drift into trees flanking the right-hand side, play overmuch to the left. And, lastly, a stand of pines makes a fine closing hole into a memorable one. Otherwise, except at the 12th, the golfer need never be beset by aerial hazards.

At one time the 12th was a straightforward short hole until various events, notably the Ryder Cup match in 1949, exposed the course as being too short for the highest class. A new green was built, making the hole swing hard right around deep woods. The daring or the strong can cut the corner from the tee, but woe betide the man who overdoes it.

The opening holes are fine examples of the admirable play made of the contours of the land: the smoothly rising 1st and the long fall of the 2nd, its green menaced on either hand by encroaching gorse, which also serves to make one concentrate on the 3rd tee. The 4th is a lovely hole with its drive to the crest of a fairway and approach across a valley to a plateau green, a creation of H. S. Colt (one of several distinguished architects who had a hand in Ganton). Yet the changing levels are never arduous. The golfer can always see what he is about; given a reasonable drive no hazards are hidden, no approaches blind.

The splendidly sited bunkers, especially those protecting the fairways, make the course a demanding test of driving, while the greens, not savagely guarded, offer a rewarding prospect. Invariably, like the rest of the course, they are in flawless condition. The club and its green-

Card of the course

No 1	370 yards	par 4	No 10	169 yards	par 3
No 2	420 yards	par 4	No 11	403 yards	par 4
No 3	330 yards	par 4	No 12	360 yards	par 4
No 4	397 yards	par 4	No 13	500 yards	par 5
No 5	153 yards	par 3	No 14	280 yards	par 4
No 6	444 yards	par 4	No 15	441 yards	par 4
No 7	427 yards	par 4	No 16	448 yards	par 4
No 8	387 yards	par 4	No 17	255 yards	par 4
No 9	496 yards	par 5	No 18	397 yards	par 4

Ganton Golf Club, Scarborough, Yorkshire

Out	3,424 yards	36
In	3,253 yards	36
Total	6,677 yards	par 72

Record: 66, Eddie Polland, Dunlop Masters 1975

The hazards of Ganton are plain for all to see, and the golfer taking risks takes calculated ones. It is an aspect of the course that becomes telling when, in a tight finish, players face a challenge such as the tee shot at the 17th. It must carry over a road, a formidable pit and heavy bunkering.

keepers have always taken an uncommon pride in cherishing their course.

Above all, there is change and variety. After the smooth sweep of the 6th out into the country, the 7th swings back, curving across a shallow fall in the land to a slightly raised green. The long 9th has a valley all its own, encouraging length and compelling straightness, while the 13th, the last par-five, is likewise inviting after a forbidding drive over great banks of gorse.

The first two short holes are most engaging; the 5th with its pool awaiting the pull, and the 10th in a wooded corner. The 17th can be formidable with its carry over the road and cross-bunker to a far green, closely trapped and exposed to all the winds. It simply demands a long, true shot, not easily achieved when the destiny of a match or score is at issue. The hole is a key part of a stern finish, beginning at the 15th with its array of sandy caverns to be avoided from the tee.

Ganton, created in 1891, has been closely linked with the story of English golf since Harry Vardon, while professional there, won the first of his six Open championships. Two years later he crushed Willie Park in a challenge match at Ganton and the foundation of a deathless fame was laid. Although the club had long been the pride of Yorkshire golfers, attracting a sub-

stantial membership from the professions and higher echelons of industry, its widest recognition did not come until the Ryder Cup match.

This was memorable for a great recovery by the Americans after losing three of the four foursomes. Inspired by their captain, Hogan, then convalescing after his accident, they produced ruthless figures in winning six of the singles. The golf of Mangrum, Demaret, Snead and others brooked no response from the British, although Rees and Adams played finely in winning their matches.

Four years later Max Faulkner became the only British golfer thus far to win the matchplay championship, beating Rees in the final at Ganton, as well as the Open and Dunlop Masters. From 1953 until 1975, when the Masters brought Bernard Gallacher his second successive victory, the course's great occasions were confined to amateur affairs. The effortless striking of Alan Thirlwell in 1955 enabled him to retain his English title, and in 1964 Michael Lunt just failed to defend the Amateur championship he had won the previous year, losing to Gordon Clark in the final at the 39th. In 1968 Michael Bonallack made an indelible mark on Ganton's history.

In the final of the English championship that year he played a round in 61, ten under the then

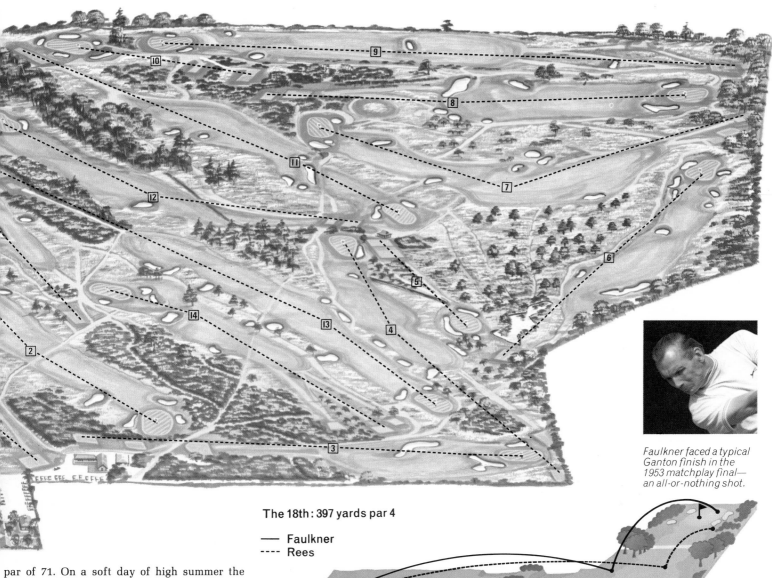

Faulkner faced a typical
Ganton finish in the
1953 matchplay final—
an all-or-nothing shot.

The 18th: 397 yards par 4

— Faulkner
---- Rees

par of 71. On a soft day of high summer the course could not have played more easily, yet even so Bonallack was superb. He missed only three greens, was home in 29 and gave an exhibition of putting the like of which has rarely been approached. His hapless opponent, David Kelley, was even par for 13 holes—and seven down. When the match ended, Bonallack had played 25 holes in 89 strokes, the most merciless golf in a British championship since Lawson Little was 82 for 23 holes in the Amateur final at Prestwick in 1934.

The distaff side has also had its hours at Ganton with various team contests and championships. During the visit of six American professionals many had their only sight of the incomparable Babe Zaharias, and in 1954 there was one of the most stirring of all women's matches. On her way to winning the British championship Frances Smith (then Stephens), the most resolute British competitor of her generation, beat Marlene Streit (then Stewart) of Canada, one of the finest of all women golfers, at the fourth extra hole of a semi-final.

Ganton has known many proud and unforgettable moments. But its enduring place in English golf is in the pleasure it has given, and will continue to give, to countless golfers from the humblest to the most accomplished.

The 18th: A death-or-glory challenge
Drive slightly to the left from the last tee at Ganton and you learn why it is one of the finest closing holes in the country. The second shot then is screened by a copse of pines which can pose the severe problem of combining elevation with length. The green, flanked by bunkers and with outer defences of gorse, can be a long iron's distance away. Max Faulkner, all square with Dai Rees in their matchplay final in 1953, found himself thus encumbered. But he felt himself to be just far enough back to make the distance and the height over the trees and braving all the perils with a death-or-glory shot, he hit a great iron to the back of the green.

This was a clear instance when the gamble was worth while. Rees was on the fairway and likely to make a four so Faulkner had to go for the shot, with the possibility that success might disconcert his opponent. As it proved Rees missed the green with his second shot, chipped short and Faulkner won the match with a four.

Matchplay tactics can vary greatly from those in a strokeplay event. The psychological effect on an opponent often justifies the taking of a chance which would not be justified in strokeplay because of the possibility of a heavier penalty. Unless it happened to be the last hole of a tournament, and a four was needed to win or tie, most golfers in Faulkner's position would probably have taken a more lofted club and played safely to the fairway, minimizing the risk of finding the trouble around the green. Calculation of risk within the limits of ability is essential at any level of competition.

A Kentish haven of history

No course is closer to the golfing heart of England than Royal St George's at Sandwich because of its association with the growth of championship golf and its distinctive character. No other English club moved so swiftly from a quiet and pleasant beginning to a lasting place in the chronicles of the game.

Since Roman times Sandwich has been a harbour. More than 1,000 years ago Wilfred, Bishop of Northumberland, arrived "pleasantly and happily in Sandwich haven"—and a haven it remains. The town, with its quaint, mysterious little streets and ancient dwellings, is snug and peaceful, and the links are wild and lonely, free to the winds and the sky as they have been since the tides withdrew countless centuries since.

The setting has changed little since one Doctor Laidlaw Purves "spied the land with a golfer's eye" from the tower of a Sandwich

The Sandwich hall of fame includes such figures as, left to right, Walter Travis, Walter Hagen and Roger Wethered. It was there in 1904 that quiet American Travis became the first overseas player to win the British Amateur title, and where the great Hagen became America's first British Open champion in 1922. In 1930, Sandwich was the first English venue for a Walker Cup match, with Wethered making the fourth of five British team appearances. But it was not enough and the Americans won for the sixth successive time

Card of the course

No 1	415 yards	par 4	No 10	377 yards	par 4
No 2	341 yards	par 4	No 11	222 yards	par 3
No 3	216 yards	par 3	No 12	364 yards	par 4
No 4	466 yards	par 4	No 13	443 yards	par 4
No 5	436 yards	par 4	No 14	508 yards	par 5
No 6	156 yards	par 3	No 15	455 yards	par 4
No 7	488 yards	par 5	No 16	165 yards	par 3
No 8	426 yards	par 4	No 17	427 yards	par 4
No 9	389 yards	par 4	No 18	442 yards	par 4
					—

Royal St George's Golf Club, Sandwich, Kent

Out	3,333 yards	35
In	3,403 yards	35
Total	6,736 yards	par 70

Record: 64, Tony Jacklin, Dunlop Masters 1967

Soft-sprung rolling fairways and yawning duneside bunkers make Royal St George's a classic links course. A good score on the outward half—much improved by Frank Pennink's recent modifications— can lay the foundations for a winning total, but this can be so easily spoiled by the long par-four 13th, the daunting 14th alongside the boundary wall, and the heavily bunkered 15th. No matter what his score the golfer can take pleasure from the beauty and seclusion of verdant fairways that run along hollows between high dunes, making golf at Royal St George's a very private pastime.

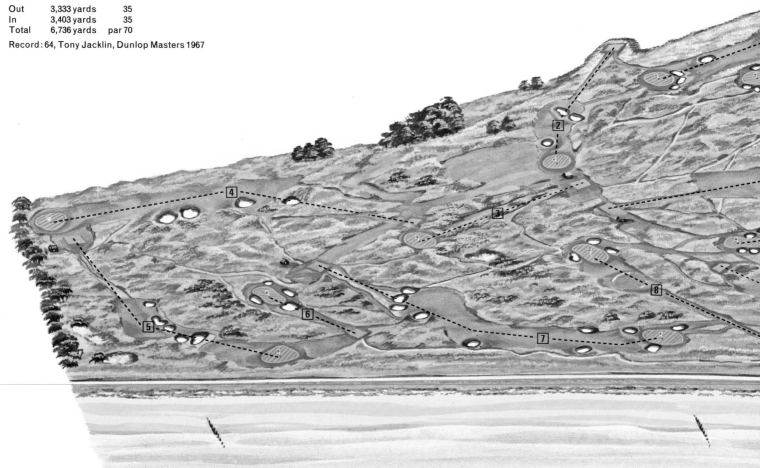

church. The sight must have stirred his imagination, and that of others. A syndicate was formed and in 1887 the club was founded.

That was the age of mighty amateurs, whose stature surpassed that of all the English professionals with only one notable exception. The Scottish had commanded the scene until 1894 when J. H. Taylor, a sturdy, flaxen-haired young professional from Winchester, won the first Open championship to be played outside Scotland. His score of 326 on the desolate and windswept links seems monumental by modern standards.

In those years there was no challenge to the supremacy of British golfers until in 1904 Walter J. Travis, described by one observer as "a little man in middle age with a black cigar and a centre-shafted putter", came to Sandwich from the United States to compete in the Amateur championship. He was, it seems, a coldly

A visible green over the sandhills of the Sahara —the short 3rd—was the first of the 1975 course changes. It used to be in a blind hollow.

determined, implacable person who played with great steadiness, winning match after match with accurate approaching and uncanny skill on the greens. His success was not popular, for the British were unaccustomed to defeat and American golf was hardly out of the embryonic stages. The chagrin that must have swept St George's when he beat Horace Hutchinson in the semi-final and the vast hitter Ted Blackwell in the final can be imagined. The centre-shafted putter was banned for years to come, but it was too late. Travis, who was born in Australia, was the first American citizen to win in Britain.

Soon after World War I, in 1922, another American came to Sandwich. He also had cigars and an enchanted putter—and more besides, for Walter Hagen was the most colourful personality that British golf had seen. He won the Open that year, the first in which native-born American supremacy was becoming ▷

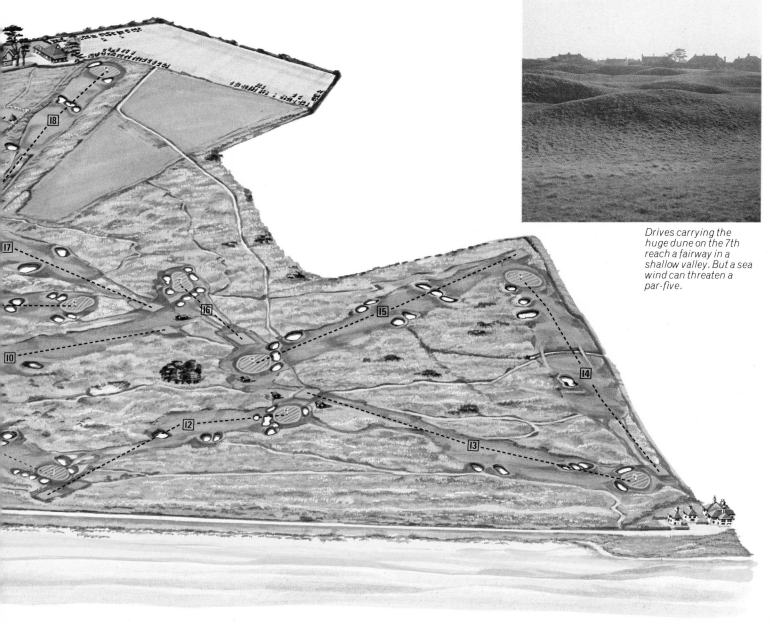

Drives carrying the huge dune on the 7th reach a fairway in a shallow valley. But a sea wind can threaten a par-five.

▷ established, and at its peak Hagen won again at Sandwich, in 1928. In 1930 Bobby Jones led his side to an overwhelming victory in the first Walker Cup match to be played in England. Then, four years later, the incomparable Henry Cotton stemmed the transatlantic tide not far from where King Canute had made his fruitless gesture a while earlier.

In a century of championships no beginning has matched Cotton's opening rounds of 67 and 65; and no golfer can have endured a greater agony of suspense than he did on the last day, when illness threatened to sabotage his triumph. In 1938 Cotton again played magnificently in one of the most ferocious gales that has ever beset an Open, but the yeoman figure of

Henry Cotton had his first big success at Royal St George's when he won the 1934 Open there, setting an Open record of 65, after which a new and now famous Dunlop ball was named. But his return there in 1938 was less happy when he lost in the gale-swept final round by going out-of-bounds at the 14th hole.

R. A. Whitcombe just prevailed. After Bobby Locke had won the first of his four Opens at St George's in 1949 the championship came no more to Sandwich; its approaches were too congested for large crowds and mounting numbers of cars. This did not affect amateur events, however. The Americans came in force for the 1959 championship and Deane Beman, sharp, earnest and mightily determined, played masterfully on a links that was burnished smooth and quick with danger to all but the most accurate and gifted of golfers.

A lasting memory of those days is the sight in 1959 of Jack Nicklaus receiving the club's great Challenge Cup, which he won before the championship began. There was the mightiest

A view of the 6th green from the Maiden. The hole is no longer played blind over the giant sandhill, but it remains a real challenge in the wind, with the green guarded by four unkindly shaped bunkers.

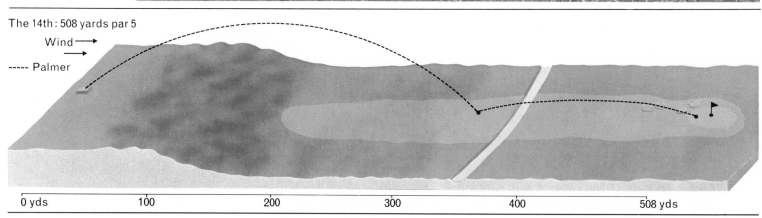

The 14th: 508 yards par 5

Wind ➝

----- Palmer

0 yds   100   200   300   400   508 yds

The 14th: The low road home in a high wind

The ability to maintain balance and rhythm of swing and to flight the ball truly in a strong wind is not given to many. Among modern golfers few have mastered the art to a greater degree than Arnold Palmer. His stance is so solid that it seems immovable; his hands so powerful that he can drive the club through the ball, keeping it so low that its flight is hardly affected, even by strong wind.

Although cross and contrary winds are the most difficult to combat, there are times when flight downwind is an important consideration. When

the ball is launched high in the air exact control of length is jeopardized. In the last round of the 1975 Penfold PGA championship at St George's the 508-yard 14th hole was straight downwind. Palmer's drive was long—not far short of Suez Canal, the broad stream which crosses the fairway, where many second shots have found watery graves.

Palmer was comfortably in range of the green which, to all intents, is a continuation of the flat fairway and therefore not a sharply defined target. His problem was to estimate the distance, making allowance for the run of the ball. As he said later he

did not want it to be blown around by the wind so he took a 3-iron, and hit a superb shot. It did not rise more than eight feet, curving gently from right to left and finishing six feet from the hole. When he left the green, having holed the putt for an eagle, he was asked which club he had taken. He grinned and said: "I just turned a 3-iron in a little," meaning that he had closed the face slightly to ensure that the ball would not rise and that it would run. This masterful shot enabled him to draw level with Eamon Darcy, his only close challenger, and he went on to win by two strokes.

young player of the generation with one of the oldest trophies in golf, first held by John Ball, supreme amateur of the old years, in 1888.

What a glorious place it is for golf. When sunlight is dancing on the waves of Pegwell Bay, the white cliffs of Ramsgate shining in the distance, the larks singing as they always seem to sing at Sandwich, and a sea wind stirring in the sand grasses, the golfer may share the famous golf writer Bernard Darwin's view that it is "as nearly my idea of heaven as is to be attained on any earthly links".

As with many another historic course, St George's was admired in its earlier days more for its charm than the quality of its golf. It was a place of mighty dunes and blind carries, and there were those who claimed that the art of the game was not hitting a ball over a sandhill and running to the top to see where it had finished. But changes were made and the course is now a rich and varied examination of golf, owing little to guessing or fortune.

The 1st, its fairway like a stormy sea of green with a cross-bunker threatening the second shot, is a perfect opening hole; a mounting crest before the 2nd green makes the approach difficult to judge. Then comes a demanding new short hole, a long iron or more over wild country to a narrow shelf of green. This hole replaced a relic from gutty days and was one of several changes by the architect Frank Pennink which came into play in 1975. Previously three short holes pursued the same direction. The 6th, alongside the Maiden, remains, as does the 16th. The 8th is now an appealing par-four with its drive to a plateau amid the crumpled land and approach down to a green in a dell of its own. It is replaced as a short hole by the 11th.

Early in the round the golfer will be aware of frequently changing levels and stances, such as the long rise of the 4th past a mountainous bunker to a sharply contoured green high on a folding hillside, and the drive from the next tee into a valley enclosed by dunes. Only if the drive is placed right is a sight of the distant green possible, for otherwise the approach is blind. This hole is typical of the course's beauty; so, too, is the 7th with its drive to a lovely, hidden expanse of fairway running clear to a green that may or may not be reached according to the wind.

Thereafter the mood of the course quietens somewhat except for the approach to the 10th high on an exposed plateau, a fiercely testing shot in a wind. Around the turn pars may not be too difficult, but the 13th is the first of a great trinity. The drive is diagonal over a long shoulder of rough country towards the clubhouse of the neighbouring Prince's, white and remote in the distance. The 14th can be the most fearsome tee shot on the course, with dunes to be carried and with out-of-bounds on the right all the way to the green. Then the golfer must decide whether or not he can carry the wide waters of the stream crossing the fairway.

A similar decision is often required at the 15th, unless the wind is helping or the fairway running fast. An array of cross-bunkers must be carried, and the narrow green is farther beyond them than it seems to be. The 16th is fringed with sand, a target shot. This is the hole that gave British television viewers their first sight of a tee shot being holed in important competition. On his way to winning the 1967 Dunlop Masters, Tony Jacklin holed out with a 7-iron. The 17th is a strong four and the approach to the 18th, from a downhill fairway, is a great finishing stroke, made by one beautifully placed greenside bunker.

Deane Beman, never a long hitter, was able to compete successfully because of his consistent putting, largely the result of maintaining a firm left wrist through the stroke. His putting was potent in the 1959 Walker Cup at Sandwich.

The power of positive putting

The defeat of the British and Irish team in the 1959 Walker Cup match prompted intensive post-mortems as to the causes. Prominent among them was the difference in putting methods. The Americans, almost without exception, struck the ball more positively, with a rapping rather than a stroking action. The basis of this was a firm left wrist which never broke during the stroke. There was no finer example that year than the putting of Deane Beman, who, after the Walker Cup match, won the Amateur championship at St George's.

Beman was not powerful but his driving to narrow, hard fairways was wonderfully controlled, and on fast, perfect greens he holed out ruthlessly from short and middle distances. It was this more than anything that enabled him to win most of his matches comfortably and to wear down Bill Hyndman in the final.

Subsequently Beman won the United States Amateur championship twice, and had a successful professional career before being appointed Commissioner of the Tournament Players Division. He was one of the game's finest putters and when asked what single point he concentrated upon when making the stroke he said that he "never allowed the clubhead to move in front of the left wrist". This helped to ensure that the blade of his putter was kept square to the intended line.

These awesome bunkers, cut into the dunes beside the 4th fairway, are typical of the hazards to be faced at Sandwich.

In 1949, Royal St George's was the scene of Bobby Locke's first Open win. It was the last Open played over the old links.

Intimacy that belies quality

An odd characteristic of seaside golf in the British Isles is that many links courses permit little more than an occasional glimpse of the sea; it can be heard, but is usually invisible. A fine exception is Royal Porthcawl, on the rock-fringed southern shores of Wales.

In the strictest sense it is not a links. There are occasional sandhills, but gorse, hummocks, heather and deep bunkers are its principal features. The land hereabouts leans down to the rocks and the smooth shining sand and from every point the golfer can look across the Bristol Channel to the long dark line of the Somerset coast. At times when wind and rain sweep in from the Atlantic he might long for the shelter of dunes, for Porthcawl is exposed to every mood of the elements, but such days are exceptional. For most of the time there are few courses as agreeable to play.

The origins of golf in Wales are by no means as ancient as those in Scotland. Most of the early clubs were formed towards the end of the last century and Porthcawl is regarded as the senior, in stature if not in age; the Glamorganshire club at Penarth is a few months older.

Porthcawl was founded in 1891 and started with nine holes laid out on common land near the sea. However, cattle on the greens, carriage wheels and camping were a constant nuisance and eighteen holes were planned afresh. Many years passed before their quality was appreciated and even now a first sight of the intimate little clubhouse would not suggest the presence of a championship course. Nevertheless a more beautiful, princely beginning could hardly be imagined.

The opening holes follow the line of the coast and when surf is foaming on the rocks, and the sky fresh and clear, the urge to play is almost overwhelming. The 1st is not severe—a tempting drive into a valley and pitch to a subtle green—but the next two holes are beautifully fashioned over gently falling ground, demanding substantial approaches to greens on the shore's edge. They are classic seaside holes. After a fine short hole the course swings inland, mounting the long 5th to a trough of green whose sides were once so steep—alas, no more—that many a wide shot would find its way unerringly and obligingly into the hole.

The golf on the uplands is more of a heathland character. Great banks of broom and gorse, a glory in early summer, threaten, but not too unkindly, the 6th and 8th. Between them is a charming little hole for which strong players hardly have a club small enough. Anyone would settle for a four at the 8th with its long second uphill over cross-bunkers, and the 9th is harder than it looks. The drive must hold a leaning fairway and huge bunkers guard a sharply sloping green which positively invites three putts unless a player thinks carefully before approaching it.

The golfer's task thus far may not have been too severe unless there is a firm wind and this proviso must be made for all British seaside courses; wind is as much a part of their character as the links turf, the dunes and the gorse. They can vary enormously in difficulty and Porthcawl is as good an example as any. Pro-

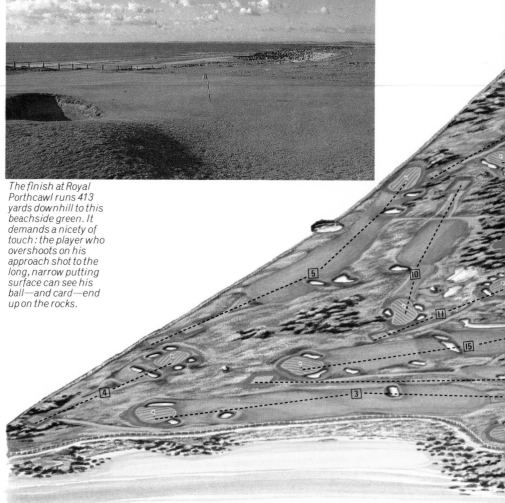

The finish at Royal Porthcawl runs 413 yards downhill to this beachside green. It demands a nicety of touch: the player who overshoots on his approach shot to the long, narrow putting surface can see his ball—and card—end up on the rocks.

fessional events are rarely played there, but in 1961 Peter Thomson had to play outstanding golf in a strong wind to win the Dunlop Masters with 284. On the other hand there has been remarkable scoring in good weather. When, after many attempts, Richard Chapman won the Amateur championship there in 1951 he produced a sequence of figures that even Charles Coe could not match. He was little over an average of threes for the last nine holes of the matchplay contest, which ended on the 14th.

From the turn the levels of the holes vary constantly. The 10th dips into a valley and offers a testing pitch to a narrow oblong of green. The short 11th is a target hole, while the 12th mounts a somewhat forbidding hill. Few can reach its green with their seconds, but the effort is worth while. From the crest of the 13th fairway the prospect is superb. The green lies at the foot of a long slope with the sea shining beyond. All around, the great basin of the course can be seen; the golfers moving out on the early holes, climbing the 5th, approaching the 10th and 11th, toiling up the nearby 12th and—it is hoped—choosing the right club at the short 14th, where nothing but a true shot is rewarded.

The 15th and 16th are similar holes, pursuing opposite directions, with drives to island fairways far below and second shots of rare quality.

The whole of the greens cannot be seen, but the distant, fluttering flags should be guide enough to the golfer who knows his course. The shot to the 16th poses the age-old problem of getting the ball airborne when there are no two ways about the need to do so. Deep cross-bunkers must be carried or a six is almost inevitable.

Whether by design or coincidence most of the famous British courses have 17th holes of great distinction. That at Porthcawl may not rank with the Road Hole at St Andrews, the Royal at Hoylake and one or two others, but it is admirable none the less. As all such good holes should, it gives the golfer who is trailing a chance to recover—if he can produce two superlative shots. Reid Jack, one of Britain's finest amateurs, did so once when playing for Scotland in a crucial match against England. His spoon shot finished six inches from the hole, a wonderful stroke considering that the green is diagonal to the line, with bunkers on its near side.

The last hole can be most exacting, tumbling gently towards the sea and a slippery, falling green. The approach over hummocks, hollows and heather demands delicate touch if it is to finish within reasonable putting distance. And, when the sun is going down and the Bristol Channel gleams like polished pewter behind the green, the shot can be the very devil.

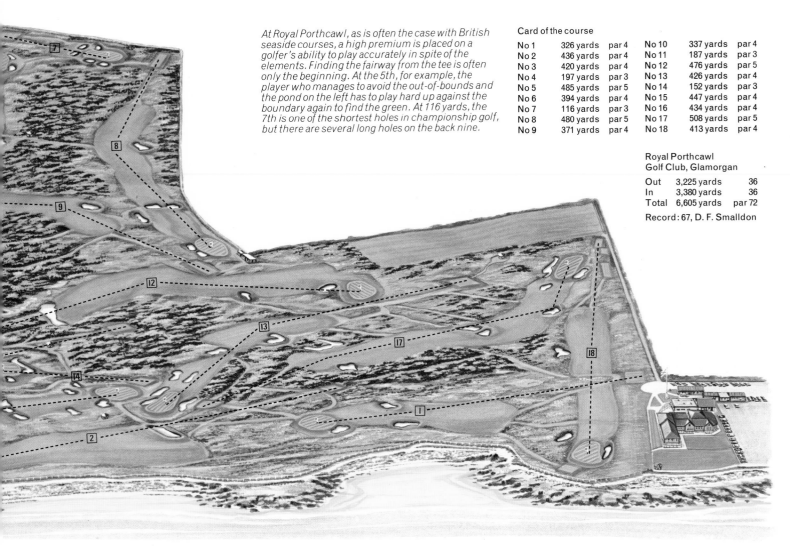

At Royal Porthcawl, as is often the case with British seaside courses, a high premium is placed on a golfer's ability to play accurately in spite of the elements. Finding the fairway from the tee is often only the beginning. At the 5th, for example, the player who manages to avoid the out-of-bounds and the pond on the left has to play hard up against the boundary again to find the green. At 116 yards, the 7th is one of the shortest holes in championship golf, but there are several long holes on the back nine.

Card of the course

No 1	326 yards	par 4	No 10	337 yards	par 4
No 2	436 yards	par 4	No 11	187 yards	par 3
No 3	420 yards	par 4	No 12	476 yards	par 5
No 4	197 yards	par 3	No 13	426 yards	par 4
No 5	485 yards	par 5	No 14	152 yards	par 3
No 6	394 yards	par 4	No 15	447 yards	par 4
No 7	116 yards	par 3	No 16	434 yards	par 4
No 8	480 yards	par 5	No 17	508 yards	par 5
No 9	371 yards	par 4	No 18	413 yards	par 4

Royal Porthcawl
Golf Club, Glamorgan

Out	3,225 yards	36
In	3,380 yards	36
Total	6,605 yards	par 72

Record: 67, D. F. Smalldon

Sight of the Bristol Channel from every hole is one of the pleasures of Porthcawl, but it is the wind from the sea that makes some of the holes so difficult to play. At the 13th, with its exposed crest of fairway, it can make the second stroke—played downhill towards the sea from a hanging lie—particularly testing.

Dick Siderowf's ease with long irons is the envy of any handicap golfer. Tom Weiskopf—who, like Siderowf, is renowned for his prowess with these clubs—feels failure is due to trying to hit too hard. The secret, he says, is "to let the club do the work".

The 13th: A battle against the wind

Most golfers regard the 1-iron with a certain awe. Because of its slight loft and the fact that it demands greater precision of strike than any other club it is not normally included in a set of irons. The development of the more lofted woods has rendered it superfluous for most golfers and it is generally used only by those of the highest class. Some, like Nicklaus, Player and Miller, use the 1-iron for tee shots when position rather than length is the criterion, and when a hole is dangerously narrow. One of its greatest virtues, in

the hands of an expert, is that it can give greater control in contrary winds than the fairway woods.

A heavy westerly wind gusted down the Bristol Channel throughout the final of the Amateur championship in 1973. The golf was so demanding that the experienced Dick Siderowf of the United States soon had a clear edge over Peter Moody, his young English opponent. At one point in the afternoon he was six up, but Moody came back at him and was three down going to the 426-yard 13th. The crest of the fairway before it swings left and begins its graceful fall to the green is a high point

of the course and that day was exposed to the full force of the hammering wind.

Moody was in trouble from the tee and Siderowf, whose drive had found the fairway, had the opening to take complete command of the match. His 1-iron shot bored through the wind with an unwavering flight to the heart of the green. He said later that it was his finest shot of the week and it proved to be conclusive. The quality of his golf is revealed not least in the accuracy of his iron play, made possible by a splendid extension of the swing through the ball.

Emerald fairways by a sapphire sea

A breathtaking backdrop of mountains and sea is reward in itself at Royal County Down, but the golfer who strays can pay devastating penalties in the fierce rough and bewildering frequency of traps that make the championship course one of Ireland's best. It is an added hazard, too, that the 2nd, 5th, 6th, 9th and 15th holes all call for blind tee shots, and others, such as the 13th, offer only markers to guide approach shots to unseen greens.

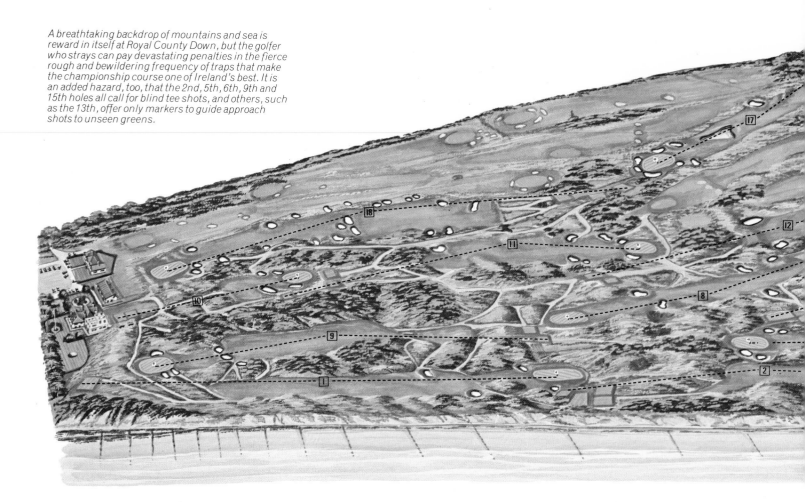

The lasting appeal of the finest British courses is their variety. County Down bears little resemblance to its great Irish companions, Portrush, Portmarnock and Ballybunion; an occasional valley hole might stir memories of Birkdale or Turnberry, but not strongly. At County Down one is, as so often, on a course with such individual character that it is among the hardest, yet most rewarding, to play anywhere in the British Isles.

It lies on a curve of Dundrum Bay, with the Mourne mountains in the background. It can be a paradise for the golfer in early summer, when sunshine turns the sea to sapphire and brings forth the golden glory of the gorse and the richness of emerald fairways and greens, with cloud shadows playing on the mountains and the quiet green hills to the west.

The club came into being in 1889 and minutes of an early meeting reveal the remarkable fact that Tom Morris was to lay out a course for a sum not exceeding £4. How far this princely sum availed the old man is not known, but within a decade the links were written of as the finest in Ireland. It was reconstructed later; Vardon gave it high praise in 1908 and the same year King Edward VII bestowed the Royal title on the club. Since then the golf has changed but little. Purists might claim that there are too many blind shots—five from the tees and others where the green is all or partially concealed—but somehow they are so in keeping with the nature

of the course that they cannot with any justice be condemned.

The opening holes head northwards along the shores of the bay, which is screened by ranges of dunes. The long 1st resembles a trough from the tee—an inviting prospect for the straight driver—but the next tee shot is the very reverse. A high ridge must be carried and against the wind it can seem insurmountable; the second shot must be steered through a divide in another ridge to a well-guarded plateau green—not a long hole, but one that can be fierce indeed. The drive down the valley of the 3rd should be held to the left, for bunkers in a spur of dunes on the right protect the straight line to the flag.

The short 4th, a medium shot over a waste of rough heather, is followed by a great 5th. The drive must be aimed to carry as much as the striker dares of a heathery outcrop of land, around which the hole swings to the right. The approach is a fine shot to a green backed against sandhills.

The 6th is a lovely hole, blind from the tee but not harassingly so, and the 7th a tricky little pitch over a gully; part of the green is behind a hummock and its sides are closely bunkered. In the Irish Open amateur final in 1933 Eric Fiddian, playing Jack McLean, holed his tee shot there in the morning round.

In the afternoon he did likewise at the 14th, a feat without parallel on an important occasion

The distant clubhouse and town of Newcastle, and the sweep of the Mountains of Mourne, provide players with a diversion so magnificent as to make concentration difficult at the 4th. The hole measures 211 yards, almost all of it carry across gorse and heavy rough. The green, much longer than it is wide, is protected by no fewer than ten bunkers, most of them positioned to catch the underhit or the sliced tee shot.

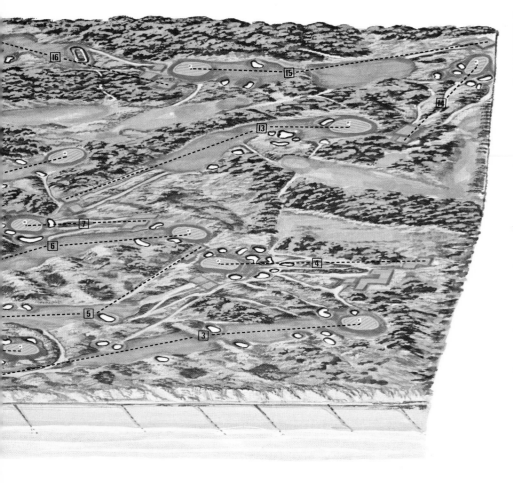

Card of the course

No 1	512 yards	par 5	No 10	200 yards	par 3
No 2	424 yards	par 4	No 11	441 yards	par 4
No 3	468 yards	par 4	No 12	503 yards	par 5
No 4	211 yards	par 3	No 13	445 yards	par 4
No 5	440 yards	par 4	No 14	216 yards	par 3
No 6	394 yards	par 4	No 15	454 yards	par 4
No 7	137 yards	par 3	No 16	267 yards	par 4
No 8	427 yards	par 4	No 17	420 yards	par 4
No 9	488 yards	par 5	No 18	548 yards	par 5

Royal County Down Golf Club, Newcastle, Down

No 1 course

Out	3,501 yards	36
In	3,494 yards	36
Total	6,995 yards	par 72

Record: 66, James Bruen, Irish Open 1939

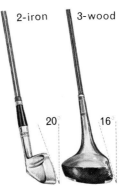

2-iron   3-wood

20   16

The Vicomtesse de Saint-Sauveur, whose fairway wood play was the equal of many good men players' long

irons. She used the less lofted 3-wood for a shot that most men would, for accuracy, make with a 2-iron.

but one that still failed to give him victory.

Into a prevailing wind, the approach to the 8th green between its embracing hills can be a taxing stroke. This is the highest point. As one drives from the next tee into a valley far below, leading to a distant plateau green, the mass of Slieve Donard, highest of the Mourne mountains, can seem menacingly close, and the spires and roofs of the town at its foot almost alpine in appearance.

The turn is by the clubhouse, blessed virtue of design, and the 10th, although short, is another characteristic hole, from a raised tee along a valley to a green where bunkers abound. The 11th leads to more open country and after the falling sweep of the 12th comes a gracefully curving hole in a valley all its own. The second shot is blind and the one swinging in over the hill has the best chance of finding the green. This is a splendid hole to watch from on high, whence its secrets are visible to the spectator but not to the player.

After the challenge of the 14th, a downhill shot over sand and gorse to a well-bunkered green, the course heads for home. The 15th demands two substantial strokes of anyone's game, and maybe more, but the 16th is fun. The strong can drive the green, but to threaten the frail a charming little pool with an island lies in the fairway below. The finish on the landward side of the big dune country is not typical of the rest but a pond, just out of driving range, must

be carried at the 17th, and the last hole is the longest of all.

Newcastle is an examination for any golfer whatever the elements, and how swiftly these can change. Once during an international meeting the seas were a tossing, angry turmoil and the wind so violent that eight holes could not be reached with two wooden club shots. So low were the clouds that one young golfer, forgetting that the sea was at his feet, asked, "How high are we here?" Mercifully such days are rare.

Many of the most memorable moments at County Down have involved women golfers, not least three from France. In 1927 the tiny Simone Thion de la Chaume (now Madame René Lacoste) became the first Frenchwoman to win the British championship. Her daughter Catherine was the most recent, remarkably also in Northern Ireland, at Portrush in 1969. The dark, lithe grace of the Vicomtesse de Saint-Sauveur (now Madame Segard) prevailed in 1950, and Brigitte Varangot, one of the most accomplished woman players of her time, succeeded in 1963.

The one Amateur championship to be played there was in 1970 when Michael Bonallack won for a third successive year. This was a record and also his fifth victory, a tally surpassed only by John Ball long ago. By an extraordinary coincidence, and one without precedent in a major championship, Bonallack's opponent in the final was Bill Hyndman, as it had been the previous year at Hoylake.

The 5th: The case for wood over iron

Fairway woods are an indispensable part of every woman golfer's game, however accomplished she may be. Few women are strong enough to achieve comparable results with the long irons, which require a swing making contact with the ball and then the turf, whereas the wooden club shot is a sweeping motion with the club sliding along the turf and not taking a divot. This swing requires less strength and less speed of hands in the hitting area. Because the lofted woods are easier to play, many men golfers, even first-class players, will carry them in preference to the long irons and the finest women players can attain an accuracy with them comparable to men using medium irons.

This skill was ably demonstrated in the final of the 1950 British championship played at Newcastle. The Vicomtesse de Saint-Sauveur (now Mme Segard) was three up at lunch on Jessie Valentine, but lost two of the first four holes of the afternoon round. The 5th at Newcastle compels the golfer to decide his line from the high tee over a ridge of heather which determines the right-hand sweep of the hole. The danger of attempting to cut off too much is obvious and bunkers guard both sides of the fairway. Both hit good drives and Mrs Valentine a fine shot to the green. Unless the Vicomtesse could match it, her lead would probably vanish and the match would be desperately in the balance. As it was she hit a superb 3-wood shot with her glorious free, attacking swing and finished a foot from the hole.

Ulster's green leagues of links

The informed golfer in search of the game in Northern Ireland may head south from Belfast to Newcastle in County Down, or north to Portrush; if he is wise he will make both journeys. When Portrush is the first choice, and there is no particular haste, he should take the Antrim coast road, not only because it is one of the most beautiful in Britain but because, as an approach to a links, it has few parallels. Soon after the road passes the ancient ruins of Dunluce Castle it turns a corner, and there below, with magic abruptness, the whole spread of the course can be seen in a sweeping glance: green leagues of tumbling, broken links falling away to cliffs of sand—the highest near any golf course—and the shining seas. The course, much changed since it was established in 1888, winds and climbs and falls over a profusion of green hills, and within their grasses are primrose, bluebell and dog-rose. To the east and west the dark headlands of Benbane and Inishowen rise from the sea, and not far off shore the long, low sprawl of the Skerries stand patient against the tide. Well distant, the faint shadows of Islay and the Paps of Jura, remote outposts of Scotland, can be seen when the air is clear, and a few miles away lies the Giant's Causeway.

The modern version of the main course, named Dunluce after the ancestral home of the lords of Antrim, evolved from the work and imagination of many men, from one McNeill, a greenkeeper who laid the greens, to the architect, Colt, who was responsible for most of the

There is no room for error at the aptly-named Calamity Corner, the 211-yard 14th. The tee shot can vary from a full-blooded drive to an easy mid iron, depending on the wind force and direction.

improvements. From a purely golfing point of view the most distinctive feature is the severe driving. There are few great courses where the erratic driver can consistently escape all consequences of waywardness; at Portrush he has less chance of doing so than on almost any other championship course, not because of particularly savage roughs or hazards but by the design of the holes. The first and last alone are straight; all the others curve, usually more than 200 yards from the tee. When the rough is allowed to grow inwards for an important occasion, and the fairways are no more than the width of a street, uncommon accuracy is essential for any golfer, let alone the long hitter who tries to carry the corners.

Another unusual aspect is the comparative absence of bunkers about the greens. Mostly these are protected by natural hills and mounds, hollows and runnels, and holding the greens can be difficult unless the drive has been rightly placed. If they are missed then the little shots can be a real test of touch. Neither are the greens enormous, and this accounted for Max Faulkner having so few putts when he won the Open in 1951: it is doubtful whether any champion has ever had fewer over four rounds. The number was said to be 108; even allowing for exaggeration it was an astonishingly low proportion of a winning total of 285.

The opening holes move along the uplands of the course. After a rise to the plateau of the 1st green, the 2nd winds down a long path through the dunes. The 4th is a lovely hole with

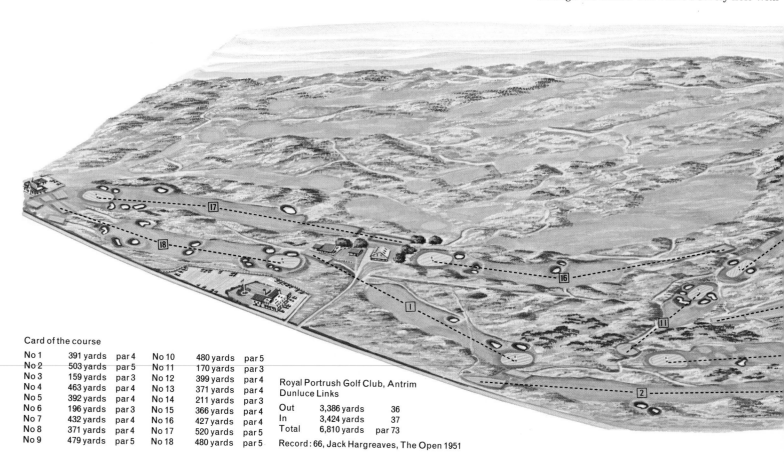

Card of the course

No 1	391 yards	par 4	No 10	480 yards	par 5
No 2	503 yards	par 5	No 11	170 yards	par 3
No 3	159 yards	par 3	No 12	399 yards	par 4
No 4	463 yards	par 4	No 13	371 yards	par 4
No 5	392 yards	par 4	No 14	211 yards	par 3
No 6	196 yards	par 3	No 15	366 yards	par 4
No 7	432 yards	par 4	No 16	427 yards	par 4
No 8	371 yards	par 4	No 17	520 yards	par 5
No 9	479 yards	par 5	No 18	480 yards	par 5

Royal Portrush Golf Club, Antrim
Dunluce Links

Out	3,386 yards	36
In	3,424 yards	37
Total	6,810 yards	par 73

Record: 66, Jack Hargreaves, The Open 1951

its drive over a stream, out-of-bounds on the right and a green nestling in the sandhills, and from the next tee the whole glory of the links can be seen. The 5th fairway cascades to a green by the sea, and an inadvertent step backwards hereabouts brings a long tumble down a precipice of sand to the beach. The 6th is a beautiful short hole calling for a long fade into the green; and now the stern stuff has begun.

The middle holes of the round swing back and forth, but in no way monotonously, for the angles of their approaches are alternately inclined, never unduly favouring the slice or hook. After a picturesque dropping shot to the 11th, the course takes a turn towards the sea again; and soon one stands on the tee of the 14th, as famous a short hole as there is in Ireland, with the singularly appropriate name of Calamity Corner. Between tee and green, 200 yards away, is a chasm of rough, and the prevailing wind does not help; often enough the stroke calls for wood. The merest slice can mean disaster, just as a pull from the next tee is a most unhelpful stroke. The 16th fairway leans left towards a grassy bank, and it was there, in the last round of the 1951 Open, that Tony Cerda's drive finished and, as it proved, his challenge to Faulkner expired. Nine years later the hole saw a memorable stroke in a semi-final of the Amateur championship. Robert Cochran, an American of middle years, was two down to Gordon Huddy when he struck a spoon shot low under the wind to within only twelve feet of the flag to win the hole.

The last two holes, lengthy and flat, are not entirely in character, but they favour the strong —as they did Joe Carr in the other semi-final against James Walker. Rarely had Carr been so pressed, though he was a different golfer the next day. All the anxiety, the straining at the leash and the tendency to steer had vanished. He drove vast distances, usually to the heart of the winding fairways; the mood of conquest was upon him and Cochran could muster no lasting response. As a beautiful May afternoon reached its zenith Carr became ten up and ten to play. Life could hold little more for a golfer and soon he was champion a third time.

Neither the Open nor the Amateur has been played at Portrush since Joe Carr's year in 1960. The course is remote for most golfers—but not, curiously enough, for the women. In 1895, Lady Margaret Scott, a handsome figure with skirts trailing the turf, won her third successive victory in the British championship. She could hardly have done more; the championship was only in its third year. The Hezlet sisters of the great Portrush family had their enduring hour, and in 1969 Catherine Lacoste, one of the greatest of all women golfers, won the British title on the way to conquering all her worlds.

Another Hezlet—Charles—was an Olympian figure of amateur golf during the years astride World War I, years in which a young caddy at Portrush, Fred Daly, was learning to become one of the longest straight drivers of his time. Daly, a great competitor, won the Open—the only Irishman ever to do so—in 1947.

The 9th: 479 yards par 5

------ Carr

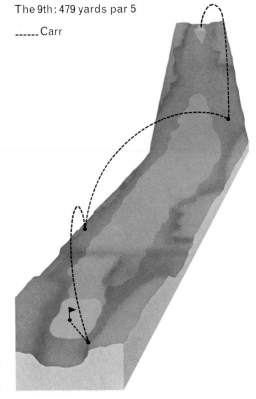

The 9th: Carr's determination proves crucial

One of the first, and often one of the hardest, lessons a successful competitor has to learn is not to cease trying even when his cause seems hopeless. In golf the unexpected is commonplace and turns of fortune so unpredictable that within the moment seeming disasters can become prosperity. The reverse also is true for often, in the words of the golf writer Robert Browning, "Just when we are safest, there's a sunset touch."

Joe Carr, the great cavalier of Irish golf, was an overwhelming favourite to win the 1960 Amateur championship at Portrush. His hardest match was in the semi-final against James Walker, an uncommonly solid, resolute Scottish golfer. At lunch Carr was two down and although he shook himself free of inhibition afterwards, Walker's implacable short game rarely failed and he was one up going to the 9th, a 479-yard par-five.

The hole bears to the right and, should the drive carry the corner, the green, like an armchair in the dunes, may be reached in two if a large hollow fronting it can be carried or traversed. For a man of Carr's great power a birdie-four was always possible, but he pulled from the tee across the elbow of the fairway into deep rough, sliced from there to a bad, hanging lie, still in rough, from where he pulled his pitch wide of the green. Then, when he seemed certain to lose the hole to a five and become two down, he holed the chip. The game was even and finally Carr outgunned Walker on the closing holes, going on to beat Robert Cochran commandingly in the final the next day.

Carr's holing of the chip revealed his flair for producing a telling thrust at crucial moments, largely because he never yielded.

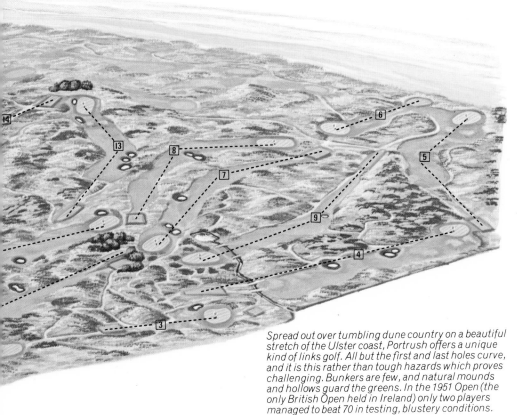

Spread out over tumbling dune country on a beautiful stretch of the Ulster coast, Portrush offers a unique kind of links golf. All but the first and last holes curve, and it is this rather than tough hazards which proves challenging. Bunkers are few, and natural mounds and hollows guard the greens. In the 1951 Open (the only British Open held in Ireland) only two players managed to beat 70 in testing, blustery conditions.

The very Irish hazard of Maggie Leonard's cow

Card of the course

No 1	388 yards	par 4
No 2	368 yards	par 4
No 3	388 yards	par 4
No 4	460 yards	par 4
No 5	407 yards	par 4
No 6	586 yards	par 5
No 7	180 yards	par 3
No 8	370 yards	par 4
No 9	444 yards	par 4
No 10	380 yards	par 4
No 11	445 yards	par 4
No 12	144 yards	par 3
No 13	565 yards	par 5
No 14	385 yards	par 4
No 15	192 yards	par 3
No 16	527 yards	par 5
No 17	466 yards	par 4
No 18	408 yards	par 4

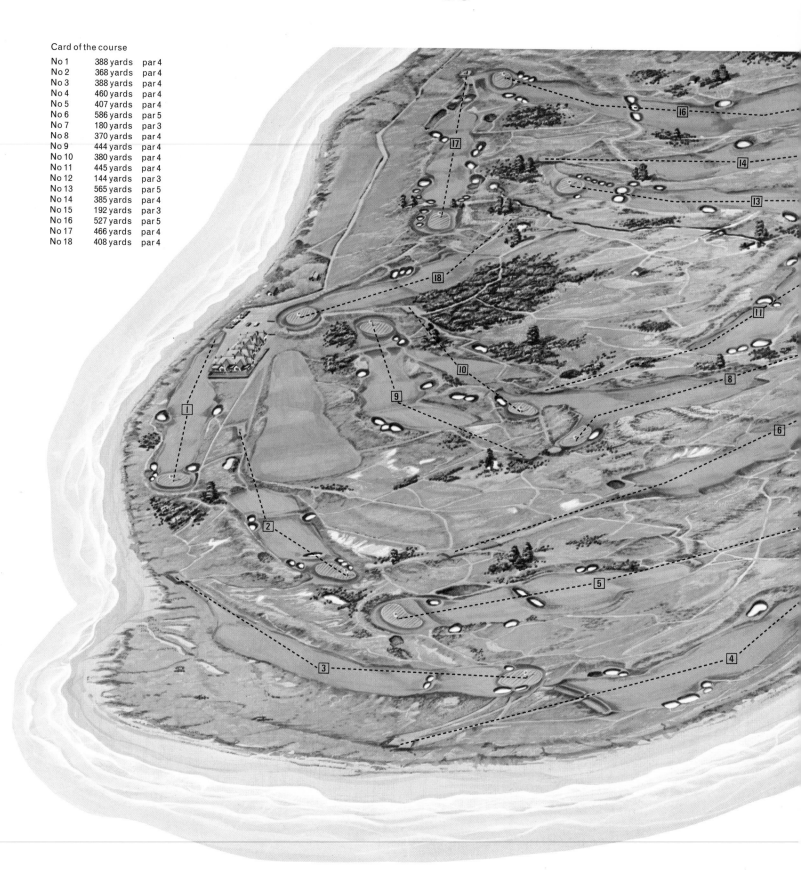

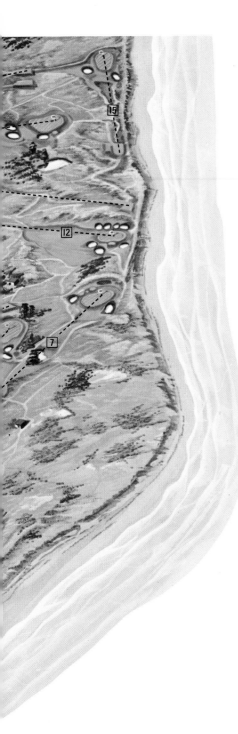

Surrounded by the sea on three sides, Portmarnock offers a genuine links course comparable with any of the great British championship links; indeed, Bobby Locke rated it among the finest in Europe. It never lacks challenge, and many of the less demanding holes become severe tests of skill and control when the wind comes in off the sea. Two in particular—the 14th and 15th—can wreck a card.

Portmarnock Golf Club, County Dublin, Dublin

Out	3,591 yards	36
In	3,512 yards	36
Total	7,103 yards	par 72

Record: 66, Christy O'Connor, Dunlop Masters 1959; Gary Player, Canada Cup 1960

In a land where beauty, poetry, conflict and passionate belief in the individual are constantly intermingled, the Irish have found golf to be a ready expression of their character and flair for games. The enthusiasm of the players, the variety of styles and the quality of courses is remarkable. Ireland is not large, but it has several of the finest tests of golf to be found anywhere in Europe.

Except in the country itself, where local feelings might influence judgement, one would be hard-pressed to find agreement as to which was the greatest course—Portrush, Portmarnock or County Down. These three are not alone, for there are Ballybunion and Rosses Point on the far Atlantic shore; Killarney, serene on its lakeside amid the mountains, and Waterville have elements of majesty.

Of all courses, few are blessed with the natural magnificence of Portmarnock. Within the fine sweep of coastline curving to an end at Howth Hill, the northern guardian of Dublin Bay, there is a long tongue of linksland between the Irish Sea and an inland tidal bay. It is thus almost enclosed by water, a private place where a man is alone with the turf, the sea, the sky and the challenge of the wind. It is brave, splendid golfing country.

Portmarnock's moods can vary from a sternness, that can be savage, to wondrous peace. In summer, with a fresh breeze sparkling the bay and stirring the dune grasses, Ireland's Eye and Lambay rising sharp from the sea, there are few more tempting places for a golfer to be. On such a day, long ago, Sam Snead was at practice, pouring a stream of flawless strokes with a 1-iron into the morning distance. Watching golf could offer little more.

Like its great Irish rivals, Portmarnock often changes direction, somewhat after the fashion of Muirfield, with two distinctive and separate trails finishing by the clubhouse, a graceful white landmark from afar. The spectacular

quality and unexpectedness of County Down are absent, but Portmarnock's problems are straightforward, even if considerable and often severe. There are no blind shots to the greens and few from the tees, no sharp changes of level yet no monotonous flatness, either. Several holes follow shallow valleys, but they are never as pronounced as they are at Birkdale. They might suggest, but certainly do not afford, protection from the wind.

The design of the course is natural rather than contrived. The 3rd, along a strath of turf, narrow and slightly convex between sandhills on one side and the marshy fringes of the bay on the other, is an example. So, too, is the one bunker guarding the pin at the 5th. The approaches to the shorter par-fours such as the 2nd and 8th, are beautifully shaped. There are only three short holes—the 7th, into a dell, the 12th, high in the dunes, and the 15th, which can be fearsome with a wind from the sea on the right. To hold the narrow table of green, it may be necessary to swing the shot over the beach—which is out-of-bounds—and back again. Even in still air the green, shelving away on either hand, is difficult to hold. Only a true stroke here will prevail.

The three par-fives can be immense. At times the 6th, along its dimpled fairway and valleys, can be three woods for the strongest, yet second shot can be as little as a medium iron when the course is running fast. The 13th has a long carry from the tee, behind which the waves pound, and there are bunkers to attract and destroy the second shot. The 16th is of similar shape, down from the sea with the approaches swinging in from the left.

These two noble holes are part of a challenging finish, for the 14th, too, is a great hole although less than 400 yards. According to the wind, the second from a rolling fairway can be anything from a wood to a pitch and must carry huge bunkers in front of a long plateau of green ▷

This insidious little pot bunker is one of two which flank the entrance to the 15th green. They and the wind are all the protection that the hole, hard by the sea, requires.

The 15th: Palmer bends with the wind

In all golf, few short holes are as severe in their classic simplicity as the 192-yard 15th, hard by the sea along the eastern fringe of the course. The tee is high in the dunes above the level of the narrow table of green, so that only a long, true shot will hold—the subject of many wagers.

When the wind is strong from the sea the only hope of hitting the green is to swing the shot in from over the beach; as this is out-of-bounds no small amount of courage is needed. Conversely, with the wind from the left, a slight fade can be magnified into a fatal slice. The approach to the green is flanked by two bunkers to catch the timid or mishit shot, but the natural quality of the hole is in itself so taxing that they are almost superfluous.

Arnold Palmer's first competitive round east of the Atlantic was in 1960, his greatest year, and probably the finest stroke he hit that day was a 3-iron across the breeze to the 15th. It died a yard past the hole, but his first putt failed to touch it. The miss was of no moment. He was round in 69 and he and Sam Snead went on to win the Canada Cup—as the World Cup was then called—with eight strokes to spare.

▷ in the dunes. Legend has it that Joe Carr, greatest of Irish amateurs, has driven the green, the ball somehow escaping the bunkers; fact in its turn states that Henry Cotton once took seven strokes there—and lost an Irish Open in the process.

As a strong par-four, the 17th takes a deal of beating. Bunkers flanking the straight fairway are cause for thought on the tee and the second demands a long, accurate shot to a closely guarded green. The 18th, a fine hole, owes less to fortune than it did when the home green was hard by the clubhouse. The hole has been shortened and the green moved to a position offering less of a threat to the constantly peppered building.

Portmarnock has been the setting for many great occasions, played in the wildest extremes of weather. When a tempest assailed the last round of the Irish Open in 1927, George Duncan—one of the greatest of inspirational golfers—was round in 74, the only player to break 80. The weather was such that, even with this historic round, his winning score was 312. Christy O'Connor took 36 strokes fewer when he won the Dunlop Masters at Portmarnock thirty-two years later.

The Dunlop tournament won by O'Connor in 1959 was memorable for the golf of Joe Carr. After three rounds, all under 70, he led a strong field by four strokes and was within sight of being the first amateur to win a major profes-

sional tournament in a generation until O'Connor passed him with a final round of 66.

The only time the Amateur championship has been played in Eire, in 1949, it was won by Max McCready. His golf had power, authority and great confidence and it disposed of the two most formidable Americans in the field, Frank Stranahan, the defending champion, in the semi-final, and Willie Turnesa in the final. Thunder prowled the distant hills as the inscrutable Turnesa became one up with four to play, but McCready won the next three holes. Ireland rejoiced that night.

None of this might have happened but for the inspiration in 1893 that impelled two men, J. W. Pickeman and George Ross, to row across the mouth of the estuary from the point where the Sutton clubhouse now stands. By some blessing of the imagination they visualized a golf course on what was then a wilderness of dune and bracken inhabited only by a remote and self-sufficient community of farming and fish folk, yet only ten miles from Dublin.

The first clubhouse was only a shack and the greatest hazard Maggie Leonard's cow, which devoured hundreds of balls. Golfers reached the course by crossing the estuary at low tide in a horse-drawn cart, at other times by boat. There is a road now at the far end of the peninsula and this delightful and very Irish way of reaching the 1st tee has gone the way of Maggie Leonard's cow.

Dublin-born amateur Joe Carr, whose excellent short game was ideally suited to Portmarnock, seemed likely to cause *something of a shock by winning the 1959 Dunlop Masters—until Christy O'Connor returned a record 66 to snatch the title.*

The 17th: O'Connor's mastery with wood

There can be no firm rule as to the ideal number of bunkers on a hole; too many imponderables, not least the whim and imagination of the architect, are involved. One bunker is often more than enough to fulfil the strategic concept of a fairway or to protect and give character to a green. Occasionally though, the dramatic and aesthetic values of a hole can be enhanced by plentiful use of bunkers. This is particularly true of the 17th at Portmarnock.

Were the hole not so fair and straightaway in its demands it could be described as penal. A pair of bunkers on either side of the fairway compel a drive of exacting straightness. If the second shot (probably with wood, because a truly helpful wind is rare) is pulled it is in danger of being trapped in one of three bunkers short of the green. A series of four more lurk on its right flank to punish the shot drifting that way.

Rarely has this beautiful hole been mastered as impressively as by Christy O'Connor in both rounds on the final day of the Dunlop Masters in 1959. Even though the day was still, the hole, at 466 yards, was the toughest par on the course. Yet O'Connor twice made three when fives were commonplace. In the afternoon he ensured victory with a 4-wood shot that feathered into the green and finished eight feet from the hole.

Although he never won the Open—an honour that belongs to Fred Daly alone of Irish golfers— O'Connor has been the most consistently successful of them all. Throughout his career he has had a wonderfully smooth rhythm, great control of the clubhead and the ability to shape all manner of shots, not least with the fairway woods.

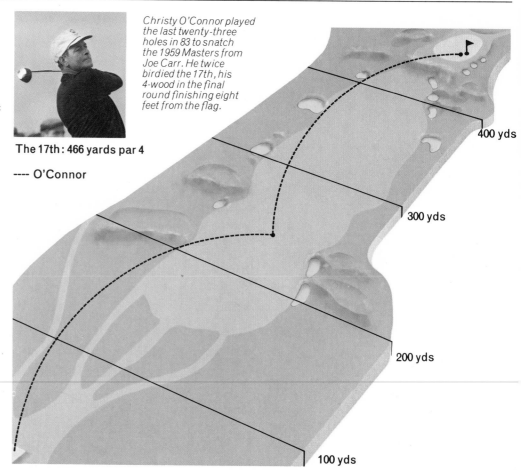

Christy O'Connor played the last twenty-three holes in 83 to snatch the 1959 Masters from Joe Carr. He twice birdied the 17th, his 4-wood in the final round finishing eight feet from the flag.

The 17th: 466 yards par 4

---- O'Connor

400 yds

300 yds

200 yds

100 yds

Ireland's gift to the world of golf

Killarney's setting exhausts superlatives. The loom of Macgillicuddy's Reeks, the blue-black depths of its lake, the changing light and moist, Atlantic-tempered climate have conjured enough ballads to drain the repertoire of a bar-room tenor. A golf course in such a setting is bound to have a magnetism for even the most prosaic of golfers, and Killarney's championship course is worthy of its incomparable surroundings.

There is at Killarney a quality and variety of golf to match the best in the British Isles, and although it does not quite come into the championship lists along with courses such as Muirfield and Birkdale, its combination of two highly challenging courses, set in spectacular surroundings, places it in a category of its own.

The success of Killarney Golf and Fishing Club stems directly from the untoward behaviour of a land agent in 1936. For forty-five years, golf had been played at Killarney on a course in Old Deer Park, owned by the Earl of Kenmare, for a token rent of only one shilling a year on the land. In 1936 the Earl's agent—obviously not a golfer—proposed to the club that the rent should be increased to £75, a 1,500 per cent increase that sent the club committee into horrified conclave. They emerged to ask the Earl if they could take over another area of his land—a wild stretch of trees and scrub on sandy soil bordering Lough Leane, Killarney's lake—where they would create a new course.

It was at this point that a new figure came into the picture—the Earl's heir, Lord Castlerosse, a larger-than-life luminary of the London social scene and a scratch golfer in his university days. He took an immediate interest in the project, seeing in it the chance to create on the shore of Lough Leane a course of beauty far exceeding in quality the modest attributes of the original parkland Killarney course.

Sir Guy Campbell was called in to design the new course and Castlerosse invited Henry Longhurst, a close friend, to add his views. The course was three years in the making but its completion and opening, in October 1939, was overshadowed (not to put too fine a point on it) by more momentous happenings in Europe. Once hostilities ended, the new location and the more challenging course began to attract visitors from all parts of the world.

The course, played and enjoyed by so many since the end of World War II, bears no great resemblance to the one designed by Sir Guy Campbell, for when Castlerosse succeeded his father as Earl of Kenmare in 1939 he spent more and more time pursuing his dream of the perfect golf course. It began with a few subtle changes to the line and shape of the holes, became more adventurous with the planting of new trees and the repositioning of tees and finished with thirteen holes substantially changed in character, no fewer than three being completely new designs.

Of the three holes which bear the unmistakable stamp of Castlerosse, the 13th (also the ▷

The 193-yard 3rd is one of the three holes at Killarney which bear the unmistakable mark of Lord Castlerosse, the larger-than-life figure whose enthusiasm took the Irish course from a golfing backwater to a championship venue. Apart from a bunker guarding the left of the green, it is completely natural—and so are the dangers of woods and lakeshore if the drive should stray.

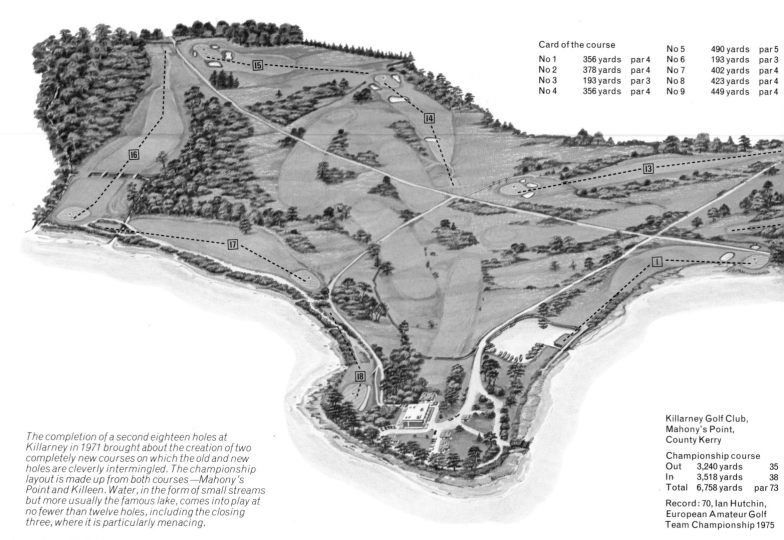

Card of the course

			No 5	490 yards	par 5
No 1	356 yards	par 4	No 6	193 yards	par 3
No 2	378 yards	par 4	No 7	402 yards	par 4
No 3	193 yards	par 3	No 8	423 yards	par 4
No 4	356 yards	par 4	No 9	449 yards	par 4

The completion of a second eighteen holes at Killarney in 1971 brought about the creation of two completely new courses on which the old and new holes are cleverly intermingled. The championship layout is made up from both courses—Mahony's Point and Killeen. Water, in the form of small streams but more usually the famous lake, comes into play at no fewer than twelve holes, including the closing three, where it is particularly menacing.

Killarney Golf Club,
Mahony's Point,
County Kerry

Championship course
Out 3,240 yards 35
In 3,518 yards 38
Total 6,758 yards par 73

Record: 70, Ian Hutchin,
European Amateur Golf
Team Championship 1975

▷ 13th on the Mahony's Point course) is perhaps the most difficult of the current 36-hole layout. A modest par-five of 478 yards from the championship tee, it demands nothing of the tee shot except that it be long and straight—for even the biggest hitters need a near-perfect second shot to hold the ball on a raised green which falls away to both sides, with bunkers, trees and a nearby road waiting for the ball which does not find its target. Even those who play short in two are faced with an extremely difficult pitch to this daunting green. The heavy penalty extracted by this hole from good shots which are not quite good enough has led to some harsh criticism over the past thirty years, but every great course should have one hole which truly rewards a perfectly struck shot and consigns the often successful mediocre to the fate it deserves.

It is typical of Castlerosse that he should include such an examination in his personal contribution to the Killarney success story. His two other gems survive as the 3rd and 9th holes of the championship course (the 3rd and the 13th of the Killeen course), a par-three and par-four both demanding accuracy and reasonable power to achieve results. His work at Killarney was unfinished at the time of his sudden death in 1943 and his plans to plant every part of the course with extravagantly

coloured shrubs, as he had seen at the Augusta National Golf Club in Georgia, regrettably died with him. A giant of a man, whose twenty stones were clad in vivid plus-fours during most of his last years at Killarney, his personality, character and enthusiasm for the game of golf are firmly etched on the ground three decades later. It is to be hoped they will always remain so. Castlerosse's prediction that Killarney would eventually need more than eighteen holes of golf was borne out in the late 1960s when the Irish Tourist Board acquired enough land for a further nine holes and the club itself reclaimed a parcel of land between the existing course and the lake. The new eighteen holes were opened for play in 1971, parts of the old course being intermingled with the new to form two completely new courses—Mahony's Point and Killeen. Not unnaturally, the changing of the old course brought protests from many quarters. But the clearing of the land close to the lake brought the water into play at many more holes and also opened up wonderful new vistas of lake and mountains.

Strangely, although the new holes present a challenge equal to much of the original course, it is the work of the 1930s which best captures the imagination. In addition to the three holes designed by Castlerosse, Sir Guy Campbell's original finishing trio remain virtually un-

touched, bringing the championship and the Mahony's Point courses to a testing and beautiful conclusion. The par-five 16th swings gently downhill to a green set against a backdrop of Lough Leane and Tomies Mountain. There is water in front of the green and along both sides of the fairway. After the tee shot, the green is at least one club farther away than it appears.

The par-four 17th runs along the lake shore, dog-legging slightly to the right, but with the safe left side of the fairway lined with trees. Bunkers are unnecessary to protect this green for the lake to the right and trees behind offer sufficient warning. And so to the 18th, a one-shotter across the corner of the lake to a narrow green—a fitting finish to a spectacular course.

Killarney has attracted only a small number of tournaments and championships in its long history, but the legendary Joe Carr scored the first of a hat-trick of victories in the Irish Amateur Close championship there in 1963 and Scotland's Eric Brown won the first of only two professional events to be staged at Killarney in 1955. Perhaps the most significant aspect of this event was Gary Player's first tournament appearance outside South Africa. He scored 84 and 76 and failed to qualify for the two final rounds. Gary Player and Killarney have come a long way since then.

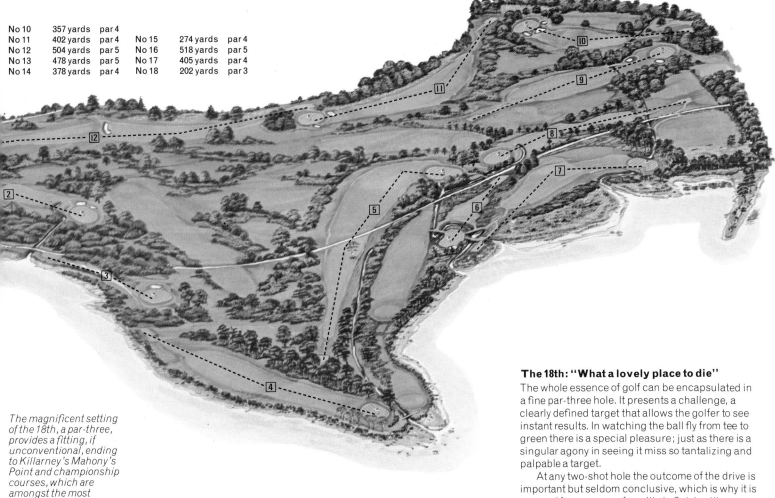

No 10	357 yards	par 4				
No 11	402 yards	par 4	No 15	274 yards	par 4
No 12	504 yards	par 5	No 16	518 yards	par 5
No 13	478 yards	par 5	No 17	405 yards	par 4
No 14	378 yards	par 4	No 18	202 yards	par 3

The magnificent setting of the 18th, a par-three, provides a fitting, if unconventional, ending to Killarney's Mahony's Point and championship courses, which are amongst the most beautiful in the world.

The 18th: "What a lovely place to die"

The whole essence of golf can be encapsulated in a fine par-three hole. It presents a challenge, a clearly defined target that allows the golfer to see instant results. In watching the ball fly from tee to green there is a special pleasure; just as there is a singular agony in seeing it miss so tantalizing and palpable a target.

At any two-shot hole the outcome of the drive is important but seldom conclusive, which is why it is unusual for a course of quality to finish with a par-three as Killarney does. Two factors save this slight architectural blemish—the Mahony's Point 18th (which also serves as the closing hole on the championship course) is both tough and spectacular. Set right on the edge of Lough Leane, it measures 202 yards from the back tee and a shot at the pin must carry across the rugged shore of the lake to a narrow green angled slightly to the right. The margin for error on the right is small: trees flank this edge and the back of the green, and the waters of the lake wait to snap up any ball which is farther off target.

The one consolation is that the prevailing wind comes off the lake, carrying the ball back towards the safe side of the green. Yet even here there is little room for error. The entire left side of the putting surface is edged by a long, thin bunker, with a road and more trees beyond. Short of the bunker on the left side lies an enormous thicket of rhododendrons. The only safe area for the shorter hitters is a small patch of grass that lies just in front of the green.

Add to this golfing challenge the magnificence of the setting, with the waters of the lake lapping beside tee and green and the backdrop of sparkling green hills and distant blue mountains, and the result is a finishing hole that will never fail to stimulate the senses. The ironic nature of the hole—its beauty and its difficulty—was perhaps summarized most succinctly by Henry Longhurst when he said of it: "What a lovely place to die."

Tumbling links amidst the Dutch sandhills

There is no finer example of seaside links on the continental mainland than the Kennemer club at Zandvoort, half an hour by car from Amsterdam. Despite the popular conception that Holland is a land of unwavering flatness, this coastal stretch is a place of wild tumbling dunes to stir the heart of any golfing architect. It must have inspired H. S. Colt when he came to create the present course in the late 1920s. The club was founded in 1910 and started elsewhere with nine holes on flat meadowland; no greater contrast to it could be imagined than this links with its glorious fairways, towering sandhills and spinneys of pine. It has no parallel in America but, at first sight, brings thoughts of problems of stance—not in a severe or arduous sense, but sufficient to test balance and control and to compel thought before striking.

One essential feature of a good course is that its attraction should be immediate. There are few more inviting prospects than the tees of the 1st and 10th holes at Kennemer; the course runs in two loops of nine, beginning and ending by the handsome thatched clubhouse poised high with a commanding view of the whole golfing scene. The 1st hole falls away to a spreading fairway, flanked by dunes with pines on their crests, the kind of drive that would appeal to the most humble performer. After an exciting short hole over a valley to a huge sloping plateau green one stands again on a high tee looking down upon another expanse of spacious fairway, gently curving to the left around a wood: a splendid hole. Even if you have not started 4, 3, 4—none too difficult down a prevailing south-westerly wind—a sense of pleasure to come and beauty all around is inescapable.

There are all the pastel shades of quiet fawns and golds and greens, and in the summertime the rough, often uncommonly tenacious, is alive with wild flowers. Buckthorn, with its savage spikes piercing the thickest trousers and vivid orange berries in the autumn is another occasional menace and delight. Pheasants nest in the long grasses and twice a year or so shoots are rewarding. Only the wild driver need fear the rough. For all normal purposes the fairways are of a generous width, but they could be narrowed, as could the entrances to the greens, to an extent that would challenge a championship field of the highest quality.

The 4th begins a fine stretch of golf. Colt considered this the one weak spot in his design and it has been converted from a par-three into a par-four. This hole apart, the course is little changed from his original concept, although it is some 400 yards longer and has a par two strokes lower. The drive from the new championship tee at the 4th through a cluster of trees, together with a tightly trapped green, makes a challenging hole. The 5th is a challenge, too, with its fairway all swales and mounds, out-of-bounds threatening the slice, and a valley before the green to confuse estimates of distance. Most of the greens are fairly large, offering a variety of pin positions; happily their undulations are slight and subtle and the surfaces of fine fescue putt swiftly and true.

The carry to the next fairway, the longest outward hole, is deceptively far and the golf hereabouts can be sterner than the card suggests; the wind, more often than not, will be leaning against the line of flight. Blind shots can be a tiresome affliction, but an occasional drive to an invisible fairway is effective for contrast. The one to the 7th is welcome, for the sight from the fairway's peak is splendid with the green set against tree-crested dunes and protected by a considerable cross-bunker. The 8th presents no great problem if a long iron is hit straight. It is followed by another tempting drive to a slightly angled, crumpled fairway, and an approach to a green in a basin below the clubhouse. Here, as on many holes, the placing of the drive determines the difficulty of the second shot as much from the question of stance as of line. In this respect Colt made memorable use of the terrain's natural features.

The drive to the 10th over a wild valley to a distant unseen fairway can be infinitely satisfying or disastrous, according to contact with the ball. The course then swings away to more open country, past the tunnel entrance to the 11th green, down the long, straight 12th, turning again for a lovely 13th with its green on rising ground, outlined against a dark cluster of pines. The long hitter may reach the deep hollow of the 14th fairway and find his view of the green obscured, but not if he holds the left side of the fairway.

At first glance the tee shot to the short 15th looks formidable, for the green is on the summit of a smooth, grassy cliff, down which the underhit or underclub will roll relentlessly into one of three traps at its foot. The high ground by the green makes a superb vantage point from which to watch the play of the last five

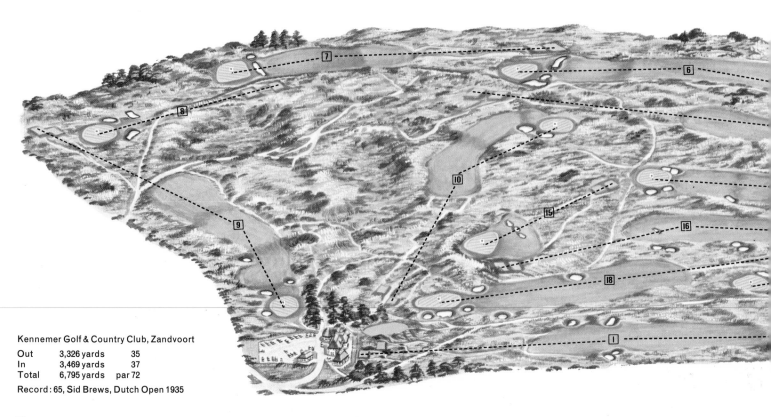

Kennemer Golf & Country Club, Zandvoort

Out	3,326 yards	35
In	3,469 yards	37
Total	6,795 yards	par 72

Record: 65, Sid Brews, Dutch Open 1935

holes—the long second away to the 16th cradled in the dunes; the last turn for home with the shot over wilderness to the short 17th, and the gradual rise of a fine finishing hole, its green between two large guardian bunkers.

Perhaps the most memorable contest at Kennemer was in the 1958 Dutch Open, soon after Peter Thomson had beaten David Thomas in a play-off for the British Open. Thomas exacted some measure of revenge, finishing five strokes ahead of Thomson with a total of 277. Three years earlier Alfonso Angelini, probably the finest Italian golfer of his day, beat Gerry de Wit in a play-off. In his time De Wit has been the best of the Dutch professionals, but victory in his own Open frequently escaped him by the narrowest margin; one year he lost after thirty-six holes of extra play to Ugo Grappasoni, another fine Italian player of the 1950s. Marcel Dallemagne, a magnificent French golfer of the 1930s, Bobby Locke, Flory Van Donck and Sid Brews, who set a seventy-two-hole record of 275 and the course record of 65 in the 1935 Dutch Open, have also won at Kennemer, so the club has a distinguished tally of champions.

However, the most shining moment in the club's history did not occur in competition but when a Canadian colonel—presumably a golfer —agreed to demolish the anti-tank wall built across the course during World War II. The area had been a defence zone, and the course virtually vanished under the concrete. By 1947 golf was again being played at Kennemer and now all recognizable traces of a massive stupidity have gone from a beautiful golf course.

Dutch links and the origin of golf

There has long been a school of thought that golf evolved from the ancient Dutch game of *het Kolven*, but the evidence is far from conclusive. Down the centuries many games have shared the aim of hitting a ball with a club towards a target, but learned researchers have failed to discover a definite link between any pursuit of the Middle Ages and the game of golf as mentioned by James II of Scotland in his famous decree of 1457. This demanded that "the fute-ball and golfe be utterly cryed downe and not to be used"; presumably the citizenry were neglecting the practice of archery and military training in those troubled times when England was a bitter enemy.

The precise origin of golf probably will never be known but the paintings by Van der Velde, Aver-

camp and others of *kolven* on ice, and not its normal form on indoor courts, stirred the imagination of historians. The indoor game was played in a walled space or court with a club and ball and involved the striking of posts at either end, but both club and ball were larger than those used for golf, as were those used on ice. The attitude of the players about to strike was the main resemblance to golf.

The ancient Flemish game of *chole* has also been suggested as an origin because of its cross-country nature. It was played to targets often miles away but both sides used the same ball. It had little similarity to golf save in the act of striking a ball with a club. This simply fulfils a fundamental human instinct from which various games have evolved. The likelihood is that golf was the form peculiar, in the beginning, to Scotland.

The continental challenge to Scotland's outstanding claims as the birthplace of golf is led by the Dutch. This painting by Adriaen van de Velde shows 17th-century Dutchmen adapting their game of kolven, normally played on an enclosed area of sand and clay with posts as targets, to winter conditions.

At Kennemer the English architect H. S. Colt was fortunate to have at his disposal an area of linksland ideally suited for golf. On it he created a marvellously challenging course with two holes, the 10th and the 15th, of particular distinction. At the 10th the drive is blind; at the 15th deep, fearsome bunkers guard a highly elevated green.

Card of the course

No 1	463 yards	par 4	No 10	370 yards	par 4
No 2	171 yards	par 3	No 11	484 yards	par 5
No 3	418 yards	par 4	No 12	555 yards	par 5
No 4	437 yards	par 4	No 13	380 yards	par 4
No 5	350 yards	par 4	No 14	407 yards	par 4
No 6	497 yards	par 5	No 15	172 yards	par 3
No 7	374 yards	par 4	No 16	513 yards	par 5
No 8	189 yards	par 3	No 17	181 yards	par 3
No 9	427 yards	par 4	No 18	407 yards	par 4

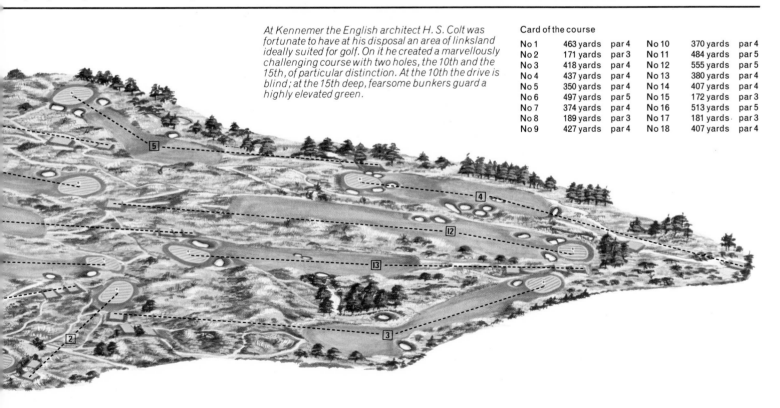

A royal course that has few peers

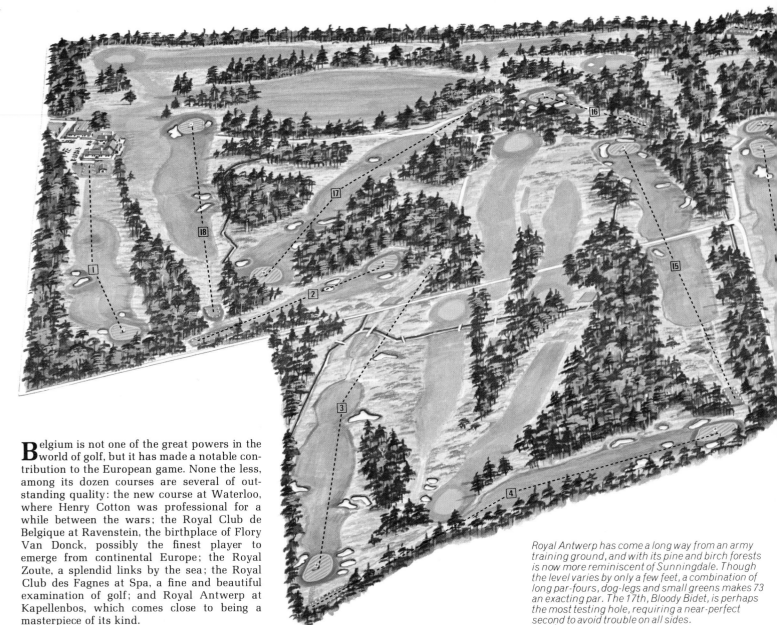

Royal Antwerp has come a long way from an army training ground, and with its pine and birch forests is now more reminiscent of Sunningdale. Though the level varies by only a few feet, a combination of long par-fours, dog-legs and small greens makes 73 an exacting par. The 17th, Bloody Bidet, is perhaps the most testing hole, requiring a near-perfect second to avoid trouble on all sides.

Belgium is not one of the great powers in the world of golf, but it has made a notable contribution to the European game. None the less, among its dozen courses are several of outstanding quality: the new course at Waterloo, where Henry Cotton was professional for a while between the wars; the Royal Club de Belgique at Ravenstein, the birthplace of Flory Van Donck, possibly the finest player to emerge from continental Europe; the Royal Zoute, a splendid links by the sea; the Royal Club des Fagnes at Spa, a fine and beautiful examination of golf; and Royal Antwerp at Kapellenbos, which comes close to being a masterpiece of its kind.

All those clubs are distinguished by the Royal title, bestowed upon them by Belgian kings. Since 1833, the British monarchy has conferred its patronage on more than sixty clubs in many different lands, but no royal family has taken a livelier interest in golf than the Belgian. King Baudouin has represented his country in international matches, a unique distinction for a reigning monarch, and his father, the abdicant King Leopold, is a true *aficionado*.

The choice of a single course from this excellent company is difficult but Royal Antwerp, twelve miles from the seaport, makes so favourable an impression that it takes pride of place. It is also the oldest club in the country, founded in 1888—the year that the St Andrews club in New York became the first in the United States. Like most of the older continental courses (only Pau is its senior on the continental mainland) Antwerp was formed by a few members of the local British settlement there.

The course at first was laid out on an army training ground. It cannot have been a particularly sympathetic site and soon after the turn of the century an area of woodland was bought some seventeen miles north of the city. Willie Park was called upon to make the new course and it was in play several years before World War I. It remained as Park designed it until, in the late 1920s, Tom Simpson created what became the ten middle holes of the main course. Within its confines nine shorter holes, including some of Park's original work, remain for those seeking relief from sterner pursuits.

In all Europe, including Britain, Antwerp has few peers for the type of course that wends its way through woods of pine and silver birch, heather and shrubs, and it has a character similar to those on that fine belt of golfing country west of London. At first sight it might appear easier than Sunningdale, Wentworth and their brethren. Its level changes hardly more than a yard or so; rarely do the trees threaten peace of mind, even that of a golfer. Yet its very flatness calls for fine judgement of distance, and the unusual disposition of some 6,700 yards makes the strict par of 73 severe even for the good player.

Few courses anywhere have so high a proportion of good long par-fours. Only the 1st, with its uncommonly billowing fairway, and the 4th, where the drive must be placed for a clear shot to the pin, are drive and pitch holes. On most, even the first-class golfer will be using longish irons to the greens—or occasionally wood, depending on the strength of the wind and the pace of the fairways. For the driver of average length the course is a great test of iron play, because the greens are not large and only that of the 16th, which is the shortest hole, is in any way set up as a target.

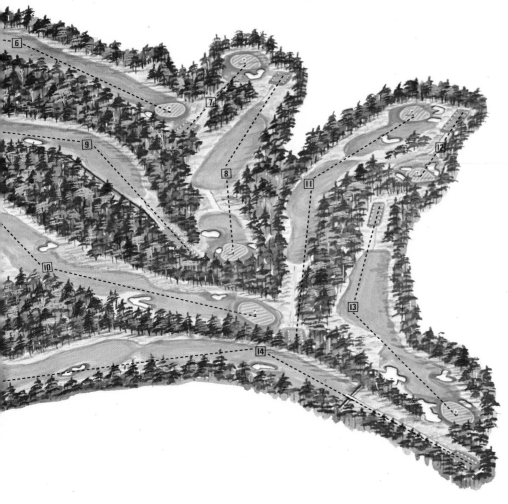

The 9th, 10th and 14th: Tackling the dog-legs

Tom Simpson, the architect of Royal Antwerp, was a great believer in the dog-leg hole and fifty years ago was something of a pioneer in this form of design. It is a conspicuous feature on the course's middle holes, seven of those between the 6th and the 14th curving markedly. Five swing to the left, favouring the right-to-left player.

Dog-legs provide variety and avoid the monotony of a sequence of straightaway holes. As at the 10th, with its narrow-waisted fairway, they stress the importance of placing from the tees. Occasionally, as at the 14th, the dog-leg is used to restrict the length of the drive, but the player with power and skill can bend his shot around the curve.

Such holes can be a snare in that they may tempt the player into attempting overmuch in order to cheat the corner, either by trying to clear it or by bending his shot around it, despite the ease with which an intentional draw can become a hook and a fade become a slice.

Architects often place bunkers within the inside of the curve, as at the 9th, and where position rather than length is essential one can visualize Hogan, for instance, aiming at the hazard and drawing or fading the shot gently away from it. In this way, when the shot's power is expiring, the ball is moving away from and not towards trouble, as the shots of humbler mortals are prone to do.

Card of the course

No 1	336 yards	par 4	No 10	412 yards	par 4
No 2	226 yards	par 3	No 11	493 yards	par 5
No 3	481 yards	par 5	No 12	164 yards	par 3
No 4	378 yards	par 4	No 13	405 yards	par 4
No 5	492 yards	par 5	No 14	478 yards	par 5
No 6	427 yards	par 4	No 15	477 yards	par 5
No 7	186 yards	par 3	No 16	148 yards	par 3
No 8	394 yards	par 4	No 17	381 yards	par 4
No 9	421 yards	par 4	No 18	398 yards	par 4

Royal Antwerp Golf Club, Kapellenbos

Out	3,341 yards	36
In	3,356 yards	37
Total	6,697 yards	par 73
Record: 68, Aldo Casera		

From a purist's viewpoint the one criticism is that the par-fives are not long enough for modern conditions. The 3rd is a lovely hole with the fairway angling away to the left, a heathery crest to threaten the second shot, and a long, narrow green. A finely placed centre bunker fifty yards short of the green makes the long, straight 5th and players can get home with an iron on the 11th—the longest and, for the ordinary golfer, one of the finest holes of all. The drive must be held left centre of the fairway and, unless the second is similarly placed, it will probably break from a shoulder of ground towards a bunker well short of the green.

The course is notable for its economy of bunkering—an admirable precept of the architects of old. The 7th, with a smooth hump protecting the line to the pin and ground falling towards a single right-hand bunker, is a beautiful short hole. The 12th has an extra bunker instead of a hump, threatening the safe way home, but the second is the stiffest of the short holes. It is a big shot, with a fold of ground making it look less than it is. Again there is only one greenside trap.

Several holes are compelling in their design and beauty. The 6th curves around an elbow of woods and narrows like an hour-glass where a long drive finishes, and a mound before the green stirs memories of St Andrews. The fairway of the 8th is almost an island of heather, from where a medium iron shot should flight to the heart of a green set against a shining stand of birch. From the back tee of the 13th the carry is considerable, and the drive must be right to open up the hole round trees to a green that is for once beset by bunkers. The 14th is a real dog-leg, swinging sharp left with cross-rough challenging the approach.

The finish is testing enough to keep hope alive in the breast of anyone who is trailing. The 15th needs two long shots, and the championship tee of the 17th would give even Nicklaus food for thought. Two big bunkers emphatically suggest that the approach should come in from the right, especially as a smaller bunker lies concealed beyond. This was the inspiration of a secretary wise in the ways of golf. At first it was known as Beatty's Bath, but its victims were so plentiful that it is now called Bloody Bidet. Bunkers await the slice on the last fairway and the hole is just short enough to quicken hopes of a saving three.

Then only memories remain and they will linger; every hole is so attractive. Always the silver of birches leavens the blackness of pine; rhododendrons bloom in the spring and in the late summer the heather is a purple glory—if a constant menace to those who stray from smooth fairways.

Classic links in a remote northern landscape

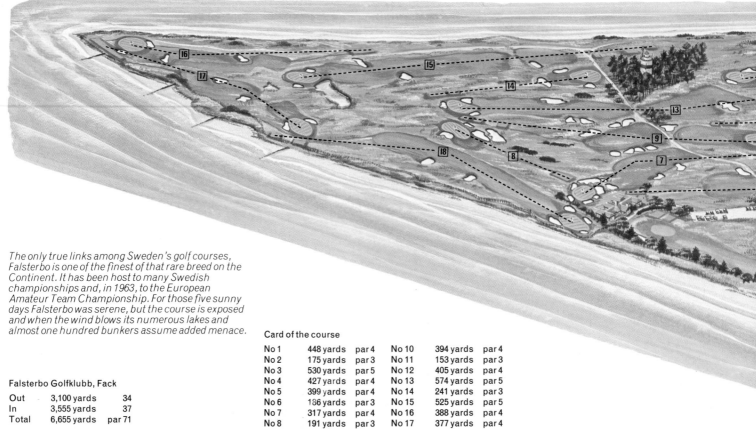

The only true links among Sweden's golf courses, Falsterbo is one of the finest of that rare breed on the Continent. It has been host to many Swedish championships and, in 1963, to the European Amateur Team Championship. For those five sunny days Falsterbo was serene, but the course is exposed and when the wind blows its numerous lakes and almost one hundred bunkers assume added menace.

Falsterbo Golfklubb, Fack

Out	3,100 yards	34
In	3,555 yards	37
Total	6,655 yards	par 71

Record: 66, John Cocken

Card of the course

No 1	448 yards	par 4	No 10	394 yards	par 4
No 2	175 yards	par 3	No 11	153 yards	par 3
No 3	530 yards	par 5	No 12	405 yards	par 4
No 4	427 yards	par 4	No 13	574 yards	par 5
No 5	399 yards	par 4	No 14	241 yards	par 3
No 6	186 yards	par 3	No 15	525 yards	par 5
No 7	317 yards	par 4	No 16	388 yards	par 4
No 8	191 yards	par 3	No 17	377 yards	par 4
No 9	427 yards	par 4	No 18	498 yards	par 5

True links courses are rare outside the British Isles. There is one at Le Touquet and a few nestle amongst the sandhills of the Low Countries, but one of the finest examples on the mainland of Europe is at Falsterbo in Sweden. It is not the oldest of Swedish courses —Hovås, near Gothenburg, came into being a few years earlier—but its very nature and its spectacular setting give Falsterbo pride of place. The course is laid out on the tip of a tiny peninsula that all but drops off the southern-most corner of Sweden—Stockholm is more than 300 miles away to the northeast, Copen-hagen a mere thirty, as the migrant geese and waders fly, across the Öresund.

In Sweden, golf's beginnings around the turn of the century were at best hesitant—the first eighteen-hole course was not built until 1929, and as recently as 1945 there were only twenty-two clubs. Now there are more than 120 courses and almost 50,000 golfers. From its start, in 1909, Falsterbo has been a pace-setter. In the year it was opened it staged Sweden's first international match between clubs (against its near neighbour, the Copenhagen Golf Club) and it became, in 1930, one of the country's first eighteen-hole courses.

Falsterbo incorporates all the links qualities of turf, natural hazards and changes of wind— now from the mainland, now from the Baltic— which can present a totally different test within a matter of hours. Such is its strength that it has been altered little over the years. It is an obvious setting for a golf course. The holes blend beautifully into natural surroundings which no amount of money could ever copy or create. The vast stretch of water that gives the 4th, 5th and 11th their menace and charm is to a measure reminiscent of the marsh holes at England's Royal West Norfolk, although only at the short 11th hole does very much of it have to be crossed.

At the excellent 4th, however, a stiff second has to skirt the water dangerously and it preys on the mind in the way that only water can. It is the feature by which players remember Falsterbo. In 1963 the men's European Amateur Golf Team Championship was staged there, and for most of that week the south of Sweden had its finest summer weather for years; the fairways turned brown and the beach, bordering the 17th and 18th, beckoned enticingly. Michael Bonal-lack, captain of the winning English team, speaks of that championship as just about the most enjoyable he has known. But Falsterbo also struck a deep note as an unrelenting test of golf, in which the water holes played a significant part—particularly in the qualifying stages of the match.

Falsterbo is invigorating rather than op-pressively daunting, but like all good courses it commands respect, calling for unrelenting con-centration, confidence and sound technique. From the moment the golfer encounters the dog-leg at the demanding 1st hole, with out-of-bounds on the right, he is confronted with the severity of Falsterbo's challenge.

The next four holes form a narrow offshoot out to the end of the marsh and back and, be-cause of their low-lying position, they have more of an inland character than the rest. The high, marshy reed grasses readily identify the edges of water hazards—which add flavour to the short 2nd, with its well-bunkered green, divide the 3rd and 4th holes and completely surround the 5th.

The 3rd is the only par-five in the outward half. It has all the hallmarks of a long hole, offering little alternative to a good drive, a good second and a good pitch. But it is probably the 4th, with its green tucked into a little alcove by the water's edge, and the 5th, where there is no margin for error with the drive, which most players will be pleased to pass without a skirmish with the water that haunts the slice. Not that the short 6th offers any respite. It has more water in front of the tee, an artificial out-of-bounds to the right and some of Falster-bo's few trees on the left. However, the 7th, a dog-leg to the left, offers the chance of a birdie and heralds the start of what the British would recognize instantly as true links golf.

With the odd exception, bunkers now take the place of water and at the 8th, the third short hole, one which is particularly well sited has to be carried from the tee. The two medium par-fours which follow do not present too much difficulty, but when the wind is against, the short 11th can only be reached with what is perhaps the most spectacular shot on the course. Although only 153 yards, it is death or glory, all or nothing, with water on all sides and the green nestling on a peninsula which looks minute from the tee.

The 12th has its fairways split into two by

Falsterbo is dominated by the old lighthouse, seen here from the 2nd green across the exquisite turf of the classic linksland course.

bunkers and the green is generously encircled by sand, but it can be child's play compared with the 574-yard 13th, known as Tipperary. Both fairway and green are closely guarded with bunkers and a substantial carry is necessary from the tee, the drive again being threatened by out-of-bounds on the right.

The 14th is the last and longest of the five short holes. The tee shot is threatened by a large cross-bunker, but it is the setting which makes this hole memorable. Beyond the green stands the old Falsterbo lighthouse, a reminder of the remoteness of the setting and the nearness of the sea. Golf's rich variety of settings

provides a powerful reason for playing and at Falsterbo there is the added delight of a vast, uninhabited stretch of shoreline, a haven for migratory birds in spring and autumn. Birds and golfers have chosen well at Falsterbo, and it is fitting that the true character of the course finds appealing expression in its finish. Shaped rather like the head of a fish, the 15th and 16th run out to the tiny peninsula's tip, where the sound and the Baltic meet, and the 17th and 18th return along the line of dunes.

The 15th and 18th are par-fives and, with the 16th and 17th among the best of the par-fours, Falsterbo certainly does not use up its

ammunition in its opening salvoes. Varying with the wind, the finish strikes a nice balance, but the splendour of the golf and the sheer pleasure of being in this remote northern landscape are exemplified by the prospect from the 17th tee. From there the views across the sound to Denmark and along Sweden's surf-fringed southern shore are positively breathtaking, but the golfer must constantly beware of letting them slacken his concentration, for it is quite possible to slice a shot far into the Baltic. To the very end Falsterbo's golfing charms refuse to be outdone by their almost excessively scenic setting.

The 18th: A finish fit for a king

The uncertainty and drama of matchplay often makes it more enjoyable than strokeplay. There is something fundamentally appealing about two men duelling their way round a golf course and it is through such encounters that many courses have become legendary.

Professionals of world class or even amateurs of international standing rarely play at Falsterbo, but in 1963 the European Team Championships brought it to the notice of golfers of many countries, and one of the matches produced a dramatic finale which can seldom have been repeated anywhere. Appropriately, the scene—as in all good matchplay plots—was the 18th.

From a tee in the sand-dunes, the hole dog-legs to the right between fairway bunkers to a deeply bunkered green some 500 yards away. On the day on which Sweden played Italy it was reachable

in two. Italy's Angelo Croce was just on the fringe at the back of the green, but Sweden's Rune Karlfeldt was short and much less likely to make the four it seemed he would need to halve the match, in which he had the support of a few hundred Swedes, including King Gustav.

The celebration, the cheering and stampeding which followed the chip with a 6-iron which Karlfeldt holed for his three is therefore not hard to imagine. Victory seemed assured, the King shook his hand and Croce, who had yet to play, somehow managed to convey that he, too, was pleased. After order had been restored, Croce stepped up to a putt which, to a man having only one shot in which to save the match, must have seemed an impossibility. But Croce duly holed it for as unlikely a half as anyone could remember. Happily he too was hailed by the Swedes and the celebrations and the handshakes were resumed.

The 18th:
498 yards par 5

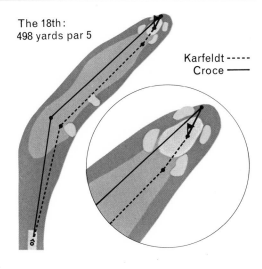

Karlfeldt -----
Croce ——

A forest where even the caddies get lost

The turn of the century was a halcyon time for golf. Adherents to the game were growing in number, especially among city dwellers seeking exercise in the open air. Cities themselves were expanding rapidly, but not yet to a degree that put the availability and cost of land at a premium—as, for example, in Japan today, where enthusiasm for the game, which almost amounts to a national obsession, is stymied by shortage of space in which to indulge it.

Bremen Golf Club, one of the oldest in Germany, was founded in the last years of the nineteenth century as the Hanseatic town was beginning its years of growth. It began with a nine-hole layout and the present course is the result of a decision by the Club Zur Vahr, which embraces a number of sports and social activities, to build a course suitable for major championships. The site chosen for the new course was the Garlstedter Heath, a setting with all the natural attributes needed to echo, in the mind of the club's president, August Weyhausen, those virtues he had found when playing the great Scottish and English courses. He sought a course where players of all standards would be forced to think, to accept their personal limitations and negotiate a tough test according to their abilities.

The course planned by Weyhausen and architect Bernard von Limburger occupies 220

The 5th at Bremen, a good example of the punishing nature of the German woodland course. The narrow fairways, deep rough and the ever-present woods make accuracy and good tactical thinking essential for a low score.

acres in thickly forested, undulating countryside. On the premise that nature itself is the best architect, the Bremen course was constructed with minimum change to the existing landscape. It is dominated by pine trees, tall and dense, crowding in from tee to green, controlling play on holes which bend narrowly to generally small targets. The strategic effect of the forest was such that it was necessary to construct only twenty-four bunkers. From the championship tees, the course measures 7,240 yards, with six holes of more than 500 yards.

Since its completion, the Garlstedter course has commanded respect from all who have played there and appreciated its disciplines. From the fine, modern clubhouse, three holes—the 1st, 7th and 9th—run over fairly level, pastoral parkland. Most of the others make their way through the forest, narrow and with sharp dog-legs which call for clear tactical thinking, since most fairways offer a choice of routes to the green. Among the trees there is thick undergrowth, with its risk of an unplayable lie and almost certainly a lost stroke.

The pressure of the natural hazards is com-

pounded by the fact that, to reach the ideal driving area, shots must be long as well as straight. When he was competing in the 1971 German Open, Roberto de Vicenzo was asked if it would help to have more fore-caddies. "No," he replied, "for then the fore-caddie is lost also."

The 7th hole is a good example of Bremen's thoughtful design, a 410-yard par-four with two completely separate routes to the green. Here the player has to weigh up the risks and make a clear choice. The good golfer drives out to the right to a fairway that begins only after a carry of 220 yards. Accuracy is essential, since there is out-of-bounds close by and the approach can be easily blocked by a copse just before the green. The second shot would normally be a 6- or 7-iron. A much wider fairway is open to the left, following a curving route around the copse. It is an easier choice, longer and over trees, but better for the handicap player.

Neil Coles, winner of the German Open in 1971 and, with Peter Thomson, joint holder of the course record of 68, knows the layout well: "I would rate it as one of the best championship

courses I have played in Europe. One could compare it to Augusta—it is a course with a big feel about it. The construction is very natural; there are not a lot of fairway bunkers off the tee, because they are not needed. The big thing about Club Zur Vahr is that it is a very good driving course—the penalties are tough if you are off line. Once you are among the trees which come right up to the edge of the fairway, you can only hope to come out sideways—assuming you find a playable lie.

"I think the par-fives are the outstanding holes. The 2nd and 6th, both of which have two routes, are particularly good. To reach the green in two, you have to take a chance off the tee and drive very close to the trees. The 10th, 547 yards and almost a right-angled dog-leg, is probably the best hole of all. You drive from the apex of a V, with tremendously tall trees on both sides. You must take a driver because you cannot play safe—you need the length, but with tall pines either side, it's quite a drive.

"The main thing about the course is that it is not only tight but long—on most holes in a tournament, you need that driver to avoid

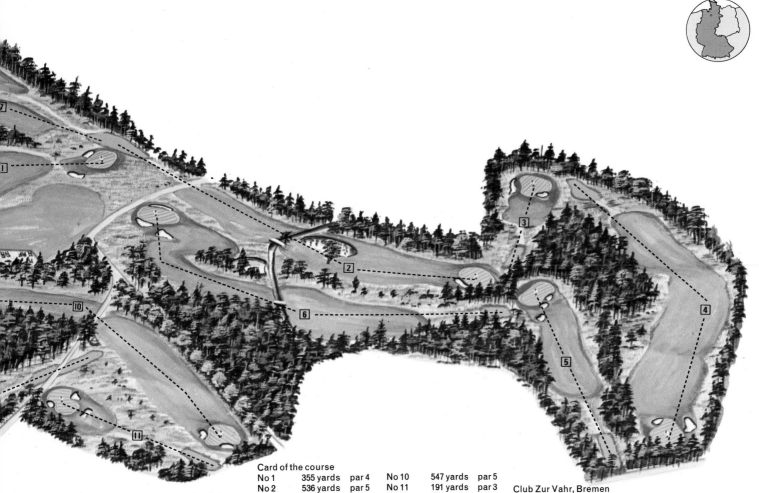

The heavily forested 220 acres of the Club Zur Vahr holds one of the most difficult layouts in Europe. The length (well over 7,000 yards including six par-fives), undulating fairways narrowing at strategic points, great patches of heather and comparatively small greens all combine to produce a real challenge. Any wayward shots are punished by dense rough.

Card of the course

No 1	355 yards	par 4	No 10	547 yards	par 5
No 2	536 yards	par 5	No 11	191 yards	par 3
No 3	208 yards	par 3	No 12	509 yards	par 5
No 4	569 yards	par 5	No 13	410 yards	par 4
No 5	334 yards	par 4	No 14	355 yards	par 4
No 6	574 yards	par 5	No 15	551 yards	par 5
No 7	410 yards	par 4	No 16	454 yards	par 4
No 8	164 yards	par 3	No 17	230 yards	par 3
No 9	427 yards	par 4	No 18	416 yards	par 4

Club Zur Vahr, Bremen
Garlstedter Heide Course

Out	3,577 yards	37
In	3,663 yards	37
Total	7,240 yards	par 74

Record: 68, Neil Coles, Peter Thomson, German Open 1971

being blocked off by the dog-legs. The 12th hole— 509 yards, par-five—is one of the narrowest, and is a good example. Even after a long drive you are still left with another long, narrow shot to the green over marshy rough and scrub. It is an easy five, but to get a four you have to take a chance.

"Another good hole is the 15th—a snaking, double dog-leg of 551 yards, lined with tall trees all the way. Again you have to keep close to the left to get the best shot in for your second. If you go right, playing safe, you really are shut out.

"Like all good courses, the finish is tough. The 16th is good, with a single, large tree plumb in the way of your drive, leaving a narrow entrance on to the fairway. The 230-yard 17th is probably the best short hole on the course. You play through a narrow avenue of tall pines to an elevated green with one large bunker front left. There is out-of-bounds just on the left; if you hit the bank, you can very easily go out. Altogether, an excellent championship test—forcing you right to the limit all the way."

Brian Huggett, another Ryder Cup player and former German Open champion, agrees: "It is like Champions at Houston, the best course that I have played in America. If you don't drive on the correct side of the fairways, you have to hook or cut your next. There is probably no harder course in Europe, not just because of length but because there are so many holes which call for skill as well."

The 2nd, 6th and 15th: The drive is critical

The strength of the Bremen course lies in the precise control needed from the tees at the long holes. There are always alternative routes to the greens, invariably safer but longer and inevitably requiring three shots to get there instead of two. The 2nd hole divides clearly to either side of a large oak tree in the centre of the fairway. If the drive can be hit close to the edge of the woods on the left, the green on this 536-yard hole is in range, but the shot has to be placed carefully since there is a small creek crossing the fairway just over 300 yards from the tee. The safer route is to the right of the tree, avoiding the lake to the left of it and aiming to reach the uphill elevated green in three. There is a strategic bunker set into the front right face of this green.

Another hole where the line and length of the tee shot is critical to the way in which the rest of the hole can be played is the 6th, which begins from a tee back in the forest known as "Napoleon's platform". The tee shot is played out to an area called "devil's island", which is surrounded by a marsh. From there, if his drive is long enough to allow a clear shot between the woods and over the swamp, the player can elect to go for the green. The alternative is to follow the narrow fairway which dog-legs to the right, avoiding trees, swamp and two bunkers, to reach the putting surface in three for a safe par.

Just occasionally a player who is not ideally placed can "beat the odds" at Bremen—but only by skill rather than luck. During the German Open, Roberto de Vicenzo cut his drive at the long, serpentine 15th. In extricating himself from the woods he hit his second shot much too strongly, going clear across the fairway and into the woods on the other side. From there he hit his third to the right, finishing in shallow heather some 250 yards from the green. Only fifteen yards in front of his ball was a large fir tree. Taking a 4-wood, Vicenzo kept his shot low to fly under the hanging branches of the fir. The ball then climbed over tall firs about one hundred yards in front of the green, faded with intentional slice and settled ten feet from the pin. Vicenzo had refused to let a series of three disastrous shots upset his rhythm or his concentration and he showed the mettle of a champion in producing a masterly shot, which enabled him to rescue his par at a critical time.

The 15th: 551 yards par 5
Vicenzo——
Normal line-----

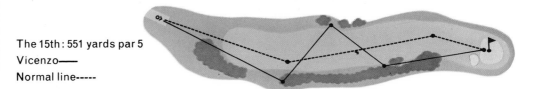

A classic course in a classical landscape

Peter Oosterhuis attacks the 16th. Though it is probably the most picturesque hole at Olgiata, nestling in a clearing by a stream, it is also one of the most difficult, demanding a perfect shot to the heavily bunkered green.

Card of the course

No 1	384 yards	par 4
No 2	213 yards	par 3
No 3	466 yards	par 4
No 4	383 yards	par 4
No 5	481 yards	par 5
No 6	410 yards	par 4
No 7	171 yards	par 3
No 8	377 yards	par 4
No 9	545 yards	par 5
No 10	394 yards	par 4
No 11	437 yards	par 4
No 12	407 yards	par 4
No 13	427 yards	par 4
No 14	161 yards	par 3
No 15	478 yards	par 5
No 16	192 yards	par 3
No 17	499 yards	par 5
No 18	437 yards	par 4

Circolo Golf Olgiata, Rome

Out	3,430 yards	36
In	3,432 yards	36
Total	6,862 yards	par 72

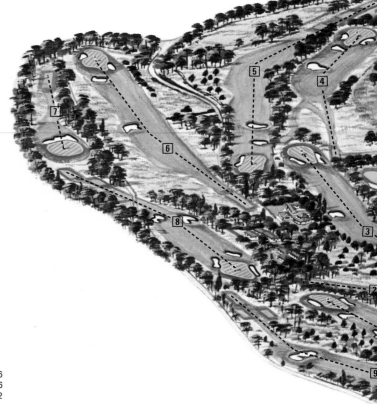

The approaches to Rome from the north pass through a gentle, rolling landscape, the home in antiquity of the Sabines and the southernmost of Etruscan lands, and the home today of Circolo Golf Olgiata, one of Italy's newer and better courses. For a long time this area has been famous for the stables of Dor-mello-Olgiata. Thus the golf course, itself a thoroughbred, is in a wholly appropriate setting. The Olgiata courses—one of eighteen holes, another of nine—were designed by C. K. Cotton, one of Britain's foremost architects, and completed in 1961. The clubhouse has the virtues of the most comfortable American country club, the architect achieving a masterly concealment of its size in a long, low building which harmonizes gracefully with the surrounding scene. The championship course frequently changes direction, moving in two separate loops beginning and ending at the clubhouse.

One of the greatest blessings a golf architect can have is ample room for the wanderings of his imagination. Cotton was fortunate in this at Olgiata: he was able to plan every hole in its own spacious setting, thus ensuring that each would be individual in character. There is no sense of congestion or monotony; the holes are easily remembered long after playing them.

The strongest impressions at first are of the large greens and the manner of their protection. Most of the entrances are narrow and between bunkers, but the attacking stroke is rarely punished severely; there is room enough behind the greens whichever one of various pin positions is used. Another feature is the changing levels; none is harsh, but all serve to tax judgement of length. The golfer is soon aware that his driving will be tested. The opening hole swings uphill to the right, and to have a

clear pitch to the green the tee shot must be long and straight between spinneys. The emphasis on placing is not always so obvious; at the 3rd and 5th it is achieved by a single tree, and a perfectly placed bunker on the left of the 6th fairway tends to encourage a fade towards woods, for the hole moves that way. The drive to the 8th is very narrow, but the spread of fairway below is enticing—as is that of the 9th. This is the longest hole, with cross-bunkers to be carried and spinneys to be threaded to a favourable position for the final approach.

Hardly a hole on the course is straight but the balance between movement to the right and left is well preserved. The drive to the 10th, like several others, is stiffened by the placing of one bunker on the opposite side of the fairway to the natural hazard of the woods that make a kind of spine to the course. Most of these bunkers are a good way out from the tees and—as Sam Snead remarked after a round of 72—they tend to make the course difficult for the good player. Lesser mortals can aim away from the major hazard without fear of reaching the alternative.

A minor criticism is that from the 11th three successive holes are blind from the tee. Yet this matters little, for the hills are not steep and all the holes are worth while. The approaches to the raised plateau of the 12th are testing strokes. Once the drive has cleared the ridge of the 13th the hole is not too difficult, and the 14th is the mildest of the short holes unless the shot is very short and fails to carry a pool. Thereafter the course yields nothing.

The 15th is forbidding because the fairway tilts steeply to the left towards a stream and woods, the end of which can cut into the line of a long second. Nothing less than a true, straight

shot has any chance of reaching the next green. The hole, narrow as the nave of a church, is the only one enclosed by trees, and a dramatic setting they make. The 17th, a great leaning curve along woods to the right, is a glorious hole and—if the final drive is not sliced—a challenging stroke remains over cross-bunkers to a green of varying levels.

All this amounts to a considerable golf course, as the players in the 1964 World Team championships for the Eisenhower Trophy discovered. Their tasks were intensified by dreadful weather, for, after an opening day when sunshine was warm on the olive hills, a strong wind gusted through the trees. The greens were, however, the real problem. Their grass was beautiful and consistent but they were very soft. Even Deane Beman, one of the world's great putters, was helpless.

On the second evening a violent storm exploded over Rome; the skies were alive with wild blue light and the course was drenched. The greens were like sponges, but the British—Michael Bonallack, Rodney Foster, Michael Lunt and Ronnie Shade—made fewer putting errors than their immediate challengers. They began the last day five ahead but suffered awful suspense before triumph was theirs.

In the dripping twilight a Canadian, Keith Alexander, slender and easy of style, could have put his side level with Britain if he had finished with five birdies. As four in succession fell to his courageous golf British agony and Canadian joy needs no imagining, but his second to the last fell away from the green. The name of Olgiata was engraved on the memories of those who watched and played that day, as it will be remembered by many who have the good fortune to play there on less earnest occasions.

Completed in 1961, Olgiata has all the advantages of a course constructed from scratch. Ken Cotton was able to design a spacious, well-balanced layout of great variety, and one to test every aspect of golfing strategy and tactics—particularly the choice of club on the shorter holes. It was impressive enough to be chosen as the venue for the World Cup in 1968, only seven years after it opened, when the Italian team of Bernardini and Angelini finished a fine third.

Canada's Al Balding took the individual honours during the 1968 World Cup with a 271 total, seventeen under par. His spectacular eagle from a bunker at the 17th sealed the fate of the American pair Lee Trevino and Julius Boros. Balding's partner was George Knudson.

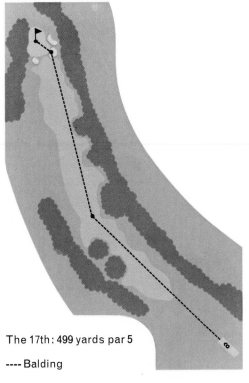

The 17th: 499 yards par 5

---- Balding

The 17th: Balding's eagle takes the World Cup

The Canadians Al Balding and George Knudson won the World Cup, the trophy that once bore their country's name, in 1968. They began the last round at Olgiata two behind Julius Boros and Lee Trevino of the United States and finished two ahead. Their play of the 17th proved decisive.

Throughout its length the curving fairway falls to the right towards deep woods, ever threatening the shot that drifts a little. On the left edge of the fairway a little cluster of trees, nature's contribution, ensures that those wary of perdition to the right do not hold up the second shot too much. Standing above the ball with a wooden club in hand does not make for the easiest shot in golf, especially when hoping to reach the green poised above a steep bank on the right.

For once the gifted Knudson was outshone. Balding's short game that day had a celestial touch that reached its climax on the 17th. He played his second with wood almost perfectly, keeping his weight back and—essential with such strokes—making a good turn, but the shot was fractionally off line, not more than five yards, and it was bunkered some fifteen yards from the flag. However, he exploded into the hole for an eagle, the ball pitching short of the pin and resting against it. Canada was ahead.

The Americans still had their chances of birdies at the 17th, but Boros floated a 4-wood over the green and Trevino cut his into the trees. Finally, they needed a birdie and a par to tie. But the birdie was not forthcoming and Balding, in his greying years as a competitor, had won a memorable victory for his country. Italy, too, did remarkably well to finish in third place, only four strokes behind Canada and two behind the United States, Roberto Bernardini shooting a splendid 279.

"...nor the slightest glimpse of an alien world"

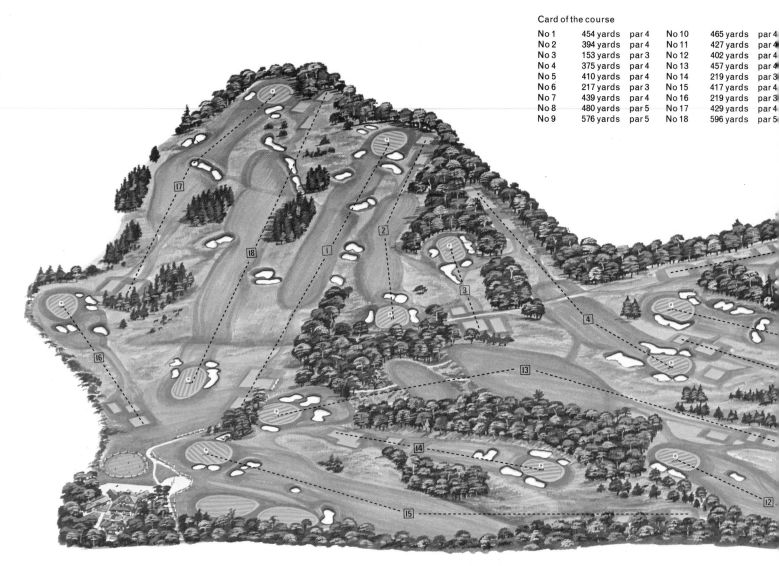

Card of the course

No 1	454 yards	par 4	No 10	465 yards	par 4
No 2	394 yards	par 4	No 11	427 yards	par 4
No 3	153 yards	par 3	No 12	402 yards	par 4
No 4	375 yards	par 4	No 13	457 yards	par 4
No 5	410 yards	par 4	No 14	219 yards	par 3
No 6	217 yards	par 3	No 15	417 yards	par 4
No 7	439 yards	par 4	No 16	219 yards	par 3
No 8	480 yards	par 5	No 17	429 yards	par 4
No 9	576 yards	par 5	No 18	596 yards	par 5

More than a century has passed since golf was first played in France. In 1856, when the Duke of Hamilton and a few of his friends formed a club at Pau, in the foothills of the Pyrenees, golf was hardly known outside Scotland; there were but few courses in England and no others on the Continent of Europe. In the last years of the old century clubs appeared in Biarritz, Cannes and the hinterland of Paris; now, the game's influence is fast growing and numerous courses have been created, as beautiful as the most fervent golfer could desire.

Eminent players often fail to agree as to the exact merits of courses. There are so many imponderables of setting, design, feature and personal taste to influence one's judgement, but few would dispute that the one in the forest of Chantilly, twenty-five miles north of Paris, stands high if not paramount in France.

Long before golf was dreamed of, Chantilly played no small part in the affairs of men. For more than 1,000 years a great castle has stood there. Save for a period of annexation by Louis XIII, the estate belonged to the Condé family. The castle, one of the most magnificent in all France, was almost destroyed during the French

Revolution, and when the last Condé, Duke of Bourbon, hanged himself in 1830 Chantilly passed to the Duke of Aumale, a son of Louis-Philippe, the last king of France. In 1897 Chantilly was bequeathed to the Institut de France, an illustrious body of learned men, and now, in woods a mile away, golfers pursue their eternal challenge.

The club was founded in 1908 under the presidency of Prince Murat, and five years later the French Open championship was played there after seven years at La Boulie, the golf course of the Racing Club de France.

Few clubs other than Chantilly have longer enjoyed the blessing of two courses. In the early 1920s Tom Simpson was commissioned to lay out a new eighteen holes, and to redesign those which form the present championship course, known as the Vineuil. Much of his work was damaged beyond reclamation during World War II and nine of the new holes were abandoned, but there is little doubt that Simpson's work on the main course, which included reducing the number of bunkers, was the foundation of its greatness.

A first sight of Chantilly gives an impression

of dignity, peace and space. Nothing is confined or cramped; there is always ample room around the greens and tees and between the holes. The course falls quietly away from the clubhouse, rather as it does at the Augusta National: all around is the great forest and nowhere is there the slightest glimpse of an alien modern world. At once the impulse to play is strong; the awareness of a beautiful and demanding course immediate. After the opening drive over a valley, a long second must avoid bunkers staggered to the right and slice traps by the green. A pull from the 2nd tee is disaster; a fade may be engulfed by a long bunker but a good shot leaves a pitch to a raised target of green. A long, flat bunker acts as a false lighthouse on the short 3rd, and the view from the 4th tee is like looking down a gun barrel. The hole is not long but the entrance to the green is tight with bunkers across and flanking the approach. When the French Open was at Chantilly in 1964 the course was playing far too short, the rough was light, and the greens true and holding.

Roberto de Vicenzo, that majestic golfer from the Argentine, and Cobie LeGrange of

Situated in beautiful woodland in one of Europe's greatest horse-racing areas, Chantilly is an outstanding course that has hosted several French Open championships. It is a pleasure to play there—not merely because of its serene forest setting but also because of its demanding qualities. Two series of holes in particular—the 9th to 11th and the 13th to 15th—provide a stern test of power and accuracy.

Chantilly Golf Club, Oise

Out	3,498 yards	36
In	3,631 yards	35
Total	7,129 yards	par 71

The 18th: A test of stamina to the end

When Peter Oosterhuis stood on Chantilly's 18th tee in the last round of the 1974 French Open he needed a par-five to retain the title he had won the previous year at La Boulie. With a following wind, the huge hole was playing short; the range of cross-bunkers which can menace the drive were no threat and Oosterhuis's one concern was to keep the ball in play and not be snared by the spinneys flanking the fairway or reach the bunkers on the right. Length was of no account and, like many another strong player, Oosterhuis used a 1-iron.

His next problem was to avoid the bunkers which tightly embrace the entrance to the green; he overcame this with a tremendous spoon shot which soared over the valley, pitched on the green and held eight yards past the flag. A moment later he had beaten Peter Townsend by two strokes.

The beauty of the hole is that the green encourages an attacking stroke because there is no trouble beyond and the ground slopes gently upwards. Yet the prospect of the second shot can be perplexing as it was at the close of the 1964 Open. Roberto de Vicenzo made his four there in the last round with a masterly little downhill pitch and run after his long second had bounded past the green. Eventually Cobie LeGrange of South Africa needed a four to win but, faced with having to hit a perfect fairway wood to reach the green, deliberately played short rather than risk being bunkered. From forty yards he failed to get down in two and lost the play-off to Vicenzo on the fifth extra hole.

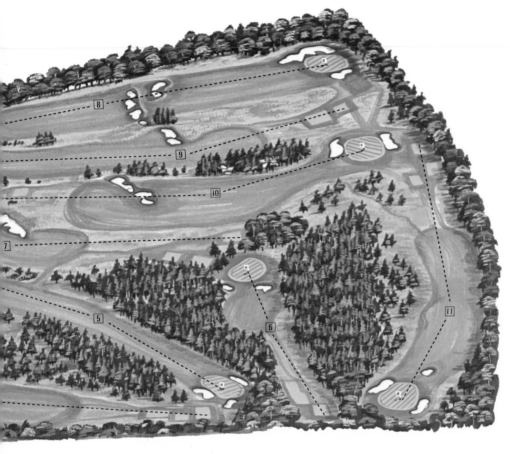

British star Peter Oosterhuis retained his French Open title at Chantilly in 1974 with a coolly executed birdie at the testing 18th, one of the longest finishing holes in Europe.

South Africa tied with totals of 272. Vicenzo, who won the play-off, toyed with the course, but more accurate statements of its quality were that in 1950 Vicenzo needed 279 to win and, a few years earlier, Henry Cotton, then the greatest British golfer, needed six strokes more to become champion.

The 5th is a fine hole, turning at a point from where the approach must be played through a neck of woods, with a cluster of pines by the green threatening the golfer who has driven too far to the left. Every instinct suggests a faded tee shot to the short 6th, but if it is played too safely pines again come into the reckoning. Although it might not appear so, there is room enough to pitch and hold after carrying the bunker guarding the green.

A compelling feature of Chantilly is its constantly changing character and, for that matter, direction as well. The holes around the turn swing back and forth across more open country. The woods may flank—as for the full length of the 8th and the 11th, curving away from the dark forest towards a green set against a backdrop of ivy-clustered trees—but they never enclose. A whole series of bunkers, quickening

memories of Muirfield, await the sliced second to the 7th. The angled curves of the 9th and 10th run parallel, but each drive and approach poses different problems. The shallow spine of the ground which divides them is alive with golden broom in the summertime.

The importance of placing the tee shot is emphasized at almost every hole and is particularly true of the 12th, where no player would wish to come into the green from the right and towards the steeply falling ground beyond. At its foot lies the 14th green in a secret dell, and a golfer can enjoy a brief, if imaginary, feeling of superiority watching those putting far below. For the next three holes the golf is spectacular, and testing indeed for the frail if they have hopes of par.

A good drive to the 13th leaves a lovely second shot over a deep, grassy chasm to a green set against a fringe of trees. The 14th is the longest of the short holes, the green an oasis in its basin. Then comes a formidable drive. The championship tee is high in woods which snare the slightest hook and, on the right-hand peak of the deep valley—which must be carried to reach the fairway—is a tall spinney

of oak and lime trees. The second shot is straight to a twin-level green.

The closing holes are sternly orthodox. Another target tee shot, to a green ringed with sand, is followed by a perfect-length 17th. A diagonal of hazards is meant to challenge the second shot; in 1964 in one round Vicenzo's drive carried it. The green, like so many of Simpson's, has bunkers for the man who does not stay with his shot.

The 18th, plunging and rising through a valley, makes a compelling climax to a noble course and was the setting for a memorable finish in that 1964 Open. Vicenzo's huge second bounded through the green, but a masterly downhill pitch made his four. Eventually LeGrange needed a four to win but decided not to risk the long, hazardous carry over the bunkers in front of the green.

He played short, failed to pitch close enough, and, after five sudden-death holes, Vicenzo was the champion. The effortless power and style of his golf may have been surpassed in this generation by the ageless, smooth-swinging Sam Snead, but not the warmth, gentleness, and charm of the man himself.

Water and sand on the grand scale

The tide of tourism in Spain and Portugal during the 1960s and early 1970s brought with it something of a boom in the construction of golf courses of a calibre high enough to mount championship events. They were a major factor in attracting visitors, especially in winter, and resort developers spared no expense in creating courses of high quality, usually in attractive settings.

One of the most outstanding is Nueva Andalucia, near Marbella on the Spanish Costa del Sol. Designed by Robert Trent Jones and opened in 1968, it is part of a vast 2,700-acre residential and holiday complex that includes, for the Hemingways among its golfers, a bullring. The course has already been used for a number of major competitions, including the 44th Spanish Open and the World Cup of 1973, won by Jack Nicklaus and Johnny Miller for the United States.

Nueva Andalucia is a typical example of Trent Jones's work. It is dramatic, difficult and controversial, attracting praise, respect—and some criticism. One of the most prolific and successful architects in the history of the game, Trent Jones believes that a course should always provide an easy alternative route for the Sunday golfer, but a tough test for the par shooter. Large, sculptured and strategically placed sandtraps, mammoth water hazards often pinching into narrow driving areas, undulating greens with variable pin positions—these are the Trent Jones hallmarks which turn what is simply a difficult course into one of true championship quality.

At Nueva Andalucia, the course follows a valley leading towards the sea from the Sierra Blanca mountains. Set on high ground and framed by a stand of pines, the clubhouse looks out across the entire course with its series of attractive but critical water hazards excavated from the valley floor. Inevitably, in a country where green turf is uncommon—and, where it exists, the product of great care and even greater expense—the course is essentially artificial, with exotic trees planted to enhance its beauty and increase its difficulty. At its far end, a grove of mature olive trees has been used to create a number of tight dog-leg holes, contrasting with the more open, undulating holes of the higher ground.

By clever use of the rolling land and the placement of hazards, Trent Jones avoided the need for virtually any rough at all. Unless a drive is placed correctly on the sloping fairways

and pitched right into the large holding greens, the ball will most certainly be in sand, water, or out-of-bounds. The penalties are visible, clear—and total.

Nueva Andalucia is a stern and testing course, combining an examination of playing skill with the distractions of beauty. It is liberally sprinkled with pine and eucalyptus, palm and almond trees, Indian figs and sugar cane and acres of orange orchards which scent the air at dusk. Vivid shades of green contrast with the crushed white marble of the bunkers and dominating it all is the stark peak of La Concha, the large white mountain which towers over the course.

The qualities that make a course a great playing test, even in perfect weather, are best seen at those holes which expose the skills or limitations of a golfer, which force him to elect to play perfect nominated shots (often at full stretch) or else settle for safety and second best. Sebastian Miguel, the club's professional, has represented Spain twelve times in the World Cup and has been in the second-placed team twice. In his opinion the best holes on this demanding layout are the 2nd, 12th and the finish from the 15th.

The second hole is a 421-yard par-four with a narrow, sloping driving area between two traps and a water hazard among trees; there is also out-of-bounds all along the right. The green, which is well protected on a high plateau, tilts sharply towards the front and can leave an almost impossible downhill putt, depending on the pin position. Another good hole in the first nine is the 8th, 530 yards with two clear routes of approach. The main feature is water, following the right-hand side of the fairway all along the hole and crossing in front of the green. The safe second is played away to the right, across the water to a fairway area leaving a simple pitch to a small green between two sandtraps. To reach the green in two, the shot must be perfectly struck, avoiding the hazards and the water which hugs the steep slope of the elevated green. Johnny Miller had an eagle there during his record round of 65. The water hazard also figured in a spectacular birdie for Mr Lu (Lu Liang Huan of Taiwan). From the water below the green, he literally splashed out to two feet.

One of the toughest and most beautiful of the short holes is the 208-yard 11th, played from a slightly elevated tee to a small green,

The 17th green at Nueva Andalucia, with the Sierra Blanca in the background. The elevated green, water hazards on three sides and the three irregular bunkers of crushed marble are typical of Jones's designs. The course has few rivals in any country for sheer magnificence.

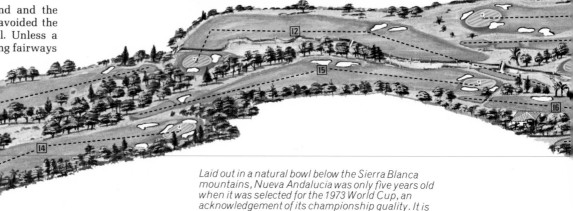

Laid out in a natural bowl below the Sierra Blanca mountains, Nueva Andalucia was only five years old when it was selected for the 1973 World Cup, an acknowledgement of its championship quality. It is a big, tough course full of long carries over water (a trade mark of Robert Trent Jones), strategically placed sandtraps and cleverly sculptured greens.

bunkered on both sides, with water stretching across the front and completely around the left-hand edge. A long iron, possibly even a wood, is needed in wind for there is no room for error here.

The 15th, at 427 yards dog-legging sharply right through the grove of mature olive trees, is not the toughest hole on the course, but it does require careful negotiation. It is also notable for having been the setting for one of the greatest nominated tee shots of all time. The hole runs straight for more than half its length, through a narrow avenue of olives, with two fairway traps on the left-hand side at the corner. An out-of-bounds fence follows the hole. During the World Cup, Jack Nicklaus aimed right and calmly knocked his drive over the olives and the out-of-bounds, completely over the corner—a full 270 yards of carry, to leave a simple approach to the small, angled green. The hole following, a 224-yard par-three, has claimed many victims and probably aroused more controversy than any other hole on the course. The steeply sloping green has two bunkers biting deeply into its surface from either side and a large water hazard across its front. It is always a long shot and often barely reachable from the back tee into a wind. Finishing above the hole, the golfer can putt straight back off the green.

The 17th is a short two-shotter of 323 yards, requiring discretion off the tee followed by an accurate pitch to a small oasis encircled by water on three sides, date palms and olives. Two large bunkers guarding the entrance and steep slopes down to the water demand a positive, accurate shot. The caddie's regular cry here is "agua" (water).

Now comes the last hole, a moderate par-four, where placement of the drive between out-of-bounds and a large, gathering water hazard is vital. The elevated green, two tiered and well bunkered, is a good deal farther away than it looks. It is an excellent finish to a demanding, unrelenting but most attractive championship challenge.

The 12th: A birdie chance for the brave

Nueva Andalucia's 520-yard 12th combines to perfection the ideal characteristics of a championship par-five. Played strictly as a three-shot hole, it offers ample room and the prospect of an easy par. However, for the player seeking a birdie and striving to reach the green in two, the margin for error is minute and the penalties for a slightly mishit shot severe.

From a tee back in the olive trees, out of sight of the green, the drive is out to an open fairway, protected on the right by two shallow bunkers in a stand of palms. The hole dog-legs left and along the left-hand side is a small watercourse. This hazard has been cunningly designed to bulge into the fairway at strategic points. To reach the green in two, the player must play down the left-hand side, avoiding the meandering water, to a fairway which slopes left and gathers the over-ambitious shot to cause substantial new problems.

The water hazard, which develops into a series of attractive descending pools with small waterfalls, continues menacingly all the way along the left side of the fairway until it crosses in front of the green. The subtly sloped putting surface is elevated, and the steep surrounding slopes ensure that any shot slightly short will run back down into the water. The green is bunkered front and back and the rear half is surrounded by olive trees. The shape of the hole dictates that the drive has to be long to prevent a small grove of tropical trees and the encircling olives from obscuring the flag, yet

it must be kept dangerously left to bring the green within range. The second shot is very tight, with no room for manoeuvre, not least because the surrounds of the green are designed to throw the errant shot away from the flag into trouble.

If the hole is played as a genuine par-five, with two solid, safe shots away from trouble, the golfer is left with an 8- or 9-iron to the fat of the green, the greenside bunkers not really coming into play. However, if he aims to be up in two a handicap player will have to hit two of the best golf shots of his life.

To make Nueva Andalucia's 12th green in two has become something of a challenge to the golfers of Europe. The second shot must carry not only water but also a huge bunker.

Card of the course

No 1	399 yards	par 4	No 10	394 yards	par 4
No 2	421 yards	par 4	No 11	208 yards	par 3
No 3	503 yards	par 5	No 12	520 yards	par 5
No 4	202 yards	par 3	No 13	383 yards	par 4
No 5	580 yards	par 5	No 14	394 yards	par 4
No 6	383 yards	par 4	No 15	427 yards	par 4
No 7	170 yards	par 3	No 16	224 yards	par 3
No 8	530 yards	par 5	No 17	323 yards	par 4
No 9	355 yards	par 4	No 18	399 yards	par 4

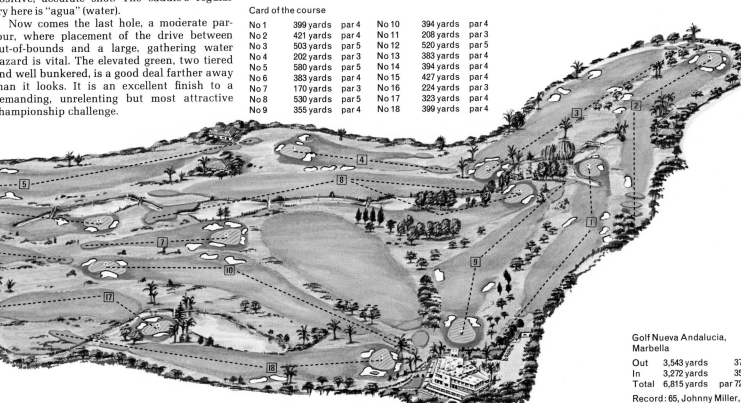

Golf Nueva Andalucia, Marbella

Out	3,543 yards	37
In	3,272 yards	35
Total	6,815 yards	par 72

Record: 65, Johnny Miller, World Cup 1973

An extravagant American entry into Europe

Card of the course

No 1	394 yards	par 4	No 10	453 yards	par 4
No 2	527 yards	par 5	No 11	373 yards	par 4
No 3	339 yards	par 4	No 12	582 yards	par 5
No 4	235 yards	par 3	No 13	214 yards	par 3
No 5	361 yards	par 4	No 14	503 yards	par 5
No 6	517 yards	par 5	No 15	426 yards	par 4
No 7	422 yards	par 4	No 16	388 yards	par 4
No 8	199 yards	par 3	No 17	174 yards	par 3
No 9	363 yards	par 4	No 18	440 yards	par 4

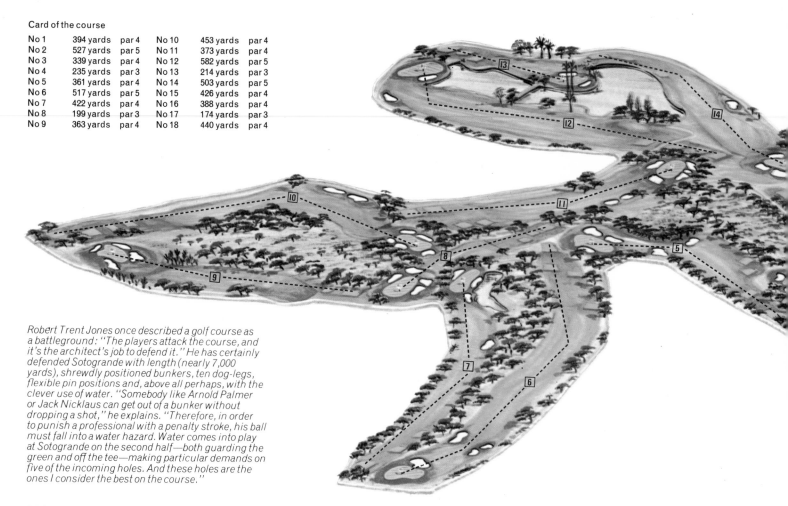

Robert Trent Jones once described a golf course as a battleground: "The players attack the course, and it's the architect's job to defend it." He has certainly defended Sotogrande with length (nearly 7,000 yards), shrewdly positioned bunkers, ten dog-legs, flexible pin positions and, above all perhaps, with the clever use of water. "Somebody like Arnold Palmer or Jack Nicklaus can get out of a bunker without dropping a shot," he explains. "Therefore, in order to punish a professional with a penalty stroke, his ball must fall into a water hazard. Water comes into play at Sotogrande on the second half—both guarding the green and off the tee—making particular demands on five of the incoming holes. And these holes are the ones I consider the best on the course."

The second shot to the 7th green at Sotogrande. This is probably the most spectacular hole on the course and certainly the tightest. The drive is into a narrow valley with out-of-bounds on the left and a large bunker on the right. The second, to a green which slopes away from the cork trees towards a bunker and the lake, is equally tight.

Club de Golf Sotogrande, Cadiz

Old course

Out	3,357 yards	36
In	3,553 yards	36
Total	6,910 yards	par 72

Record: 66, Roberto de Vicenzo, Spanish Open 1966

A Lancashire-born American, Robert Trent Jones has designed or helped to remodel more than 300 golf courses around the world— among them Dunes, Spyglass Hill and Mauna Kea in the United States, and Moor Allerton in Yorkshire. Sotogrande was his first venture in Europe ("nobody believed that we could build a golf course on sandy ground") and the fusion of the environment and Jones's style proved attractive and successful.

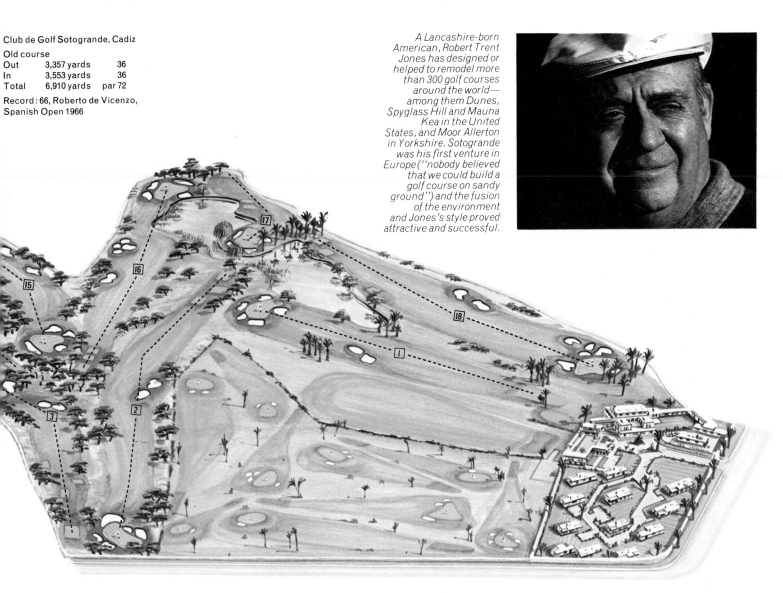

The courses at Sotogrande, on the Spanish Costa del Sol, lie twenty-two miles from Gibraltar, a massive silhouette on the western horizon. Designed by Robert Trent Jones—the Old course, completed in 1965, was his first venture in Europe—they are outstanding for their design and beauty of setting.

American influence is clear in every aspect of the design of the Old course. The tees are long, sleek quadrangles of turf allowing great variation in the length of the holes. The greens are large—perhaps excessively so—but they allow for a variety of pin positions, and as putting surfaces their contours are subtly fashioned. The bunkers and traps gleam white, made of crushed marble from Andalusian quarries because the local sand was not considered good enough. No spectre of economy haunted the architect's plans.

The turf itself is probably the strongest reminder of America. This was the first time Bermuda grass was used on a course in Europe, and two sacks of seed from Tifton in Georgia proved sufficient for a nursery from which all the fairways were sown. These are superb to

the tread and for the lie of the ball; there is no such thing as a bad lie on the fairways of Sotogrande. At first the Bermuda was used on several greens, but eventually all were sown with Pencross bent, and beautiful putting surfaces they are.

The golfer fresh from the courses of Britain has to accustom himself to pitching approaches right up to the flag in the true target manner, otherwise he will forever be short. All the greens hold; so, too, do the fairways, for an automatic electric system feeds almost 500 watering points. For a course to survive throughout the long, dry summers constant watering is essential, but unlike the desert courses in America and elsewhere one has no impression of playing on an oasis. The dark green of the cork trees, the fertile valley of the Guadiaro River, the Mediterranean itself, all serve the cause of richly contrasting colours, but the long savage outlines of the sierras beyond the foothills on which the course lies quicken memories of Nevada.

The sea does not enter the golfer's reckoning at Sotogrande except as a background. The graceful clubhouse and its clusters of neighbour-

ing villas stand a spoon shot or more inland and the course flows quietly away towards the hills. The 1st hole runs parallel to a splendid practice ground, with its sentinel palm trees, so there is no excuse—especially in a land where haste is no part of civilized life—to start the round cold: a good drive and a medium iron will suffice. The 2nd calls for much more. It is a beautiful, long hole, rising and curving to the left with bunkers to trap those who would cut the corner, little spinneys to threaten the erring second, and a raised green to tax the final pitch.

Contrast is immediate, for the 3rd and 5th holes each offer hope of threes, given a well-placed drive and an accurate pitch. If the pin is placed on any of the petals at the 3rd the approach must be most delicately judged, but this is fair because the hole is only 339 yards. Meanwhile, the short 4th has demanded a long, straight stroke over a valley to a green above the level of the tee—few twos are scored at this hole—and as one stands on the 6th tee there is the feeling that henceforth the tasks will be real and earnest. The hole swings uphill to the right, and only a long drive to the left centre of a ▷

▷ dimpled fairway will give a sight of the green; except for the strong, this is a fine par-five.

Most people will settle happily for their pars at the 7th, a spectacular hole. The drive plunges into a valley cleared from a forest of cork trees, and the second from a downhill stance looks alarmingly narrow. The green is a shelf sloping from woods on the left towards a lake and, even with merely pitching club in hand, the shot would give anyone cause for apprehension. The green of the short 8th, another hole across a valley, is typical of hundreds on the other side of the Atlantic. Its fall from back to front is considerable, and an overhit from the tee probably means three putts. At the 9th the drive is tight between trees to a ribbon of fairway, and now the highest point of the course has been reached, without awareness of effort.

As if in celebration, the ground falls away from the 10th tee, leaving a tempting carry over woods for those who wish to shorten the hole, and a line for others content to play it safe. The 11th green is another of the pulpit target variety and is followed by the first of two fascinating loops. The 12th pursues the side of a large lake, which looks far more natural than it is. Those who try to get home in two court danger, for the green is tucked away behind a far corner of the lake, two arms of which make the 13th a beautiful short hole. The attacking shot that errs in any direction will usually splash from sight. From any tee the 14th is the hardest five of all. However much the lake's edge is trimmed only a second of tremendous order, shaped to draw into a tree-cloistered green angled against a hillside, has any chance of getting home.

A long drive should give a sight of the 15th green, otherwise the second over a crest on the fairway is the one blind shot of the round. A slice from the tee will descend in a stone-walled paddock. A similar stroke to the 16th is threatened by another artificial lake, which enables the next green to be sited on a little peninsula similar to that at the 13th. The tee shot, although shorter, is more testing; if aimed at the flag most of its flight must be over water. These short holes, an instance of the imaginative use of water in which American architects are so skilled, contrast pleasantly with those on the outward half. The gentle rise of the last hole is an invitation for two satisfying long shots towards a finely bunkered, crested green, and for the cool drinks beyond. As the relaxing golfer looks out across the broad acres to the green hills, and the mountains turn black against the fading light, there is a sense of peace and beauty and fulfilment that few other golf courses in Europe can match.

Time may tell, but down the years discussion will echo as to whether the New course, opened in the summer of 1975, matches the quality of the Old. Similar in length, it shares the same rolling land and cork forest for its character and the same superb views to inspire or soothe the golfer. It is a demanding test of driving in its emphasis on placing from the tees. The greens are subtle and by no means the least of its blessings is that it is under the direction of Henry Cotton, the imperishable old master himself.

Trent Jones responds to target conditions

Robert Trent Jones has been criticized on occasion for the severe contours of his greens. He defends them by claiming, with some justice, that leading players have become so accurate in the target conditions usually prevailing that they should be able to hit the part of the green most favourable for an approach putt or, conversely, avoid the three-putt area.

The 8th green, with its steep fall from back to front, is a good example; a tee shot finishing past the flag can cause a major putting problem. The 3rd green, where he allowed himself a moment of whimsy in design, can also be maddening. Shaped like a four-leaf clover, it offers numerous tricky pin positions. If the pin is on one of the petals the pitch needs the most subtle touch. But the demands of the hole are not excessive; a drive of good length will bring the green within accurate pitching range.

Sotogrande's 8th green slopes steeply back towards the tee and often, in an effort to carry the upslope of the fairway, a golfer will hit too strongly and find trouble behind. Even hitting the green is no guarantee of a par because the putt down the slope is wicked.

The 3rd: 341 yards par 4

---- Normal tee-shot

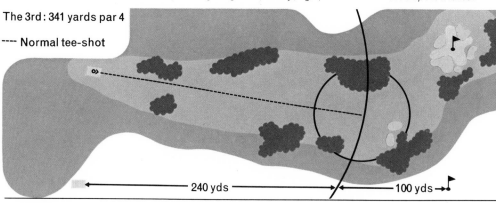

240 yds   100 yds

The 14th: Vicenzo unleashes all his power

Throughout his great career Roberto de Vicenzo has been basically a right-to-left player, hitting all his long shots with a slight draw. Such was the uncommon strength of his hands and arms, and so rocklike his stance, that his simple swing was always under control. The hitting of thousands upon thousands of shots in practice and play for thirty years or more made the whole process of striking, so absolutely free of frills or mannerisms, appear as if it were second nature to him.

Few golfers in the game's history (Sam Snead, of course, was one and Tom Weiskopf is another) have generated power comparable with Vicenzo's, with so little apparent effort. Rarely has it shown to finer advantage than in the 1966 Spanish Open, the first important event to be played at Sotogrande. On the second day the breeze was fresh—setting considerable problems

of flight even for short approaches—and most of the greens were wickedly fast. But Vicenzo made the course seem absurdly simple. In spite of taking three putts from ten feet on the last green he was round in 66, the foundation of a commanding victory the following day.

He drove vast distances, easily mastering the par-fives, and his play of the 14th still lives in the memory. The hole, more than 500 yards long, curves gradually to the right along the shore of a lake and can be shortened by those able to carry a substantial segment of it. The wind was exactly as Vicenzo would have it, behind and slightly from the right. He swung the ball out across the water in a great booming arc and back to the fairway. His partner, Sebastian Miguel, one of the soundest golfers ever to emerge from the Continent of Europe, hit a solid drive which was nevertheless eighty yards short of Vicenzo.

The 14th: 506 yards par 5

—— Vicenzo's tee-shot
---- Normal tee-shot

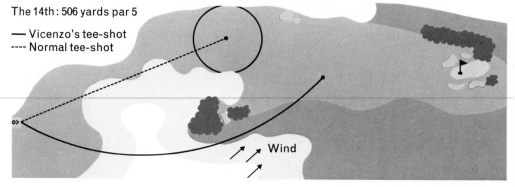

Wind

A test of finesse high above the Atlantic

Until the mid-60s, the sunny Algarve coast in the south of Portugal—a beautiful stretch of white beaches, rugged, red cliffs and tessellated villages—was a well-kept holiday secret enjoyed by only the few: a place apart, rich in orange, olive and fig trees, fish and flowers. There was not a golf course to be seen. Even now, despite its popularity as a high-class resort, the Algarve retains the essential charm and character that are the legacy of its history, its situation and its climate. It also now offers some outstanding golf.

All the early courses, although intensely scenic and kept in immaculate condition, were of high championship quality and, even off the forward tees, much too difficult for the average holiday visitor. Not that golfers have been in any way deterred, relishing as they do a really stout challenge. And on all the Algarve

coast, no course offers that challenge more surely than Vilamoura.

It was designed by Frank Pennink on and around a ridge of high ground as part of an extensive 4,000-acre development, and opened for play in January 1969. Pennink's original brief was to create a course closely resembling the beautiful but testing courses of England's Berkshire, and this is what he indeed achieved. Using the steeply sloping land as well as the more level areas, and judiciously siting his fairways through mature umbrella pines, he produced a flowing succession of fine golf holes that are vividly reminiscent of Swinley Forest or of the Berkshire club itself. From the outset he planned it as a championship course, but in the event it turned out to be even tougher than he intended.

Although basically a holiday centre, Vila-

moura has seen two professional events in its short history—the Algarve Open of 1970, in which the winner, Brian Huggett, set a course record of 69, and the Portuguese Open (with Penina) in 1973, won by Jaime Benito of Spain after a tie with Bernard Gallacher. In 1975 the record was lowered to 68 by the little-known professional Jimmy Hume. Because of the particularly tough, tight holes on the course, it is interesting to note that at the time Hume was having trouble not with his game through the green but with his putting. A friend advised him to line up his putt and then close his eyes before striking the ball—the result was a five-under-par score on a course where very few professionals have ever broken par.

From the beautifully appointed clubhouse at one end of the ridge, the course spills down either side in green ribbons between the attractive but punishing umbrella pines. Four holes occupy the high-level ground, from where there are fine views out over the rolling Algarve countryside. Vilamoura is an attractive course, with no blind shots and much variety in the holes and in the recently relaid greens. The strength of the par-threes registers immediately. Each is totally different, each intensely visual and attractive; all require careful club selection and control if a par is to be scored. For the rest, a crucial role is played by the trees which line the fairways and often encroach strategically to block off a long approach. There is little or no rough under the umbrella pines—merely bare sand and rocky ground, just as there always was before the golf arrived. But try to play a golf shot up through one of the trees and you discover why they are such an effective hazard—the pine needles clutch at the ball and kill its flight immediately. In the trees, a player must accept the fact that the only sensible shot is a chip out sideways back to the fairway.

Despite its situation at the centre of a popular coastal resort, Vilamoura has a unique feeling of quiet isolation. This is partly due to its setting, high on one of the few pieces of elevated ground on this part of the coast. With holes rising, curving and dipping down through a billowing green sea of bushy-topped pines, the course has eighteen quite separate holes presenting widely varying problems. On the long holes, bunkering is minimal and strategic —the main hazard being the trees which line the narrow, sloping fairways. There is no need for semi-rough; a shot under the trees is a stroke that is lost.

The best long holes come in the tough back nine, a rugged, 3,690-yard par 38. The 12th is 536 yards from the back tee and curves sharply to the right around a large hill. It is an excellent hole, since a player cannot bite off too much from the tee—there are trees on the right coming into play, and he has no view of the green wherever he reaches the fairway. The hole narrows for the second shot, which is all uphill with concealed bunkers waiting to catch the errant approach. A tilted, elevated green has out-of-bounds immediately behind. The next long hole is the 571-yard 16th, a great driving hole with the ideal landing area pinched between a large bunker and some trees which ▷

Vilamoura's longest par-three—and its most famous—is the 6th, where the downhill sweep to the green presents an encouraging target. But there is danger on all sides: a deep bunker placed on the right of the green, the ever-present umbrella pines on the left and, for those who over-club—an easy thing to do when hitting downhill—behind the green, too.

At only 298 yards, the par-four 9th can seem an easy birdie. But the drive straight to the green is turned into a gamble by two pines in the line of flight, with a bunker in between to snare anything that just fails to clear them. Large bunkers around the tight green, right, will catch any shot hit slightly off line.

lurk on the right. The hole follows a gentle curve to the right, partly downhill, requiring exact placement of each stroke and—like all good par-fives—it leaves no room at all for error to the birdie-shooter. There is a duck-festooned water hazard left of the fairway, with further traps and strategic trees; the kidney-shaped green is well bunkered, offering a narrow target, with steep fallaway on all sides. Finally, the last hole—a mere 542 yards. This hole, which probably has the widest fairway, is made by three trees. Drive slightly left and the second shot is blocked by a large, lone umbrella pine. Play it too far to the right and two trees on the very edge of the green deny the route to the flag. Simple, but highly strategic.

Bernard Hunt, experienced European tournament player and former winner of the Algarve Open, has great respect for Vilamoura: "It is one of the hardest courses in Portugal. In the opinion of many professionals it is one of the toughest because there is no let up. It is a very tight driving course, demanding mastery of all the shots in the bag, and it is the sort of course that the longer you go on the more certain you are that you will have a disaster somewhere.

"For me, the three short holes are outstanding. I believe a good short hole should be a test of finesse. I would criticize any course or any par-three hole where you have to fire a wood to a large green with big bunkers. The modern, American style of golf tends towards this. But I think the short 4th, 10th and 15th at Vilamoura, which are all mid irons or less, yet still very difficult par-threes, represent the ideal test. They also happen to be the most attractive holes at Vilamoura. One of the big problems at these holes is picking the correct club. The greens are

Vilamoura is memorable for the umbrella pines which line each hole, providing a beautiful backdrop and creating an atmosphere of seclusion. Its taxing par-threes are well known, but Vilamoura also has five par-fives, three of them more than 500 yards long. Even here judiciously sited single bunkers, inconvenient trees or the fierce dog-leg of the 12th put the premium on accuracy, not length.

Vilamoura Golf Club, Algarve

Out	3,184 yards	35
In	3,690 yards	38
Total	6,874 yards	par 73

Record: 68, Jimmy Hume, 1975

It is easy to underclub at the 10th, where the view from the tee gives no hint of the ravine which fronts the green.

The 4th, 10th and 15th: Accuracy is all

One of the most striking features of Vilamoura is the quality of its par-threes—the long downhill 6th, which must be one of the most photographed holes in Europe, and more expecially the 4th, 10th and 15th, three precise gems where finesse takes priority over length.

The 4th is very picturesque, its tee tucked back under large umbrella pines and with a large water hazard, complete with island, dividing the 168 yards to the raised two-level green. Partly obscured by trees, the green is well protected by a deep trap on the right and a smaller one to the left. Only a precisely judged shot will do.

The 10th presents a very clear problem. The shallow green is exactly 176 yards from the tee and is on the same level. But between the two is a deep ravine. There is no need for much bunkering here, for anything short runs right back down the steep slope. Hit too strongly, the ball will run downhill on to hard, stony ground among trees.

The 15th presents something of the same problem: an extremely attractive shot across a small valley sloping left to another level green only eleven yards deep. The green is wide, allowing some margin for error in direction, but there can be no mistake in length. There are two deep bunkers on either side in front, and at the foot of a very steep downhill bank at the back is a further bunker. The hole calls for careful club selection and, the decision once made, the courage not to hold up on the shot.

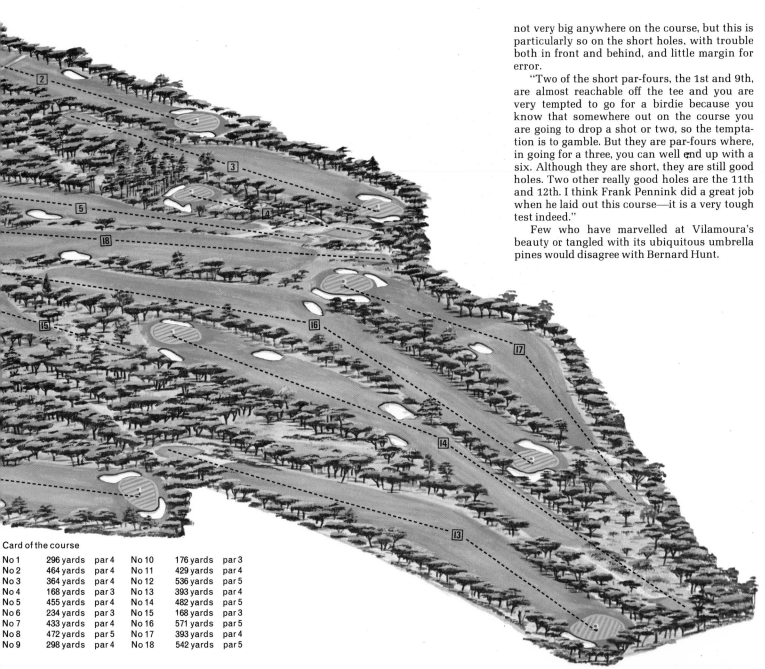

not very big anywhere on the course, but this is particularly so on the short holes, with trouble both in front and behind, and little margin for error.

"Two of the short par-fours, the 1st and 9th, are almost reachable off the tee and you are very tempted to go for a birdie because you know that somewhere out on the course you are going to drop a shot or two, so the temptation is to gamble. But they are par-fours where, in going for a three, you can well end up with a six. Although they are short, they are still good holes. Two other really good holes are the 11th and 12th. I think Frank Pennink did a great job when he laid out this course—it is a very tough test indeed."

Few who have marvelled at Vilamoura's beauty or tangled with its ubiquitous umbrella pines would disagree with Bernard Hunt.

Card of the course

No 1	296 yards	par 4	No 10	176 yards	par 3
No 2	464 yards	par 4	No 11	429 yards	par 4
No 3	364 yards	par 4	No 12	536 yards	par 5
No 4	168 yards	par 3	No 13	393 yards	par 4
No 5	455 yards	par 4	No 14	482 yards	par 5
No 6	234 yards	par 3	No 15	168 yards	par 3
No 7	433 yards	par 4	No 16	571 yards	par 5
No 8	472 yards	par 5	No 17	393 yards	par 4
No 9	298 yards	par 4	No 18	542 yards	par 5

The 4th, left, and the 15th, right, look deceptively easy. The 4th is most difficult when the pin is set on the right side, the trees interrupting the line and a hidden bunker awaiting the slice. An unseen bunker also comes into play at the 15th, where it is very easy to over-club in avoiding the front traps only to find a steep downslope which ends in a nasty bunker.

North America

Golf in North America is statistically overpowering. In the United States there are almost 12,000 courses and 13,500,000 players, most of whom enjoy a round at least once a month—a feast of golfing indulgence that far exceeds that of all other countries put together. Moreover, any figures are quickly obsolete; hundreds of new courses are built each year. There is a breathtaking diversity of settings for the game, from the Monterey Peninsula on the west coast, where cypresses weep over the shot that is sliced into the Pacific, to South Carolina, where the new course at Harbour Town, on the Atlantic shore, has achieved instant greatness. The science of agronomy has made golf possible in deserts where previously grass could never grow; and shrewd businessmen, together with brilliant architects, have bulldozed forests and drained swamps to create resort golf in the islands of the Caribbean and elsewhere. Linksland courses in the manner of the Old Country do not exist, but other true tests of golf are there in profusion. The game in America had its tentative beginnings in the old Colonial states of the Atlantic seaboard during the latter years of the eighteenth century, but records are fragmented and discontinuous. The first authenticated club was St Andrews at Yonkers, New York, founded in 1888 (here, the United States must give precedence to Canada, where the Royal Montreal began life fifteen years earlier). Within twelve years the United States had more than 1,000 courses—including the first outside Britain for public use, at Van Cortlandt Park in New York City (1895). From that time on, golf in America passed through well-defined phases. There was an early period in which the Scots still dominated all things to do with the game, from course design to the winning of championships. The free-spending, freewheeling twenties saw considerable growth, much of it due to the luminous talents of Bobby Jones. The next dramatic boom coincided with the rise of Arnold Palmer, one of the most compelling of all sporting heroes.

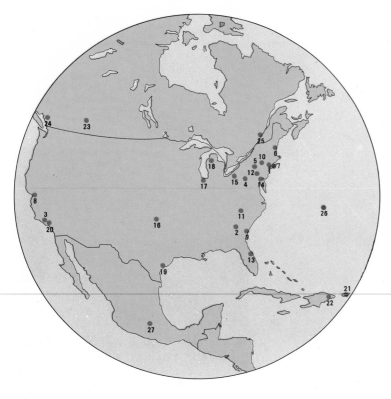

1 Shinnecock Hills
2 Augusta
3 Cypress Point
4 Oakmont
5 Baltusrol
6 The Country Club
7 The National
8 Olympic
9 Harbour Town
10 Winged Foot
11 Pinehurst
12 Merion
13 Seminole
14 Pine Valley
15 Firestone
16 Southern Hills
17 Medinah
18 Oakland Hills
19 Champions
20 Pebble Beach
21 Dorado Beach
22 Cajuiles
23 Banff
24 Capilano
25 Royal Montreal
26 Mid Ocean
27 Club de Golf Mexico

Evening shadows heighten the drama of the approach to the 18th green at Olympic's Lakeside, which is rare among American courses in having no water hazards and only one bunker. Here, trees form a natural hazard so pervasive that architect Sam Whiting saw no need to elaborate when he built the course in 1924.

Golf takes root — among the burial mounds

More's the pity, but it is next to impossible to find in America the kind of pristine golfing conditions that exist on the historic seaside links of Great Britain. There are a few approximations, however, along the northeastern seaboard facing the Atlantic Ocean, and of these nothing of finer quality than Shinnecock Hills, which has a claim to being the first "formalized" golf club in the United States and also the first eighteen-hole course. Part and parcel of the stylish summer resort of Southampton at the eastern end of Long Island, Shinnecock's superb playing qualities have largely been overshadowed by the exclusive "social" panache that attached to it through the years.

Because of the club's seniority, the genesis of Shinnecock Hills is of considerably more interest than that of most other clubs, for it epitomizes the almost casual manner in which golf planted its roots in the United States. During the winter of 1890–1 William K. Vanderbilt, the prominent sportsman and son of the founder of the Vanderbilt dynasty, was travelling through southern France with a couple of his friends. At Biarritz they came across Willie Dunn, one of the early Scottish professionals who were then beginning to export their native game to foreign countries. Dunn was building a course at Biarritz, so he staged an impromptu exhibition of his skills for the visiting Americans, who were fascinated.

Within a few months, the Americans were back home and excitedly discussing the possibility of building a golf course at Southampton. By the early summer of 1891 they had imported Dunn from Europe and taken him on a tour of the Southampton area in search of an appropriate locale. Eventually, they settled on some low-lying sandhills a couple of miles from the seashore and within a few minutes' driving time of most of the houses in this small summer colony. Equally important, the land adjoined the railroad line from New York City, giving those golfers who would be making the two-and-a-half-hour journey from the city in the years to come easy access to the club.

With the help of 150 Indians from the neighbouring Shinnecock Reservation, Dunn set to work on his pioneering project. His primitive methods are best described in his own words, as he recalled the event some years later. "Except for several horse-drawn roadscrapers," he said, "all the work was done by hand. The fairways were cleaned off and the natural grass left in. The rough was very rough with clothes-ripping blueberry bushes, large boulders and many small gullies. The place was dotted with Indian burial mounds, and we left some of these intact as bunkers in front of the greens. We scraped out some of the mounds and made sandtraps. It was here that the Indians buried their empty whiskey bottles, but we did not find this out until later when playing the course. One never knew when an explosion shot in a trap would bring out a couple of firewater flasks, or perhaps a bone or two."

Thus twelve holes were laid out and ready for play by late summer, and there is little argument that this was then the most sophisticated golfing facility in the country. Forty-four mem-

Amongst the oldest (some claim the oldest) golf clubs in the United States, Shinnecock Hills is—despite Dick Wilson's later changes—the American course closest in style and spirit to the links of Britain.

Jim Foulis, who won the second US Open title at Shinnecock Hills in 1896 with 78 and 74.

bers had already been enrolled at several thousand dollars apiece, and the eighty acres on which the course had been laid out were purchased for $2,500, a sum that would today scarcely buy a half-acre of that same property. Stanford White, the most fashionable and prominent architect of the day, was commissioned to build a clubhouse in the shingled style of the region, with such modern appurtenances as a grill-room, lockers and shower-baths. Although there have been additions in subsequent years, White's original building, which was ready for use by the summer of 1892, is still the nucleus of the great rambling white structure that today sits atop Shinnecock Hills, dominating the surrounding landscape and serving as the most prominent landmark in the Southampton area.

Within a year of its founding, the Shinnecock Hills course had been enlarged to eighteen holes. Golf quickly became a fad among the wealthy and prominent figures who summered at Southampton, and the club became a thriving vortex of the social whirl, the members adding to the splendour of it all with their red blazers, monogrammed brass buttons and white flannel trousers.

In 1894, the fourth summer after golf was first played at Shinnecock Hills, an attempt was made to conduct a national championship (for amateurs, of course) at Newport, Rhode Island. It ended in some unhappy bickering, as

did another attempt a few weeks later at the St Andrews Golf Club in Yonkers, but an open championship that was appended to the Newport event was won by Shinnecock's Willie Dunn, giving him just, but unofficial, claim to having been the first US Open champion. As a result of the bickering, the United States Golf Association was formed with Shinnecock Hills as one of the five founding clubs.

The USGA's first official championship was held at Newport in 1895, and the following July the championship was brought to Shinnecock Hills. In the Open championship that was played over 36 holes on the day after the Amateur championship was completed, so many of the professionals broke 80—a feat that was not to be commonplace in championship golf again until the introduction of the rubber-cored ball a decade later—that some second thoughts were prevalent regarding the quality of the Shinnecock Hills course. At less than 5,000 yards, it was obviously not of championship calibre, and so the first of a long series of alterations and improvements was undertaken.

It was not until 1931 that the course finally emerged as it now exists. Largely the work of the late Dick Wilson, who was to design many of the better southern courses, Shinnecock Hills fully utilizes the outstanding features of the area—the strong prevailing winds off the Atlantic to the southwest, the sandy and rolling terrain and the thick, reed-like grasses that

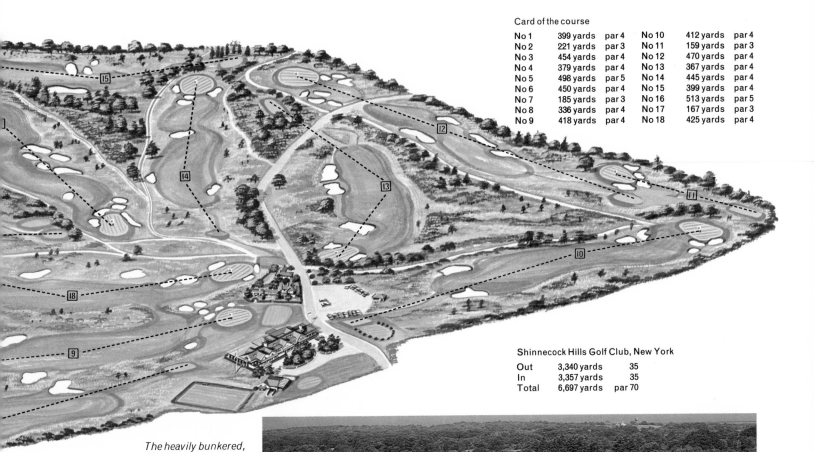

Card of the course

No 1	399 yards	par 4	No 10	412 yards	par 4
No 2	221 yards	par 3	No 11	159 yards	par 3
No 3	454 yards	par 4	No 12	470 yards	par 4
No 4	379 yards	par 4	No 13	367 yards	par 4
No 5	498 yards	par 5	No 14	445 yards	par 4
No 6	450 yards	par 4	No 15	399 yards	par 4
No 7	185 yards	par 3	No 16	513 yards	par 5
No 8	336 yards	par 4	No 17	167 yards	par 3
No 9	418 yards	par 4	No 18	425 yards	par 4

Shinnecock Hills Golf Club, New York

Out	3,340 yards	35
In	3,357 yards	35
Total	6,697 yards	par 70

The heavily bunkered, 399-yard 15th is typical of Shinnecock's short but difficult par-fours.

border the fairways. While not truly linksland —the grass of the fairways and greens is more of an inland texture—the ambience and windy bleakness of Shinnecock Hills on an average day evoke feelings of the British seaside links.

At 6,697 yards Shinnecock Hills is not long by the standards of today's championship courses, yet it is a course that brings one's long and middle irons out of the bag quite often enough. Virtually all the shorter par-fours play into the wind, and the longer ones with it. The true playing qualities of the course are never more evident than on the parallel closing holes of the front and back nines, both dog-legs with the wind blowing strongly from the right and the long roughs on either side that are bound to cost a stroke or two, if the ball can be found at all. The fairways are undulating, much in the Scottish tradition, so the placing of the drive is half the battle. The second shots off a good drive are in each case entirely reasonable, yet the price of a misplay is very high indeed. In fact, that might be said to be the predominant nature of Shinnecock Hills. The fact that the competitive course record is 68 after nearly fifty years attests to its difficulties.

As Ben Hogan remarked after playing it in the early 1960s: "Each hole is different and requires a great amount of skill to play properly. You know exactly where to shoot and the distance is easy to read. All in all, I think Shinnecock is one of the finest courses I have played."

Only the good driver will succeed

It goes without saying that any great course (Augusta may be the only exception) is a strong test of driving. This is conspicuously true of Shinnecock. Whatever one's standard may be, to drive indifferently from either the members' or the back tees is to court unavailing struggle for the remainder of the hole; but drive solidly and far and the rich rewards of a glorious course are there for the playing. In one sense, although certainly not in setting, Shinnecock is reminiscent of Augusta in that the ability to carry crests on the fairways sets up the approach nicely. Otherwise, it can be most demanding. In this respect holes like the 9th, where it is essential to carry a great mound in the fairway (otherwise the second to an uphill semi-blind green is most taxing), and the 15th come immediately to mind. If the drive from the 15th

tee, poised high in a wilderness of scrub, can carry into a valley the next shot to an island target of green is comparatively easy.

But Shinnecock is far from being only a driver's course. The short holes are splendidly varied in their challenge and length, from the long shot over a valley to the tightly trapped 2nd green, to the target of the 11th and the beautiful 17th. Not to be outdone by its neighbour, the National, in the use of the ancient Scottish names, the hole is known as the Eden. Although it bears no resemblance to the 11th at St Andrews, the tee shot is no less exacting. The line to the flag is guarded by three large bunkers and, according to the wind, long iron or wood must carry all the way and not fade; another bunker lurks for that very shot. The man who plays Shinnecock in the low 70s has played good golf—of that there is no question.

115

Dream course in a dream setting

It was characteristic of the uncommon grace, the high intelligence and ordinary horse sense which had marked all his too-brief career that, when it came time for Bobby Jones to build his dream course, he employed a wisdom far beyond his years by enlisting the aid of a professional architect.

After all, he was certainly well qualified in his own right to build any kind of course he wanted and people would have bowed to it. In eight Olympian years he had won more than 60 per cent of the national championships he had entered, winning thirteen national titles in all. And he had won them on some of the most hallowed fields in golf—St Andrews, Merion, Hoylake, Oakmont, Winged Foot. At the age of twenty-eight, he retired from competition. He played every note there is to play in the symphony of golf, capping it all with a Beethovian burst by winning the Open and Amateur championships of both the United States and Great Britain in the single triumphant year of 1930. It was a feat so far beyond the imagination of the public that people did not even have a name for it until months after, when a New York

Bobby Jones, one of the truly great figures of golf, achieved a unique combination of old Southern charm and pure golfing challenge at Augusta National.

Needing three birdies in the last four holes to tie the Masters, Gene Sarazen sank his 4-wood second at the 15th, a 520-yard par-five, for a double-eagle. This remarkable shot brought Augusta National and the Masters tournament instant fame.

Augusta National is one of the most idyllic of golf courses. It is at its best in the spring, when flowering shrubs are a blaze of colour among the trees that bring seclusion to almost every hole. But the inviting width of its lush green fairways is deceptive, for it is a course on which cutting corners in a bid to beat par can bring severe trouble.

newspaperman tagged it the "Grand Slam", picking up the parlance of the day when contract bridge was the great indoor pastime.

Having performed his masterpiece, Jones walked off the stage of competitive golf forever. He had decided never to play professional golf, and that was that. Naturally, there was a call for an encore by the genius from Georgia, for his audience reached to every continent where grass will grow. Jones refused to leave the wings, but he did leave a legacy. This is the Augusta National Golf Club—easily the most famous American course, quite possibly the best and, for a certain period each year at least, simply the most beautiful golf acreage anywhere in the world.

Jones could not have made the course more universally appealing, and it remains so today as it has since its inception more than forty years ago—and as it undoubtedly will do a century from now. It is one of the few courses anywhere which even the tweediest of pro-

fessionals will play tight-lipped and then go home and rave about.

Despite the force of his personality, his golfing background, his intelligence, Bobby Jones's 365 acres did not come into being in a final, perfected form. The Augusta National as it is now is far different from the course he had visualized and—as Jones would have been the first to admit—it is far better today. The architect he chose and with whom he worked side by side was Alister Mackenzie, a Scottish-born physician who had recently emigrated to America and who abandoned medicine in order to concentrate on his first love—golf.

In Mackenzie, Jones could not have picked a more adept partner for the venture, particularly for the venue he had chosen for the course of his dreams. The site was on rolling hills ablaze with fruit-bearing trees and flowers—the kind of scene any lesser architect might have ruined by building a good golf hole at the sacrifice of its beauty, or else a bad hole in order to maintain

Augusta National Golf Club, Augusta, Georgia

Out	3,510 yards	36
In	3,520 yards	36
Total	7,030 yards	par 72

Record: 64, Lloyd Mangrum, 1940, Jack Nicklaus, 1965

Card of the course

No 1	White Pine	400 yards	par 4
No 2	Woodbine	555 yards	par 5
No 3	Flowering Peach	360 yards	par 4
No 4	Palm	220 yards	par 3
No 5	Magnolia	450 yards	par 4
No 6	Juniper	190 yards	par 3
No 7	Pampas	365 yards	par 4
No 8	Yellow Jasmine	530 yards	par 5
No 9	Carolina Cherry	440 yards	par 4
No 10	Camellia	485 yards	par 4
No 11	Dogwood	445 yards	par 4
No 12	Golden Bell	155 yards	par 3
No 13	Azalea	485 yards	par 5
No 14	Chinese Fir	420 yards	par 4
No 15	Fire Thorn	520 yards	par 5
No 16	Red Bud	190 yards	par 3
No 17	Nandina	400 yards	par 4
No 18	Holly	420 yards	par 4

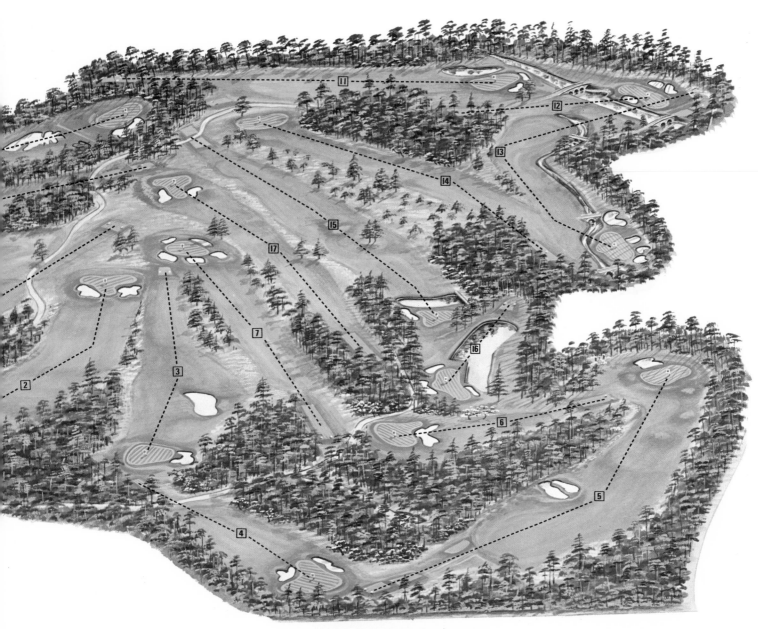

it. Mackenzie best showed his self-discipline in this respect at the spectacular Cypress Point in California. So an architect who had an artistic bent for hewing a golf course out of exciting terrain joined forces with a designer who knew more about shot values than anyone in the history of championship golf since the great Harry Vardon.

Like many of America's great courses, the Augusta National is not exactly at the centre of things. The city of Augusta is hardly the crossroads of the United States or even of the southeastern part of it—or, for that matter, of Georgia. Its history had been that of an ante-bellum resort which Jones, as an Atlantan, often visited. He married an Augusta beauty named Mary Malone and it was at Augusta that he made the acquaintance of a well-to-do New Yorker, Clifford Roberts, who often wintered there. Soon after his retirement from golf, Jones had expressed to Roberts his desire to found a very private golf club which his many friends

Most people know only the Augusta of the Masters, with its vast crowds. Then the 12th green, scene of this leisurely play, becomes the focus of world attention as the heart of Amen Corner, the scene of so much drama.

throughout the world could join, or just visit to revel in—a course that he himself would design with the master's touch clear down to the roots.

Roberts, who always had a knack for knowing when to buy and sell things, had got wind of a famous nursery in Augusta, named Fruitlands, that was for sale. It had been owned for three-quarters of a century by the family of a Belgian baron, Louis Edouard Mathieu Berkmans, whose son Prosper became a renowned horticulturist. Almost single-handedly, Prosper had popularized the azalea, now so common all over the southeastern stretches of the United States. The setting was practically perfect for Jones's wishes. It has the gentle hills he wanted for his inland "links", which would capture the spirit—but not imitate the characteristics—of the British seaside courses he loved so much. What with its almost endless flora, the property would be ablaze with the colours of so many flowers that it later became no problem at all to name each hole after a different one—dog- ▷

Amen Corner—where even golfing gods pray

The Masters championship has been won or lost so often between the 11th and the 13th that this three-hole stretch, menaced by the waters of Rae's Creek, has become known as Amen Corner. Nobody knows the origin of the name but in the opinion of Dave Marr, "It's called that because if you get around it in par, you believe a little bit more in God." When Byron Nelson won in 1937 and 1942 it was mainly because of his sub-par barrages at Amen Corner, where possibly his most memorable shot was a gently chipped 3-iron for a fifty-foot eagle-three at the 13th in 1937. Five years later he birdied all three holes to defeat Ben Hogan in a play-off. Hogan did the same thing many years later when, at the age of fifty-four, in one of the most emotional moments in golf, he tamed Augusta's back nine in a remarkable thirty shots. In 1954, a little-known amateur, Billy Joe Patton, muffed his great chance to win out over the great Hogan and Snead when, after making up a five-shot deficit, he hit into the creek at the 13th and wound up with a disastrous double-bogey seven. Arnold Palmer, four times Masters champion, first won in 1958 after a superb eagle on the 13th. The following year a 7-iron splashed into Rae's Creek at the 12th, costing him the title, but in 1962 he defeated Gary Player and Dow Finsterwald in a play-off, largely because of a crucial birdie at the same fateful hole.

Augusta's famous Amen Corner, which has had a decisive influence on the outcome of so many Masters. The 11th, a long par-four, emerges from the trees on the right. The 12th is played from the shadow of the central grove of trees across Rae's Creek to a shallow, well-bunkered green. The tee shot at the 13th, played over the creek from alongside the 12th green, should follow the gentle leftward curve of the fairway.

The 11th: Strategy for winners

No golfer can win the Masters without a carefully planned strategy for every hole. Gary Player, twice a winner, and Doug Ford, who took the title in 1957, both regard the 11th—a 445-yard par-four—as a hole where planning the attack is just as important as how the strokes are played.

The instinct of most golfers is to take the shortest route to the green, and on the 11th this means driving up the right-hand side of the fairway. This leaves a 5- or 6-iron into the green, but it also means that the approach must be aimed directly at the water lying menacingly beyond. The shot is made even more difficult by the lie of the ball on an upslope, which is liable to induce a hook into the water on the left.

Player's method is to aim down the left of the fairway and take a 4-iron for his approach, which can then be played away from the water. Ford played up the centre of the fairway, but hit a low second shot deliberately aimed at the banking on the right of the green so that it would kick on and roll up towards the flag. In his final winning round he played his approach perfectly with a 2-iron. His shot came off the bank to finish no more than ten feet from the hole.

The 11th: 445 yards par 4

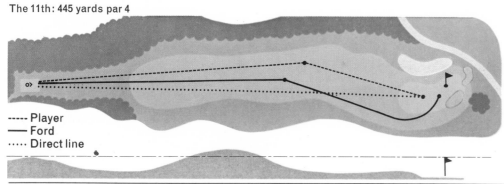

----- Player
—— Ford
····· Direct line

▷ wood, redbud, magnolia, and so on. Furthermore, it seemed to have just the right cluster of trees through which Jones would want his fairways to meander. To top it all off, the highest point on the property was dominated by a pre-Civil War mansion that could form the nucleus of a clubhouse. Bobby Jones looked no further. Fruitlands would be his Augusta National.

In essence, the course Jones and Mackenzie finished in 1933—with Jones playing thousands of experimental shots off every potential tee and to every possible green site—is almost the same today. The original front nine is now the back nine; Jones reversed them in 1935 because he thought that the original 9th was a far more demanding finishing hole than the old, shortish 18th, which could not be lengthened without giving the player an unconscionably difficult shot off a downhill lie to an elevated green. One thing Jones wanted Augusta National to have was flexibility, to be a course that would not overpower his 90-shooting members or be a push-over for his par-busting visitors. It remains so to this day.

By and large Augusta National remains, despite numerous changes since, what Bobby Jones wanted it to be: an elegantly flexible course with fairways so broad they seem impossible to avoid, with greens so huge they seem impossible to miss, with bunkers so sparse they seem impossible to get into. The course has a mere forty-four sandtraps, only ten of which are in the fairways. Although its tantalizingly beautiful trees are as inviting as Greek sirens, there is no rough in the ankle-deep American sense and certainly not in the knee-deep British sense. As for its putting surfaces, there isn't one a player couldn't hit and hold with a wood.

So what makes it so great? It is great because Augusta National is a thinking man's golf course, the least obvious championship layout in America, perhaps matched nowhere in the world except by the Old course at St Andrews. Like all great courses, it must be played mentally from the green back to the tee before a single shot is hit. Since the greens are so fast, three-putting is a very real hazard, no matter where the flagstick is placed. A shot to the green must be finely gauged and truly struck, else it will bounce and roll unimpeded across yards of green, making three-putting a staggering reality. Since getting close to the flagstick with approach shots is not only the easiest way of getting a par

The 12th: No place to gamble

No man is better qualified to assess the problems of Amen Corner than Jack Nicklaus, who in 1975 won his fifth Masters title, a record. In his estimation the short 12th, only 155 yards long, is "the most demanding tournament hole in the world"—a hole where even a player of his calibre can ill afford to gamble. Depending on pin placement and wind conditions he has used every iron from a 4 down to a 9 on this deceptively simple-looking hole, the shortest on the course.

On those days when a gentle breeze blows down the hill behind the tee it is for Nicklaus a 9-iron shot. When the wind blows from right to left and the pin is placed on the extreme right of the green, even he might need a 4-iron from the back of the tee. Under those conditions Nicklaus has been happy to settle for a chip out of the swale that runs along the back of the green. He never plays for the pin but goes for the centre of the green, his aim being to make sure of clearing the water while staying out of the back bunkers.

The 13th: 475 yards par 5

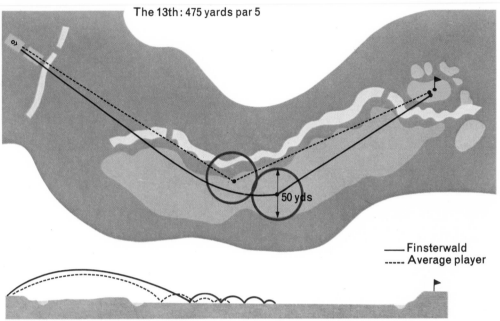

—— Finsterwald
----- Average player

The 13th: Safety in distance

The 13th, a par-five lengthened by ten yards in 1976 to 485 yards, provides a classic illustration of the advantages enjoyed by the game's long hitters. Here the average golfer's only chance of reaching the green in two and possibly setting up a birdie is to hit his drive dangerously close to the creek at the left corner of the fairway. For the big hitter there is a safe margin between his drive and the creek; he can hit his ball well around the corner and make it easy to get home in two.

Dow Finsterwald, never noted for his long driving, always felt he could compensate for his lack of length at the 13th by an accurate drive hit with a controlled hook, or draw. To do this he allowed the left hand to dominate in control of the clubhead, kept his right elbow close to his body and, by assuming a closed stance, hit from the inside out. The topspin naturally generated by the draw gained as much as twenty-five extra yards.

This type of shot gave Finsterwald another advantage. A drive down the middle allowed a margin of error of only twenty-five yards on each side; with his controlled draw he could aim to the right side of the fairway, confident that his drive would land within its fifty-yard width.

---

but very often the only way, the angle at which the green is approached is a constantly critical problem. It requires the player to spot his tee shot judiciously—not an easy task to discipline himself to, when the fairways are so prosaically wide and so free of hazards. In other words, Augusta National has made many a mere ball-hitter look and feel a fool. For the first time he discovers that a golf course can hit him back.

All these subtleties, all this foresight and golfing technicality, might have gone for nothing. Augusta National might very sadly but easily have remained one of the great untested championship courses in America—such as Shinnecock Hills on outer Long Island or Prairie Dunes in deepest Kansas—were it not for the almost incidental invention of the Masters tournament.

Soon after the course was finished, Jones decided to hold an informal get-together, a tournament of sorts, with all his amateur and professional friends. He agreed to play himself, but only under the condition that he was participating as host. Even though he had lost his amateur standing, he refused to accept any prize money: that, he said, belonged to the "pros". Despite the fact that for eight years he had handled them on the course like yo-yos, off the course he deeply admired them. And they, in turn, revered him. Bobby Jones was probably the most genuinely loved golfer who ever lived.

This tournamental get-together would be by invitation only, he decided, and without anyone giving it much thought it was tagged the Augusta National Invitation. The title did not last past the four days it took to play it. News-

papermen almost immediately began calling it the Masters.

Among all the reasons behind the evergreen success of the Masters as a golfing saga, none approaches that of its gift for supplying the unexpected. Like all larger-than-life stories, the history of the Masters has always been strong on character—in this case, the superb quality of the field. But its greatest strength lies in its plot, in its unique ability to supply each year another chapter of almost unendurable suspense, bordering on the impossible and stopping just short of the implausible, as though it had been written by Saki or Maupassant.

Since the tournament started in 1934, there remains not a hole that hasn't been eagled. Two of its four par-fives have been shot in two, and three of its four par-threes have been ▷

The lovely 16th hole, set in a verdant glen, epitomizes the elegant tranquillity of Augusta. The tee is set back in the shadows of tall pines and in April, at the time of the Masters, pink azaleas bloom amongst the trees and sunlight sparkles on the long lake. Finding the green from the tee is no guarantee of a par. Three putts here sealed Ben Hogan's fate when he went down to Sam Snead in the 1954 play-off.

The 16th: Lovely but lethal

In Mackenzie's original design the key to the 16th hole—then 150 yards long—was a tall pine at the edge of a narrow creek. The green lay directly to the left of it and had two steeply terraced levels. It was approached from two different tees, one to the left and one to the right of the 15th green.

In 1947 the hole was completely redesigned by Robert Trent Jones. He kept the tee on the left but, along with the original green, abandoned the other. He then turned the innocuous creek into a lake that runs virtually the entire length of the hole, thus forming a classic hazard. A new green, to the right of the pine and about twenty-five yards beyond the original, was constructed.

Trent Jones made the green kidney shaped, the length of it facing the player. To the right front he placed a smallish bunker, a large one along the right side, and a striptrap back on the left. The green has no distinct terrace, but it slopes sharply from right to left and from front to back, the lowest points being the left front and left rear. As a final bit of dash, he placed two grassy mounds directly behind the green.

"All these revisions", says Trent Jones, "give the hole more definition. It now has a green that has a more receptive landing area for the kind of shots required to carry the water."

He might have added that his revisions gave the 16th infinitely more beauty, the spectators a million new thrills, and some of the contestants cause for a heart attack. "Usually", Bobby Jones once wrote, "the hole will be cut on the narrow neck on the far left and it will be a daring competitor indeed who will go for this pin position."

One of the very, very few twos that have been made when the flagstick has been there was scored by Arnold Palmer. In the last round of the 1960 Masters he was battling it out with Ken Venturi and Dow Finsterwald. Palmer played the hole straightaway, favouring the right side. His ball rolled over the putting surface on to the fringe. Palmer then played a gentle chip shot with a pitching wedge which lodged itself between cup and rim.

In 1971, again in the final round, Johnny Miller apparently found the burden of a two-shot lead too much and made a fundamental error. Instead of aiming safely for the centre of the green he took a 6-iron and went for the pin, set at the back on the right. He caught a bunker and wound up with a bogey. He lost the lead and the Masters; Charles Coody, the eventual winner, made a birdie.

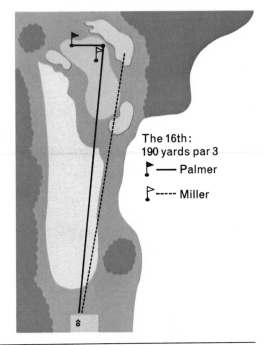

The 16th:
190 yards par 3

⚑—— Palmer

⚑----- Miller

---

scored in one. The ringer score for the event is a fantastic 35—37 strokes under par. But back in 1935, professional Frank Walsh needed twelve strokes to play the uphill, par-five 8th. Herman Barron, another professional, took an eleven on the par-three 16th in 1950, and the following year Dow Finsterwald took twelve on the par-three 12th. In 1951, again, Sam Snead started the last round tied for the lead and, after having shot a 68 the day before, took 80. That same day, William "Dynamite" Goodloe, leading the amateur field after a third-round 72, completed the course in 88.

In 1935 Craig Wood was in the clubhouse, the apparent winner. Out on the par-five 15th Gene Sarazen gambled on carrying across the water which fronts the green. He knew he needed three birdies to catch Wood and he hadn't much to lose. He chose a 4-wood for the 220-yard shot he had left, caught the ball flush and watched it soar over the water. To the astonishment of Walter Hagen, his playing partner, and Bobby Jones, who had wandered down from the clubhouse to see what was going on, the ball rolled slowly on to the putting surface and trickled into the hole for a double-eagle. In one shot he had caught Wood, and he won the play-off the next day. It remains one of the most famous golf shots ever hit.

It is difficult to name a hole at Augusta on which something spectacular hasn't happened. Take the 400-yard 1st hole, a slight dog-leg to the right. (There are eleven dog-legs at Augusta National, but only the first and the last bend to the right.) In 1968, after a booming tee shot, Roberto de Vicenzo holed a 9-iron for an eagle to catch the lead—which he later tragically lost by signing an incorrect scorecard.

In 1966 Jack Nicklaus engaged in a play-off with Tommy Jacobs and Gay Brewer. On the second hole—a 555-yard downhill par-five—neither Jacobs nor Brewer could reach the green

The second shot into the 10th green, beautifully framed by majestic pines, can be no more than a medium iron if the drive has been kept to the left to take full advantage of the slope.

with their drivers and their best fairway woods. Nicklaus hit a 3-wood off the tee to give himself a level lie. Then, again using his 3-wood, he hit the flagstick on the fly! He won the play-off handily for his third Masters.

During one particularly windy tournament, Cary Middlecoff elected to use a driver on the par-three 4th, the tee-markers set only a shade over 200 yards since the hole was playing into the teeth of the near-gale. At the instant Middlecoff struck the ball, the wind died. His ball was a hundred feet in the air when it reached the green, carried clear over the gallery standing behind it and sailed off the confines of the golf course.

The fifth hole—a 450-yard monster, par-four, with an uphill second shot—has a two-level green which is lightning fast. Sam Snead once left himself on the lower level fifty-five feet from the flagstick, which was on the upper level. His approach putt just barely made the crest of the upper level, turned left, and then rolled down the crest leaving him sixty-five

feet away from the hole. He then proceeded to sink that one!

On the par-three 6th, 190 yards to a gigantic green from off a high hill, amateur Billy Joe Patton in 1954 took sole possession in the last round after some spectacular recovery shots all week, by the simple expedient of making a hole in one. That year he also birdied the uphill 9th—par-four, 440 yards—in all four rounds.

And so it goes through the gorgeous 10th—485 yards, par-four—where Bruce Devlin once went three over par after having played the par-five 8th in three under, the second double-eagle in the history of the Masters. Then there is Amen Corner—the gorgeously treacherous 11th, 12th and 13th holes. And finally the exciting finishing holes where all sorts of drama has taken place. Art Wall won in 1959 by making birdies on six of the last seven holes. On the 18th, in 1961, Arnold Palmer lost to Gary Player by skulling his third shot out of a bunker; Doug Ford had won in 1957 by holing out of a bunker.

In 1956 Jack Burke won over Ken Venturi by picking up a clear nine strokes in the last round. "I have always said", Bobby Jones once declared, "that this can be a very easy course or a very tough one. There isn't a hole out there that can't be birdied if you just think. But there isn't one that can't be double-bogeyed if you stop thinking. A lot of the difference has to do with the weather."

Some proof of this came in 1965, when Nicklaus shot the tournament record of 271—seventeen under par—winning by nine strokes from Palmer in near-perfect weather. The following year he ballooned to 288, even par, under less than ideal conditions. He still won. In 1976 conditions were again perfect and Ray Floyd managed to equal Nicklaus's record 271 but only eight players beat par and Floyd's closest pursuer, Ben Crenshaw, finished eight shots back.

"The best seventeen-hole course in the world"

Cypress Point Club, Pebble Beach, California

Out	3,309 yards	37
In	3,155 yards	35
Total	6,464 yards	par 72

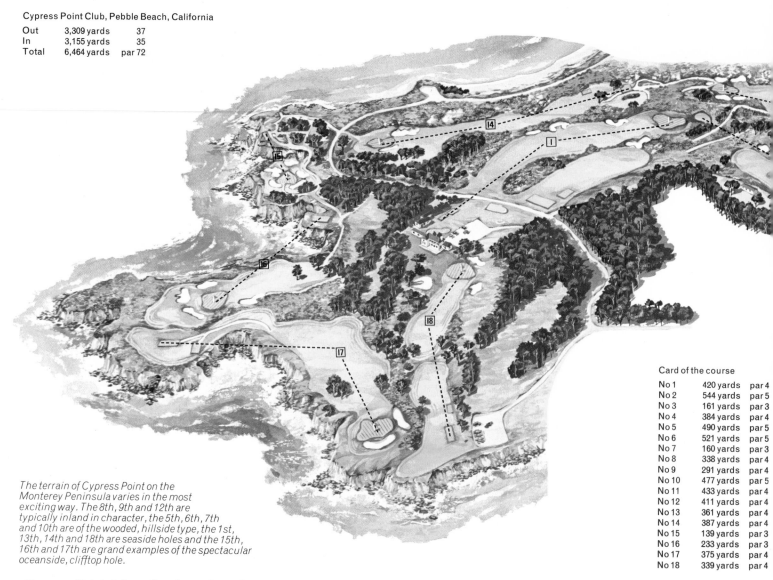

The terrain of Cypress Point on the Monterey Peninsula varies in the most exciting way. The 8th, 9th and 12th are typically inland in character, the 5th, 6th, 7th and 10th are of the wooded, hillside type, the 1st, 13th, 14th and 18th are seaside holes and the 15th, 16th and 17th are grand examples of the spectacular oceanside, clifftop hole.

Card of the course

No 1	420 yards	par 4
No 2	544 yards	par 5
No 3	161 yards	par 3
No 4	384 yards	par 4
No 5	490 yards	par 5
No 6	521 yards	par 5
No 7	160 yards	par 3
No 8	338 yards	par 4
No 9	291 yards	par 4
No 10	477 yards	par 5
No 11	433 yards	par 4
No 12	411 yards	par 4
No 13	361 yards	par 4
No 14	387 yards	par 4
No 15	139 yards	par 3
No 16	233 yards	par 3
No 17	375 yards	par 4
No 18	339 yards	par 4

Cypress Point, it has often been claimed, is perhaps the loveliest golf course ever built. If anything, that is an understatement. Cypress Point is not just lovely; it is dazzling. Situated on the palisades of the Pacific at the tip of the Monterey Peninsula, it is one hundred miles or so south of San Francisco and barely a mile from its more famous neighbour, Pebble Beach.

"Pebble", says Julius Boros, "has six great holes—all those that lie on the coastline. Cypress has eighteen of them, whether they lie on the coast or not."

For a championship course—and nobody would deny that it is—Cypress Point has several anachronisms. For one thing it has never had a major championship played over it. The most important event is the Bing Crosby National Pro-Amateur every winter, and it shares this with Pebble Beach and its other famous neighbour, the relatively new but gorgeous Spyglass Hill. For another thing, it has two par-threes and two par-fives back to back. No other golf course in the world could get away with such architectural anomalies. To top everything off, the course is only 6,464 yards

long, the kind of length you would expect of a public links. Cypress Point is anything but: its clubhouse, one of the most conservative in America, is barred to all but its small number of members, even at tournament time.

One thing the great architects have all understood is the dictum best expressed by "Nipper" Campbell, one of the pioneering Scottish architects in America: "The best golf course is built into the landscape you've got." Consider, then, the landscape Alister Mackenzie, Cypress Point's architect, got when he was assigned the job by the club's promoter, Marion Hollins, the 1921 Women's Amateur champion.

Cypress Point sits at the foothills of the Santa Lucia mountains where, when the tide is out, the land drops sixty feet or more straight down into the Pacific. When the seas are high they batter the edge of the course with the immense waves and awesome roar you would expect to see or hear only in the North Atlantic. Just offshore, sea-lions bask in the sun atop gigantic rocks. The ocean is dotted with fishing smacks plying between the nearby fishing grounds and the canneries of Monterey. And the

course itself is set within the Del Monte Forest, 5,200 acres of private land developed by the late Samuel Morse into one of the world's most stunning seaside resorts—complete with deer that roam freely across the course.

The turf at Cypress Point is rather special—springy and sparkling. In the dusk or in the light of dawn, when the deer come out of the woods to romp upon the fairways, the dew gives the grass an emerald brilliance that contrasts vividly with the chalky sand of the dunes and bunkers. Bordering the fairways and many of the greens are Monterey cypress, bewildering picturesque trees. To O. B. Keeler, the Atlanta newspaperman who was Bobby Jones's Boswell, they were "the crystallization of the dream of an artist who had been drinking gin and sobering up on absinthe". The real wonder of Cypress Point is how anybody can keep his mind on playing golf over it.

Given the spectacular site, Dr Mackenzie's work at Cypress Point was a monumental work of conservatism. There are a hundred places where he might have sacrificed the principles of sound golf course architecture to show off the

The 16th: The ultimate in water hazards

The 16th at Cypress Point is quite possibly the most beautiful golf hole in the world. Both tee and green are perched above the ocean and the roar of the surf drowns all other sounds as the sea surges in to foam white against the grey rocks below. The green is lush and circled by sprawling traps of dazzling white sand and beyond, all the way to the horizon, is the blue Pacific.

Officially, the 16th has a par of three. But everybody who has ever made a par on it has walked off the green feeling he has made a birdie. It should be a par-four, it can be a par-eight. In the half century since it was designed, only two holes in one have been made on it. Dramatically, one of them was by Bing Crosby, a long-time member and mentor of the Bing Crosby National Pro-Amateur, played annually over Cypress Point and neighbouring Pebble Beach and Spyglass Hill. He would not trade that scorecard for another Oscar.

The hole stretches 233 yards from the back tees; there are no front ones. Every inch of that distance is complete carry. Fall short and it can mean disaster, as a professional named Hans Merrell well knows. In the 1959 Crosby tournament he failed to make the carry and wound up taking nineteen strokes. The dangers of the hole are obvious and members and even some of the professionals use the alternative route to the left, settling for a drive and a pitch for a bogey-four. In this way they avoid the possibility of picking up, and a severe loss of face.

Against the wind—and it usually is—the hole calls for a full driver. Even with the wind, only hitters with the power of Jack Nicklaus would use an iron. To compound the problems of this devilish hole, going over the green can present even worse trouble—more rocks, or the ultimate in water hazards, the swift tides of the Pacific. As Jimmy Demaret once said about overshooting the green: "There is no relief. The only place you can drop the ball over your shoulder is in Honolulu."

natural beauties of the property—to make a hole badly in order to make it look good. The miracle is that not once did he succumb to such a temptation, although it usually takes several rounds to realize that you are playing a traditional, marvellously strategic course as well as a thrilling one, and not just moving within a playground of the gods.

The 1st hole at Cypress Point starts from atop a hill and drops into a valley with a turn to the right that cannot truly be called a dog-leg; you can see the green quite easily from the tee. The hole goes inland, so there is no sight of the sea. Just a glimpse of it comes into view on the magnificent 2nd—a par-five but only 544 yards long—and over the next three holes. From there on, the course winds its way through eight holes of sandy dunes and sylvan glades and past Fanshell Beach until, at the 15th, it reaches the point from which it derives its name.

Now the golfer faces the first of the back-to-back par-threes. It is a mere niblick shot across the booming surf of a deep rocky inlet; a lovelier 9-iron has never been called upon. Then comes the 16th, 233 yards long from the cham-

pionship tee. The carry is again across the water, but this time it holds real menace and a large bunker may well temper the pleasure of those relieved at just making it to the other side.

The 17th is the hole most admired by the professionals. It measures a mere 375 yards. The drive from the elevated tee high above the steep cliffs behind the 16th green carries across the Pacific to a wide fairway. This is only the beginning. The second shot must bypass a strategic pine to the right front of the green, not in itself the least tricky but backed and flanked by massive bunkers and a tangle of cypresses.

If there is a weak hole at Cypress Point it is the 18th, which ordinarily should be the strongest hole on any golf course. It is a par-four dog-leg going right and uphill to a green where it is hard to know where the flagstick is, leaving grave doubts as to what kind of putt must be faced. However, an iron off the tee will still leave only a niblick. Over this hole alone Jimmy Demaret takes issue with Julius Boros's assessment of Cypress Point. In Demaret's view, "Cypress Point is the best seventeen-hole course in the world".

The toughest golf course in the world?

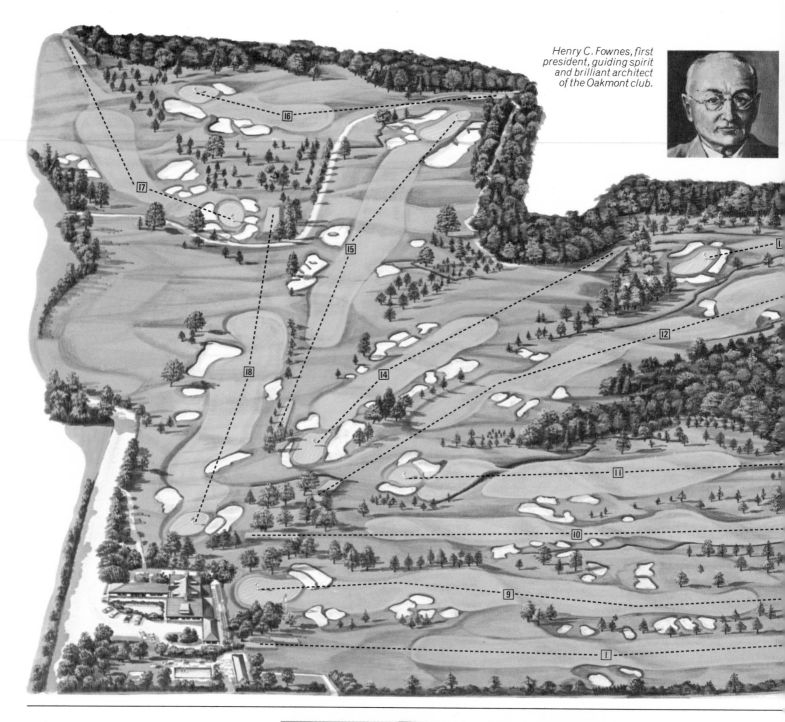

Henry C. Fownes, first president, guiding spirit and brilliant architect of the Oakmont club.

The Pennsylvania Turnpike is America's oldest super-highway. It wends its way westwards from Philadelphia, connecting the heavily industrialized eastern coast with Pittsburgh, the coal and steel capital of the nation. It bends across the northern section of the city and through the suburb of Oakmont, a lovely stretch of flatlands that lies at the foothills of the Alleghenies.

When the turnpike was being constructed it had to go directly across a dream of a golf course that had been fathered by a steel magnate, Henry C. Fownes, in 1904. Luckily for Fownes and the rest of the golfing world the course had already been sliced in two by a railroad whose tracks formed a gorge. The Pennsylvania Turn-

The famous Church Pews bunker, which will catch any hooked drive at the 3rd and 4th holes, has come to epitomize the terrors of Oakmont. The tapering trap, almost forty yards wide at its broadest point, takes its name from the seven grassy ridges that run across its sixty-yard length.

Oakmont is torn in two by highway and railroad and scarred by nearly 200 bunkers. It can be a cruelly punishing course, boasting as it does such fearsome hazards as the mammoth Church Pews bunker separating the vast 3rd and 4th fairways. For those who succeed off the tee, torment and anguish can be found on the lightning-fast greens. The strength of any golfer will be sapped by the 12th, a huge par-five of 605 yards which ends in a typically treacherous green.

Oakmont Country Club, Oakmont, Pennsylvania

Out	3,479 yards	36
In	3,442 yards	35
Total	6,921 yards	par 71

Record: 63, Johnny Miller, US Open 1973

Card of the course

No 1	469 yards	par 4	No 10	462 yards	par 4
No 2	343 yards	par 4	No 11	371 yards	par 4
No 3	425 yards	par 4	No 12	603 yards	par 5
No 4	549 yards	par 5	No 13	185 yards	par 3
No 5	379 yards	par 4	No 14	360 yards	par 4
No 6	195 yards	par 3	No 15	453 yards	par 4
No 7	395 yards	par 4	No 16	230 yards	par 3
No 8	244 yards	par 3	No 17	322 yards	par 4
No 9	480 yards	par 5	No 18	456 yards	par 4

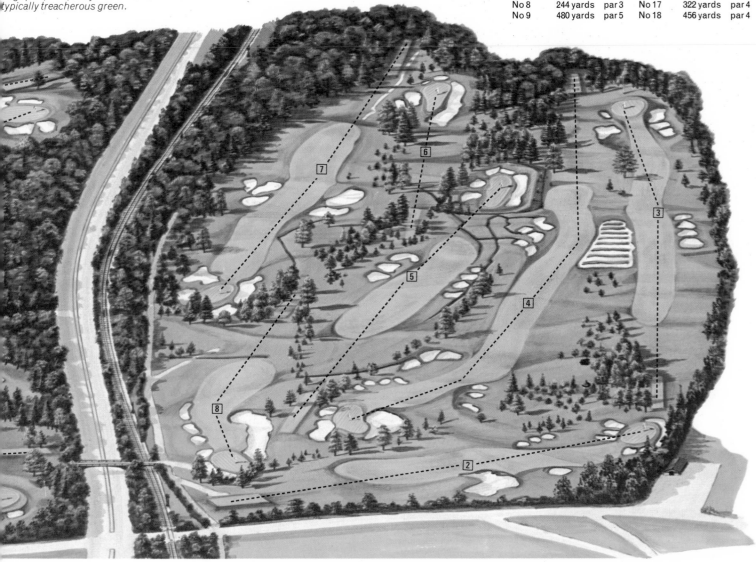

pike was also laid through the gorge, leaving the Oakmont Country Club course practically intact. Bobby Jones, Tommy Armour, Sam Parks, Ben Hogan, Jack Nicklaus and, finally, Johnny Miller might have given their heartfelt thanks, for it was there that all six wrote some of the finest chapters in America's golf history. Oakmont might well be the toughest golf course in the entire world, barring the weather as a factor. It is a course that will humble a golfer like no other, even on a lazy day in May. Bobby Jones played there in the 1927 US Open and never broke 76. That year Armour won over 898 entries, without even breaking par. In 1935 Sam Parks—who knew every blade of grass on the course—was the only player to break 300

on the way to his surprising Open victory. Hogan won the Open there in 1953 with ridiculous ease by breaking par—by one stroke. Nine years later, Nicklaus tied Arnold Palmer with an identical score—283—and then won the play-off simply by matching the scorecard. In contrast Johnny Miller won the Open at Oakmont in 1973 by playing the last round in 63. It has been said that it was the finest round of golf ever played, and there is not a member at Oakmont who would disagree.

What makes Oakmont so tough? To begin with, it once had 220 bunkers (it now has some thirty fewer, five times more than Augusta National). Each was raked in furrows two inches deep and two inches apart, a process carried

out with the rake specially designed by Henry Fownes. "You could have combed North Africa with it," says Demaret, "and Rommel wouldn't have got past Casablanca."

Then there are the greens, originally rolled with barrels of sand weighing a quarter of a ton each. After that was done, they were cut to a sixteenth of an inch and an area within six feet of the cup to one thirty-second of an inch. They were not watered in any way, by sprinklers or otherwise, during the early years. In 1935 Jimmy Thomson drove, on the fly, the par-four 17th. Thomson was then justifiably known as America's longest hitter, though not as one of the country's best putters. Tied with Sam Parks at that point, he proceeded to four-putt the ▷

At 379 yards the 5th is, for Oakmont, a relatively short par-four. The three fairway traps, positioned to catch the hooked drive, are matched by a series of four on the right side. But, like the ditches running diagonally across the front of the green, they should not present too much of a problem. The real difficulty in this hole is in mastering the heavily trapped and severely undulating green. In the final of the 1951 PGA championship Sam Snead managed to circumvent any putting problems by sinking his wedge shot from the hillside rough above the green. His birdie-three gave him the hole and helped him defeat Walte Burkemo 7 and 6.

▷ green. Thomson recalls, "I could have six-putted. When the ball got to two feet from the hole, I thought I had an eagle. Then it took off again. I had to hole a three-footer for my bogey. On the 5th green I had spotted my ball with a dime so Parks could putt out. When I got back to the ball, the dime was gone. It had slid off the green!"

Under championship play—and Oakmont comes close to holding the American record—no other course has more big greens or more narrow fairways than Oakmont. "These greens are so slick", said 1947 US Open winner Lew Worsham, "that nobody I know uses any kind of putter except a blade. If you used a mallet-head —well, that's like getting a back-rub with a sledge-hammer."

All that has been said about Oakmont might seem as though it were some sort of tricked-up golf course. The opposite is true. Oakmont has character, the quality that separates the men

from the boys, the players from the ball-hitters. A player can have the time of his life—or spend four hours of torture. The first hole is so easy that par is changed from five to four for a tournament. The par-five 9th is so short that a professional can easily reach the green in two shots. The problem is that he might have a putt more than one hundred yards long. The 9th green is not the biggest in the world (although it comes mighty close), but some idea of what it is like—for the golfer who has never played there —is that, in addition to the cup itself, it also contains seventy-two holes of a putting clock. The local rule says that if a player is on the clock, he may drop off the putting surface, without penalty, and play back to the cup— thereby breaking the Rules of Golf of the USGA and the R & A without so much as a frown from either body. Rules are rules. At Oakmont the golfer is not playing off grass, but off an altar cloth and he had better treat it as such.

In 1919 Bobby Jones, then a lad of 17, los to an Oakmont member named Davey Herro by the rather lopsided margin of 5 and 4. Si years later he returned for the US Amateur an won his matches 11 and 10, 6 and 5, 7 and 6, an in the final, 8 up. All this was done with hickor shafts, iron heads that were drop-forged, driver that had a hole in the centre of the swee spot, and a putter—later to become famou as "Calamity Jane"—that looked like a toy.

Now, as the years have passed, the tools o golf are improved immeasurably. The ball i gaining a distance of approximately a yard year. Steel has replaced hickory in the shafts and it in turn will eventually be replaced b graphite. Had Jones played out the last fou holes of the 1925 Amateur final against a bette match, he would probably have gone roun Oakmont in 66, hickory clubs and all. It was performance to be surpassed only by Johnn Miller's in 1973.

----- Hogan

Ben Hogan, far left, won the 1953 US Open by six strokes, largely because of his brilliant play over Oakmont's difficult finishing holes. His closest pursuer, Sam Snead, left, blew up in that same stretch to finish with a 76.

Oakmont's finish fails to humble Hogan

All great courses have great finishing holes. Sometimes it may only be the last, sometimes the last two. Oakmont has four, and they are positively heroic. The 15th—a par-four—is a backbreaking 453 yards to an elevated green. There are two key bunkers, the first lying to the right of the landing area to catch the errant drive, the other guarding the left side of the green. The par-three 16th is 230 yards, which is just about as long as a par-three can be without becoming ridiculous. The 17th is a short par-four of 322 yards—but every inch of it goes uphill and bunkers are everywhere, the key one guarding the left front of the green. The 18th is a 456-yard par-four. The tee is elevated, but the second shot plays uphill. How these four holes play is best illustrated by the way they were tackled by Ben Hogan in 1953, the year he won every tournament he entered, including the Masters, the British Open, played at Carnoustie, and the United States Open, played that year at Oakmont. Hogan's closing round 71 gave him a winning margin of six strokes.

During the last round Hogan came to Oakmont's 15th tee with a slender lead over Sam Snead, playing a few holes behind him. Hogan, who often plays an intentional fade to offset an earlier tendency in his career to hook unintentionally, this time let his fade get away from him. The ball bounded into that key fairway bunker.

He marched into the sand and stood, hands on hips, studying the possibilities for his second. Going forwards towards the green was ruled out by the bank of the bunker in front of him. He had to choose between pitching out sideways into the fairway, or going backwards into the rough, which was not a very exciting prospect. He shook his head, plucked out his wedge, and then almost nonchalantly played a light sand shot on to the fairway. He then hit a soaring long iron twenty feet from the flagstick, and holed the putt for his par.

On the 16th he elected to use his 4-wood. He wanted height on the shot so the ball would drop, which it did—about twenty-five feet to the left of

The green at the par-three 16th as it was when Hogan played his memorable 4-wood to the very centre, twenty-five feet from the pin, which was placed on the extreme right. For the 1973 Open a bunker was added to the front right-hand corner and this has made the flighting of a high fade over the left corner even more crucial than it was for Hogan.

the flagstick, which had been placed precariously far to the right. Two putts. A par-three.

The 17th in those days was thirty yards shorter than it is now. Hogan slashed a drive that hit a few yards short of the green and bounded on, leaving him about thirty-five feet away. Two more putts, this time for a birdie three.

At the 18th he hit a towering drive that left him with only a 6-iron to the flagstick, which was situated towards the rear of the putting surface. Hogan struck the shot six feet to the right of the hole. The championship was over, because in the meantime Snead had faltered badly and, as it turned out, Hogan could have taken five putts and still won. Yet for some unknown reason Hogan stood so long over the meaningless putt that anyone might have thought the title hung on it and that his nerves had frozen—except that everybody knew that in those days Hogan didn't have any nerves. After an unconscionable wait, he finally stroked the putt. It fell in for his third straight three.

A golfer plays out of the Big Mouth bunker at Oakmont's lethally ringed 17th. The tee is 322 yards away, deep in the distant trees.

The reluctant legacy of Mr Baltus Roll

The curious distinction of having won a major championship—the US Open—by playing two different courses in his winning round belongs to Ed Furgol, a consistent if until then not markedly successful competitor on the American circuit.

Furgol's never-to-be-forgotten year was 1954, the course—or courses—Baltusrol, New Jersey. Named oddly after a local farmer, one Baltus Roll, whose life was brought to an untimely end by a murderer in 1825, Baltusrol has two courses, the Upper and Lower. The Lower course was chosen for the 1954 championship and for the most part was used by Furgol.

At the end of the third round Furgol was four under par, leading Dick Mayer by a stroke. Not far behind were Lloyd Mangrum and Gene Littler, at that time the boy wonder of the American circuit.

Baltusrol is an architectural oddity in that the last two holes are both par-fives. The 17th is a 623-yard monstrosity that is half sand—a lot of which is left unraked—and with a green as high as a house. The 18th is much shorter—542 yards—with a downhill tee shot that can be hit so far that reaching the green in two is foremost in the mind of any professional player as he stands on the tee.

Playing in front of Furgol, Mayer hit himself out of the championship with a wild push to the right into some Jersey jungle to finish with a horrendous eight. Furgol, in his turn, hit a darting hook off the tee into the woods which line the fairway to the bottom of the hill where he had hoped to land. He had a nasty lie with no possible access back to the fairway. Looking to

The 623-yard 17th, the longest par-five in the history of the US Open. The drive has to be threaded between two towering banks of trees; should a player find trouble off the tee he may not be able to carry the Sahara Desert, which splits the fairway at the 375-yard mark.

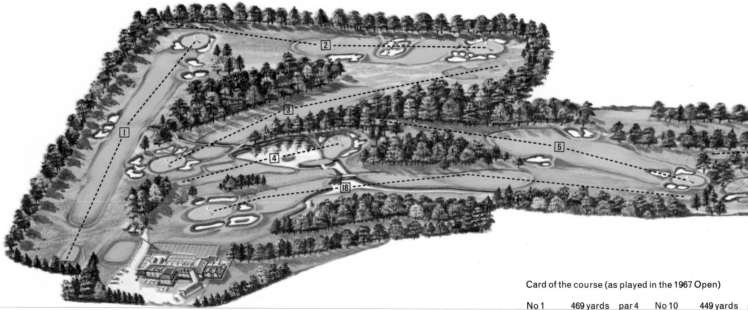

Card of the course (as played in the 1967 Open)

Baltusrol Golf Club, Springfield, New Jersey

Lower course (1967 Open)
Out   3,390 yards   34
In   3,632 yards   36
Total   7,022 yards par 70
Record: 65, Jack Nicklaus, US Open 1967

No 1	469 yards	par 4	No 10	449 yards	par 4
No 2	390 yards	par 4	No 11	410 yards	par 4
No 3	438 yards	par 4	No 12	193 yards	par 3
No 4	194 yards	par 3	No 13	383 yards	par 4
No 5	388 yards	par 4	No 14	399 yards	par 4
No 6	470 yards	par 4	No 15	419 yards	par 4
No 7	470 yards	par 4	No 16	214 yards	par 3
No 8	365 yards	par 4	No 17	623 yards	par 5
No 9	206 yards	par 3	No 18	542 yards	par 5

is left, he found an opening, no bigger than a doorway, to a patch of fairway on the Upper course. He called for an official, and asked if he could play to it. Baffled, the official called another official, who in turn called for another.

Finally, they decided that, since the fairway of the Upper course had not been staked off as out-of-bounds, Furgol could go ahead and play there if he wished. He took his 8-iron, punched the ball through the doorway, used the same club to leave the ball eight feet past the flagstick, and holed the putt.

Golf first came to Baltusrol when the land once owned by the ill-fated Baltus Roll eventually found its way into the hands of a New York socialite, Louis Keller, the owner and publisher of the *New York Social Register*. He had been one of the first enthusiastic golfers when the game hit America in the 1890s, playing it in Newport and Southampton, where the rich spent their summers. In the early nineties he laid out a nine-hole course of his own and formed a club of friends that was soon 200 strong. Keller then added on another nine holes and gained 200 more members. For a professional he hired a transplanted Scotsman, Willie Anderson, the first man to win four US Opens (a record since matched only by Bobby Jones and Ben Hogan).

The courses today bear no resemblance

The second shot at the 419-yard 15th must carry two large traps guarding a fast, undulating green. The fairway bunker on the left is not visible from the tee set among trees.

to the original. They were both laid out by the ubiquitous A. W. Tillinghast during the Roaring Twenties, when everybody was getting rich and when Bobby Jones and Walter Hagen were converting golfers out of flappers and fast-talking opportunists who didn't know the difference between a bunker and a brassie.

The Lower course has a great deal of variety, playing to what would seem a monotonously long 7,069 yards and the standard par of 72 (reduced to a par of 70 and a length of 7,022 yards for the Open). The 1st hole is a very short par-five, only 479 yards (for the Open it is played as a par-four). It is followed by a slightly up-hill par-four 379 yards long. Out-of-bounds are to the left of both holes, but very few weekend players hook a tee shot before they are warmed up. Now there is another fairly sharp right turn to face a longer par-four of 432 yards, downhill off the tee.

Then all hell breaks loose. The 4th is 194 yards long, every inch over water, to one of the most diabolical greens ever made. The 5th is a relatively short par-four, but requires a very exacting drive. Then comes a long par-four followed by a short par-five (both played in the Open as par-fours of the maximum length of 470 yards), a short par-four and a long par-three.

The course goes much on the back nine as on the front nine: a teasingly short hole here, an ▷

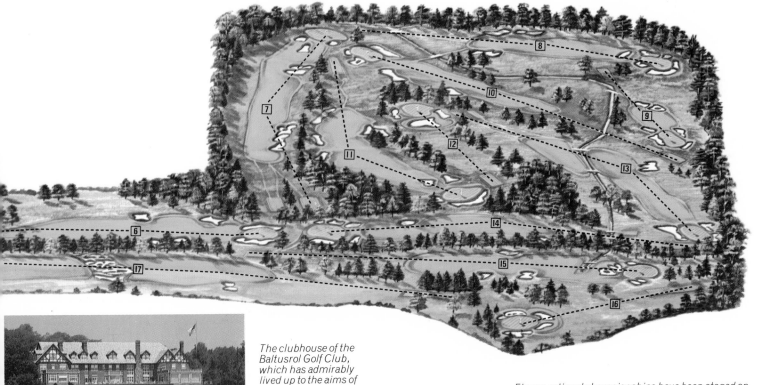

The clubhouse of the Baltusrol Golf Club, which has admirably lived up to the aims of its founders who, in Article II of their original constitution, declared: "The object of this club shall be the playing, cultivation and advancement of the royal and ancient game of golf."

Eleven national championships have been staged on Baltusrol's Lower course, where every hole presents a unique challenge. For championship play the par-five 1st and 7th are shortened to long par-fours, leaving only two par-fives, both at the finish. The shorter holes offer no refuge; the difficult 4th is well protected by water and at the 12th the tee shot is aimed towards a semi-blind green sheltering behind an expanse of sand.

The 4th: 194 yards par 3

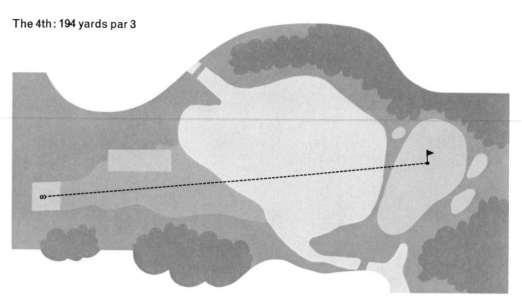

The 4th: An heroic hole made by an ace

The 4th: An heroic hole made by an ace

When golfers start choosing the greatest holes they have ever played, their minds invariably turn to par-threes and, in America, almost inevitably to the 4th at Baltusrol. It is not a strategic hole in the sense that there are a dozen different ways to play it. It is more along heroic lines, meaning that it takes one good shot to get anywhere near the flagstick and then the courage to try to do it. It also means that if a player does not bring the shot off, he just has to grit his teeth and re-tee.

The 4th at Baltusrol is simply a water hole, water hazards being almost a trademark of American courses for a variety of reasons, not the least of which is that they feed the sprinkler systems when Artesian wells cannot be found or when piped water is simply too expensive.

The shot to the green can be anywhere from 150 yards to almost 200, depending upon where the tee markers are set. It must be all carry, because the entire front edge of the putting surface is faced with a stone wall. The green itself is about four times wider than it is deep. It slopes down from left to right and from back to front. To the left, guarding the high side, is a fair-sized bunker. Guarding the entire rear are three other bunkers side by side. Thus if you over-club you end up in one of those, thereby facing a delicate sand shot to that down slope which might well take you back into the very water you were trying to avoid.

The hole was redesigned over Tillinghast's original by Robert Trent Jones, the architectural specialist almost every club calls upon when they want their course toughened for a championship, in this case the 1954 Open. When Jones got through with the job, the members protested that it was too tough. Jones disagreed. He offered to pay for any necessary changes out of his own pocket and to settle the issue he, Johnny Farrell, the club's famous pro, the club president and the chairman of the Open Committee went to play the 4th. Jones stood by while each of the others played their shots. Now it was his turn. He struck a lovely shot that hit short of the flagstick, bit the green, and gently rolled into the cup for a hole-in-one.

Jones shrugged. "As you can see, gentlemen," he said, "this hole is not too tough."

The daunting view from the forward tee over the lake to the 4th green.

▷ agonizingly long one there. The cloth of the course has been so cut that it seems to have no pattern at all, which may account for a golfer wanting to come back again and again.

Like the whole course itself, the bunkers have the variety of shapes and sizes, flatness and depth that can put a frown on a brow or a smile on a face. Tillinghast did some of his finest bunkering at Baltusrol. There are not too many and each one seems always to be in just the right place.

The contours of his greens were masterpieces of restraint. There are no steep terraces to drive a putt up to or, on the other hand, feather a putt down from. There are no ninety-foot putts across half an acre of putting surface and no six-footers with three feet of break. To be sure, a

A ditch crosses the 13th fairway from 180 to 250 yards out and the trap on the left catches any

long drive to the safe side. A well-placed drive will open up the entrance to the green.

player has to borrow something here and something there, for the greens are not just eighteen pancakes. But they are, in a word, subtle.

In keeping with the greens and bunkers, Tillinghast's fairways are just as decorous. They do not bend in those ridiculous right-angled dog-legs to which contemporary architects are so prone, thus creating more home sites for the real estate developers who underwrite them. There are no downhill lies where the right foot is as high as the left knee. Nor are there sidehill lies where the ball seems to be up to the waist, or a yard below the feet. Tillinghast's fairways just roll along, like miniature Mississippis, with just a slight bend every now and then. Baltusrol, in the final analysis, is simply aristocratic.

The definite article — despite its extra hole

The schisms that were to split the United States into the warring factions of North and South were appearing when The Country Club, in the Boston, Massachusetts, suburb of Brookline, was chartered in 1860. In the definite article of its title, The Country Club stresses its ascendancy over all other country clubs; it was the first of its kind, as befits a city whose links with the founding fathers are impeccable.

Golf was a long way from the minds of its first members, who bought the land merely to exercise their horses and take the air, en famille, in their carriages, "free from the annoyance of horse railroads".

It was twenty-two years before the club put the site to the use for which it was purchased,

and thirty years before it laid out some of its spare land for six holes of golf. Nevertheless, on the basis of this somewhat fragile start, the club was one of the five to form the American Golf Association, later to be renamed the United States Golf Association.

The original six holes were extended in 1910 to eighteen, setting the stage for an event three years later that was to prove a watershed in American golf—the victory of a young unknown, Francis Ouimet, in a play-off for the US Open title. The twenty-year-old former caddie at The Country Club beat two British immortals, Harry Vardon and Ted Ray.

The manner of Ouimet's victory over Vardon and Ray—his steady game waited for them to

make mistakes, which they duly did—is enshrined in the histories of golf. Ouimet's subsequent career as one of golf's outstanding amateurs and best-loved characters received unique recognition in 1951, when he became the first non-Briton to be elected captain of the Royal and Ancient.

The value to American golf of his win was inestimable. It marked the first real loosening of the grip which players from the British Isles had seized upon the game in the New World. More, it showed Americans that success was not limited to those with a high and esoteric talent, or to those with deep pockets.

Francis Ouimet is not the only champion that The Country Club has produced. The club ▷

The 17th: The hole that decided two Opens

Quite apart from the geography of the course itself there were quite a number of reasons for the stratospherically high scores of the 1963 US Open, played at The Country Club to commemorate Francis Ouimet's famous victory there fifty years earlier. They were so high that even Jack Nicklaus failed to qualify for the last thirty-six holes.

The championship was staged, as usual, in June, but the weather was unseasonably cold—so cold that two sweaters were the order of the day and, for those who had the uncommon foresight to bring them, windbreakers. The cause of all this was a freakish storm blowing from the northeast off the North Atlantic, and the winds made the greens like slate. Sitting as it does so far inland and protected by its numerous ancient trees, the course is not ordinarily a windy one. But that week it was more like the British than the US Open.

However, the wind brought into the reckoning

two holes in particular—the 1st and the 17th, which had been redesigned by the New England architect Geoffrey Cornish. The 1st hole, already 455 yards, now played into the teeth of the wind. But it was the 17th, regarded for years as one of the pushover holes, which had the decisive influence. It turned out to be the most difficult hole to par.

The 17th, only 365 yards long and slightly dog-legged to the left, had already influenced the result of one Open. In the crook of that dog-leg was a small but deep bunker—the key hazard to the

hole—and it was there that the 1913 Open was effectively won by Francis Ouimet or, more accurately, lost by Harry Vardon. In the fourth round, Ouimet hit a fine drive safely to the right of that bunker, hit a jigger twenty feet past the hole on a green that is long and extremely narrow, and made the birdie-putt that enabled him to tie with Vardon and Ted Ray. In the play-off the next day Ouimet came to that same hole with only a stroke advantage over the seemingly invincible Vardon who, realizing he had to make a birdie quickly, bit off too much of the dog-leg and landed in the bunker. He took a bogey-five. Ouimet played the hole precisely as he had the day before, including another downhill putt for a birdie.

Fifty years later Geoffrey Cornish enlarged that bunker, added two more to the left of the green and re-contoured the putting surface, giving it multitudinous breaks. The hole still required no more than a spoon off the tee (as against Ouimet's hickory-shafted driver) and a niblick pitch to the green (against Ouimet's jigger) but, half a century later, it was still baffling. The late Tony Lema bogeyed it to lose the chance of a tie and Arnold Palmer's bogey cost him the opportunity to win the championship outright. And Jacky Cupit, needing only a par and a bogey to win, took a double-bogey six. Julius Boros took only one putt at the 17th to join Cupit and Palmer in a play-off. He won handily with a one-under-par 70. Once again the 17th had been instrumental in deciding an Open championship.

Francis Ouimet and caddie Eddie Lowry in the 1913 US Open at The Country Club. A former caddie himself, the 20-year-old Ouimet snatched the title from Vardon and Ray.

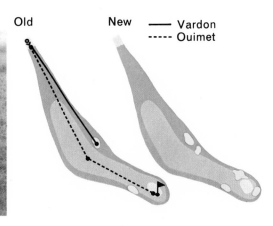

Old   New   —— Vardon
                          ----- Ouimet

Already drenched in tradition as the first-ever country club, Brookline became even more famous with tantalizing finishes in the two US Opens held there, won by Francis Ouimet in 1913 and Julius Boros half a century later. Narrow, tree-lined fairways and exceptionally small greens make accuracy off the tees and fine chipping essential for a low score.

Bunkers short of the green exact their toll on gambling second shots at The Country Club's 505-yard par-five 9th.

▷ has an ice rink, and six members—one of them Tenley Albright (now Dr Tenley Gardiner), an Olympic gold medallist—have won a total of forty-one United States figure-skating championships. Its world-class tennis players have included Hazel Wightman, winner of fifty-three national tennis titles and donor of the famous Wightman Cup.

The golf course over which Ouimet played and won was later the scene of a US Women's Amateur championship and three Men's championships. In 1927 a third nine holes was added "for ladies, children and beginners".

The championship course now draws holes from all three nines, one of them, the 11th, is composed of two holes ordinarily used by members—a short par-four and a par-three over water. Combined, they make a brute of a par-four, particularly since the golfer must drive through an avenue of oaks and maples.

There are probably a hundred golf courses in America that are tougher to play than The Country Club and perhaps fifty that are more artistically designed. From the extreme back tees it measures 6,870 yards, playing to a par of 71—something of a joke by today's standards, when anything under 7,000 yards is regarded as a "drive and a kick" course. It is neither over

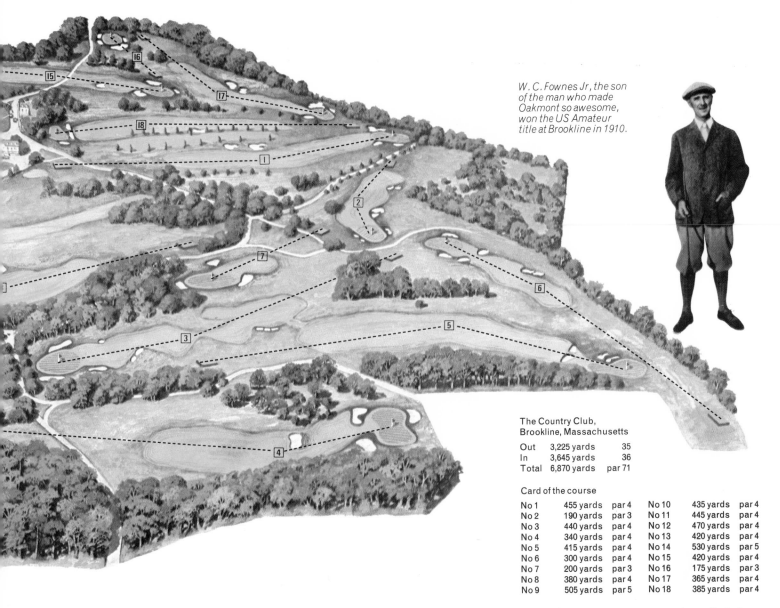

W. C. Fownes Jr, the son of the man who made Oakmont so awesome, won the US Amateur title at Brookline in 1910.

The Country Club,
Brookline, Massachusetts

Out	3,225 yards	35
In	3,645 yards	36
Total	6,870 yards	par 71

Card of the course

No 1	455 yards	par 4	No 10	435 yards	par 4
No 2	190 yards	par 3	No 11	445 yards	par 4
No 3	440 yards	par 4	No 12	470 yards	par 4
No 4	340 yards	par 4	No 13	420 yards	par 4
No 5	415 yards	par 4	No 14	530 yards	par 5
No 6	300 yards	par 4	No 15	420 yards	par 4
No 7	200 yards	par 3	No 16	175 yards	par 3
No 8	380 yards	par 4	No 17	365 yards	par 4
No 9	505 yards	par 5	No 18	385 yards	par 4

Julius Boros, who in 1963 emulated Ouimet by winning the US Open at Brookline in a triple play-off. The wind which had earlier played havoc died in the play-off and Boros, with superb chipping on a course renowned as a test of short play, beat Cupit and Palmer with a 70.

bunkered nor severely dog-legged and its greens average about 6,000 square feet, about half that of most modern greens. Wind is only an occasional factor and while there are a number of trees, the course was certainly not hacked from a forest; all in all, playing it is rather like playing through a park.

If these seem modest credentials, they are deceptive. When the US Open was played there in 1963 to commemorate the fiftieth anniversary of Ouimet's famous victory, it produced the highest winning score for eighteen years, Julius Boros's nine-over-par 293. The previous highest was Sam Parks's eleven-over-par 299 at Oakmont, which was then more of an obstacle course than a golf course. The Country Club's greens are of bent grass and are feathery-fast. If the golfer misses them he is bound to chip—or, more likely, pitch—out of ankle-deep rough of rye grass. At tournament time the fairways are like ribbons in a schoolgirl's hair and the nineteen holes that are chosen from the twenty-seven available (remembering that two holes form one for championship purposes) are certainly not the easiest.

The 1st hole runs straightaway down an old polo field with a stretch of The Country Club's old racecourse on the right. It is a routine par-four of 455 yards; the 2nd, an uphill par-three of 190 yards to an ample green, is also un-remarkable. The 3rd becomes demanding, for the rough intrudes on the fairway at about 260 yards, leaving a long iron to a green over-shadowed by ancient oaks and guarded from every conceivable angle by sand.

From the 3rd to the 8th, the course is again nondescript—no more demanding than a thou-sand other holes in the USA: the 9th is where the golfer really has to start to play. If he is not under par at that point his chances of finishing in par are remote. The 9th measures 505 yards, nothing to speak of as par-fives go. Drives off the elevated tee must be hit comfortably short to avoid rolling into a stone-filled cliff, or hit hugely long to carry it. It is a do-or-die hole—an easy par or a muscular birdie, the decision has to be made on the tee.

Now the course narrows. The 10th, 11th and 12th are long and hazardous par-fours—435, 445, and 470 yards in turn—and the 12th is one of the most rugged par-fours anywhere. Even a long hitter must use a wickedly long iron or a wood shot to reach the green, which is not only elevated but hidden from view. All access to the green is cut off by five bunkers in front of it, and too much club lands the ball in either of two bunkers behind.

The remainder of the course is deceptively simple—even the 18th, which is straightaway to an elevated green guarded by an enormous and very obvious bunker and shadowed by an enormous oak that was something to be avoided even in Ouimet's day.

In its lifetime, The Country Club has been host to a dozen international events, including the Walker Cup (twice); its members, too, have a special international distinction—their annual contest with Royal Montreal, first played in 1898, was the world's first golf match between teams from different countries. Added to Ouimet's famous victory, they give The Country Club a pedigree of which it is justly proud.

Charles Blair Macdonald's ultimate design

The National Golf Links of America, New York

Out	3,227 yards	37
In	3,518 yards	36
Total	6,745 yards	par 73

Record: 68, Arthur F. Lynch, 1946

Bernard Darwin, a late replacement in the 1922 Walker Cup team, described The National as "a truly great course".

On the eastern seaboard of the United States, National Golf Links, known simply as the National, has attained something of the status of an institution of golf, comparable in its way with Pine Valley in New Jersey and the Augusta National in Georgia. Some such destiny must have been in the mind of its founder, the late Charles B. Macdonald, to have given the club such an imposing, almost presumptuous, name.

Macdonald was a most complex and controversial figure. Although his home was in Chicago, he attended the University of St Andrews in his youth, and there he grew enamoured of the great Scottish pastime. Returning to the American Middle West, he was easily the outstanding player of a game that was just beginning to take root among the well-to-do. In the year 1905, he travelled east to Rhode Island and won the first National championship, then an amateur event.

In the course of time, Macdonald became obsessed with the notion of building the ultimate golf course in his native land. Starting in 1902, he made an annual visit to Britain, taking meticulous notes on all the greatest links and measuring what he considered to be the best holes in England and Scotland. It was a labour that lasted through five summers.

A great many sites along the Atlantic coast were carefully considered by Macdonald as a possible location for his golf course and rejected for a variety of reasons, not least among them being the cost of the real estate. He finally settled for a parcel of some 250 acres of gently rolling landscape on the shore of Peconic Bay in eastern Long Island, a mere three miles from the Southampton railroad station and one hundred miles from New York City. Construction began on the course in 1907, and it was first played two years later. As originally laid out, the National was relatively short at 6,100 yards, but subsequent changes and modifications have stretched it to its present moderate length of 6,745 yards from the back tees. Distance, however, is not the yardstick by which one measures the quality of the National. There is scarcely a day, even in midsummer, when the air is thin and the fairways hardened by the sun, when either the outbound nine or the incoming holes are not stretched formidably by the winds blowing off the Atlantic from the south or from Long Island Sound on the north. It is these elements that bring out the ingenuity and forethought of Macdonald's design, for virtually every two-shot and three-shot hole offers an alternative route or two to suit the elements as well as the strength and nerve of the player, and there is seldom any agreement on the best line to a hole in any given wind.

Of the five holes at the National which are close imitations of celebrated holes in Britain, three are encountered almost at the start of a round. The 2nd is modelled after the old 3rd at

Royal St George's, a short par-four with the direct route from the tee requiring a carry of 200 yards over a wide, deep bunker that presents a bold choice at a moment when one is not yet sure of one's strength and timing on a given day. The 3rd reproduces the problems of the Alps at Prestwick. It is a 426-yard hole with a blind second shot hit over a sharply rising hill to a very wide and steeply contoured green, protected from end to end by a bunker front. Only a strong, well-placed drive leaves any hope of reaching this harrowing green in two. The 4th is a copy of North Berwick's Redan, a middle iron par-three with a long green falling off diagonally to the left. Here the direct shot to the green flirts with a deep bunker on the left that can destroy any chance of a par. The more cautious shot to the right will leave a long and delicate downhill chip or putt.

Two remaining holes, the 7th and 13th, were both designed to recreate something of two classic moments on the Old course at St Andrews. The former is more suggested by than modelled after the famous Road Hole, where so many championship hopes have died. However, the absence of the railroad sheds, which are represented only by a large expanse of scrub-filled bunkers, removes a great deal of the terror once implicit in the tee shot at St Andrews. Yet the plan of attack remains much the same, and the third shot into the green asks for a most delicate touch if it is not played from a perfect position. It can impose some grievous mental hardship when it must carry the pot bunker at front left towards the gaping deep

bunker that runs half the length of the green to the right rear. The 13th is a splendid hole of medium iron length across a pond with deep bunkers protecting the green to both right and left. While by no means a copy, it is very much reminiscent of the 11th at the Old course, where the green lies alongside the River Eden. So there would be no mistaking its origins, Macdonald even named the 13th after the famous St Andrews river.

Although the National has so many features reminiscent of the finest British seaside links, it is not strictly a links course in the British sense. The soil on which it is built is of inland texture, and the fairways and greens are of the softer inland quality. Only the great sprawling bunkers, some 500 in number, and stretches of sandy hazards filled with huckleberry bush and other cloying scrub reproduce the playing characteristics of linksland, and the frustrations involved in extricating oneself from their grasp.

Despite the character and diversity of the National, the first Walker Cup match, played in 1922, was the only occasion when an event of international interest has taken place there.

The splendid days of the National, when members arrived by private yacht, are long gone—although the telescope on the front porch by which arriving members' yachts were identified still stands as a reminder. But the club itself and its magnificent course continue to serve a generation of prominent, if less pretentious, golfing enthusiasts with a taste for perfection.

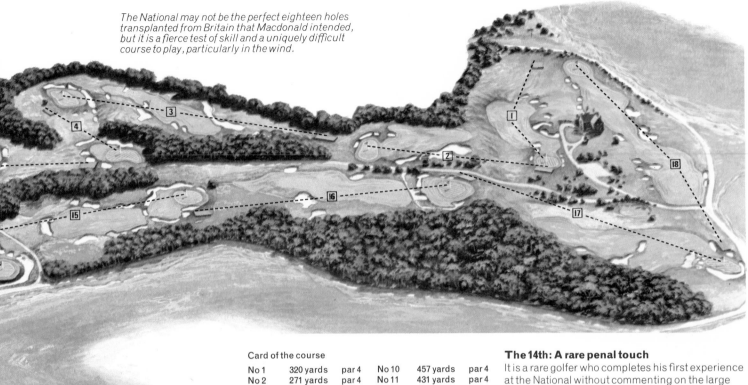

The National may not be the perfect eighteen holes transplanted from Britain that Macdonald intended, but it is a fierce test of skill and a uniquely difficult course to play, particularly in the wind.

Card of the course

No 1	320 yards	par 4	No 10	457 yards	par 4
No 2	271 yards	par 4	No 11	431 yards	par 4
No 3	426 yards	par 4	No 12	437 yards	par 4
No 4	196 yards	par 3	No 13	170 yards	par 3
No 5	476 yards	par 5	No 14	359 yards	par 4
No 6	130 yards	par 3	No 15	392 yards	par 4
No 7	478 yards	par 5	No 16	401 yards	par 4
No 8	390 yards	par 4	No 17	368 yards	par 4
No 9	540 yards	par 5	No 18	503 yards	par 5

Though Macdonald usually concentrated on strategic rather than penal design, the carry over water and very tight second shot make the 14th at The National a real test of accuracy.

The 14th: A rare penal touch

It is a rare golfer who completes his first experience at the National without commenting on the large and sharply contoured greens. Through the years they have acquired a deep matting of grass and the subtle little borrows that come only with age. But their original undulations, as conceived by Charles Blair Macdonald, supply their true personality, so it is worth pausing to hear his explanation of how he designed them. "I take", he said, "a number of pebbles in my hand and drop them on a miniature space representing a putting green on a small scale, and as they drop on the diagram, place the undulations according to their fall."

For some years after the National was opened for play in 1909, Macdonald was busy altering the holes, both in length and bunkering. "I am not confident", he said once in a rare moment of self-doubt, "that the course is perfect and beyond criticism today."

On another occasion Macdonald expressed at greater length some of the philosophy behind his most notable creation: "It is", he said, "to endeavour to make the hazards as natural as possible. I try not to make the course any harder but to make it more interesting, never forgetting that 80 per cent of the members of any golf club cannot on average drive more than 175 yards, so I always study to give them their way out . . . by taking a course much as a yachtsman does against an adverse wind, by tacking."

Macdonald certainly was the first American architect to appreciate the subtleties of design, for instance the difference between penal and strategic. Mostly he used the latter but the 14th is a rare example of a hole where the player has no alternative but to hit a reasonably straight shot. The carry over the water is not too formidable but it must be made, and having found the fairway the options are negligible. The approaches form a narrow waist of fairway flanked by water and bunkers and the green itself has a wide collar of sand around its back and sides.

A course that was built in reverse

Although short by modern American standards, Olympic's Lakeside plays long because the moist San Francisco climate limits roll and carry. Narrow fairways and small greens strengthen its challenge.

The 4th from the tee. It is typical of the tough par-fours at Olympic, a narrow dog-leg with a small target for a tee shot menaced by trees.

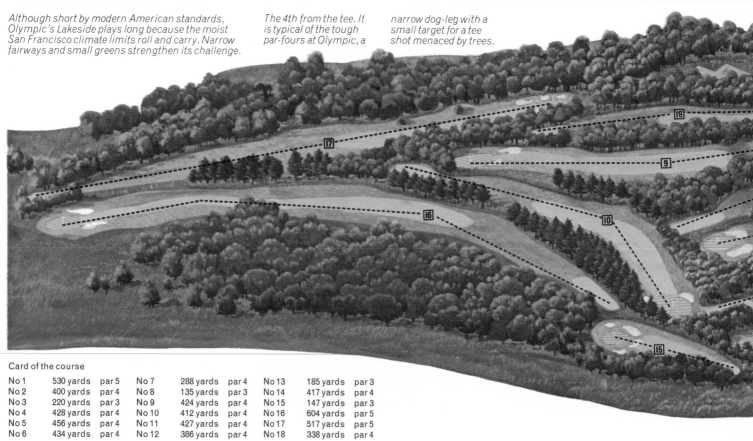

Card of the course

No 1	530 yards	par 5	No 7	288 yards	par 4	No 13	185 yards	par 3
No 2	400 yards	par 4	No 8	135 yards	par 3	No 14	417 yards	par 4
No 3	220 yards	par 3	No 9	424 yards	par 4	No 15	147 yards	par 3
No 4	428 yards	par 4	No 10	412 yards	par 4	No 16	604 yards	par 5
No 5	456 yards	par 4	No 11	427 yards	par 4	No 17	517 yards	par 5
No 6	434 yards	par 4	No 12	386 yards	par 4	No 18	338 yards	par 4

San Francisco's reputation for beauty and charm is so widespread one tends to forget many of its less celebrated assets—the great University of California just across the Bay, the influence it has had on the literature of the Far West and, by no means least, the fine sportsmen and athletes who have been sent out from time to time to spread fame in foreign lands. The first of the international-class golfers was Lawson Little, and a generation later came Harvie Ward, winner of US and British amateur titles in the 1950s, and Ken Venturi, the 1964 US Open champion. It is appropriate and perhaps significant that Venturi played much of his junior golf at a course known far and wide as Lakeside, although that is not its formal and proper name. Actually, it is the Lakeside course of the Olympic Club Country Club, a clumsy designation deriving from Lakeside's rather untidy and varied history.

Almost all American cities of any size contain some organization akin to San Francisco's Olympic Club. These are athletic clubs with a membership numbering many hundreds, and their facilities usually include a sizeable clubhouse in the downtown area with a swimming pool, gymnasium, squash and handball courts, Turkish baths and pleasant common rooms in which to dine and drink or just read and relax. The Olympic Club, whose origins go back more than a century, is such a place. It fosters teams in almost every sport that Americans enjoy, and just after World War I it expanded into golf.

In 1922, the Olympic Club bought a golf course on the western edge of San Francisco alongside the Pacific Ocean. The course had been built by the then floundering Lakeside Country Club and, as its name implied, it bordered a lake—Lake Merced, which is a small fresh-water lake less than a mile long and separated from the sea by a spine of low sandhills. The course had been built on the bare inland side of the hill, and its principal feature was the canted topography of practically all its holes as they sloped abruptly from the crest of the hill to the lake. The Olympic Club promptly planted a mass of eucalyptus, pine and cypress trees to frame all eighteen of the holes in a veritable forest as the trees reached full maturity some twenty or twenty-five years later.

Thus the course was, in a sense, built in reverse. For it is the towering trees that now give Lakeside its unique character and make it so different from the club's other eighteen holes, the Ocean course, which is built on the seaward side of the hill. The nearby Pacific and its enormous dunes play no part in the personality of Lakeside except for the prevailing wind that blows off the sea most afternoons throughout the year and the fog that comes rolling in from the ocean most evenings to wrap the course in its silent, cottony moisture, keeping it soft and damp and green even during the hot, dry months of early autumn. When the winter rains begin around December, Lakeside tends to become much too heavy for real enjoyment, and it stays that way during the wetter winters until the early springtime of northern California begins to dry it out a bit in March and April.

By June, the course is almost always in its

30,000 pines, cedars eucalyptus and cypress trees dominate the *Olympic course and are always a hazard. This is the 400-yard 2nd hole.*

ideal playing condition, a lovely and noble-looking arboreal parkland. It is not surprising, then, that the USGA has twice chosen Lakeside as the site of its Open, always a mid-June affair, and so made it one of the only three courses in all of sports-minded California ever to play host to its premier championship, Riviera and Pebble Beach being the others.

By modern standards, Lakeside appears to be short for a major championship, measuring ▷

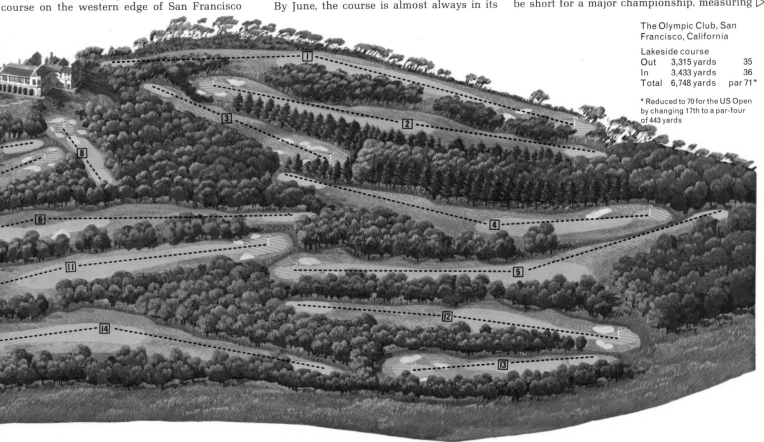

The Olympic Club, San Francisco, California

Lakeside course
Out	3,315 yards	35
In	3,433 yards	36
Total	6,748 yards	par 71*

* Reduced to 70 for the US Open by changing 17th to a par-four of 443 yards

▷ only a little over 6,700 yards from its back tees and only 6,400 yards or so from the members' tees. In this case appearances are most deceiving, for Lakeside plays long—very long. During the 1955 Open, with the 17th hole reduced from a par-five to a par-four (the USGA prefers to play all its Opens at par 70 to give uniformity to its records), only six rounds were played in sub-par figures, the lowest being Jack Fleck's closing 67 that brought him a 72-hole tie with Ben Hogan. The only other Open to be played at Olympic was eleven years later and this also resulted in a tie and a horrendous turn of fortune for Arnold Palmer: he lost a seven-stroke lead in eight holes to Billy Casper, who then beat him in the play-off by four strokes.

Except for the short holes there is no such thing as a straight line at Lakeside. The course winds and bends its way through the trees in such a way that the second shot on at least half its holes is dictated entirely by the terrain and little, if any, advantage is to be gained by the big drive. It is, in addition, a course that plays havoc with the hooker, or with the player who likes to draw big, long drives from right to left for added roll. Those who would take a shortcut on the bent and crooked holes find their route frustrated by the towering trees that close in on both sides of every fairway. Off many of the tees, the shot must be played as out of a chute because of overhanging branches at the front edge of the tee or just beyond, thus further confining the leeway available on the drive. Finally, Lakeside's use of the sloping fairways and the dog-leg has been so artfully contrived that the very shot designed to defeat the purpose of the hole will bring on the most severe penalty; for example, if a golfer tries to cut the corner on the right with a fade and misses the trees, he will probably find his shot slipping downhill off the fairway and into the scrubby rough, with his next shot a rather humiliating little recovery into a playable area.

The course starts out docilely enough with a par-five that can be reached comfortably in three strokes while one is untying the kinks. The 2nd hole, however, abruptly indicates the sort of trouble ahead. The hole feels as if it moves leftwards, and the fairway slopes sharply to the left towards the lake, yet the two big shots must be moved from left to right—against the contour of the land. The 3rd is a longish par-three, with bunkering that is typical of Lakeside. It is a very sparsely bunkered course, with only three holes, two of them short, in which there is no opening to the green for the player who prefers to run the ball on to the putting surface rather than hit directly for the pins and hope to hold the green. This is just as well, for the greens are relatively small by today's standards, averaging approximately 5,000 square feet or so, and in many instances it is simply foolhardy to hit long irons directly at them.

It is at the 4th hole that one first confronts the problems of hitting a drive out of a chute. The exit from the tee is extremely narrow because of the overhanging branches from the tall trees on either side, and there is no choice but to drive the ball straight to the target area

on the fairway, some 220 to 250 yards distant. From there, a long, uphill iron or fairway wood is the proper shot. As is so often the case on this course the trouble is on the high side of the fairway, forcing one to favour the side that will bounce the ball into the rough and the trees. This same problem exists in reverse on the 5th hole, where the trouble is on the right, and the fairway slopes to the left.

The 6th hole, a slight dog-leg left, is one more longish par-four, but it is notable because it provides the only fairway bunker on the entire course—a large sandtrap on the left—that will catch any shot trying to shave some distance off. The 7th is an unusually short par-four; again a drive out of a chute to a small fairway from which there is just a little flip of a pitch shot to a green that falls away if one plays the shot too boldly to the back portion. The 8th would be a rather easy par-three were it not for the overhanging branches again, not only in front of the tee but also overhanging the entrance to the green on the right.

The 9th through the 12th are all longish par-fours, the last three directly into the prevailing wind, and in all of them there is the problem of the precisely hit drive between the trees and the carefully hit second shot into greens that offer only a minimum target. The turn for home really begins at the 13th, where two par-threes and a par-four now border a deep culvert on the left that is played as out-of-bounds, except in major tournaments such as the Open. However, anything hit into the impenetrable foliage of this culvert is virtually unplayable and might just as well be out-of-bounds.

The 16th is extremely long—more than 600 yards—and it is said that nobody has reached

The 3rd: A lucky hole for Jack Fleck

With one exception, Lakeside's par-threes do not make severe demands on length. The 3rd alone is over 200 yards but even then tends to play shorter because it is played from an elevated tee, some fifty feet above the level of the green. Strong players can reach the green with an iron, but for most, with the prevailing wind from left to right, a substantial wood will be needed. The hole is unusual for an American course in that the approaches are open, the fairway flowing into the green. This could be a welcome sight to British eyes, for the shot can be pitched short and allowed to run on to the green. This is small and protected by five shrewdly placed bunkers.

Jack Fleck, winner over Ben Hogan in the play-off for the 1955 Open, considered the 3rd his "lucky hole". In that play-off Hogan, playing first, placed a 2-iron about a yard from the pin. Fleck then enjoyed the good fortune which prompted his description of the hole. His shot bounced off the edge of a bunker on to the green to finish some twenty feet from the hole. Fleck got his par but Hogan missed his birdie. Fleck gained in confidence, recalling later that the episode had shown him that "Hogan was only human after all"

Some critics claim that the 3rd's fame rests on the view from the tee, *but it is a trying par-three with a green that is difficult to hold.*

this green in two, even though it is played with the prevailing wind at one's back, since Bobby Jones did it many years ago. The trees on the left were smaller then and no doubt he took a shortcut over them, for the hole bends in a seemingly endless crescent to the left. The drive needs to be played to the centre of the fairway, with a 3- or 4-wood for the second shot to the right side, avoiding a large tree on the left. Then a 6- or 7-iron is needed for the approach.

It is at the 17th hole that a good deal of the excitement usually develops at the Open, for it is shortened for that tournament only from a 517-yard par-five to a 443-yard par-four simply by using a shorter tee. It is uphill all the way, and even at the distance used for the Open the very biggest hitters among the professionals can seldom reach the green in two shots playing directly into the teeth of the prevailing wind. The 18th hole, a very short par-four at 338 yards, is a driving problem. The trouble is on the left, but the fairway slopes so sharply to the right that one is always tempted to flirt with the left rough. On the other hand, if the ball carries to the right side of the fairway, the pine trees and their overhanging branches completely cut off any entrance to the green, which leans steeply forwards and seldom offers a simple, straight putt. Hogan had to sink a thirty-foot putt for a six here in his play-off with Jack Fleck for the 1955 Open, and that was the *coup de grâce* to any chance he had for an unprecedented five Open championships.

Nobody who hits the ball straight and can play a well-controlled left-to-right fade should have any large problems at Lakeside, but the hooker would be well advised to take a long look at it, drink in its arboreal, park-like beauty and then go find somewhere else to play golf.

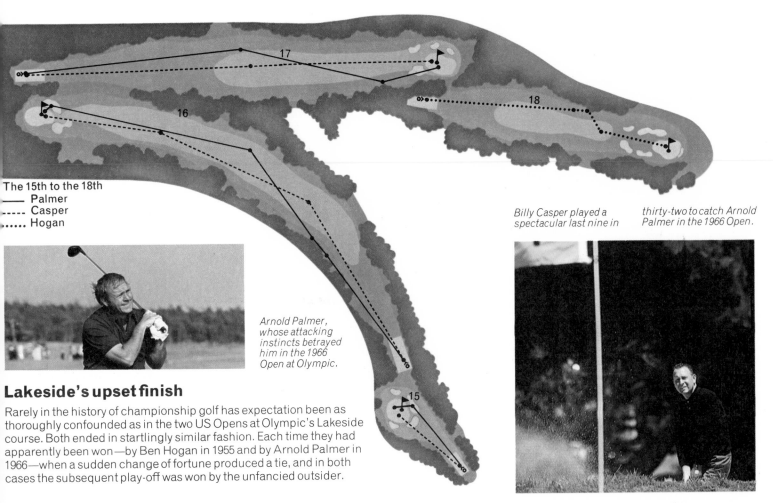

17

16

18

The 15th to the 18th
—— Palmer
---- Casper
····· Hogan

Arnold Palmer, whose attacking instincts betrayed him in the 1966 Open at Olympic.

15

Billy Casper played a spectacular last nine in *thirty-two to catch Arnold Palmer in the 1966 Open.*

Lakeside's upset finish

Rarely in the history of championship golf has expectation been as thoroughly confounded as in the two US Opens at Olympic's Lakeside course. Both ended in startlingly similar fashion. Each time they had apparently been won—by Ben Hogan in 1955 and by Arnold Palmer in 1966—when a sudden change of fortune produced a tie, and in both cases the subsequent play-off was won by the unfancied outsider.

The 15th to the 18th: Hogan and Palmer fail

Late one June afternoon in 1955 all the world was convinced that Ben Hogan was assured of a record fifth Open victory; one radio broadcast actually announced it as a fact. But as a weary Hogan waited in the locker-room, his task complete, the news came that Jack Fleck, hitherto quite unknown, needed a birdie-three on the last hole to tie. Hogan dreaded the prospect of a play-off. Since the accident which nearly destroyed him in 1949, he had to husband his resources with great care.

His strategy for a championship was confined to seventy-two holes and as he waited he said that he hoped Fleck would make two or four. Fleck did neither. He holed from seven feet for the tie. Even then nobody dreamed that he could beat the almost invincible Hogan the following day. But Fleck was in an exalted state of confidence, seemingly unafraid of the implacable presence beside him or of the prospect of victory, and he was playing the golf of his life.

After seventeen holes he was one ahead. Then, on the last tee, Hogan's foot slipped, he hooked into a patch of vicious rough from which he needed three strokes to recover and Fleck had achieved the seemingly impossible.

If ever there was an instance of a golfer being betrayed by the very qualities that made him the most compelling sporting figure of his time it was Arnold Palmer's failure to win the 1966 Open. For all that Billy Casper played one of the great last

rounds, Palmer should never have allowed him to tie. On the 10th tee he was seven strokes ahead and surging to victory. Casper was forgotten and Palmer was intent on beating Hogan's record score of 276, but Casper was playing superb golf and he had regained two strokes by the time they reached the short 15th. The flag was close to a bunker which Palmer's shot, just failing to hold the green, found. He took four while Casper holed for a two. On the huge 16th Palmer strove for length after driving into heavy rough and "the finest six I ever made"

was of no avail. Casper's flawless birdie had gained him two more strokes. When Palmer again pulled his drive into the rough from the next tee Casper had drawn level.

One of the greatest of attacking golfers had attacked when it seemed that prudence decreed a conservative approach, but had Palmer been a prudent golfer he would never have been the idol of millions. Again in the play-off Casper came from behind, two strokes at the turn, and even Palmer's resistance was spent.

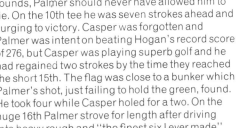

The climax of two great chases, and ties, in US Opens—Jack Fleck after Ben Hogan in 1955 and Billy Casper after Arnold Palmer in 1966— the short par-four 18th at Olympic has tempted many players to flirt with the rough on the left. Most wish they had gone for accuracy and safety—the golden rule of the course.

America's oldest club finds a fine new home

The 4th at Harbour Town is a beautiful hole, but it calls for a carefully controlled shot to a green jutting out into a creek and backed by a long, fearsome bunker.

Harbour Town Golf Links, Hilton Head Island, South Carolina

Out	3,283 yards	36
In	3,372 yards	35
Total	6,655 yards	par 71

Record: 63, Jack Nicklaus, Heritage Classic 1975

Only a week after Harbour Town Golf Links was opened its name was known around the world. Before even a round had been played there, it was chosen as the site for the 1969 Heritage Classic. That tournament was won by Arnold Palmer, his first victory in fourteen months, and all the world heard the news.

Harbour Town's fame has proved to be lasting. The course is spread out among the trees and along the inland coast of Hilton Head Island in South Carolina. The nearest city is Savannah, Georgia, which is twenty-five miles away. It is one of the most beautiful golf courses in America, but it owes its reputation not so much to its undoubted scenic attractions as to its genuine quality, as players of the calibre of Lee Trevino, Gary Player and Tom Weiskopf have testified.

On paper, its credentials are unimpressive. It is only 6,655 yards long from its extreme back tees. It has a par of 71, which has been broken once by eight strokes, twice by seven and a number of times by five and six. Even more unlikely for a championship course, the landing areas of its fairways are forty-two yards wide, far above USGA standards.

The course has only fifty-six bunkers, eight of which are off the fairways. Every bunker lies

At a time when the trend in American course design was very definitely towards length and large greens, architect Pete Dye, working closely with Jack Nicklaus, created a refreshingly different course at Harbour Town. The greens are smaller than usual, the bunkers fewer but more thoughtfully placed and designed. The premium is on accuracy and a thoughtful approach to a short, subtle course.

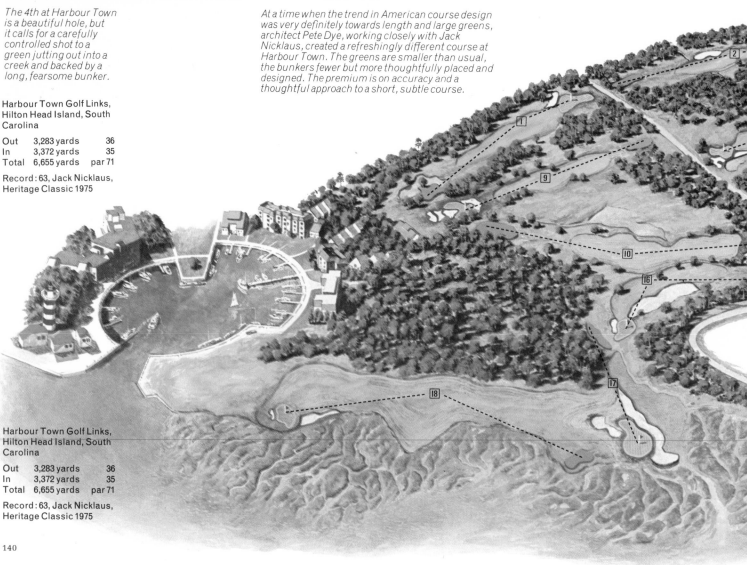

Harbour Town Golf Links, Hilton Head Island, South Carolina

Out	3,283 yards	36
In	3,372 yards	35
Total	6,655 yards	par 71

Record: 63, Jack Nicklaus, Heritage Classic 1975

bsolutely flat; not one is banked, so it is almost impossible to get a buried ball. Fully a third of he bunkers are set up behind or to one side of a green, simply to make the green a better arget. There are a dozen bunkers at Harbour Town that nobody has ever been in.

The greens are small and so lacking in undulations that three-putting is more a matter of incompetence than a geographic survey hat went awry. For every long par-four there is a short par-four. For every dog-leg left there is one to the right, and only two of them are so bent that you cannot see the green from the tee. There are no uphill or downhill lies on the course because of the nature of the land, which is so flat that the highest point on the course is only six feet above the lowest.

The course was bulldozed and chain-sawed through sub-tropical vegetation, but Pete Dye, the designer, and Jack Nicklaus, Dye's consultant, went to extraordinary pains to leave trees just where they could come into play: palmettos, towering pines, magnificent magnolias and oaks draped in Spanish moss, thick as tinsel on a Christmas tree. Where the trees stand in groves, they encroach upon the fairways so closely that they make the landing areas look much smaller than they really are. In any

event, there is little excuse for missing a forty-two yard patch of fairway.

The 1st hole is a straightaway par-four, calling for about a 5-iron to the green. The 2nd is typical of the par-fives, short but reachable only by two very exacting shots. It calls for a drive down the extreme left side of the fairway, flirting with a bunker on the way. Only from this position is it possible to hit the green with the second shot, for a long bunker and a gigantic oak stand sentinel over the right side.

The 3rd is like the 1st, a drive and a 5-iron. Although the fairway is wide, the green is very small. The 4th is one of the most diabolically beautiful par-threes a golfer is ever likely to face. It is 180 yards of pure carry, because water fronts the green and lies to the left and to the rear. A flurry of pampas grass lies to the right and, to make matters worse, the green is banked right to the edges with railroad ties between the pampas grass and the water. It is impossible to roll the ball on to the green.

Like the 2nd, the par-five 5th can also be reached in two, and again both shots have to be played down the left-hand side to bypass trees near the green—which, to make the second shot even tougher, banks from left to right.

Two of the more interesting holes on the

front nine are the 7th and the 9th. At the 7th, a 167-yard par-three, the green is surrounded by sand except for a spit of land to the rear which provides access. The 9th is one of the shortest of par-fours—a mere 324 yards. A long bunker protects the front of the horseshoe-shaped green, which is wrapped around yet another bunker; land on the wrong side and the golfer will have to three-putt purposely to find a way around it.

The 10th and the 11th bend to the left away from the clubhouse, and the 12th makes a quick dog-leg to the right with, unusually on an American course, a double green. It is impossible for any golfer to putt from one part to the other in two without holing at least a thirty-footer for his second.

The 13th is a fascinating hole. It is only 358 yards long but it is wise to leave the driver in the bag. Unless the narrow fairway is hit, there is no shot to the green because oak trees narrow the approach. The green itself is Y-shaped, with the stem protected by a bunker that seems to be half an acre in size. More, the elevated green is banked with boards.

The 152-yard 14th, like the 4th, is a par-three that is water from tee to green—all of it banked with railroad ties and sawn-off telegraph poles. ▷

At Harbour Town the golfer has to contend with water at fifteen holes, one of which is the 14th. Typically this hole follows the line of a creek, with a forced carry all the way to the ample, round green.

Card of the course

No 1	380 yards	par 4	No 10	453 yards	par 4
No 2	492 yards	par 5	No 11	418 yards	par 4
No 3	383 yards	par 4	No 12	405 yards	par 4
No 4	180 yards	par 3	No 13	358 yards	par 4
No 5	521 yards	par 5	No 14	152 yards	par 3
No 6	403 yards	par 4	No 15	562 yards	par 5
No 7	167 yards	par 3	No 16	378 yards	par 4
No 8	433 yards	par 4	No 17	188 yards	par 3
No 9	324 yards	par 4	No 18	458 yards	par 4

One tournament pro has advised that the best way to play the 17th is to "use your 2-iron and pray". That remark was made after Jack Nicklaus had hit numerous balls from this spot and repeatedly failed to hold the green, which is guarded front and left by an eighty-yard-long bunker. The tee is now to the left and about fifteen yards farther forward.

▷ The four finishing holes then present some of the most thoughtful shotmaking a golfer will ever be asked to countenance. The par-five 15th is the longest hole on the course, yet it is only 562 yards. Even so, it has never been hit in two shots in competition and only twice in practice —once by Jack Nicklaus and once by Larry Ziegler. Although the tee shot is straightaway, close to the tiny green the fairway dog-legs around a small lake. Consequently, even touring pros often lay up with their second shots.

The 16th is a shortish par-four, sharply dog-legged to the left. The tee shot must avoid three lonesome pines scattered down the middle of the fairway and the start of a mammoth bunker, fully 130 yards long, on the left. The narrow 17th green widens to the rear, but a strip-trap about eighty yards long skirts the left side and becomes, at the rear, a huge basket trap. For two-thirds of its flight the tee shot must carry water, which continues close along the left side all the way to the green.

A par-four of 458 yards, the 18th is unforgettable. Both shots must carry the tidal salt-marsh along the shores of Calibogue Sound. Played bravely the hole is absolutely straight, with the tee, the fairway landing area and the green jutting out into the marsh. It is one of the great finishing holes in golf, as events in the Heritage have proved.

This tournament was so named in recognition of the fact that the South Carolina Golf Club—whose home Harbour Town became— is the oldest golf club in North America, having been founded in 1786 at Charleston. In its eight years the Heritage has been won only by truly gifted golfers, irrefutable testimony to the worthiness of the course over which it is played. Victory has gone twice to both Johnny Miller and Hale Irwin, and to Bob Goalby, Arnold Palmer, Hubert Green and Jack Nicklaus who calls it "a thinking man's golf course".

The 18th: An Olympian finish across a marsh

There are some people who think the 18th hole at Harbour Town the best hole on the course. There are others who think it is the worst.

Whatever it may be, it is one of the most Olympian finishing holes in golf—not excluding the famed 18th at Pebble Beach, which it somewhat resembles. Calibogue Sound (pronounced Cali-bogey) runs from tee to green along the left, as the Pacific Ocean does along the 18th at Pebble Beach. Both finishing holes have out-of-bounds along the right.

The 18th at Pebble Beach is a par-five—the 18th at Harbour Town is not, although a lot of people think it ought to be. At 458 yards, it is not quite long enough to meet the USGA's recommendation for a par-five. But it certainly plays that way, particularly if the wind is against you. The left-hand edge of the fairway snakes along the tidal salt-marshes of the sound. The tee, the landing area for the drive and the green are all on promontaries, which means that both the drive and the approach must be hit across the marsh if the player entertains any hope of a par. The second shot must also carry a sinuous bunker that curls along the shore, stopping at the edge of the green. It is at least one hundred yards long.

There are three ways in which the hole can be played. The hardest is from what has become known among the members as the "Nicklaus tee", for it requires a gigantic drive simply to carry to the peninsula of fairway. The hole is so rugged from that tee that even the PGA very seldom uses it during the Heritage Classic.

Another tee, forward and to the right, confronts the player with a drive of somewhat less carry. But even from there it is in all probability still a wood to get home, and that shot will have to carry the full length of the long bunker in order to hit the green, which, although relatively small, will hold a wood shot with surprising ease.

The third alternative—and one which most members employ—is to hit two woods straight up the fairway. Two well-struck shots will leave the ball about hole-high on the right. From there, there is always the chance that the pitch will be close enough that one putt will suffice. Many, however, will settle for a bogey.

In the 1969 Heritage, Arnold Palmer drove from this second tee. The ball almost ran through the landing area, stopping just three feet short of the water. From there he hit an 8-iron, one of the shortest clubs ever used on this hole, and landed on the right-hand fringe of the green. For his third shot Palmer used his putter. The ball hit the back edge of the cup and bounced in. A typical Palmer finish. It was one of the very few birdies made at the 18th that week—or, for that matter, any week.

Looking back over green, salt-marsh and fairway on the remarkable 18th.

Two great shots over water are essential for a chance of a par-four.

"Give us a man-sized course..."

In that vast Manhattan bedroom known as Westchester County, golf courses are almost as numerous as car service stations and, like them, they frequently lie side by side. Many of them are undeniably of championship calibre, but Winged Foot, in the town of Mamaroneck, is undoubtedly the best. It has two courses, the East and the West, both designed in 1923 by an eccentric but highly imaginative architect named A. W. Tillinghast. He was one of America's truly great designers, whose creations include Baltusrol, San Francisco Golf Club, Quaker Ridge, Ridgewood, Five Farms and Fresh Meadow. The winged foot from which the club takes its name is from the emblem of the New York Athletic Club, in mid-town Manhattan, a number of whose members banded together to form the suburban golf club. Later, the affiliation between the two was severed but the emblem stayed.

It has long been a locker-room debate among the members as to which course is the better.

The entrance to the 3rd green is little more than sixty feet wide. With the flanking bunkers and out-of-bounds just over the back, this hole, 216 yards long, calls for both length and control.

But most professionals who have played both would probably agree on the longer, somewhat more treacherous West, particularly since in 1972–3 it was toughened up in some places for the 1974 US Open. As usual, par for a tournament is dropped from 72 to 70. In the 1974 Open, Hale Irwin won with a 287, seven over par. In 1959 Billy Casper had won the same championship with 282, one-putting thirty-one greens in the process. And way back in 1929 Bobby Jones and Al Espinosa tied at fourteen over, Jones winning a thirty-six-hole play-off by the humiliating margin of twenty-three strokes.

It is not difficult to see why these scores came close to being stratospheric even by Open championship standards. The reason lies in the par-fours, as everybody learns to their dismay when they first play the course. There are twelve of them, fully ten measuring more than 400 yards. This means that even the good amateur club player capable of hitting a drive 220 yards straight down the middle of the fair- ▷

Winged Foot's 10th green and the house that prompted Ben Hogan's description of the hole as "the 3-iron into some guy's bedroom".

The 17th: 444 yards par 4

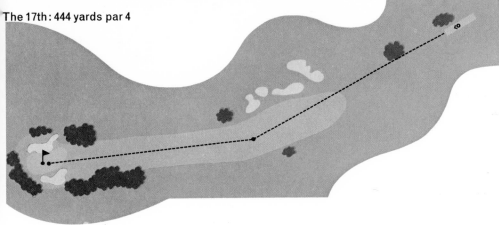

The 10th and 17th: Tillinghast's finest

Two holes, the 10th and the 17th, stand out at Winged Foot. Jack Nicklaus describes the 444-yard 17th as "one of those text-book tests of golf—a hole that really pits the player against the designer". The hole is a slight dog-leg to the right, the crook of which contains four huge bunkers. On either side of a slim, curving green are long, well-like bunkers. In Nicklaus's words, "A straight tee shot is a definite necessity. The second shot requires a long iron, which again must be hit with great accuracy to a well-trapped, extremely narrow green."

Two of Winged Foot's four short holes are at least two club lengths longer than the 10th, but it is a superior hole. Seen from the tee, the hole is not all that imposing. At 190 yards it cannot be called short. The broad, deep green tilts invitingly towards the tee. Directly in front is an opening between the two flanking kidney-shaped bunkers. The third bunker, on the left centre of the fairway, is so short of the green as to be practically out of play, although the handicap golfer must be conscious that it has to be carried.

It is only at the green itself that the hole becomes imposing. One look at its smooth, subtle undulations brings worries not of two-putting but of three-putting. With the flagstick at the front of the green and the ball well behind it, comes the possibility of a chip back or, worse, playing from one of those bunkers, both of which are deeper than a man is tall. A shot out of either of these, played not quite tenderly enough, can easily see the ball back into the other one. When the flagstick is to the rear of the green, a club too many could result in hitting into the out-of-bounds area, which is no more than thirty feet behind the putting surface. The hooked shot will land in a pack of trees on the left.

The hole requires precise judgement in club selection, the shot must be hit truly after that and then the putt must be stroked, not jabbed. All the hazards and other trouble are in plain view from the tee. There is nothing tricky about the 10th. The greatest endorsement the hole ever received came from A. W. Tillinghast himself. He considered it the finest par-three he had ever built.

▷ way—good distance for any non-tournament player—is faced with a wood shot on all ten, on seven of which he won't be able to reach the green at all. And even the other three are doubtful, for all the greens are elevated and each is protected by bunkers that are not only big but very deep. Tillinghast once explained his design philosophy on bunkers: "I think that I always will adhere to my old theory that a controlled shot to a closely guarded green is the surest test of any man's golf."

In all, Winged Foot has sixty bunkers and every one of its greens has at least two of those deep bunkers carved out about as close to the putting surface as you can get without actually being on it. Claude Harmon, an astute teacher and professional there for more than thirty

years, claims there is not a low-handicap member there—and there are lots of them—who is not an excellent bunker player. It is impossible to chip from them or even to pitch out. A sand-iron must be used with a finely timed swing for an explosion shot or, if one has the nerve, a semi-explosion. Alternatively, if the ball is buried in the sand, an outright blast with plenty of muscle is called for.

Many of the finer players among the members have learned from Harmon and other professionals a good way of dealing with a ball buried in sand. They leave their sand-iron in their bag and instead use a pitching wedge or even a 9-iron. The flange on the sand-iron more often than not will not permit the clubhead to cut through the sand. The club just bounces off,

thereby moving the ball only a few feet. The thinner flange of the pitching wedge or 9-iron will cut through the sand like a knife. One thing more: they suggest closing the face slightly, for the force of the blow will almost surely open it out to a square position at impact.

The Winged Foot membership list has always been something to talk about, as have the professionals who have worked there. At one time the club had both the Open and Amateur champions of the country. Member Dick Chapman won the Amateur in the autumn of 1940 and the following spring the head professional, Craig Wood, won the Open. Harmon, who became head professional six years later, won the Masters in 1948 and three years later member Joe Gagliardi (later Judge Gagliardi) was runner-

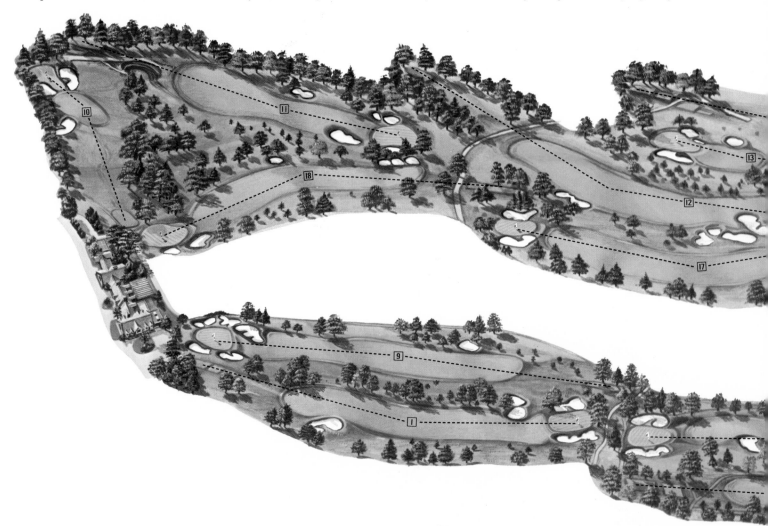

Card of the course

No 1	446 yards	par 4	No 10	190 yards	par 3
No 2	411 yards	par 4	No 11	382 yards	par 4
No 3	216 yards	par 3	No 12	535 yards	par 5
No 4	460 yards	par 4	No 13	212 yards	par 3
No 5	515 yards	par 5	No 14	435 yards	par 4
No 6	324 yards	par 4	No 15	417 yards	par 4
No 7	166 yards	par 3	No 16	452 yards	par 4
No 8	442 yards	par 4	No 17	444 yards	par 4
No 9	466 yards	par 4	No 18	448 yards	par 4

Winged Foot Golf Club, Mamaroneck, New York

West course

Out	3,446 yards	35
In	3,515 yards	35
Total	6,980 yards	par 70

Record: 64, Jug McSpaden, Goodall Tournament 1946

Tillinghast's stunningly tight West course unfolds along two distinct, parallel arms. The lower front nine includes a deceptively easy looking, long par-three, the 3rd, which caused so much trouble in the 1959 US Open. The inward half starts with another impressive short hole, the 10th, which precedes a succession of seven dog-legs and concludes with the infamous 18th, where the narrow fairway leads into a fiendishly undulating green.

up in the Amateur. Among the former assistants to Harmon have been Jack Burke, who won both the Masters and the PGA championship in 1956, Dave Marr, winner of the PGA in 1965, and Mike Souchak, long a star on the tournament circuit who shares the record for the low round on tour at 61. Dick Mayer, who won the Open in 1957, was a member at Winged Foot before turning professional.

It is certainly no accident that so many fine players have emerged from Winged Foot or chosen to work there. The course perfectly exemplifies the design philosophy of Tillinghast, which he himself succinctly sums up this way: "In planning holes there are thousands of combinations, each offering a mute appeal for recognition. It is necessary to decide on the collection which will work out economically and satisfactorily from many angles. But this is sure: every hole must have individuality and must be sound. Often it is necessary to get from one section to another over ground which is not suited to easy construction, but that troublesome hole must be made to stand right up with the others. If it has not got anything about it that might make it respectable, it has got to have quality knocked into it until it can hold its head up in polite society."

There can be no doubts about Winged Foot's social standing or of Tillinghast's confidence in his own workmanship, as his assessment of the course shows: "As the various holes came to life they were of a sturdy breed. The contouring of the greens places a premium on the placement of the drives, but never is there the necessity of facing a prodigious carry of the sink-or-swim sort. It is only the knowledge that the next shot must be played with rifle accuracy that brings the realization that the drive must be placed. The holes are like men, all rather similar from foot to neck, but with the greens showing the same varying characters as human faces."

Looking at those lush, velvet greens and emerald fairways, it is difficult to believe that Tillinghast had to move 7,200 tons of rock and cut down 7,800 trees to create them. The magnitude of his task was in stark contrast to the brevity of the instructions he received from the gentlemen of the New York Athletic Club: "Give us a man-sized course," they said. Tillinghast's response was a Herculean achievement.

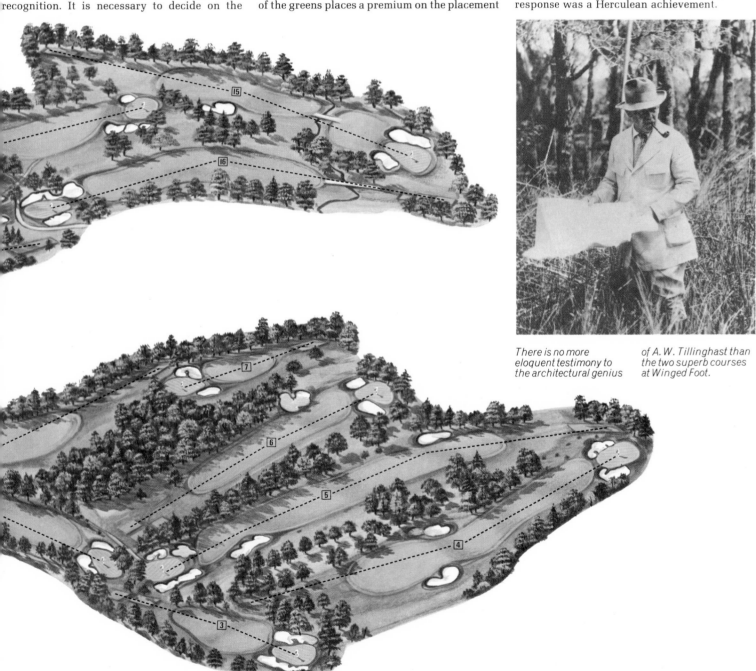

There is no more eloquent testimony to the architectural genius of A. W. Tillinghast than the two superb courses at Winged Foot.

Donald Ross creates his masterpiece

Card of the course

No 1	414 yards	par 4
No 2	454 yards	par 4
No 3	345 yards	par 4
No 4	532 yards	par 5
No 5	438 yards	par 4
No 6	216 yards	par 3
No 7	398 yards	par 4
No 8	464 yards	par 4
No 9	162 yards	par 3
No 10	596 yards	par 5
No 11	434 yards	par 4
No 12	423 yards	par 4
No 13	378 yards	par 4
No 14	444 yards	par 4
No 15	206 yards	par 3
No 16	504 yards	par 5
No 17	187 yards	par 3
No 18	433 yards	par 4

Pinehurst was the first resort to offer seventy-two holes of golf, but it was Donald Ross's Number 2 course that brought it world renown. Ross created a masterpiece, blending visual harmony with a balanced array of hazards: mounds guarding the greens, wire grass and pine needles waiting off the fairways, and greens falling away on all sides. As Sam Snead put it after one North and South Open: "You've got to hit every shot on old Number 2."

There is no resort in America that is quite so saturated with golf as Pinehurst, a charming little New England-style village located incongruously in the South—or, at least, in the northern part of the South. Quite fortuitously, and long before anyone had golf in mind, a pharmacist from Boston named James W. Tufts conceived the notion of starting a modest winter resort in the South so that other New Englanders of modest means and advancing years could escape the bitter winter weather. He finally chose the Sandhills of North Carolina because of the mild climate and the reasonable price of $1 an acre then being asked for this rather barren, cutover timberland. Nobody but an incorrigible optimist or an oaken-hearted New Englander would ever have had the temerity to think he could create anything habitable and attractive on such desolate land.

The North Carolina Sandhills are a geological phenomenon dating back to some ice age. They reach a hundred miles inland from the Atlantic and, except for the thick stands of pine forest, they provide much the same sort of terrain as is found on the linksland of Great Britain. Thus, when James W. Tufts and his pioneering neighbours of Pinehurst suddenly found themselves intrigued by this peculiar new game of golf somewhere around the years 1897 and 1898, they had the ideal landscape on which to build an experimental course.

The year 1900, however, provided the two events that shaped Pinehurst's future. In March Harry Vardon stopped by and played four rounds over the rather primitive eighteen holes of Pinehurst Country Club's Number 1 course. Just watching the great Vardon was enough to whet the appetites of the locals for this game. In December Donald J. Ross arrived in Pinehurst to assume the duties of resident professional.

At the time of his arrival in Pinehurst, Donald Ross was a young man, a Scot from Dornoch who had taken his apprenticeship under Old Tom Morris at St Andrews and then served a few years as professional and greenkeeper at Royal Dornoch. His youthful enthusiasm and natural gift for the "feel" of the game were just what the budding new resort needed. Within his first year at Pinehurst, Ross started to build the first nine holes of what is now the justly famous Pinehurst Number 2 course, and he completed the original eighteen holes in 1907. So great was the artistic triumph of Pinehurst Number 2, even in those paleolithic times of sand greens, scruffy fairways and only 5,860 yards, that Ross eventually became the Standford White of American golf architecture.

Through the years, Ross was continually altering and improving Pinehurst Number 2 as equipment and technique required until he arrived at the course we know today, one of the masterpieces of golfing architecture of its particular genre. That is to say, Pinehurst Number 2 is a kind of idealization of the old-fashioned parkland courses that characterized American golf architecture until World War II—tree-lined, following the natural terrain, with small greens and ample but not profligate use of bunkers. It is the kind of course that puts the emphasis on the planning and precision of the golf shot rather than the great strength that the more recent courses demand, although, as it stands today, Number 2 measures an imposing 7,028 yards from the back tees. It is also a course that is calculated to call forth the use of every club in the bag during the progress of a round. In addition to these qualities, Number 2 has the added advantage of being located on the Sandhills, thus giving it something of the playing qualities of a linksland course.

In the seventy-one years since James W. Tufts first began to develop his resort, the timberlands of Pinehurst have grown back to their full maturity. As a result, nearly every one of the eighteen holes of Number 2 is a separate aesthetic entity unto itself, completely surrounded by the tall pines and shut off from the rest of the course. Except for those who may be engaged on the same hole, a player has the feeling of being entirely isolated from the rest of the world, golfing or otherwise. Aside from whatever one's problems may be on the golf course—and at Number 2 they can often be most humiliating—there is an atmosphere of peace and solitude that is seldom found in golf or any other social game. The course opens with

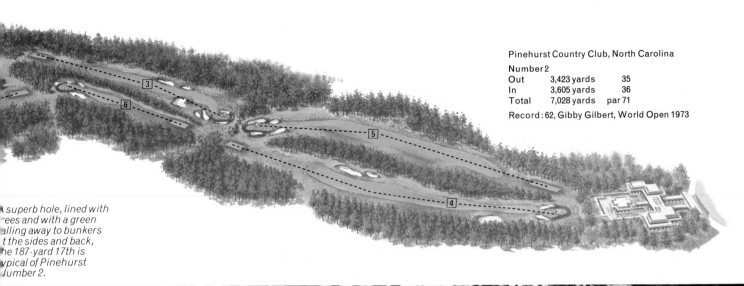

Pinehurst Country Club, North Carolina

Number 2
Out	3,423 yards	35
In	3,605 yards	36
Total	7,028 yards	par 71

Record: 62, Gibby Gilbert, World Open 1973

A superb hole, lined with
trees and with a green
falling away to bunkers
at the sides and back,
the 187-yard 17th is
typical of Pinehurst
Number 2.

▷ a rather uncomplicated hole of 414 yards, which places no great premium on distance and with plenty of fairway space on which to unlimber. The only really serious trouble is the boundary fence that runs the length of the 1st and 2nd holes on the left but not unduly close to the line of play.

At the 2nd the distance begins to build, and here is a hole requiring a strong second shot. At the 3rd, a shortish two-shotter, finesse suddenly comes into play, and the emphasis is on strategy, with a birdie awaiting those who have their shots under control. The 4th and 5th are played over the only hilly portion of the course, the 4th providing the first of three par-fives that can be reached in two with a couple of very well-executed shots. In fact, the 10th is the only one of the four three-shotters that the big player cannot expect to reach in two if he is on his stick. The length of Number 2 is not to be found in the par-fours nor even in unusually long par-threes (the longest of these is 216 yards) but in the two-shotters, most of them calling for a big drive and a powerful second.

Unlike so many of the better American park-

When the World Golf Hall of Fame was opened at Pinehurst in 1974 Walter Hagen was an automatic choice by the Golf Writers of America as one of the thirteen initial members. Winner of four British Opens, two US Opens and five USPGA titles, the extrovert Hagen was without peer in the ranks of professional golf in the 1920s.

land courses, Pinehurst is virtually without water. The only water hole is the 16th, where a small pond in front of the tee requires a carry of no more than 180 yards on the proper line of play, yet the water does serve to fashion the tee shot and increase the problems of mound and bunker beyond. This is the second of a stretch of

four closing holes that make Number 2 one of the most exciting courses for tournament play that exists in America.

Probably because it is somewhat off the beaten path and remote from any of the large population centres, it has not entertained nearly the amount of national championship and international golf that it deserves. Its first major championship was the 1936 PGA, which was a matchplay event in those days and neither dependent on, nor expectant of, large galleries. The Ryder Cup matches brought international golf in 1951, and in 1962 the Amateur championship was played there for the first and only time thus far.

Since 1901, however, the North and South championship, an amateur tournament ranking in prestige only just below the national Amateur championship itself, has been played annually at Pinehurst, first on the rather short Number 1 course but since 1909 on Number 2. In 1903, the North and South Open was inaugurated there too, but as the purses and galleries of professional golf became the paramount concern following World War II, the latter event was

The 5th and the 8th: Fairest of the fair

Although the 438-yard 5th is not the longest par-four on the course, the player is probably more aware of distance there than at the longer 8th, and it is certainly more demanding. The drive, over a quietly rising crest of fairway towards a gentle valley beyond, is the only blind one on the course, but is in no way distracting because of it. According to the length of the tee shot the second can be anything from wood to medium iron and is a most exacting stroke. The green, which leans towards the player, is angled away to the left on rising ground with large bunkers on either hand. Unless the approach is played from the right side of the fairway there is no clear entrance to the green, and the shot must carry the forward of the left-hand bunkers. The 5th is a truly beautiful hole, as indeed are all the par-fours, not one of which is similar to the others.

The 8th hole, a par-four of 464 yards from the championship tee, plunges into a long valley from where the fairway rises smoothly to a green which,

because of its slight elevation above the surrounding land, will only hold a truly struck shot. Such greens are a notable feature of Donald Ross's design. His intention was that a good shot should always be rewarded but that the fractionally erring one, leaking a little either way, would tend to slip off the putting surface. Punishment for missing his greens usually is not too severe but recovery can involve a variety of shots and decisions as to the most effective one to use—chips, little throw-up pitches, even bumbles with a putter. Ross had no call to protect his greens with thick fringes, common to many American courses, which can harshly penalize a good shot which is no more than a matter of inches too strong or too wide.

Pinehurst Number 2 is a monument to the genius of Ross, who spoke of it as being "the fairest test of championship golf I have ever designed". Even the most carping of professional golfers could hardly disagree, and the 5th and 8th holes are striking examples of Ross's skill.

The drive at the 5th left, is blind, but should be long because of the exacting second into an angled green.

bandoned. It will be remembered in the record books largely for the 1940 renewal, which was the first professional tournament won by Ben Hogan at the start of his fabulous string of victories that were to extend for the succeeding fourteen years. The World Open was played here for the first time in 1973 and for it the par-five 8th hole was shortened by some twenty yards to make it a par-four of 464 yards. Gibby Gilbert set the record of 62 for this par 71 course. His score was equalled by Tom Watson, the eventual winner.

Nowadays the golf at Pinehurst is largely social. Particularly in the fall and spring when the Carolina climate is propitious, groups of friends will travel to Pinehurst from all over the eastern and southern part of the country to spend a few days in the soothing environs of Pinehurst's peaceful little village, living quietly in one of the numerous little inns or the large and stately Hotel California, playing golf by day and talking golf well into the evening. For aside from the splendid testing qualities of Number 2, there are currently five other excellent eighteen-hole courses of considerably less rigour fanning

Patty Berg, right, and "Babe" Zaharias were the first women elected to the World Golf Hall of Fame. Four times world champion, Miss Berg has been a leading figure in women's golf ever since she first reached the final of the US Amateur in 1935 at the age of seventeen. Glenna Collette Vare and Joyce Wethered were elected in 1975.

out from the pleasant clubhouse on the hill.

Since James W. Tufts first conceived this semi-paradisical retreat for winter-bound New Englanders, four generations of the Tufts family have taken an active part in the development of the community. To the world of golf, the best-known of these is James W's grandson, Richard

S. Tufts, a man who has served the USGA selflessly for several decades in numerous capacities, including the presidency. Among his many great services to amateur golf was his contribution to the unification and standardization of the USGA and Royal and Ancient versions of the Rules of Golf and the inauguration of the World Amateur Team Championship, known as the Eisenhower Trophy.

In the late 1960s the Pinehurst Country Club was purchased by the Diamond Head Corporation, a real-estate company with holdings all over the country. The resort continues to be developed but its character has not been altered. There has been one notable addition. In view of its association with the early years of golf in the United States, Pinehurst is a fitting site for the World Golf Hall of Fame which was opened in September 1974 by President Ford. The building is an imposing structure, colonnaded and massive but pleasingly simple in design. Embraced by pools and fountains, it stands in the tranquil pine forest close to the Number 2 course, an enduring monument to the most eminent figures in the history of the game.

The 10th: Ward finds Hogan at his peak

For a golf course so famous and so hallowed, Pinehurst Number 2 has played host to surprisingly few major golf events. The most prestigious competition ever held there was the 1951 Ryder Cup, which the United States won over Great Britain and Ireland by nine to two. In the singles, always played over thirty-six holes, it became the unhappy duty of Charley Ward to face Ben Hogan, then at the absolute peak of his game. Everything went along swimmingly for Ward until they reached the 10th hole—par-five, 596 yards—during the second round. Ward stood only one down and, when Hogan hit a darting hook into the thick pines on the left, it looked very much as though he would draw level or even pick up a badly needed point for his side.

Hogan stomped into the trees, grim as ever. It appeared as though his only hope would be to chip out, take a bogey, and lose the hole. But no, not Ben Hogan. Somewhere in those trees he found an opening no wider than a rain-barrel. He took out

his wedge, stuck his ball through that opening and so advanced forty yards. However, he still stood 280 yards from the green, two-thirds of which is guarded in front by a bunker. Hogan crushed a 2-wood that drew into that one-third of the green which is open, leaving himself a sixty-foot putt. He holed it to not only save the hole but to win it. Ward threw up his arms in despair: "What", he seemed to be saying, "do you have to do to win a hole from this man?" Hogan won the match three and two. Under the circumstances, that four on the 10th has to be counted as a very fine birdie, even by Hogan's exacting standards.

The 10th provides a good example of the Pinehurst finish: an elevated, contoured green prefaced by carefully placed bunkers. As Sam Snead remarked: "You won't see any pitch-and-putt scramblers winning here."

Scottish-style mounds are a distinctive feature of the green entrances on Number 2, the result of Donald Ross's years

at Dornoch, while the penalizing rough lurking off the fairways (this is on the 13th) puts a real premium on accuracy.

A flawless setting for high drama

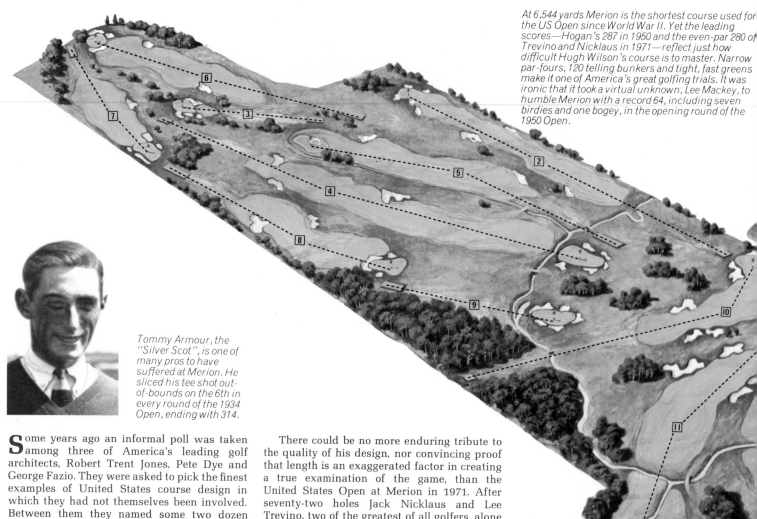

At 6,544 yards Merion is the shortest course used for the US Open since World War II. Yet the leading scores—Hogan's 287 in 1950 and the even-par 280 of Trevino and Nicklaus in 1971—reflect just how difficult Hugh Wilson's course is to master. Narrow par-fours, 120 telling bunkers and tight, fast greens make it one of America's great golfing trials. It was ironic that it took a virtual unknown, Lee Mackey, to humble Merion with a record 64, including seven birdies and one bogey, in the opening round of the 1950 Open.

Tommy Armour, the "Silver Scot", is one of many pros to have suffered at Merion. He sliced his tee shot out-of-bounds on the 6th in every round of the 1934 Open, ending with 314.

Some years ago an informal poll was taken among three of America's leading golf architects, Robert Trent Jones, Pete Dye and George Fazio. They were asked to pick the finest examples of United States course design in which they had not themselves been involved. Between them they named some two dozen courses, but agreed unanimously on only six: Pine Valley, Augusta National, Seminole, Pebble Beach, Pinehurst Number 2 and Merion.

Ironically enough, four of those six had been designed by complete architectural amateurs. Pine Valley had been almost wholly laid out by a Philadelphian, George Crump; Augusta National was Bobby Jones's first try at architecture (although with the inestimable counsel of Alister Mackenzie); Pebble Beach was designed by Jack Neville and Douglas Grant, two amateur players from California; and Merion was the first effort of a transplanted Scot, Hugh Wilson, a member of the old West course when it was affiliated to the Merion Cricket Club, whose members at the time wanted a championship layout. They dispatched young Wilson to Scotland and England to take a post-graduate course in British linksland before transforming a section of Philadelphia's Main Line—the long stretch of the city's socially élite suburbs—into a "golf links" no proper Philadelphian would be ashamed of. Since that time Wilson's parkland course has been host to more USGA championships—fourteen—than any other course. It remains the only complete course that Wilson was to write his name to, for he died at the relatively young age of forty-six and was never able to pursue his newly found vocation.

There could be no more enduring tribute to the quality of his design, nor convincing proof that length is an exaggerated factor in creating a true examination of the game, than the United States Open at Merion in 1971. After seventy-two holes Jack Nicklaus and Lee Trevino, two of the greatest of all golfers, alone had matched the par of 280 in conditions that were uniformly fair throughout.

For that Open, Merion measured 6,544 yards, only twelve yards longer than the shortest course used for the championship since World War I, and hundreds shorter than most of the others. Out of that length, 1,135 yards were contained in the only two par-fives, the 2nd and the 4th. Merion is a classic example of a course that encourages attack but rewards only those with the skill to hold its fairways and strike the ball truly from them—as well as the nerve to putt greens that are as swift as ice.

The greens are, of course, the heart of the matter. In 1971 they were superbly prepared by Richard Ballantine, who succeeded his father as course superintendent—in sixty years the club has had only the two. Only approaches struck with maximum spin would check on the flawless surfaces, and this was not possible from the rough. As always at Merion, accuracy and touch were of the essence, and they made for a well-nigh perfect championship.

Bobby Jones played in his first Amateur championship at Merion, leading the field after the first of the two qualifying rounds. This happened in the autumn of 1916 when Jones was a lad of fourteen, standing all of five feet four inches but weighing a chunky 165 pounds

(in contrast to the spindly, sickly boy who had been practically pushed on to his neighbourhood golf course—East Lake near Atlanta—because his father had feared he would be forever frail). Young Jones led the field after the first round, played over the old West course. He shot a 74, ridiculously high by today's standards, but it was good enough. He was playing speedy bent grass greens, not the coarse and harsh Bermuda green of his native south, for the first time in his life.

The speed of the old West course's greens set a standard that Merion has had ever since

Olin Dutra (left) made up eight shots over the last thirty-six holes to win the 1934 Open at Merion.

Card of the course

No 1	355 yards	par 4
No 2	535 yards	par 5
No 3	183 yards	par 3
No 4	600 yards	par 5
No 5	426 yards	par 4
No 6	420 yards	par 4
No 7	350 yards	par 4
No 8	360 yards	par 4
No 9	195 yards	par 3
No 10	312 yards	par 4
No 11	370 yards	par 4
No 12	405 yards	par 4
No 13	129 yards	par 3
No 14	414 yards	par 4
No 15	378 yards	par 4
No 16	430 yards	par 4
No 17	224 yards	par 3
No 18	458 yards	par 4

Merion Golf Club, Ardmore

East course		
Out	3,424 yards	36
In	3,120 yards	34
Total	6,544 yards	par 70

Golf Course Road in Ardmore, which borders the Merion course, is now often referred to as "Beman's Road" since Deane Beman slashed his tee shot over it on the 15th during the third round of the 1966 US Amateur. The hook began a slide that cost the former champion a five-stroke lead and, finally, the title itself.

Touches that mould tradition

In his determination to make Merion East a course apart, Hugh Wilson concerned himself with the kind of detail that so many other architects ignore. Over the years these touches have conspired with momentous golfing events to create a tradition at Merion that is rare among American courses. One of Wilson's ideas, which he picked up from Sunningdale in Berkshire during his long pilgrimage to Britain, was to do away with flags and to mark the holes with wicker baskets atop the usual flagsticks. For many years the baskets were woven in the maintenance shop at Merion.

Although now out of favour elsewhere, wicker baskets were once widely used in Britain because they could be seen from any angle and did not aid a player in judging wind direction and strength. In the unlikely, but not entirely inconceivable, event of a ball lodging in a basket, the Rules of Golf permit the player to remove the ball and, without penalty, place it on the edge of the hole.

The 6th of the West was a short par-four, which Jones hit with a drive and a mere pitch with his niblick. The ball ended thirty feet past the flagstick. Forgetting that he was no longer playing on his home greens, Jones hit a horrifying putt that sailed back past the cup, over the green, and into a brook in front of it. That afternoon, the "Kid from Dixie" had to play the newer East course. Suffering from stage-fright, he shot 89, with every golf fan in Philadelphia and every sports-writer in America peering over his shoulder at every stroke.

Jones went out of the competition in the quarter-final, defeated by Bob Gardner, the reigning champion. Eight years later, again at Merion, he won the first of his record five US Amateur titles and in 1930 the last of them, achieving the Grand Slam in the process.

If the years of Jones were enough for any course to achieve immortality, 1950 brought a new drama to the old links—an unknown, Lee Mackey, broke the US Open record with a first round of 64. But a colossus, Ben Hogan, was to bestride the stage that year like some golfing Caesar, casting Mackey's moment of glory into deep shadow.

Little more than a year before, Hogan had been badly hurt when the car in which he and his wife were travelling collided head-on with a bus. Only a man of indomitable fortitude could have returned to golf as quickly as Hogan did and he was still in considerable pain when the Open began at Merion in 1950.

He played through the competition in great discomfort, at one time stopping the car taking him back to the hotel because he felt so ill. On the final day, the Open reached its climax and Hogan reached for his astonishing reserves of courage. There were two rounds left, thirty-six ▷

▷ holes. Hogan managed the first round with a 72, suffering no ill effects. As a precautionary measure during the afternoon round, he had his caddie pick the ball out of the cup for him so he would not have to aggravate the pain in his legs by bending over.

He made the turn in 36; par on the back nine would give him a winning score of 282, four under the 286 which he had anticipated would be enough to triumph.

As he started the final nine he was seized by an extreme cramp in his left leg. By the time he reached the 13th green near the clubhouse, the pain had become so acute that he thought about withdrawing—not because he did not think he could win, but because he didn't think he could walk, much less play.

That he did not withdraw is now history, and he stumbled home with a total of 287, level with George Fazio and Lloyd Mangrum. When he won the play-off next day it was an anticlimax, the dénouement taking place on the 16th green when Mangrum was penalized two strokes for blowing a bug off his ball. Hogan then rang down the curtain by scoring a birdie-two on the 230-yard par-three 17th with a 4-wood and a sixty-foot putt, for the second and greatest of his four Open wins.

Ten years later Jack Nicklaus, then a young amateur, shot the course over four rounds in 269, eighteen strokes better than Hogan had scored in 1950. American golf history has marched on at Merion.

In a sense Merion is old-fashioned. It covers no more than 110 acres, compared with the 250 acres most American courses take in order to

An aerial view of the front nine. The 9th, (lower left) is typical of Wilson's tight greens, guarded by brook, lagoon and several bunkers.

accommodate the trappings now needed to back a golf course project financially.

There are 120 bunkers, which may seem a lot until compared with the 280 that Oakmont once had and to those on the Old course at St Andrews. Hugh Wilson placed each one exactly where it ought to be. When Chick Evans won the US Amateur there in 1916, he nicknamed them the "white faces of Merion" after the glaring sand from a nearby quarry with which they had been filled.

Merion straddles Ardmore Avenue, and the first hole goes directly towards it. Eleven holes—the 2nd to the 12th—lie on the other side. There are only two holes at Merion, the 2nd and the 4th, which play to a par of five. On the back nine there are none—hence the par of 70.

The first hole is a short par-four—as an opening hole should be—bending slightly to the right but not quite enough to be classified as a dog-leg. The green is clearly visible from the tee, but so are nine bunkers, most of them on the right side of the fairway to snare a slice. Once they are bypassed only a pitch to the green is left.

Across Ardmore Avenue there is a completely different style of hole: a skinny, 535-yard par-five uphill, with out-of-bounds all the way along the right side. Then follows a fairly long par-three—not quite 200 yards—to a large green that is hard to miss. This, in turn, is followed by the longest hole on the course, a par-five of 600 yards. It is straightaway and bunkered only for the most errant shot—two pleasant, straight woods followed by a 6- or 7-iron across a thin stream to a very deep green. It is guarded to the rear and on both sides by six bunkers to trap the foolhardy who try to reach the green in two.

Four par-fours follow. All are of medium length, the longest being the 5th, 426 yards but with very little bunkering, and the shortest the 7th, a mere 350 yards. The 6th and 7th present no sand problems off the tee, but they are very strategically trapped around the greens. Hugh Wilson never put a single extraneous bunker into Merion; despite the fact that there are 120 of them, every single one is for play, not display.

The 8th hole is a perfect example of his use of sandtraps. There is a bunker short to the right of the fairway for the slicer and another far to the left for the hooker. In other words, the short hitter has to be aware of the first trap and the long hitter, ignoring the first, has to be aware of the second. If both are avoided only a short iron is left, since the hole is only 360 yards long. Here, Wilson formed a snake-like trap to protect the entire front of the panhandle green, the handle of which faces the player. If the pin is on the handle, it is one of the most challenging and

Chick Evans followed his 1916 Open win with the Amateur title when he coined the phrase, the "white faces of Merion" for Hugh Wilson's traps.

nerve-racking par-fours to be found anywhere.

The par-three 9th is some 195 yards long, but the tee shot is from a hill to a green in a small valley so it requires less club than that distance usually calls for. A brook, and a lagoon which spurs off it, have to be carried; but they lie well short of the huge green, which is guarded by six bunkers to the left, right and rear.

From the 9th green there is a walk up a hill to the 10th tee. At 312 yards and a par of four, it falls just short of being a joke—until played. Big hitters have often driven nearly hole-high, only to find themselves with a pitch as delicate as picking up a teacup filled to the brim. Both sides of the green are edged by sand, and the oblong green has a dozen varieties of pin positions.

The golfer now faces the 11th, which is played in the opposite direction and, at 370 yards, is really not much longer than the 10th. The tee shot is into a slight valley and the pitch, although not overly long, is across a creek to a green banked with rocks. In 1930 Bobby Jones —having won the British Amateur at St Andrews, the British Open at Hoylake and the US Open at Interlachen—then stood dormie-eight on Eugene Homans, needing only a niblick shot to the green to be the first and only man to have won all four championships in a single season. He flicked the ball upon the green, took two putts to halve with Homans and so won, 8 and 7, to ensure himself a place in golf history. It took a body of marines to protect him from the slaps on the back and the handshakes of the immense gallery.

The 11th was also the scene of a moment of comedy during the US Open four years later. Bobby Cruickshank—the "Wee Scot", as he affectionately came to be known in America— was very much in contention. After a good drive into the valley he had to carry the brook in front of the green. He hit his approach to the green a little "fat"; the ball plopped into the water.

To everyone's astonishment it hit a rock in the brook and bounded on to the green. Cruickshank was so elated that he threw his niblick into the air and turned to the gallery in disbelief. As everybody cheered the club fell and ▷

The 1st: 355 yards par 4

0 yds   100 yds

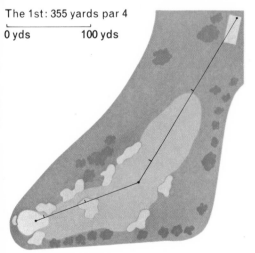

The 1st: An elusive touch of poetry

Almost anyone can design a par-five or a par-four that can only be reached in regulation figures by the supremely long hitters and seldom by the average player. The same holds true for a par-three that will accept only one shot. But it takes a touch of the poet to lay out a short par-four like the 1st at Merion, a mere 355 yards long but one of the great opening holes in golf.

It is a dog-leg to the right, in which the only problem for the average golfer lies in his tendency to slice. The hole has no fewer than nine bunkers, only three of which are on the left, two alongside the fairway and one beside the green. A solitary trap lies in the middle of the fairway, but it is far out of reach of the amateur.

All the others line the right side of the fairway clear to the green, which is so exquisitely contoured that it contains half a dozen different pin positions. The putting surface is pear shaped and slopes

gently from right to left and from the front to the back, where there is a tiny, shallow trap. Thus, while the second shot may be nothing more than a mere pitch, it must be very exact. For the professional the problems from the tee are somewhat different. He must see that he does not drive into the two bunkers on the left, since he is more prone to hook, or right through the very broad fairway into the rough, which contains a series of mounds from which it is a near impossibility to pitch anywhere near the flagstick.

Many of the holes at Merion have more instant appeal but the golfer who plays there regularly finds that he appreciates more and more the subtleties of the 1st. It combines the two most difficult objectives sought by a master architect: a great opening hole, and a great short par-four. That achievement alone shows why Hugh Wilson was able to build such intricate poetry into the design of the Merion course.

The 18th: A fitting finale for a superb course

From the back tee deep in the woods the 18th at Merion is like looking along a gun barrel. The distant crest of the fairway falls to a valley and then rises to a hump-backed green, its entrance protected on both sides by bunkers. Some 460 yards long, it is a supreme finishing hole. Legend has it that Paul Runyan, realizing that he probably would not reach the championship tee (a carry of more than 200 yards), pitched to one of the forward tees. From there he played a fairway wood: a unique way of tackling a long par-four.

The lovely hole has been the setting for two of the greatest iron shots ever struck in the clutch of a championship. In the 1950 US Open Ben Hogan limped out of the shadows to the sunlit fairway knowing that he needed a four to tie with Lloyd Mangrum and George Fazio. From a slightly downhill stance he struck a perfect 1-iron to the green. It was the last time he ever used the club. A golf bandit stole it while Hogan was signing his card and his caddie was not looking.

Years later an English writer somewhat daringly asked Hogan whether he had any doubt that he would not strike the shot well. The reply was the briefest of negatives, followed by the comment that he had meant to fade the shot but it flew straight. Doubtless Hogan, the ultimate technician, planned for a winning birdie, as Jack Nicklaus certainly did in the Open twenty-one years later.

Nicklaus needed a four to tie with Trevino. So vast was the drive that rocketed out of the woods that he was left with a much steeper downhill stance than he would have liked but, like Hogan, he hit a flawless stroke. Had the 4-iron pitched a foot or so from where it did it would have finished very close to the hole, instead of a dozen feet away. The putt just missed and a great round by Trevino was justly rewarded.

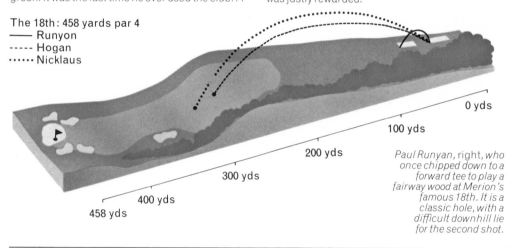

The 18th: 458 yards par 4
—— Runyon
----- Hogan
······ Nicklaus

0 yds
100 yds
200 yds
300 yds
400 yds
458 yds

Paul Runyan, right, who once chipped down to a forward tee to play a fairway wood at Merion's famous 18th. It is a classic hole, with a difficult downhill lie for the second shot.

▷ hit him squarely on the head, knocking him to his knees. "Aye," said Bobby as he rubbed his head, "that's the first time I've made a par hitting two rocks on the same hole."

The 12th is again a drive off a high tee, with no drastic situations for the moderately straight driver. There are bunkers to the left but they are of no concern to the long hitter—mainly because they serve as hazards for the short hitter off the parallel 11th. The hole is a dog-leg to the right where there are trees which cannot be carried and which therefore dictate the placing of the drive. The second shot is uphill, thus compensating for the downhill tee shot, and the long green now facing the golfer is bounded everywhere except in front by bunkers, all of which drop off quickly into rough.

The green sits alongside Ardmore Avenue and may be unique in that it is probably the only putting surface that lies not two feet from out-of-bounds. Walter Hagen, one of the most delicate putters who ever lived, once overhit his putt and rolled it into the street—thus leaving him with another improbable record: the first important player in a major contest to hit a putt out-of-bounds!

Next to the 7th at Pebble Beach, where the wind is always a major consideration, the 13th at Merion—only 129 yards long—may be the most stringent par-three in America. It is a mere pitch to the green, but it has to be perfect because there is no margin for error whatsoever. Directly in front of the green is one of those "white faces" and to the left and behind it are three more, staring like ghosts. The putting surface is wide but not deep, and a misjudged shot or mishit is certain to find one of them. Since the first is so deep and the others slanted, getting out and on to the green presents an even more tender shot than that which has to be played off the tee.

The next two holes, both par-fours, are tightened by a road down the left side which is out-of-bounds. For the 1971 Open the 14th played at 414 yards, some thirty yards shorter than its full length. The hole dog-legs left and from the back of the tee the trees on the left emphasize the need to draw the ball round the corner and clear of the traps on the right. The second shot requires only a mid iron to an oval green, protected by three sprawling traps. The 15th is another drive and a mid iron. It dog-legs to the right and the well-placed drive has to carry two traps on that side to open up the green, which is angled diagonally across the line. Two traps flank the left side and a large bunker eats into the front, making it very difficult to go for the pin when it is placed anywhere on the right side of the green.

The last three holes at Merion provide a great championship finish. The "quarry hole"—the 16th—is 430 yards long off an elevated tee through a valley which stops at an old overgrown quarry which, fortunately, cannot be reached with the drive; the second is the worrying shot—anything from a 4-iron to a 4-wood is needed and the golfer has to succeed in carrying the green on the fly.

The 17th, played in the reverse direction, is the 224-yard par-three where Hogan made his momentous two in the play-off for the 1950 US Open. The quarry lies at the foot of the tee, but does not have to be taken into account any more than it does at the 18th, which again comes back across it. The 18th is 458 yards long, calling for a wood shot—or at least a long iron—to the green. It is immortalized in a photograph of Hogan making his second shot to the green with a 1-iron. It was the last time he used the club, for as he signed his card it was carried off by a souvenir hunter.

One of the men Hogan beat in that historic play-off was George Fazio, now a noted golf architect and course adviser to the United States Golf Association. Nobody is more qualified than he to assess Merion, which he rates alongside Pine Valley as the kind of course he most admires. Why? "It has character," he says. "It is challenging, without being backbreaking."

The deepest South gets its first great course

The Atlantic Ocean and the Florida beach provide a magnificent backdrop to the 13th, left, and 16th greens at Seminole. Both are slightly elevated and guarded by some of the most awkward of the course's numerous sandtraps. The tight approach shot at the 16th—the second half of a sharp dog-leg—is made even more difficult by the breeze off the sea, which can become quite strong in the afternoons. The greens, subject to a constant barrage of salt spray, are some of the truest to be found anywhere in the golfing world.

Golf in the tropical climate of southern Florida is a seasonal thing except to a few natives who are so addicted to the game that they will forsake their air-conditioning for the Turkish-bath atmosphere of the months from May through October. This is particularly true in such purely resort towns as Palm Beach, where all the expensive shops are locked and shuttered shortly after Easter, not to reopen again until after Thanksgiving in November. During the dead months, when their members are in the northern states or the spas of Europe, clubs like Seminole tend their courses only just enough to prevent them from running to seed. It is, then, something of a miracle that the best of these courses—and there is none better than Seminole—can be brought to such a peak of perfection for the short winter season.

It is a characteristic of many truly superior golf courses that one dedicated man will have given an immense amount of his time and energy to the pampering and nursing and cosseting of his special favourite as if it were an overly precious child. For many years, Seminole was so pampered by a singularly devoted golfer named Christopher J. Dunphy, who had been a close friend of and uncompromising competitor against just about all the leading amateurs and professionals of his time. In fact, when one thought of Seminole, one thought of Chris Dunphy.

Dunphy's love affair with golf began in earnest soon after World War I. He was employed at the time by Mr Edward B. McLean, the wealthy Cincinnati newspaper publisher who was himself a golfer of great enthusiasm, so in his younger days Dunphy was able to spend a good deal of his leisure on the famous courses of America and Europe in company with his employer. After McLean's death, Dunphy and his wife settled down in Palm Beach, and Dunphy began to spend more and more of his time playing at Seminole.

The club had been built in the 1920s during that ripe period in American life when it seemed that millionaires bloomed like wild flowers and money flowed as bountifully as the Mississippi. The course was laid out by Donald Ross, who was the architect for so many of the outstanding courses on the East Coast of the United States when golf was first attracting the fancy of the leisure class. With assistance from a former ▷

The 15th: Safe way for those lacking strength
Seminole, although measuring nearly 6,800 yards, makes a far greater demand on accuracy and intelligence than brute strength. This, undoubtedly, was why Hogan, when asked which was his favourite course, said that he thought Seminole gave him most of what he sought in a course. With his ruthlessly precise approach to golf he would appreciate the emphasis on placing the shots, the beautifully defined targets and the fairness of the challenge.

From the tee, one can cut off as much distance as one feels capable of across the pond that separates the tee from the fairway on the crescent-shaped, rightward-turning hole. The very short hitter has been given a narrow strip of fairway to the

left of the pond requiring no carry over the water at all, but the premium is offered to he who will gamble on carrying the greatest expanse of water. The second shot, too, is over water that separates the fairway from the green, but again there is a safe—and much longer—route to the left of the water. Thus, he who will risk the water with two very long shots has a good chance to reach the green the short way in two, but the more cautious who wish to avoid the water may find it takes them four shots before they begin their putting. It is one of the triumphs of Seminole's design that it almost always offers a safe way of avoiding the trouble to anyone who lacks either the strength or the nerve to battle its hazards. But, for the truly brave, the rewards can be sweet indeed.

The 15th green can be reached in two shots, *both over water, or, by the safe route, in four.*

▷ Tennessee mountaineer, T. Claiborn Watson, Ross designed a true linksland course over the Florida sand ridges adjacent to the Atlantic Ocean some fifteen miles north of the exclusive Palm Beach winter colony, where the new millionaires from the industrial north had erected their suitably sumptuous pleasure domes. At the time, the club was no more than a half-hour's drive from the colony over an uncrowded highway.

Ross and Watson's course was the first truly fine test of golf in that southernmost part of America, but the exclusive and expensive nature of the club was such that only a few of the very rich ever had a chance to play it. From the back tees it was a long course, but its principal feature was its profligate use of large bunkers covered with snow-white sand. Even today, Seminole's bunkers, which have grown to more than 200 in number, are the most

Typically, this long, irregular bunker—one of three guarding the 9th green—offers some chance of escape.

Dominated by 200-odd bunkers and traps, a large central lake and swaying palms, Seminole is one of the most attractive of America's courses. It is also one of the most exclusive and it is unfortunate that the claims made for it by regular visitors like Armour and Hogan have never been really tested in tournament conditions.

Seminole Golf Club, Palm Beach, Florida

Out	3,458 yards	36
In	3,320 yards	36
Total	6,778 yards	par 72

Record: 60, Claude Harmon, 1948

conspicuous feature of the course. They are everywhere, and on some holes one seems almost to be playing from island to island of grass across an ocean of sand.

As was the case with so many of the enterprises of America's wealthy businessmen, the fortunes of Seminole declined during the great Depression, but the club survived through the attention of a few deeply devoted members. When World War II left it with virtually no patronage, there was some question whether it would survive. It was at the end of this bleak period that Dunphy appeared on the scene and restored the Seminole course and club to its former glory—and then some.

The war over, members began to drift back to Palm Beach, and a whole new generation of the rich started to discover the area as a winter playground. It was then that Dunphy assumed the role of Seminole's *ex officio* ringmaster. He introduced the new to the old. He made sure that anyone who appeared on the scene at lunchtime was certain of a good match that afternoon. More important, however, he spent countless hours with Watson, who had remained on as

greenkeeper ever since the course was first built, restoring and improving Seminole. New hybrid grasses of the Bermuda strain were added to the fairways and greens to give them added firmness and depth and to keep them in first-class playing condition during the latter part of the season when the less hardy grasses begin to die out. As a result, the ball sits up on the Seminole fairways as if it had been ever so gently placed on a soft cushion. The greens, with their Bermuda base, are large with subtle borrows, averaging around 7,500 to 8,000 square feet, and they are as true as any greens can be in that humid region with its constant spray of salty mist from the ocean.

Life at Seminole during the "season" has a most opulent feel to it. The large, Spanish-style clubhouse is most attractively furnished, and the lunchtime meals are on a par with anything at the finest metropolitan restaurants. The men's locker-room is a model of its kind and has been imitated by other clubs around the country. The lockers, which are built into the walls, are made of a darkly stained wood, and there is comfortable, heavily upholstered furni-

ture in the centre of the room where the golfers like to gather for their drinks and post-mortems. A small bar at one end of the room takes care of the needs of the inner man.

In this setting on an average day one is apt to find a great many of the captains of American industry and a sizeable collection of the most celebrated names of wealth and society, as well as innumerable presidents of large corporations. Bing Crosby is apt to be there from time to time and, during March each year, one used to find the indestructible Ben Hogan practising relentlessly morning and afternoon for his first competitive appearance of the year—at the Masters tournament.

Although the use of the course is confined almost entirely to that very exclusive list of the privileged from which its membership is drawn, most of the leading professionals had a shot at it until the club's annual professional-amateur tournament was discontinued in 1960. It was a fascinating event in several ways, not the least of which was the large Calcutta pool that preceded the two-day event. Although no records are kept on such matters, it was

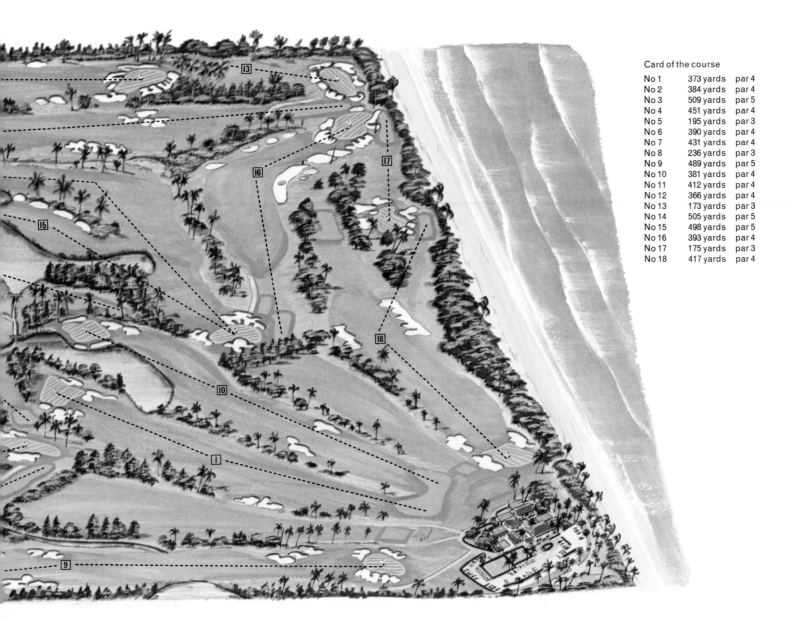

Described by Ben Hogan as "the best par-four in the world", the 6th at Seminole has a daunting array of strategically placed fairway bunkers.

generally regarded as the largest pool connected with any tournament in the country during its time, invariably reaching several hundred thousand dollars.

It was always interesting, however, to see the professionals struggling with Seminole's complex design of sand and water, and it should be noted that few of them ever dominated it. None the less, the course will—as all good courses should—give way to superior golf. Claude Harmon, who was for many years the distinguished resident professional at Seminole in the winter months, once scored a 60 there for the course record. A map of his remarkable round hangs on the clubhouse wall.

The sight of the Seminole course on a balmy winter day with a brisk afternoon wind blowing in off the Atlantic is one to be cherished. The lovely sweep of the rolling green fairways, punctuated by the multitude of dazzling white bunkers and the tall palms leaning with the breeze, is one of the most spectacular vistas to be found in this flat, tropical country, the highest point of which is only sixty-five feet above sea-level. It is a wide open course with very

little of the tough, scrubby underbrush that characterizes so many Florida courses. The stray shot is far more likely to come to grief in a bunker than anywhere else, but the tall palms and the stubby palmettos are nevertheless a hazard on many of the holes.

Finally, there is an unforgettable pair of closing holes running alongside the dunes that separate the course from the sea. The 17th, a par-three, plays almost always into the wind from an elevated tee to an elevated green with a vast amount of sand falling away on three sides and the thick tangle of sea-grape bushes on the ocean side. As Dunphy once put it, "It is a rare sight to see all four balls of a match on the green at once." The 18th is a very long shot from an elevated tee to the elbow of the fairway below, and then a long iron or fairway wood uphill to a splendid green nestling against the sea-grapes atop the dune. A par is dearly bought here, too.

The strength of Seminole and its fascination to dedicated golfers was summed up by Ben Hogan when he said: "If you can play well there, you can play well anywhere." Every golfer finds that kind of challenge irresistible.

George Crump's 184-acre bunker

Pine Valley's reputation as the toughest inland course in the world has never been tested in a major professional tournament, since there is virtually no room for spectators. But the evidence of visiting players is there: all testify to the constant pressure, the severe penalties, the unique challenge of every hole. One pro, after a disastrous encounter in its sandy soil, called it "a 184-acre bunker".

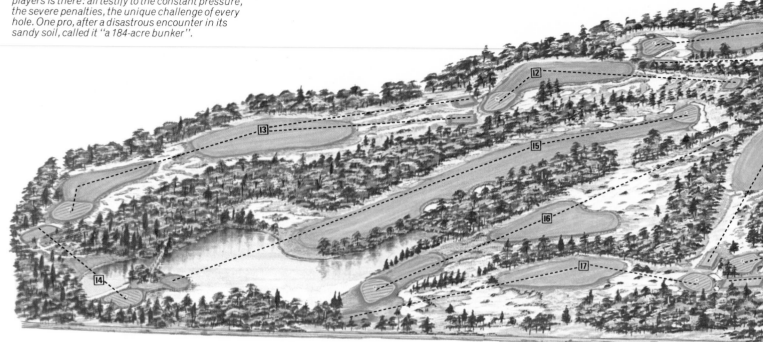

Pine Valley is the perfect example of penal architecture, the ultimate test for the giants of golf. It lies on the New Jersey side of Philadelphia and it is hard to believe that what is reputed to be the toughest course in the world could be located in such nondescript countryside: desolate enough in itself, and a wasteland of filling stations and billboards, dusty and tawdry and almost treeless—an environmentalist's nightmare.

Pine Valley may not be as tough to play as some British championship courses in a forty-knot wind, nor tougher than Pebble Beach in the near-gales which so often sweep that seaside course in winter. Yet it is assuredly the world's most challenging inland course—perhaps inevitably, when it was fashioned from such a landscape as this.

Each hole is a separate and distinct entity. No hole parallels another, and each is protected by huge tracts of pines, bushes, shrubs and jungle-like undergrowth. During the 1936 Walker Cup matches (the only championship ever played at Pine Valley, because it cannot accommodate spectators) a member of the British squad—P. B. "Laddie" Lucas, then only twenty-one years old—hit a wild slice directly into the woods.

"Watch it! Watch it!" he yelled at his caddie.

"You don't have to watch 'em here," the caddie replied nonchalantly. "Just listen for 'em."

Uniquely, Pine Valley has no fairways, no rough, no chipping surfaces, and no sandtraps in the accepted sense. The course itself is in effect one huge, 184-acre bunker. Since the whole Chinese Army couldn't keep it raked—

Philadelphia business-man George Crump, the prime mover behind Pine Valley.

even if it was available for a task of such capitalist decadence—nobody bothers to. On it are eighteen tees and eighteen greens, the more distant sets reached via islands of immaculate fair-green. Once off these verdant oases the player is either in the trees or inside a part of that apparently endless sand that has been designated a trap. The par-threes have nothing between the tees and the greens; the greens are hit on the fly—or else. Surrounding the greens and running right up against the putting surfaces are countless little potholes of sand,

some so steeply faced that it is often necessary to play away from the green in order eventually to get on to it.

Pine Valley took seven years to build. It was the brainchild of a Philadelphia hotelier, George Crump, who died in 1918 with only fourteen holes finished and the remaining four only roughly sketched out. It was completed in 1919. Notwithstanding its appalling penalties, it is not as tough a course as its reputation would suggest. Although the official course record has stood for many years at 67, one pro has shot it twice in 66. He did not mention the scores to any of the members for fear of not being invited back.

The chief reason most golfers fail at Pine Valley to score within ten or even twenty strokes of their regular game is psychological —the course simply terrifies them. For years they have heard of its fiendish hazards. After a few holes they discover they are even more frightening than they had been led to believe and desperation enters their play—backswings became as fast as a snap of the fingers, and follow-throughs do not pass the hip.

One story which Pine Valley members have been telling for years illustrates how easy, and yet how terrifying, the course can be. The late Woody Platt, a gifted local amateur who knew Pine Valley well, started off the 1st hole with a birdie-three, no easy task since the hole bends sharply to the right after the tee shot to a green that drops steeply into trouble on both sides and to the rear. Platt had hit a 4-iron for his second stroke.

The 2nd hole, which changes direction sharply to the left, is not long—only 367 yards.

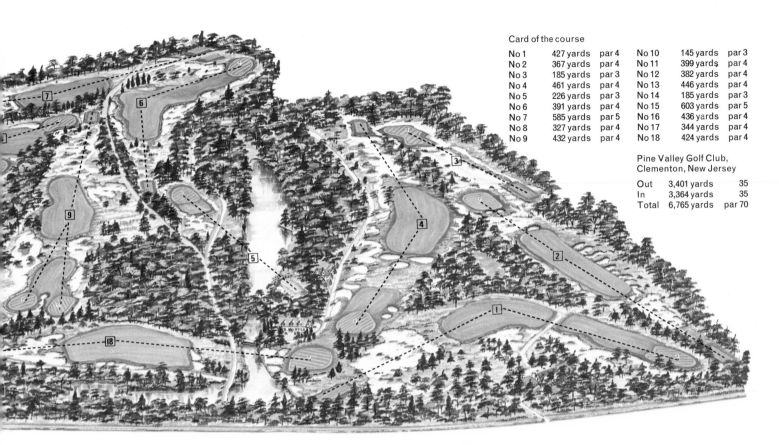

Pine Valley's 3rd hole is sand all the way from the tee down to a green which slopes from right to left. "The first time I played this hole," recalls golf writer Peter Allen, "I'd just got to the top of the swing as an Atlantic City express came by and the engineer pulled the whistle-cord for the level crossing; I topped it and took eleven to the hole without hitting another bad shot." Such is the penalizing power of the Pine Valley course.

But the tee shot—no topped shots here—must carry over 180 yards of sand peppered with lash traps completely along its right side. The green is highly elevated and, being almost completely surrounded by a wasteland of sand, it resembles a miniature Mount Suribachi. Platt hit a 7-iron into the hole for an eagle two.

The par-three 3rd is, like all the short holes at Pine Valley, strictly a one-shotter. There is nothing between the player and the green but sand. The green lies below the level of the tee and tilts sharply from right to left downhill.

Missing the green may mean six more shots to get back on to it. Platt solved the problem by the simple expedient of a hole in one.

The 4th hole is very long for a par-four: 461 yards. The tee shot is blind and the hole swerves slightly to the right. Sand is everywhere, as on every hole at Pine Valley, but it is not much of a factor here, lying just in front of the tee and way short of the green. Platt hit a driver and a 4-wood, and then holed a thirty-footer for a birdie. He was now six under par after only four holes of the roughest test of golf in the world.

The first four holes make a full circle back to the clubhouse. Platt now faced the prospect of playing the 5th, which juts out from behind the clubhouse and is easily one of the most stringent par-threes in the world. A huge bunker lies well short of the green, falling steeply to the right into saplings and undergrowth. If Platt's ball had bounced there, his main problem would have been in trying to find it. Since the hole is 226 yards long, the problem was compounded by the fact that he would have had to play a wood—probably a driver—off the tee.

Before facing the task, he decided to bolster his spirit with a drink in the clubhouse while he contemplated the dual problem of maintaining a pace of six under par and tackling the devilish 5th.

He never came out of the clubhouse.

At Pine Valley, golfers find their games falling apart with absolutely nothing at stake. People who are used to playing golf for hundreds of dollars find at Pine Valley that they cannot get their games in gear playing for matchsticks. The pines and oaks, firs and birches—which are actually well away from the trajectory of anything but a completely uncontrolled shot—now seem to form a corridor. The patches of fair-green, which will accept any moderately hit drive, now look as though they could not contain a 9-iron. And the greens, most of which cover a third of an acre, begin to look like watch crystals.

On precisely which hole this terror begins to strike the heart nobody ever knows. But it happens, almost invariably. Knowing this so well, the members at Pine Valley have a stand- ▷

The 7th: The evils of Hell's Half-Acre

George Crump was not the only architect to work on Pine Valley, for he had had the experienced guidance of the British architect H. S. Colt, whose most famous course in England was Sunningdale, near London. But it was Crump who drew up the first basic outline and the master plan, not to mention pouring $250,000 of his own money into it. Colt simply added the final touches that made it into a masterpiece of the macabre. When he died, Crump had not finished his outlines for the 12th to the 15th holes; that was done by Hugh Wilson—whose own masterpiece had been Merion—with the help of his brother Allen.

Nobody can be sure if there is even one hole which was Crump's work alone, but there is little doubt that the 7th is the hole of which he would be most proud. It may be the most exacting par-five in the world. Absolutely no mistakes may be made if that par is to be equalled, and it takes a minor miracle to score a birdie. At 585 yards, there are plenty of par-fives that are much longer. There are many that are much trickier. But there is none that requires three shots of the difficulty of those

needed to reach Pine Valley's 7th green in regulation figures.

The length of the drive is limited by an area of sand and scrub so diabolical in nature and of such frightening dimension that it is known as Hell's Half-Acre. It begins some 285 yards from the tee and does not end for more than a hundred yards. This means that the drive and the second shot must travel at least 385 yards, the last hundred yards on the fly, just to be clear of trouble.

In other words, if the tee shot is missed it leaves the golfer with no choice but to play short of Hell's Half-Acre. If he hits a good drive and a poor second shot, he is in it. Nobody can make a par from there.

Even after two perfect wood shots the golfer is faced with an equally difficult problem for his third shot, which could very easily be a mid iron. The fairway comes to an end some twenty yards short of the green, which virtually sits in a huge bunker. The green, not overly large and crowded by trees on both sides, falls away steeply at the rear.

Is it any wonder nobody has ever hit that green in two?

The 7th: 585 yards par 5

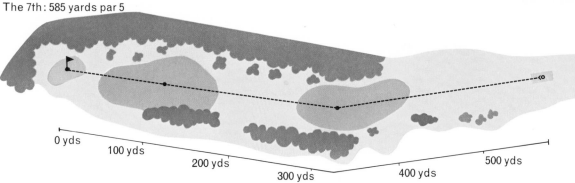

0 yds 100 yds 200 yds 300 yds 400 yds 500 yds

Regarded by many as the most awesome par-five in the world, the 585-yard 7th is dominated by the aptly-named Hell's Half-Acre, a monstrous expanse of sand and scrub beginning 285 yards from the tee and stretching for a further 150. Even with two well-placed wood shots the third is a problem, the green sitting in another great sea of sand and falling away steeply at the back.

▷ ing bet that nobody can break 80 on his first try at the course. One man who did was Arnold Palmer, in 1954, when he was US Amateur champion. "I was desperate for money at the time," Palmer recalls. "I was about to be married. So I collected all the bets I could find. I don't know what I would have done if I had lost—it was far more money than I could afford. But everything turned out all right. I shot a 68." One more record for the spectacular Palmer.

But there are few Arnold Palmers. Not many really good players can get around the course without a few triple-bogeys, or worse. Many rounds that might have otherwise been under par have been marred along the line by a nine or a ten—or worse. For this reason, Pine Valley is in a class by itself as a test of matchplay. A golfer can be three down and four to play and win easily, simply by watching his opponent suddenly discover that he has been walking on water. Woody Platt made his discovery at the 5th, but Pine Valley offers no respite and even if he had completed the 5th in respectable fashion he would then have been faced with a crucial decision on the tee of the 6th.

This hole is a medium-length par-four, 391 yards. The pay-off shot is the drive, for an enormous bank of sand runs along the bias of the fairway as it turns right. The player is therefore faced with deciding how much of the sand

he wants to bite off. Just the right amount and he will have only a pitch to the green, but too much and he will be shooting uphill off a mountainside of sand.

Now comes the "Sahara", a horror of sand all along its 585 yards, with much lying around the green. Nobody has ever hit it in two shots because of the huge belt of sand (from which the hole derives its name) which crosses the fairway

At 130 yards, the 10th is the shortest of Pine Valley's four marvellous par-threes. Although it requires only an 8- or possibly a 7-iron, the undulating green is small and treacherous sand is all around. The real danger, however, is the steep trap in front, whose unprintable name testifies to its difficulty. It is all too easy for a pitch, or even a putt, to roll off the green into it, and there is only one possible way out—backwards.

and stifles all hope of a really long drive.

By contrast, the 8th is only a drive and a pitch, being a mere 327 yards downhill. But what a pitch! Many a player has hit what he thought was a perfect wedge to within a foot of the flagstick, only to watch in disbelief as the backspin on the ball started it creeping down the steep slope to end up in the deep bunker in front of the putting surface.

The 13th: Where a par is a triumph

The 13th, a par-four, is one of the four holes finished off by Hugh and Allen Wilson after George Crump's death. It follows his basic plan and may very well have exceeded his grand ideas of what a hole at Pine Valley ought to be. The 13th is the epitome of the heroic hole in golf, though it also incorporates elements of the penal and strategic styles of architecture.

It takes the heart of a heavyweight to play the hole successfully. It can be punishing to the point where a player might not be able to finish it. And yet, it can be played strategically if it is viewed as a par-four-and-a-half.

At 446 yards it is, by the card, a par-four. It is a single dog-leg to the left if it is played bravely. It is a double dog-leg if the player is content to seek only a bogey.

There are two tees, but the difficulty of the drive and the length of the hole remain the same from

both. A forest of pines obscures all view of the green from the tee. But the patch of fairway you are supposed to hit is in plain view. It begins about 175 yards from the tee. Providing the drive is not short and to the right, the green can be seen from the fairway. However, also in full view is a bunker lining the entire left side of a second patch of fairway which leads into the green from the right. The second shot, most certainly a wood, must carry the full length of that bunker, hit the green on the fly, and hold. Running downhill to the left of the bunker is that forest of pines, and behind the green lies yet another bunker.

Those who prefer discretion to valour can play the second shot short and to the right of the green with an iron. From there it is a simple pitch and, with two putts, a bogey-five.

Of course, there is always the possibility of a par. Most players are more than content to complete the 13th in the regulation four.

The 13th: 446 yards par 4

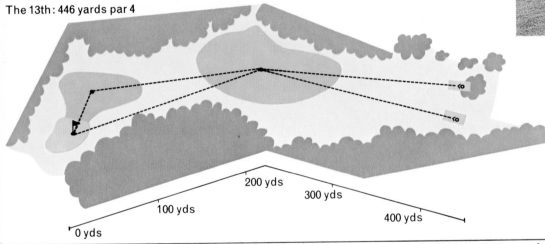

100 yds 200 yds 300 yds 400 yds 0 yds

The 439-yard 13th is yet another hole which gives the impression that Pine Valley is a great bunker with fairways appearing at all too infrequent intervals. The drive must land on the first patch of fairway; the second must carry a huge sandy area on the left of a curving fairway. Par is a major achievement, and many players prefer to play safe with a short second, leaving a simple pitch.

The 9th is a long par-four—432 yards—with two greens. Behind the left one is a cliff, not just a slope. The man brave enough to even attempt finding a ball down there would need to climb down a rope to do so.

The 10th is just an 8- or possibly a 7-iron, but the green is protected all round with what can best be described as sandpits, one of which is cone shaped and has been nicknamed after an unprintable part of the Devil's anatomy. The 11th is a fine two-shotter, at 399 yards one of those rarities in golf architecture: a great short par-four. It is followed by another four, so short that the player can drive hole-high then pitch to the green from the fairway as it turns sharply to the left.

The par-four 13th is another story altogether. It requires a tremendous drive and, because the 446-yard hole is a dog-leg, almost certainly another wood, all of it sheer carry, to get home.

At 185 yards, the par-three 14th does not play that long because the green lies well below the tee. But, again, it is a hit-or-miss one-shotter. Fifty feet of water lies directly in front of the green and a bunker to the left of it.

The 15th hole, which sits at right angles to the 14th green, carries over this same body of water, but any fair tee shot will easily carry it. At 603 yards it is the longest hole at Pine Valley and, to make matters worse, it goes straight

The longest hole at Pine Valley, the 15th is a carry over water and a big trek up a narrowing fairway, one of the longest in existence. As at the long 7th, the other par-five, the green has never been reached in two shots.

uphill into a narrowing fairway. Like the 7th, nobody has ever hit this green in two shots.

The par-four 16th—436 yards—plays long although it travels downhill. It has a tiny patch of fair-green, guarded in front by a minor desert, and then plays over more sandy wasteland to a green strategically bunkered on the left and guarded by water on the right.

The 17th is a shortish par-four, only 344

yards, but it is uphill all the way. By Pine Valley standards the green is small but it is protected all around by sandtraps, which begin a full fifty yards in front of it.

Oddly, the final hole is not as heroic as might be expected at the Pine Valley finish. At 424 yards it is not short, but a drive off the high tee can easily carry the 180 yards or so of sand which lies in front of it, and this to a very wide patch of fair-green. The second can easily carry a brook lying well short of the green, provided it can be truly struck from a downhill lie. But the green is mammoth and the key here lies in the choice of the correct club for the approach. The route is uphill, so it is difficult to see where the cup is, and if the wrong club is chosen avoiding three putts presents a real problem.

Despite its unprepossessing environs, Pine Valley is one of the most beautiful golf courses in the world. It has no backdrop of mountains, no craggy coastlines with waves lapping at its shores. It is simply gorgeous in its own right. Trent Jones likes to tell the story of Lowell Thomas, an avid golfer and traveller for many years. After playing his tee shot safely across the water at the 15th, he turned to admire the scenery around him. "In all my travels", he said to Jones, "I do not think I have seen a more beautiful landscape. This is as thrilling as Versailles or Fontainebleau."

A rubber man's long, long stretch

They are fortunate sportsmen indeed whose employer provides that ultimate in off-duty amenities—a golf course for their own use. Firestone Country Club, at Akron, Ohio, began in this way, the gift to his workforce in 1928 of Harvey Firestone, the millionaire industrialist. Now approaching its half-century, it has become much more than an amenity for Firestone people; it is a challenge to the best in golf, rating as one of the toughest courses on the American tour.

The first of the club's two courses, Firestone South now bears little resemblance to its original plan, having been altered beyond all recognition by Robert Trent Jones in 1959. As a result of his work it is now the longest championship course in America: 7,180 yards, to a par of only 70. Despite its extreme length, even medium-hitting professionals regard it as

The comeback story of Bobby Nichols, the head professional at Firestone, rivals that of Ben Hogan. At sixteen he was injured in a car crash and told he would never walk again. Spurred on by letters of encouragement from Ben Hogan, he became a successful amateur and, twelve years after the accident, won the USPGA title at Columbus, Ohio.

Trent Jones's finest piece of work. Firestone is also the golf course with which American enthusiasts are most familiar; it has been the site of more televised tournaments than any other course. Its television exposure began with the 1960 PGA Championship, for which Trent Jones carried out his drastic surgery—to say merely that he redesigned it would be an understatement. He added fifty bunkers, two ponds and two greens; the remaining sixteen greens were enlarged to two and three times their original size, so that a knee-buckling eighty-foot putt, across typically sharp-breaking undulations, is an ever-present reality.

This is never more typified than at the 17th —at 390 yards one of the shortest par-fours on the course—where there is a ripple running right through the spine of the green. Getting down in two putts may well be the most difficult feat on the entire course.

Bobby Nichols, Firestone's head professional and still a top player on the PGA circuit, declares that it takes a subtle blend of strength and accuracy to win at Firestone. "You don't use 9-irons and 8-irons out here, as a pro can expect on at least a few courses on the tour. At Firestone almost all your approaches to the par-fours and par-threes call for long irons, or maybe even wood shots."

The 1st is a modest opening par-four of 400 yards to a narrow fairway. It is followed by one which Nichols has described as "a gambler's hole", a 500-yard par-five uphill, with deep woods on the left and a heavily bunkered green.

Completely redesigned by Robert Trent Jones for the 1960 USPGA tournament, Firestone is now the longest championship course in America. It is especially notable for its succession of tough par-fours (particularly the 4th and 9th, which proved the most testing over eleven years of World Series play) and for the 625-yard 16th, named "The Monster" by Arnold Palmer after his triple-bogey eight there in the 1960 USPGA competition.

Card of the course					
No 1	400 yards	par 4	No 10	405 yards	par 4
No 2	500 yards	par 5	No 11	365 yards	par 4
No 3	450 yards	par 4	No 12	180 yards	par 3
No 4	465 yards	par 4	No 13	460 yards	par 4
No 5	230 yards	par 3	No 14	410 yards	par 4
No 6	465 yards	par 4	No 15	230 yards	par 3
No 7	225 yards	par 3	No 16	625 yards	par 5
No 8	450 yards	par 4	No 17	390 yards	par 4
No 9	465 yards	par 4	No 18	465 yards	par 4

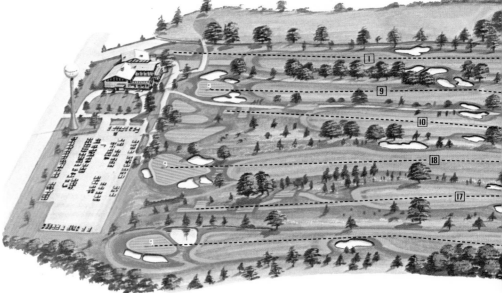

Two woods will give the chance of a birdie, but those who want to play safe will hit short and wedge it into the green.

Now begins the first of the lengthy par-fours, one of five on the front nine and measuring exactly 450 yards. After a 250-yard drive, the second must carry 200 yards on the fly over a pond in front of the green. The 4th is a par-four dropping just short of a par-five. There are only three bunkers: one to the right of the fairway, the others on either side of the green. Despite a prosaically easy green to putt, the 4th remains the most bogeyed hole on the course.

The bone-jarring 5th—a 230-yard par-three —is almost certainly a wood shot to players short of the calibre of Nicklaus. There follows a 465-yard par-four, bunkered only around the green; a 225-yard par-three, bunkered broadly to both the right and left; the downhill 450-yard par-four 8th, severely trapped around the green; and the magnificently bunkered 9th, first downhill and then uphill for 465 yards to the green. It is considered by Nichols to be the second-toughest hole on the course and tournament statistics back him.

The 10th is a bit of a breather. Only 405 yards, it nevertheless calls for a well-nigh perfect tee shot to split the fairway between two finely placed bunkers. The 11th is perhaps the easiest hole on the course, a good drive to a trapless fairway and a pitch to a well-trapped but broad green. The golfer looking for birdies at Firestone had better make one here.

The 12th is the shortest par-three on the

course, 180 yards and nothing to speak of by Trent Jones's standards. Yet it is, as Nichols has pointed out, "fickle". The green is elevated, guarded to the front and on both sides by big bunkers and with lots of trees, the most intrusive of which is a gigantic oak to the rear. The 13th is another 460-yard hole, but Tommy Bolt once scored an eagle-two on it—using a 3-wood for his second shot.

Television has made the last five holes at Firestone the most familiar. The 14th is just 410 yards, but the tee shot is made difficult by two deep bunkers on the right and another on the left which very much tighten the landing area. Most pros choose to lay up off the tee and then play a mid iron for their second shot, which is slightly uphill, to a relatively flat green. If there are such things as birdie holes at Firestone, the 14th is one. But that is the last.

The 15th does not look an exciting hole, because although it is the highest on the course it is long and flat. Club selection is all important because of the winds which swirl off the flatlands of Ohio and around the elevated green, from which the ground drops away sharply on both sides. The two large bunkers on both the left and right and a much smaller one to the front-right help to make this the most disturbing one-shotter on the course. Many tournaments played at Firestone have been won with a birdie at the 15th.

The 16th is not the longest par-five in the world, though it is all of 625 yards. That length seems impossible in print but the hole is en-

Firestone Country Club, Akron, Ohio

South course

Out	3,650 yards	35
In	3,530 yards	35
Total	7,180 yards	par 70

Record: 63, Bruce Crampton, PGA Championship 1975

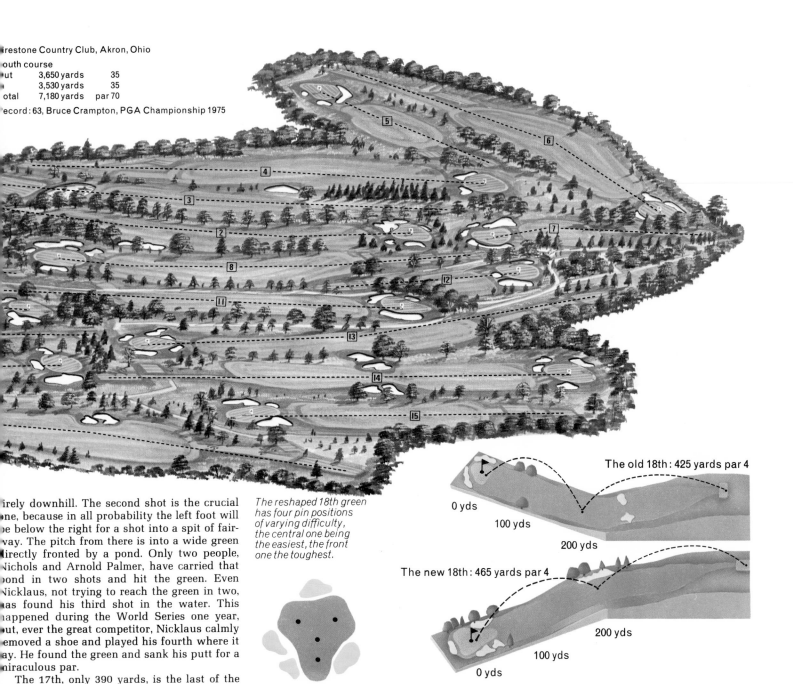

The reshaped 18th green has four pin positions of varying difficulty, the central one being the easiest, the front one the toughest.

The old 18th: 425 yards par 4

0 yds
100 yds
200 yds

The new 18th: 465 yards par 4

200 yds
100 yds
0 yds

irely downhill. The second shot is the crucial one, because in all probability the left foot will be below the right for a shot into a spit of fairway. The pitch from there is into a wide green directly fronted by a pond. Only two people, Nichols and Arnold Palmer, have carried that pond in two shots and hit the green. Even Nicklaus, not trying to reach the green in two, has found his third shot in the water. This happened during the World Series one year, but, ever the great competitor, Nicklaus calmly removed a shoe and played his fourth where it lay. He found the green and sank his putt for a miraculous par.

The 17th, only 390 yards, is the last of the shortish par-fours, but it is uphill and four bunkers—two of them on either side—dictate such a tight tee shot that most long-hitters use an iron off the tee. This leaves them with a medium iron shot to the green with its notorious rippled surface.

The 18th is another of those long par-fours which have given Firestone its reputation. It is 465 yards long from an elevated tee, from which you must play to the right of the fairway to open up the tightly bunkered green. The drive is threatened on the left by a thick grove of trees and on the right by two huge bunkers that will catch any slice or push. The second shot is yet another long iron to a huge green virtually surrounded by bunkers. Three putts are not unusual here. The 18th is the signature hole for the entire Firestone layout—long and tough, but truly great.

The 18th: Finishing in championship style

When Robert Trent Jones redesigned Firestone South in 1959 it was with a view to turning it into a championship course. Not unnaturally, he paid great attention to the 18th, making it into a much stiffer test. As befits the closing hole it still offers the chance of a birdie to the player who badly needs to score one—though it will not be easy to come by. Statistics compiled by the club show that in more than 5,000 tournament rounds, the professionals managed only 415 birdies while registering 1,432 bogeys.

Jones changed the direction of the dog-leg and lengthened the hole by some forty yards by moving the tee back. This had the important effect of reducing the length of the drive by keeping it at the crest of the fairway and denying it the advantage of the downhill roll. He then replaced the flanking fairway traps, which were too close to the tee to cause any anxiety, with two large bunkers on the right side some 240 yards from the tee. He retained the trees which guarded the left side and built a new and larger green which he virtually surrounded with traps. He then plotted four tournament pin positions, three of which were so sited as to make it a chancy business to aim the second shot at the pin. Then, as if he had not created problem enough, Jones gave the hole his own characteristic finishing touch; he toughened the rough by recommending that it be cut with gradually increasing severity and that within a matter of feet of the fairway it be no less than four inches in length.

There can be no doubt that Firestone's new 18th is of the championship calibre that the club sought. The rest of the course is no different.

Rough like steel wool, sand like talcum powder

Southern Hills Country Club, at Tulsa, Oklahoma, was built in 1935, during the depths of the Depression. It was an act of enlightened self-interest by a group of wealthy Tulsans at a time when one in five of the nation's workforce was unemployed.

Tulsa had made its money from oil, and its better-off citizens put up the money for a club of which the state could be proud—and one which, in its construction, would provide employment. In the event, course and clubhouse cost no more than a new locker room at today's inflated prices.

For their architect Southern Hills chose Perry Maxwell, and their choice could not have been a wiser one. Although he lived in Oklahoma his golf knowledge was universal: examples of his architecture are to be found all over the mid-west. The excellence of his work has been carried on by his son, J. Press Maxwell.

Southern Hills is fundamentally a driver's course and thus the key to it is the tee shot. While an accurate drive is an absolute necessity for any course with championship pre-

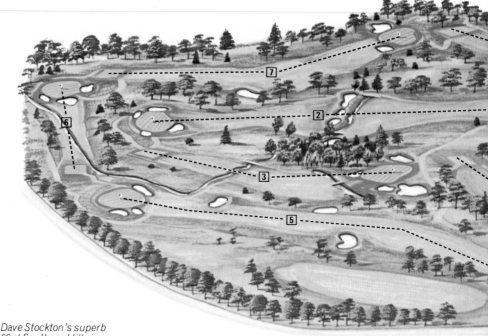

Set in gently undulating parkland, Perry Maxwell's Southern Hills course is one of the great driving tests in American golf. The figures of the first major competition played there (the 1958 Open) illustrate difficulties: only three men, winner Tommy Bolt, Gary Player and Julius Boros broke 290.

Dave Stockton's superb 66 at Southern Hills in the third round of the 1970 USPGA was enough to give him his first major title— despite a three-over-par 73 on the last day.

tensions, it is absolutely crucial at Southern Hills. Nobody ever won anything there who did not drive the ball with extreme accuracy and abundant length.

The reason is that Southern Hills, despite its tournament par of only 70, plays close to 7,000 yards. Furthermore, most of the holes are flat— the club's name is misleading, for there is no help from nature, such as a downhill roll, in driving. The only holes with any real elevation are the 9th and the 18th, and they go uphill to the clubhouse sitting majestically at the top of a hill that is, on the plains of Oklahoma, a minor mountain.

The emphasis on driving is all the more pronounced because all but two of the par-fours and two of the par-fives dog-leg either to the left or the right, each presenting a tight little corner to be negotiated—if, indeed, the corner can be reached at all.

Adding to these difficulties is the tough Bermuda grass with which the entire course is planted; any other type of grass could not survive the sizzling heat in which matches at Tulsa are often played. When the USGA holds one of its championships at Southern Hills—it has held five of them there, and the Open championship comes up again in 1977—the Bermuda grass is allowed to grow in the rough to an ankle-height of almost three inches. It is

like playing from a surface of steel wool so tough that Ben Hogan had to withdraw from the 1958 Open after hurting his wrist trying to extricate a ball from it.

Because of the baking sun and long periods without rain, the sprinkler system at Southern Hills often works night and day in the summer, and even while a tournament is in progress. In the course of one day Southern Hills may use up 400,000 gallons of water. Its greens (most of them are steeply banked from back to front and are rife with undulations) often have to be syringed twice a day. All this works back to the tee, for without an excellent drive through Southern Hills' thick trees it is impossible to get in position for a second shot that leaves any kind of putt.

The bunkers add yet another premium to the drives. While they are numerous, they are not over-abundant alongside the fairways. They are filled with a sand called "Number Six Wash" culled from the nearby Arkansas River. It is not unlike talcum powder, and buried lies are common enough. It is far from the thick quarry sand preferred by professionals, and so a recovery out of the bunkers is never much better than an outside possibility.

The most heavily publicized championship ever held at Southern Hills was the 1958 US Open. It was played in heat that would have

made a camel faint and was won by Tommy Bolt, a temperamental man famed more for throwing clubs than playing shots with them. Bolt won by a very comfortable four strokes from Gary Player, who admitted afterwards that he had played some of the best golf of his career. Bolt missed only thirteen of the seventy-two greens in regulation figures, yet he was three over par; Player was seven over. Asked what had won the championship for him, Bolt just pointed to his driver.

Southern Hills has an extremely long opening hole, a par-four of 459 yards. It is off an elevated tee near the clubhouse and dog-legs to the left with deep bunkers to the right of the green. At the next two holes, both par-fours, a stream must be carried. Along with two bunkers across the fairway it affects the drive at the 450-yard 2nd, but presents no real problem for the approach at the shorter 3rd. The 4th, a short par-four of 360 yards to a slightly elevated green, provides some respite before the rigours of the monstrously long par-five 5th—a full 630 yards, with a heavily bunkered green backed by trees as thick as they are high.

The 6th is a fairly easy par-three and the 7th little more than a 3-wood, for position, and a short iron. The 8th can be unnerving. At 218 yards it is a long par-three with three bunkers.

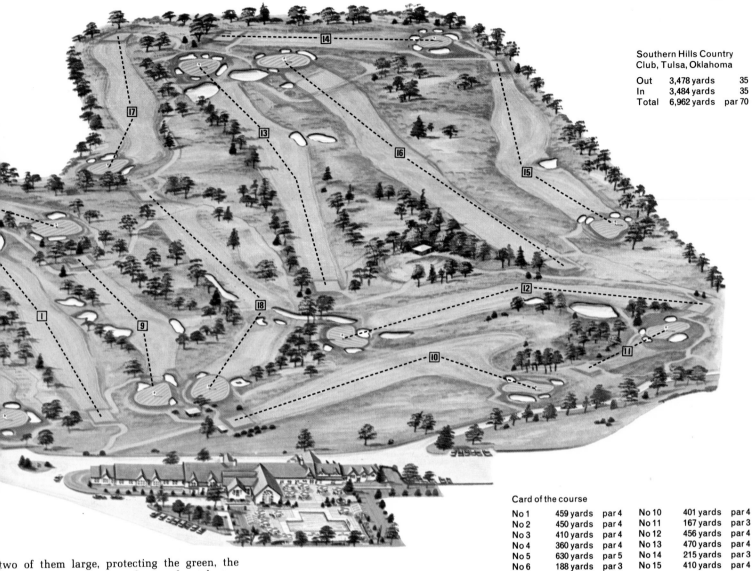

Southern Hills Country
Club, Tulsa, Oklahoma

Out	3,478 yards	35
In	3,484 yards	35
Total	6,962 yards	par 70

Card of the course

No 1	459 yards	par 4	No 10	401 yards	par 4
No 2	450 yards	par 4	No 11	167 yards	par 3
No 3	410 yards	par 4	No 12	456 yards	par 4
No 4	360 yards	par 4	No 13	470 yards	par 4
No 5	630 yards	par 5	No 14	215 yards	par 3
No 6	188 yards	par 3	No 15	410 yards	par 4
No 7	385 yards	par 4	No 16	552 yards	par 5
No 8	218 yards	par 3	No 17	355 yards	par 4
No 9	378 yards	par 4	No 18	458 yards	par 4

two of them large, protecting the green, the back part of which cannot be seen from the tee. The uphill 9th is a mere 378 yards.

From the elevated tee of the 10th the course descends, playing through flatlands until it hits the 16th tee, just about the lowest point on the course. In that stretch are two particularly tough holes—the 12th, described by Ben Hogan as the "greatest par-four 12th hole in the United States", and the 13th.

Trees, rough and a big bunker strategically placed in the crook of the dog-leg make the tee shot especially demanding at the 12th. The long second shot is complicated by a blind water hazard in front of the green and down its right side, and by bunkers and trees to the back and along the left side.

For tournament play the 13th is shortened from its usual par-five 551 yards to a par-four of 470 yards. The short hitter is faced with a blind second shot over two lakes to a smallish green surrounded by five bunkers.

A late dog-leg to a green heavily trapped in front imparts difficulty to the 17th, at 355 yards the shortest par-four on the course. The drive at the 18th, complicated by water on both sides of the fairway landing area, has to be precisely positioned to open the way uphill to the last green. This is a strong finishing hole, and a tough one by any standards.

The 18th: A tough one to finish

The 18th at Southern Hills is not the most technically perfect finishing hole in golf. It may not even be technically the best hole at Southern Hills, but it is certainly the toughest.

It has the trees, the curves, the bunkers, and the insufferable rough which make par so very, very difficult to break at Southern Hills. What is more—for tournament play—its green presents a magnificent view from the clubhouse, which overlooks it from atop a hill so steep that cart paths have to wind their way up it because carts do not have the power after eighteen holes to go straight up. All this provides a perfect viewing platform from which the spectator can watch the contestants play their second shots. For player and spectator alike this is either a thrilling or a gruesome experience, depending on just how well the ball has been driven off the tee. In other words, the 18th is the most characteristic of all the holes at Southern Hills.

From the championship tees, the hole is 450 yards long, which while not an excessive length could hardly be considered short. The drive goes down a slight slope, with trees on both sides, the thicker grove being on the right, the direction in which the hole bends. There is a narrow pond right at the crook of the dog-leg and two fairway bunkers lie just around the corner, which means that anybody who tries to cut it might well rue his ambition. A stream and another bunker lie straightaway, but it requires an enormously long drive to reach them from that championship tee. Accurate placement is absolutely vital.

If the hole has any flaw, it is the lie which results from a perfectly safe and sane tee shot. It is downhill. As if that were not enough of a problem, from it one has to hit uphill to the green—and that shot might very well call for a wood. That is not the sort of shot any golfer, amateur or professional, wants to face if he has any money on the line.

The green is very wide and chock full of breaks. A huge, banked bunker lies to the left front of the green and another, for the slicers, lies to the right. The opening between them is wide enough but, regardless of where the flagstick is placed, that second shot calls for a controlled draw. And when your lie is downhill and the prize is the US Open that must rank as one of the most difficult final approaches on any championship course.

Chicago's controversial golfing shrine

Medinah, twenty miles from downtown Chicago, is an American country club in the most dramatic sense of the term. Its clubhouse, built by the Shriners—members of the Ancient Arabic Order of Nobles of the Mystic Shrine, an association not unlike Freemasonry—is a mock-Moorish structure at once imposing and lavish. It was built in the easy-money 1920s with three golf courses, a polo field, ski-slopes, toboggan runs, an amphitheatre, riding stables and a gun club.

Today, its Number 3 course is considered by many golfers to be the finest in the Chicago area and by its more dogmatic partisans to be the finest in America. However accurate these opinions are, one thing is certain—it is too tough for women, for whom it was originally designed by an expatriate Scot, Tom Bendelow.

It is not known how Bendelow came to serve the big-spending Shriners. He had arrived in America to work as a compositor for the old *New York Herald*, but in 1895 joined Spaldings as an architectural consultant. From then on, he laid out some of the most abominable examples of golf landscaping ever seen, some of which he designed in a day for twenty-five dollars.

Medinah Number 3 has been changed out of all recognition from Bendelow's original conception. The process of change was sparked off by Harry Cooper, who shot the course in 63 on his way to winning the 1930 Medinah Open. Five new holes were built immediately and in 1935 Cooper won there again, this time with a less spectacular 289. Since that time, the course has been revamped many times, most recently by George Fazio in time for the 1975 United States Open. This contest was won by Lou Graham with 287, three over par, which for the Open was 71, a stroke less than usual.

Twenty-five years after being beaten by Ben Hogan and Lloyd Mangrum in the 1950 US Open play-off, George Fazio (as course adviser to the USGA) revamped Medinah for the same championship, won after a play-off by Lou Graham with a 287 total, three over par.

The Medinah championship course tracks through a landscape of oaks, elms, hickories and other trees whose leaves blend into a palette of greens, golds and ambers in the autumn. Much of the course is in sight of Lake Kadijah (named after Mohammed's wife, in the best traditions of the Arabic Order) and two holes, the 2nd and the 17th, are played across it. For the rest, the course has nine dog-legs, two of which swing through a full ninety degrees.

Until 1975 Medinah had been the site of only one US Open, in 1949, when Cary Middlecoff won; it is surprising, because it measures 7,032 yards, holds a very high course rating of 74.8 (one of the highest in the land), has sixty-four artfully placed bunkers—and all Chicago to draw on for spectators. Furthermore, its greens are large if not immense, and are contoured and slanted for the most delicate of putters.

The first hole is dead straight and on the short side, as an opening par-four ought to be. There then follows a first trip across Lake Kadijah, a 187-yard par-three, followed by the slight dog-leg of the 3rd, again over a spur of

Lake Kadijah but presenting no problem, to an elevated green protected on both sides by bunkers. Like the 3rd, the trees on both sides of the 4th fairway are the principal difficulties although its contoured green is not easy to master either. At 527 yards, the par-five 5th is a birdie hole (if there is such a thing at Medinah) although there are two fairway traps, one to the right for the slicers and the other straight down the middle for the really long hitters. The second shot then must carry over two gaping traps on both sides of the rolling green.

What might have been gained on the 5th could very well be lost on the 442-yard 6th which has five bunkers, one of which lies to the left-middle of the fairway, in the landing area. Out-of-bounds is behind the green.

Then comes the formidable 7th, a dog-leg par-five playing to just under 600 yards. In the 1975 Open it yielded far more bogeys than birdies. Since the hole bends right, the tee shot should stay left but it must be carefully placed to avoid an inconveniently placed bunker. The second must carry through groves of trees on both sides and miss another fairway bunker on the left. The third goes to a pear-shaped green, heavily bunkered, with an almost infinite number of pin positions.

At this stage the golfer begins to wonder when Medinah is going to show any mercy. As he makes the turn—from the 8th to the 12th—he finds out that it doesn't. And by the time he reaches the 453-yard par-four 13th—Cary Middlecoff described it as the most difficult hole on the entire course—he is apt to clasp his

Originally built as a private course for members of the Shriner organization, Medinah has been the venue for the US Opens of 1949 and 1975. It has violent dog-legs and dense woods, crowding right to the fairway edge, border all but the first and last holes and make the course seem narrower than it really is. Of all the US Open courses, Medinah probably inspires most controversy.

Card of the course

No 1	390 yards	par 4
No 2	187 yards	par 3
No 3	421 yards	par 4
No 4	446 yards	par 4
No 5	527 yards	par 5
No 6	442 yards	par 4
No 7	594 yards	par 5
No 8	205 yards	par 3
No 9	435 yards	par 4
No 10	583 yards	par 5
No 11	402 yards	par 4
No 12	384 yards	par 4
No 13	453 yards	par 4
No 14	167 yards	par 3
No 15	318 yards	par 4
No 16	452 yards	par 4
No 17	220 yards	par 3
No 18	406 yards	par 4

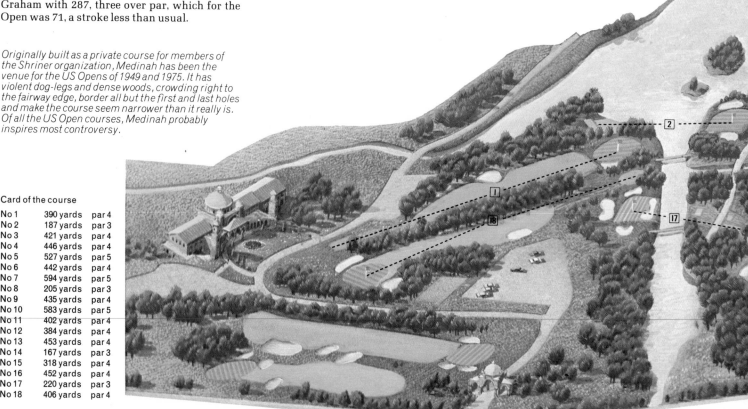

hands to his head. It turns abruptly to the left at 200 yards from the tee and the player has to lay up on his first shot or play an intentional hook with his driver—not a shot any pro relishes. From that point on he may have another wood shot to the small plateau green. On both shots the golfer is playing between thick woods; there are woods everywhere at Medinah.

The 14th is prosaic as Medinah goes, a 167-yard par-three. And the par-four 15th is so short—318 yards—that in the 1930s Jimmy Thomson once drove the green, but the string of bunkers which now gird the front half make this an unlikely event today. The 16th is rather uninteresting although the drive is through a narrow chute of trees. There are no bunkers, just length—452 yards of it.

The 17th—par-three at 220 yards—is easily the toughest hole on the course. The tee shot must carry the lake and a long narrow green-side bunker right on the bank and then hold a shallow green with bunkers on all four sides. The 18th is heavily wooded down the right side and a large bunker on the left means that the drive must thread a narrow neck of fairway. Dense woods on the left leave little margin for error on the second shot.

It has been said that when Bendelow originally laid out the course he designed all his bunkers in the shape of a camel, in keeping with the Moorish theme. The story is probably apocryphal but—to make a bad pun—after playing Medinah the golfer certainly feels as though he has been over some kind of a hump.

The 17th: Contenders kill their chances

The par-three 17th, a full 220 yards long, is the most decisive hole on Medinah Number 3. The tee shot, almost certainly a wood, must carry over the waters of Lake Kadijah. As if that were not enough, it must also carry over a kidney-shaped bunker which lies on the bank between the water and the green. Finding that bunker makes the chances of a par extremely remote. A hook or a sliced tee shot will in all probability find one of the flanking bunkers. Playing safe by over-clubbing is not the answer either: there is another huge bunker to the rear.

Like the 12th at Augusta National, there is one chance and only one chance. Even if that comes off, putting woes have still to be avoided on a green full of tremendous borrows. The green is in a natural amphitheatre, and during the major events hordes of spectators park themselves there by the hour, like ghouls waiting to see the players kill all their chances. They have certainly had their money's worth in past years.

In the 1949 US Open, Clayton Heafner and Cary Middlecoff came to the 17th tee tied for the lead. Middlecoff parred and Heafner bogeyed, and then sadly missed an eight-foot birdie putt at the last to lose. Playing behind them was Sam Snead, looking for the US Open victory that always eluded him. He, too, was tied coming to the 17th. He pushed his 1-iron but miraculously avoided the bunker. With the flagstick on the right, not too far from him he inexplicably elected to run the ball up to the cup through the thick grass around the edge of the green instead of to chip—and he is one of the greatest chippers in the game. The ball, not unexpectedly, pulled up about eight feet short of

the hole. Snead missed, to lose yet another Open.

Asked in the locker-room afterwards by Jimmy Demaret why he hadn't chipped, Snead replied, "Man, if I'd chipped with a wedge, I might have left the ball at my feet. Then where would I be? Right back where I started."

That is the kind of hole the 17th at Medinah Number 3 is. More often than not it makes a man want to go back and start all over again.

Fronted by an eight-foot-deep bunker and with another one to the rear, the 17th green demands a perfectly judged shot.

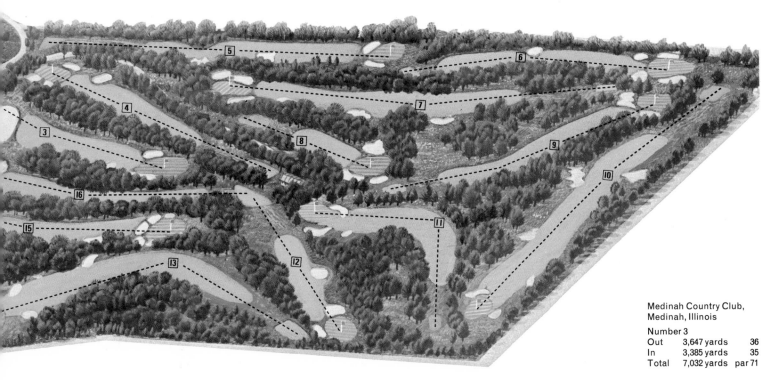

Medinah Country Club, Medinah, Illinois

Number 3

Out	3,647 yards	36
In	3,385 yards	35
Total	7,032 yards	par 71

A course more mellow than monstrous

Though no longer the frightening spectre it was for the famous Open in 1951, when Ben Hogan battled with Robert Trent Jones's changes, Oakland Hills remains a stern test with awkward dog-legs, plentiful bunkers and notoriously undulating greens. Gary Player, who won the PGA title there in 1972, claims only Carnoustie rivals it as the world's toughest.

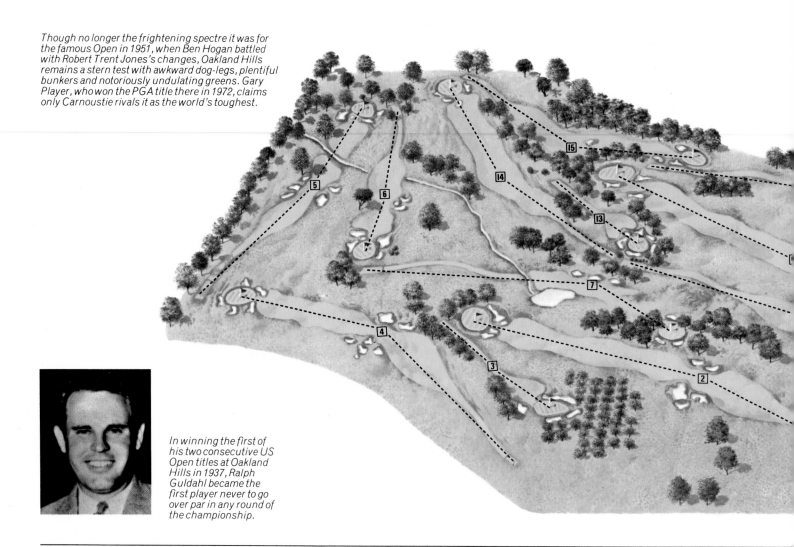

In winning the first of his two consecutive US Open titles at Oakland Hills in 1937, Ralph Guldahl became the first player never to go over par in any round of the championship.

The most overworked nickname for an American golf course is "The Monster". Press agents use it weekly (and weakly) to describe any course where the touring professionals happen to be setting up their nomadic camp, and more often than not it is applied to some harmless sequence of eighteen holes that are as drab as they are undistinguished. The original and authentic "Monster", however, is Oakland Hills, so christened by Ben Hogan after winning the US Open there in 1951.

Prior to that championship, Oakland Hills had twice before played host to the Open—in 1924, when it was won by an obscure little golfer named Cyril Walker, and again in 1937, when Ralph Guldahl was a surprise winner over Sam Snead. That was quite a different course, though, than the one on which Hogan scored his third Open victory. It had been designed in 1917 by Donald Ross, the George Washington of American golf architecture, who said of the rolling woodland when he first saw it, "The Lord intended this for a golf course."

When the time for the 1951 Open approached, the USGA hired Robert Trent Jones to modernize the work of the Lord and Donald Ross. "The game had outrun architecture," Jones has since explained in describing his work

at Oakland Hills, and he set out to give the world's best players what he called "the shock treatment". The philosophy behind his rebuilding programme was to create two target areas on each of the par-four and par-five holes, one on the fairway for the tee shot and another at the green. The result was a series of wasp-waisted fairways, formed by bunkers on either side, and greens surrounded by wide and deep bunkers and overhanging lips—a total of 120 bunkers in all containing some 400 tons of so-called medium-sharp sand.

On his first round of the 1951 Open, Hogan spent a great deal of his time in this sand, and bogeyed five of the first nine holes to bring in a 76 that apparently spoiled any chance he might have had to win the championship twice in a row. The next day was a slight improvement—a 73 that left him five shots behind Bobby Locke, the leader at the half-way point. Despite three bogeys and a double-bogey in his morning round on Saturday, Hogan was able to wring four birdies out of the course for a one-over-par 71, leaving him two strokes behind Locke and Jimmy Demaret, who were now tied for the lead.

There are those who still call Hogan's final round on Saturday afternoon "the finest eighteen holes of golf ever played by anyone". To escape

English-born Cyril Walker held off defending champion Bobby Jones to win the US Open at Oakland Hills in 1924—the first championship in which steel-shafted putters were permitted.

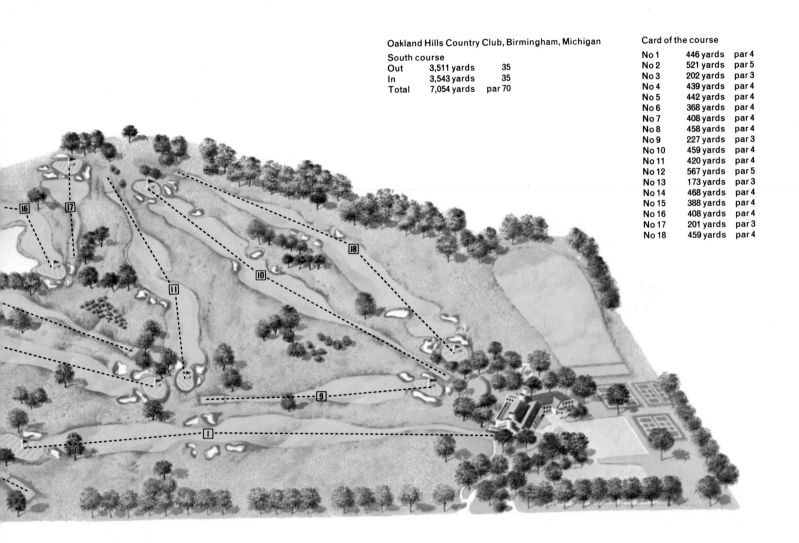

Oakland Hills Country Club, Birmingham, Michigan

South course

Out	3,511 yards	35
In	3,543 yards	35
Total	7,054 yards	par 70

Card of the course

No 1	446 yards	par 4
No 2	521 yards	par 5
No 3	202 yards	par 3
No 4	439 yards	par 4
No 5	442 yards	par 4
No 6	368 yards	par 4
No 7	408 yards	par 4
No 8	458 yards	par 4
No 9	227 yards	par 3
No 10	459 yards	par 4
No 11	420 yards	par 4
No 12	567 yards	par 5
No 13	173 yards	par 3
No 14	468 yards	par 4
No 15	388 yards	par 4
No 16	408 yards	par 4
No 17	201 yards	par 3
No 18	459 yards	par 4

the trouble on the fairways that had bothered him so much in his early round, Hogan often used his brassie off the tee and once even his spoon. He played the first nine holes in even par 35. At the 448-yard 10th, Hogan hit a 2-iron to the green, a shot that travelled more than 200 yards and stopped five feet from the pin. "It was one shot that went exactly as I played it every inch of the way," Hogan said afterwards. He sank the putt for his birdie-three and a few minutes later a fifteen-foot putt for a birdie-two at the 13th hole. A bogey-five at the long 14th cost him a stroke when his second went over the green, but he got it back with a birdie-three at the 15th. Standing on the 18th tee, Hogan knew he had at least a two-stroke lead over the field, but he still refused to play safe. He hit a drive that even today is held in wonder by those who saw it—well over the bunkers guarding the elbow of this 459-yard dog-leg right, leaving him only a 6-iron uphill to the green. He played his second shot perfectly to within four feet of the hole and sank the putt for his fourth birdie in the final nine holes and at that time a competitive course record of 67. "I'm glad", he said at the presentation ceremonies, "that I brought this course, this monster, to its knees." And thus the much-

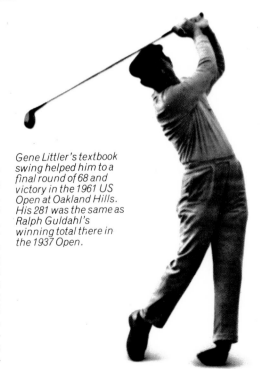

Gene Littler's textbook swing helped him to a final round of 68 and victory in the 1961 US Open at Oakland Hills. His 281 was the same as Ralph Guldahl's winning total there in the 1937 Open.

abused phrase was born. Locke, incidentally, finished with a 73 to drop into third place behind Clayton Heafner, whose closing 69 was the only other sub-par round of the entire tournament.

The open returned to Oakland Hills ten years later to be won by smooth swinging Gene Littler, but the Monster had lost a great deal of its bite. "The course has matured," explained Al Watrous, the club professional. But the USGA had mellowed too. The rough was not nearly as severe as it had been during the Hogan victory, and architect Jones had even removed seven of the 1951 bunkers while preparing the course for the championship. Still, the large, undulating greens were there and are today, somewhat reminiscent of the North Atlantic during a mid-winter storm. Littler's winning score was 281, and eleven players finished with 287 or better, the score that had won for Hogan. There were a number of sub-par rounds during the tournament, and on the second day three players tied Hogan's. During the first Carling World championship in 1964, much the same kind of field scored even better. Even so, and taking into account the understandable pride of the designer, it is only a slight exaggeration when Jones calls it "the greatest test of professional ▷

The 16th: Player goes for glory

Every great champion has had the capacity to make a telling stroke in the heart of crisis, but few more so than Gary Player. Three instances come to mind. There was the spoon shot to within two feet of the 14th hole at Carnoustie in the last round of the 1968 Open. The superb eagle stayed the challenge of Jack Nicklaus who, strive as he did, could not catch the little man.

Then there was a 9-iron shot stone dead on the 71st hole at Augusta which well-nigh ensured his second Masters victory in 1974, and two years earlier he played an even more remarkable

stroke with the same club at Oakland Hills.

Player was pursuing his second PGA title with all his intense tenacity and with three holes to play was even with Jim Jamieson, who was on the 18th. The 16th curves elegantly but sharply to the right around a long lake with the green set so close to it that any approach has to cross it. Weeping willows on the near side discourage those who think of trying to cut the corner, as Player discovered when he sliced from the tee. His ball lay well in rough trampled by spectators, but he faced a blind shot of 150 yards, the willows and the lake between him and the flag. The carry was huge for a 9-iron but

Player felt he needed that much loft to clear the trees. A seat stick left on the ground under the trees helped him decide the line. It was a carefully calculated death-or-glory shot; the slightest mishit, or if the 9-iron were not enough club, and he would probably take five or even six. He struck it perfectly and the ball came to rest only four feet from the hole.

Down went the putt and, as Jamieson had missed a short one on the last green, Player had an insurance stroke in hand. He did not need it, thanks to one of the finest pressure shots that has ever been struck in a championship.

The 16th: 408 yards par 4
----- Player

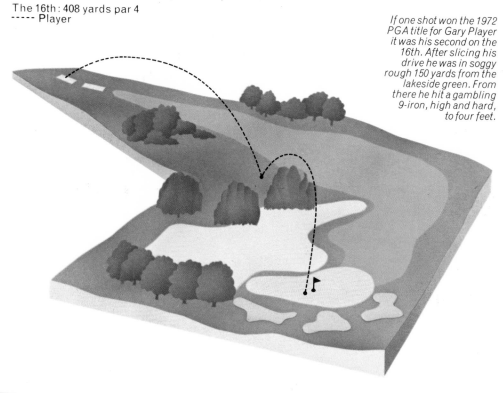

If one shot won the 1972 PGA title for Gary Player it was his second on the 16th. After slicing his drive he was in soggy rough 150 yards from the lakeside green. From there he hit a gambling 9-iron, high and hard, to four feet.

▷ tournament championship golf in the world. The player with the best shots, swing and nerve control has the best chance to win."

Lying as it does in a Detroit suburb and less than an hour's drive from the heart of that great city, it is fitting that Oakland Hills should be an offspring of the motor industry. The property belonged originally to a printer and an accountant who were connected with the Ford Motor Co. They played golf together at the nearby Bloomfield Hills Country Club, which even then was a gathering-place for car makers, and eventually decided to see if Ross could fashion an exciting course on their land. They opened for business in a modest way during the summer of 1918, and Walter Hagen, who lived near by, was their first professional.

Hagen had a favourite anecdote to illustrate the pastoral debut of Oakland Hills. "There was a big red barn on the left-hand side of the first fairway," Hagen recalled. "We used to hang our coats on a nearby crab-apple tree to practise. Very few of the members could hit the barn from the practice tee. I got a lot of practice taking

their clubs from them and showing them how to hit the barn."

In due course, it was decided to build a clubhouse for the rather impressive sum of $275,000. The result was the huge neo-colonial structure that now dominates the entire course from the crest of the hill overlooking the 1st, 9th, 10th and 18th holes, certainly one of the most spacious clubhouses to be found anywhere and a marvellous spot from which to watch the golf unfold at the start and finish of each nine holes. The clubhouse presented only one problem at the time it was built, however: due to innumerable changes and modifications during its construction, it cost $650,000 instead of the anything-but-modest amount which was originally budgeted for it.

Although its length of 7,054 yards is not unduly long as championship courses are measured today, Oakland Hills concentrates a great deal on its more hazardous yards and more trying problems in the closing holes where they test the nerves as well as the ability. The 14th at 468 yards requires two very long shots. The

15th, at 388 yards, is uphill all the way with a large bunker in the middle of the fairway just where it turns left towards the green. The second shot at the 16th is a medium iron across a large pond that cuts right into the middle of the green. The 17th, with the deeply undulating green in a plateau some thirty feet above the tee, allows no margin for error since the green is completely surrounded by yawning bunkers. The 18th hole, the aforementioned dog-leg, with its bunkers to the right to guard against the shortcut and rough to the left to inhibit the long approach and a hump-backed green that has only the smallest entrance between protecting bunkers in front, is the kind of hole where tournaments are far more often lost than won— as many know to their cost.

Oakland Hills has undergone some drastic changes in character. It started out merely as a good course, falling short of greatness. It was then transformed by Trent Jones into a course too severe even for the élite among professional golfers. It has now mellowed with age into one of America's finest and fairest tests of golf.

The largest and finest — of course!

According to 1967 US Masters champion Gay Brewer, the 418-yard 6th at Cypress Creek can "turn into a disastrous hole." If the drive is hooked, the only way to recover and still have a chance of par is to hook the second around the single tree and over the lake which skirts the right side of the green. The 6th begins the first of two three-hole stretches which leave a lasting memory of Champions: the other group is the 12th to 14th, demanding holes which can give a real lift at a vital stage—or destroy a round.

A golf club like Champions could really only be found in the State of Texas, where superlatives are not only commonplace but also, as often as not, quite justified as well. It has not just one but two championship courses, Cypress Creek and Jackrabbit, a clubhouse that has almost every amenity imaginable, and a membership roll that even includes six astronauts.

As if all that were not enough, the men who own and run it are champions too. Jimmy Demaret, winner of more than fifty tournaments, was the first man to conquer in the US Masters three times; Jackie Burke, his partner, took both the Masters and the USPGA championship in 1956, two years after being the first to take four consecutive PGA tour events.

Slighter qualifications, it would seem, might not have sufficed for Houston, with its mighty sports arena, the Astrodome, the NASA Space Center and, so it is claimed, millionaires who are more numerous than policemen. Many Texans have made their mark in golf. Apart from Demaret and Burke, Texas has produced Ben Hogan, Byron Nelson, Lloyd Mangrum, Ralph Guldahl, Babe Didrikson Zaharias, Harry Cooper, Lee Trevino, Mickey Wright, Don January, Charles Coody, Miller Barber . . . the roll of honour is seemingly endless. Considering the size of Texas (it is twice as big as the British Isles, for instance) and the number of great golfers it has produced, it is surprising that it should have so few really memorable

golf courses. Texas does, of course, have a number of good courses, among them Colonial at Fort Worth, Pecan Valley, Preston Trail at Dallas and the Dallas Athletic Club. But none has the charisma of Champions, as those who have played in tournaments there—the 1967 Ryder Cup was one, the 1969 US Open another —will readily testify.

When Demaret and Burke decided to build Champions in 1957, they not uncharacteristically announced that it would be "the world's largest and finest" course. "When you do something in this town, you have to do it on a grand scale," says Demaret. "So we decided to model our holes after the world's classics. We weren't going to imitate them; rather, we were going to blend their characteristics into the terrain we had. We wanted a golf club right here in our home town that would become to Houston and Texas what Augusta National is to Georgia, or Pinehurst to North Carolina, or St Andrews to Scotland."

Burke adds: "While we wanted an ample clubhouse, we wanted it strictly for golfers. We didn't want to build some barn of a place and then put the course on what was left over, meanwhile going broke with a lot of idle waiters standing around an empty ballroom. Furthermore, Jimmy and I decided we would run the club our way. You can't run a club smoothly through a board of directors, however brilliant each member may be in his own field. One wants

a swimming pool, one some tennis courts, while another wants to fix up a couple of holes. So everything suffers."

The only concession they made was to construct a swimming pool, because most of Champions' members are wealthy young men in their thirties and forties, with children.

The site Demaret and Burke decided to buy was 500 acres, heavily wooded with oaks, pines and sweet-gums in an otherwise threadbare northern section of the town. Later, members bought a further 1,500 acres around the course for future home sites. Although the course is twenty miles from downtown Houston, it can be reached by one of the city's network of freeways in twenty minutes.

Knowing their architectural limitations (as few professional golfers do), Demaret and Burke hired Ralph Plummer to lay out a master plan. Two of Plummer's most successful previous efforts had been the Dallas Athletic Club course and Shady Oaks, near Forth Worth, where Ben Hogan had localized his golf activities after retiring. After Plummer had finished, he would indicate the possible location of a tee or green to Demaret and Burke, who would then hit hundreds of balls to make sure the shots would play as projected.

At first, no bunkers were built. Instead, grass-covered mounds were bulldozed into shapes that could eventually be removed if unwanted or converted into carefully shaped ▷

Card of the course		
No 1	452 yards	par 4
No 2	452 yards	par 4
No 3	397 yards	par 4
No 4	228 yards	par 3
No 5	513 yards	par 5
No 6	418 yards	par 4
No 7	428 yards	par 4
No 8	180 yards	par 3
No 9	510 yards	par 5
No 10	448 yards	par 4
No 11	466 yards	par 4
No 12	230 yards	par 3
No 13	544 yards	par 5
No 14	430 yards	par 4
No 15	428 yards	par 4
No 16	180 yards	par 3
No 17	420 yards	par 4
No 18	440 yards	par 4

Champions Golf Club, Houston, Texas

Cypress Creek course

Out	3,578 yards	36
In	3,586 yards	35
Total	7,164 yards	par 71

Record: 64, Bob Rosburg,
Champions International 1968

The brainchild of two of America's finest golfers, Jimmy Demaret and Jackie Burke, Champions can claim to be one of the best courses in Texas. More than 70,000 trees dominate Ralph Plummer's layout, which has quickly become a regular venue for major events.

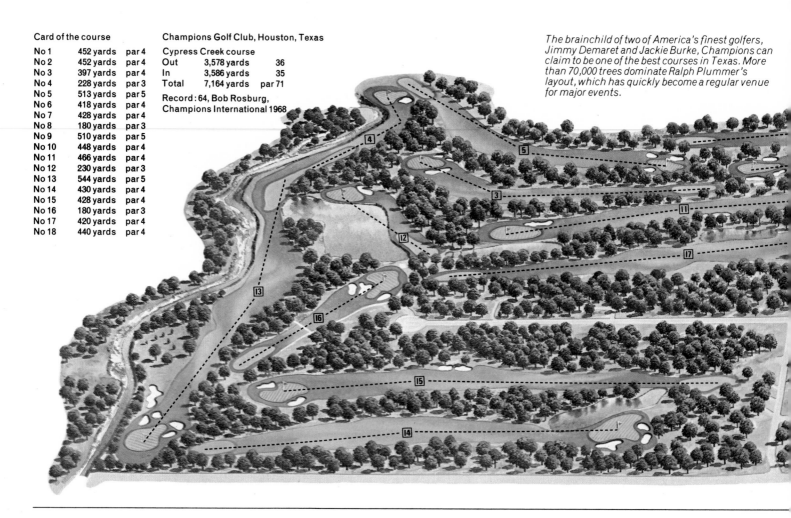

bunkers. Most bunkers are on the shallow side, especially those on the fairways. "We felt", Burke explained, "that if a player hits into a bunker, he should still be able to scramble his way to a par if necessary. There is no prettier shot in golf than a well-executed shot out of sand, particularly a long shot."

While the Jackrabbit course, designed later by George Fazio, is just as stringent as the Cypress Creek, it is utterly different. It has narrower fairways, smaller greens and deeper and more numerous bunkers. Cypress Creek, on the other hand, has wide fairways, tremendous greens and bunkers that are more strategically placed. Both are about the same length, around 7,100 yards.

Choosing the best hole at Cypress Creek is not easy, but two stretches of holes have impressed the professionals particularly: the 6th through the 8th, and the 12th through the 14th.

The 6th and 7th are both medium-length par-fours with big, inviting greens. Gay Brewer has said of the 418-yard 6th that "the drive is the key shot. The hole is wooded both right and left. Under normal conditions, I'll play a 6- or 7-iron at the big green, which is guarded on the left by a sandtrap. The great fear and problem on this hole is hooking the drive, for then the player is going to have to try to recover by hooking his ball out over the big lake which guards the right side of the green. It can turn

into a disastrous hole." The 7th, only ten yards longer, can be difficult if the wind is against and, according to Ben Hogan's protégé, Gardner Dickinson, "hugging the right side of the fairway can be dangerous and aiming to the left makes the hole play longer. The green is large and has a big dip, and this invites three-putting. If you don't select the right club for your second shot, you can leave yourself a hundred-foot putt. Another reason for avoiding the trees on the right is that a ditch comes into play in front of the green, although it is well short of the green."

In the opinion of Bobby Nichols the 8th, a par-three of 180 yards, is a lot like the 12th at Augusta National. "You want to take plenty of club and hit deep on to the green. I'd rather risk the long putt than land in the lake in front of the green. There's not much penalty if you go over. All the trouble is to the front and to the left."

The second group of holes makes no great demands on length but they come at a vital time in a round. Scoring well here can give the lift that every golfer needs to finish in style. The three-hole stretch starts with a par-three and a par-five back to back. The 12th is 230 yards long and, says Jackie Burke, "a good player will use anything from a 3-iron to a 4-wood, depending on the wind. The green is rather large, well guarded on the right by sand and in front by a lake that runs practically from tee to green. We call it Bob Hope Lake because he was the first

person to hit a ball into it. He's hit a whole lot more since then."

In the opinion of Bob Goalby, the 1968 Masters winner, the 13th, 544 yards long, "is a treacherous hole, and it must be played sensibly and safely. This is no place to gamble. Off the tee you don't try to cut that right corner because it's simply not worth the chance: the trees there can block the second shot. A 2-iron may be the best second shot, because unless you're an extremely long hitter you'll never make the green. The bunkers to right and left make the entrance too narrow."

The 14th is a par-four of 430 yards. "This is the hole that has been the consistently toughest to par," says Jack Nicklaus. "The oddly shaped green is bunkered tightly to the left, right and rear, and a small lake directly in front of the green must be carried. Arnie Palmer says this is the finest 14th hole he has ever played. I'm inclined to agree with him."

After everything has been said about Champions as a golf club, what makes it special are the two ebullient men who run it. During his time on the tour the good-humoured Jackie Burke was one of the most popular players amongst his fellow professionals and Bob Hope, adhering to the principle that only a superlative is adequate to describe a Texan, has called Demaret the funniest amateur comedian he ever met.

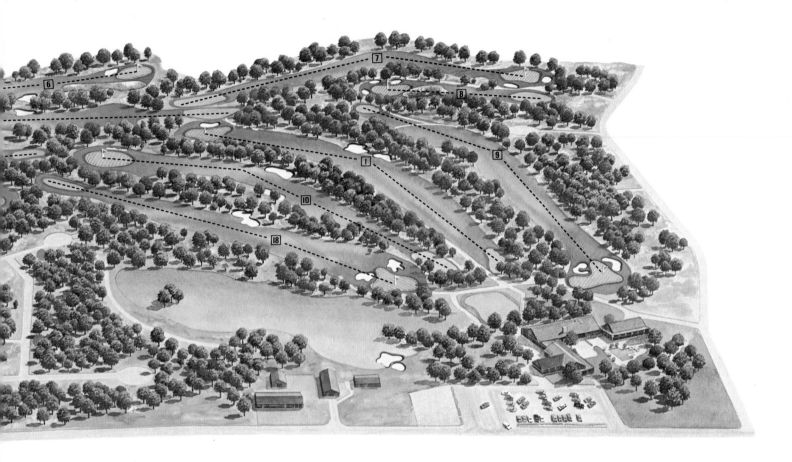

*Arnold Palmer and Jack
Nicklaus both rate the
430-yard 14th one of the
best holes they have met
at that stage of a round.*

The 4th: The hole that was too much for Hogan

Many maintain that the 4th on the Cypress Creek
course at Champions is amongst the toughest
par-threes in the world. At 228 yards from the
extreme back tees, it also comes close to being the
longest.

Its tee, which looks long enough to land a small
aircraft on, allows the markers to be set at 190
yards or so—170 yards for members and 140 yards
for women. Regardless of where the markers are
set, though, the tee shot must carry over a deep
gulch that barely has any water in it except after a
heavy rain. It is so deep and so steep and so full of
rocks and unimaginable undergrowth that it takes
bravery to climb down into it, luck to find a ball and
then sheer foolishness to play the shot.

Lee Trevino hit his tee shot into the gulch
during the first round of the 1969 Open. He had the
nerve to climb into it, somehow found the ball,
slipped as he played the shot, injured himself and
failed to make the cut.

In the 1971 Champions International, now
defunct but then worth $100,000 in prize money,
Ben Hogan came out of retirement to play as a
favour to his old friend and four-ball partner
Jimmy Demaret. He hit four successive shots into
the gulch, not daring to aggravate his weakened
legs by climbing down into it. He ended up with an
eleven on the hole. He apologized to his playing
partners and at the end of nine holes withdrew.
As he walked off the 9th green for the clubhouse,

he turned to one of them and said simply: "Never
grow old."

"To play this hole successfully," says Demaret,
"it is necessary to keep the ball high. A low shot
faces the danger of being embedded in the bank
in front of the green. With that gulch running all
the way from the tee to the green on the left, I find
it best to hit either a 3-iron or a 4-wood with a slight
draw, depending on the wind. If the wind is out of
the southwest, the 3-iron is the best shot. If it is
from the south, I usually go for the 4-wood."
Demaret might have added that he is one of the
all-time great iron players and quite possibly the
best ever with a 4-wood.

To add to the severity of the hole, to the right
of the green—for the slicers or those who lack the
nerve to try to carry the full width of the gulch—
there is a flat bunker that surrounds a sweet-gum
tree. But a player is better off in that, even if he is
stymied by the tree, than he is in that gulch!

But not even these problems alone can make
any hole rank amongst the toughest in the world.
The green, too, must pose some problems. This
one is outsized even by Cypress Creek's standards,
and it is full of tiny undulations. As if they are not
tricky enough, some of the pin positions,
particularly those on the front and on the right side,
make it impossible to aim anywhere close to them.
In fact it is possible to hit a full driver over the
gulch, avoid the tree and the bunker, end up ten
feet from the hole—and still take a bogey.

Where the old-fashioned still reigns supreme

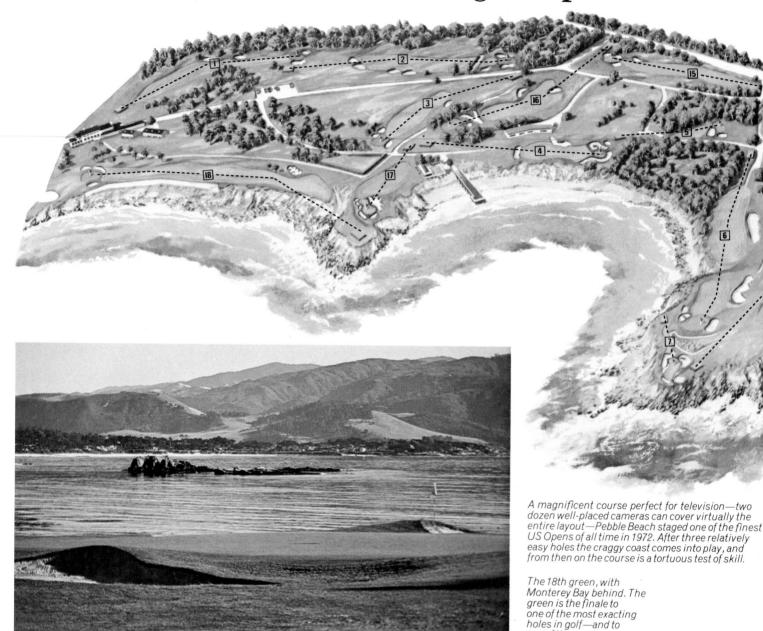

A magnificent course perfect for television—two dozen well-placed cameras can cover virtually the entire layout—Pebble Beach staged one of the finest US Opens of all time in 1972. After three relatively easy holes the craggy coast comes into play, and from then on the course is a tortuous test of skill.

The 18th green, with Monterey Bay behind. The green is the finale to one of the most exacting holes in golf—and to one of the most challenging courses.

Without any argument, the supreme golf course in the western United States is Pebble Beach, twice the site of the US Amateur and, for the first time in 1972, the Open, despite the reluctance of the USGA to hold its championship so far from a major city. Stretching for several miles alongside the rocky shore and steep cliffs of Carmel Bay, some 120 miles south of San Francisco, Pebble Beach has gained, thanks to television, a fame—indeed, even a notoriety—far beyond the immediate world of golf. Each January it is the scene of the two closing rounds of the Bing Crosby National Pro-Amateur Championship, a tournament that attracts a larger television audience than any other event of the golfing calendar, due in no small part to the reputation of the host. It is almost axiomatic that once "The Crosby" goes on the air, the climate of the Monterey Peninsula goes into a frenzy, and Pebble Beach becomes a ruffian that intimidates and manhandles the

world's finest professional golfers. In 1955, the lowest score there on a windy, rainy Saturday was 76, and only a handful of the professionals broke 80.

By American standards, Pebble Beach is an

Bing Crosby, who plays off a two-handicap, started his Pro-Am in 1936. Television has given it the largest audience of all golf tournaments— including the US Open— and made Pebble Beach world famous.

old-fashioned course. At slightly more than 6,800 yards it is not particularly long; nor is it heavily bunkered. But the greens are small by present-day standards; many of them are well contoured, and when the course is in its best playing condition they can be as slick as any in

the world—including notoriously speedy Oakmont.

The unique quality of Pebble Beach, however, is to be found on its stretch of seaside holes. Beginning at the 4th, a shortish par-four, and continuing through the 10th, it presents one of the loveliest and probably the most severe succession of seaside holes to be found on any American course of championship calibre. The vista of these holes, particularly as viewed from the upper part of the 6th fairway and looking down the shoreline to the 10th green, is one of the loveliest sights of a sport that is by no means short of beauty. More than that, the last three of these holes, even on the balmiest of days, are enough to unsettle the strongest players and take the momentum from a round that seems on its way to something memorable.

Take the 8th hole, the first of the vicious triumvirate. A mere 425 yards on the card, it begins with a blind drive from a slightly

Jack Neville was hired by Sam Morse in 1918 to lay out Pebble Beach, and with Douglas Grant (like Neville a former amateur champion) as consultant, he produced one of the most magnificent and testing of all courses.

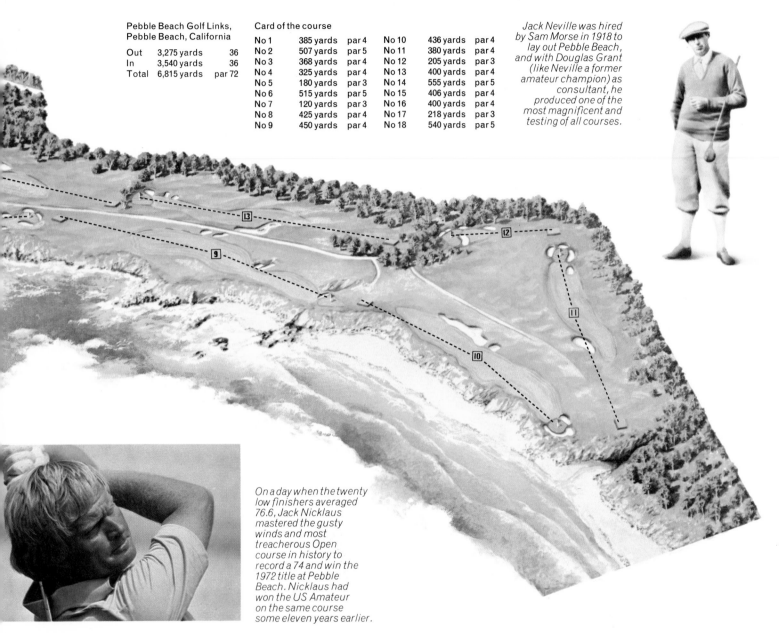

On a day when the twenty low finishers averaged 76.6, Jack Nicklaus mastered the gusty winds and most treacherous Open course in history to record a 74 and win the 1972 title at Pebble Beach. Nicklaus had won the US Amateur on the same course some eleven years earlier.

depressed tee perched on the side of a cliff that falls away some fifty feet to the sea below. The well-hit uphill drive of some 200 yards to the middle of the fairway leaves an awesome shot across an elbow of the bay that cuts into the fairway approximately 250 yards from the tee. There is an absolute carry of 180 yards across the bay to a small green that is liberally trapped on three sides. A scrubby bank rises up on the left side of the green to catch the overhit shot, and one would prefer not to be there either. Probably half the pars achieved here during a major tournament are made with one putt.

The 9th has been described by more than one tournament professional as the toughest par-four in golf. That could be an overstatement, but not by much. The hole runs downhill all the way to the green, and the fairway slopes towards the sea, so the tendency is to keep the ball to the left and thus lengthen the hole beyond the 450 yards it measures on a straight line. With the wind blowing in from the sea, as it so often does, only the very strongest hitters are going to reach this green in two.

The 10th, although a little shorter at 436 yards, still poses the same forbidding problems —the sea on the right and the green tucked up against the side of the cliff. On a day when "Crosby weather" is on the rampage, anyone who can go par-par-par along this stretch is playing virtually perfect golf.

Pebble Beach turns inland from there, but it returns to the sea at the 17th and 18th, two holes where a match or a tournament are more likely to be lost than won. It was at the 17th, a 218-yard tee shot—usually into the wind—to a large, two-level green with the sea to the left and behind, that Arnold Palmer took his horrendous nine during the 1964 Crosby and thereby failed to qualify for the closing round, for one of the few times in his brilliant career. Misjudging the wind, Palmer hit his tee shot too hard and found himself trying to play back to the green off the wave-swept rocks. At the 18th, a 540-yard hole that curves to the left along the beach, the temptation is always to cut off more ocean than one's strength or the wind will allow. In one Crosby, the wind off the sea was so strong that Arnold Palmer hit his second shot at least thirty or forty yards out to sea and then watched the wind bring it back to within a few yards of the green.

Until 1966, Pebble Beach was, to all intents and purposes, a public golf course designed for the use of visitors to Pebble Beach Lodge, the large resort hotel overlooking the 18th green and the sea. It was built in the early 1920s as part of the newly organized Del Monte Properties, which had undertaken to develop a remote and exclusive resort community in the wild pine forests of the Monterey Peninsula. Until World War II few but the very rich were attracted to the Pebble Beach area. For the most part it was ▷

the weekend and summer playground of the corporation presidents and their wives from Los Angeles and San Francisco, with a sprinkling of just enough Middle Westerners and Easterners to give the area and its expensive houses an aura of eastern sophistication.

The Pebble Beach course was too splendid to go unnoticed, however. California state championships were played there, and its reputation grew to the point where the USGA finally brought the Amateur championship there in 1929—the first national championship ever played west of the Mississippi. The tournament is remembered nowadays largely because it was the only Amateur championship during the last seven years of his active career in which Bobby Jones failed to reach the final round. On five of the other six occasions he was the winner, but

The 7th: 120 yards par 3

The 7th: An eloquent plea for delicacy
When, in the 1973 British Open, Gene Sarazen holed his tee shot at Troon's 8th hole, the famous Postage Stamp, only 126 yards long, it was seen by millions and commanded welcome attention to the virtues of the short short hole. There is no finer, or more beautiful, example of this than the 7th at Pebble Beach. After mounting the crest of the 6th the golfer turns towards the ocean. There below him on a promontory, bounded with rocks where the surf spills silver, lies a tiny green of 2,000 square feet embraced by sand. The hole measures only 120 yards and is downhill. In calm air a wedge or 9-iron is the club, but when the wind is strong from the Pacific golfers may be fingering medium irons to keep the ball low on line. Normally the shot offers no problem to the expert, but the distance is not all that easy to judge and there are no marks for being too bold. The heaving tumult of the waves awaits. Short the hole may be, but even great players must thrill to the sight of the ball flighting high against the sky and falling softly near the flag. This requires the utmost precision because the green lies directly along the line of approach and offers a target of no more than eight yards in width.

The hole must be the shortest on any major championship course in America, but nobody scorns it because of that. For the player seeking a birdie it demands a more sensitive touch than most shots of similar length from the fairway. Rightly, therefore, it commands its place in the heart of the most compelling stretch of seaside golf in the world. Pebble Beach has become the yardstick against which all new seaside courses are measured. It is a matter of regret that more

at Pebble Beach he lost his first-round match to unknown Johnny Goodman, probably the biggest sports upset of the entire year.

The impact on American golfers can be imagined. As an amateur Jones was supreme to an extent that no other has ever been, and who on earth was Goodman? Although he lost to Lawson Little later in that championship, he was soon to make an enduring mark. In 1933 he was the last amateur to win either the US or British Open, but that morning at Pebble Beach the great crowd was stunned. Goodman, unafraid of what he was about, took the lead at the 14th, halved the remaining holes and Jones was beaten. In time, the only golfer of his generation who conceivably might have assumed the mantle of Jones also came to Monterey, but his journey was infinitely more rewarding than that

architects have not been inspired by this short but memorable 7th hole.

Sadly, though, such holes are rare. The increased power of golfers in recent decades has led to short holes being made longer and longer. Often the average player is blinding away with wood or long iron, concerned mainly with making the distance and not finessing the shot to the most favourable part of the green. Every course should have at least one truly short hole, where delicacy rather than strength is of the essence. No architectural genius is needed to make it extremely testing—and hugely enjoyable.

of Jones. The words Pebble Beach should be engraved on the heart of Jack Nicklaus.

In 1961 progress to his second US Amateur title was little short of massacre. Eleven years later he walked in triumph up the last long fairway by the ocean towards his third Open victory. In all golf there can be no more beautiful walk for a champion about to be crowned. His victory was assured when a magnificent 1-iron shot, drawn into the strong breeze, almost went into the 17th hole, gently hitting the pin and finishing inches away. He became the first and most probably the last American golfer to have won both US championships on the same course. In Britain, Jones alone has accomplished the feat with his victories at St Andrews in 1927 and 1930.

In addition to his Amateur and Open

At 120 yards Pebble Beach's 7th is one of the shortest holes in golf but one of the most difficult, particularly in a wind, when it may take as much as a 3-iron to hit the tiny green, only eight yards wide and tightly trapped. After a punched 7-iron Nicklaus holed a birdie putt of twenty-five feet here in the final round of the 1972 Open.

Nicklaus had won the Crosby tournament three times and a fourth seemed likely in 1976 when he was sharing the lead after the last turn. Then suddenly it was revealed that Nicklaus could be as human a golfer as any humble hoper. On the 13th, after a big drive, he hit an inexcusably bad iron shot and made seven on the par-four hole. A good tee shot to the 17th was harshly bunkered and led to another triple-bogey and, in trying to get home in two at the last, he pulled into what Bing has called the "mollusc country" and took seven. Nicklaus, smiling disbelief, was back in 45 for an 82 and golfers everywhere were comforted by the thought that even the mightiest of the age, if not of all the ages, could be as vulnerable as they.

The post-World War II prosperity and the jet age drastically changed the character of Mon-

terey Peninsula and, in turn, brought Pebble Beach to its present fame. The new-rich built houses in the area by the hundreds, and the nation's growing population of golfers could afford to fly there from anywhere on the continent in a matter of hours. Almost adjacent to Pebble Beach was the small and exclusive Cypress Point Club with its lovely links-like course built in 1930, and it was there that most of the better-connected golfers played, if they could arrange it, leaving Pebble Beach to the general public and the visitors at the Lodge. Bing Crosby moved his tournament to the area in 1947, and as it grew in size he used not only Pebble Beach and Cypress Point but a third course farther along the beach belonging to the Monterey Peninsula Country Club. By 1966, a fourth course called Spyglass Hill, designed by

the eminent Robert Trent Jones, was in operation, assuming the burden of the public play; and Pebble Beach became a club, yet still available to the guests at the Lodge.

No description of Pebble Beach would be complete without some mention of the professional who ran the course with as autocratic a hand as any medieval monarch's. A Scotsman whose powerful voice and style seemed never to have left the heath and heather, Peter Hay was as much a part of Pebble Beach as the misty rain that blows in from the Pacific. Some claimed they built the course around him. There are still some grandfathers playing around Pebble Beach today who learned their first golf under Peter Hay's stern commands, not the least of which was "Play your shots quickly and don't complain."

The 9th and 10th: A classic test of technique

Never were golf architects more richly blessed in a setting than were Jack Neville and Douglas Grant when they came to create Pebble Beach. With scarcely a second glance they must have visualized the great sequence of holes along the coast. By right of its place in the round the 18th is the most famous; the 7th is the most beautiful and the 8th the most spectacular but, in pure golfing terms, there cannot be two successive par-fours anywhere of greater quality than the 9th and 10th. Both are classics of their kind, rolling along the jagged coast, their greens hard against it and the land

leaning towards the ocean all the way. If ever holes reward, indeed demand, true striking these do. Few shots test a golfer's technique more precisely than those which compel him to hold a true line when the elements are from left to right, whether they be wind or, as on these holes, falling ground. The man who fears the slice or push towards the ocean and holds his shot overmuch to the left may be bunkered or, at best, face a fearsomely long approach to the green with all the perils that lie beyond. In the final round of the 1972 Open Jack Nicklaus twice found the beach at the 10th to wind up with a six that almost cost him the title.

The 9th and 10th holes complete one of the toughest trios of consecutive par-fours in golf. When the wind is up even the big hitters struggle to make the green with two woods on the 450-yard 9th, "The Old Heartbreaker", where Dale Douglass took nineteen in the 1963 Crosby. The shorter 10th, with a sloping fairway, needs perfect accuracy.

Trent Jones transforms a swamp

The luxurious sprawl of Dorado Beach, its hotels and golf courses conjured out of a tangle of fruit plantations and mangrove swamps on the Puerto Rican seashore, offers the apparent incongruity of a resort only the wealthiest can afford in a place where it can do some good for a poor society. Whatever the altruism involved, Puerto Rico is now a sunlit paradise for golfers—so long as they can afford it.

Dorado Beach was built in the late 1950s and early 1960s by Laurance Rockefeller, who retained Robert Trent Jones to design the four golf courses that it now has (two are at nearby Cerromar Beach). Jones has a rare grasp of the economics of resort golf. Why, he asks, build a hotel with a gorgeous view of the ocean from the front and a view of the parking lot from the back? Build a golf course in the rear and you can charge as much for those rooms as you do for the ones overlooking the ocean.

His singular talent for creating resort golf could not have found a better canvas on which to work, nor one which would require more landscape engineering. Tens of thousands of tons of earth and rock were shifted to create lagoons, well stocked with fish—and, by the same token, to drain the swampy ground. The spoil was used to contour the course. Tired trees were uprooted, new ones planted. Dense mangrove scrub was cleared; where the man with a mower now walks, the man with the machete did the donkey work. The result is a masterpiece that is maturing with the years.

Perhaps the most significant factor at Dorado Beach is the Atlantic, forever within sight and sound of the golfer as it combs the glorious beaches. And the sea breezes, changing in direction as the sun passes through the heavens, shape the golfer's shots as though under the personal direction of Trent Jones himself. At the end of the day there is Dorado Beach's clubhouse, the former Spanish colonial estate house and one of the few reminders left of the splendours of Castile; within an hour, by limousine, are the fleshpots of San Juan, the island's capital.

Dorado Beach is well away from the mainstream of golf and as a consequence has not staged many important contests. It has been the site of two televised tournaments and two top events—the 1961 International Golf championship and the 1961 World Cup (then the Canada Cup). The Canada Cup was won by Sam Snead and Jimmy Demaret, whose combined ages were then ninety-nine years. They scored a joint total

Chi Chi Rodrigues's rise as a world player helped promote golf in his native Puerto Rico.

of 560, sixteen under par, winning by a clear twelve strokes. Demaret, whose game had grown rusty from lack of competition, was a last-minute replacement—but he still managed to score an even par of 288. Snead won the individual title with a 272—the sixteen strokes under par that won the team title.

The World Cup matches were staged over a composite course, for only nine holes of the East course had then been completed. Major events are now played over the East course, which is considered the tougher of the two.

The first four holes are pleasantly challenging, the sea sparkling away to the golfer's left as he drives from the first tee. Like the 4th it is a par-four; with the par-three 3rd the three holes call for no more than a 6-iron to the greens. At the 2nd, a par-five of 530 yards, the golfer must hit two long woods to stand any chance of a birdie.

The par-five 5th, 570 yards, is the longest hole on the course. Palms flank either side of the hole from tee to green and the tee shot is threatened by a glaring trio of bunkers and two large mangrove trees. The second is no easier, with three more bunkers standing sentinel on the left and a fourth on the right. The third shot is to an elevated green, from the rear of which the player is faced with a harrowing putt. One bunker lies to the left of the green, another directly in front of it.

There follow two par-fours of moderate length and then the 195-yard par-three 8th, where the chief difficulty lies not in hitting its immense green but in getting down in two putts. The 9th is altogether another matter; it is the most demanding par-four on the course, although at 440 yards its length is not backbreaking. Three bunkers demand accuracy from the tee and the second shot is menaced by trees on either side. It is almost certain to be a long

Over a million cubic yards of earth was moved to fashion the East course at Dorado Beach, the best of five fine courses situated just east of San Juan. Shortly after it opened it was host to the 1961 World Cup, when Sam Snead won the individual title with a sixteen-under-par 272.

iron—perhaps a 4-wood—and the green, which is hemmed in by two giant bunkers, is deep and narrow.

The 10th is a shortish par-five, the beach keeping it company throughout its entire length. The 11th is only 215 yards long, but it is moated about by water and the green is not one to miss. The short par-four 12th plays longer than it looks because the prevailing wind is in the player's teeth and the two lakes of the 13th, 540 yards, pose a fascinating dilemma for both long and short hitters. The 14th, a par-three going away from the ocean, presents no special problem if the golfer does not slice or push his tee shot. Four bunkers embrace the green and water comes into the reckoning on the right.

The last four holes are all par-fours, only the long 16th calling for real power hitting. The 15th requires extreme authority off the tee and in the approach to the green. The fairway is narrow and the elevated green has two tiers, with traps lying to the left, right and front. At 455 yards the 16th is the longest par-four on the course, but the wind is now following. The long, narrow green rises to the rear and is surrounded by bunkers. The dog-leg 17th is made

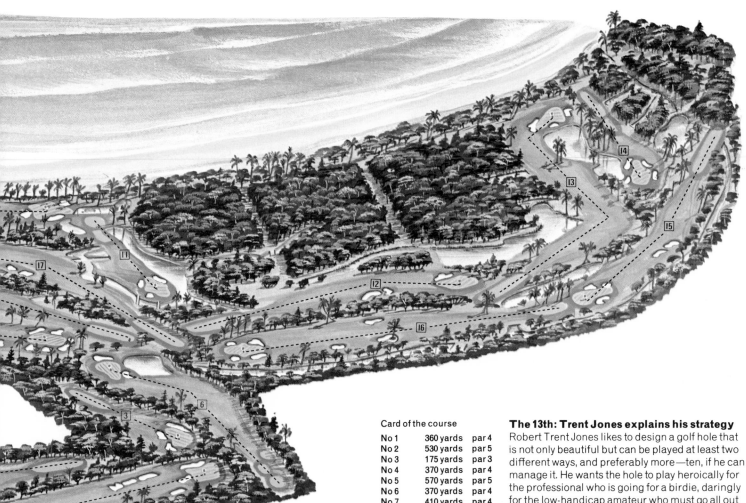

Card of the course		
No 1	360 yards	par 4
No 2	530 yards	par 5
No 3	175 yards	par 3
No 4	370 yards	par 4
No 5	570 yards	par 5
No 6	370 yards	par 4
No 7	410 yards	par 4
No 8	195 yards	par 3
No 9	440 yards	par 4
No 10	520 yards	par 5
No 11	215 yards	par 3
No 12	390 yards	par 4
No 13	540 yards	par 5
No 14	205 yards	par 3
No 15	430 yards	par 4
No 16	455 yards	par 4
No 17	415 yards	par 4
No 18	415 yards	par 4

Dorado Beach Hotel Golf
and Tennis Club,
Puerto Rico

East course
Out   3,420 yards   36
In   3,585 yards   36
Total 7,005 yards   par 72

Record: 64, John Buczek,
International Pro-Am 1975

The 13th : 540 yards par 5
— Scratch player's
  bold line
--- Scratch player's
  safe line
···· Handicap
  player's
  alternatives

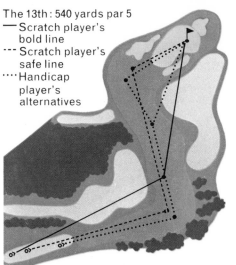

more difficult by trees and by two bunkers just beyond the corner. Double bunkers guard the front of the green. The finishing hole provides a challenging finale, with two large fairway traps to be sidestepped and two more barricading the green. A strong breeze gusting in from the ocean stiffens the challenge.

When the late Ed Dudley first went to Dorado Beach as head professional in 1958, from the Augusta National course, he called the original eighteen holes "the toughest test for the top professionals of any course I have played". The second eighteen is regarded as even tougher!

On paper, the course sounds attractive rather than tough. Seven of its ten par-fours are less than 420 yards long; the longest of the par-threes is only 215 yards and the longest of its par-fives only 570 yards. The secret of Dorado Beach lies in the ever-present Atlantic winds. Trent Jones has cleverly made full use of them by laying out the course in such a way that the player has to cope with the wind from all quarters. Thus it is a perfect resort course, offering a tough challenge to the high-handicap player and, at the same time, giving nothing away to the professional.

The 13th: Trent Jones explains his strategy

Robert Trent Jones likes to design a golf hole that is not only beautiful but can be played at least two different ways, and preferably more—ten, if he can manage it. He wants the hole to play heroically for the professional who is going for a birdie, daringly for the low-handicap amateur who must go all out for his par with the possibility of a birdie, safely for the high handicapper to whom par is a victory, and not overly long for the ladies.

In this respect, the 13th at Dorado Beach is one of his favourites. It is a double dog-leg par-five that twice bends sharply around a water hazard, first to the left and then, near the green, to the right. The green is elevated and, in addition to the protection of the seventy-five-yard-wide lake, is surrounded by traps. Behind the green, about thirty yards away, is the Atlantic. The courageous and capable golfer can reach the green, but he will have made two thoroughly superb shots.

The hole embraces four possibilities. The confident golfer can hit over both lakes to reach the green in two strokes, thereby cutting off a hundred yards of the hole's 540-yard length through the fairway. Or he can elect to play to the right of the first lake and to the left of the second, leaving himself a short pitch to the length of the green. The handicap golfer also has two choices. He may drive safely to the right of the first lake and follow this with a straight second before deciding on whether to gamble by going for the green with his third or settling for the fourth alternative, the safe four-shot route to the green. The ladies have the same options.

In the words of its designer, the hole is "fair to all, demanding all to be sure, but it demonstrates clearly all the rewards and penalties that should be innate to all great golf holes".

Tradition inspires a peerless original

Whenever a new seaside course is constructed, if it uses ocean, beach and cliff to any effect, it is inevitably compared with Pebble Beach, which to most golfers is the ultimate in this type of course. Pete Dye's marvellous creation, Campo de Golf Cajuiles, on the southeast coast of the Dominican Republic, is no exception. But there is one big difference—Cajuiles is worthy of the comparison.

The accolade is intended to be complimentary, but it might offend the quiet-spoken, affable Dye because it implies that the course lacks an identity of its own. Nothing could be farther from the truth. Curving past azure sea and coral reefs, and threading its way through tall Guinea grass and groves of coconut, sea grape and cashew trees (Cajuiles is Spanish for cashew), it is simply one of the most stunning and original of all golf courses. It is not long, at only 6,843 yards from the championship tees, but in any kind of breeze—and the eastern trade winds blow along the coast—only players of the top flight will master its conventional par of 72. Nowhere on the course is the golfer unaware of the sea, and for six holes he may find himself all too conscious of it—for he must hit over it. In all, two glorious stretches of four holes are played beside the ocean. Their impact is so overwhelming that they tend to diminish the remaining holes, though not one of these is in any way dull.

The 1st is pleasantly undemanding, but the next three holes, all on the inland side of the course, are of greater interest, largely because of the inspiration that lies behind them. Dye is very conscious of the qualities of the best traditional Scottish links—"all golf course design is derived from the original Scottish courses"—and he modelled the 2nd at Cajuiles on Prest-

Aptly nicknamed The Doughnut, the 170-yard 13th is perhaps the most sculptured hole at Cajuiles. It is hit-or-miss here, as one holiday golfer found: on a three-day trip, he eventually stayed a week "to hit a green on one of those damn par-threes with my first shot".

wick's 18th. Here, too, the pitch shot is critical because of the bushes, knolls and bunkers that surround the green. The 3rd, a par-five of 536 yards which usually plays somewhat longer because of the wind, has an elevated green that in the words of Dye "simulates the style of Charles Blair Macdonald". The 4th, a tantalizing short par-four slightly downhill, was inspired by the 3rd hole of Donald Ross's masterpiece, the Number 2 course at Pinehurst. Bunkers surrounding the green, slightly offset to the right, call for a courageous and precise approach.

The 5th marks the beginning of the first stretch of seaside holes. Its 215 yards are reduced by at least two clubs by the prevailing following wind. At the 6th the bold drive is rewarded by a green which has been carefully contoured to invite the lofted iron approach. The 195-yard 7th consists of little more than a tee and a green, the distance between being wholly taken up by one long, broad expanse of bunker and, of course, the seashore. The 8th is a fiendishly difficult 385-yarder from a peninsula tee, one of four at Cajuiles that jut out into the ocean.

The second stretch of oceanside holes begins at the 500-yard 14th and all are played into the prevailing wind. The 14th green is artfully placed behind a long, sinuous bunker and an expansive lagoon which make a daunting shot of the gambling second in search of a birdie. Dye describes the 15th, with its tee perched high on the cliffs, as "the longest 380 yards in golf". The hole was designed for a drive and a wedge, so the green is heavily protected. The 16th is a delightful par-three played across the waves which beat lazily against the low cliffs to a sizeable green circled by six traps. The drive at the 17th is again over the sea and, as is so

Cajuiles architect Pete Dye, his own most severe critic, who continues to improve his much-acclaimed design.

often the case at Cajuiles, the player prepared to gamble on his strength and accuracy can earn a birdie.

The course now turns away from the sea for the final hole. But the player still has to contend with water, for a long lagoon thrusts its way into the left side of the fairway to isolate the green, making Cajuiles a test of nerve to the end.

Cajuiles is a remarkable course, but the story of its genesis is possibly even more amazing. It is part of a luxury resort complex of 7,000 acres near the town of La Romana. The resort, known as Costasur, was the brainchild of a Cuban-born naturalized American, Alvaro Carta, and it was he who in 1970 invited Dye to construct a 'special course''. Dye did just that after spotting a likely piece of coastline from an aircraft. It was a mixture of stark rock and impenetrable underbrush. The course was virtually built by hand; Dye and Bruce Mashburn, a North Carolinian who had learned course-building under the tutelage of Donald Ross, marshalled a 300-strong workforce for the task. They not only cleared the site with machetes but made their own top-soil—a mixture of sand, dirt and cachaza, an organic residue from the sugar-refining process. This was spread and raked before the grass was planted, sprig by sprig. They then built the neat little walls which accentuate the teeing areas and some of the bunkers. For this they used a coral called dientes del perro, "teeth of the dog", yet another name that has been bestowed on Cajuiles.

Dye, who has since built a second course at Costasur, described his work at Cajuiles as "a chance of a lifetime to create a seaside course where so much of the sea—almost three miles of it—came into play". Not that it matters to Dye, but that is more than at Pebble Beach.

The view from the tee at the 5th, above, leaves no doubt as to the fearsome possibilities that await the mishit tee shot. However, hitting the small green, right, is only half the problem; it is well contoured and sharply tilted and only a carefully feathered iron shot will hold it.

The 5th: The problem is avoiding the obvious
After the 4th the Cajuiles course reverses direction so that the 5th is not only the first oceanside hole but also the first played with the prevailing wind. The wind at least eases the task of reaching a green 215 yards distant, but club selection is a headache. The green is contoured away from the sea and to hold it the shot must be hit right to left. All the trouble is on the left and can be plainly seen from the tee—all that a player has to do is avoid it!

Although he several times turned down the commission to build a course near La Romana in the Dominican Republic, architect Pete Dye, renowned for his ability to impart a feeling of great naturalness to the courses he builds, finally found an ideal location on a wild stretch of coast. There he built, largely by hand, a distinctive course with tees, some greens and even bunkers walled with coral. It has become his favourite course.

Campo de Golf Cajuiles, La Romana

Out	3,375 yards	36
In	3,468 yards	36
Total	6,843 yards	par 72

Record: 70, George Burns, Jerry Pate, Jaime Gonzales, 1974 World Amateur Golf Team Championship

Card of the course

No 1	380 yards	par 4	No 10	380 yards	par 4
No 2	380 yards	par 4	No 11	548 yards	par 5
No 3	530 yards	par 5	No 12	430 yards	par 4
No 4	320 yards	par 4	No 13	170 yards	par 3
No 5	215 yards	par 3	No 14	500 yards	par 5
No 6	450 yards	par 4	No 15	380 yards	par 4
No 7	195 yards	par 3	No 16	185 yards	par 3
No 8	385 yards	par 4	No 17	435 yards	par 4
No 9	520 yards	par 5	No 18	440 yards	par 4

Mind the bunkers — and the bear cubs!

It was once suggested to no less qualified a judge of golf course beauty than Bobby Locke that Banff Springs occupied one of the most spectacular settings in the world. To which Locke replied: "Not really. It's *out* of this world." So striking is the setting of Banff Springs, in the Canadian Rockies, that it has few visitors who can concentrate only on their golf.

Banff's first course, of only nine holes, was created by the Canadian Pacific Railway Company in 1911 as an added attraction for its huge, turreted Banff Springs Hotel. During World War I a further nine holes were built by German prisoners of war. Stanley Thompson, the Canadian architect with whom Robert Trent Jones served his apprenticeship, was commissioned to redesign the course in 1927. He was assisted by Casper McCullough, a turf expert who was to become the course superintendent for the next forty-four years.

Capitalizing on the setting, Thompson's artistry leaves no suggestion of an altered landscape. There is no evidence that tons of rock were quarried, that hundreds of trees were felled and trainloads of topsoil transported from an experimental farm on the Prairies, a hundred miles to the east. None the less, maintenance problems remain legion. Golf course greenmasters in southern Alberta wage an endless battle with the ravages of alternate freezing and thawing, caused by the sub-zero temperatures and mild Chinook winds of winter, and by the warm, sunny days and sub-zero nights of spring.

Measured against the exacting standards of today's top players, Banff Springs is a true championship test. Yet its 6,729-yard challenge has never been used for a major competition, perhaps because of its remoteness. The course is a maze of bunkers—144 in all. Twenty-eight

of them come into play at the 18th, an imperious finishing hole running parallel to the Bow River and only a few hundred feet from thundering Bow Falls. The surrounding mountains induce an optical illusion; distances appear reduced, tempting the use of a short club where a longer one is necessary. Conversely, links golfers tend to use too much club, forgetting that the ball travels farther in the thin mountain air.

The 1st tee, immediately below the clubhouse pavilion overlooking the often torrential confluence of the Bow and Spray rivers, presents a breathtaking vista. A precipice drops to the Spray tributary directly in front of the tee and, although the carry across it is less than a hundred yards, the churning river has been known to unnerve the most composed of scratch players. The drive should carry a crest 200 yards distant and avoid a mound on the right, fronting dense forest. Now the green opens up, but accuracy is still essential for a safe par of four, because six narrow traps crowd tightly around the sides and rear.

The 2nd and 3rd are both short, undemanding par-fours. They contrast sharply with the 4th, the course's longest hole, where mounds and bunkers are neatly stacked on the fairway. The drive must clear a cavernous bunker snaking from the left; a sound second, across a nest of mounds and traps, leaves a fairly open avenue home. From a straightaway par-four of undemanding length, the route swings south towards the steep face of Mount Rundle, which so dominates the course. The short 6th is conventional, requiring an iron shot to a raised green imprisoned by traps, but the par-five 7th, aptly named Gibraltar, is unusual. The tee gazes out on a rather lean strip of greensward, bounded on the right by the rising cliffs of Mount Rundle and on the left by a series of

traps. A precise shot is required to reach the green in two, for it is tucked away to the right, partially hidden, and the approach must thread between the precipice on the right and the sand that lies to the left.

An easy climb to a high lookout affords a heart-stopping view of the par-three 8th, known as the Devil's Cauldron. This famous hole calls for a most difficult shot, complicated by swirling wind, from an elevated tee across a lake to a tiny, heavily bunkered green. This is followed by a short walk over the road and through a pleasant forest glade to the 9th, a dog-leg par-four sliced out of dense woods. The fairway curves and slopes left, guiding hooked shots into bunkers which lie beyond an awkward trough. A prodigious second shot is required to reach the green, trapped heavily to the right. The relatively routine 10th, straight but to an elevated and well-trapped green, leaves one at the farthest point from the clubhouse as the course angles north towards the Bow River and a panorama of cliffs beyond, webbed with pillars of clay, sand and gravel known as the Hoodoos. A network of bunkers surrounds the green on the downhill par-five 11th, which, if the two

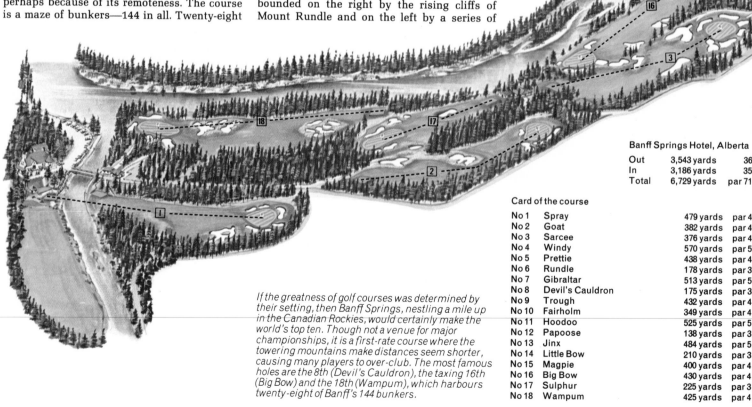

If the greatness of golf courses was determined by their setting, then Banff Springs, nestling a mile up in the Canadian Rockies, would certainly make the world's top ten. Though not a venue for major championships, it is a first-rate course where the towering mountains make distances seem shorter, causing many players to over-club. The most famous holes are the 8th (Devil's Cauldron), the taxing 16th (Big Bow) and the 18th (Wampum), which harbours twenty-eight of Banff's 144 bunkers.

Banff Springs Hotel, Alberta

Out	3,543 yards	36
In	3,186 yards	35
Total	6,729 yards	par 71

Card of the course

No 1	Spray	479 yards	par 4
No 2	Goat	382 yards	par 4
No 3	Sarcee	376 yards	par 4
No 4	Windy	570 yards	par 5
No 5	Prettie	438 yards	par 4
No 6	Rundle	178 yards	par 3
No 7	Gibraltar	513 yards	par 5
No 8	Devil's Cauldron	175 yards	par 3
No 9	Trough	432 yards	par 4
No 10	Fairholm	349 yards	par 4
No 11	Hoodoo	525 yards	par 5
No 12	Papoose	138 yards	par 3
No 13	Jinx	484 yards	par 5
No 14	Little Bow	210 yards	par 3
No 15	Magpie	400 yards	par 4
No 16	Big Bow	430 yards	par 4
No 17	Sulphur	225 yards	par 3
No 18	Wampum	425 yards	par 4

cross-bunkers can be avoided, offers chances of a birdie.

The course now turns back along the Bow River towards the distant battlements of the hotel. The drive at the tree-sheltered 12th, the 138-yard Papoose, carries a long strip of tee and a backwash of the river. The 13th green, hidden from the tee, is accessible in two with an exacting drive that will stand some pull out of a chute of trees to the more elevated left side of the fairway.

An arm of the river severs the 14th, which is lengthy for a par-three: the temptation is to use a wood to reach the green, but the fairway banks sharply in the direction of the water and any slight fade or short shot is doomed. It makes the 14th a score-wrecking hole. Two cross-bunkers and nine greenside traps make the 15th tough, yet it is the 16th, another par-four, which boasts the toughest rating at Banff Springs. It is a slight dog-leg to the right with a series of bunkers off the tee and a fairway that rolls and heaves, pinching in to the right and trees and sand to the left. The green is long and narrow. Accuracy with the middle irons is vital.

The shadow of nearby Tunnel Mountain looms directly above the 17th, a flat, long par-three with severe traps flanking the green. The 18th, another slight dog-leg right, has two massive clusters of bunkers, one of which must be carried. The fairway traps, which stretch to 185 yards off the tee, can only be avoided by courting the trees down the narrow right side, but this only makes for an extremely difficult shot across the second nest of traps.

The Banff Springs course lies within a National Park game reserve; deer and even a bear cub or two can be seen from time to time. But these distractions merely add to the charm of the course which, although rooted in a mountain fastness, asks no unnecessary climbing of its players. It does, however, make demands on their game, calling for thoughtfulness and accuracy. Banff Springs is indeed out of this world.

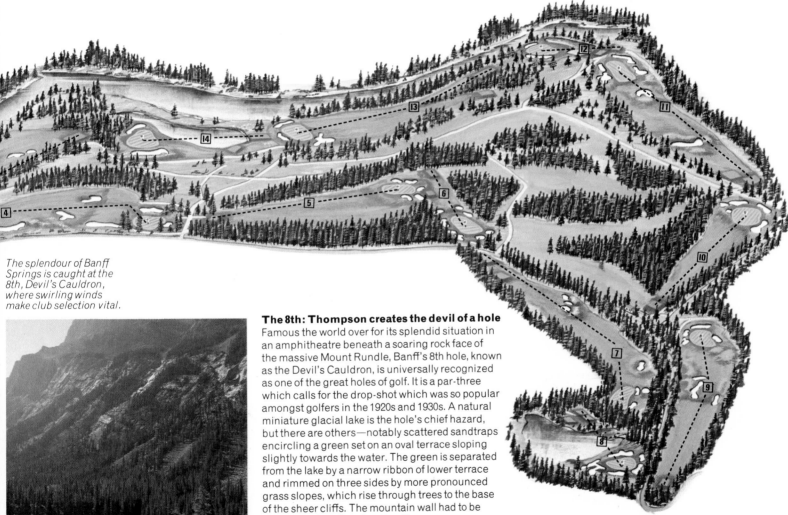

The splendour of Banff Springs is caught at the 8th, Devil's Cauldron, where swirling winds make club selection vital.

The 8th: Thompson creates the devil of a hole

Famous the world over for its splendid situation in an amphitheatre beneath a soaring rock face of the massive Mount Rundle, Banff's 8th hole, known as the Devil's Cauldron, is universally recognized as one of the great holes of golf. It is a par-three which calls for the drop-shot which was so popular amongst golfers in the 1920s and 1930s. A natural miniature glacial lake is the hole's chief hazard, but there are others—notably scattered sandtraps encircling a green set on an oval terrace sloping slightly towards the water. The green is separated from the lake by a narrow ribbon of lower terrace and rimmed on three sides by more pronounced grass slopes, which rise through trees to the base of the sheer cliffs. The mountain wall had to be blasted to clear the site when the course was reconstructed in 1927.

From the championship tee, high above the lake to the west, a 175-yard iron shot is required. Pin placement dictates the degree of risk to be considered from the tee. Wind, though sometimes a factor, is rarely excessive because of the sheltered setting. The usual pin position is to the front, making for the greatest degree of difficulty.

The putting green is not unduly large, but normally soft enough to hold a shot with a steep trajectory. However, because of the danger of the downslope, the temptation is to carom the shot off the steep side-slopes so that the ball rolls in an arc to the putting surface. Over-clubbing is a natural mistake from the elevated tee. From its lofty level, the lake appears larger and the green more distant. Long shots will disappear into the trees or strike high on the bank and rebound, on occasion to the very edge of the water.

"The decision must be made at the tee and then it's a matter of precision," says head professional Malcolm Tapp, who terms the Cauldron "an ideal example of Stanley Thompson's uncanny knack for producing marvellous holes in rugged terrain".

A course worthy of its glorious setting

The visitor's first impression of Capilano is of its almost Olympian setting. Buttressed to the north and east by the coastal mountains of British Columbia, it overlooks the not unpleasing sprawl of urban Vancouver with Mount Baker beyond, south of the 49th Parallel; to the west is a misty Vancouver Island, across the Strait of Georgia. It is a vista decidedly distracting to the concentration, even for those club members most used to it.

A glorious setting does not in itself make a great golf course. But while the views at Capilano may distract, they do not detract from the course's true golfing qualities. This course, in which no two holes are remotely similar, would be outstanding wherever it were set down.

Capilano is exceptional in this part of the world as one of the few courses—if not the only one—which has not been drastically remodelled since it was opened. It was designed and constructed in 1937 by Stanley Thompson, the well-known Canadian golf course architect and creator of many other exquisite courses, among them Banff Springs. The course was part of a

huge project embarked upon in the early 1930s by Guinness Estates. The scheme was for a high-class residential development and golf course at West Vancouver, isolated from the city proper by the Burrard Inlet but to be linked to it by a mile-long bridge. It was a huge undertaking by any standards, not least in the construction of the course itself.

Capilano had to be shaped from a hillside tangled with the stumps of Douglas firs, cedar and hemlock, a forest of second-growth trees and massive outcrops of rock. The result, nevertheless, is a gem. It is not difficult for the player of average ability who keeps his drives in the fairways. The championship course measures 6,538 yards but it can be stretched by more than 300 yards for special events.

The 1st is downhill all the way—453 yards, but closer to 500 from a seldom-used championship tee, within a whisper of the men's bar. It is a hole where the par of five feels more like a bogey to the scratch player. The par-four 2nd, a drive and medium iron, is followed by a blind uphill tee shot at the 451-yard 3rd, a par-

four that is littered with bunkers. Sprayed wood shots here create problems in reaching the relatively small and well-guarded green in regulation figures. A mid-iron will suffice to carry a pond safely to the double-tiered green of the par-three 4th, though insufficient club leaves a nasty putt if the pin placement is on the upper level.

Then comes yet another par-five, a dog-leg right over more water which, from one of the upper tees, demands a flush and perfectly placed drive. The second shot, hit downhill towards the city, must also be accurate to the vicinity of an undulating, treacherously fast green. The stroll down the 6th is a divine pleasure; the spectacle below of the Lions Gate Bridge, linking Vancouver with the North Shore across the sparkling waters of Burrard Inlet, is simply entrancing. By the time the golfer is putting on the 6th green he has descended almost 300 feet from the 1st tee, 672 feet above sea-level. Many handicap players have negotiated these first six holes well under par figures.

But there are pitfalls ahead, for now the course flattens out and Capilano begins to catch up on the careless golfer. The next two holes are both fine par-fours. The climb back towards clubhouse level begins from the 9th tee. The hole is a troublesome, 183-yard par-three on which club selection varies according to the weather. It usually requires a low iron or spoon to reach the elongated green guarded by gaping bunkers, from which only the top of the flagstick is visible.

The beginning of the second nine offers some relief—a possible birdie at the 10th. It is less than 460 yards long, a dog-leg left calling for accuracy with the second shot to an elevated, narrow-necked entrance to the green. The next hole is a sheer delight. From the elevated tee it is nothing more than a 6- or 7-iron over a man-made pond, but the slick green undulates like an oily sea in a swell.

On the last seven holes birdies are uncommon and pars require considerably more finesse

The downhill 1st hole at Capilano, with the clubhouse, the highest point on the course, and the coastal mountains in the background. The course, built on a steeply sloping hillside, drops through some 300 feet to its lowest point. As a result many fairways were built across the slope and uphill and downhill lies are common.

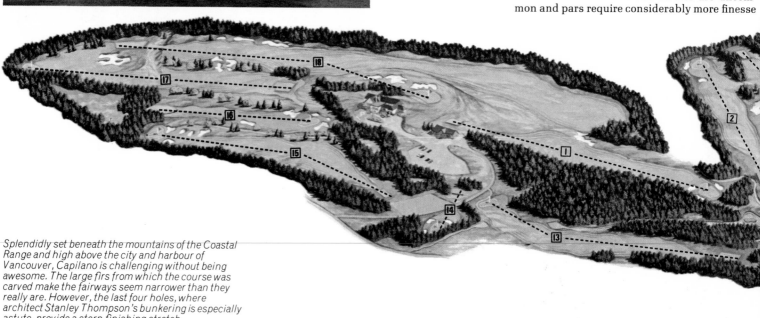

Splendidly set beneath the mountains of the Coastal Range and high above the city and harbour of Vancouver, Capilano is challenging without being awesome. The large firs from which the course was carved make the fairways seem narrower than they really are. However, the last four holes, where architect Stanley Thompson's bunkering is especially astute, provide a stern finishing stretch.

and thought than has hitherto been necessary. The exception, perhaps, is the short 14th, a pitch over the main driveway from another elevated tee. The 12th and 13th, both par-fours, call for well-placed drives followed by precise shots over a stream at the 12th and a gully at the longer 13th.

The 15th, like the 7th, cannot be manipulated without two exceptional shots. It is an ominous 420-yarder, directly into the face of the mountains and slightly uphill to the green. Short hitters can only hope to chip and one-putt to achieve par here. At the 16th a par-three, even on the calmest of days, is utter victory. From the back tee it is 254 yards to the green, which sits immediately beneath the clubhouse. With any kind of opposing wind it is nothing less than a full wood.

At the 17th, slightly over 400 yards long, the main difficulties lie in club selection and in avoiding an awkward lie among the fairway mounds while steering clear of a long bunker and the obtrusive trees on the left. The green is in a beautiful setting, softened by the shadows of tall trees and the mountains.

The home hole is a classic, 575 yards long and uphill all the way to a green set on the side of a hill scattered with a network of bunkers. The safe way to approach this monster is to lay up short of the three diagonal bunkers fronting the green, leaving a mid-iron approach over the inviting sand to the elevated but reasonably flat green. Few long hitters have ever reached this green in two. It is a feat requiring a "Sunday best" drive and a gambling brassie over the narrow, upper portion of the fairway, which is flanked by the bunkers and out-of-bounds stakes.

The elevation and the nearness of the mountains make Capilano vulnerable to rain, and umbrellas are an essential item throughout the winter and spring. But few golfers—no matter what the weather or their final scores—have ever left Capilano without singing the praises of this truly magnificently set course.

The 4th and 11th: Thompson at his fiercest

Stanley Thompson, Capilano's Scottish-born architect, made something of a specialty of creating fascinating short holes. Among the more celebrated are the Devil's Cauldron at Banff Springs and, at nearby Jasper, the 150-yard Bad Baby and the slightly longer Colin's Clout. At Capilano Thompson maintained his tradition of colourfully named, tough par-threes.

Two of them, the 4th and 11th, are across stretches of water after which they have been named. Paradoxically these names imply a certain ease and benevolence on the part of the architect. Indeed, the water at the 4th, known as Lily Pond, is intimidating only to the handicap golfer who might otherwise find the hole relatively easy. It is only from the extended championship tees, which can stretch the hole to almost 200 yards, that the 4th becomes in any way fierce. Then, because of three huge traps which guard the front half of the

With a carry over one of the three natural lakes at Capilano and a two-tiered green surrounded by firs, the 168-yard smallish, two-tiered green, the drive must be absolutely accurate, particularly when the pin is on the farther, upper level.

4th is one of the most attractive holes on this beautiful course. Traps in front and on both sides call for precision.

The 11th, called Wishing Well, is an entirely different proposition. It embodies all the characteristics that have made Thompson's short holes so feared. Typically, it is only 155 yards long but the green, wonderfully sited amongst stately pine trees, is fast and heavily undulated and tightly enclosed by hazards. Immediately in front is a small lake and around the back and sides are four long, sprawling bunkers. Anything other than the most precise medium iron shot will find severe trouble. Fittingly, this beautiful hole is the architect's favourite.

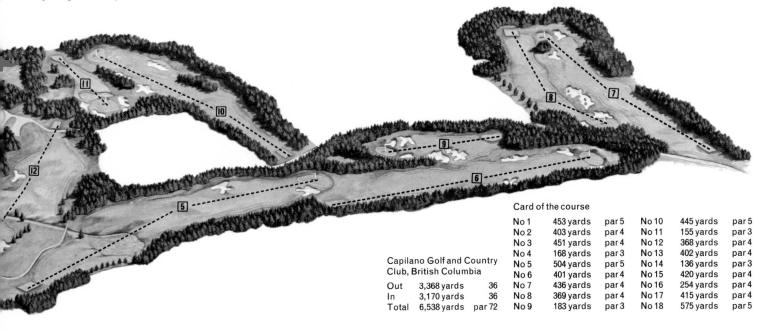

Capilano Golf and Country Club, British Columbia

Out	3,368 yards	36						
In	3,170 yards	36						
Total	6,538 yards	par 72						

Card of the course

No 1	453 yards	par 5	No 10	445 yards	par 5
No 2	403 yards	par 4	No 11	155 yards	par 3
No 3	451 yards	par 4	No 12	368 yards	par 4
No 4	168 yards	par 3	No 13	402 yards	par 4
No 5	504 yards	par 5	No 14	136 yards	par 3
No 6	401 yards	par 4	No 15	420 yards	par 4
No 7	436 yards	par 4	No 16	254 yards	par 4
No 8	369 yards	par 4	No 17	415 yards	par 4
No 9	183 yards	par 3	No 18	575 yards	par 5

Fit for the next fifty years

Though rarely used for major competitions, the Blue course at Royal Montreal is regarded by many experts as the finest in Canada. It became better known after the 1975 Canadian Open, when Tom Weiskopf and Jack Nicklaus broke the record by three shots in the opening round. The most notable feature of this beautiful course is the size of the greens—averaging 12,000 square feet, almost twice the usual size.

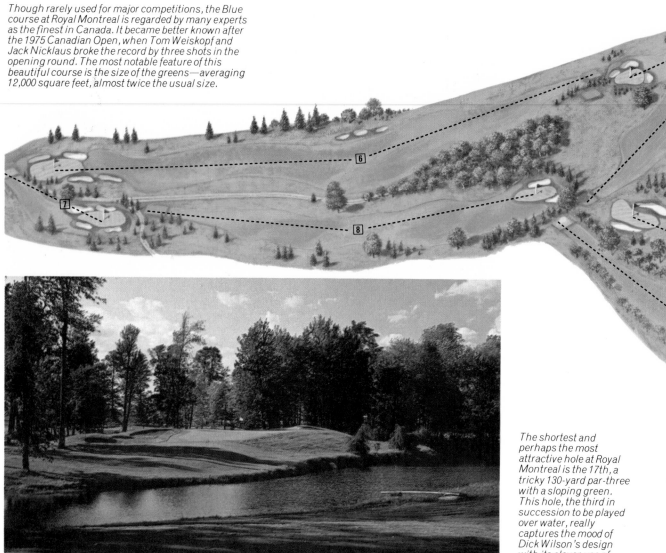

The shortest and perhaps the most attractive hole at Royal Montreal is the 17th, a tricky 130-yard par-three with a sloping green. This hole, the third in succession to be played over water, really captures the mood of Dick Wilson's design with its clever use of sand, trees and water.

Whatever insubstantial traces of golf there are to be found in the history of North America before the late nineteenth century, pride of place in seniority must go to Canada and in particular to the Royal Montreal Club, which celebrated its centenary in 1973. It was the first properly constituted club on the continent, predating the first in the United States—St Andrews at Yonkers, New York— by fifteen years.

Golf in Canada is older than in the United States probably because Canada attracted the larger proportion of Scottish immigrants. Toronto Golf Club, Royal Quebec and Brantford Golf and Country Club, Ontario, though marginally younger than Montreal, are older than any of their counterparts across the border.

Royal Montreal's beginnings were those of countless clubs throughout the world—a group of Scots getting together to recreate, in alien surroundings, their national sport. They were led by a bearded giant, Alexander Dennistoun, whose name was proof enough of his antecedents. The medal he gave for competition

(upon which, by means of a little Scottish finagling, he managed to have his name the first to be engraved) is still played for as the symbol of the club's championship.

Fletcher's Field, a public park on the slopes of Mount Royal, was the club's first site. The joining fee was five dollars, the annual dues half as much; a wooden club would set a member back two dollars. The site was adequate to begin with, but in time the game attracted more players and, moreover, Montreal was growing rapidly. In 1896 a new site was found at Dixie, ten miles to the west of the city, and here the club was to remain for the next sixty-three years.

The Dixie course saw the first Canadian national championships, the women's amateur in 1901 and the men's a year later. The club also staged the world's first "international", the first of an annual series between Royal Montreal and The Country Club of Brookline, Massachusetts. The contest predates by four years the England–Scotland series, which began in 1902 and is still played.

Dixie was to be the venue for five Canadian Opens, won by J. H. Oke (1904), Albert Murray (1908 and 1913), Macdonald Smith (1926) and Jim Ferrier (1950). It was played by those legends of the links Harry Vardon and Ted Ray; and by the Prince of Wales (later King Edward VIII) and Lloyd George.

The tentacles of the urban octopus that had squeezed the club from its first home reached out again in the 1950s. A site was found on Ile Bizard in the Lake of Two Mountains, and the late Dick Wilson was fetched from Florida to design the course.

Wilson, an outstanding golf architect, was the second choice. The Royal Montreal had first sought the services of Robert Trent Jones, but he was otherwise committed.

Trent Jones and Wilson made much of their professional rivalry and were never slow to damn each other's work with faint praise. The two were as different as a driver and a sand-iron. Trent Jones brings to his work a background that is almost academically perfect for the job of golf course design. At Cornell he

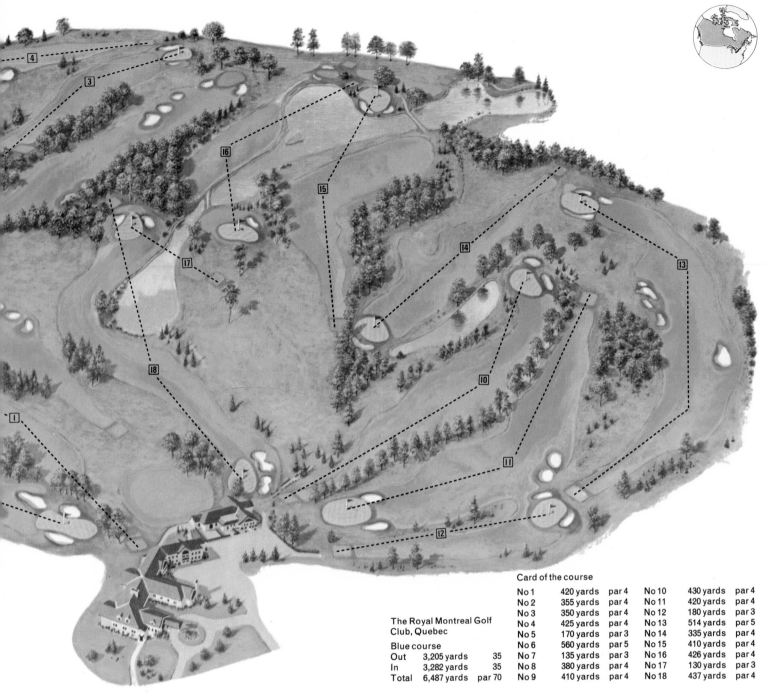

Card of the course

No 1	420 yards	par 4		No 10	430 yards	par 4
No 2	355 yards	par 4		No 11	420 yards	par 4
No 3	350 yards	par 4		No 12	180 yards	par 3
No 4	425 yards	par 4		No 13	514 yards	par 5
No 5	170 yards	par 3		No 14	335 yards	par 4
No 6	560 yards	par 5		No 15	410 yards	par 4
No 7	135 yards	par 3		No 16	426 yards	par 4
No 8	380 yards	par 4		No 17	130 yards	par 3
No 9	410 yards	par 4		No 18	437 yards	par 4

The Royal Montreal Golf Club, Quebec

Blue course

Out	3,205 yards	35
In	3,282 yards	35
Total	6,487 yards	par 70

successively studied engineering, architecture and agriculture, taking in the essential disciplines of surveying, hydraulics and landscape architecture, among other things. He is an urbane man and his courses reflect this.

Dick Wilson, a down-to-earth, blunt-spoken man, was a fully fledged civil engineer who went to college on a football scholarship. To him, a Jones course was too contrived, paying too little attention to the nature of the land on which it was built; he believed that it took a better man to build a course than to lay one out. Trent Jones is equally succinct: the heart of a good golf course is its design, he believes—any good engineer can do the rest.

How Royal Montreal's Ile Bizard courses—two of eighteen holes, the Red and the Blue, and a nine hole—would have differed had Jones and not Wilson designed them is mere speculation. They certainly needed Wilson's constructional talents. There were rocks, boulders, tree stumps to be removed, swamp to be drained and lakes to be created, all in a climate in which snow and ice put paid to any work for months on end.

All forty-five holes were completed for play in just over two years, finishing in May 1959. Wilson was proud of his creation. On a visit to the club before his untimely death he remarked: "There is a sweep and dimension to this layout which can only be described as exciting. That vista of the Lake of Two Mountains is the perfect backdrop to these courses. Don't ever shut off the view with too many trees.

"I have designed these courses for the present and the future. With the improvement in players' abilities and training and with better equipment, older courses will become old-fashioned and inadequate in the next fifteen years. The Red and the Blue courses will remain modern and can be made even more challenging for the next fifty years."

Both Red and Blue courses are formidable assignments and are distinctive in that they are among the few in Quebec which, for handicap purposes, are rated higher than their par. Both courses have a par of 70 but are rated at 72. It is generally accepted that a Royal Montreal player can play to his handicap anywhere.

The greens—to which Dick Wilson paid particular attention—are enormous, averaging 12,000 square feet in size, nearly double the conventional size in North America. It means that from the same patch of fairway, under comparable wind conditions, the approach might call for anything from a 3-iron to a 5-iron, depending on where the pin is placed.

Putts of extraordinary length are often called for, up to 120 feet in extreme cases. Pat Fletcher, the professional at Montreal for twenty years, says: "The secret is to hit your approaches a little longer rather than a little shorter. While some of the entrances are narrow, they all widen out considerably towards the back. The greens also putt deceptively."

Unlike many challenging courses, Royal Montreal is not renowned for its fairway bunkering; there are only eleven on the Blue course. But closer to the scoring areas, no fewer than forty-eight traps—deep gouges filled with heavy sand and with diabolical contours—guard the greens themselves.

The thoughtfully placed and artistically ▷

Tom Weiskopf took his second Canadian Open title in 1975 by edging out Jack Nicklaus in a play-off. The tie-breaker was the 15th, where his approach shot finished two feet from the pin. This play-off was only the third in the history of the Canadian Open, first contested in 1904.

▷ moulded bunkers are typical of Dick Wilson's design. Indeed, Royal Montreal could well be described as the archetypal Wilson course. It has the bunkers, the gently contoured greens and the winding fairways, softly mounded to blend superbly with their surroundings. The hand of man is unobtrusive, the beauty of the course is muted and, despite the changes in the landscape wrought by Wilson, there is not jarring artificiality, only a serene naturalness.

Regular players regard the Red course with more respect as a test of all-round golfing skills. The "Blue Monster" is far more celebrated, largely because of the four finishing holes that throw out a direct challenge to the player, daring him to take on their vast expanses of water.

Nobody in tournament play was able to peel more than two strokes from par before the 1975 Canadian Open, when both Nicklaus and Weiskopf opened with 65s. Nicklaus let the title slip from his grasp when he hooked his tee shot into the water on the dog-leg of the finishing hole, and was forced into a play-off.

The tie-breaker took place on the 15th, a 410-yarder distinguished by a lake that bites into the fairway and protects the green. Because of the water, both Nicklaus and Weiskopf had to hold back off the tee, but both were left with only 7-iron approaches. Weiskopf's stopped two feet from the pin, Nicklaus's almost hit his rival's ball, but was carried back eight feet by the backspin. Nicklaus missed the putt, Weiskopf did not.

Nicklaus had come face to face with the realities of the philosophy espoused by both Trent Jones and Dick Wilson: "A golf hole should be a hard par and an easy bogey." At Royal Montreal that is true of all the holes.

The 16th: Determination gains immortality

The 16th hole on the Blue course at Royal Montreal is perhaps the most intimidating par-four in Canada. At 415 yards from the regular tee-markers and no more than 430 yards from the very back, it is not inordinately long. It has only one sandtrap—but that is all it needs.

The challenge is that the normal flight of the ball between tee and green is almost wholly over water. The drive is across a lake which the approach has to recross to reach an elevated pear-shaped green. The wind is almost always against and the second shot is invariably a long iron shot or even a wood hit low.

The lake is contoured so that the safer the line a player takes from the tee—in other words the farther to the right—the more difficult his approach becomes, because the carry over the water in front of the green is lengthened.

It is not uncommon for a proficient player to pump two or even three balls into the lake from the tee and then follow them with two or three more negotiating the approach. Scores in the low twenties have been recorded on the hole. In one tournament played by Canada's premier senior players flooding made the hole unplayable and it was assigned an arbitrary rating of 5.5, the figure being added to everybody's card.

The hole was also the setting for a memorable par-four by an intense young tour regular named Pat Fitzsimons in the 1975 Canadian Open. In the

The 16th tee, from which Pat Fitzsimons hit his memorable drive, lies between the two greens on the right-hand side of the large lake.

The 16th: 426 yards par 4

Fitzsimons ———
Normal line -----

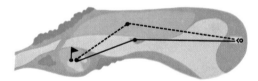

second round his drive was struck off line to the left, straight towards the water. Fitzsimons was preparing to reload when the ball came down on a raft-sized island some ten yards from the shore. The ball was plainly visible but seemingly inaccessible. Or was it?

Nobody had ever tried it before, but there was nothing in the rules of golf to stop Fitzsimons from attempting to reach the island. He climbed on to his caddie's back but proved to be too much of a load and the two of them tottered and nearly went under. Fitzsimons then ventured out alone. The water turned out to be no more than waist deep.

He completed the crossing, lofted a 4-iron to the green, made the return trip without incident, partially dried himself and two-putted from thirty feet for his par. The inconsequential island now has a name. It is called after Fitzsimons.

Golf with a mid-Atlantic accent

The name of Mid Ocean has a faraway, compelling sound. It is one of the remotest of all the British Commonwealth courses in the northern hemisphere, yet the golfer is rare who has not heard tell of its fame. It lies on the southern shores of Bermuda, that entrancing island in the western reaches of the Atlantic,

The approach to the 11th green, dominated by Trott's Pond. At 487 yards this dog-leg left, considered to be the easiest of Mid Ocean's three par-fives, provides a welcome relief from the rigours of a demanding course.

and has become familiar to legions of Americans; New York is only ninety minutes away by scheduled airliner.

Mid Ocean has no close parallel; in some aspects it might resemble Cypress Point, because while the ocean plays little part in its design, it provides a glorious background to

the beginning and the end. The greater part of the course is laid over beautiful inland country of rolling hills and crests, gentle vales and valleys, coursing through deep woods of casuarina and innumerable flowering shrubs. One might be miles from the sea, but no point is more than a few substantial golf shots from the coast.

The course was designed in 1924 by the great pioneer of American golf Charles Blair Macdonald, who had matriculated at St Andrews and seemed determined to spread the gospel of Scottish golf wherever he could. There are no outstanding signs of this at Mid Ocean; it bears no resemblance to any course in Scotland, but the skill of the bunkering shows an imagination that had its roots in the old concepts of architecture. In 1953 the course was revised in some measure by Robert Trent Jones. It is a lasting compliment to both men.

Even in December it can be a joy, with the trade winds standing firm off the ocean, a marvel of deep blue, amethyst and turquoise, and the encircling reef making a distant chain of silver. The impact of a wondrous setting does not diminish respect for the quality of the golf. It begins with a magnificent par-four, curving to the left and rightly called Atlantic; it is simple enough to pull the second away from the raised green down to the rocks below. The 2nd swings down into the woods and up again to make a hole that is harder the longer one looks at it. From tee to green the short 3rd is a perfectly straight offering; it seems no greater problem than a thousand others of its length, until suddenly one is aware of the long fall to the ocean on the left and the garden on the right.

The 4th is another plunge-and-rise affair, narrow between trees and not altogether ▷

The 5th: A play upon courage, fear and greed

Fortunately there is no way that golfers, even Nicklaus, can walk on water, although some of his rivals might suspect he is sometimes possessed of such powers. Unless the distance across lakes, ocean inlets and wide rivers has previously been measured the player must rely on the evidence of his eyes. This practice is becoming increasingly rare in an age when most leading golfers, or their caddies, pace the distances to the greens and the various pin positions and write them down for future reference. Without these, many would seem to be lost.

Sport holds few more ridiculous sights than that of an eminent golfer striding down the fairway like a trainee surveyor, looking for the bush, tree or whatever his distance marker may be, and then pacing one way or the other—often as little as a few yards—to his ball. On one famous occasion a player finished far over a green with an admirably struck shot and then realized he had added instead of subtracted.

As an amateur, Nicklaus was one of the first to bring pacing into prominence. It suits his precise, infinitely methodical approach and nobody could say that he has suffered as a result. But few of the great golfers before him did it. Hogan never did, saying that it would have disturbed his concentration; neither did Locke, Cotton or Thomson. They relied on their own distance

perception and feel for the shot, as must any golfer standing on Mid Ocean's 5th tee preparing to play across Mangrove Lake.

The hole, 433 yards long, is a perfect example of how an architect can play upon courage, fear and greed. The fairway curves around a lake which is at its widest on the direct line to the green. The timid can play safely to the right, from where there is little or no hope of reaching the green with the next shot; the alternative is to attempt to drive over as much of the lake as he can or dares. The longer the carry made, the shorter and easier the approach.

From the tee high above the lake the distance across to the fairway looks shorter than it is, as distances invariably do over water. And so, until the golfer knows the limits of his skill and nerve, usually from the chastening experience of seeing a well-struck drive splash from sight forever, far short of where he thought it would finish, discretion is the better part.

The principle of being invited to bite off as much as one can reasonably hope to do is a basic of good design, and not by any means confined to water holes. The drive to the 6th at Pine Valley, where a wilderness slants across the line to the fairway, has deceived many into thinking they were stronger than they were, or has taught them not to be greedy. But then water is the classic hazard for such purposes. It has a dreadful finality.

The view from the back tee at Mid Ocean's 433-yard 5th. Despite the fact that the green seems closer than it is, the temptation is to try to cut off too much of the gentle dog-leg.

The Atlantic plays little part in the design of Mid Ocean, but it provides a magnificent backdrop to a course which is given something of a cathedral-like atmosphere by tall, elegant pines. Although length is important at Mid Ocean (the par-three 13th is 238 yards long, and six of the par-fours measure more than 400 yards), there is some compensation in the size of the greens. The course is the best of four excellent ones on an island twenty-one miles long.

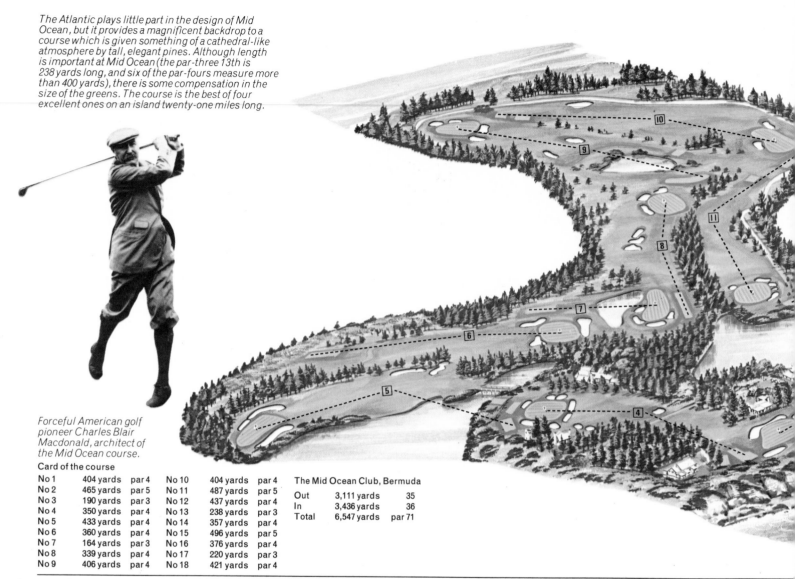

Forceful American golf pioneer Charles Blair Macdonald, architect of the Mid Ocean course.

Card of the course

No 1	404 yards	par 4	No 10	404 yards	par 4
No 2	465 yards	par 5	No 11	487 yards	par 5
No 3	190 yards	par 3	No 12	437 yards	par 4
No 4	350 yards	par 4	No 13	238 yards	par 3
No 5	433 yards	par 4	No 14	357 yards	par 4
No 6	360 yards	par 4	No 15	496 yards	par 5
No 7	164 yards	par 3	No 16	376 yards	par 4
No 8	339 yards	par 4	No 17	220 yards	par 3
No 9	406 yards	par 4	No 18	421 yards	par 4

The Mid Ocean Club, Bermuda

Out	3,111 yards	35
In	3,436 yards	36
Total	6,547 yards	par 71

appealing. But what rewards await the climb; the 5th is one of the world's unforgettable holes. Far beneath a gun platform of a tee spreads the shining expanse of Mangrove Lake and, in a manner of speaking, one sips as much of it as one can swallow. There is a way to the right for the frail of heart, but any carry over the water is considerable. The next three holes are a quiet interlude before the stern tasks really begin. Solid drives to the 6th and 8th leave only pitches, but these are to greens above eye level. This is a feature of Mid Ocean, making distances—even of little shots—difficult to judge precisely. The greens are not too small, but the slopes protecting them are often steep and recovery of an erring approach can be difficult. The greens are not watered artificially, but the ample rain and sunshine permit two growths of grass each year—Bermuda in the summer, rye and bent for the winter. The greens therefore are good the year around, although their pace and contours need knowing.

The 7th is a medium pitch over a pool and so far par has not been too exacting; the golfer, on his first visit, may wonder whether the course is as demanding as he has been led to expect. But the hard part is at hand. From the back tee of the 9th the carry is disturbingly long, with no easy alternative, over a wilderness of rushes that would not be out of place at Westward Ho! on the north Devon coast. The drive down the 10th, after ice has tinkled in glasses at the turn, seems spacious enough, but only one of exact placing will leave a clear shot to the green. A huge bunker guards its right side, and usually the pin. This is a splendid hole except that the over-bold shot is likely to be punished too severely. After a drive over a crest the 11th is a fair par-five, the 12th nobody's easy four with the tee shot across a leaning shoulder of hillside, and the 13th a long short hole to a green ringed with traps.

The bunkers on the left of the 14th are suggestive of Muirfield in their clustered insistence on trapping a pull to the fairway that tilts in their direction. Two good hits to the 15th should leave an easy pitch over rising ground to the green. Then follows a menacing uphill drive between trouble on the left and a great green basin, into which anything but the truly

struck drive will roll. From there the second, naturally enough, is blind; but even from the fairway—and the hole is not long—the green on its high place, free to all the wind's force, can be elusive. And now the ocean is in sight again and a splendid 17th awaits. It was named Redan—presumably after the famous 15th at North Berwick, although there the similarity ceases. The shot is downhill, but into wind many golfers will be feeling for a wooden club.

The 18th pursues the line of the beach and the tee is situated high above it. Behind are the cliffs with pink and white houses clustered about their edges; ahead the handsome white mass of the clubhouse, where Churchill and Eisenhower once conversed of matters other than golf. The long driver must beware here because the fairway narrows abruptly. But the hole is beautifully shaped, and as one holes out there is a feeling that an enduring memory has been made. Beyond the green is the little practice ground where Archie Compston, so long the professional at Mid Ocean, gave his lessons; a memorial to him stands near by.

Golf in Bermuda is not confined to Mid

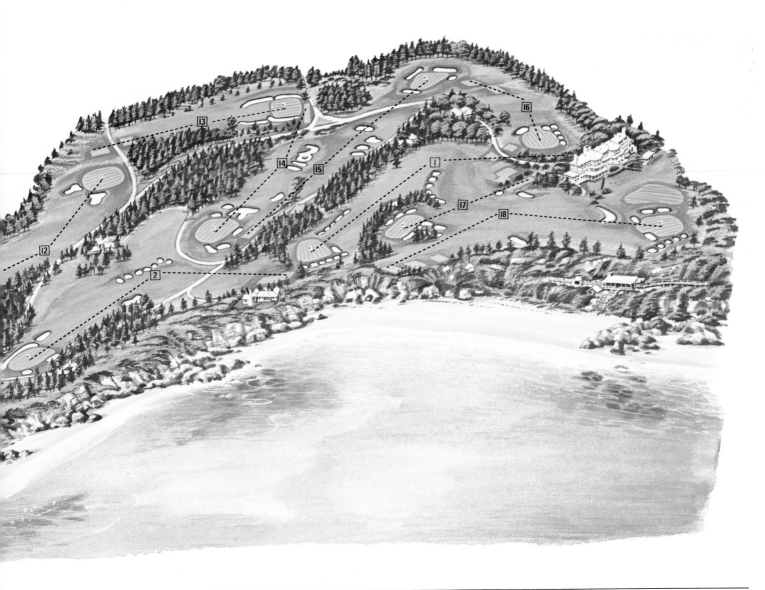

The trees backing the 17th green nestle into the dog-leg of the 1st, with its intimidating arc of old-fashioned, but decidedly effective, cross-bunkers. Any golfer hooking his second shot will find out for himself how the hole came to be called Atlantic.

Ocean; far from it. There are four other eighteen-hole courses, two of nine holes and a par-three—remarkable riches for an island of only some twenty-two square miles. Castle Harbour, with the most beautiful 1st tee imaginable, and an abundance of hills and valleys, is quite an experience to play. Belmont Manor is of a quieter undulating kind, and Riddell's Bay is charming. It flows along a green tongue of land with inlets of the Great Sound, where the ships glide by to Hamilton, testing the golfers from time to time. It is all gentle and appealing after the splendours of Mid Ocean.

Finally, and most recently, Port Royal is another Trent Jones creation. It makes fine strategic use of water and sand; the land is sharply contoured and some 200,000 trees and shrubs were planted over a period of about seven years. There are, too, some challenging holes, not least the 16th, hard by the ocean. Everywhere there is stunning beauty, that precious part of the golfer's legacy; and the island, a minute speck in the northern Sargasso Sea, makes a background for the game that very few places on earth can match.

High-altitude golf amongst the cedars

From the 18th tee the way to the green looks clear, but 250 yards out a creek crosses the fairway.

Golf is a long, long way from replacing the *fiesta brava* or *futbol* in the hearts of the Latin Americans, but it is making good progress as a sport for the privileged minority. This is especially true in Mexico, which affords a great many more opportunities to play than most of its Pan-American neighbours to the south, although the game had trouble taking roots until the dust finally settled following the 1910 revolution. By the middle 1920s interest in the game had revived—thanks largely to an influx of Britons and Americans in pursuit of oil—and some rather primitive courses began to appear around Mexico City, as well as in petroleum areas like Tampico and resort villages such as Cuernavaca. Yet it was not until the late 40s that the Club de Golf Mexico was formed, giving the country its first course of truly international calibre. Since its fairways were opened for play in 1951, the club has played host to a great many of the world's leading golfers and international events, including the Canada Cup matches of 1958 and the World Amateur Team Championships of 1966.

Club de Golf Mexico emerged from the imagination and determination of Percy J. Clifford, six times amateur champion of Mexico and six times runner-up. With the sponsorship of President Aleman, Clifford found just the terrain he wanted at a place called El Cedtal, a lovely grove of cedar, pine, eucalyptus and cypress trees on the outskirts of the town of Tlalpan, less than an hour's drive south of Mexico City. The course was carved directly out of this grove of trees, which extends in symmetrical rows over several hundred acres and stand like silent sentinels on either side of most of the fairways. Through the heart of the grove runs a deep, usually dry, creek that comes into play in interesting and varying ways on nearly half the holes.

Designed by Clifford and American architect Laurence Hughes, Club de Golf has a par of 72 and plays at an imposing 7,250 yards from the back tees. However, Mexico City's altitude of 7,500 feet lends a great deal of distance to the longer shots. A drive of 230 to 250 yards at sea-level will travel anywhere from 10 to 20 per cent farther in this rarefied atmosphere de-

pending on the temperature and climatic conditions, a circumstance that makes the proper selection of clubs a distinct problem to the golfer who plays here for the first time. While he may be agreeably surprised at the new distance he has acquired off the tee, he may similarly find that his well-hit 7-iron to the green ends up in serious trouble ten or twenty yards past the target.

Due largely to the thousands of trees guarding its fairways, Club de Golf Mexico is principally a driving course with a secondary premium on long irons and fairway woods. While not heavily bunkered like so many of the newer courses north of the border, the target areas off the tees are generally narrowed and confined by at least one strategically placed sandtrap. The real punishment for the stray drive is, however, the trees themselves. From amongst them, it is seldom possible to do more than nudge the ball back to the centre of the fairway. Even the sides of the fairways are apt to cost a

stroke now and then, for the overhanging branches will quite often block a straight route to the green.

The second-shot problem is easily grasped by a glance at the yardage figures for the individual holes. Only four of the par-fours measure less than 425 yards, and one of them is a full 470 yards. All four of the par-fives extend over more than 550 yards, and two—the 2nd and the 6th—offer but a minimal entrance to the green for even the finest second shot. Only one of the short holes is less than 200 yards and all four are extremely tight, either because of the crowding trees, the enclosing bunkers or the confining boundary of the club property. Of medium size in terms of the newer golf courses, the greens have only the subtlest borrows, but they are well protected by bunkers where it matters without being unduly surrounded. Club de Golf is, in short, a course where the straight golfer will be rewarded by honest pars, while the birdies are bought at peril.

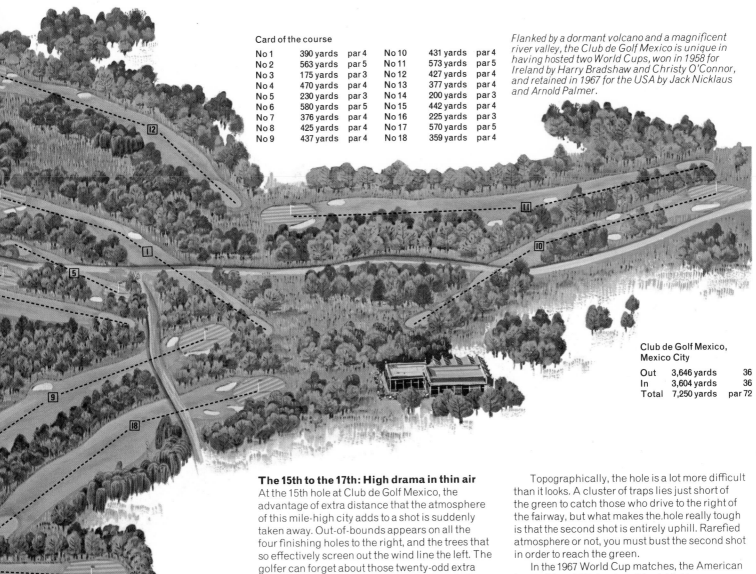

Card of the course

No 1	390 yards	par 4	No 10	431 yards	par 4
No 2	563 yards	par 5	No 11	573 yards	par 5
No 3	175 yards	par 3	No 12	427 yards	par 4
No 4	470 yards	par 4	No 13	377 yards	par 4
No 5	230 yards	par 3	No 14	200 yards	par 3
No 6	580 yards	par 5	No 15	442 yards	par 4
No 7	376 yards	par 4	No 16	225 yards	par 3
No 8	425 yards	par 4	No 17	570 yards	par 5
No 9	437 yards	par 4	No 18	359 yards	par 4

Flanked by a dormant volcano and a magnificent river valley, the Club de Golf Mexico is unique in having hosted two World Cups, won in 1958 for Ireland by Harry Bradshaw and Christy O'Connor, and retained in 1967 for the USA by Jack Nicklaus and Arnold Palmer.

Club de Golf Mexico,
Mexico City

Out	3,646 yards	36
In	3,604 yards	36
Total	7,250 yards	par 72

As with all fine courses of championship quality, Club de Golf offers an imposing sequence of finishing holes that test not only the skill but the nerves of a player. The 15th demands a most carefully placed drive to avoid the impinging trees on both sides of the fairway, thus inhibiting the temptation to hit all-out and shorten the approach to the green. The 16th is either a very long iron or a wood off the tee with no room at all for error, since the course boundary is only a few yards to the right from tee to green, while overhanging trees will catch the off-line shot to the left. The 17th, with an immensely long, uphill second shot over threatening bunkers, must be played safe by all but the very longest hitters. And finally, the creek that splits the 18th fairway will catch the overly long drive, putting everyone on an equal footing for the approach to the green. Considering that it has been played often by the best professionals, the record of 66 indicates how difficult it is to bring this course to its knees.

The 15th to the 17th: High drama in thin air

At the 15th hole at Club de Golf Mexico, the advantage of extra distance that the atmosphere of this mile-high city adds to a shot is suddenly taken away. Out-of-bounds appears on all the four finishing holes to the right, and the trees that so effectively screen out the wind line the left. The golfer can forget about those twenty-odd extra yards and concentrate on accuracy. Thus Latin Americans, who glorify length, learn that the second shot is just as important as the first.

The 15th, a par-four, is very demanding off the tee, automatically making the shot to the green either easy or, if you get in the trees, impossible. The 16th offers no room for error all the way from tee to green. And then comes the 17th. Stretching 570 yards, it is a mighty par-five even in this rarefied atmosphere. For once the golfer finds a bonus in a thick grove of trees—they prevent him from hitting out-of-bounds.

Topographically, the hole is a lot more difficult than it looks. A cluster of traps lies just short of the green to catch those who drive to the right of the fairway, but what makes the hole really tough is that the second shot is entirely uphill. Rarefied atmosphere or not, you must bust the second shot in order to reach the green.

In the 1967 World Cup matches, the American team of Arnold Palmer and Jack Nicklaus was so far in front of the rest of the field (at nineteen under par) that the championship had become a formality. They finally won by thirteen strokes over New Zealand. Palmer won the individual title with a twelve-under-par score of 276, and Nicklaus, driving poorly for once in his life, ended up seven under. But together they played that 17th hole for four rounds in a total score of five under par. That is to say, one or the other birdied the hole every time they played it and, in the third round, Palmer made an eagle-three.

All but the big hitters must play a safe second to the well-protected green of the long, uphill 17th, but in the 1967 World Cup Arnold Palmer and Jack Nicklaus totalled five under par here, with Palmer making a superb eagle in the third round.

Asia

Golf arrived in Asia in the early nineteenth century, its vectors the garrisons and administrators of the British Empire. Far and away the oldest golf club in the world outside the British Isles—far older, even, than most of them there—is the Royal Calcutta, founded in 1829. In course of time golf spread to all the countries of the East where the European presence was strong—even into China, where there were courses adjoining the now-vanished European cantonments. For more than a century, golf was essentially a game for the representatives of Colonial power, and a club of any standing rigorously excluded even the most important locals from membership. Colonialism and its trappings have now vanished, but the game has survived. It flourishes in India and Southeast Asia generally, in the Philippines and Taiwan (thanks to American influence), and—most remarkably of all—in Japan, the one country that had not come under the Colonial influence. The number of golfers there (well over a million, and growing) now outstrips that of all other nations except the United States—and, furthermore, it far outstrips the capacity of Japan's 800 courses. New courses are being built constantly, but the popularity of the game has another edge: land is at a premium in Japan, and strong opposition has grown against the use of what land there is for the pleasure of the few. Entrepreneurs and course designers have been literally driven to the hills in order to find sites for which permission will be granted—some so hilly that players travel by escalator from one hole to another. Near the cities, a player may have to give six months' notice to play a round, and even then consider himself lucky; there are ten million would-be golfers who have to make do with practice ranges and who will never play a real course. It is a measure of the modern fortunes of Japan that one of its consortia has already built new courses overseas—in the United States. The game is now wholeheartedly embraced in the continent where it first took tenuous root so long ago.

1 Hirono
2 Kasumigaseki
3 Fujioka
4 Royal Calcutta
5 Royal Hong Kong
6 Singapore Island
7 Royal Selangor
8 Bali Handara

Alison's restrained but inspired architecture

The tree-lined 9th fairway runs like a broad boulevard straight to the Hirono clubhouse. The hollow in front of the green and the flanking bunkers are the classic trademarks of the course's architect, Charles Alison.

The Westernization of Japan, a breakneck process during the early decades of this century, was most marked in and around the great maritime cities like Tokyo and—farther west on the island of Honshu—the international port of Kobe. It was in centres such as these, with their cosmopolitan communities, that the game of golf first took root and at Kobe, Japan was to acquire one of the world's most superb courses—Hirono. It was to set a standard by which all the courses of the Orient would subsequently be measured.

The site chosen for Hirono was in every way ideal. Twelve miles to the northwest of the port it was, in a contemporary description, "dotted with many pretty ponds, winding streams, running rivulets, pine woodlands, ravines and gentle undulations". The materials were at hand for an architectural artist, the Englishman Charles Alison. And the course he designed in 1930 remains unaltered to this day.

At Hirono Alison took advantage of the terrain to arrange, as at Sunningdale and St George's Hill (where he had worked with Harry Colt), several splendid carries from the tees. He planned intriguing greens at the end of generous fairways and sprinkled the course with bunkers of the type that in Japan bear his name to this day. In every way it was a piece of Berkshire transplanted in the Orient.

Charles Alison was a skilful draughtsman.

His maps and drawings showed an outstanding clarity. In addition he had an unusual talent for sketching the end result in an illustrative picture easily understood by the constructors, none of whom could have had any idea of what a good golf course should look like. He left, among other things, an exquisite pen sketch of the 5th hole, a 150-yard par-three, that shows all the beauty of an oriental painting. There are also marvellous pencil drawings of scenes and

impressions. It was a talent that would have appealed to the Japanese. The holes, hazards and greens in Alison's drawings were produced with amazing accuracy after he departed, a tribute to his skill in designing and to the high esteem in which he must have been held by all those with whom he came into contact.

Hirono measures 6,950 yards from the back tees and 6,100 yards from the forward ones; Alison gave it all the length a championship ▷

The 15th: Alison's inspiration

At 555 yards, the 15th is Hirono's longest and most interesting hole, a perfect example of the way in which the architect Charles Alison made use of natural features in the days before earth-moving machines made it so easy to turn fairways into freeways. All Alison had at his disposal were hundreds of willing farm workers. Thus he was constantly on the lookout against the destruction of valuable hills and swales.

On the 15th he has put two shallow gullies to good use. The first, at the halfway mark, has been left in something like its natural rugged state, and the second one, just short of the green, has, of necessity, been prepared as a useful arena. Then, in the most natural way, he has cut his trademark bunkers into the steep farther slopes by the green so that they loom large and look threatening. The club has kept faithfully to his concept of naturalness and those lovely, single-file paths through the ravines, so reminiscent of the rabbit

tracks of Alison's native Berkshire, still follow the easiest walking path.

The hole is in every way inspiring. The tee shot should carry the first gully and land safely in a wide expanse of perfect fairway. At the 250-yard mark there is a pine tree which may not have been a part of Alison's original concept. Such trees are much liked by Japanese golfers, who see companionship in a stately pine. Whatever its origin, the tree must be avoided and the second shot thrashed across the big gully towards the green. There, another less frightening depression is encountered, together with greenside traps that frame the target. The difficulties, so carefully created or retained by Alison, combine with length —555 yards is just right for a par-five of this severity —to make the 15th into a most satisfying hole to play. The remaining holes at Hirono are difficult, but they are shorter and birdies are easier to come by. However, to get past the marvellous 15th hole in par figures is an accomplishment.

The second shot at Hirono's 15th must avoid a lone tree and carry a well-bunkered, lethal gully.

The 15th: 555 yards par 5

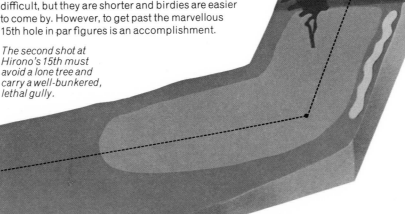

With subtle bunkering and a delightfully varied use of water, Charles Alison created Japan's best test of golf at Hirono. The pine trees which flank the fairways do not intrude into play, but provide instead a decorous frame for the rolling terrain broken by strategically placed natural gullies. The water comes effectively into play at the short holes—the 5th, 13th, and 17th—and at the long 12th, a 550-yard par-five where the drive must carry an awesome combination of rough and water to gain the safety of the fairway.

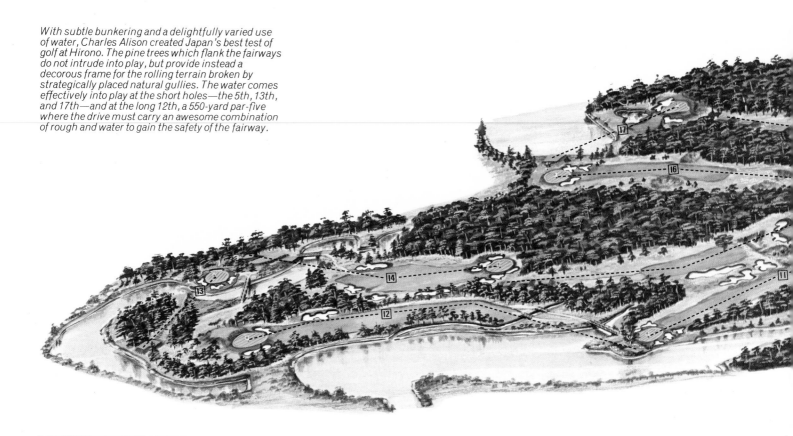

▷ course should need. Nowadays too much importance is attached to playing a course of 7,000 yards or more, especially in Japan. There is generally thought to be some inadequacy in a layout that measures less. More monstrosities have been constructed in the name of length than would be thought possible; a look at Hirono provides an answer to the argument, for 6,950 yards of this kind of architecture is worth 7,400 yards of most other kinds.

Few courses outside Britain have the striking difference and variety in each hole that Hirono possesses. Each is named after its peculiarity—Lake End, Fiord, Wee-Wood, Devil's Divot, Boulevard and Quo Vadis? We can assume that Alison had a hand in the naming, which is thoroughly appropriate. In playing or just walking the course, the titles immediately strike home. Devil's Divot, for example, is a par-three across a huge gouge in the earth, in the shape of a giant divot. Fiord is another par-three, across an inlet of a lake resembling a small Norwegian harbour. Some of the names commemorate people associated with the club's founding, but most announce a hole's feature or situation.

At first the greens were all of creeping bent grass but it was soon found that the ten-times more virile Japanese Bermuda grass encroached and took over, in spite of all efforts to stem its advance. A fine variety of korai grass—of the same family as the fairways—was substituted, and properly maintained and mown short is a suitable enough putting grass even though it browns off in winter and goes dormant. It does, however, have a wiry texture that baffles nearly all golfers who are new to its acquaintance.

Varieties of American seed grasses make up the rough grass together with some local flora. The trees are almost entirely pines indigenous to the area, and they are lovingly cared for.

The whole is a vista of beauty and naturalness that changes colour through the seasons. In summer it is a rich green with only the sand-traps offering a contrast to the softness mirrored in the lakes and ponds, while in autumn and winter it changes to the light brown of hibernation. At all times it is an inviting golf course of outstanding dignity and class.

Like Sunningdale, which in many ways it resembles, Hirono starts off with a par-five hole. It is straight, narrow and flat and clear of obstacles all the way to the flagstick, which can

The 7th at Hirono from the forward tee. With the ravine forming a huge natural hazard in front of the green the hole is challenging enough from here, but from the championship tee, which makes it 200 yards long, it becomes almost frightening, particularly in wind.

be clearly seen from the tee though 500 yards away. Two shallow depressions cross the fairway at the 100-yard and 400-yard marks. Alison placed his traps for the wayward drive at the 200-yard range on the right and at 220 yards on the left, a pattern that has been almost universally adopted by all students of his work in Japan. Two plain and modest bunkers guard the green, which inclines enough to drain itself. Here, as throughout the course, natural features are used to their best effect. Two man-sized par-fours follow, the blank spots of which are filled with large-scale moundwork that suggests something of a linksland course. The 4th hole requires a spectacularly long tee shot and the green is raised high behind a typical Alison

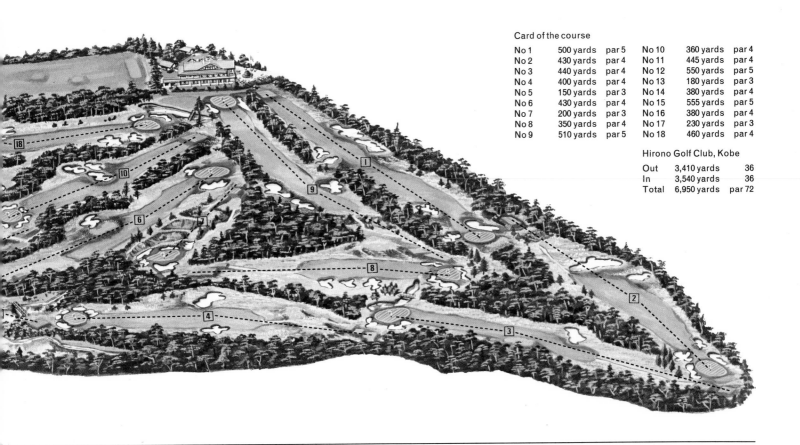

Many a good player finds himself in the bunkers after crossing the bridge at the short 13th. The 180-yard drive off the championship tee must go over both the water and the traps to a small, tight plateau green. Alison's clever use of limited water at Hirono became famous.

sandtrap. The 5th hole is a picture postcard par-three of outstanding merit high across a large lake. Fearsome-looking sandtraps guard a modest-sized green so that even at 150 yards length the hole is a difficult one for golfers of all classes and experience.

The course turns inland then by way of another first-class par-three of 200 yards. A natural, well-cleared ravine courses diagonally across it and, against a wind, it is farther than most people can hit, but the regular tee is set at 170 yards so that from this distance it is a pleasure for all golfers to play. The 8th hole uses a small pond by the green to effect. The second shot must skirt or carry the pond to an interestingly shaped green. For club golfers it is

fun and a terror, the choice of shot never easy.

The 9th takes the route straight to the clubhouse. A par-five of 510 yards, the tee shot is all carry across brush and pathways to a generous fairway that disappears into a natural grassed and cut hollow in front of the green. The 10th and 11th holes are two pleasant fours that take the golfer out to the lake again. The 12th hole is one of the course's best—and also one of the best par-fives in Japan. Its tee shot is across an inlet of the lake, beyond which there is a small natural ditch, reminiscent of Carnoustie, to worry about. The shot is fearsome for lesser players, and difficult enough for professionals. To all except the very longest and straightest hitters the green is still two shots

away. The tee shots at the 13th and 14th holes both have to carry water of marvellous proportion and beauty, giving pleasure to the player who makes it but no offence to those who don't. These two shorter holes lead to another outstanding par-five in the 15th, at 555 yards, Alison's longest hole. The 16th climbs farther away from the lake to a high plateau green seemingly set against the sky. From the back tee, the 17th is a 230-yard par-three across the margin of another lake with plenty of open space to be aimed at by those who are not ambitious or strong enough. Here Alison could have made the mistake of duplicating his 5th and 13th holes but sensibly he offered something different; water plays a lesser part but sheer length is used to compensate.

The 460-yard 18th is in every way a rewarding final hole. First there is the carry across a gully to the fairway. Then the fairway turns left for the long slog to the green. Again there is an area of mounds and hollows and sandtraps off to the right, more to distract than to impede, but the greenside traps have been sited in earnest. Eighteenth greens are almost always given the best attention, by constructor and maintainer alike, and this one is no exception. Alison never even dreamed of television but made a marvellously spectacular finish.

Hirono was host to the Japan Amateur championship in 1933 and the Japan Open in 1939, but since then there has been nothing of national or international importance staged there. This is to be regretted because there is much to show off and, as far as champion golfers are concerned, much to test them.

Bunkers gain an Englishman immortality in Japan

As a game that has more than its share of ritual and etiquette, golf might be expected to appeal to the Japanese. There has been an explosion of interest in recent years—too big an explosion, in fact, for the good of the Japanese themselves, for there are far too few courses for the army of enthusiasts who would dearly love to play eighteen holes—or any number of holes, for that matter—on a real course. There may well be many a Nipponese Nicklaus condemned to play out a lifetime of golf on one of Japan's proliferating practice ranges. And for those who are club members, fees are hideously high.

Tokyo, one of the world's greatest conurbations, has a number of the country's principal clubs within its immediate area. One is Kasumigaseki, the country's most famous club. The course was built in a matter of months by a group of enthusiasts and opened in October 1929. The design was by a talented local player, Kinya Fujita, but it soon became clear that the possibilities of the site had not been exploited to the full. The English architect Charles Alison was called in and in his subsequent work at Kasumigaseki he was to achieve a curious immortality.

Alison was drawn particularly to the par-three 10th, a medium-length pitch across a deep ravine. He introduced several deep sandtraps into the side of a steep slope leading up to the green, and their depth was an innovation to the Japanese. Since that time, every deep sandtrap or bunker on a Japanese course has been known as an Alison—or "Arison".

The English architect stamped his personality on other holes also, and although some innovations have since been added the championship course is fundamentally his work. Alison was an outstanding golf course designer and his ideas place him amongst the giants of the profession. His simple principle was that hazards should be offset to catch the wayward stroke and that the path to the hole along the straight and narrow should be smooth and unencumbered. Alison's pattern of design has been adopted almost everywhere in Japan, but it has also given birth to some very dull and stereotyped reproduction.

The climate of Japan is one of extremes and at Kasumigaseki, as elsewhere in Japan, the soft English bent grasses recommended for putting greens could not survive the heat and oppressive humidity of summer; the grass just expired. The Japanese solution was to build two greens, one sown with conventional bents regrown each year, and the other with the hardiest grass they could find—a species from Korea called, appropriately enough, korai. It survives harsh winter conditions and although it turns light brown in its dormancy, it revives to a rich greenness with the warmth and sunlight of spring. Finely developed strains make adequate putting greens, while the stouter grades make fairways of firm bristle.

The use of korai as a second green inevitably distorted the architecture by adding a considerable space to the green area. It also influenced the bunkering round the greens, the standard pattern being to have one trap to the extreme left, one to the right and another at the rear. This arrangement became the safe method of design and few local planners dared depart from it. Even today, when a number of carefully bred hybrid grasses are available (all developed in the USA to overcome conditions similar to those in Japan), the Japanese still stay with the two-green system, one for winter and one for summer. Few clubs dare offer their members anything else.

Kasumigaseki has the well-kept, well-prepared look about it that has become customary in Japan. A ground staff of more than 200, many of them women, ensure that no weeds grow anywhere and not a dead leaf can be seen. Trees are wrapped in hessian and twine to protect them from the cold of winter; many have stays or cables to hold them upright in the wind. Paths and bridges are guttered and well drained, like miniature avenues. Flower beds around the clubhouse would do justice to the Chelsea Flower Show.

On course, the flora and the grasses receive the same meticulous attention, with the same impressive results. The expensive white river sand of the bunkers, prepared to an exemplary smoothness, as elsewhere in Japan, with toothless wooden rakes, have a tidiness which defeats their purpose. This fact first came to light in the 1957 Canada Cup matches, when the Japanese winners demonstrated a hitherto unknown skill at escaping from the sand after poor shots had trapped them. Torakichi "Pete" Nakamura, individual winner by a convincing seven-shot margin, proved particularly adept. In the four days of the event he holed out from the sand four times, and never failed to get down in two when he was caught—as he often was.

The success of Nakamura and his partner, Koichi Ono, sparked the golf boom in Japan that shows no sign yet of collapse. At that time there

Kasumigaseki Country
Club, Kasahata, Saitama

East course

Out	3,455 yards	36
In	3,479 yards	36
Total	6,934 yards	par 72

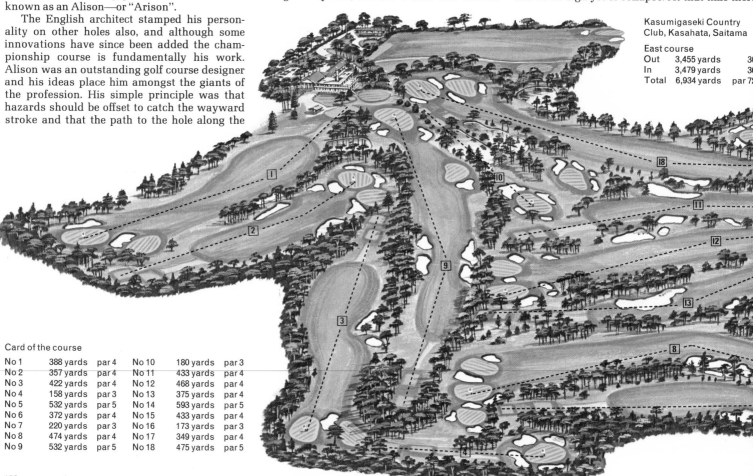

Card of the course

No 1	388 yards	par 4	No 10	180 yards	par 3
No 2	357 yards	par 4	No 11	433 yards	par 4
No 3	422 yards	par 4	No 12	468 yards	par 4
No 4	158 yards	par 3	No 13	375 yards	par 4
No 5	532 yards	par 5	No 14	593 yards	par 5
No 6	372 yards	par 4	No 15	433 yards	par 4
No 7	220 yards	par 3	No 16	173 yards	par 3
No 8	474 yards	par 4	No 17	349 yards	par 4
No 9	532 yards	par 5	No 18	475 yards	par 5

were seventy-nine courses in Japan. Today there are about 800, with applications before the authorities for building hundreds more.

Because the demand for courses quickly outstripped the availability of suitable land, golf took to the mountains. Consequently most modern Japanese courses are hilly, even mountainous. Some border on the absurd. Fairways shoot up one hill to tumble down the next. Greens are often placed out of sight over the brow so that only the flagstick is visible, and fairways are sometimes laid through ridiculously narrow cuts on the hillside. Yet such courses are popular because in Japan sport, and golf in particular, is a physical exercise.

Kasumigaseki, which still has a few of the traditional female caddies, has no such architectural absurdities. Its standing in Japan is assured by Alison's masterly creation and consolidated by Fujita and Seichi Inoue, who collaborated on a second excellent course, completed in 1931. They faithfully followed Alison's lead.

Despite Charles Alison's marvellous creations and the desire of Japan's golf founders to produce courses with all the classic features, sandtrap design and maintenance in Japan make them vastly different from the less-manicured courses they seek to emulate. Nevertheless they are much to be admired in every other respect, and Kasumigaseki, which combines something of the ruggedness of a golf course with the beauty of a Japanese garden, sets the standard. Few can match it.

The 10th: The case for intimidation

Charles Alison's timely intercession in the layout of the East course at Kasumigaseki had many benefits to the club and subsequently to golf in Japan. He was able to see at a glance the natural potential of the 10th, something which had apparently eluded the club's planners. Perhaps a natural timidity on their part stayed their hand, for to the Japanese, who had until then only second-hand knowledge of the game, a sand bunker of a depth above one's head must have seemed quite out of proportion. History tells us that only small "scratches of sand" formed the hazards on this 180-yard par-three until the persuasive Alison brought about the profound terrors that have made it a classic. Credit must go to those gentlemen of the club who realized the strength of his argument. If Kasumigaseki was to be a golf course of international standard, it must have hazards of international proportions—even if, as must have

A Charles Alison course, marked by restrained bunkering and superb grooming, Kasumigaseki came to the fore in 1957 when the World Cup was played there. Japan's success in team and individual competitions sparked off an astonishing golf boom there. It later spread through much of Asia.

been the case, new golfers spent many strokes in frantic efforts to escape.

Kasumigaseki has the look and feel of a golf course of especial high quality and harmony. Careful maintenance of grass and trees, ponds and flowers suggest this, but it is the sandtrapping that confirms it; that of the 10th makes an immediate impact because it can be seen from the clubhouse. On facing up to par-three holes it is impossible to ignore the obvious consequences of missing the target. In the case of those par-threes now recognized as superior, this intimidation is the overwhelming feature. Holes across valleys can hold severe terrors, but those across water, such as this one, have this special challenge in an obvious way. It is important that the green be just a little firm so that the ball bounces at least once before well-applied backspin takes its grip. When in this condition, the small green is exactly the right size for the hole's length.

One of the finest par-threes in Asia, the 10th calls for a tee shot over water to a small, formidably bunkered green. The hole was transformed by Alison's tough trapping.

Sam Snead was one of the 1957 World Cup players strong enough to risk getting home in two at the long 18th.

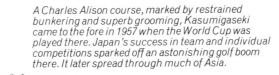

The 18th: Sophistication brings joy

Kasumigaseki's planner arranged a layout of outstanding variety, a feature of which is a sterling finish in the modern manner. A par-five of sporting length with enough dog-leg to make the best of golfers draw on his brain and brawn, the 18th makes a perfect finale to an exciting round. The drive is straightforward enough, sensibly trapped and yet wide enough to invite overstretching. There is of course every temptation to do so, for the green, some 475 yards away, can be reached in two shots. Thus when Sam Snead, Roberto de Vicenzo and others of the same power stood on this last tee in the 1957 World Cup with an eagle in mind, it made for enthralling viewing.

The second shot, though, is the spectacular one. From the perfect drive, the direct line is across

the deepest part of a valley and over the large, deep traps which guard the entrance from that angle. If the traps were not smoothed with a toothless rake, the whole exercise would take even more courage. The same sand left footmarked and unraked would make for an extremely punitive hazard of real championship calibre but unfortunately only Pine Valley amongst the world's great courses maintains this principle. This last hole at Kasumigaseki would be fearsome indeed if the penalty for falling into one of the traps was two or even three strokes. At present, because of the invariably immaculate condition of the greenside bunkers, the penalty is most often only one, and, in a significant percentage of cases, none at all. Nevertheless, this hole is a marvellous example of sophisticated architecture and a joy to play.

Golfing innovations in a land of traditions

As one of Japan's newer golf courses, Fujioka's reputation is still in the making. It came into being in 1970–1, and is one of the more successful manifestations of the golf fever that had reached plague proportions throughout the country—a plague that eventually resulted in legislation to check the rape of open land by speculative golfing developments.

Fujioka was the brainchild of Mr A. Furukawa, the owner of land to the north of Nagoya, hard by the vast Toyota motor manufacturing complex. He set out to build a course in the established traditions of Kasumigaseki and Hirono, of modern design and to international standards, but with its membership strictly limited to the manageable number of 450.

Peter Thomson was invited to become the "name" professional and to advise the appointed course architect, Tameshi Yamada. The practice of having a player of international repute associated with a new course had become

commonplace in Japan—lucrative enough, but not without its risks for the player's reputation if the course should prove a failure.

The site was 180 acres of moderately hilly land made up of tea plantations, a large lake and a pine forest. The layout used all the lower-lying land and valleys, leaving the higher pines intact. Drainage to and from the lake and beneath the fairways was used with great imagination by Yamada. Pipes beneath the fairways were of one-metre diameter, an apparently extravagant size that was to prove its worth a year after the course was completed: a typhoon devastated and flooded the region, but the course was left intact.

A feature of Fujioka is its lakes, reminiscent in treatment of those at Augusta National. At the time they were a radical departure in Japan, where lakes are usually used only timidly as hazards. Greens are hardly ever placed right against the water, as at Augusta, although on

most Japanese courses, with their abundance of water, the golfer is invited to hit over it.

A double green was made for the 4th, a long climbing par-four, and the 7th, a par-three played at right angles to it. This is probably the only double green in Japan. At Fujioka it was not built simply to be distinctive, but to solve a construction problem and conserve valuable space in a tight corner.

At one point there was some disagreement over whether the 12th green should be flush against a small lake or higher up and well away from the water. In the end a compromise was reached: both were built. The one beside the lake, which makes the hole into a dog-leg, resembles the 11th at Augusta in its setting, and the other is straight ahead. The lakeside green sits slightly below the fairway driving spot, from which the flag placement and the water surrounding the green can be seen. The alternative is blind; only the top of the flagstick and surrounding traps can be seen. These two greens are alternated in play and only time will tell which is the more popular.

Alison-type bunkers were included at various holes, although Yamada modified their depths, knowing from experience that amongst his countrymen deep bunkers with straight faces are not universally popular. The sandtraps are flexible in their depth—for ordinary club play they can be shallow and not particularly penal, but they can be deepened to suit the more prestigious occasion. Thus Fujioka, like all great courses, is flexible enough to be enjoyed not only by champions but by golfers of all abilities.

The course has a one-green system along modern lines, with modern trappings. The grass

A tee-to-green view of the 190-yard 15th. The main feature of the hole is the unusually shaped bunker which defends the whole green and rivals it in size.

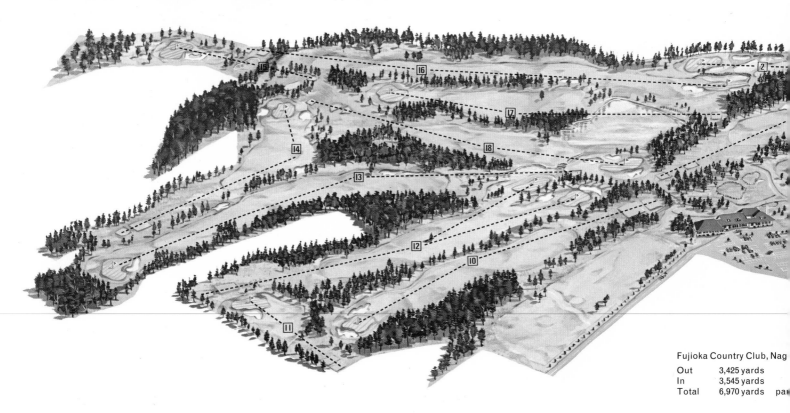

Fujioka Country Club, Nag

Out	3,425 yards
In	3,545 yards
Total	6,970 yards

pa

is a fine variety of korai, the safest type for the climate and the most familiar to Japanese golfers, although there are more suitable hybrids available. The fairways are of a coarser and tougher variety of korai, grown on turf farms and transported to Fujioka in two-foot squares, the standard method of turf culture in the southern and western parts of Japan. The squares are laid and pegged in with small bamboo stakes to frustrate the crows which otherwise lift them, looking for worms, before they settle down. The turfing of Fujioka took about five months and kept almost 6,000 workers fully employed during that time.

The whole construction took less than a year and most of it was completed in only nine months. Because it is so new, Fujioka Country Club has yet to achieve wide fame. Yet those who have played there acknowledge it as one of Japan's outstanding courses, modern but nevertheless reflecting architectural links with older more venerable courses. Other new courses in Japan are following the same lines and Japanese golfers are learning to enjoy what are to them wholly new challenges in the way they play their game.

As befits a course that looks so much to Japan's golfing future, Fujioka's last three holes were designed with television in mind. Each is spectacular and in the way in which they bring into play a large, attractive lake they rival even the famous water holes of Augusta, both in their beauty and in their difficulty. For the members, many good scores are ruined over this final run in, yet there is much pride in their existence, just as there is in the way that Fujioka has pioneered a golfing challenge that is new to Japan.

The 16th: A man-sized par-five

The huge par-five 16th is a real monster, playing every inch of its 605-yard length. The back tee is never used in club golf because the first shot involves a drive uphill—always a difficult task for a golfer of little experience. Although the fairway is not generously wide, every encouragement is left for the sliced drive to hit the bank on the right side and bounce back to the fairway, even though this cuts length from the shot. The left side plunges down to an out-of-bounds fence and hooking is something to be avoided. From the top of the hill, where a good drive will finish, it is still not possible to see the green, though the second shot is framed by some pines on either side and the V-shaped fairway makes the direction unmistakable.

It is really only with the third shot that the hole's true worth is revealed, for the task before the player is below him in the shape of a massive green curving along the side of a small lake, with a steep forested hill as a backdrop. A large sandtrap guards the entrance without blocking it off, but such is the large scale of everything, including green and trap, that the distance is deceptively long. When the flag is cut in the championship position at the far back of the green, a player can be faced with a putt of some thirty-five yards. The green becomes progressively narrower as it recedes and there are two smaller traps at the back

The 16th fairway seen from behind the green. The hole is a massive par-five which plays every inch of its 605 yards, with the green, which narrows considerably, only visible after the second shot.

to catch those who—mindful of the water on the left—overshoot. The shot into the green varies according to the wind; when there is none, and when play is from the back tee, the third shot must be a 7-iron for most people. The 16th is a man-sized par-five and is one worth watching in a championship, particularly when the going becomes tense.

No 1	400 yards	par 4	No 10	400 yards	par 4
No 2	190 yards	par 3	No 11	165 yards	par 3
No 3	540 yards	par 5	No 12	440 yards	par 4
No 4	420 yards	par 4	No 13	550 yards	par 5
No 5	350 yards	par 4	No 14	370 yards	par 4
No 6	445 yards	par 4	No 15	190 yards	par 3
No 7	195 yards	par 3	No 16	605 yards	par 5
No 8	500 yards	par 5	No 17	395 yards	par 4
No 9	385 yards	par 4	No 18	430 yards	par 4

The 17th: The unusual proves deceptive

The par-four 17th at Fujioka has some unusual characteristics which together make it unique and unrivalled anywhere in the world. The tee shot is a drive across the lake; at 200 yards, the carry is long enough but not especially difficult. The fairway, divided by a solitary pine tree, is made in two levels. These are complemented by two areas of green, which are themselves divided by a central ridge rising up to a small pine tree beyond. Thus, depending on the flagsetting and the side from which it is made, the approach is either straightforward or blocked off. The green has no sandtrap. Instead, the small thin copse on the front left side has formed a bed of pine needles which acts as a trap and imposes the same penalty.

At first sight this hole may look easy, but it proves a worrying prospect when a player wants only two pars for a good score. Landing on the wrong side of the green and having to putt over the ridge can make getting down in two an unlikely occurrence. If ever there was one, this is a "strategy hole", requiring a definite plan of attack if a par is to be made.

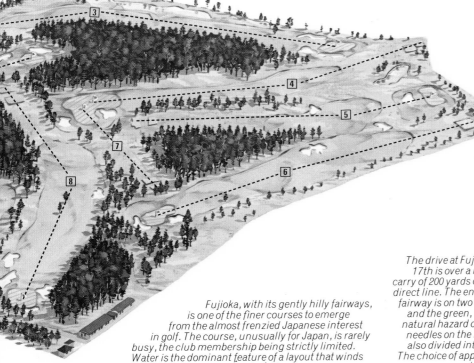

Fujioka, with its gently hilly fairways, is one of the finer courses to emerge from the almost frenzied Japanese interest in golf. The course, unusually for Japan, is rarely busy, the club membership being strictly limited. Water is the dominant feature of a layout that winds sedately through groves of pine trees.

The drive at Fujioka's 17th is over a lake, a carry of 200 yards on the direct line. The ensuing fairway is on two levels and the green, with a natural hazard of pine needles on the left, is also divided into two. The choice of approach is vital.

Vintage legacy of the British Raj

Older than any club in the world beyond the British Isles—older, indeed, than most of those in Britain itself—the Royal Calcutta has antecedents stretching back to the days when the power of the British Raj was gaining strength, beyond the beginnings of Victoria's reign. The Royal Calcutta was founded in 1829 and first used a site at Dum Dum, where the city's international airport now stands. After a series of moves the Dum Dum Golfing Club, as the Royal Calcutta was originally called, settled finally towards the end of the century in the city's southern suburbs.

The eighteen holes making up the present course are all that survive of the thirty-six club once possessed but could not afford to keep up. The land farthest from the clubhouse was sold to the Bengal government to provide some much-needed recreational space for the refugees who have crowded the club's boundaries since the partition of Bengal in 1947.

The refugees still invade the confines of the course, giving it a colour and atmosphere found nowhere else in the world. They walk single-file along the well-worn track that crosses the course. The women wash their saris and their children in the ponds formed where fill was taken to build the tees and greens, which are the highest points on a course that is never more than six feet above the level of the River Ganges. Small boys swim in each pond and wait for a wayward ball, for which they will dive to hand back to the owner in return for a few coins. The golfers are often clad in white shorts and frequently in colourful turbans. They pause under umbrellas held by caddies dressed in khaki. And above everything are the birds—squawking ravens, buzzards gliding in the hot air and the vultures, circling monotonously or peering balefully down from their nests in the trees by the 3rd.

Despite the distractions, golf continues to thrive in Calcutta as it does in the rest of India, which now has some eighty courses. Some of the more august clubs died with the Raj, others have been created, enjoying a particular popularity among members of the armed forces, where the affectations of the old English—particularly their phraseology—lingers in an odd post-colonial twilight.

Almost until independence, Indians were rigorously excluded from membership of Calcutta. A Sikh, Sardar I. S. Malik, was the first, and the first Indian to play in the all-India Amateur championship. Years later, his son Ashok won the title five times and with his partner, P. G. Sethi, represented India in every Eisenhower Trophy event from 1958 to 1968. "Billoo" Sethi, the outstanding Indian golfer of his generation, made history when he won the Indian Open in 1956, twice equalling his own course record of 68 in the process.

Royal Calcutta is immensely proud of its origins, its connections with the Royal and Ancient and with its influence on the game in India, where, until lately, it was the champion of the rules and etiquette of golf. Perhaps more importantly, there is another way in which this ancient club has exercised an influence on the game. Golf as a world-wide sport and particu-

From the tees the flat Royal Calcutta looks easy, but good medium and long irons are needed for a low score, and water hazards affect most holes.

larly as a game played in tropical and sub-tropical climes owes a debt to Royal Calcutta for a special reason. It was the first course to be built in the tropics and as such had to make use of whatever indigenous grasses there were available. The most suitable, if not indeed the only one, was dhoob.

Dhoob grass covered Calcutta's first fairways, and golf on grass became a reality in the tropics. Since then, in all probability because of the Indian experience, dhoob and related grasses such as hariali, Bermuda, Australian couch and creeping dog's-tooth, have become the standard grasses, in pure, dwarfed or hybrid form, on thousands of golf courses all over the world. Without it, golf in all but the temperate zones would be played on sand.

The eighteen holes that now make up Royal Calcutta's championship course are each a solid par of modern length and difficulty, in a flat parkland setting, with gorgeous trees and innumerable lakes or ponds (known, because they are used to store water, as tanks), drainage channels and gutters. The course can justifiably claim to be the best in the subcontinent.

The profusion of water hazards removes the need for many sandtraps and, since they are below ground-level, the course at first glance gives the impression of being easy and wide open. Nothing is farther from the truth.

Its best holes are the 2nd and 14th, neither of which has a sandtrap. The stiff 2nd is a gentle dog-leg of 440 yards, curving around huge trees of thick, shady foliage. The boundary wall runs along the left side and against it, at the 230-yard mark, is a lotus-filled tank that acts like a magnet. A drive that strays too far to the right lands behind the trees and so the placement of the tee shot is critical. The 14th follows the same pattern, but in reverse. It is a little shorter at 438 yards, but requires big hitting when the fairways are soft after the monsoon.

The 450-yard 10th is also a testing hole. Two large tanks split the fairway, and an out-of-bounds wall lines the entire left side. From the tee the bold line is straight over the first tank, a shot that must carry a full 230 yards. The safe shot down the right side leaves a long second over the other tank, which is all of a hundred yards wide, to a small, heavily trapped green. Other first-class holes are the par-three 3rd and 13th, both of which are entirely flexible in length; they can be played from 230 yards down to 150 yards. On both there are daunting water hazards, worrying to the golfer but a never-ending source of fun and funds for the small boys.

The Calcutta club has always enjoyed close ties with the Royal and Ancient, thanks no doubt to the many Scots who served in the Indian Army and Civil Service. In 1882, a group of members presented the Royal and Ancient with what is known as the Cashmere Cup, as a gesture of goodwill. To take advantage of their handsome new silver trophy, the Royal and Ancient introduced a new form of competition, the world's first handicap event. It was one which was to revolutionize club golf everywhere, although the first Silver Cashmere Cup (now known as the Calcutta Cup) tournament stayed with the traditional form of play, matchplay, with the handicaps in the form of "hole" starts.

In return for their new trophy the Royal and Ancient gave a silver tankard to the Calcutta club. This is still played for and it provides an annual reminder of the club's origins and, now that the gospel of golf has been spread throughout the world, Royal Calcutta's status as the first mission established overseas.

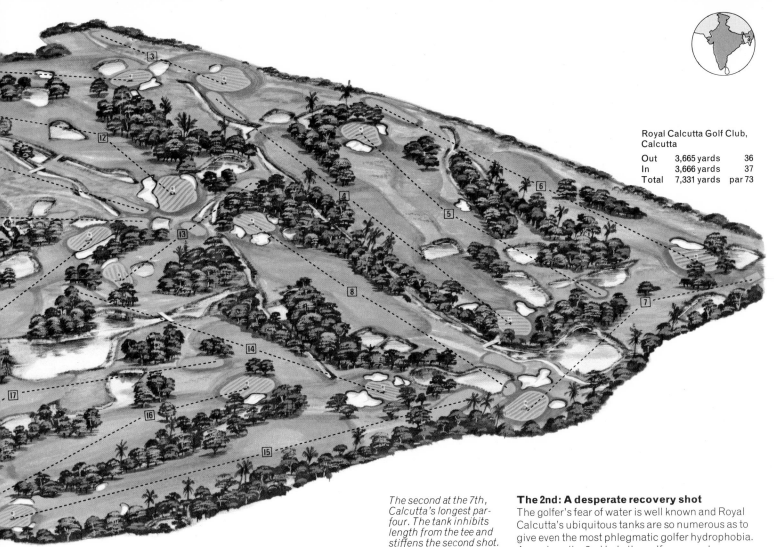

Royal Calcutta Golf Club,
Calcutta

Out	3,665 yards	36
In	3,666 yards	37
Total	7,331 yards	par 73

The second at the 7th, Calcutta's longest par-four. The tank inhibits length from the tee and stiffens the second shot.

Card of the course

No 1	Island	408 yards	par 4
No 2	Tank Ahead	440 yards	par 4
No 3	Bull's Eye	173 yards	par 3
No 4	The Long One	525 yards	par 5
No 5	Madras Thorns	427 yards	par 4
No 6	The Fields	421 yards	par 4
No 7	The Jheels	457 yards	par 4
No 8	Ditchers	407 yards	par 4
No 9	Dhobi Ghat	407 yards	par 4
No 10	Long Pal	450 yards	par 4
No 11	The Nullahs	476 yards	par 5
No 12	Dog-Leg	373 yards	par 4
No 13	Chota	235 yards	par 3
No 14	Right of Way	438 yards	par 4
No 15	Far and Sure	498 yards	par 5
No 16	Mutt and Jeff	367 yards	par 4
No 17	Thomson's Tank	416 yards	par 4
No 18	Pimples	413 yards	par 4

The 7th: Terrors that prey on the mind

Royal Calcutta's 7th hole, 457 yards par-four, has long been the terror of Indian golf. In dry or monsoon weather it wreaks havoc, the merest slip frequently resulting in an eight or a nine. Its reputation is such that some players become mesmerized by its awful possibilities, which are all too apparent from the tee.

The drive must carry one tank but stop short of a second, a vast stretch of water the full width of the fairway. Its nearside is some 250 yards from the tee and this means that a full-blooded drive is extremely risky, especially in the dry season between December and May when a drive will often run too far and find a watery grave. However,

holding back can leave an unnecessarily long shot to the green, perhaps with a 2- or 3-iron—quite a proposition, since it is largely over water.

The green has two sandtraps guarding the entrance, the right-hand one being the more formidable. The putting surface slopes downwards from back to front, so that cross-green putting or chipping from side-on require considerable allowance to the higher side. The green is perilously close to the boundary wall and a ball overshooting or hooking left on the second shot often ends up unplayable. It is the threat of this disaster that preys on the mind and which, together with the huge tank, makes the 7th as much a test of nerve as technique.

The 2nd: A desperate recovery shot

The golfer's fear of water is well known and Royal Calcutta's ubiquitous tanks are so numerous as to give even the most phlegmatic golfer hydrophobia. As early as the 2nd hole the golfer comes to understand the extent of his problems. Here he has to negotiate five tanks, three of which affect the drive, together with some cunningly sited trees and, on the left, an eight-foot-high boundary wall.

It is one of the game's oddities that for right-handed players trouble on the left side of a tee shot has a seemingly irresistible attraction which very few golfers can completely ignore. In this regard the 2nd provides a special subtlety, in that the fear engendered by the tank so clearly visible some 230 yards away on the left side can lead the golfer to overcompensate and thus fall victim to the trees on the right. They block the golfer's direct route to the green, and whilst they can be cleared the golfer cannot possibly hit with enough power to get more than halfway there. His only chance is to slice around these trees—a manoeuvre that brings him into conflict with the two tanks on the left of the green. An obtrusive tree near the green and just to the right of the perfect line is the real guardian of the target, and it takes its toll of poorly struck approach shots. No traps lodge against the putting green, which has just enough undulation to drain it in the monsoon.

Just as any well-designed par-four should, Royal Calcutta's 2nd offers the chance of a birdie, but straying from the ideal line can result in a six or a seven. However, recovery is possible, as Raj Pitambur, the well-known Indian amateur, has proved. In the final of the 1975 Indian Amateur his tee shot left him stymied by the trees. He then played a remarkable stroke, a long, curling hook around the right side of the trees to find the edge of the green. He said later: "I would never pull it off again in a thousand years. It was a desperate matchplay shot."

Fairways haunted by Chinese ancestors

In the years after World War I there were six golf clubs in China, at Amoy, Hankow, Shanghai, Tientsin, Canton and Hong Kong. Today only the Royal Hong Kong Golf Club survives, as Hong Kong itself is the lone survivor among treaty posts implanted on the China coast and interior in the nineteenth century. The Shanghai course survives in recognizable form, but is now a public park.

Today the Royal Hong Kong has three full-size courses sharing the same clubhouse at Fanling, close to the frontier with mainland China, as well as a nine-hole course at Happy Valley, on Hong Kong Island, where the club began in 1889. Here a handful of enthusiasts were forced to share the only flat and open space with other sports, including polo, with the result that the course's architect, Captain H. N. Dumbleton of the Royal Engineers, was not allowed to construct bunkers or holes. Instead, at such times as golfers had the run of the land, close mesh netting was used for bunkers and small granite setts served as holes —they had to be hit by the ball to "hole out".

It was effective enough, and popular. In May 1890, a six-a-side match was played between the club and the Argyll and Sutherland Highlanders, which the club won easily. The match attracted a number of spectators and the membership reached one hundred the following year.

The first course that was more or less for the exclusive use of golfers was sited at Deep Water Bay on the eastern side of Hong Kong Island, where a tiny sixteen-and-a-half acre triangle of flat land by the beach became available. It was reached from the city by circumnavigating the island in a launch, and had only to be shared with some cricketers who visited it occasionally.

The links was a criss-cross affair, but enough to serve the membership. A modest single-storey clubhouse was built and, five years later, another storey was added. The building stands today, and with its nine holes it is as popular as ever, a sort of "annexe" to the club's principal amenities on the mainland.

In time, the popularity of the game and a growing membership led to further expansion and the acquisition of a piece of land large enough to accommodate a full-size course, or even two. It was found at Fanling, on the mainland near the Chinese border. Fanling and its neighbouring villages were at the time beyond the reach of the Kowloon railway, and the journey to the course entailed a two-man rickshaw ride into the hills above Kowloon and then a walk down the other side to Shatin, where it was possible to be taken by police launch to the other end of the bay at Taipo. From Taipo to Fanling the journey was completed by pony, chair or rickshaw, depending on the weather. Mercifully the railway was completed to the border in 1911.

The first course at Fanling, now the Old, sufficed until 1923, when the membership reached 800. Permission was sought to build the second course, but the members rejected their committee's recommendation and voted instead for a bigger and better clubhouse.

Whether the clubhouse or the courses should be improved is a debate that has raged in most clubs at one time or another. In the case of the Royal Hong Kong, the committee blandly ignored the rank and file and went ahead with the New course. It was opened in November, 1931, by the Governor of the Colony, Sir William Peel. In time it was to become the more popular of the two and a credit to its designer and supervisor, L. S. Greenhill.

The courses suffered from general neglect and dilapidation during the Japanese occupation from 1941 to 1945, and it required a huge effort and an equally large overdraft to put them back into working order. It was not until 1953 that all the holes of the Old and New courses and the club's third course, the Relief, were restored. Early in the 1960s it again became apparent that the two larger courses at Fanling were bursting at the seams. The answer was to upgrade the Relief course and add more land, to turn it into a course of modern dimensions and difficulty.

Land was acquired from the Royal Hong Kong Jockey Club and, under the creative supervision of Michael Wolveridge—who, along with John Harris, conceived the design—began to take shape. Numerous lakes and other water hazards were constructed to drain areas subject to flooding, and these became such strong features of the course that it could quite felicitously be called "The Lake"—as one entrant in the naming competition suggested.

As with the construction of earlier courses at Fanling, numerous old and forgotten Chinese

Card of the course

No 1	439 yards	par 4
No 2	155 yards	par 3
No 3	530 yards	par 5
No 4	295 yards	par 4
No 5	198 yards	par 3
No 6	425 yards	par 4
No 7	385 yards	par 4
No 8	192 yards	par 3
No 9	475 yards	par 4
No 10	377 yards	par 4
No 11	464 yards	par 4
No 12	530 yards	par 5
No 13	391 yards	par 4
No 14	416 yards	par 4
No 15	191 yards	par 3
No 16	382 yards	par 4
No 17	412 yards	par 4
No 18	417 yards	par 4

Golf is rarely played in a setting more beautiful than that of Royal Hong Kong, set against the mountains of China.

Royal Hong Kong Golf Club, Fanling

Championship course
Out	3,094 yards	34
In	3,580 yards	36
Total	6,674 yards	par 70

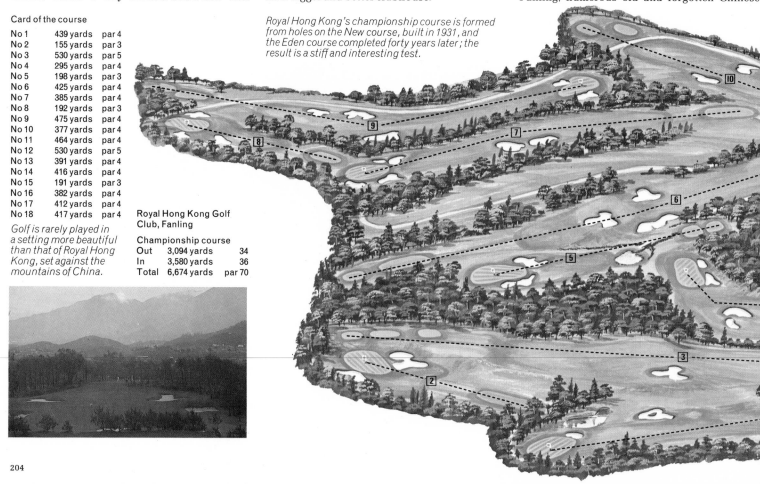

Royal Hong Kong's championship course is formed from holes on the New course, built in 1931, and the Eden course completed forty years later; the result is a stiff and interesting test.

graves were unearthed and compensation had to be paid to the families whose ancestors were disturbed. Ancestors continue to lurk in the hillsides around the course and on Ancestor Worship Day the golf course is crowded with people of all ages visiting their now long departed forebears.

On completion, the new course was named the Eden—the name of the third course at St Andrews. Of necessity it was squeezed into the corners of the last available land, which gives it some tightness. But this limitation comes where it serves a good purpose—when holes are unavoidably short for par-fours. This applies to the 10th and 11th holes, which are at the point farthest from the clubhouse. The rest of the course rolls smoothly, with adequate width and stretch, and includes some holes of undoubted world class, notably the 3rd and 18th.

To counter the severe monsoon rains the greens are mostly built up off the ground. Hitting to these raised targets is an additional test of enterprise and skill, making the Eden course quite different from the other two courses.

The Hong Kong Open is played on a composite course of the New and Eden, choosing the convenient best of each to form a course that provides very nearly the ultimate in challenge for the competitors of many nations.

The 3rd: A par-five that is a revelation

Rare is the par-five that reveals all its secrets from the tee. The 3rd hole on Royal Hong Kong's championship course does, and it is a gem. Like a Chinese scroll, it unfolds, full of detail, towards the white-walled clubhouse and the mountains of China in the blue distance. Small, trimmed trees must be carried from the elevated tee. At the 250-yard range, still short of the foot of the slope, is a large white expanse of sand with a high, thin tree standing sentinel beside it. This is the first obstacle to avoid and it dominates the scene. But there is more trouble on both sides. Down the left flank is a dense wood, on the right a pond and open ditches. It is a fearsome drive, and the elevated tee accentuates the difficulty. Driving from a high tee is exhilarating but, because curved shots have considerably farther to fly before they hit the ground, fairway widths are effectively reduced.

The second shot must run a gauntlet of sand and water, features that are typical of this fine course. The sand is on the right, a large lake beckons on the left. Shirking the challenge and playing short leaves a near-impossible third shot because, as befits a par-five, the green is none too big and it is angled to the right. Because the green is built up in table-top style the difficulty of the pitch is increased. However, by approaching from the right at an angle of some 45 degrees, which is possible with the second shot, the traps fronting the green can be avoided.

For its entire length this hole is carefully carved out and constructed to be of championship calibre. Sixes and sevens are not uncommon and a par is well earned. It is truly one of the outstanding holes in Asian golf.

The 18th: A brilliant shot to snatch the title

The last hole on any course should be capable of creating drama in a championship. This the Royal Hong Kong 18th does with a vengeance. Scores on this par-four can go as high as ten, for trouble and obstacles abound. First, the tee shot presents the challenge of driving through a narrow lane of sandtraps and trees. Laying up will do no good at all, because the green is surrounded with trouble and the nearer one can get to it from the tee the better. A drive of good length should reach a spot on high ground which presents the player with a clear view of his target. In front of him and to the right is a lake. Just beyond it is the elevated green with a deep trap in front and steep slopes all around: a difficult green to pitch or chip on to. The putting surface has two levels, separated by a small step.

It is all too easy to hook or slice the drive into the trees and find the lake with the recovery. The golfer also has to contend with a steep trap at the front of the green and, should he overshoot, a steep downslope from which recovery is well-nigh impossible.

Spectators at the Hong Kong Open witness these catastrophes annually. In 1973 they also saw a brilliant shot that clinched the championship. Australia's Frank Phillips needed a birdie-three to beat Filipino Ben Arda, who sat in the clubhouse waiting. From the right side behind the wall of trees Phillips sliced a powerful 3-iron around the branches into a strong wind to find the green. He then holed a thirty-foot putt from the top step to snatch the title from Arda's grasp.

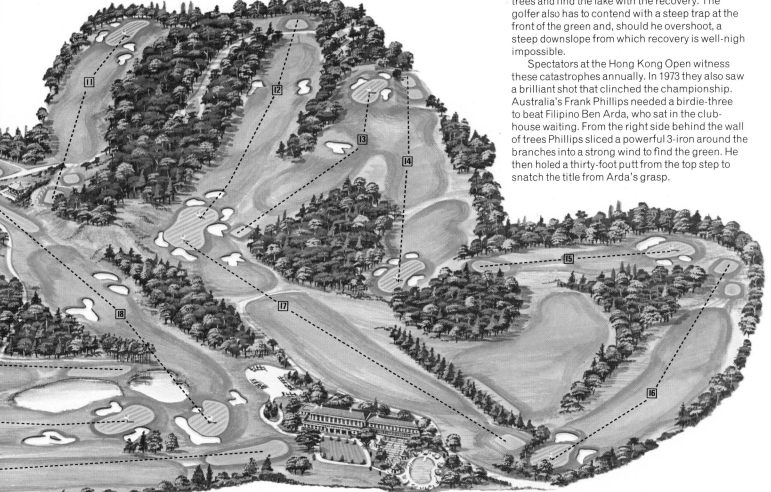

A cool oasis of peace

There is no more cosmopolitan meeting place, outside the United Nations building in New York, than the Singapore Island Golf Club. Once the exclusive preserve of colonial administrators—the city was founded by a giant among empire builders, Sir Stamford Raffles—the club now reflects the island-state itself, an international entrepôt set at the heart of all eastern trade. Every tongue of the East is heard there, and all the European.

There are four courses: the Bukit (6,645 yards); the Island (6,365 yards); the New (6,874 yards) and the Sime (6,314 yards). They are grouped attractively around the Pierce and MacRitchie reservoirs, which help, in a humid climate, to generate refreshing breezes. In such a tiny, populous state, the club is an important centre for relaxation, for it has those increasingly common appurtenances to the golf itself—a bowling alley and swimming pool, among other attractions. The club has 7,000 members, 2,000 of whom are active golfers—including 120 players with single-figure handicaps.

All four courses are exceptionally beautiful, by any standards. The green fairways twist and turn their way across the hills and dales of the catchment slopes, between the huge native trees that were left in place when the course was made. In the background are the immense stretches of the reservoirs, invariably as placid as mill ponds, and beyond them the jungle.

To anyone who spends most of his life in a Singapore office looking at others doing the same thing, the golf courses are a verdant paradise: the greenery suggests a pleasant coolness in what is one of the world's stickiest climates. To play golf there in the early morning, just after sunrise, when the fairways are still wet with dew, is a delight. To tee off late in the day, coming in as the sun disappears, is another unforgettable golfing experience. At any other time, whatever the course's virtues, the golfer can be sure of a considerable sweat.

Each of the four courses has its own personality and qualities. Bukit is the parent course, built by the Royal Singapore club in 1924 after thirty-three years at a site on the old racecourse. It is the most popular, as well as the most important, of the present four courses. It is an undeniably hilly course, so some of its holes either plunge awkwardly downhill or else climb steeply. They require a special judgement which many golfers find exasperating.

Yet each hole is a worthy challenge in its own right. The par-threes are especially difficult, even for champions. The fours are all strong, featuring either length, narrowness or canny trapping, and sometimes all three. The par-fives are an invitation to disaster, three of them coming near the end of the round when the legs are apt to be wobbly.

The greens, built on local clay, are hard for the approach shot and fast for the putt, a combination that provides the most difficult of all championship conditions. The Bermuda strain of grass in use can reduce the most stolid of golfers to a nervous wreck. Once understood and respected they make for enjoyable—if rarely entirely successful—putting.

The Bukit course was chosen as the venue

Orville Moody helped the USA regain the World Cup at Singapore in 1969.

for the World Cup when it was first played in Southeast Asia in 1969. The course was dressed for the occasion in its best, and improvements were made by the English architect Frank Pennink. The event was a great success, the United States team of Lee Trevino and Orville Moody predictably winning the team prize. Trevino just pipped the smallest of the competitors, Sukree Oncham of Thailand, for the individual honours. Oncham won the popularity contest and although he never again rose to such heights, he showed Asian galleries that those of short stature from places far distant from St Andrews or Augusta can match the best, given the opportunity.

The Island course was that originally occupied by the old Royal Island Club, whose membership took in those golfers excluded by the socially conscious Royal Singapore. It was built in 1927, three years after the Bukit course, and soon gathered the broad, cosmopolitan membership enjoyed by the present club, which

was formed when the two clubs merged in 1963.

The Island course is on the short side and some of its fairways are rather hilly on the transverse, making driving extremely difficult in dry weather. Its first nine holes wander around the reservoir shore and return to the foot of the clubhouse. The inward half is farther inland and uphill, but it is wider and longer. Both nines finish with attractive par-three holes across the valley below the clubhouse. It is a frightening prospect when results of matches—and a lot of money—depend on the final effort.

The merger of the two clubs in 1963 brought a boom in membership and resulted in the building of the fourth course, the New, starting from the old Island clubhouse and taking the last space along the shores of the reservoirs. It was originally designed by the English partnership of John Harris and Frank Pennink and is a massive and imaginative layout, with many fine and memorable holes on modern length lines. It makes a splendid course for the pro-

A recreational haven amongst the bustle of Singapore, the Island Country Club boasts four good eighteen-hole courses. The best, Bukit, was chosen as the venue for the first World Cup held in Southeast Asia.

Singapore Island Country Club, Singapore

Bukit course

Out	3,360 yards	35
In	3,285 yards	36
Total	6,645 yards	par 71

Card of the course

No 1	407 yards	par 4	No 10	379 yards	par 4
No 2	205 yards	par 3	No 11	425 yards	par 4
No 3	408 yards	par 4	No 12	220 yards	par 3
No 4	537 yards	par 5	No 13	563 yards	par 5
No 5	175 yards	par 3	No 14	194 yards	par 3
No 6	448 yards	par 4	No 15	472 yards	par 5
No 7	450 yards	par 4	No 16	412 yards	par 4
No 8	366 yards	par 4	No 17	132 yards	par 3
No 9	364 yards	par 4	No 18	488 yards	par 5

essionals who follow the Asian circuit through March and April.

The original layout was adjusted to accommodate changes in the lake level, but little was lost and the New course, with its tiny clubhouse, is outstanding in its own right. It may yet turn out to be the pride of Singapore.

The Sime course is the shortest and hence is regarded as being the most appropriate for women, although it is not theirs exclusively. It occupies a section of the Bukit, using up, as it were, the ground the bigger course does not need. The first nine holes rush over hilly ground, while the second nine is a longer excursion with even more ups and downs, following more or less in tandem with the inward nine of the Bukit.

The Sime is an enjoyable and more than usually scenic club course. Nothing more is claimed for it. But the Singapore Island Club's members are proud of the strength of their championship course, the Bukit—and they have every reason to be.

The 1st: The start that could be the end

Singapore Island's Bukit course has few holes that could be called strategic. The real difficulty of the layout, and consequently its merit, lies in its awkwardness. Most of the fairways are inclined and sloping lies are the principal challenge. The opening hole, 407 yards long, is something different, however. It descends a slight slope towards the reservoir, which makes a most beautiful background. On the left are some traps to catch the hooked drive and several large trees which effectively block the line. Clearly visible on the right side are two more traps, from which escape as far as the green is highly unlikely. Farther downhill and only fully in view after a big drive is a large, level green surrounded by traps. The whole structure is built high, like a giant step.

Allowing for the usual gentle breeze and the extra carry of the downhill slope, the approach is extraordinarily tricky and not even the perfectly struck shot heads for the green with the striker's complete confidence that he has calculated correctly. To miss the target means a scramble from deep sand or, worse, the runaway slope down towards the water. Even amongst the top players sixes are not uncommon here in the Singapore Open, the tally usually starting off with a hooked drive. Further problems come on the green because of its size and the coarseness of the grass. A thirty-foot putt usually requires the power of a sixty-footer on bent grass. It would be a worthy finishing hole but coming at the start it is formidable indeed.

The 18th: Two Texans live up to their image

The best of finishing holes are made to provide drama and the ultimate hurdle. The Bukit course's 18th hole has few equals in that respect. It is a par-five, but it makes an excellent end to a round because it has awkwardness and, at 488 yards, length. The well-struck tee shot carries across a huge valley into a fairly steep uphill slope. It is from this slope that the most awkward of second shots— with wooden club if shooting at the green—must be executed. When swinging hard on a steep slope it is all too easy to forget about balance while altering the plane of the swing to a flatter one. The ball is considerably higher than the feet and this means that full power in the execution of the stroke is not possible because the club's full length must be curtailed to accommodate the lie.

Yet the target of the green seems tantalizingly within range and, given the golfer's usual optimism, it is tempting to have a go. A line of massive trees blocks out the left side so that more often than not the shot must be bent around them with a long draw. The slope actually helps this but disaster is always possible. At the green range are deep traps and a small out-of-bounds wall, over which most tour regulars have sailed at one time or another. A slice of any magnitude can end in the locker-room. It was on this hole that Lee Trevino and Orville Moody tied up the 1969 World Cup. Somehow, using high power and skilful manipulation to devour the hole daily in birdies is appropriate to a couple of Texans. This hole always provides fascinating entertainment.

Grave problems in a burial ground

Rescued and revitalized after the war, during which time it had been used for growing crops and as an army training school, Royal Selangor has become the regular venue of the Malaysian Open. Toughened and improved recently by the English architect Frank Pennink, it is now one of the best courses in Asia.

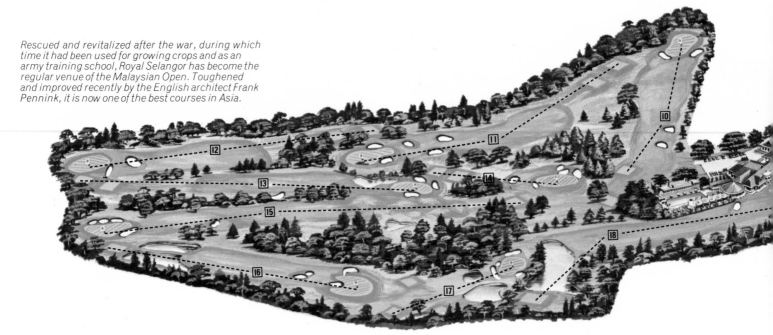

The founder-members of Malaysia's second oldest club, the Royal Selangor, must have been a singularly phlegmatic species of golfer. Sonorously, their early rules stated: "You cannot ground your club in addressing the ball, or move anything, however loose or dead it may be, when you find yourself in a grave."

For graves, on a course that included an old Chinese burial ground, were declared to be a hazard. No special mention was made of the long grass, despite the fact that to this day it is hung with bloodsucking leeches when the weather is humid. Unlike most Asian clubs of long standing, Selangor, which serves the Malaysian capital of Kuala Lumpur, has had only one change of address in its eighty years of existence. And this was not painful, because the Government, in acquiring the site of the first course after World War I, provided a more convenient and attractive alternative.

For four years during World War II the club served as the command headquarters for the Japanese Army of Occupation. During that time the clubhouse suffered no real structural damage, but the two golf courses reverted back to jungle, except for patches of tapioca and a small airstrip. "The first impression on inspecting the property", reported a member in 1946, "was that golf would never again be played there."

He reckoned without the club's professional, Yorkshireman Tom Verity, and the members. After months of backbreaking work the main course was reopened for play by the end of the year. By mid-1947 a third nine was cleared and by March 1948 both full courses were in play. Verity, an outstanding character, was appointed professional in 1937 and he was to hold the post for twenty-seven years, leaving only to build new courses and to teach up-country. Some intangible quality departed from the club when he left.

The Royal Selangor Golf Club today is a hive of sporting activity. Besides its thirty-six holes, there are twelve grass tennis courts, an Olympic-size swimming pool, a squash court,

restaurant and entertainment facilities for hundreds of people. It is something of a diplomatic listening post; the ambassadors of the United States and, most unexpectedly, the Soviet Union battle for the honours of lowest handicap, and two kings have graced the premises with almost daily attendance.

Thirty members founded the club at Petaling Hills, outside the city area, in 1893. No clubhouse was available for the first handicap competition, and notice was sent from a refreshment tent that "St Andrews Rules, of course," would be used—a reminder that in 1893 the game had no set of standard rules. Leading clubs in Britain and elsewhere drew up their own until 1897, when it was agreed that those made by the Rules Committee of The Royal and Ancient Golf Club at St Andrews would be applied universally.

In 1918 Selangor State took over Petaling Hills and paid for the construction of a new course and clubhouse. Few clubs have ever been blessed with such official help. Work began on the new site in 1920 and within a year nine holes of the main course were ready, together with the clubhouse. In the next year four grass and two hard tennis courts were laid down; the swimming pool did not appear until 1937.

The greens on both the Old and New courses were at first laid with an indigenous growth known derisively as "cow grass", a dwarf species that proved suitable for animals but which left much to be desired when used on greens.

Bermuda was used for the greens of the Old course for eleven years in the 1920s and 1930s, but the strain was never satisfactory and it was replaced in 1935 by serangoon, a species that had proved itself at Singapore. A hybrid Bermuda strain, a world away from the original "cow grass", has now been put to use.

Maintenance difficulties are enormous in a country that, apart from its heat, has an annual rainfall of 160 inches. Green surfaces have the shape of upturned saucers—a characteristic of

courses in the monsoon regions—to drain off the immense quantities of water that will flood a course in a matter of minutes.

Golf events in Malaysia are often held up or cancelled because of rain, but one way to ensure protection is to hire a "Bumu", a specialist in keeping rain away—sometimes apparently with good effect. During the 1975 Malaysian Open championship at Kuala Lumpur heavy rain was forecast and arrived on schedule. The Asian hockey championships, held in a stadium less than a mile away, suffered badly

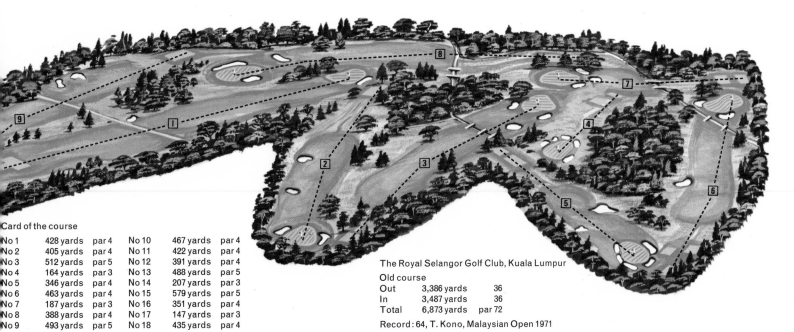

Card of the course						
No 1	428 yards	par 4	No 10	467 yards	par 4
No 2	405 yards	par 4	No 11	422 yards	par 4
No 3	512 yards	par 5	No 12	391 yards	par 4
No 4	164 yards	par 3	No 13	488 yards	par 5
No 5	346 yards	par 4	No 14	207 yards	par 3
No 6	463 yards	par 4	No 15	579 yards	par 5
No 7	187 yards	par 3	No 16	351 yards	par 4
No 8	388 yards	par 4	No 17	147 yards	par 3
No 9	493 yards	par 5	No 18	435 yards	par 4

The Royal Selangor Golf Club, Kuala Lumpur
Old course

Out	3,386 yards	36
In	3,487 yards	36
Total	6,873 yards	par 72

Record: 64, T. Kono, Malaysian Open 1971

and finished three weeks behind schedule. The golf championship had its Bumu. He came just after dawn on each of the four mornings and set up his stand beneath a simple shelter behind the 17th tee. No one spoke to him, nor he to them. He burned a few sticks, chanting the while in an undertone, except when he ate or took a short sleep. No rain fell for four days, until the Malaysian Prime Minister presented the first prize to Australia's Graham Marsh. Then the heavens opened. In a matter of minutes the course and clubhouse precincts were awash.

The 17th is usually a demanding par-four, but at Royal Selangor it is the shortest hole on the course, measuring only 147 yards. However, on a course where sand is the most common hazard, the bunkers being used sparingly but to good effect, it makes menacing use of water.

Had it fallen an hour earlier it would have been impossible to complete the event.

Royal Selangor is almost dead flat, which makes for easy walking, and the golf is particularly pleasant when the sun is not high. But giant trees provide shade and the small stream which runs through the course adds its own cooling hint of freshness.

One gets the feeling that it is an easy course. This may be because each hole is a birdie proposition, or seems so. In the course of a championship the fortunes tend to fluctuate unpredictably and the explanation is often found in the grass on the fairways and greens.

Fairways are well grassed and when freshly cut provide excellent lies. Greens require special preparation because of the rain, but at their best rival anything other than the softest bent grass. Despite the flatness of the fairways, the thick-bladed local grass gives a wide variation in lies. The way the ball sits very often determines its flight and destination, the influence of the grass overriding the skill and planning of the striker. For all that, championship golf at Selangor calls for special skills at the short end of the game, as a list of winners of the Malaysian Open shows. Inevitably, there is a lot of chapping and putting where greens are wiry and grainy. The winners deserve special praise and the course its full due.

Most holes dog-leg around the massive trees. Numerous bunkers, strategically placed, provide the obstacles. In all, the Royal Selangor is a course in the highest category. In terms of architecture it is as the best-designed courses should be—all things to all golfers. It is a fearsome test from the back tees for the champions who come around once a year for the Malaysian Open, and at the same time real fun and pleasure for those with lesser gifts.

The 6th: For the cautious rather than the bold
At 463 yards the 6th at Royal Selangor is really neither par-four nor par-five. Of course in championships this does not matter, since par has no meaning in a strokeplay scratch event except perhaps to rate the total score. The hole is barely reachable in two shots into a wind unless the fairway is dry and hard, which it seldom is. Downwind, of course, it is not the same problem. During the Malaysian Open, played each March, it is usually a drive and a 3- or 4-iron hole. But it is advisable to approach timidly: it is easy enough to get down in two from just short, but less likely from beyond.

The green is unusually narrow, being no more than ten paces wide. This makes a tiny target, especially when fired at from 200 or more yards. It is guarded by a trap on either side, the right-hand one being a little shorter than the left. The green is elevated and of two levels, rising quite high at the back. It has gained something of a reputation because of the grain of its grass, which makes putting a chancy business. Knowledge of this makes the tee shot somehow more difficult, since the player feels the need to gain as much length as possible in order to shorten the second shot. This has destroyed thousands of drives.

The tee shot is aimed at slightly higher ground and there is one yawning trap on the left which is not particularly threatening unless the shot is hooked violently. On the right side is a line of thin trees, under which the broad-stemmed indigenous grass grows lush and thick. Running diagonally across the fairway about thirty yards from the green is the course's main storm drain, which catches plenty of over-ambitious second shots. Its stone and concrete lining can sometimes be spectacularly beneficial and many a second shot nose-diving to destruction has rammed the hard rock and rebounded high in the air to safety. However, for most it means a certain one-stroke penalty, which often leads to more as desperate recovery attempts overshoot the green in the effort to get too close. Sanely played, though, it is a hole of immense challenge and, once parred, great satisfaction.

The golf boom reaches an idyllic island

Card of the course

No 1	500 yards	par 5	No 10	412 yards	par 4
No 2	180 yards	par 3	No 11	194 yards	par 3
No 3	450 yards	par 4	No 12	410 yards	par 4
No 4	180 yards	par 3	No 13	410 yards	par 4
No 5	400 yards	par 4	No 14	180 yards	par 3
No 6	410 yards	par 4	No 15	500 yards	par 5
No 7	400 yards	par 4	No 16	432 yards	par 4
No 8	411 yards	par 4	No 17	442 yards	par 4
No 9	527 yards	par 5	No 18	572 yards	par 5

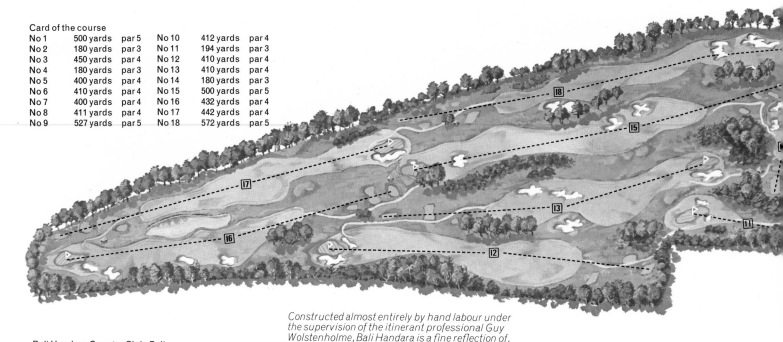

Bali Handara Country Club, Bali

Out	3,458 yards	36
In	3,552 yards	36
Total	7,010 yards	par 72

Constructed almost entirely by hand labour under the supervision of the itinerant professional Guy Wolstenholme, Bali Handara is a fine reflection of, and response to, the golf boom in the Far East. The main problem in building a course on this beautiful island was the rainfall: up to an inch can fall every day during the two wet seasons.

Even if it were possible to uphold the dubious claim that the Dutch invented golf, there is no evidence that they took it with them to the outposts of empire, as did the British. Rather, the game arrived in Indonesia—then under Dutch suzerainty—as an appendage to the tea and rubber plantations owned by British commercial interests.

Until after World War II there were fewer than a dozen courses throughout the 2,500-mile chain of islands that make up Indonesia, and all but two belonged to the plantations. The Djakarta club, in the capital, was the most thriving and successful. Its eighteen holes were spread comfortably over 150 acres or more of park-like grounds not far from the city centre.

After the war the club suffered a cruel blow. Half its property, nine holes beyond a road, was compulsorily acquired for a new university and the club is now confined to the seventy-five acres which originally contained only nine holes. Its holes are crowded in more ways than one and the total length of the course barely reaches 6,000 yards.

Other clubs, as well as a somewhat primitive municipal course, are now springing up in the Djakarta area and the golfing bug seems to have found fertile ground at last in which to thrive. The election to President of General Suharto brought to power an enthusiastic golfer and many of his ministers and senior army officers have dutifully followed his example. This growing interest in the game led, as it has done elsewhere in the world, to the need for a course of truly international quality and design. Djakarta Golf Club could never be that, because of its limited land space.

The choice for the site—and there could not have been a happier one—was Bali, at the eastern end of the Indonesian archipelago.

Bali is an island of legendary beauty, little more than an hour's flying time from Djakarta, a volcanic structure sloping down through green forests and palm groves to the white sand of reef-protected beaches. It is the home of two and a half million Balinese who lead a peaceful, carefree life in an idyllic environment.

General Ibnu Sutowo, the moving spirit

The Indonesian-style clubhouse nestles in the trees, 4,000 feet up in the Balinese hills.

behind the scheme, found his site high in the mountains where, at 4,000 feet, the weather is cool and the rainfall adequate for growing the best golf grass. The land included a dairy farm, on a gently sloping tract between two large and splendid lakes near the small town of Bedugal.

Thomson Wolveridge Fream and Storm were engaged as architects and Guy Wolsten-

holme, the expatriate English professional, took on the task of supervising the construction. He arrived in a downpour of rain in September, 1973. The only earth-moving machinery that Wolstenholme had at his disposal was an old-fashioned Russian steam-roller, converted into a bulldozer that crept along at less than walking pace. There was no other machinery available on the island, but there was something better—the wholehearted co-operation of the entire local population.

Altogether 1,500 people, many of them women, worked on the course construction. The fairways were staked out, cleared up by the villagers and finally hand-sown. Under Wolstenholme's careful supervision greens were built entirely with hand labour, frequently in heavy rain.

Bali has two wet seasons. During February–March and September–October rains fall almost every day, in the higher altitudes arriving punctually at one o'clock in the afternoon and continuing until four, during which time an inch might fall. The natural patterns of water drainage on the site were carefully noted, and the course now has a drainage system second to none. It is possible to play less than half an hour after the afternoon rain has finished, or to get at least a few holes in before the sun disappears at six o'clock.

The course took its final shape in six months. Ron Fream of California selected the grasses, flown in from the USA, and an elaborate watering system arrived from Australia. The clubhouse is a beautiful building in the Indonesian style and all about it are small cottages in the same style to complete the setting. In every way the course fits in with its surrounding environment. From the clubhouse there is a view over the course and beyond it to the lake.

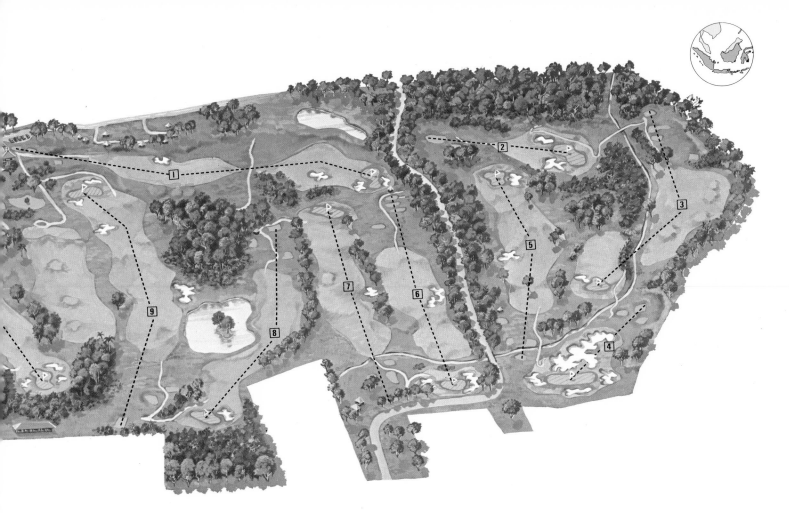

its far side lost in the distance. Everything is a rich green except for the red tile roofs of the far village and the blue sky reflected in the lake.

From the course, the clubhouse is dwarfed by a forest-clad mountain, its heights wispy with cloud. Monkeys, deer and pigs descend occasionally from the forest to cross the course, or to stop and feed before racing for cover at the approach of man.

The fairways, a superb blend of imported Kentucky bluegrass and the local Bermuda strain, roll out like an expensive carpet at every hole. Bluegrass, as its name implies, has a gentle hue distinguishing it from other vegetation. When close clipped it is crisp and firm, ideal for iron play or long wood shots. In truth, fairways so perfect take something from the play. To handle the infinite variety of lies and stances on a seaside links, by contrast, is a much more challenging task.

At Bali Handara the ball bounces and rolls truly, with a variation in proportion to the amount of rain that has fallen beforehand. The greens stand out as inspiring targets emphasized by the white sand of the bunkers, though these have not been overdone. Craters of sand would look extraordinarily inappropriate in a mountain setting; Bali Handara, like other courses in similar situations, is not a seaside links and should not be made to look like one. Golf is playable anywhere. It is one of an architect's jobs to arrange an arena for golfing in whatever natural circumstances there are, and to get the best from them without destroying their character.

The trees, the flowers, the streams and lakes at Bali Handara are unique to the course and are its real features, with the golf holes running over and between them. Bali Handara turned out even better than its designers' dreams.

The 3rd: Beauty sweetens the challenge

The 3rd hole at Bali Handara was the toughest to build, but in the end proved to be the most rewarding. It is a 450-yard par-four, dog-legging left, its fairway divided by a stream that rushes off the mountain behind. From a high teeing ground, the drive is over a garden of wild shrubs and flowers into a wide, safe field of fairway. The stream winds its way along the right of the 1st fairway, cutting it off from the shorter 2nd fairway, which is offset to the right. The second shot must then be hit across the water to the long green, which is well beyond. An imposing trap of white sand cuts into the green on the right side. When the flag is set on this side its base is hidden by the sand because a gentle dividing ridge spurs out from the trap.

This is a hole of beauty and pleasure, presenting a basic challenge to players of all standards. To tempt the long hitter there is a short stretch of fairway, partially obscured by trees. This is the direct line to the green, but the penalties of failure are severe. There is the stream to worry about and some thick trees and undergrowth to trap the slice.

From the charming single-file track that leads to the tee, to the little wooden bridge across the stream and the walk away from the green through the trees, this hole epitomizes the magic and the fascination of Bali Handara.

The 15th: Built to confound the reckless

At Bali Handara's 15th the golfer can look past the green to the shining lake beyond. As at every other hole on this lush course the view is breathtaking. But the 15th, a noble par-five of 500 yards, is memorable for one intriguing feature—a bunker right in the middle of the fairway that is modelled on the famous Principal's Nose on the 16th of the Old course at St Andrews. It is one of the few sandtraps on this delightful course and, like all the others, it serves a purpose. It is there to confound the reckless tee shot.

Those who criticize bunkers should always reflect on the gap left by their absence and no more conclusive argument can be made for their existence than Bali Handara's 15th. But for this penal feature the first half of this hole would be empty indeed. There is in any case room enough to the left, although by design the route down that side is longer—in all probability too long to reach home in two shots, always the hope of the scratch player.

Even by the direct route it is not easy to make

Modelled on the famous Principal's Nose at St Andrews, the fairway *bunker at the 15th turns a simple par-five into a demanding hole.*

this one in two shots, although the big hitter may manage the distance. Subtle slopes and bumps in the green area make it a risky business blazing away, and to get caught short of the green in the big central trap makes for the hardest shot in golf—the long explosion.

Australasia

Sport is king in Australia, a land where top-class tennis players are taken for granted and an endless succession of pubescent Olympic hopes cleave the water like dolphins. In such a climate, golf—a game that can be played from youth to near-dotage—was bound to find enthusiastic support. Estimates of the number of Australians who play golf range from 350,000 to twice that number, with the lower figure representing at least the solid nucleus of devotees. Either way, support for golf in Australia is every bit as great as in the United States and twice as great, *per capita*, as in Britain, which despatched to the southern continent its first exemplars of golf during early Colonial days. There are now rather more than 1,300 courses in Australia, most of them concentrated in the populous southeast corner of the continent where the nation's first settlements were established. The antecedents of the earliest clubs are a little confused, for there were a number of false starts in Adelaide and Sydney. The Royal Melbourne, slipping through where others were stumbling, is the club with the longest unbroken existence, since 1891. The Royal Sydney and the Royal Adelaide soon followed and by 1895 there were clubs in Perth and Tasmania. The best of Australia's courses are among the best in the world. There is a particular quality about those in the neighbourhood of Melbourne, where the soil of the Sand Belt and the talents of architects like Alister Mackenzie and Dick Wilson have shaped testing golf in surroundings of great character. They have played their part in the breeding of great players who have made their mark around the world—Norman Von Nida, Peter Thomson (five times winner of the British Open), Jim Ferrier, Kel Nagle, Bruce Devlin, Bruce Crampton and others. In New Zealand, where the game got off to a start—albeit in a limited manner—about the same time as in Australia, golf has made great strides in recent years. With 370-plus courses it has rather more than Ireland, where the population is about the same.

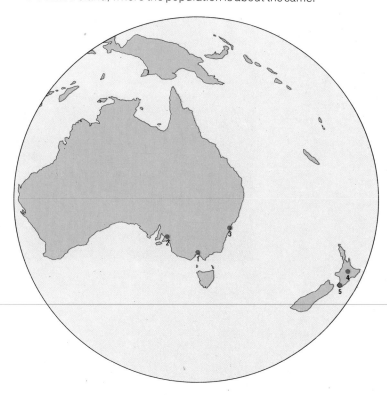

1 Royal Melbourne
2 Royal Adelaide
3 Royal Sydney
4 Wairakei
5 Paraparaumu

A course to humble even the giants

Something outstanding and exceptional was bound to emerge from the formation of the Royal Melbourne club. There was, to begin with, a dedication to the traditions of the game that stemmed through its earliest members and officers directly from St Andrews. Later, after two changes of location to the site it now occupies, it was fashioned from a duneland setting closely akin to the old Scottish links. And finally there is simply the inspired architecture of its two courses, the East and the West.

Championship events are now played over a composite eighteen holes, a beneficial expedient forced upon the organizers of the 1959 Canada Cup to avoid busy roads which cross both courses. This composite course, taking in the best of both East and West, is unquestionably the finest in Australia and by any judgement must have strong claim to equal anything on earth. It is a course that tests the most proficient golfers to their utmost, yet at the same time excites and thrills the club's members.

The necessary acreage of sandy dune left behind by a retreating sea, studded with native she-oaks and tea-trees, dwarf reed, heather and bracken, had been acquired by 1924, when it was decided to secure "the best expert advice" —with no limit to cost—to alter and finish the course to the club's satisfaction. The choice of adviser was Dr Alister Mackenzie, the celebrated Scottish golf architect. Mackenzie arrived in October 1926 and started work immediately with Alex Russell, Australian Open champion of 1924, as his partner.

Mackenzie's written philosophy of golf architecture and the courses he planned mark him as a designer of the highest skill, and the Royal Melbourne was in many ways his masterpiece. This is not to overlook Russell's contribution—evinced by the quality of the East course, which he designed and built after Mackenzie's departure. Six holes of this course are included in the composite and two, the 3rd and 18th, are among the best. It would be fair to say, then, that Royal Melbourne is the result of the best ideas of both men.

As significant as the layout and overall design of the Melbourne championship course is the scale and speed of its greens, the credit for which belongs to the former head green-keeper Claude Crockford, who joined the staff in 1934. In many ways the course is as much his as it is Mackenzie's or Russell's.

Crockford himself undertook to rebuild ▷

Surrounded by sand, heather and bracken, the sloping 5th provides a perfect example of a Royal Melbourne green. Renowned for the superb pace and texture of its greens, Australia's premier course ranks with any in the world, and the variation in championship scores there (from Sam Snead's record 65 up to 105) is a good indication of the demands it makes even on the greatest of players. The course gained immensely in stature through the skills of its masterly head greenkeeper, Claude Crockford, who battled against flood and drought to maintain and even improve upon the designs of Alister Mackenzie and Alex Russell.

▷ the short, uphill 7th hole to the concept of the then best player of the club, Ivo Whitton, after the original Mackenzie hole proved unsatisfactory. Mackenzie may have been fond of building par-threes where the green was higher than—and therefore blind to—the tee ground, but it was a design that eventually brought unpopularity and its replacement with a green somewhat lower, where it could be seen.

Crockford's 150-yard 7th is a rare gem of planning and construction. To stand by it during a championship is endless entertainment because scores from the best players vary in quick succession from two to five or even seven. It was built on the sandy hill by horse and scoop like the rest of the course. It slopes in an intriguing line from back to front although there is adequate flat, or nearly flat, territory for

the flagstick in one or two spots—a deception not always discovered until it is too late by players in awe of its glassy surface. It is surrounded by traps of good depth and formidable sides, with a foreground like a miniature natural park of small indigenous flora to add to its rugged appearance.

But Crockford's real memorials are the Melbourne greens; there are no truer or faster putting surfaces on earth. Players either love them or detest them, although it must be said the latter reaction is often the result of a player being unnerved by their speed and slope. The real art of golf greenkeeping is not growing grass but keeping it down, and Crockford did this to perfection. The greens are basically dry and firm and the grass sparse compared with the dense growth of most other courses.

Every fifteen years or so, the turf is carefully cut into lengths of six feet by one foot across, then gently lifted away to expose the rootmat and the lower six inches of soil, the home of almost all grass diseases. This potential breeding ground is scraped away and replaced by newly prepared sterile soil. Then the turf is relaid, keeping perfectly to the original contour. The greens always have a faint patchwork appearance, effected by reversing the grain of the grass when relaying the turf. This has a lot to do with the general health and trueness of all the greens.

To follow the Melbourne championship course is to experience a kaleidoscope of obstacles and emotions. The 1st is a 424-yard par-four of huge width and openness. It is hardly possible to miss this fairway. The second

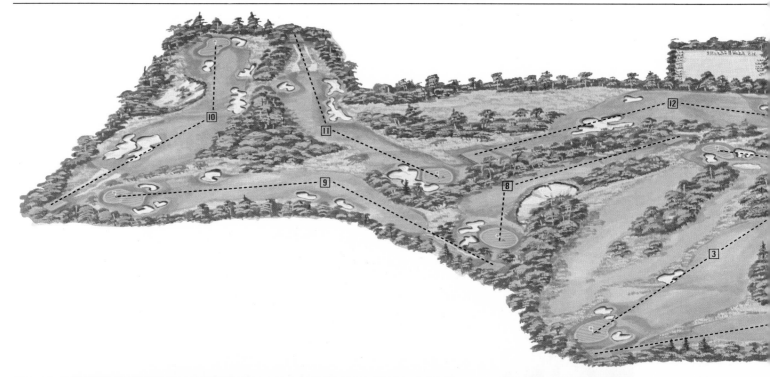

The extraordinary bunkers—these lie between the 1st and 8th fairways—provide the most lasting image of Royal Melbourne. Scoured out of the sand by horse and scoop (as was the whole course) they have none of the delicate manicuring which lessens the penalty of hazards on so many other courses.

shot—assuming one can reach the green—would be no harder if it weren't for the need to get somewhere near the flag to make the task of getting down in two a more reasonable proposition. As on every green at Melbourne, this is easier said than done.

The 2nd hole is a par-five of excellence, especially when the wind is from south of west. The tee shot must carry a formidable sand bunker on the short line and a player cannot hope to get home in two or near it unless he does. The second—if it reaches the green—runs past a crater of sand on the left and the green that looks so benign can be a holy terror when putting from a distance.

The 3rd hole is a Russell creation of 330 yards. Few holes of this length anywhere have its class. The tee shot aims out to a wide expanse except for a spread of sand on the right at the crown of the hill. Beyond, the fairway rushes down to a hollow before a two-tiered green that steps down from right to left, the third stage dropping into a final huge trap at its lowest and farthest left point. In addition the player is faced with a pitch over another deep monster on the right to get at the flag on the top right step—where it nearly always is on championship day. This can be a frightening hole and in many ways epitomizes the whole course.

There follows a dog-leg par-four, again by Russell, that climbs uphill to a green, two-tiered on the crown. The 5th is the first of the ingenious par-threes that make this course so distinctive. It is a 170-yard shot across a small valley to a green that forms a step on the farther slope. Surrounding the green is a sea of sand, heather and bracken and the slope before the green is so steep and "shaved" that a shot just feeble enough to land on the bevelled front edge inevitably trickles back down to the foot of the slope. The green is deceptively fast and sloped from the back; holing out in two putts requires a keen eye and a steady hand.

The 6th hole is one of the world's best and a thriller to watch during a championship. It is a dog-leg, starting from a high tee; the fairway turns at almost right angles around a wide area of perfectly natural ground scrub and sand, which can be crossed with sufficient power and direction. The invitation is ever to bite off more than can be chewed. From the fairway there is a gentle slope up to a green set in a natural amphitheatre that is guarded by a massive, deep ▷

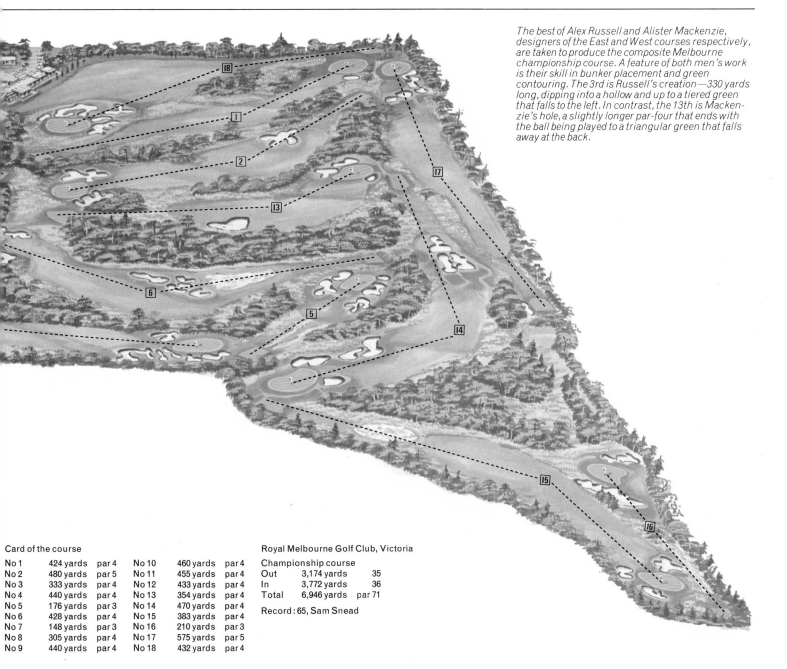

The best of Alex Russell and Alister Mackenzie, designers of the East and West courses respectively, are taken to produce the composite Melbourne championship course. A feature of both men's work is their skill in bunker placement and green contouring. The 3rd is Russell's creation—330 yards long, dipping into a hollow and up to a tiered green that falls to the left. In contrast, the 13th is Mackenzie's hole, a slightly longer par-four that ends with the ball being played to a triangular green that falls away at the back.

Card of the course

No 1	424 yards	par 4	No 10	460 yards	par 4
No 2	480 yards	par 5	No 11	455 yards	par 4
No 3	333 yards	par 4	No 12	433 yards	par 4
No 4	440 yards	par 4	No 13	354 yards	par 4
No 5	176 yards	par 3	No 14	470 yards	par 4
No 6	428 yards	par 4	No 15	383 yards	par 4
No 7	148 yards	par 3	No 16	210 yards	par 3
No 8	305 yards	par 4	No 17	575 yards	par 5
No 9	440 yards	par 4	No 18	432 yards	par 4

Royal Melbourne Golf Club, Victoria

Championship course

Out	3,174 yards	35
In	3,772 yards	36
Total	6,946 yards	par 71

Record: 65, Sam Snead

▷ trap on the left-hand side. The shot looks easy and receptive but there is a major problem of getting down in two from the back edge. Canadian Al Balding took four putts in the Canada Cup by the classic fault of not getting the first putt at least to the hole. Putting across the green is no less examining, because the "line" is apt to turn almost the length of the putt. Most of all, a good accurate second shot is paramount.

Following Crockford's new 7th, which offers no respite, is another jewel. The 8th is only 305 yards long but devilishly difficult. The green can be driven and often is, but in this lies the seeds of destruction. The fairway crosses a large valley and winds its way by circuitous route to the right until, having reached the hilltop, it turns back left to the small green surrounded

by mild wilderness. Playing safe is no guarantee of four because even after a curtailed tee shot the pitch from below the hill is blind and therefore risky. It is a fine example of old-fashioned adventure, with consequences to be suffered, come what may.

The 9th hole is a man-sized par-four which dog-legs left to the horizon and a green of alarming undulation and fiendish speed. The 10th is one of the best holes on the course. It must have started its life as a par-five because, instead of a straightforward fairway and green, the route winds away to the right and a higher level, drawing the play with it and so adding to the length and interest. The tee shot carries some large-scale Mackenzie traps and the second an expanse of Royal Melbourne native rough, thinned sufficiently for the ball not to

be lost, but rugged enough to make escape an uncertain business.

Another beautiful par-four is found at the 11th. The drive fires out on to a level area back-dropped by a forest of tea-trees, and there is no hint of what lies ahead until a hill is breasted at the 250-yard mark to reveal a spectacular target some 200 yards away across a shallow valley. The 12th (the 18th on the West course) leads back to the clubhouse. It is a par-four of much merit, presenting a drive over a hill that is characterized by typical Mackenzie sand and a sharp dog-leg turn to the right where the green is viewed, framed in several ominous white sandtraps.

The 354-yard 13th is a clever drive and a pitch made to a triangle green in which the apex points to the striker and the slope falls

The 8th: The ultimate in temptation

It is a stiff test of a golf architect's skill to ask him to make something out of a hole of only 300 yards; few holes on earth of this length can be reckoned to be anything more than stop-gaps. The par-four 8th hole on the Royal Melbourne championship course is a grand exception. Granted the designers, Alister Mackenzie and Alex Russell, had a perfect piece of land to work with but the result nevertheless is quite unique. It makes the sternest demands on good and bad players alike, and no matter what the weather conditions scores here can vary from two to ten.

In golf course design two interesting themes run counter to each other. The one rather standard principle, that the farther one hits and the nearer one approaches the target the finer becomes the margin of error, is cleverly offset by the axiom that the more finely judged second shot gets progressively more difficult the farther one falls short of the green. Architects often attempt to incorporate these two themes into their design, but few succeed.

The sporting length of the 8th, which is often played thirty yards short of its full length of 305 yards, offers the ultimate in temptation—that of driving on to the green and perhaps holing the putt for an eagle. But the very real likelihood and the dire consequences of failure on a shot of that particular line and length are apt to inhibit the free swing and bring disaster.

The hole crosses a pleasant valley from one crest to the next. In the ordinary way this would present no problems to the modern professional, except that on the direct line to the flag is a cavernous bunker. However, the designers have cleverly led the player towards the right where they offer a safe shot, provided it is not too long, to a generous expanse of fairway. Failure to reach the top of the crest leaves a shot to the flagstick which is to some degree blind and, should the green be firm and fast, as it usually is, the pitch requires the utmost accuracy to reach and hold the green. All around there is sand, except for a tiny apron in the form of a hollow, the excavation of which helped to form the green. The main feature of the hole is the enormous chasm of bunker which must be carried by the brave player who elects to go for the green. A man feels small indeed standing in there trying to play out.

The real art of a short par-four is found in the 8th at Melbourne. It is a bold and confident player who attempts to drive the enormous bunker in the hope of leaving a short pitch to the green for the chance of a birdie.

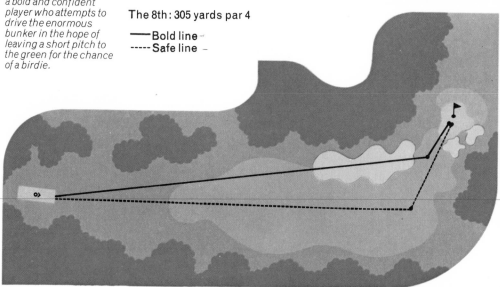

The 8th: 305 yards par 4

—— Bold line –
----- Safe line –

gently away to the back edge. The "falling away" technique was used again by Mackenzie at the 3rd at Augusta National. In the early days there was no doubt a choice of a high pitch or a run through a preceding small valley and steep bank close-shaved like the green. Nowadays— alas—everyone opts for the pitch. Perhaps the most powerful hole on the course, the 14th is 470 yards, and more a par-five than a par-four. The tee shot must carry over a hill with a savage seaside trap; the second shot, across a valley of sand and scrub, runs the gauntlet of steep-faced traps at the greenside. Again the fairway runs intriguingly to the left of the target and for once the green is comparatively flat. It was here that Lee Trevino took a nine that cost him a win in the 1974 Chrysler Classic championship.

Lined along the right side with trees and the course boundary fence, the 15th is a dog-leg sliding to the left with a green of fiendish undulations. It is, perhaps, the only place at which it is possible to go out-of-bounds. The 16th is a Russell par-three of 210 yards up a gentle hill. The back of the green, to the left, is more like 230 yards distant, a factor to remember when selecting clubs. Australia's Bruce Crampton ran up a six here just when he and Bill Dunk looked to have the World Cup won in 1972.

At 575 yards the 17th is Melbourne's longest, but—incredibly—it was twice reached in two shots in 1958, first by Sam Snead, then by an Argentinian giant, Leopold Ruiz, with a drive and a 7-iron! There are cross-bunkers at the 400-yard mark and little else in the way of obstacles.

The last hole, 432 yards and invariably into wind, is one of the world's best finishing holes. With the green an island in a sea of sand it makes a formidable par-four. It has characteristic undulation and ever-increasing speed when the chips are down. It makes the task of getting down in two little less than heroic—and sometimes beyond one's capability, as the Scot Ronnie Shade found in the Eisenhower Trophy matches of 1968. From a yard or two short of the putting green and about twenty-five yards from the cup, his run-up swung away to the left and Britain lost the contest to the USA.

There are few, if any, courses in the world where the scores for a championship vary as much as they do at Melbourne. Sam Snead's 65 is the best—and 105 by Sam Surrudhin of Indonesia the worst. It is a course to humble the giants or confirm their greatness.

The fearsome view from the tee on the 14th, generally regarded as the toughest of the twelve par-fours at Royal Melbourne. The blind drive over Mackenzie's massive traps is followed by a long second hit from a sloping fairway over rough and three deep, awkward bunkers. Finally, the generous green is a mass of subtle slopes. This is a hole where making par brings all the satisfaction of a birdie.

The 14th: Fairways that wander to deceive

The most difficult hole on the Royal Melbourne layout comes at a critical stage in the round—the 14th. It is a 470-yard par-four that both twists and rolls spectacularly. It rises over a substantial hill before descending through a long, 200-yard valley and ending on about the same elevation at which it started. If one shoots straight for the green the hole also turns some 45 degrees after the tee shot; otherwise the approach must be planned to avoid the obstacles and then the line of attack can vary considerably.

But first there is one of those classic blind tee shots over a complex of Mackenzie traps on the skyline. This must have been a fiendish hazard in the 1930s, when the balls flew shorter distances than they do now. Those who could not carry the bunkers must have been forced to go around them to the left, thus increasing the length of the hole to over 500 yards. Beyond the bunkers the fairway slopes downwards, complicating the stance for the long second, which is daunting enough, but the clear view from there of the various obstacles—and therefore possibilities—is frightening. There is rough to carry for the first part, and then the fairway twists and turns through three huge, deep bunkers that can bring disaster. Lee Trevino was caught in the heather overhanging the trap on the left side

in the 1974 Chrysler Classic and ended up with a nine! Here again we see Mackenzie cleverly leading the golfer astray with a fairway that wanders away from the direct route, forcing him to play over the trouble.

The green is a subtle complex of gentle slopes that are almost invisible, but most often seen, alas, too late. For most golfers this hole is more of a par-five than a four, and when the south wind blows strongly it becomes a par-five for even the strongest. Before the tea-trees grew high along the way, the hole traversed a sea of natural white sand. It is a pity that was lost; however, the trees make the hole more attractive if no easier.

The 14th: 470 yards par 4

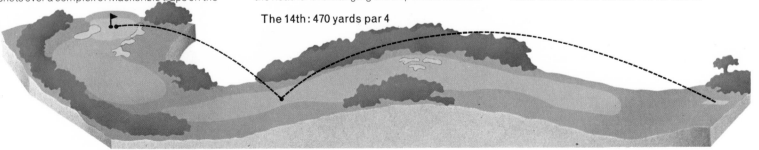

Taking on the teetotallers — and the bishop

Golf came to Adelaide in 1869, among the steamer trunks of South Australia's new governor, the Scotsman Sir James Fergusson. There were Scots enough already in residence (the administration of empire was a talent in which they were particularly distinguished) to help him establish the club with a small membership within a year of his arrival.

The early years were, at best, chequered. The golfing governor departed, having completed his term of office, and six years after it had been opened the first nine-hole course—now lost beneath the Victoria Park racecourse—was abandoned as unsuitable.

The club remained in limbo for sixteen years. A new course was found, but it was an expedient, replaced in 1896 when the club merged with the palindromic Glenelg, in the southern suburbs of the city.

The new club retained the name of Adelaide but used the Glenelg course, nine holes that were soon extended to eighteen with the advice of another expatriate Scots golfer, Francis Maxwell, whose brother Robert won the British Amateur championship in 1903.

In 1904, the club moved to its present site at Seaton, twenty-five minutes by train from the city centre. The single-track railway line is still there but the station, beside which the clubhouse was built in the centre of the 204-acre property, has been closed.

Soon after it acquired the Seaton course, Adelaide appointed its first professional—not surprisingly a Scotsman, Jack Scott, from Carnoustie. The appointment of a talented professional was critical to a young club, particularly one so far from Scotland, source and inspiration of all golfing mores. He made and repaired clubs, not the least of his functions in a climate which played havoc with woodwork; he taught, and in teaching laid the groundwork for the club's reputation; and he was the final arbiter on the game's rules and etiquette.

Scott remained at Adelaide for nearly twenty years and had the pleasure of seeing one of his protégés, Rufus Stewart, become the first South Australian to win the Australian Open in 1927.

The hazards of golf are not always just those of the sandtrap and the water. The Adelaide club had to contend with the prim city fathers—led by a bishop—who deplored the club's use of youngsters as caddies on the Sabbath. It drove off an attempt by two of its members—presumably a teetotal fifth column—to stop the sale of alcohol at the club, and itself banished one of its member's free-range turkeys from the course.

To make worth while all their strenuous efforts to keep going, Alister Mackenzie arrived in 1926 to advise on modifications to the course. The work he carried out forms the basis of the present championship route, although in subse-

Card of the course

No 1	378 yards	par 4
No 2	500 yards	par 5
No 3	301 yards	par 4
No 4	421 yards	par 4
No 5	402 yards	par 4
No 6	436 yards	par 4
No 7	156 yards	par 3
No 8	381 yards	par 4
No 9	540 yards	par 5
No 10	382 yards	par 4
No 11	382 yards	par 4
No 12	224 yards	par 3
No 13	422 yards	par 4
No 14	442 yards	par 4
No 15	515 yards	par 5
No 16	176 yards	par 3
No 17	525 yards	par 5
No 18	427 yards	par 4

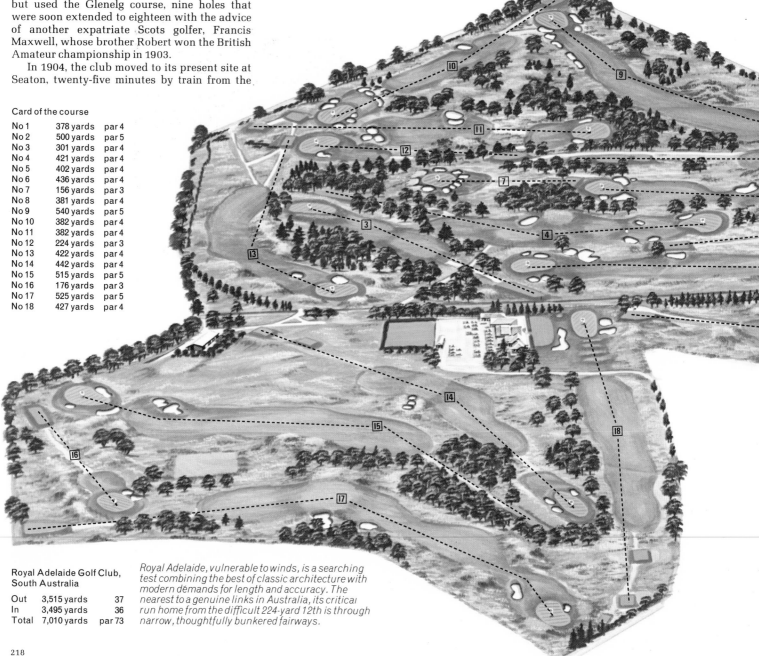

Royal Adelaide Golf Club, South Australia

Out	3,515 yards	37
In	3,495 yards	36
Total	7,010 yards	par 73

Royal Adelaide, vulnerable to winds, is a searching test combining the best of classic architecture with modern demands for length and accuracy. The nearest to a genuine links in Australia, its critical run home from the difficult 224-yard 12th is through narrow, thoughtfully bunkered fairways.

quent years the holes were constantly improved and upgraded. Among Mackenzie's innovations was the removal of the need to play across the railway line, and the introduction of the sand-dunes as features of the championship course.

Royal Adelaide (it acquired its Title Royal in 1923) is the nearest course to a links that Australia has among its top championship venues. Its sand is in many places the natural hazard and rough. The 1st, 6th, 13th, 17th and 18th holes have lately been upgraded to give them more of the "seaside" character than they formerly had.

The whole layout has the flat appearance of a links, except for a rise in the centre of the site where two tees, the 8th and 12th, are placed. Two huge craters of bare sand have been preserved to enhance the course's distinctive character.

By the mid-1970s Royal Adelaide had been the venue for the Australian Open championship eight times, the Australian Amateur championship twelve times and the South Australian Amateur championship on forty-one occasions.

Jim Ferrier, who attained world fame first as runner-up in the British Amateur in 1939 and

later as a professional in the US, won the double crown of Open and Amateur national titles at Royal Adelaide in 1938. Gary Player won the second of his seven Australian Open championships there in 1962 (an event in which Jack Nicklaus made his first appearance in Australia, finishing fifth). Player won with 278, five less than Ferrier's score twenty-four years earlier, but Ferrier was under no pressure for he won by the enormous margin of fourteen strokes from his contemporary, Norman Von Nida.

The final of the Australian Amateur in 1932 provided the most exciting contest in the championship's history. The defending champion, a seventeen-year-old left-handed prodigy, Harry Williams, was opposed by Dr Reg Bettington, a triple Oxford Blue and captain of the New South Wales cricket team. Williams appeared to have his title safely in keeping when, two up, he hit his tee shot to six feet at the par-three 12th, the 30th hole of the contest. Bettington followed to twenty feet and courageously holed the putt before stepping back to watch Williams miss. Bettington birdied the next two holes in threes, taking the lead. He stymied Williams on the 33rd green and birdied the 34th. A half in par-fives down the long 35th gave Bettington an incredible victory; Williams was on par through the last seven holes, yet lost four of them.

Scoring of this kind was unknown in Australia in 1932. Both players were of the highest international standard and Williams, who won the championship again in 1937, was recognized as the best player Australia had produced until then. He played little if any golf after 1939 and died suddenly at the age of 46. Bettington left Australia shortly afterwards to settle in New Zealand and died in a car accident.

Although the match between Williams and Bettington was one of the most remarkable in the club's history, Royal Adelaide has seen much other quality golf. It has been the venue of the Australian Open seven times, and the winners have twice included Ivo Whitton, a giant among Australian golfers. Jim Ferrier, another Australian and Open star who became an American citizen, won the USPGA title in 1947, the Canadian Open in 1950 and 1951 and was runner-up in the 1950 US Masters. Gary Player took the first of his Australian titles in 1958 with a stunning 271—a record at the time.

The tussocky marram grass, so difficult to fight clear of, makes Royal Adelaide's short par-four 3rd a difficult hole. Norman Von Nida once found the rough here and made a ten.

The 3rd: Unfair perhaps, but intriguing

Royal Adelaide's 3rd hole was devised not by man but by nature. Alister Mackenzie saw the unique possibilities and pounced on them. All he did was to arrange its participation in the layout, smooth its passage and prepare its green. This 300-yard par-four is a real gem. Norman Von Nida once took ten, it is said, straying disastrously from its narrow fairway, where the tough marram grass is high and the sharpest niblick barely bends it.

Some claim that the tee shot is too blind to be fair. They are right. But then golf never has been fair. Ever since it began on the wrinkled linksland of Scotland the luck of the bounce has been an important element in the game. It certainly comes into play at the 3rd and, although the tee shot is blind, there are all sorts of guidelines to show the way, but very little margin for error either side.

In championships people sit around on shooting sticks waiting like vultures for victims who hook or slice. Then they watch with glee the rueful efforts to escape the punishments. However, they do give due credit to the rare golfer who successfully takes it all on and, heart in mouth, goes for the green. He will not see his shot succeed. The news will come from those sitting high on the hill. Clapping means success but if he sees them fold their seats and clamber down, he knows it means the worst. This is one of the holes that makes Royal Adelaide such a great championship experience.

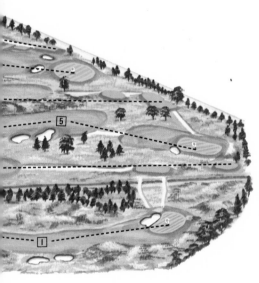

The 11th: An echo of Scotland's best

When the property at Seaton was chosen as the permanent site of the Adelaide Golf Club, much of it was white sand left stranded by the receding sea. After the fairways and greens had been made, little was left except an exciting-looking crater—the perfect natural feature around which to build a golf hole. Indeed, it became the 11th. Alister Mackenzie must have enthused over it because it was, and thankfully remains, the type of golfing feature to be found in his native Scotland.

Modern requirements have stretched the hole to 382 yards, making it into a fairly long par-four. Although it is effectively shortened by the prevailing wind from the southwest, it requires a healthy hit from the tee to reach the crest of the hill from where the green can be viewed—set tidily

and invitingly beyond the crater of wild sand that waits there so menacingly.

Two well-hit and accurately directed shots must be executed to find the target. Crafty players skirt the danger of the second by edging to the right. This might avoid the ultimate woe of a six or even a seven, but nobody can ever count on getting down in two from off the green and this route usually leads to a bogey-five. But to pass this hole without taking on the carry is to miss what golf is all about, particularly at Royal Adelaide.

The 11th has wrecked uncounted hopes of a good card. Its features are so precious but, perhaps because it comes too early in the round, it has not received the recognition it deserves. It would have been ideal as a 17th hole, where its influence would have brought it fame.

The second shot to the 11th intimidates some golfers into playing down the right, in hopes of being able to chip close enough for a par.

Seaside golf in a city saucer

A city whose premier golf course is little more than a ten-minute drive from its commercial and social heart is one where a dedicated golfer might be glad to live. The Royal Sydney is such a course, retaining the rugged look of a true links and set about by the houses of a fashionable suburb.

In a land where sporting and athletic distinction is a matter of pride, the club is as much a feature of its city's life as the famous bridge and the billowing Opera House. Its membership roll reads like a Who's Who of New South Wales. Although formed as a men-only golf club in 1893, it is now a golf, tennis and social club with 5,000 members and a waiting list of frustrating length.

The whole of the property is in the shape of a huge saucer, dominated on three sides by the higher rises upon which suburban Sydney has grown. The centre of the area is inclined to be wet and the course was laid out on the drier and sandier rim of the saucer, where good use was made of some useful undulations. The layout has peculiarities not found elsewhere. Many tees are sited against the club boundary on the higher grade with the fairways spread below and the greens in full view in the distance.

In its formative years the course was of nine holes and "rooms were taken at Mrs Ebsworth's cottage for the use of members". In 1896 James Scott joined the club as its professional, his arrival coinciding with the extension of the course to eighteen holes, taking in some of the lower-lying area, and in 1897 the club received the title Royal. It went from strength to strength as the course improved in quality and it soon became host to the Australian Open, hitherto held only at the Royal Melbourne Golf Club.

Royal Sydney is at its best on those clear, blue, hazy days that are characteristic of Sydney. Autumn and winter are particularly pleasant, when the course is at its greenest. In summer it browns somewhat—as indeed does the lower half of the Australian continent

—but even then a soft sea breeze invariably ensures that outdoor activity is still enjoyable. Like most courses by the sea, there is rarely a day when the wind is completely absent. This is a precious commodity for golfers as it adds that extra dimension to the course, enhancing its adventure.

The wind varies from morning to afternoon —not quite with the tides as in Britain but more because of the effect of hot sun on the bare continent. In October thunderstorms can wreck the golf. This almost happened in the 1969 Australian Open when Gary Player was struggling desperately to keep a narrow lead over Guy Wolstenholme. The skies to the south darkened in the late afternoon when Player was six slow holes from home. Lightning could clearly be seen some miles away and amid the turbulence of the wind and the first shower Player and Bruce Devlin took shelter; they stayed there until ordered to resume. Wolstenholme played through it and lost by one stroke. Devlin and Lee Trevino finished close behind. That was the eighth time that Royal Sydney had hosted the Australian Open. On an earlier occasion, in 1956, a youthful local, Bruce Crampton, emerged into prominence by pipping Kel Nagle after the latter had made a thorough mess of the final hole.

Nobody has won at Royal Sydney without a knowledge and command of the low, wind-

escaping shot. Members may play it instinctively, but visitors are sometimes lost in playing high shots which are at the mercy of the wind. In the spaciousness of the vast bowl, distance, too, is deceptive.

Except for five holes the course runs north and south, so that the shots called for have a repetition that can be destroying if the golfer is not particularly adept at playing into, or half across, a stout breeze. Most of the greens are small targets surrounded by large bunkers designed by Alister Mackenzie and cut deep into the bare sand underneath. The ball will often plug into the soft white sand.

The course begins with a drive-and-pitch hole. Originally it was almost driveable—at least with today's clubs and balls—but the tee grounds have crept back uphill until now there is a back tiger tee by the clubhouse door. Skirting the rim of the saucer, the course makes its way outwards with three superb par-fours and a par-three from a high tee, until it turns about at the 6th, another par-three from a high tee. The 7th is a stern par-five and the 8th and 9th, two similar par-fours, complete the half.

The best holes on the first nine are the 4th and 5th, both par-fours. With the wind against they can be as much as a wooden club second shot for all but the mightiest hitters. The tee grounds are higher than the fairways and the greens of both demand a long shot gently uphill

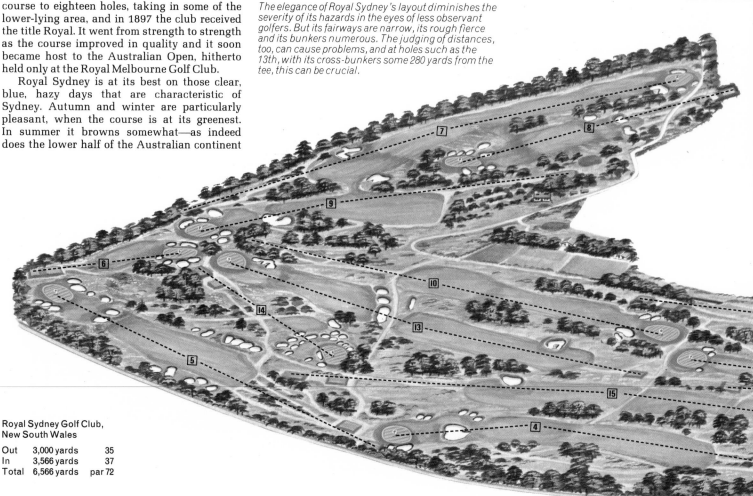

The elegance of Royal Sydney's layout diminishes the severity of its hazards in the eyes of less observant golfers. But its fairways are narrow, its rough fierce and its bunkers numerous. The judging of distances, too, can cause problems, and at holes such as the 13th, with its cross-bunkers some 280 yards from the tee, this can be crucial.

Royal Sydney Golf Club,
New South Wales

Out	3,000 yards	35
In	3,566 yards	37
Total	6,566 yards	par 72

without being blind. These two holes are truly memorable and amongst the best in the world.

This first half is the shorter but by far the more interesting in the way of undulations and features. With a wind from the north it is very short, but never easy. There are many shots to the greens that have to carry all the way.

The second nine contains the longer holes, three par-fives that run more or less straight either north or south, so that no matter which way the wind blows one or two of them are into it and therefore out of range of two shots by anyone. From the 10th tee the course descends into the lower area and only rises again at the last green in the shadow of the clubhouse.

These holes are plainer than the outward ones, but because most of them are straight they become a hard test of a golfer's technique. Stunted trees of indigenous variety separate these fairways and provide a savage penalty for waywardness.

The best holes inward are the long, par-five 13th, the 14th and the final hole, which is aptly one of Australia's best. The 14th is a long par-three of nearly 200 yards. The green is surrounded by sand and, depending on ability, the aspect is either inspiring or wholly terrifying. The final hole is a thrilling climax, a dog-legging par-four of 406 yards to a redan green, from which it is but a short step into the huge clubhouse and all it offers.

The 13th: The essence of golf course hazards

The 13th hole at Royal Sydney is an outstanding par-five that comes at a crucial stage of a round. A birdie here can lead on to victory and a low total: a six, or worse, can herald more woes later. The hole, some 504 yards long from the back tees, heads in a southerly direction, whence the fiercest winds blow. It begins on the flat part of the course and climbs slowly to finish on the high rim of the property, giving it the trajectory of an aircraft at take-off. Along the way there are obstacles in plenty to negotiate and a high green with enough slope to cause putting complications. Trees along the left side will catch the hooked drive from the player intent only on length. On the slice side is a healthy growth of rough grass, not long enough to hide a ball but awkward enough to penalize.

The player is next confronted with a barrier of cross-bunkers and mounds of the classic style (Mackenzie's stamp is apparent here). The bunkers are cut into the foot of the slope at the 400-yard mark, just where they will cause every golfer to worry. The traps yawn like a hippopotamus and they are deep enough to rule out any escape as far as the green. There is a poorly thought out contention, possibly influenced by modern professional play, that bunkers are somehow unfair and inappropriate unless the skilful player can escape from their clutches with little or no penalty of length or, at the greenside, get down in two shots. These marvellous old-style arrangements at Royal

The final shot at the par-five 13th, probably the toughest hole at Royal Sydney. The unkempt appearance of the bunkers is part of a plan to retain the feel of a true links—despite the course being right in the city.

Sydney are precious examples of what golf and its hazards are really all about.

Whether a player chooses to carry over the barrier or lay-up short, the approach shot is still something of a special challenge. The putting surface is all but blind, hidden behind yet another brace of intimidating traps cut into the slope before the green. Once gained, the green is blessed relief, but not until the putts are completed. Then it is possible to stand on the green and look back thankfully along the toughest hole on the course.

The 18th: No place for the nervous

The moment of truth in golf comes when a match is all square on the last tee. Every golfer is affected by the situation, the more so when he knows the 18th will test his stamina and nerve in the manner of Royal Sydney's closing hole. It is one of the best finishing holes in Australia. It is a par-four of good length, dog-legging to the left around a small copse of trees. The well-trapped green is set above the fairway on a kind of redan below the giant clubhouse. It slopes gently forwards and, like the home hole on the Old course at St Andrews, has just enough subtlety to make putting a

performance that is always worth watching.

The dog-leg puts the slicer at a disadvantage since his shot curls away from the hole. However, the hooker can gain ground if he can hit the 235 yards to the corner. There is a temptation to bite off too much, which, in matches, can lead to over-caution if the second player to hit is intent on avoiding at all costs the mistake of his opponent. The approach presents an invitation to mishit in an instinctive effort to hit the shot high so that the green will receive it sympathetically. There is seldom the need. The green is large and usually soft enough to hold most shots.

The placing of the tee shot is critical at the 18th, where trees on both sides narrow the entrance to the green.

No 1	264 yards	par 4	No 10	420 yards	par 4
No 2	445 yards	par 4	No 11	418 yards	par 4
No 3	161 yards	par 3	No 12	370 yards	par 4
No 4	402 yards	par 4	No 13	504 yards	par 5
No 5	399 yards	par 4	No 14	190 yards	par 3
No 6	138 yards	par 3	No 15	495 yards	par 5
No 7	536 yards	par 5	No 16	546 yards	par 5
No 8	295 yards	par 4	No 17	217 yards	par 3
No 9	360 yards	par 4	No 18	406 yards	par 4

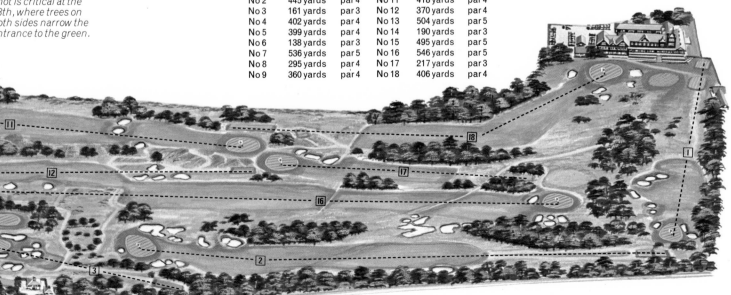

Golf among the geysers

*Wairakei, a splendidly natural course set amidst a
spectacular thermal region of the North Island, was
built in response to the growing clamour of the early
1950s for a true championship course in New
Zealand. It is long—but not too long—and imaginative
in the siting and construction of its greens and traps.*

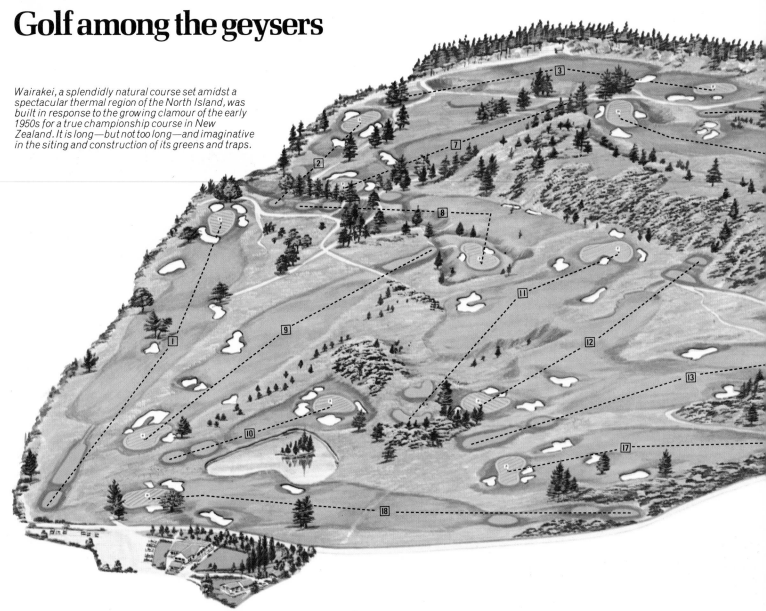

Wairakei is the most modern of New
Zealand's major golf courses, implanted
by the government's Tourist Hotel Corporation
in the heart of lovely countryside, bubbling with
geothermal activity, midway between Auckland and Wellington. It is not in fact a club
at all, but a green fee facility open to all who
spend their holidays in the neighbourhood of
the huge, trout-filled Lake Taupo and the hot
thermal springs of Rotorua.

The popularity of the game in New Zealand
was not reflected in the quality of courses
available until Wairakei was built. Even the
early Scots settlers who introduced the game at
Dunedin, in the South Island, in 1871 were ill-
served by the venues they found and there is
still no wholly satisfactory course there. Again,
until Wairakei, there was nothing to compare—
either in size or intrigue—with courses in the
United Kingdom, America or Australia. Visiting
golfers were aware of it, and said so. In 1953 the
NZGA met to approve courses for the New
Zealand championships and only four came
anywhere near international standards—Titi-
rangi, Belmont, Paraparaumu and Shirley. Even
these had their critics.

It was clear that changes had to be made if
New Zealand wanted seriously to contest inter-

national honours like the Eisenhower Trophy
and the Canada Cup—or, more importantly, to
stage them.

Every course with pretensions to status
burst into activity. Architects were called in,
courses were lengthened (there was nothing,
until Wairakei, approaching 7,000 yards),
bunkering was modernized and the game as a
whole was tightened up. The benefits were
immediate, but the perfect course was still no
more than a dream. Finally, H. T. (Dooley)
Coxhead, an accomplished golfer and a member
of the Tourist Hotel Corporation, persuaded his
colleagues that what their hotel at Wairakei
needed was a championship golf course, after
the manner of Gleneagles or White Sulphur
Springs.

The man he found to do the job was Commander John Harris, a civil engineer and
England's leading and most travelled golf course
architect, whose father had constructed Moor
Park, Wentworth and Sunningdale in Britain.
The possibilities of Wairakei must have appealed to him.

The course is set in gently rolling countryside with a few majestic spurs and a lattice of
gullies and creeks. Harris's layout made excellent use of the natural features and his sym-

pathetic handling of the terrain made all but
a little earth-moving unnecessary, apart from
green-building and general fairway preparation.
The construction was supervised by Michael
Wolveridge, an Englishman whose keen appreciation of the subtleties of golf architecture
had been enriched by a spell on the US professional tour. When completed, Wairakei
lacked only a fairway watering scheme, a
benefit excluded until later by the budget.

In its first year Wairakei came under heavy
fire from the New Zealand Conference of Greenkeepers, who were "appalled" at the subsidence
of the greens—which, like the rest of the
course, were built on pumice, the "froth" of
ancient volcanic lava. The subsidence was
soon cured.

Wairakei makes few physical demands on
the player. Walking is easy and mostly on the
flat, with an occasional climb to the higher tees.
The variety of holes, however, calls for a high
degree of skill to match par—a skill beyond the
reach of an average player. Many small creeks
have to be cleared along the front nine and
open-shouldered hitting is needed on the run
in, making the course, from the championship
tees at least, a handicap contest.

Whoever plays at Wairakei is conscious at

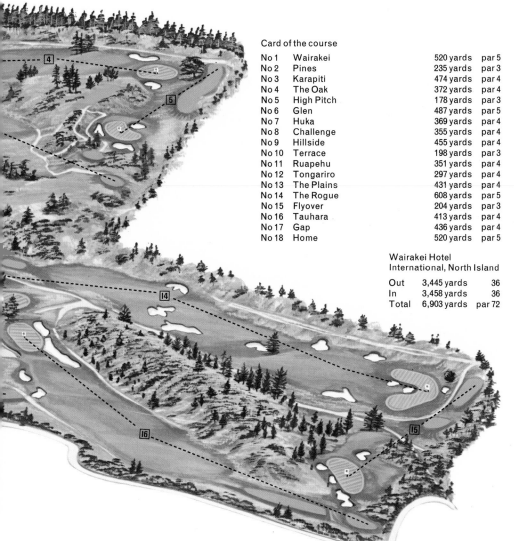

The 8th: A challenge all too rare

Well named as Challenge, Wairakei's 8th was designed to offer the golfer a great deal of adventure and amusement. A huge natural depression runs from the front of the tee almost in a direct line to the very edge of the putting green area before dividing and surrounding the green. When finances permit it is planned to fill this chasm with water, to be used in irrigating the golf course. At the left side of the chasm, inviting the prudent, the wary and the large majority of tee shots, is the fairway. Normally the tee shot will carry to the fairway and leave a shortish pitch back across the chasm to the well-guarded green. The challenge is to try for the green from the tee— an adventurous shot even without water, though not quite the splendid achievement of nerve, accuracy and length it might yet become. A hole of this length is often scorned as being just a ''drive and pitch'', as indeed the 8th is, and as a result modern golf displays very few such holes. The secret is in the degree of difficulty of the second shot, which reflects right back to the decision from the tee. The opportunity to gain or lose shots to par is ever present. Every course should have at least one such bold challenge.

From the back tee the dog-leg 8th is 355 yards long, but by the direct route it measures some 280 yards.

all times of a living earth, for above the enclosing pine forests there rises the endless vapours of the Karapiti and Rogue bore holes. The Rogue is particularly awesome, its clouds of steam and spray rising to heights of 300 feet and more. It has given its name to Wairakei's most impressive hole, the 14th—608 yards long from the back tee. The building of this hole exemplifies the importance of the construction supervisor's role in the creation of a golf course. Wolveridge improvised considerably as Wairakei was taking shape and for the end of the monster he dreamed up a banana-shaped green which is naturally set into a steep hill above the long, dog-legged fairway. It poses permanently for brochure photographers.

The course as a whole can be played in three lengths—the Championship (6,903 yards), the Regular (5,960 yards) and the Hotel (5,193 yards). Par for the Championship and Regular routes is 72, and for the Hotel, 70.

As a course without a club (and members to do the donkey work), Wairakei has yet to stage its first Open championship, but many amateur events have already been held there. New Zealand waits hopefully for the day when the giants of world golf take on this attractive, challenging course.

The 14th: 608 yards par 5

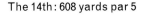

Known as The Rogue, the marathon 14th is probably the most controversial hole in New Zealand.

The 14th: The Rogue with a reputation

Flanked by soft hills and forestland, the long par-five 14th aims directly up a narrow valley towards a natural rogue borehole which belches forth clouds of sulphurous steam. Aptly named The Rogue, the hole has a reputation as the chief wrecker at Wairakei and it is an undoubted test of strength as well as skill. Its fairways wind past well-placed bunkers and beneath a tall pine tree towards an unusual green some 600 yards distant.

The main interest lies in the third shot to the green, which is large, elevated and horseshoe-shaped; its left side is fraught with bunkers and hollows. The tougher pin spots are to the left and centre and they demand a fairly lofted approach. This means, of course, that if a par-five is to be attained in the usual manner, two mighty wood shots are needed before the final approach.

The Rogue is a special hole, vociferously attacked and defended with equal passion, but always memorable.

Man conspires with nature to create adventure

Since its completion in 1951 Paraparaumu has made a great contribution to New Zealand golf, hosting several national opens. It is a links course situated on a stretch of rolling dune land very much exposed to winds. Bob Charles, 1963 British Open champion, rates the 5th as "equal to any short hole in the world".

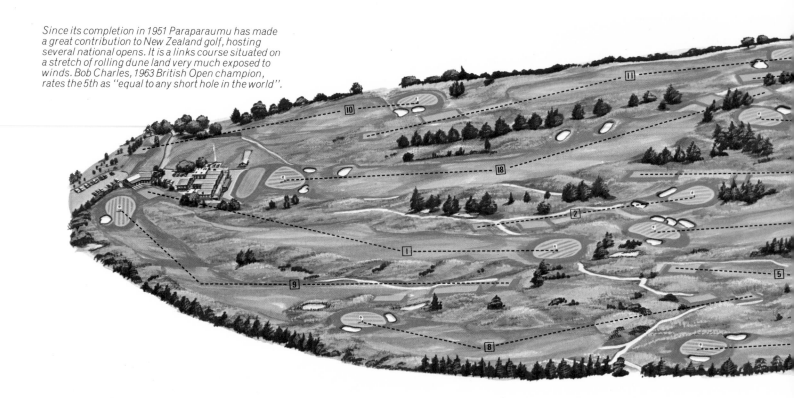

Paraparaumu Beach is an antipodean phenomenon—a real seaside links. Thirty-five miles north of Wellington in New Zealand's North Island, it is reached by a winding, circuitous route overlooking the Tasman Sea and the sentinel off-shore island of Kapiti.

The founder of the club, Stronach Patterson, and his colleague, D. O. Whyte, were attracted to Paraparaumu Beach and its linksland because in the 1920s no course of its kind existed in New Zealand or, for that matter, anywhere beyond the British Isles and the western fringes of mainland Europe. By 1930, Patterson, Whyte and their colleagues had the support necessary to build their ideal links and Alex Russell, co-architect with Alister Mackenzie of Royal Melbourne, was chosen to design it.

Only a bare minimum of land could be afforded, but it was enough for Russell. Within its 130 acres he filled every square yard, either with natural, undulating fairways and carefully constructed tees and sandtraps, or with rough he left on the high dune tops. It says much for Russell's flair for architecture that the course bears no similarity at all to his work at Melbourne. The temptation must surely have been to duplicate the wide fairways and huge rolling greens that make Royal Melbourne such a distinctive course. Here they would have been out of place and Russell must have known it.

Instead he drew upon his own experiences and observations in Britain, where he had travelled and played. The result must rank with Carnoustie or one of those happy courses along the Strathclyde coast, like Troon or Western Gailes. It is, nevertheless, different again from each of them—more a clever mixture of old and new, nature's sculpture and man's talent.

The 5th: The beauty of simplicity

Paraparaumu can boast a par-three to rival the Postage Stamp at Troon and the 11th at St Andrews. It is not the type of par-three that is at all fashionable; it requires much more of a golfer than brute strength. Instead, Paraparaumu's 5th is in the older style—now, alas, disappearing from championship play. Such holes are apt to bring out the best in golfers or to uncover any faults that are inherent in their game. Whatever the conditions the 5th, only 155 yards long, is always interesting and challenging. Into a gale it can take a 3-iron; with the wind from the sea it can require no more than a 9-iron. A birdie-two is no less difficult either way, and a par always satisfying.

The hole was created simply: all architect Alex

Russell did was to level off the top of a small dune that rose to a pinnacle above deep troughs. The result looks innocent and defenceless, invitingly close. Indeed, players facing it for the first time often find it easy, for it is not until they have experienced the fright of missing the green and going through the recovery from the surrounding depths that fear comes into their reckoning at all. The hole, one of the truly inspired par-threes, is named after Norman Von Nida, a pioneering Australian professional who saw it first in 1948 and lauded its attributes. Many have since agreed with him while others have disliked it enough to want to change it, to make it longer and add some sandtraps. But embellishment would only spoil it. Many architects might learn much from its simplicity.

Paraparaumu looks the way Troon would probably look if it had been built recently, instead of eighty years ago.

To play the course in calm and sunny weather, or to battle gales from one quarter or another, is a satisfying and exciting adventure, but it is best when the wind blows with moderate strength from the west. This is the prevailing wind, helping or hindering every stroke to some extent.

It is a mark of the course's excellence that, like St Andrew's, those holes played downwind are more difficult than when heading out into the wind.

Bunkering is mostly on a small scale—a sharp contrast to Russell's work on other courses, but here appropriate and sensible. There is a certain practicality in the creation of pot bunkers instead of the larger beach type. On some holes there are no artificial traps at all, for the steep, close-cut slopes of the dunes serve

a similar purpose, and constitute hazard enough.

The 1st hole, a 413-yard par-four, heads off towards the mountains that form a distant backdrop. There is a hundred-yard carry through a gap in the dunes leading to a large arena of fairway, with a gentle downslope giving a clear view of the green formed by low mounds and soft gathering undulations. The 1st green is typical of Paraparaumu: its small undulations, their crests only a yard or two apart, make putting a chancy business from a long way off. The small depressions tend to be lusher than the higher spots, creating variations in speed, and if a hole is cut on the crest of a bump, putting becomes an exceedingly difficult proposition.

The 2nd hole is difficult, a par-three cleverly placed on the dune tops, the green having been made by ironing one into a suitable flatness. The target is not large, shyly hiding its shape behind a bump left judiciously on the apron.

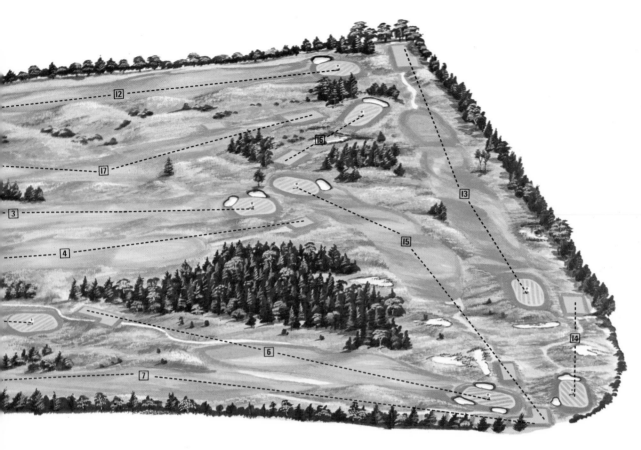

Card of the course

No 1	413 yards	par 4
No 2	195 yards	par 3
No 3	420 yards	par 4
No 4	446 yards	par 4
No 5	155 yards	par 3
No 6	310 yards	par 4
No 7	496 yards	par 5
No 8	368 yards	par 4
No 9	380 yards	par 4
No 10	312 yards	par 4
No 11	426 yards	par 4
No 12	490 yards	par 5
No 13	450 yards	par 4
No 14	147 yards	par 3
No 15	380 yards	par 4
No 16	140 yards	par 3
No 17	440 yards	par 4
No 18	470 yards	par 5

Paraparaumu Beach
Golf Club, Wellington

Out	3,183 yards	35
In	3,255 yards	36
Total	6,438 yards	par 71

Record: 62, Bob Charles,
Caltex 1968

Downwind from the back tee, the shot requires a 4- or 5-iron. Against the wind it can be a wood, and either way it is a par gratefully scored.

The 3rd fairway is reminiscent of the crumpled links of St Andrews. The green is at eye-level with a sunken bunker hidden at the left front corner. Inevitably, it catches most shots pulled from the uneven lies. The real hazard of the 3rd, though, is in overhitting, because just beyond the centre of the green is a steep, shaven slope which leads into a deep depression from which it takes luck to emerge without penalty.

The 4th is a 446-yard par-four which runs along the foot of the highest ridge of the course. The 5th is a gem. Only 155 yards long, it rivals the famous Postage Stamp at Troon and Russell must have enjoyed creating it.

On the fairway of the 310-yard 6th, massive undulations can throw a straight drive off to right or left, adding to the adventure of such a short shot. The 7th is a par-five of quality requiring some stout hitting if the green is to be reached in two and the birdie thus gained. At the short 8th penalty, in the form of strong rough, awaits on either side of the plateau green. The second shot invites an inspired iron shot through a gap in the sandhills to a green nestling at the foot of the clubhouse hill; a large wild water channel runs alongside the left. Then follow three par-fours and a par-five reachable in two powerful shots.

At 450 yards the par-four 13th is one of the best holes in this part of the world. Nothing less than two perfect shots will get to the green. Of all holes the 13th, unique and thrilling, is the one that epitomizes Paraparaumu Beach. A golfer either loves or hates it; if he hates it he

Paraparaumu's 13th hole is typical of the course. Its fairway undulates severely and it requires two precisely placed shots for a par.

cannot like the links at all. Tantalizingly short, the 14th is a little drop shot par-three made trickier by even a moderate wind. The 15th is a lovely par-four, traversing between dunes up to a step-like green which is difficult to hit from any line except the straight one.

The 16th is a gem of a three. It is cut into the side of a small hill with no bunker to guard it, but plenty of slope. The 17th, like the 13th, is magic. It has a split fairway on two levels offering a choice of routes. The lower, more direct route is easier for the first shot but fiendish for the second. The upper level is by far the best

The 13th: Nature's thrilling invitation

As at many other holes at Paraparaumu, nature has played a great part in the creation of the 13th. Just like the very oldest courses on which the game of golf was born, it has many humps and hollows—some of them massive. It is most spectacular. On a sunny day the view from the tee ground is unrivalled in golf. The rough is splashed with the green and yellow of broom and the green can be seen against a backdrop of distant snow-capped mountains. The invitation is there to enjoy it and thrill to its stout golfing challenge.

The appeal of this hole can depend on a golfer's skills or, more pertinently perhaps, the distance he can hit. It is 450 yards long and it takes a massive drive from the back tee to reach the plateau halfway to the green. This is the ideal spot, offering a good view of the slightly elevated green, about a 3-iron's carry across a huge hollow of fairway. Originally the green was a prepared saddle on the ridge without the back wall which members demanded. Its addition has taken something away from the hole's uncompromising challenge but enough remains to make it unique.

from which to approach, but it is necessarily more difficult to get there. From it, the passage is open to the green, still some 200 yards off and a daunting target. There is a steep and shaven slope off the left side, and the right is all traps and depressions; into a westerly wind it is often out of the reach of even the best players. But Gary Player played it in three into a gale in 1958, before he had become a world figure. He made another three, an eagle, at the final hole, too.

The course record is 62, scored by Bob Charles. This is a phenomenal score, because Paraparaumu is a course of real quality.

Africa

Most of Africa is a golfing void: the terrain alone sees to that. Beyond
a sprinkling of courses in countries bordering the Mediterranean, such
as Morocco (with its new, royal jewel at Rabat) and Tunisia, golf in
Africa has thrived where the British influence was at one time strong—
in Kenya, Rhodesia and, above all, in South Africa. The outstanding
performances of South African golfers over the last fifty years bears
witness enough to the quality of golf in their homeland and the
attractive and testing courses on which they can hone their game.
South Africa ranks about eighth in the world in the number of its golfers,
but is amongst the van in their quality, with men like Sid Brews, Bobby
Locke, Gary Player and Harold Henning. Within the boundaries of the
Republic there are about 350 courses of all types, ranging from true
linksland challenges on the coastline of Natal to the many high veldt
courses (there are at least eighty within a sixty-mile radius of
Johannesburg) where, in the thin air, the ball flies like a space shot
and every man is a superman when he drives from the tee. Golf travelled
to Africa by troopship in the confused and unhappy decades before the
Boer Wars. A six-hole course was laid out by a Scottish regiment near
Cape Town in 1882 and the Cape Golf Club, the senior in South Africa,
was born a few years later with a Scottish general as the midwife.
Scotsmen, both professional and amateur, were in almost total charge
of South African golf trophies for thirty years. Conditions in those early
days were far removed from those of Scotland. Greens were more often
than not compacted sand, and grass was a luxury only a few clubs
could boast. Modern strains of grass and year-round automatic
watering systems have long since overcome the drawbacks of an
unreliable rainy season and, with courses of the calibre of Durban
Country Club on the Indian Ocean coast and Royal Johannesburg,
thousands of feet up in the Transvaal, South Africa can now lay claim
to some of the most challenging layouts in the world.

1 Durban Country Club
2 Royal Johannesburg
3 Royal Rabat

The thrill of anticipation and uncertainty

Since the time it was first shaped from the bush and dunes of the Natal coast during the early years of the 1920s, the Durban Country Club course has achieved and maintained an excellence that keeps it at the forefront of South Africa's 250-odd courses.

The decision to build it grew largely from the misfortunes of the Royal Durban, South Africa's oldest club, which was host to the 1919 national championships: the course became so water-logged that the winner took 320 squelching strokes to finish. There was no guarantee that the low-lying course would not flood again and so Durban, one of the great cities of South Africa, was in danger of losing its place on the national tournament circuit.

There was already a need for a new course at Durban and pressure mounted after the 1919 debacle. A site was found and in 1920 George Waterman and Laurie Waters, four times winner of the South African Open, began its design. The course was opened in 1922 and two years later Durban Country Club staged the first of its many South African Opens. Much of the history of the game in South Africa has been enacted there, and most of the great players have made ▷

The 182-yard 2nd, left, reflects the demanding nature of Natal's finest course, the Durban Country Club. The strong sea breezes add to the difficulty of playing across the valley to the green, situated on a plateau and surrounded by banks, trees, shrubs and four bunkers.

The 18th: Where boldness can bring glory
The 18th at Durban Country Club is a remarkable finishing hole, offering spectacular reward to the bold player who might be looking for a three, and often bringing disaster to anyone playing safe. At 276 yards the green is in reach of a driver in favourable conditions, and yet in the slightest breeze a tendency to slice the ball can assume nightmare proportions should one fail to hold the rim of the valley, for it is a long way down a grassy bank to the practice tee and the road below.

Of all the golfers who have stood on the 18th tee staring glory in the face, the man who must have felt most pressure is Sewsunker "Papwa" Sewgolum, a former Durban caddie who became the first player of colour to compete in and win a South African provincial open championship.

Sewgolum, who was the only person affected at the time, was banned from playing in Whites Only tournaments by government decree after two victories at Durban Country Club, in the Natal Opens of 1962 and 1965. The ban has since been relaxed, but although there are now several Black players in South African tournaments, there have been no more winners.

In both his victories Sewgolum stood on the 18th tee wanting fours to win, and each time he cut his ball down the bank and into a clinging, hanging lie. Each time he wedged into the heart of the green to make sure of his par with two putts, revealing one of the most sensitive touches in the game, in spite of—or perhaps because of—his left-over-right-hand grip. The spectator most concerned with that winning wedge in 1965 was the runner-up, Gary Player.

There have been more spectacular finishes,

the most memorable being that of Jock Brews in the 1928 South African Open. The margin of his victory was a stroke. The man he beat was his brother, Sid. The way in which he won was magical. He drove the green and sank a fifteen-foot putt for an eagle-two.

The clubhouse beckons the brave for a birdie-three on the 18th, below. Making the green is not impossible, but many a player has lost a title here by overhitting.

One of the largest memberships in the world enjoys the trials of the Durban Country Club course, automatic choice when the South African Open is held in Natal. At first sight it seems undemanding, but many hazards are apparent only when the wind gusts off the ocean—across the sandhills which support the elevated tees and greens, and over the undulating fairways on the lowland part of the course.

Card of the course

No 1	390 yards	par 4	No 10	550 yards	par 5
No 2	182 yards	par 3	No 11	456 yards	par 4
No 3	506 yards	par 5	No 12	147 yards	par 3
No 4	172 yards	par 3	No 13	337 yards	par 4
No 5	459 yards	par 4	No 14	514 yards	par 5
No 6	349 yards	par 4	No 15	166 yards	par 3
No 7	383 yards	par 4	No 16	375 yards	par 4
No 8	498 yards	par 5	No 17	392 yards	par 4
No 9	424 yards	par 4	No 18	276 yards	par 4

Durban Country Club, Natal

Out	3,363 yards	36
In	3,213 yards	36
Total	6,576 yards	par 72

Record: 64, Gary Player, South African Open 1969

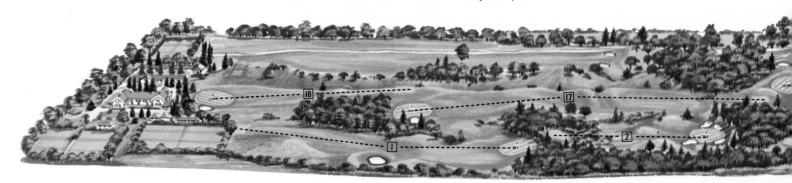

their pilgrimage to it. Sid Brews, Bobby Locke and Gary Player have had some of their greatest moments at the Country Club—and others they will want to forget.

The course saw Gary Player's first South African Open success in 1956, with 286. He returned in 1969 (having won the title another five times in the intervening thirteen years) to score 273, which included a record round of 64.

The Country Club is not long at 6,576 yards, and this was Arnold Palmer's only criticism of it after his first experience there in 1963: "It would", he said, "be a much better course with the big ball." Palmer, with 71, lost his encounter to Player that time by a stroke, after Player had been out in 34 and Palmer had returned 34 for the second half.

To see the Country Club course at its best, it must be experienced in all its moods—especially in the wind, which blows often and puts a green out of reach of two shots when it could have been hit with a 7-iron only a matter of hours before. Suddenly all the bunkers then begin to make sense.

The course has been updated on occasions—most recently by Bob Grimsdell in 1959, and before him by the English architect, Colonel S. V. Hotchkin, whose suggestions were adopted in 1928. Several tees have been resited and some holes have been renumbered, but basically the Durban Country Club has remained unchanged since 1922.

From the outset there was very little interference with the natural terrain but rather an accentuating of some of the site's original features. Grimsdell says: "The player is not shown everything at a glance, but is given the thrill of anticipation and uncertainty."

There are two distinct features—the holes on the dunes where either tee or green is elevated and surrounded by the natural bush, and those on the flatland, where trees still help shape the fairways but where the chances of a hanging lie are minimal—typically at the 5th, 6th, 7th, 10th, 11th, 14th and 15th. They are no easier, but are not likely to cause so much apprehension.

The course's difficulties commence at the very first hole, where the golfer who flinches from the out-of-bounds on his right hand risks a hanging lie on the hump to his left. From it he can be out of sight of the green, set into a huge tree-covered dune. From the plateau green at the 1st there is a climb to the tee on the 2nd, where the shot is played from one ridge to another, over a deep, grassed hollow.

The 3rd is everybody's favourite hole, played from an elevated tee at the highest point of the course into a valley. The ground rises again through a series of mounds, reaching like fingers on to the valley floor, to a green in the shadow of a tree-covered dune. Two shots are possible, but getting home with the second depends on the perfect placement of the first—and an ability to shut out the hazards lurking in the bush on both sides.

At the short 4th the golfer is coming off the dunes on to flatland, with the green, surrounded by slopes and mounds, looking deceptively small from the elevated tee. The 5th, 6th and 7th take the corner on the flat, taxing neither the golfer's endurance not his talents to any great extent, provided he is placing his shots well from the tee.

The 8th journeys back alongside the 3rd, playing in the opposite direction and with the high ground now causing more than a little concern: a 3-wood might not get the distance nor the height to hold the conical green, which is only partly visible. On the same level, the 9th tee looks down at a broad expanse of fairway—the green is somewhere to the right, out of sight. But for a time the pressure lifts.

The 10th and 11th are again on the flat, and length is the greatest prerequisite. There is a climb to the short 12th and the biggest concern again is to hold the green, for it is a long way back up the dune in the event of failure. Here Edward, Prince of Wales cut a ball down the bank and legend has it that he took another sixteen shots before he finally holed out.

Still on the parkland, the 13th tee is elevated —a pitch with the wedge for most players. A big

second is required at the 14th and the 15th demands another short iron. None of the three is a really memorable hole. Now the player is back in the dunes, close to the sea. The 16th is a steep climb to a green high amongst them, and they also provide the tee for the 17th. This is a spectacular hole requiring a carefully placed drive to the rim of the valley on the right, for otherwise there is no sight of the green from the bottom of a deep basin in the fairway.

One can almost drive the 276-yard 18th in favourable weather. Whatever the conditions, the temptation to hit beyond one's capacity is always there and this makes it a fine finishing

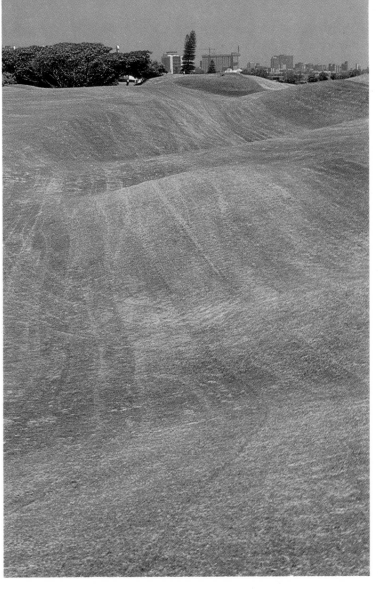

hole, demanding accuracy even from the faint-hearted. The way into the green is left, but a big pull finishes below the level of the fairway; a quick hook is dead in dense bush and a slice is invariably headed down a steep bank to the practice area below. Durban's 18th is amongst the shortest finishing holes in championship golf, but this does not make it easy to play.

"A little longer and the hole would be mediocre—just another drive and pitch," says Grimsdell. "But at this awkward and tempting distance it is just the finish needed for a course which rewards good golf but ruthlessly exposes all our weaknesses."

Edward, Prince of Wales, once took seventeen to conquer the short 12th, above; this view from behind the green shows some of its problems.

The swooping undulations of Duban Country Club's 17th fairway, right, give some indication of the problems of stance and siting of the greens which will confront the golfer during a round.

The joy of golf on the high veldt

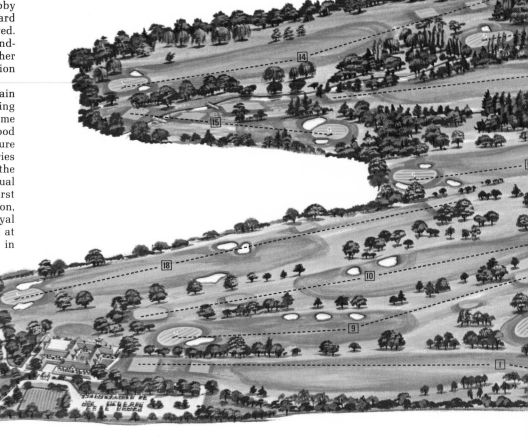

To most golfers any mention of South Africa brings to mind Gary Player and Bobby Locke, who have borne their country's standard in almost every land where the game is played. Since Locke emerged as an amateur of outstanding skill in the late 1930s they have together preserved the name of South Africa as a nation capable of producing golfers of world class.

Compared with the United States, Britain and Australia, the most powerful golfing nations, South Africa is small, with only some 250 courses, but the fact that so many good players have emerged from them is a measure of their quality. In common with most countries the gospel of golf reached South Africa in the closing years of the last century, and as usual the missionaries were Scotsmen. The first appearance of the game, in an organized fashion, was on a six-hole course, laid out by the Royal Scots Regiment on rough and stony ground at Wynberg in 1882. Thereafter golf spread in

The tricky nap of Johannesburg's greens held no terrors for Bobby Locke.

fairly swift succession to the principal cities, but the South African Golf Union was not formed until 1910.

Johannesburg was only a mining camp when the first course was laid in 1890. It was rough and windswept, enthusiasm soon waned, and within the next few years the course was moved several times. This was not as great a problem as might be imagined; the ground was cleared for fairways, leaving all the natural hazards, of which rocks were a feature, and a tin was sunk wherever a hole was required; the sand greens followed later.

Meanwhile Johannesburg was expanding so swiftly that not until 1906 was the club able to find land free from the covetous reach of builders. Money was advanced by Sir George Farrar and Sir Abe Bailey for the purchase of a site, part of which is still in use. The construction of grass greens and tees, the first in Johannesburg, was a great step forward; a mule bus carried the members to and from the terminus of the trams into the city, and the club settled to a generation of steady progress. As golf gained in popularity, and the membership increased, it was decided to have two courses, East and West. In 1933 more land was bought and construction began under the guidance of R. G. Grimsdell, a golf architect of rare skill. There were many problems, not least ridding the ground of the coarse kikuyu grass which threatened the fairways and greens.

The East was recognized as the more difficult, but a gradual improvement in scoring, notably

Royal Johannesburg's 13th, a short par-four, is lined with vast bunkers, deep enough to make the loss of a stroke almost inevitable.

by Harold Henning in the Transvaal Open in 1955, prompted changes. These included the reshaping of fairways; the creation of new tees on many holes so that fairway bunkers would threaten the long driver; and new bunkers and hollows tightening some of the approaches. Now the course was a true championship test; Gary Player ranks it as one of the very best.

Its length of almost 7,300 yards may seem exceptional, but at the high altitude of the Rand (more than 6,000 feet) the ball flies much farther

than at sea-level, where a similar course would probably play about 6,700 yards. Thus the golfer new to South Africa need have no alarm that the distances will be beyond him, and soon he will know the joy of seeing the ball fly as he never would on the finest courses elsewhere.

The course wanders quietly over wooded parkland. After the great sweep of the 1st, and a long short hole to a green plentifully trapped on the fade side, one is soon aware that this is a driver's course. The fairway bunkering at times is tight at around 250 yards, but one shrewdly placed bunker on the right side of the 3rd fairway is enough to make the golfer think on the tee. The 4th, the first of seven holes that curve to the right, and the 8th are outstanding driving holes, demanding length and exact placing for approaches to tightly guarded greens.

The short holes are of a high quality and vary in their demands; the 5th is a pitch which must carry to a slightly raised green embraced by bunkers, and so must the long iron to the 12th —beautifully set against a backdrop of willows —because the entrance to the green is angled to the line of flight. The 15th is possibly the most testing, for the plateau green makes the distance hard to judge.

Length is by no means the only criterion in the difficulty of a hole, and the 13th is a fine example. It swings to the left and, given a good drive, needs only a pitch to the green, though the entrance is narrow between bunkers; a spinney on the right threatens the approach to that side of the green, and a mishit to the left may be

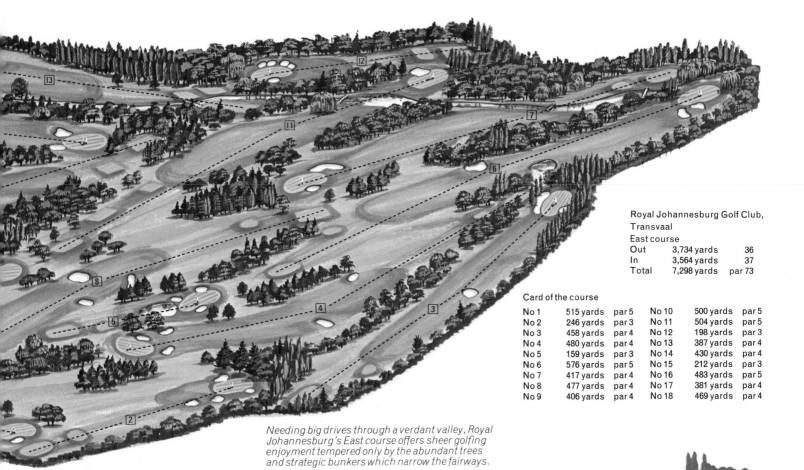

Needing big drives through a verdant valley, Royal Johannesburg's East course offers sheer golfing enjoyment tempered only by the abundant trees and strategic bunkers which narrow the fairways.

Royal Johannesburg Golf Club, Transvaal
East course

Out	3,734 yards	36
In	3,564 yards	37
Total	7,298 yards	par 73

Card of the course

No 1	515 yards	par 5	No 10	500 yards	par 5
No 2	246 yards	par 3	No 11	504 yards	par 5
No 3	458 yards	par 4	No 12	198 yards	par 3
No 4	480 yards	par 4	No 13	387 yards	par 4
No 5	159 yards	par 3	No 14	430 yards	par 4
No 6	576 yards	par 5	No 15	212 yards	par 3
No 7	417 yards	par 4	No 16	483 yards	par 5
No 8	477 yards	par 4	No 17	381 yards	par 4
No 9	406 yards	par 4	No 18	469 yards	par 4

caught by a pool that cuts into the line. Of the par-fours only the 17th is shorter and this is the one hole where there is the slightest danger of becoming short of breath, for the drive must carry a steep crest. Elsewhere the ground is gentle in its undulations, like the falling fairway of the splendid 11th hole. The drive must be placed as near as possible to a lone wattle tree, guarding the inside curve of the right-handed dog-leg, for the most favourable position from which to carry a stream in front of the green.

The stream that winds its way across the northern part of the course also comes into play at the 7th, where it slants across the fairway and must be carried from the tee. It can quicken fear in the mind of the golfer prone to hook because, as he stands on the 16th tee, he is aware that it follows the line of the hole too closely for comfort. Then at the last comes the challenging finish.

The design of the holes is not necessarily the greatest problem, particularly if the player comes from a country where nap on the green is uncommon. The greens demand most careful reading because often the nap will more than counter the natural breaks of the ground. For a man to become a successful golfer in South Africa he must develop a firm putting stroke and a courageous attitude—and be a diligent observer of the greens.

Regardless of whether the visitor to Royal Johannesburg can manage this, he is sure to agree that the East course has few peers as a challenging and beautiful place to play golf.

Cole's recovery at the 11th led to a birdie and an Open title at Johannesburg in 1974.

The 11th: Cole's gamble pays off

The 11th, 504 yards long, is perhaps Royal Johannesburg's best hole. It is a gentle dog-leg to the right, with a long carry from the tee but without fairway bunkers to inhibit the drive. At a strategic distance in front of the green a stream crosses the fairway diagonally. Closer to the green the fairway narrows considerably and towards the bank on the left side is a solitary bunker. The hole demands placement as opposed to the length so often required on many of the other holes. Yet, curiously, one of the best shots ever made there was also the longest—Bobby Cole's second from the rough in the second round of the 1974 South

The 11th: 504 yards par 5
----- Cole

African Open, which Cole started in fourth place.

Played by a lesser player it would have been a desperation shot, a careless gamble in pursuit of a cause already lost. It was undeniably adventurous but it was the only shot with which Cole could be sure of a four after his drive had leaked left into the rough. His approach to the green was blocked by the stream and by some willows, some 220 yards distant. Cole knew that to reach the green from there his approach would have to be long and high enough to clear them.

Using wood, he hit the perfect shot to make his four. He was on his way to a 65 and a record-breaking total of 272.

Bravura golf — close to the casbah

As a broad generalization, golf course architecture falls into two schools, the "natural" and the "artificial". Like most labels, these words, with their emotive overtones, must be heavily qualified in each individual case. The designer whose instinctive approach is to leave the landscape looking as nearly undisturbed as possible must compromise when he works with terrain which is alien to the golfing ideal. Compromise is always at the designer's elbow raising insuperable objections: "The client insists . . . the budget does not permit . . . the land does not allow. . . ."

Compromise is the last word to be applied to the work of Robert Trent Jones, the founder of the "artificial" school of architecture and the man who conceived the Royal Rabat course in Morocco's capital on the Atlantic coast. Jones is a visionary whose imagination conjures up mountains and lakes. He shapes his landscape and does not undertake a commission unless he is guaranteed the batteries of earth-moving machinery, the train-loads of topsoil and the torrents of water that are needed to execute his bravura designs.

As a result, his courses are stamped with a personality as distinctively as a signature. The vast, aircraft carrier tees, the sadistically moulded greens, the extravagantly shaped bunkers and torture by water are the loops and flourishes by which his name is inscribed.

The specification for Royal Rabat exactly matched his style. It was to be a course fit for a king—Hassan II of Morocco, the most enthusiastic golfer among contemporary royals. The championship layout, the Red course, was completed in 1971 and was the first of three courses at the club to come into play.

The tingle of anticipation which every true golfer feels on approaching a course begins at Rabat with the salute from the guard at the imposing mosaic gatehouse. The drive to the clubhouse makes its way through the stands of cork oak from which Jones carved the course, and the visitor's first feeling of anticipation is tinged by a more guarded feeling, almost of trepidation; he will come to an intimate familiarity with the cork oak, with its drab, olive-green leaves, gnarled branches and trunks that are stripped annually of their outer layer of bark, leaving them smooth, pink and bare. (They are blushing for their nakedness, as the Spanish saying has it.)

Between the trunks of these trees the visitor catches glimpses of brilliant green fairways and seemingly excessive blue expanses of water. The colours are exaggerated by the sombre tints of the cork oak foliage and the twinge of fear that has attacked the visitor is soon confirmed by the view from the first, and subsequent, tees.

Trent Jones clearly has a high regard for the cork oak, since he spared far too many of them in cutting out his avenues of fairways.

Every golfing instinct screams for an iron—or at most a 3-wood—off the tee, but the mathematical reality of the yardage demands that courage and driver be taken in both hands. What is more, the driving must be of high quality. The standard, unthinking boom straight down the middle may come to grief, for Jones slopes

The strong participating interest of King Hassan II and the need to attract tourists now means Morocco has over a dozen courses. By far the best is Royal Rabat, a long and demanding layout by Robert Trent Jones in a superb setting near the capital.

Sloping fairways, lined with cork trees, guide the poor shot towards well-placed traps, typifying the exacting nature of Trent Jones's Rabat courses. It is a tribute to his skills that 70 was broken only four times by the pros in the four years following Rabat's opening in 1971.

his fairways cunningly to deflect the ball towards his hungry bunkers. On nearly every hole the drive must be shaped, with draw or fade, if the ball is to finish in the prime position for an attack on the green.

Deception is the key to Jones's design and if he has failed to outwit the golfer with the demanding nature of the drive he has another trick in store for the approach. It looks fairly simple. His greens are invitingly large and will hold a well-struck shot. How can such targets be missed? To ask the question is to provide the answer, for any suspicion of complacency can send the ball away on a wayward course. But the cunning of the trick is that even if the ball finds the green it is by no means a formality to get down in two putts.

The two-putt zone on a Jones green is usually a small area and anything in the nature of an "outer" will need exceptional skill, or luck, if

the ball is to be caressed over those glassy undulations to within holing-out range.

And so it goes for eighteen tormenting holes. Some of them appear superficially to relax the challenge as the course moves into more open country, but it is an illusion. Artificial lakes are brought into play and, where they do not actually impinge on the target areas, their threatening proximity often induces the golfer to choose a "safe" line which turns out to be the road to some hazard from which his eye has been decoyed by the harmless water.

It is small wonder that the world's most skilled professionals have failed to beat the par of 73 by more than five strokes in the most favourable conditions in five championships, and 70 has been broken only four times. Many good players have been thankful to break 80—and that without having hit a bad shot. As on all Trent Jones courses, it is the easiest thing in the

Royal Dar-es-Salam,
Rabat

Red course

Out	3,735 yards	36
In	3,727 yards	37
Total	7,462 yards	par 73

Record: 69, Sam Snead,
Moroccan Open 1971

Card of the course

No 1	409 yards	par 4	No 10	483 yards	par 5
No 2	233 yards	par 3	No 11	464 yards	par 4
No 3	454 yards	par 4	No 12	567 yards	par 5
No 4	424 yards	par 4	No 13	389 yards	par 4
No 5	569 yards	par 5	No 14	210 yards	par 3
No 6	443 yards	par 4	No 15	396 yards	par 4
No 7	430 yards	par 4	No 16	430 yards	par 4
No 8	574 yards	par 5	No 17	225 yards	par 3
No 9	199 yards	par 3	No 18	563 yards	par 5

world to drop a stroke at every hole without the suspicion of a mishit. Without showing some dazzle, the player will simply fail.

For lesser players, even off the extreme forward tees, Rabat provides a humbling if unforgettable experience. There are, however, rewarding compensations for the eights and nines which blemish the scorecard, for this is golf at its most exotic. Where most clubs manage with a staff of a dozen, and often fewer, to maintain the course, here 500 men are kept busy grooming the fairways, raking the bunkers and cosseting the greens. Their labours have produced a herbaceous wonderland of flowering shrubs as a foil to the cork oak and eucalyptus background. Walter Hagen's famous advice of "Never hurry, never worry and always take time to smell the flowers" might have been coined for Rabat. Mimosa, Bougainvillaea, fuchsia and orange blossom provide splashes of colour as dazzling as an impressionist's palette.

Geographically, the casbah seething with poverty and all manner of social deprivation is just down the road, but in every other sense it is a million miles away—another world, albeit still a Moroccan world. It would be a soulless golfer who could shrug off this juxtaposition with untroubled conscience, but in the narrow and unashamedly selfish context of golf, Royal Rabat represents an ideal which few inland courses can approach.

The 9th: A drug to make you hook

Water is the most powerful hallucinatory drug known to golf. The sight of it anywhere near the target area causes an involuntary tightening of the grip, a slight acceleration of the normal speed of swing and, as often as not, a premature raising of the head in anxiety to see the ball pitch safely on dry land. Even the simplest pitch shot over a stream acquires a potential for disaster because of the destructive influences of the drug, which few holes in the world dispense in such a powerful dosage as the 9th at Royal Rabat.

It is also one of the most picturesque holes to be found anywhere. The tee is set on the bank of a large lake with duck, geese and flamingos in noisy regatta. Far across the lake—some 200 yards, but seemingly farther since water deceives the eye—the island green assumes minute proportions. It is connected to the mainland by two hump-backed wooden bridges irresistibly reminiscent of a willow pattern plate. The golfer who is in serious action may be excused if he does not absorb the beauty of the scene.

The casual tourist whose prime aim is enjoyment may play from one of the shorter tees, a mere 7-iron shot, and he may linger to appreciate the view. But the true competitor, pitting himself against the full ferocity of the course, must march steadfastly to that farthest tee and select a 3-iron at least and, if the wind is against, possibly even a driver. The urge to make

The 9th hole may be Rabat's shortest, but it is water all the way to *an island green. Nothing but the most accurate iron will suffice.*

certain of the carry often results in a forcing of the shot and consequently a hook. The ball may splash into the water left of the island or, even more maddeningly, pitch short on the upslope and roll back into the water. One contestant in the annual Moroccan Grand Prix, a professional with a notable tournament record, doggedly persevered with his idea of how the shot should be played and hit six balls into the lake before finally getting down in fourteen strokes.

Royal Rabat offers few more rewarding satisfactions than retracing one's footsteps across the wooden bridge with a three safely marked on the card—not that the golfer can afford to relax his concentration, for there are four more water holes still awaiting him and plenty of other problems besides.

South America

South American golfers—players of the stature of Tony Cerda and
Roberto de Vicenzo—are better known to the world of golf than golf is
in the continent where they learned their game. Of all the continents,
South America has the slenderest golfing resources and most of them
are concentrated in Argentina, where there are some hundred clubs,
and Brazil, with about thirty. A scattering of courses have been built or
are under construction in countries on the Caribbean shore like
Venezuela, where Dick Wilson and Joe Lee laid out the taxing course at
Lagunita Country Club as part of the sunlit circle of resort golf that now
loops through the islands of the Spanish Main. But away from these
areas, golf fades away almost to nothing. There is a handful of clubs
in the Andean capital of Colombia (where the El Rincon course is a
Trent Jones design), in Chile, Bolivia and in Peru where, high in the
thin air of the Andes, the visiting golfer from less dramatic altitudes is
likely to exhaust himself merely teeing up. Golf arrived by railway in
South America; to be exact, by railways in the making. The English and
Scottish engineers who went to Argentina and Brazil to lay down the
tracks at the turn of the century also laid down the first golf courses, in
the neighbourhood of Buenos Aires in Argentina and São Paulo in
Brazil. Since that time the game has enjoyed steady rather than
spectacular growth in popularity, although the facilities that there are
—mostly for the better-off citizenry—possess outstanding qualities.
The Jockey Club at Buenos Aires is a typical example. It has two
courses dating from 1936, designed by the redoubtable Alister
Mackenzie; the better known of the two, the Colorado (Red) course,
was the venue for the World Cup in 1962 and 1970. It was fitting that,
in the 1970 competition, the individual prize was won by Argentina's
greatest golfing son, Roberto de Vicenzo, a man who had won his first
Argentine Open in 1944 and gone on to add as much lustre to the game
as any of its finest champions.

1 The Jockey Club
2 Lagunita

A superbly groomed playground for the rich

Golf is a sport for the well-to-do in Argentina and at the best known of its hundred or so courses, the Jockey Club at Buenos Aires, it is merely an additional attraction to horse racing and polo. Its two courses at San Isidro are, however, none the worse for that; they were designed by Alister Mackenzie, whose imaginative flair has stamped the hallmark of greatness on golf courses in both northern and southern hemispheres.

The exclusive nature of golf in South America makes it the more surprising that the continent should have produced so many fine professionals—men like Martin Posé and Mario Gonzales of Brazil and José Jurado, Tony Cerda and, the greatest of them all, Roberto de Vicenzo.

Vicenzo is a folk hero among the golfers of Argentina and something of a demi-god at the Jockey Club. A fairly tall, heavily muscled man, Vicenzo none the less swings at the ball with supreme grace. When he first went to the USA, at the age of twenty-four, he could not speak a word of English. He did not have to; his driver spoke for him. His length astounded even Sam Snead and Ben Hogan, and he achieved it without even bothering to tee the ball up. He simply dropped the ball to the ground, pushed it with the clubhead of his driver on to a tuft of turf, and then smashed the ball into the atmosphere with a hook that was under complete control.

Born of poor parents, Vicenzo learned the game at a golf course in Buenos Aires—not the Jockey Club—where he caddied with his four brothers (who are now also professionals), and turned professional at the age of eighteen. By the time he retired at the age of fifty-two, he had won more than 140 tournaments, a record not even the evergreen Sam Snead has been able to approach. Among them have been more than twenty national championships won in

fourteen different countries, an unapproachable record. Vicenzo's quest for the British Open is something of a saga in itself, quite apart from his story-book life. After ten fruitless tries at the title, during which he had finished second once and third twice in his first three attempts and coming close on several occasions, he finally won at mighty Hoylake in 1967, leading Jack Nicklaus home with rounds of 70-71-67-70 for a total of 278. Cheers were heard throughout the golfing world, not because people enjoyed seeing Nicklaus being beaten but because Vicenzo, who now speaks a delightful fractured English, is a hugely popular man.

The next spring, however, tragedy struck when he seemingly tied with Bob Goalby for the Masters title, only to be denied a chance at a play-off because his playing partner had inadvertently put down on the scorecard a par-four on the next to last hole when in fact Vicenzo had scored a birdie-three. Unwittingly, Vicenzo signed the card and, under The Rules of Golf, the score had to stand as it was. The dignity with which he accepted this disappointment earned Vicenzo the Bobby Jones Award for "distinguished sportsmanship" in 1970.

If he needed to Vicenzo marked his place in Argentina in that same year when the 1970 World Cup matches were staged at the Jockey Club. (Among his many other records, Vicenzo has played in more of these matches than any other man.) Now he won the individual title for the second time, winning by a stroke over Australia's young David Graham with a total of 269, nineteen strokes under par. His partner was Vicente Fernandez, whose score was sixteen strokes higher than Vicenzo's, and Argentina finished second, ten strokes behind Australia. It was a fitting climax to a career whose course was not yet run. In 1976, Vicenzo

was invited to become an honorary member of the Royal and Ancient Golf Club of St Andrews.

The Red course of the Jockey Club, which was used for those 1970 World Cup matches, is not really suited for a game of Vicenzo's immense strength. At 6,699 yards, it has not nearly the length with which he can ordinarily overpower his opponents. Yet it is in superb condition all year round, for Buenos Aires has no harsh winters nor summers—sitting as it does about as far south of the equator as Atlanta is north of it—and, being a port, it lies practically at sea level.

The 1st hole shoots directly away from the rear of the stately, U-shaped clubhouse and belies what is yet to come. At 437 yards it is long by the standards of any opening hole. Starting at about 150 yards from the tee and running nearly to the green on both sides of the fairway is what the members refer to as a *pared de pinos*, or a wall of pines. Approximately 260 yards from the tee, on the left—very strategically placed for professionals—is a large, banked bunker. This must be avoided at all costs, for it is well-nigh impossible to reach the green from out of it. Thus, it is wise to favour the right-hand side of the fairway off the tee. There is still another reason for doing so. All the trouble about the green lies on the left-hand side. First comes a cross-bunker lying slightly short of the green to the left, making any successful recovery from the fairway bunker all the more improbable. And running the length of the long, narrow green are two more thin bunkers, recovery from which with any hope of single putting is made more difficult by the undulating putting surface.

At 345 yards, the 2nd hole is more in keeping with the cunning of the course. A gigantic eucalyptus, not one hundred yards to the right ▷

The two courses at the Jockey Club were laid out by Alister Mackenzie, the architect of such famous courses as Augusta National, Royal Melbourne and Cypress Point, and were opened in 1935, a year after his death. Working mainly on very flat land, he introduced mounds and contouring and this, combined with subtle bunkering, has made the short course a tricky one to negotiate.

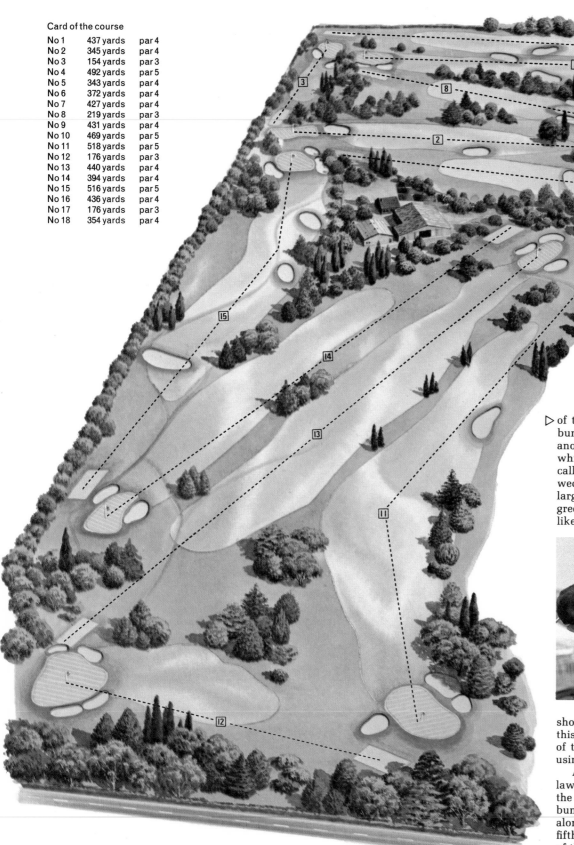

Card of the course

No 1	437 yards	par 4
No 2	345 yards	par 4
No 3	154 yards	par 3
No 4	492 yards	par 5
No 5	343 yards	par 4
No 6	372 yards	par 4
No 7	427 yards	par 4
No 8	219 yards	par 3
No 9	431 yards	par 4
No 10	469 yards	par 5
No 11	518 yards	par 5
No 12	176 yards	par 3
No 13	440 yards	par 4
No 14	394 yards	par 4
No 15	516 yards	par 5
No 16	436 yards	par 4
No 17	176 yards	par 3
No 18	354 yards	par 4

Although, as its name suggests, the Jockey Club's main interest is racing—the racetrack (and polo fields) adjoin the golf courses—it hosted the World Cup in 1970, when only nineteen players finished under the Red course's par of 292 for seventy-two holes.

▷ of the tee, makes the hole half blind. A cross-bunker lies to the left at the landing area and another lies to the right just short of the green—which is small, as it should be, for the hole calls for nothing more than a 3-wood and a wedge. The 3rd, a 154-yard par-three, is largely a matter of proper club selection. The green bends from right to left around a bunker, like a boomerang. Another trap sits slightly

Australia's rising star David Graham shot 270 to finish second in the individual contest of the 1970 World Cup and with Bruce Devlin (third on 284) took his country to a convincing victory.

short of the putting surface to the right, but this can easily be cleared. The one in the crook of the green must be avoided—and can be by using the proper club to carry the pin position.

At 492 yards, the 4th hole is short by the laws of any par-five, but the entire left side of the fairway is out-of-bounds. There are five bunkers on the hole, four of them scattered along the right-hand side of the fairway. The fifth protects the left side of the green. None of them presents a problem for three soft shots or two hard ones. This is the place for an early birdie. The 5th hole is one of those rare holes that only an architect of Mackenzie's imagination could bring off: a good, short par-four.

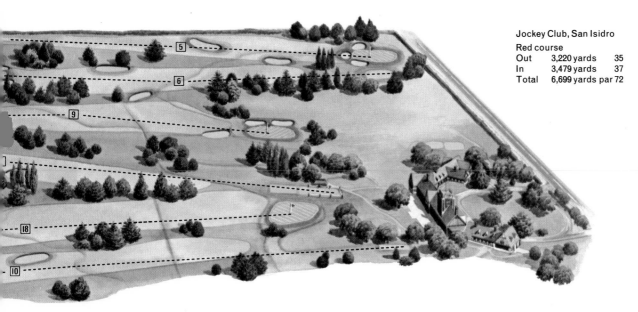

Jockey Club, San Isidro
Red course
Out   3,220 yards   35
In   3,479 yards   37
Total   6,699 yards par 72

Veteran Roberto de Vicenzo finished with a 269, nineteen under par, to take the individual honours in the 1970 World Cup, an event in which he had first competed in 1953 when Argentina won the title.

Only 343 yards long—a mere drive and a niblick or wedge—the hole must nevertheless be treated with respect. The entire left side is out-of-bounds and the tee shot must carry a cross-bunker jutting into the fairway at the 220-yard mark. A sliced drive finds itself in another *pared de pinos*, ending with an ombú tree, a foliage typical of Argentina's pampas. The second shot, though short, must be precise, because the green is tightly guarded in front with three bunkers; the green is slickly undulated. The 6th, at 372 yards, lacks length and despite the small green is another promising birdie hole. The 7th is something else again, a full 427 yards and tightly bunkered off the tee. Two cross-bunkers intrude upon both sides of the fairway a good 230 yards off the tee and another lies to the right some forty yards beyond them. The green is large and has a pot bunker which bites into its left side. To the right lies a mound covered with shrubs and trees that can leave an all but unplayable lie.

The par-three 8th is most notable for its beauty and its length—219 yards. Even professionals are sometimes obliged to play a 4-wood off the tee. The green is very deep, widening considerably at the rear. As it widens, two bunkers lie to the left and the right, along the slants it takes. There is no birdie here.

Next comes the swing—the crucial 9th and 10th holes which can make or break a round. The first is a very long par-four, the second a short par-five. After the 10th green the course makes an abrupt turn to the left. The 11th is another par-five, but much more severe. For one thing, it is fifty yards longer than the 10th and, for another, it presents a much more severe dog-leg, this time to the left. Bunkers to the right and left of the green are the main problems once the bend in the fairway has been cleared.

The 12th, at 176 yards, is a one-shotter to a very wide green full of curves, and any shot not reasonably close to the cup makes three-putting a distinct reality. At 440 yards, the 13th hole stands as the longest and probably the roughest par-four on the course. The fairway is ex-

tremely narrow, as is the green. This, together with the fact that it is long and rises sharply to the rear, makes it difficult to hit and hold. Two bunkers to the left and another to the right mean that the second shot is not only long but must be accurate. The 14th is a straight-forward par-four just under 400 yards long. The 15th, a 516-yard par-five, is much stiffer. Out-of-bounds lies along the entire left side of the hole and the right side is well bunkered. Three more traps flank the green. The 16th—par-four, 436 yards—is an oddity in that it has only one bunker, lying right across the fairway, slightly beyond the 200-yard mark. While the green has no traps, it nevertheless is sharply banked on all four sides. The 17th presents a similar

Vicente Fernandez was Vicenzo's partner in the 1970 World Cup. His final round of 67 gave Argentina a total of 554 and pushed them into second place behind the Australians.

problem with its raised green and, although only 176 yards, is as tough a par-three as there is on the course. The green is very large and deep and two beautifully placed bunkers on the left make the shot a delightful challenge.

The 18th is something of an anticlimax for people who are used to heroic finishing holes. It flies in a direct line towards the clubhouse and has not a single bunker on it. What is more, it is a mere 354 yards long; a 9-iron or a wedge will hit the green easily after an accurate drive. But weak as the last hole is, it cannot diminish the stature of the Jockey Club, which alone among South American courses conceived before World War II has any claims to greatness.

The 9th and 10th: Vicenzo turns things his way

In almost every competitive round of golf the 9th and 10th holes (known variously as the swing or the turn) are crucial. Golfers have a habit of becoming tense on the 9th hole as they strive to complete a good nine-hole score. At the 10th they tend to become lackadaisical, either because they have scored well on the front nine or because they have given up, having scored badly.

With this thought in mind, Alister Mackenzie laid out the Red course of the Jockey Club with a rugged par-four for the 9th and a deceptively easy par-five for the 10th. To score well a player cannot sail through the 9th but must be at his best, and at the 10th, a hole which requires careful thought, he cannot afford to ease up.

At 431 yards, the 9th can hardly be regarded as a birdie hole despite the absence of fairway bunkers. A good deal of length is called for off the tee, a not inconsiderable undertaking since the fairway is very narrow. A large bunker lies fifty yards short of the green, coming into play when a long second has to follow a short drive. Two more traps lie to the left of the green, which must be reached with at least a 5-iron. Trees and bunkers lie on three sides of the green.

Although only 469 yards long, the simplicity of the par-five 10th is deceptive. It is a dog-leg to the right—a sharp one with a big bunker just where the fairway turns. It is impossible to cut the hole short, particularly since that right-hand side has a file of trees along it. Thus, discretion dictates that the golfer favour the left-hand side of the fairway. However, a bunker lies forty yards or so short of the green to the left, which means that it must be carried with the second shot. The green is very wide in front, but it rises steeply to the rear and requires a very delicate third shot when the flagstick is placed to the right because guarding the entire right side and the elevation to the rear is a huge bunker.

The significance of the 10th was apparent when Roberto de Vicenzo won the World Cup individual title in 1970. His winning margin over Australia's David Graham was one stroke but, crucially, he was able to birdie the 10th in all four rounds.

237

South America's busiest course

There are three outstanding country clubs in the vicinity of Caracas, a sprawling oil-rich city of more than two and a half million people. The Caracas Country Club is for the Venezuelan upper crust; the second is Valle Arriba, with a membership of American businessmen and foreign diplomats; the third is the relatively new Lagunita Country Club, in the suburb of El Hatillo, and its membership is a combination of the other two, mainly Spanish-speaking but with a high percentage of English-speakers, too.

The Lagunita golf club is part of a real estate development which includes expensive housing and covers more than one and a half square miles. It was bought by a group of local businessmen in 1956. The club now has 1,100 members, of which 700 are active golfers with handicaps —a high number by South American standards. Although the club is strictly private it is, nevertheless, the "buzziest" golf course on that continent, according to Freddy Alcántara, an authority throughout the Americas both as player and official.

"Lagunita is not a very long course by British or American standards," says Alcántara. "It is only 6,895 yards at its extreme back tees. But, despite this, it is a tough course and it is beautifully designed. It is a true and fair test for championship players. For example, there is not a blind shot on the entire course, so you always know where you are going. Furthermore, the greens are very big, slick and fast-breaking. I

would say the lack of length in its par-fours is more than compensated by its par-threes. They are long and very difficult and there are five of them. Hence the total par of only 70. They are the key holes on the course."

Lagunita was designed by Dick Wilson during the latter part of his career and was for the most part constructed under the supervision of Joe Lee, then Wilson's assistant. It was completed in 1962.

Lagunita has been host to four of Venezuela's National Amateur championships and to the Simon Bolívar International Trophy, which was founded and organized by Alcántara. Its grandest day came in 1974 when it was chosen as the site for the twenty-second World Cup and Sr Alcántara's views of his home course turned out to be a bit conservative. Only three players in the entire field—Bobby Cole of South Africa, Hale Irwin of the United States and Masashi "Jumbo" Ozaki of Japan—were able to break par over the seventy-two-hole route; despite the fact that the official course record of 64 had been set by one of Lagunita's assistant professionals, Noel Machado (who also once unofficially shot the course in a startling 61). Machado is one of only three assistants to head pro Tommy Fonseca, and all are excellent players.

The course at Lagunita is dominated by a large, modernistic clubhouse complete with ballroom and mandatory swimming pool. From

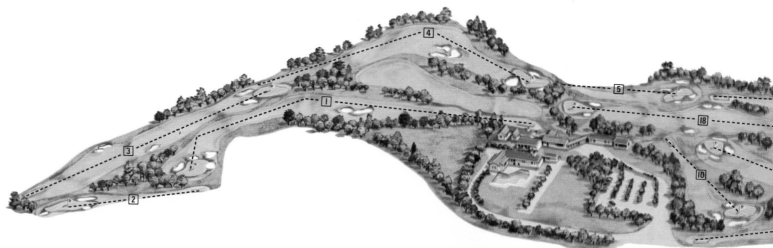

The high-rise blocks of Caracas's sprawling hillside suburb of El Hatillo form a backdrop to the Lagunita club, the newest and best known of the three excellent courses in the Venezuelan capital. Designed by Dick Wilson, it was completed in 1962.

Lagunita Country Club, Caracas			Card of the course		
Out	3,450 yards	35	No 1	535 yards	par 5
In	3,445 yards	35	No 2	205 yards	par 3
Total	6,895 yards	par 70	No 3	470 yards	par 4
			No 4	455 yards	par 4
			No 5	190 yards	par 3
			No 6	405 yards	par 4
			No 7	380 yards	par 4
			No 8	220 yards	par 3
			No 9	590 yards	par 5
			No 10	210 yards	par 3
			No 11	510 yards	par 5
			No 12	445 yards	par 4
			No 13	420 yards	par 4
			No 14	435 yards	par 4
			No 15	425 yards	par 4
			No 16	170 yards	par 3
			No 17	390 yards	par 4
			No 18	440 yards	par 4

its position on a hill, five holes can be seen, together with the practice range. The course fans out both to the left and to the right of the clubhouse, bending back on itself at the 2nd and 3rd and again at the 13th and 14th.

The 1st hole starts away from the left of the clubhouse and is a bit of an oddity in that it is a par-five of 535 yards. Out-of-bounds lies along the left side—which is just as well, since the land has been turned into a quarry pit from which nobody could possibly play. The hole is a double dog-leg with two cross-bunkers at the 220-yard mark, after which the fairway bends left for an easy second if the player chooses not to go for the green. Few players do, for the green is completely cut off in front and on both

sides by bunkers. The quarry is avoided by laying up and playing into the green from the second dog-leg. The 2nd is the first of those five treacherous par-threes. It is 205 yards to the large, deep green, and that quarry still lies on the left. In a delightful understatement, the course notes describe the 2nd as "dangerous". The most difficult thing about the 3rd hole is its length: it is 470 yards, the maximum for a par-four hole. Again, out-of-bounds lurks ominously on the left.

The 4th hole is one of the most interesting par-fours on the course. It is 455 yards and demands a full-out drive to get past a dog-leg that turns a complete ninety degrees and which cannot be cut because of three fairway bunkers ▷

A green-to-tee view of the dog-leg 15th, right, shows the need for an accurate second to clear the large trap in front but still hold the fast-breaking green, a feature of Lagunita.

The 18th green, left, has an awkward, narrow entrance and is well guarded by bunkers on both sides. It is a straight last hole, but uphill all the way and into the prevailing wind.

The 13th: A perfect par-four

The 13th is not the toughest hole on Lagunita. The 1974 World Cup matches confirmed the 12th in that role. When he was leading the individual competition in the third round Roberto de Vicenzo took a seven there and the following day Masashi "Jumbo" Ozaki's eight cost him the title. However, the 13th more or less typifies the grace and artistry Dick Wilson and, especially, Joe Lee built into the course.

It is a par-four. 420 yards long, with a fairway which slopes gently up to the green. On that slope no fewer than seven bunkers stare back to the tee. Only two of them can snare a drive. These are set at the 200-yard and the 220-yard range. A full 270 yards from the tee is a third bunker which is only within range of the likes of Nicklaus and Vicenzo.

For the last two-thirds of the hole out-of-bounds, a pervasive hazard at Lagunita, lies to the right, as does a concrete drainage ditch, played on this hole as a hazard. Some dubious but none the less welcome relief comes in the form of a thin protective file of trees which presents something of a problem of its own, but one thankfully less severe than the others.

Any mishit drive means that another bunker lying one hundred yards or so short of the green has to be contended with. The green itself, which is narrow and very deep, is protected by two small bunkers fronting the right side and a long one which skirts the left. Thus the demands of the 13th are classically simple: length and accuracy off the tee and a very exacting second shot. What more can a golfer ask of a par-four?

Though Lagunita is not particularly long by modern championship standards, the club's confidence in its course was justified by the scores in the World Cup, held there in November 1974. Only three players among more than ninety broke the seventy-two-hole par, all of them men in form: South African Open champion Bobby Cole, US Open title holder Hale Irwin and Japan's Masashi Ozaki, who led the world stroke averages that year.

A superb 66 by Bobby Cole, left, put him on the road to individual honours in the World Cup at Lagunita in 1974, while Dale Hayes, above, returned a steady 283 to help Cole take South Africa to victory, five shots ahead of Japan and nine clear of USA's Irwin and Trevino.

▷ and trees to the right. The green is shaped like a frying pan, with the handle protruding in front and guarded on either side by bunkers, with a flash trap to the rear. The 4th is not an easy par and no place to try to pick up a birdie.

The green of the 5th, a par-three of 190 yards, is beautifully bunkered all around and to the left is another gravel pit. The 6th and 7th holes, both shortish comparatively uninteresting par-fours, are followed by the longest par-three on

Crowned five months earlier as US Open champion, Hale Irwin recorded three sub-par rounds after a poor 73 to pull up behind Cole and "Jumbo" Ozaki of Japan at Lagunita in the 1974 World Cup.

the course, the 220-yard 8th. It is the green which makes the hole, for it sharply inclines towards the approach and is well protected to the front and on both sides by bunkers. The prevailing wind at Lagunita blows across this hole from right to left. The 9th is a par-five of 590 yards, the last third of which is uphill. There are no fairway bunkers and the hole needs none. The second shot must be played around a slight dog-leg and requires something of a gargantuan effort to get anywhere near the green, which has two bunkers on either side. It is a truly fine par-five.

The 10th tee, which sits just below the club-house, takes a long iron to carry 210 yards across a dip in the ground to the green, which slopes severely towards the tee. The fairway of the 510-yard par-five 11th is very wide, but out-of-bounds runs the entire length of the right side. The green is very narrow, long and extremely fast. A cross-bunker sits just short of it for a lazy second shot and three more skirt the edges of the green. The 12th is one of the most treacherous holes on the course. A par-four, 445 yards long, it is a sharp dog-leg to the right with out-of-bounds all the way from tee to green. Three little bunkers and a copse at the angle of the dog-leg make cutting it un-feasible. There are no bunkers around the huge green, but it is protected in front by a lake which runs clear to the putting surface. The second shot must carry the lake all the way.

The 13th and 14th, both medium-length par-fours, are beautifully bunkered. At 435 yards, the 14th has plenty of length and no fewer than eight traps, three of them on the left side of the fairway in the landing area, where it bends slightly to the left. The ever-present out-of-bounds lies the complete length of the hole on the right. The elevated green is full of slopes and is practically encircled by five bunkers. The 15th—a favourite among the members—marches directly towards the clubhouse, as do the remaining holes. It is 425 yards long, par-four and has three fairway bunkers to the left and close to the landing area. However, a gulley crosses the fairway and is played as a hazard. Out-of-bounds lies to the right of the fairway but can easily be avoided off the tee. A lateral water hazard, almost hidden, lies to the left of the green, which has but a single bunker directly in front of it. Also to the left of the green is another drainage ditch which is played as a hazard. All in all, it is a devious par-four.

At only 170 yards, the 16th is the shortest hole on the course. However, the green is very large although fast and all but surrounded by bunkers. The 17th is short as par-fours go, only 390 yards, but it dog-legs to the right with two fairway bunkers lying short of the bend.

Lu Liang Huan had steered Taiwan to an historic win in the 1972 World Cup in Melbourne, but at Lagunita he could never quite break par and finished fourth on 283, level with countryman Kuo Chi Hsiung.

Three more, front, right and left, stand sentinel over every possible approach to the green. The 18th is a strong finishing hole, as it should be, 440 yards uphill to the clubhouse and against the prevailing wind. The fairway is wide, but bunkers lie on both sides of the landing area off the tee. The pear-shaped green is heavily bordered with rough and bunkers lie on both sides of its narrow entrance.

Lagunita, then, is a testing course and one that breeds a high degree of skill among those who play it regularly: in 1974 the club had four scratch players, which locals believe may be something of a record.

Gazetteer: 100 outstanding courses from around the world

1   Nairn
2   Gullane
3   Gleneagles
4   Troon
5   Prestwick
6   Royal St David's
7   Southport and Ainsdale
8   Formby
9   Little Aston
10 Saunton
11 Royal North Devon
12 Burnham and Berrow
13 West Sussex
14 Royal Cinque Ports
15 Prince's
16 Walton Heath
17 Wentworth
18 Berkshire
19 Royal Worlington and Newmarket
20 Hunstanton
21 Royal West Norfolk
22 Woodhall Spa
23 Notts
24 Lindrick
25 Moortown
26 Alwoodley
27 Lahinch
28 Ballybunion

29 Halmsted
30 Rungsted
31 Falkenstein
32 Frankfurter
33 Haagsche
34 Royal Belgique
35 Royal Waterloo
36 Saint-Nom-La-Bretèche
37 Crans-sur-Sierre
38 Seefeld-Wildmoos
39 Glyfada
40 Rome
41 Pevero
42 El Prat
43 La Manga
44 Estoril
45 Penina

46 Doral
47 Jupiter Hills
48 Sea Island
49 Peachtree
50 Palmetto Dunes
51 Dunes
52 Country Club of North Carolina
53 Cascades
54 Congressional
55 Baltimore
56 Quaker Ridge
57 Concord
58 Oak Hill
59 Canterbury
60 Scioto
61 Inverness
62 Chicago
63 Butler National
64 Prairie Dunes
65 Colonial
66 Cherry Hills
67 Spyglass Hill
68 Riviera
69 Mauna Kea
70 Princeville
71 Hamilton
72 St George's
73 Jasper
74 Vancouver
75 Vallescondido
76 Port Royal

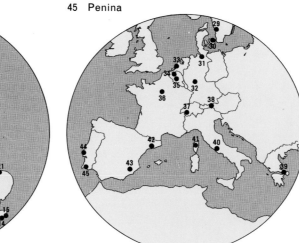

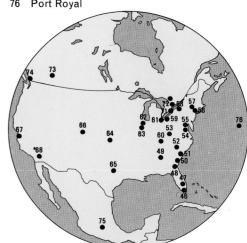

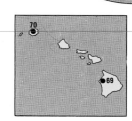

77 Lucayan
78 South Ocean
79 Cerromar
80 Fountain Valley
81 Tryall
82 Tobago
83 Club Lagos de Caujara
84 El Rincon
85 Bogotá

86 Karen
87 Chapman
88 Houghton

89 Kasugai
90 Nasu International
91 Yomiuri
92 Wack Wack
93 Navatanee
94 Delhi
95 Australian
96 New South Wales
97 Lake Karrinyup
98 Kingston Heath
99 Auckland
100 Christchurch

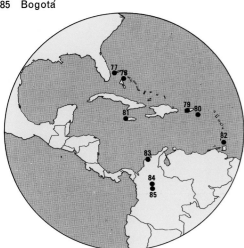

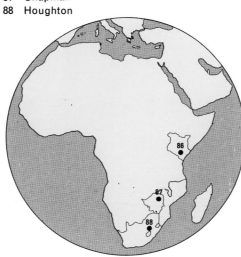

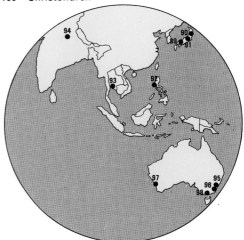

Scotland

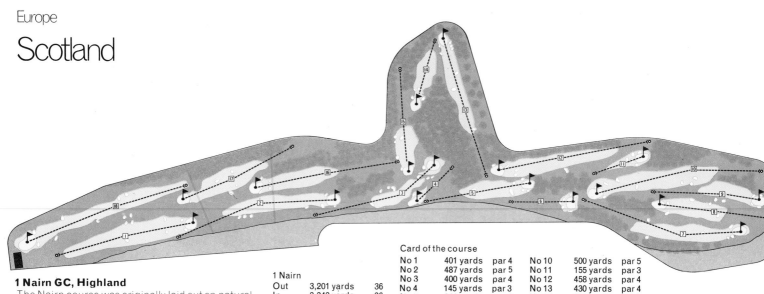

1 Nairn GC, Highland

The Nairn course was originally laid out on natural linksland by Archie Simpson in 1887 and modified two years later by Old Tom Morris and James Braid. It features large, undulating greens and deep bunkers, with panoramic views across the entrance of the Moray Firth to the mountains of Caithness. The sea plays its own part in the hazards at Nairn, and nowhere more than at the 5th—called Nets after the salmon nets on the shore. The tee shot over the beach needs judgement—and a long carry of 175 to 200 yards—to set up the best line for an exacting second shot to a semi-plateau green that is protected by bunkers to the front and side. The Scottish Professional Championship has been played here four times, with that famous pair John Panton and Eric Brown among its winners. In 1899 it became the first Scottish club to make an admission charge for a golf match.

2 Gullane GC, Lothian

Gullane No 1, the best of this small village's three fine courses, is often claimed to be the equal of nearby Muirfield. Certainly it has the same fine turf and true greens, plus the bonus of breathtaking views over the Firth of Forth to the hills of Fife. The 7th hole starts from the top of Gullane Hill, the course's highest point, and falls to the green 400 yards away. The back nine starts with a series of long, exacting holes. The 10th and 11th are both par-fours—of 470 and 472 yards—and they are followed by a very short par-five of 478 yards set at cliff height, which is the lowest point on the course. Golf was played at Gullane from the start of the seventeenth century, and seven holes were laid down by 1844. Forty years later a full eighteen holes were in play, with two courses completed by 1900 and three by 1910.

3 Gleneagles GC, Tayside

Designed by the legendary James Braid and Major C. K. Hutchinson, the King's course is one of three set on a sheltered moorland plateau. It is carved out of superb natural golfing country of rising hills splashed with purple heather and golden gorse, with sculptured bunkers that sparkle against tall stands of dark pine. The firm turf and immaculate greens combine to form a sequence of well-designed, memorable holes. The best is probably the 451-yard 13th, Braid's Brawest, where the fairway rolls narrowly away from the tee like an ocean swell between heather and bracken, demanding a long, straight drive to carry a ridge set with two deep bunkers. The approach to an elevated, well-trapped plateau green is deceptive, and par is an elusive reward.

Card of the course

1 Nairn

Out	3,201 yards	36				
In	3,343 yards	36				
Total	6,544 yards	par 72				

Record: 66, Ian Hutcheon, N. Scotland Amateur Stroke Play 1975

No 1	401 yards	par 4	No 10	500 yards	par 5
No 2	487 yards	par 5	No 11	155 yards	par 3
No 3	400 yards	par 4	No 12	458 yards	par 4
No 4	145 yards	par 3	No 13	430 yards	par 4
No 5	381 yards	par 4	No 14	199 yards	par 3
No 6	189 yards	par 3	No 15	311 yards	par 4
No 7	501 yards	par 5	No 16	421 yards	par 4
No 8	332 yards	par 4	No 17	365 yards	par 4
No 9	365 yards	par 4	No 18	504 yards	par 5

At Gullane's 17th, Lawson Little hit a drive that carried bunkers 340 yards from the tee.

Card of the course

No 1	304 yards	par 4
No 2	378 yards	par 4
No 3	498 yards	par 5
No 4	142 yards	par 3
No 5	445 yards	par 4
No 6	313 yards	par 4
No 7	400 yards	par 4
No 8	329 yards	par 4
No 9	152 yards	par 3
No 10	470 yards	par 4
No 11	472 yards	par 4
No 12	478 yards	par 5
No 13	165 yards	par 3
No 14	430 yards	par 4
No 15	538 yards	par 5
No 16	187 yards	par 3
No 17	384 yards	par 4
No 18	359 yards	par 4

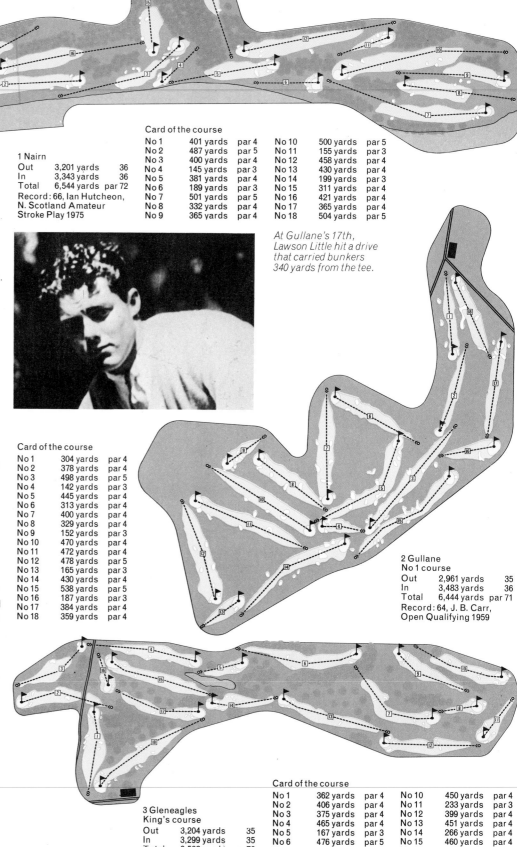

2 Gullane No 1 course

Out	2,961 yards	35
In	3,483 yards	36
Total	6,444 yards	par 71

Record: 64, J. B. Carr, Open Qualifying 1959

Card of the course

3 Gleneagles King's course

Out	3,204 yards	35
In	3,299 yards	35
Total	6,503 yards	par 70

Record: 65, Eric Brown, Dunlop Masters 1960

No 1	362 yards	par 4	No 10	450 yards	par 4
No 2	406 yards	par 4	No 11	233 yards	par 3
No 3	375 yards	par 4	No 12	399 yards	par 4
No 4	465 yards	par 4	No 13	451 yards	par 4
No 5	167 yards	par 3	No 14	266 yards	par 4
No 6	476 yards	par 5	No 15	460 yards	par 4
No 7	429 yards	par 4	No 16	135 yards	par 3
No 8	170 yards	par 3	No 17	374 yards	par 4
No 9	354 yards	par 4	No 18	531 yards	par 5

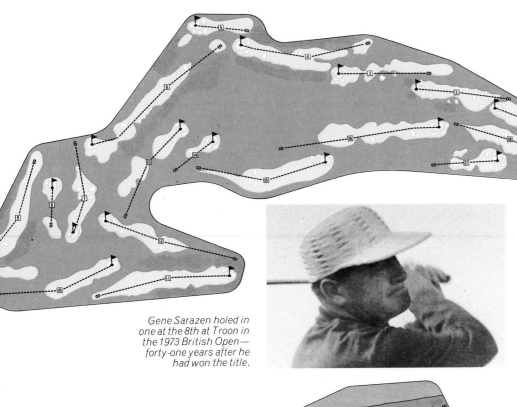

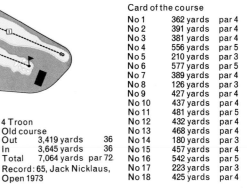

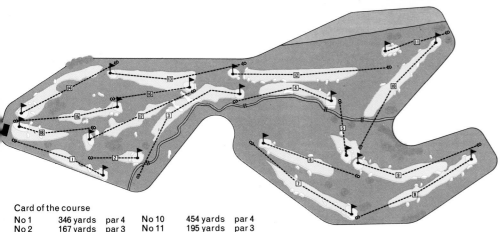

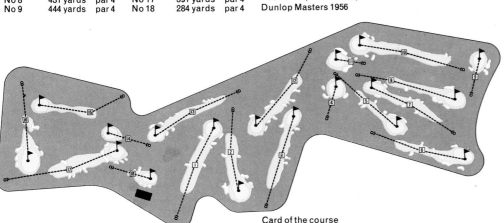

Gene Sarazen holed in one at the 8th at Troon in the 1973 British Open— forty-one years after he had won the title.

Card of the course

No 1	362 yards	par 4
No 2	391 yards	par 4
No 3	381 yards	par 4
No 4	556 yards	par 5
No 5	210 yards	par 3
No 6	577 yards	par 5
No 7	389 yards	par 4
No 8	126 yards	par 3
No 9	427 yards	par 4
No 10	437 yards	par 4
No 11	481 yards	par 5
No 12	432 yards	par 4
No 13	468 yards	par 4
No 14	180 yards	par 3
No 15	457 yards	par 4
No 16	542 yards	par 5
No 17	223 yards	par 3
No 18	425 yards	par 4

4 Troon
Old course

Out	3,419 yards	36
In	3,645 yards	36
Total	7,064 yards	par 72

Record: 65, Jack Nicklaus,
Open 1973

4 Troon GC, Strathclyde

The Old course at Troon is one of the Open venues —an excellent test, especially in a stiffish breeze. The championship record of 276, twelve under par, by Arnold Palmer in 1962—equalled by Tom Weiskopf in 1973—underlines the fact that only a performance of extraordinary quality will conquer its hazards. Started as five holes by twenty-four local enthusiasts in 1878, it offers some very long and rugged pars, with the natural, untamed contours of the land deciding the strategy. The 126-yard 8th, the Postage Stamp, is a subtle, demanding challenge. Its deep traps menacing a small green have upset many great golfers, including Walter Hagen in 1923 when he lost the Open title by one stroke. Another great hole is the 481-yard 11th, which offers a narrow driving line plus the challenge of a green tucked up against the railway wall.

5 Prestwick GC, Strathclyde

Prestwick Golf Club was host to the first Open championship in 1860 and twenty-four more thereafter, the last in 1924. There is a fascination in tackling these fabled holes, many of them little changed since those early days; the ghosts of Young Tom Morris, Braid, Taylor and Vardon seem to stalk its narrow fairways still. The course lies on typical hard, humpy linksland, with deep bunkers, wild rough, a winding burn and many blind shots over sandhills to the tiny greens. The most famous hole is probably the 482-yard par-five 3rd, the Cardinal. Its main feature is a massive bunker set right on the dog-leg, which has to be carried in the face of a solid revetment of uncompromising railway sleepers.

Card of the course

No 1	346 yards	par 4	No 10	454 yards	par 4
No 2	167 yards	par 3	No 11	195 yards	par 3
No 3	482 yards	par 5	No 12	513 yards	par 5
No 4	382 yards	par 4	No 13	460 yards	par 4
No 5	206 yards	par 3	No 14	362 yards	par 4
No 6	362 yards	par 4	No 15	347 yards	par 4
No 7	430 yards	par 4	No 16	288 yards	par 4
No 8	431 yards	par 4	No 17	391 yards	par 4
No 9	444 yards	par 4	No 18	284 yards	par 4

5 Prestwick

Out	3,250 yards	35
In	2,294 yards	36
Total	6,544 yards	par 71

Record: 67, Eric Brown,
Dunlop Masters 1956

6 Royal St David's GC, Harlech, Gwynedd

Overlooked by the magnificent Harlech Castle, on reclaimed land of links-like character that is separated from the sea by sandhills, the Royal St David's course is renowned for its beauty and its superb, large greens. The finishing stretch includes two of the finest holes, the 15th and 17th, both measuring 435 yards but requiring contrasting strategies. The 15th, with Mount Snowdon in the background, is bunkerless. The fairway is slightly dog-legged right, winds between sandhills and narrows towards a hollow just short of the green; it takes two good shots to get there against the prevailing wind. The 17th, usually downwind, needs extreme accuracy from the tee because of bunkers on the right of the narrow fairway and cross-bunkers that guard the green. The club has twice staged the Home International.

6 Royal St David's

Out	3,417 yards	36
In	3,189 yards	33
Total	6,576 yards	par 69

Record: 66, John Morgan,
St David's Gold Cross 1951

Card of the course

No 1	451 yards	par 4	No 10	470 yards	par 4
No 2	378 yards	par 4	No 11	150 yards	par 3
No 3	470 yards	par 4	No 12	451 yards	par 4
No 4	182 yards	par 3	No 13	458 yards	par 4
No 5	385 yards	par 4	No 14	225 yards	par 3
No 6	380 yards	par 4	No 15	435 yards	par 4
No 7	484 yards	par 5	No 16	360 yards	par 4
No 8	507 yards	par 5	No 17	435 yards	par 4
No 9	180 yards	par 3	No 18	205 yards	par 3

England

7 Southport and Ainsdale GC, Merseyside

Embedded amongst the magnificent sandhills that reach down much of the South Lancashire coast are several courses of championship quality. The Southport and Ainsdale, or S and A links, is one of them. In 1906 there were nine rather undistinguished holes, but sixteen years later, with the help of James Braid, a tournament-class arena was built on a new site. Its challenging and demanding character is most apparent at the 16th, Gumbleys. This is a 510-yard par-five, almost invariably played into the prevailing wind and requiring a tee shot between tight fairway bunkers to avoid the out-of-bounds railway area on the right. The second shot must clear the towering sandhills, or else an enormous, sleeper-faced bunker. The opening hole is unusual, a 200-yard par-three, where the ball must be shot to the heart of the green: anything short sticks in the encircling sandtraps. In 1933 the British won a rare Ryder Cup victory on this course and more recently it has been host to a qualifying tournament for the Open.

Card of the course

No 1	200 yards	par 3
No 2	520 yards	par 5
No 3	418 yards	par 4
No 4	316 yards	par 4
No 5	447 yards	par 4
No 6	386 yards	par 4
No 7	480 yards	par 5
No 8	157 yards	par 3
No 9	482 yards	par 5
No 10	160 yards	par 3
No 11	447 yards	par 4
No 12	401 yards	par 4
No 13	157 yards	par 3
No 14	383 yards	par 4
No 15	353 yards	par 4
No 16	510 yards	par 5
No 17	443 yards	par 4
No 18	355 yards	par 4

8 Formby GC, Merseyside

When golf started at Formby in 1884 the membership was limited to twenty-five, who paid one guinea a year for the privilege of playing nine completely natural holes. The site remains basically unchanged apart from the addition of nine more holes. It is a fine, sandy stretch between railway and sea and it is the sea that is forcing changes now. Erosion of the coastline is eating away the 8th, 9th and 10th holes, and they are to be replaced in 1978. The first hole is typical of the course: the drive is menaced by an out-of-bounds railway on the right and the second shot requires extreme accuracy to find a flat, well-bunkered green. It was here that Sam Snead won his second World Senior title in 1965 by beating Charley Ward at the 37th hole. Formby has twice played host to the Amateur championship, with Reid Jack and American Bob Dickson taking the honours in 1957 and 1967.

Card of the course

No 1	405 yards	par 4
No 2	381 yards	par 4
No 3	510 yards	par 5
No 4	313 yards	par 4
No 5	162 yards	par 3
No 6	405 yards	par 4
No 7	495 yards	par 5
No 8	346 yards	par 4
No 9	182 yards	par 3
No 10	513 yards	par 5
No 11	388 yards	par 4
No 12	407 yards	par 4
No 13	382 yards	par 4
No 14	420 yards	par 4
No 15	403 yards	par 4
No 16	124 yards	par 3
No 17	472 yards	par 4
No 18	392 yards	par 4

9 Little Aston GC, Birmingham

As a true parkland course, set in splendid isolation within a few miles of the centre of Birmingham, Little Aston offers more room for error from the tee than most courses of championship standard. This does not mean it presents a lesser test of golf, for the course demands accuracy of iron play to achieve anything like a good score. The holes were laid out in 1908 by Harry Vardon, who made full use of the excellent subsoil of sand and gravel. The 17th sums up its challenge, for although the second shot is no more than a pitch it is to a plateau green surrounded by bunkers and flanked by a lake on the left. Three fine two-shotters, the 6th, 7th and 8th, zig-zag through the course, providing a challenging run to even the most accomplished of golfers. The 368-yard 7th is a classic short par-four where both fairway traps and severe bunkering in front of the green must be avoided. The Dunlop Masters has been held here five times, with such celebrated winners as Harry Weetman in 1958 and Bernard Hunt in 1963.

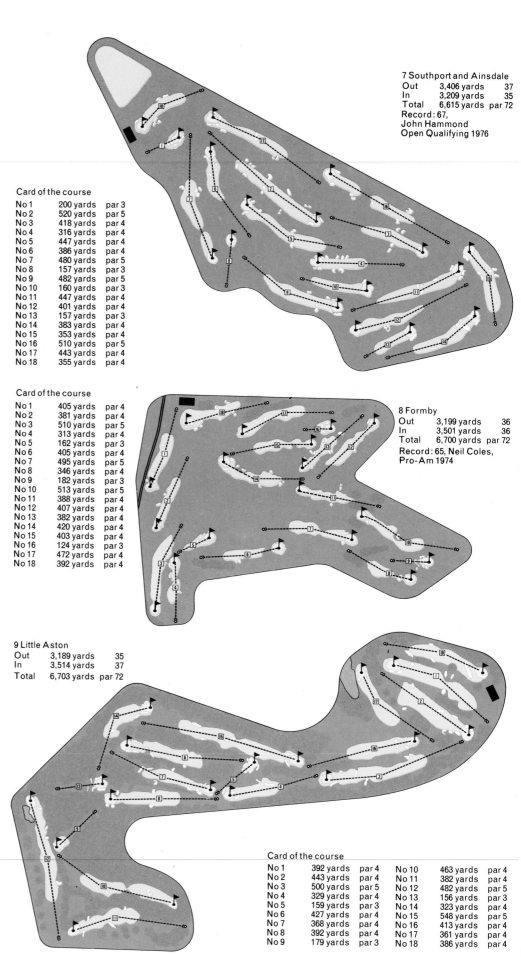

7 Southport and Ainsdale
Out	3,406 yards	37
In	3,209 yards	35
Total	6,615 yards	par 72

Record: 67,
John Hammond
Open Qualifying 1976

8 Formby
Out	3,199 yards	36
In	3,501 yards	36
Total	6,700 yards	par 72

Record: 65, Neil Coles,
Pro-Am 1974

9 Little Aston
Out	3,189 yards	35
In	3,514 yards	37
Total	6,703 yards	par 72

Card of the course

No 1	392 yards	par 4	No 10	463 yards	par 4
No 2	443 yards	par 4	No 11	382 yards	par 4
No 3	500 yards	par 5	No 12	482 yards	par 5
No 4	329 yards	par 4	No 13	156 yards	par 3
No 5	159 yards	par 3	No 14	323 yards	par 4
No 6	427 yards	par 4	No 15	548 yards	par 5
No 7	368 yards	par 4	No 16	413 yards	par 4
No 8	392 yards	par 4	No 17	361 yards	par 4
No 9	179 yards	par 3	No 18	386 yards	par 4

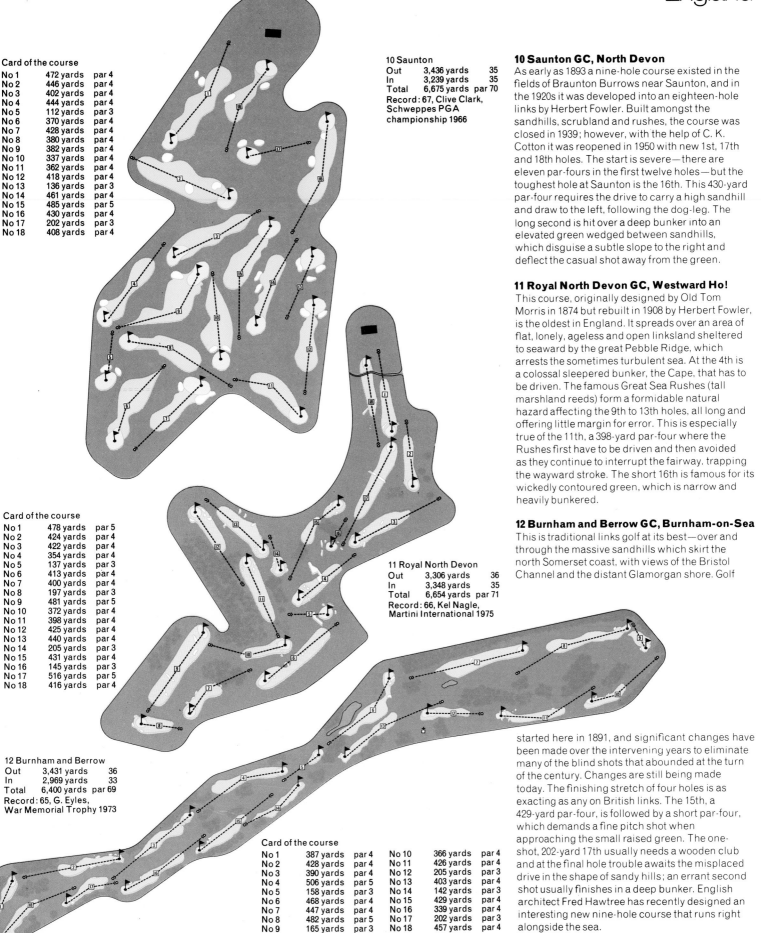

Card of the course

No 1	472 yards	par 4
No 2	446 yards	par 4
No 3	402 yards	par 4
No 4	444 yards	par 4
No 5	112 yards	par 3
No 6	370 yards	par 4
No 7	428 yards	par 4
No 8	380 yards	par 4
No 9	382 yards	par 4
No 10	337 yards	par 4
No 11	362 yards	par 4
No 12	418 yards	par 4
No 13	136 yards	par 3
No 14	461 yards	par 4
No 15	485 yards	par 5
No 16	430 yards	par 4
No 17	202 yards	par 3
No 18	408 yards	par 4

10 Saunton

Out	3,436 yards	35
In	3,239 yards	35
Total	6,675 yards	par 70

Record: 67, Clive Clark,
Schweppes PGA
championship 1966

10 Saunton GC, North Devon

As early as 1893 a nine-hole course existed in the fields of Braunton Burrows near Saunton, and in the 1920s it was developed into an eighteen-hole links by Herbert Fowler. Built amongst the sandhills, scrubland and rushes, the course was closed in 1939; however, with the help of C. K. Cotton it was reopened in 1950 with new 1st, 17th and 18th holes. The start is severe—there are eleven par-fours in the first twelve holes—but the toughest hole at Saunton is the 16th. This 430-yard par-four requires the drive to carry a high sandhill and draw to the left, following the dog-leg. The long second is hit over a deep bunker into an elevated green wedged between sandhills, which disguise a subtle slope to the right and deflect the casual shot away from the green.

11 Royal North Devon GC, Westward Ho!

This course, originally designed by Old Tom Morris in 1874 but rebuilt in 1908 by Herbert Fowler, is the oldest in England. It spreads over an area of flat, lonely, ageless and open linksland sheltered to seaward by the great Pebble Ridge, which arrests the sometimes turbulent sea. At the 4th is a colossal sleepered bunker, the Cape, that has to be driven. The famous Great Sea Rushes (tall marshland reeds) form a formidable natural hazard affecting the 9th to 13th holes, all long and offering little margin for error. This is especially true of the 11th, a 398-yard par-four where the Rushes first have to be driven and then avoided as they continue to interrupt the fairway, trapping the wayward stroke. The short 16th is famous for its wickedly contoured green, which is narrow and heavily bunkered.

12 Burnham and Berrow GC, Burnham-on-Sea

This is traditional links golf at its best—over and through the massive sandhills which skirt the north Somerset coast, with views of the Bristol Channel and the distant Glamorgan shore. Golf

Card of the course

No 1	478 yards	par 5
No 2	424 yards	par 4
No 3	422 yards	par 4
No 4	354 yards	par 4
No 5	137 yards	par 3
No 6	413 yards	par 4
No 7	400 yards	par 4
No 8	197 yards	par 3
No 9	481 yards	par 5
No 10	372 yards	par 4
No 11	398 yards	par 4
No 12	425 yards	par 4
No 13	440 yards	par 4
No 14	205 yards	par 3
No 15	431 yards	par 4
No 16	145 yards	par 3
No 17	516 yards	par 5
No 18	416 yards	par 4

11 Royal North Devon

Out	3,306 yards	36
In	3,348 yards	35
Total	6,654 yards	par 71

Record: 66, Kel Nagle,
Martini International 1975

12 Burnham and Berrow

Out	3,431 yards	36
In	2,969 yards	33
Total	6,400 yards	par 69

Record: 65, G. Eyles,
War Memorial Trophy 1973

started here in 1891, and significant changes have been made over the intervening years to eliminate many of the blind shots that abounded at the turn of the century. Changes are still being made today. The finishing stretch of four holes is as exacting as any on British links. The 15th, a 429-yard par-four, is followed by a short par-four, which demands a fine pitch shot when approaching the small raised green. The one-shot, 202-yard 17th usually needs a wooden club and at the final hole trouble awaits the misplaced drive in the shape of sandy hills; an errant second shot usually finishes in a deep bunker. English architect Fred Hawtree has recently designed an interesting new nine-hole course that runs right alongside the sea.

Card of the course

No 1	387 yards	par 4	No 10	366 yards	par 4
No 2	428 yards	par 4	No 11	426 yards	par 4
No 3	390 yards	par 4	No 12	205 yards	par 3
No 4	506 yards	par 5	No 13	403 yards	par 4
No 5	158 yards	par 3	No 14	142 yards	par 3
No 6	468 yards	par 4	No 15	429 yards	par 4
No 7	447 yards	par 4	No 16	339 yards	par 4
No 8	482 yards	par 5	No 17	202 yards	par 3
No 9	165 yards	par 3	No 18	457 yards	par 4

England

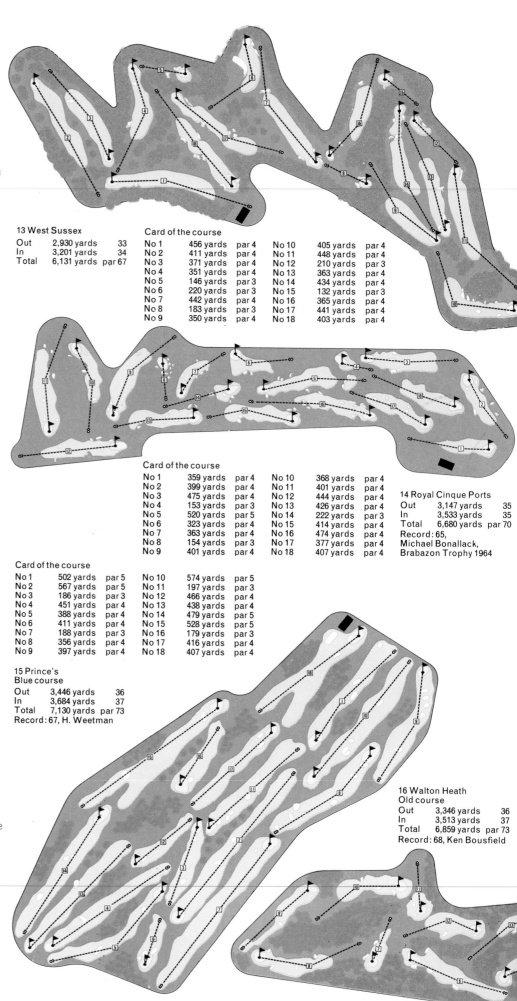

13 West Sussex GC, Pulborough

This delightful inland course in a secluded area of woodland countryside was designed by Major Hutchinson and Sir Guy Campbell and opened in 1930. The bunkers are filled with silver sand, contrasting magnificently with the pine and birch trees that line the fairways. Lack of length and the conspicuous absence of any par-fives does not reduce the quality of play. Indeed, the 5th and 6th are two fine par-threes which aptly illustrate the ingenuity of the architects. The essence of the 5th—146 yards—is to avoid the large sandtrap guarding the left side of the green. The 220-yard 6th can be a lethal hole, where an expanse of marshland and scrub must be carried to make the green. The hole may be played as a dog-leg by the timid, avoiding the soft ground at the probable cost of a stroke.

14 Royal Cinque Ports GC, Deal

This superb natural links, one of the most challenging courses in Britain, opened in 1895. It has heavily bunkered fairways and well-protected greens. The only major alteration to the original layout occurred in 1938–9, when the direction of the 4th hole was reversed. Minor changes were also made to the 5th, 9th and 14th holes. But the 16th, a 474-yard par-four, is considered to be the best hole. The drive is uphill, requiring a carry of 150 yards to clear strategically placed fairway bunkers. An accurate approach shot must then be struck to pass through a channelled entrance on to the well-elevated green. The course was the setting for two early British Opens; J. H. Taylor won his fourth Open victory there in 1909 and, in 1920, George Duncan carried off the title by two strokes after starting the final round thirteen strokes behind.

15 Prince's GC, Sandwich

Prince's, lying alongside Sandwich Bay, is a deceptive, stark links that is characterized by its flatness and the scarcity of sandtraps. Originally designed by Sir H. Mallaby-Deeley and P. M. Lucas, it was first played in 1907 when a large ridge of dunes—the Himalayas—dominated the course. World War II interrupted the golf and 1948 saw twenty-seven new championship holes, designed by J. S. F. Morrison and Sir Guy Campbell, come into play. The Blue is the championship course, no longer menaced by the dune ridge, but the wide, flat fairways make distance difficult to judge and the fast greens demand the greatest respect.

16 Walton Heath GC, Tadworth

The Old course was designed by Herbert Fowler in 1904, and his additional nine holes were later extended to become the New course. Both resemble seaside courses in design and quality of turf, even though forty miles from the English Channel. The bunkers are large and deep, while the greens are big and consistent in pace in all weathers. The short and gentle first hole of the Old course belies the trials which follow, and the finish from the 14th is daunting. The 16th, a 499-yard par-five, is critical, needing a long drive down a narrow, heather-lined fairway and then a full-blooded shot to a green that is cut into a left-to-right slope, with a large bunker eating into the right-hand edge.

13 West Sussex

Out	2,930 yards	33							
In	3,201 yards	34							
Total	6,131 yards	par 67							

Card of the course

No 1	456 yards	par 4	No 10	405 yards	par 4
No 2	411 yards	par 4	No 11	448 yards	par 4
No 3	371 yards	par 4	No 12	210 yards	par 3
No 4	351 yards	par 4	No 13	363 yards	par 4
No 5	146 yards	par 3	No 14	434 yards	par 4
No 6	220 yards	par 3	No 15	132 yards	par 3
No 7	442 yards	par 4	No 16	365 yards	par 4
No 8	183 yards	par 3	No 17	441 yards	par 4
No 9	350 yards	par 4	No 18	403 yards	par 4

Card of the course

No 1	359 yards	par 4	No 10	368 yards	par 4
No 2	399 yards	par 4	No 11	401 yards	par 4
No 3	475 yards	par 4	No 12	444 yards	par 4
No 4	153 yards	par 3	No 13	426 yards	par 4
No 5	520 yards	par 5	No 14	222 yards	par 3
No 6	323 yards	par 4	No 15	414 yards	par 4
No 7	363 yards	par 4	No 16	474 yards	par 4
No 8	154 yards	par 3	No 17	377 yards	par 4
No 9	401 yards	par 4	No 18	407 yards	par 4

14 Royal Cinque Ports

Out	3,147 yards	35
In	3,533 yards	35
Total	6,680 yards	par 70

Record: 65,
Michael Bonallack,
Brabazon Trophy 1964

Card of the course

No 1	502 yards	par 5	No 10	574 yards	par 5
No 2	567 yards	par 5	No 11	197 yards	par 3
No 3	186 yards	par 3	No 12	466 yards	par 4
No 4	451 yards	par 4	No 13	438 yards	par 4
No 5	388 yards	par 4	No 14	479 yards	par 5
No 6	411 yards	par 4	No 15	528 yards	par 5
No 7	188 yards	par 3	No 16	179 yards	par 3
No 8	356 yards	par 4	No 17	416 yards	par 4
No 9	397 yards	par 4	No 18	407 yards	par 4

15 Prince's
Blue course

Out	3,446 yards	36
In	3,684 yards	37
Total	7,130 yards	par 73

Record: 67, H. Weetman

16 Walton Heath
Old course

Out	3,346 yards	36
In	3,513 yards	37
Total	6,859 yards	par 73

Record: 68, Ken Bousfield

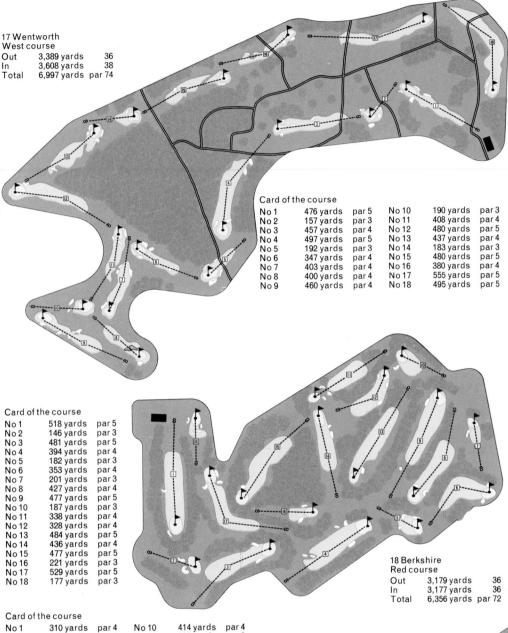

17 Wentworth
West course

Out	3,389 yards	36
In	3,608 yards	38
Total	6,997 yards	par 74

17 Wentworth GC, Virginia Water

Rolling woodland and sandy subsoil create great golf courses and Wentworth, in Surrey's exclusive Virginia Water area, is an outstanding example. Designed by H. S. Colt, the East course opened in the early 1920s and was followed soon after by the West, the championship course. Playing it requires a combination of length and accurate placement of the tee. The 17th, a 555-yard par-five, which curves off to the left from the tee, is rated by Arnold Palmer as one of the best long holes in Britain. The Ryder Cup (1953), the World Cup (1956) and the Piccadilly World Match Play are among the major events staged here.

18 Berkshire GC, Ascot

In 1928 Herbert Fowler built thirty-six splendid holes for the Berkshire club, in the heart of rural England. The Red and Blue courses wind over rolling heathland and through quiet woods of pine, silver birch and chestnut. The Red is unusual in that it has six short holes, the finest of which is the 221-yard 16th, where the outstanding plateau green can only be reached and held with a tightly controlled shot to its centre. The 8th is the most difficult of the longer holes. The drive must be faced around the pines to leave the way clear for the second over a shallow valley on to the green. Holes from both courses are used to form the championship course.

19 Royal Worlington and Newmarket GC, Suffolk

Acclaimed as the best and most distinguished nine-hole course in the country, this inland gem was constructed in 1890 under the guidance of Captain A. M. Ross, a local golfer, on a base of light sandy soil reminiscent of a links. This has enhanced the quality of the turf and led to true and unusually fast greens. The 5th is a stunning, bunkerless short hole which can be played with anything from a 5- to a 9-iron, and where the over-long shot is punished by the trees behind the green. The 7th is another fine par-three, with a classic saucer green leaving only the top of the pin visible from the tee. In 1907 J. F. Ireland achieved the rare double of an ace at both the 5th and the 7th in the same round.

Card of the course

No 1	476 yards	par 5	No 10	190 yards	par 3
No 2	157 yards	par 3	No 11	408 yards	par 4
No 3	457 yards	par 4	No 12	480 yards	par 5
No 4	497 yards	par 5	No 13	437 yards	par 4
No 5	192 yards	par 3	No 14	183 yards	par 3
No 6	347 yards	par 4	No 15	480 yards	par 5
No 7	403 yards	par 4	No 16	380 yards	par 4
No 8	400 yards	par 4	No 17	555 yards	par 5
No 9	460 yards	par 4	No 18	495 yards	par 5

Card of the course

No 1	518 yards	par 5
No 2	146 yards	par 3
No 3	481 yards	par 5
No 4	394 yards	par 4
No 5	182 yards	par 3
No 6	353 yards	par 4
No 7	201 yards	par 3
No 8	427 yards	par 4
No 9	477 yards	par 5
No 10	187 yards	par 3
No 11	338 yards	par 4
No 12	328 yards	par 4
No 13	484 yards	par 5
No 14	436 yards	par 4
No 15	477 yards	par 5
No 16	221 yards	par 3
No 17	529 yards	par 5
No 18	177 yards	par 3

Card of the course

No 1	310 yards	par 4	No 10	414 yards	par 4
No 2	447 yards	par 4	No 11	190 yards	par 3
No 3	285 yards	par 4	No 12	371 yards	par 4
No 4	453 yards	par 4	No 13	516 yards	par 5
No 5	395 yards	par 4	No 14	520 yards	par 5
No 6	400 yards	par 4	No 15	415 yards	par 4
No 7	176 yards	par 3	No 16	499 yards	par 5
No 8	485 yards	par 5	No 17	176 yards	par 3
No 9	395 yards	par 4	No 18	412 yards	par 4

18 Berkshire
Red course

Out	3,179 yards	36
In	3,177 yards	36
Total	6,356 yards	par 72

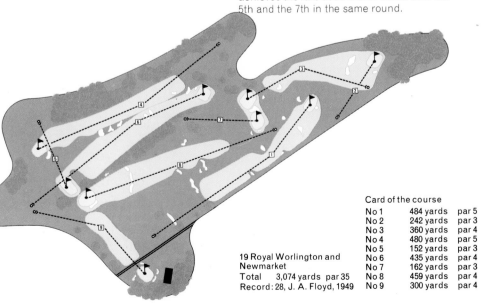

19 Royal Worlington and Newmarket
Total 3,074 yards par 35
Record: 28, J. A. Floyd, 1949

Card of the course

No 1	484 yards	par 5
No 2	242 yards	par 3
No 3	360 yards	par 4
No 4	480 yards	par 5
No 5	152 yards	par 3
No 6	435 yards	par 4
No 7	162 yards	par 3
No 8	459 yards	par 4
No 9	300 yards	par 4

England

20 Hunstanton GC, Norfolk

This is an excellent example of open seaside golf, especially when played in the brisk winds common to this northern Norfolk coast. The course, laid out over gentle undulating linksland between the river Hun and the shores of the Wash, was first played in 1892. Improvements over the next fifty years, mainly under the guidance of James Braid and James Sherlock, brought it up to championship standard. The front nine includes a fine short hole—the 7th—where the ball is driven from a raised tee, 162 yards over a deep hollow to a small, exposed plateau green guarded by an enormous forward bunker. On the back nine, sandhills cradle the fairways and punish any mishit stroke. The 13th, a 387-yard par-four, is a testing hole where the dog-leg to the left must be conquered by two long shots—the first from the tee and the second to carry some very rough country to an island target. The 16th needs a dropping shot over a large diagonal sandtrap invitingly positioned just short of the green. On May 31, 1974, and on the following two consecutive days, this hole was aced three times by a club member, R. J. Taylor.

21 Royal West Norfolk GC, Brancaster

The vast, sleeper-faced bunkers, unyielding greens and savage rough at this Brancaster course suggest all the elements of early links golf. A mixture of tidal marsh and undulating sand-dunes threaten the often windswept fairways and form a formidable array of hazards for the erring shot. Horace Hutchinson and Holcombe Ingleby laid down the course in 1891, and despite alterations to their design, by C. K. Hutchinson in 1928, its character remains little changed. The start is from an ancient rambling clubhouse out along the shoreline to its most easterly point, where the turn is taken. The 8th is on islands in the marsh; the harder and straighter the tee shot, the shorter and easier the second will be. At 485 yards, this par-five needs heroism and strength. The 9th is a fine right-hand dog-leg, a 402-yard par-four, again played over the marsh, but this time with the added hazard of a creek short of the green. The back nine is exactly 400 yards shorter than the outward half, but is generally played into a strong wind, which compensates for the lack of length.

22 Woodhall Spa GC, Lincolnshire

One of the finest British inland courses, Woodhall Spa is built on sandy soil and abounds in heather, silver birch and pine trees. It features some of the most formidable bunkers in the country, particularly those which guard the three short holes, the 5th, 8th and 12th. Against the wind, the 560-yard 9th is doubly severe, for the fairway is completely cut by a line of bunkers set 340 yards from the tee. Failure to clear this hazard, or playing short and safe, means that it is nearly impossible to reach the closely guarded green in three. Many championships have been held here, including the Brabazon Trophy and the ladies' home internationals, played between the countries of Great Britain and Ireland. The original Harry Vardon layout of 1905 was altered by H. S. Colt in 1912, and completely redesigned in the late 1920s by the owner, Colonel S. V. Hotchkin.

Card of the course

No 1	343 yards	par 4	No 10	372 yards	par 4
No 2	532 yards	par 5	No 11	439 yards	par 4
No 3	443 yards	par 4	No 12	356 yards	par 4
No 4	165 yards	par 3	No 13	387 yards	par 4
No 5	424 yards	par 4	No 14	216 yards	par 3
No 6	332 yards	par 4	No 15	476 yards	par 5
No 7	162 yards	par 3	No 16	188 yards	par 3
No 8	483 yards	par 5	No 17	446 yards	par 4
No 9	508 yards	par 5	No 18	398 yards	par 4

20 Hunstanton
Out 3,392 yards 37
In 3,278 yards 35
Total 6,670 yards par 72
Record: 65,
Malcolm E. Gregson,
Schweppes PGA
championship 1967

Card of the course

No 1	400 yards	par 4	No 10	150 yards	par 3
No 2	443 yards	par 4	No 11	480 yards	par 5
No 3	401 yards	par 4	No 12	375 yards	par 4
No 4	125 yards	par 3	No 13	195 yards	par 3
No 5	410 yards	par 4	No 14	430 yards	par 4
No 6	168 yards	par 3	No 15	190 yards	par 3
No 7	477 yards	par 5	No 16	336 yards	par 4
No 8	485 yards	par 5	No 17	375 yards	par 4
No 9	402 yards	par 4	No 18	380 yards	par 4

21 Royal West Norfolk
Out 3,311 yards 36
In 2,911 yards 34
Total 6,222 yards par 70

Card of the course

No 1	359 yards	par 4
No 2	408 yards	par 4
No 3	417 yards	par 4
No 4	415 yards	par 4
No 5	155 yards	par 3
No 6	500 yards	par 5
No 7	435 yards	par 4
No 8	193 yards	par 3
No 9	560 yards	par 5
No 10	333 yards	par 4
No 11	442 yards	par 4
No 12	152 yards	par 3
No 13	437 yards	par 4
No 14	489 yards	par 5
No 15	325 yards	par 4
No 16	398 yards	par 4
No 17	322 yards	par 4
No 18	491 yards	par 5

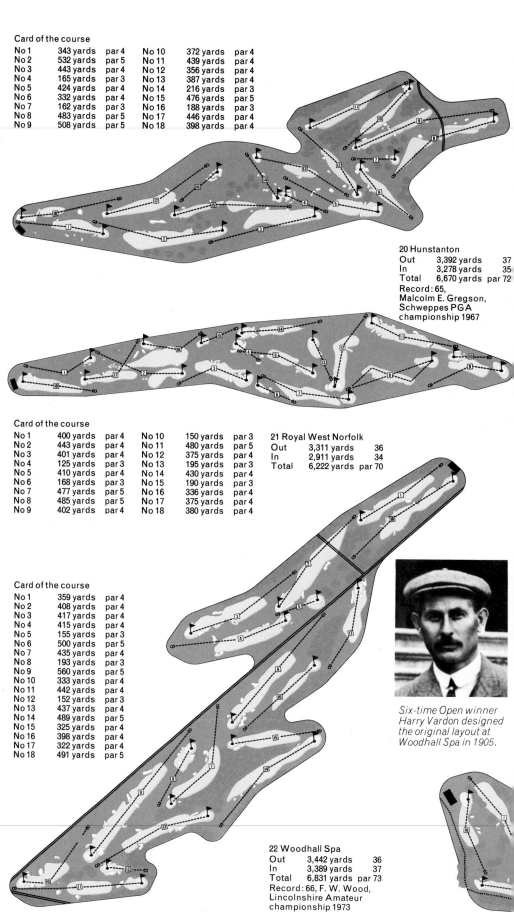

Six-time Open winner Harry Vardon designed the original layout at Woodhall Spa in 1905.

22 Woodhall Spa
Out 3,442 yards 36
In 3,389 yards 37
Total 6,831 yards par 73
Record: 66, F. W. Wood,
Lincolnshire Amateur
championship 1973

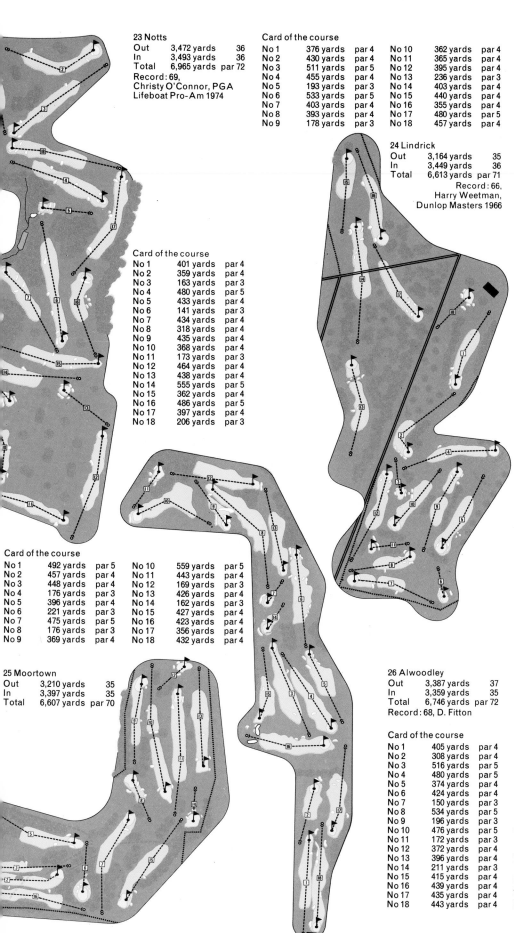

23 Notts

Out	3,472 yards	36
In	3,493 yards	36
Total	6,965 yards	par 72

Record: 69,
Christy O'Connor, PGA
Lifeboat Pro-Am 1974

Card of the course

No 1	376 yards	par 4
No 2	430 yards	par 4
No 3	511 yards	par 5
No 4	455 yards	par 4
No 5	193 yards	par 3
No 6	533 yards	par 5
No 7	403 yards	par 4
No 8	393 yards	par 4
No 9	178 yards	par 3
No 10	362 yards	par 4
No 11	365 yards	par 4
No 12	395 yards	par 4
No 13	236 yards	par 3
No 14	403 yards	par 4
No 15	440 yards	par 4
No 16	355 yards	par 4
No 17	480 yards	par 5
No 18	457 yards	par 4

24 Lindrick

Out	3,164 yards	35
In	3,449 yards	36
Total	6,613 yards	par 71

Record: 66,
Harry Weetman,
Dunlop Masters 1966

Card of the course

No 1	401 yards	par 4
No 2	359 yards	par 4
No 3	163 yards	par 3
No 4	480 yards	par 5
No 5	433 yards	par 4
No 6	141 yards	par 3
No 7	434 yards	par 4
No 8	318 yards	par 4
No 9	435 yards	par 4
No 10	368 yards	par 4
No 11	173 yards	par 3
No 12	464 yards	par 4
No 13	438 yards	par 4
No 14	555 yards	par 5
No 15	362 yards	par 4
No 16	486 yards	par 5
No 17	397 yards	par 4
No 18	206 yards	par 3

Card of the course

No 1	492 yards	par 5	No 10	559 yards	par 5
No 2	457 yards	par 4	No 11	443 yards	par 4
No 3	448 yards	par 4	No 12	169 yards	par 3
No 4	176 yards	par 3	No 13	426 yards	par 4
No 5	396 yards	par 4	No 14	162 yards	par 3
No 6	221 yards	par 3	No 15	427 yards	par 4
No 7	475 yards	par 5	No 16	423 yards	par 4
No 8	176 yards	par 3	No 17	356 yards	par 4
No 9	369 yards	par 4	No 18	432 yards	par 4

25 Moortown

Out	3,210 yards	35
In	3,397 yards	35
Total	6,607 yards	par 70

26 Alwoodley

Out	3,387 yards	37
In	3,359 yards	35
Total	6,746 yards	par 72

Record: 68, D. Fitton

Card of the course

No 1	405 yards	par 4
No 2	308 yards	par 4
No 3	516 yards	par 5
No 4	480 yards	par 5
No 5	374 yards	par 4
No 6	424 yards	par 4
No 7	150 yards	par 3
No 8	534 yards	par 5
No 9	196 yards	par 3
No 10	476 yards	par 5
No 11	172 yards	par 3
No 12	372 yards	par 4
No 13	396 yards	par 4
No 14	211 yards	par 3
No 15	415 yards	par 4
No 16	439 yards	par 4
No 17	435 yards	par 4
No 18	443 yards	par 4

23 Notts GC, Hollinwell

The spacious and testing Notts course was designed by Willie Park Jr, with the bunkers added by J. H. Taylor. The typical heathland course, opened in 1900, winds among silver birch, oak, gorse and heather. At the difficult 8th, a 393-yard par-four, the drive is crucial, requiring a 200-yard carry across Hollinwell lake and through a funnel of trees. The 236-yard 13th is played from an elevated tee down into a valley to a heavily bunkered green. Notts has been host to several British competitions in the last decade, including the Dunlop Masters and the John Player Classic in 1970, when the £25,000 offered as first prize was a world record.

24 Lindrick GC, Worksop

It was at Lindrick in 1957 that Britain won the Ryder Cup for only the third time, giving the course a kind of immortality. It started life in 1891 as the Sheffield and District Golf Club and the only major change has been the resiting of the 2nd and 18th holes. The course is laid out across beautiful heathland, with the River Ryton meandering through it, vast, threatening areas of gorse and an abundance of trees. The limestone subsurface means that the course drains quickly and remains in excellent condition throughout the year. The greens are fine in texture and very fast; the 4th lies in a natural amphitheatre which was once used for prize-fights and cockfighting. Both the new holes offer exacting golf. The 2nd, a 359-yard par-four, is played around a sharp left-hand dog-leg that leaves the green hidden from the tee. The drive must be at least 200 yards to set up the best lie for the approach shot.

25 Moortown GC, Leeds

Designed by Alister Mackenzie in 1909, this Yorkshire moorland course was the venue for the first Ryder Cup match played in Britain—and the first to be won by the British—in 1929. The short 8th, Gibraltar, is a superb hole; the shot is 176 yards to a plateau green built on a foundation of rock and set against the ever-present birch wood. At 559 yards, the 10th provides a stiff test when starting on the longer back nine. Scrub, heather and general rough interrupt the fairway at the 250-yard mark, putting a premium on accuracy with the first two strokes. Flanking sandtraps guard the green and suck in the wayward shot.

26 Alwoodley GC, Leeds

With crisp moorland turf menaced on all sides by heather and bunkers, this fine inland Yorkshire course was laid out by H. S. Colt in 1907; it also bears the hallmark of his partner Alister Mackenzie, who became the club's first secretary. An indication of Alwoodley's challenges comes as early as the 2nd hole: the tee shot must carry 100 yards of gorse, uphill to an unseen fairway. Of the many fine dog-legs, none is better than the 516-yard, par-five 3rd, a unique long hole with only one bunker placed on the left of the fairway to narrow the landing area for the drive. The absence of sandtraps makes the final approach deceptive. The 415-yard par-four 15th is another classic dog-leg. Trees on the right force the short line to be taken to the large, undulating green. The homeward run is slightly the more difficult.

Eire/Sweden

27 Lahinch GC, County Clare

A barometer without hands hangs in the entrance to Lahinch Golf Club. Across its face is a message which reads "See goats"—for if they are in the lee of the clubhouse foul weather is on the way and barometric pressures are neither here nor there. Laid out in 1893 by Old Tom Morris and remodelled thirty-three years later by Alister Mackenzie, it is characterized by massive sandhills, views of the ocean and the dramatic Cliffs of Moher. Oddly, the most celebrated hole, the 156-yard 6th, The Dell, is probably the worst of a course that is stern yet essentially fair. From the tee the green is totally hidden and a mid iron shot must be played over a hill. Judge the distance correctly and the ball is on the green in the hollow beyond; short or long and the next shot is from a precipitous bank. Club member John Burke was eight times Irish Amateur champion, an Irish international from 1930 to 1949 and a member of the Walker Cup side in 1932.

28 Ballybunion GC, County Kerry

Nestling on the southern shore of the Shannon estuary, Ballybunion is a wild and magnificent golf course. Its new clubhouse now offers greater facilities and its position has forced a change in the order of play so that the dull, slogging finish of two undistinguished par-fives now reappears as the 4th and 5th. Although the holes remain unchanged they are tackled with a livelier mental and physical approach early in the round. The course boasts the biggest sandhills of any links in the British Isles— and certainly the closest proximity to the sea. After a modest opening this becomes apparent at the 7th, a 417-yard par-four, laid out along the shore with a small plateau green clinging precariously to the dunes above the Atlantic. The 10th, 356 yards, dog-legs its way left, back to the very edge of the ocean, and the 443-yard 11th has the twin threat of sandhills to the left and Atlantic to the right. Founded in 1896, the club was the scene of James Bruen's incredible emergence at the age of seventeen as Irish Amateur champion in 1937.

29 Halmstad GC, Tylosand

Halmstad Golf Club, in the picturesque west coast town of Tylosand, mid-way between Malmö and Gothenberg, is a fine inland course not unlike Wentworth in Britain. The challenging eighteen-hole course, designed by Rafael Sandblom of Stockholm in 1938, and the less demanding nine-hole layout, are cut through predominantly pine forest on relatively flat, quick-drying sandy soil. Well-designed dog-leg holes, such as the 6th, 8th, 9th and 10th, four exceptional par-fours, perceptive bunkering and the ever-present trees combine to present a fine test of golf. An extremely comfortable and well-equipped clubhouse commands a central position and floodlit night putting competitions are a feature of the club's friendly, relaxed atmosphere. In 1958 it hosted the Scandinavian Amateur and Ladies' championships and there are frequent competitions to which visitors are encouraged, particularly during "Tylosand Week" in August, when the welcome is even warmer than usual.

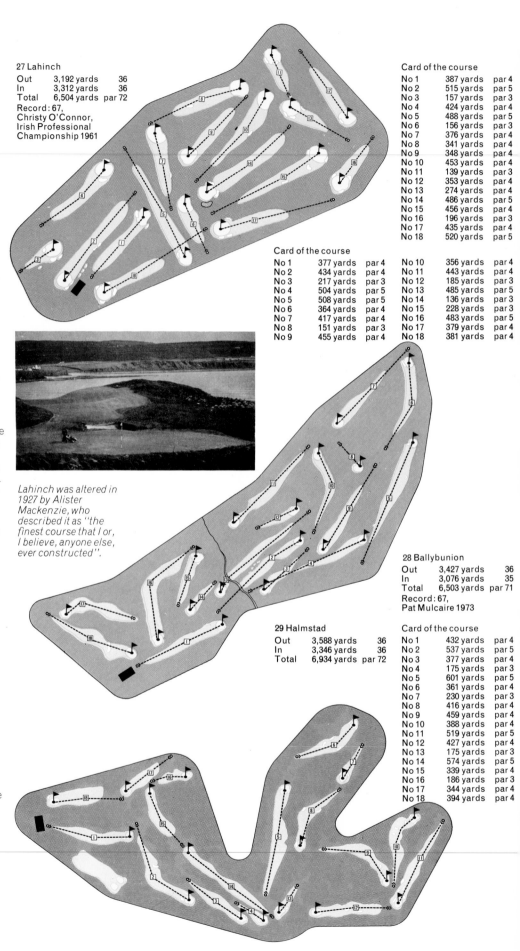

Lahinch was altered in 1927 by Alister Mackenzie, who described it as "the finest course that I or, I believe, anyone else, ever constructed".

27 Lahinch

Out	3,192 yards	36
In	3,312 yards	36
Total	6,504 yards	par 72

Record: 67, Christy O'Connor, Irish Professional Championship 1961

Card of the course

No 1	387 yards	par 4
No 2	515 yards	par 5
No 3	157 yards	par 3
No 4	424 yards	par 4
No 5	488 yards	par 5
No 6	156 yards	par 3
No 7	376 yards	par 4
No 8	341 yards	par 4
No 9	348 yards	par 4
No 10	453 yards	par 4
No 11	139 yards	par 3
No 12	353 yards	par 4
No 13	274 yards	par 4
No 14	486 yards	par 5
No 15	456 yards	par 4
No 16	196 yards	par 3
No 17	435 yards	par 4
No 18	520 yards	par 5

28 Ballybunion

Card of the course

No 1	377 yards	par 4	No 10	356 yards	par 4
No 2	434 yards	par 4	No 11	443 yards	par 4
No 3	217 yards	par 3	No 12	185 yards	par 3
No 4	504 yards	par 5	No 13	485 yards	par 5
No 5	508 yards	par 5	No 14	136 yards	par 3
No 6	364 yards	par 4	No 15	228 yards	par 3
No 7	417 yards	par 4	No 16	483 yards	par 5
No 8	151 yards	par 3	No 17	379 yards	par 4
No 9	455 yards	par 4	No 18	381 yards	par 4

Out	3,427 yards	36
In	3,076 yards	35
Total	6,503 yards	par 71

Record: 67, Pat Mulcaire 1973

29 Halmstad

Out	3,588 yards	36
In	3,346 yards	36
Total	6,934 yards	par 72

Card of the course

No 1	432 yards	par 4
No 2	537 yards	par 5
No 3	377 yards	par 4
No 4	175 yards	par 3
No 5	601 yards	par 5
No 6	361 yards	par 4
No 7	230 yards	par 3
No 8	416 yards	par 4
No 9	459 yards	par 4
No 10	388 yards	par 4
No 11	519 yards	par 5
No 12	427 yards	par 4
No 13	175 yards	par 3
No 14	574 yards	par 5
No 15	339 yards	par 4
No 16	186 yards	par 3
No 17	344 yards	par 4
No 18	394 yards	par 4

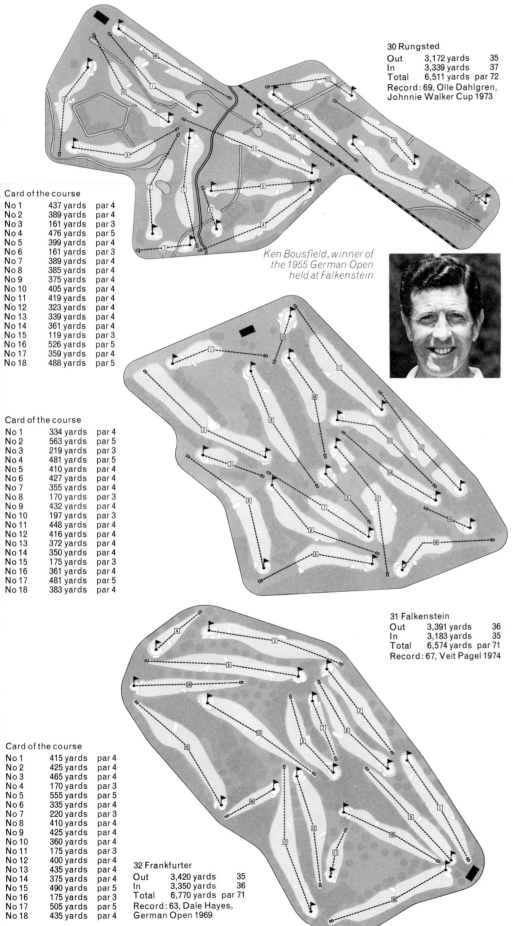

Card of the course

No 1	437 yards	par 4
No 2	389 yards	par 4
No 3	161 yards	par 3
No 4	476 yards	par 5
No 5	399 yards	par 4
No 6	161 yards	par 3
No 7	389 yards	par 4
No 8	385 yards	par 4
No 9	375 yards	par 4
No 10	405 yards	par 4
No 11	419 yards	par 4
No 12	323 yards	par 4
No 13	339 yards	par 4
No 14	361 yards	par 4
No 15	119 yards	par 3
No 16	526 yards	par 5
No 17	359 yards	par 4
No 18	488 yards	par 5

30 Rungsted

Out	3,172 yards	35
In	3,339 yards	37
Total	6,511 yards	par 72

Record: 69, Olle Dahlgren, Johnnie Walker Cup 1973

Ken Bousfield, winner of the 1955 German Open held at Falkenstein

Card of the course

No 1	334 yards	par 4
No 2	563 yards	par 5
No 3	219 yards	par 3
No 4	481 yards	par 5
No 5	410 yards	par 4
No 6	427 yards	par 4
No 7	355 yards	par 4
No 8	170 yards	par 3
No 9	432 yards	par 4
No 10	197 yards	par 3
No 11	448 yards	par 4
No 12	416 yards	par 4
No 13	372 yards	par 4
No 14	350 yards	par 4
No 15	175 yards	par 3
No 16	361 yards	par 4
No 17	481 yards	par 5
No 18	383 yards	par 4

31 Falkenstein

Out	3,391 yards	36
In	3,183 yards	35
Total	6,574 yards	par 71

Record: 67, Veit Pagel 1974

Card of the course

No 1	415 yards	par 4
No 2	425 yards	par 4
No 3	465 yards	par 4
No 4	170 yards	par 3
No 5	555 yards	par 5
No 6	335 yards	par 4
No 7	220 yards	par 3
No 8	410 yards	par 4
No 9	425 yards	par 4
No 10	360 yards	par 4
No 11	175 yards	par 3
No 12	400 yards	par 4
No 13	435 yards	par 4
No 14	375 yards	par 4
No 15	490 yards	par 5
No 16	175 yards	par 3
No 17	505 yards	par 5
No 18	435 yards	par 4

32 Frankfurter

Out	3,420 yards	35
In	3,350 yards	36
Total	6,770 yards	par 71

Record: 63, Dale Hayes, German Open 1969

30 Rungsted GC, Rungsted Kyst

The scene of many Scandinavian championships, Rungsted is distinguished by the problems of hilly terrain with deep ravines and encroaching beech woods. Its greatest weakness is the imbalance caused by the easiest holes, the 12th to the 15th, occurring together. At this point the play is building to a tough climax and these four cause a break in concentration before the final challenge, of which the centrepiece is the 17th. The drive here is threatened by out-of-bounds on the left and, as the ball loses height, it clears a belt of sheltering trees and may be caught by the prevailing westerly wind and carried into deep rough or the woods that lie on the right of the narrow fairway. Pinpoint accuracy from the tee is essential for any chance to attack the target with the second shot, which must negotiate trees short of the raised green. Ravines on either side await any ball that is slightly off the target, which is pear shaped with possibilities for very difficult pin placings. Rungsted was designed by C. K. Mackenzie and opened in 1937. O. Bojensen made slight alterations to the course in 1969.

31 Falkenstein GC, Hamburg

A fine natural course showing obvious signs of the game's Scottish origins, Falkenstein was laid out in 1930, by architects Alison and Morrison, on gently undulating ground with quick-draining sandy subsoil which encourages the growth of heather, pines and silver birch. Alterations were made later by Dr Bernard von Limburger. The course features many well-contrived dog-leg holes, with the sparing but intelligent use of sandtraps. The massive 2nd, more than 560 yards, swings to the left past a giant bunker and presents the handicap golfer with a difficult third shot to a green that is guarded by sand on both sides. The 17th, another par-five, is eighty yards shorter yet has vast areas of heather in front of the tee and crossing the fairway short of the green. In the German National Amateur of 1973, Rainer Falge scored an eagle-three, only to lose the hole and the match to a spectacular holed second shot by Jens Harder, the eventual runner-up.

32 Frankfurter GC, Frankfurt

With a total length of just under 6,800 yards, the Frankfurter Golf Club is decidedly short by modern championship standards. The difficulty here is in overcoming the very large greens, which demand second-shot accuracy to get near the pin. The course is essentially flat, but the fairways are carved through forest and the problems set by the trees add to the scoring difficulties. The best hole is probably the 7th, a 220-yard par-three that is flanked on the lip of the green by left and right bunkers; it requires a full-blooded tee shot into the heart of the target. Little has been done to the original H. S. Colt and John Morrison layout of 1928, and the course attracts a great international following because it is within easy reach of the city. The German Open has been held here six times since 1938, when Henry Cotton won the second of his hat-trick of victories. It was also the scene of South African Dale Hayes's German Amateur triumph in 1969.

Netherlands/Belgium

33 Haagsche GC, Wassenaar

The Dutch coastline is similar in many places to the best links country of the British Isles, and the Haagsche course is ideally sited for capitalizing on the best features of seaside golf. Designed in 1939 by British architects Colt, Alison and Morrison, it has needed very little change. The 481-yard par-five 6th is the best example of the course's exacting qualities. From the championship tee there is a hundred-yard carry to the fairway target area left of centre. The correct lie then allows a glimpse of the distant green past a huge sandhill on the right. One large bunker cutting into the left face of the green is sufficient protection. It was here, during the 1972 Dutch Open, that eventual winner Jack Newton hit a spectacular shot. His massive second rolled across the green and into the cup for a double-eagle. His total of 64 equalled the course record set earlier in the day by Peter Oosterhuis, who repeated his feat a year later.

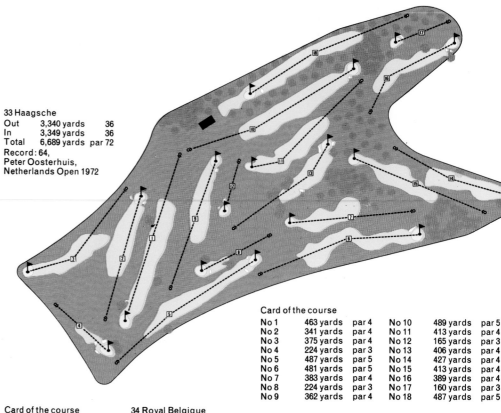

33 Haagsche

Out	3,340 yards	36
In	3,349 yards	36
Total	6,689 yards	par 72

Record: 64,
Peter Oosterhuis,
Netherlands Open 1972

Card of the course

No 1	463 yards	par 4	No 10	489 yards	par 5
No 2	341 yards	par 4	No 11	413 yards	par 4
No 3	375 yards	par 4	No 12	165 yards	par 3
No 4	224 yards	par 3	No 13	406 yards	par 4
No 5	487 yards	par 5	No 14	427 yards	par 4
No 6	481 yards	par 5	No 15	413 yards	par 4
No 7	383 yards	par 4	No 16	389 yards	par 4
No 8	224 yards	par 3	No 17	160 yards	par 3
No 9	362 yards	par 4	No 18	487 yards	par 5

34 Royal Belgique GC, Tervuren

With a clubhouse that is a national monument and a course that was built by royal command, the Royal Golf Club de Belgique indeed does justice to its auspicious origins. Tom Simpson laid out the eighteen holes on a clay subsoil in an area of parkland in 1904. He constructed nine short par-fours, making club selection for the second shot a critical decision. Of the long par-fours, the 17th is the most difficult. Dog-legged right, and with the entrance to the fairway flanked by two large sandtraps, it demands a drive which must be as long as possible to line up the second with a clear shot. The spacious, stepped green is menaced by two bunkers guarding the front; three putts are certainly not uncommon here for the average golfer. After the rigours of the 17th, the final hole is a welcome relief. A short par-four of 302 yards, the last hundred yards downhill, it is easily driven with the help of the prevailing wind by carrying a small hill at 200 yards and keeping to the left of the fairway to avoid a greenside trap. The royal connection is upheld to this day, with King Baudouin as honorary president.

Card of the course

No 1	488 yards	par 5
No 2	422 yards	par 4
No 3	155 yards	par 3
No 4	417 yards	par 4
No 5	514 yards	par 5
No 6	194 yards	par 3
No 7	377 yards	par 4
No 8	361 yards	par 4
No 9	337 yards	par 4
No 10	350 yards	par 4
No 11	398 yards	par 4
No 12	183 yards	par 3
No 13	525 yards	par 5
No 14	328 yards	par 4
No 15	509 yards	par 5
No 16	331 yards	par 4
No 17	437 yards	par 4
No 18	302 yards	par 4

34 Royal Belgique

Out	3,265 yards	36
In	3,363 yards	37
Total	6,628 yards	par 73

Record: 65,
Flory van Donck,
Belgian Open 1935

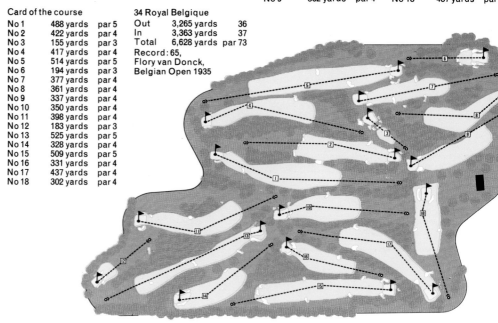

35 Royal Waterloo GC, Ohain

The first of Henry Cotton's three British Open victories, in 1934, came when he was the professional at the original Royal Waterloo Golf Club, whose course had been laid out eleven years earlier. In 1960 a new eighteen holes were designed by Fred Hawtree on a site at Ohain near Brussels. The greens are consistently slow, and the course is split into two distinct playing sections: the first ten holes and the finishing pair run over a wide, undulating plain with a scattering of small trees, but the 11th to the 16th climb and drop through a high beech wood. The dramatic contrast is best seen at the 13th, a 396-yard par-four dog-leg running through a wooded valley—a claustrophobic hole after the open plains. The course record is 67, set by Donald Swaelens, for many years the club's professional until his untimely death while still in his thirties.

35 Royal Waterloo

Out	3,376 yards	36
In	3,437 yards	37
Total	6,813 yards	par 73

Record: 67, Donald Swaelens

Card of the course

No 1	405 yards	par 4
No 2	362 yards	par 4
No 3	538 yards	par 5
No 4	190 yards	par 3
No 5	519 yards	par 5
No 6	415 yards	par 4
No 7	173 yards	par 3
No 8	363 yards	par 4
No 9	411 yards	par 4
No 10	401 yards	par 4
No 11	422 yards	par 4
No 12	195 yards	par 3
No 13	396 yards	par 4
No 14	399 yards	par 4
No 15	165 yards	par 3
No 16	479 yards	par 5
No 17	492 yards	par 5
No 18	488 yards	par 5

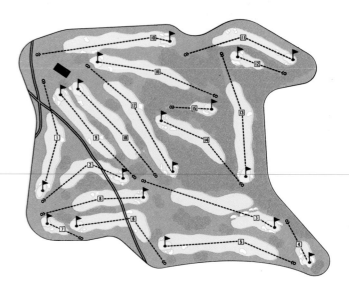

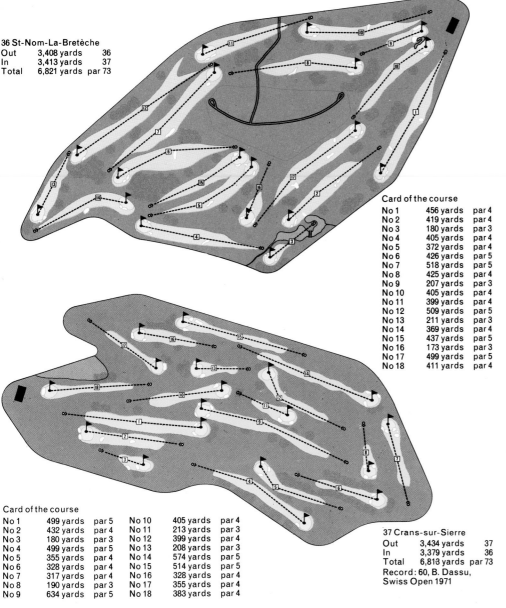

36 St-Nom-La-Bretèche

Out	3,408 yards	36
In	3,413 yards	37
Total	6,821 yards	par 73

Card of the course

No 1	456 yards	par 4
No 2	419 yards	par 4
No 3	180 yards	par 3
No 4	405 yards	par 4
No 5	372 yards	par 4
No 6	426 yards	par 5
No 7	518 yards	par 5
No 8	425 yards	par 4
No 9	207 yards	par 3
No 10	405 yards	par 4
No 11	399 yards	par 4
No 12	509 yards	par 5
No 13	211 yards	par 3
No 14	369 yards	par 4
No 15	437 yards	par 5
No 16	173 yards	par 3
No 17	499 yards	par 5
No 18	411 yards	par 4

Card of the course

No 1	499 yards	par 5	No 10	405 yards	par 4
No 2	432 yards	par 4	No 11	213 yards	par 3
No 3	180 yards	par 3	No 12	399 yards	par 4
No 4	499 yards	par 5	No 13	208 yards	par 3
No 5	355 yards	par 4	No 14	574 yards	par 5
No 6	328 yards	par 4	No 15	514 yards	par 5
No 7	317 yards	par 4	No 16	328 yards	par 4
No 8	190 yards	par 3	No 17	355 yards	par 4
No 9	634 yards	par 5	No 18	383 yards	par 4

37 Crans-sur-Sierre

Out	3,434 yards	37
In	3,379 yards	36
Total	6,813 yards	par 73

Record: 60, B. Dassu,
Swiss Open 1971

38 Seefeld-Wildmoos

Out	3,356 yards	36
In	3,396 yards	36
Total	6,752 yards	par 72

Record: 68,
Gerhard König, Seefeld
Pro-Am 1975

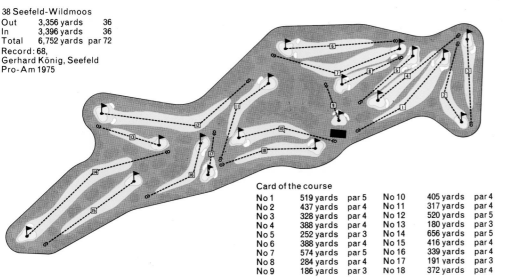

Card of the course

No 1	519 yards	par 5	No 10	405 yards	par 4
No 2	437 yards	par 4	No 11	317 yards	par 4
No 3	328 yards	par 4	No 12	520 yards	par 5
No 4	388 yards	par 4	No 13	180 yards	par 3
No 5	252 yards	par 3	No 14	656 yards	par 5
No 6	388 yards	par 4	No 15	416 yards	par 4
No 7	574 yards	par 5	No 16	339 yards	par 4
No 8	284 yards	par 4	No 17	191 yards	par 3
No 9	186 yards	par 3	No 18	372 yards	par 4

36 Saint-Nom-La-Bretèche GC, Versailles

There are many fine and exclusive golf clubs in the area that surrounds Paris, and Saint-Nom-La-Bretèche rates with the highest. Situated twelve miles west of the city in the pleasant countryside of La Tuilerie, it has a magnificent eighteenth-century manor house that overlooks its two excellent courses—the Red and the Blue. Both were designed in 1959 by Fred Hawtree, on lightly wooded, undulating terrain; the Red course is the higher of the two. The championship layout, first played in 1963, takes the 1st from the Blue and the remainder from the Red. Its most memorable feature is the small horseshoe lake that separates the 9th and 18th greens. The World Cup was the inaugural event and it has since been followed by two French Opens, in 1965 and 1969, and since 1970 by the annual Lancôme Trophy.

37 Crans-sur-Sierre GC, Valais

Few major championship courses are better known for their surroundings than their quality, but Crans-sur-Sierre, set on a high green mountain plateau 5,000 feet up in the Berner Alps, offers one of the most spectacular settings for golf anywhere. Completely encircled by high, snow-capped peaks, the course has been the venue for seven Swiss Opens. Although unplayable for half the year, in summer it offers ideal conditions, its fairly level greens standing out against the tall stands of pines. The holes undulate gently and are reasonably wide open with minimal rough and a few strategically placed evergreens. The 6th, a 328-yard par-four, is enveloped on all sides by pines and demands a well-judged approach shot to a long, elevated green that is set among a confusion of large bunkers. At 6,813 yards the course is full by European standards, but this is compensated for by the high altitude which lets the ball fly far. In the 1971 Swiss Open, Baldovino Dassu scored a massive thirteen-under-par 60 and captured the course record.

38 Seefeld-Wildmoos GC, Tirol

A major ski resort needs steep mountain slopes at high altitude, often densely wooded, with the longest possible snow season. Seefeld not only meets these criteria but also boasts a spectacular new golf course. Designed by British architect Donald Harradine and located at 4,300 feet, it is carved out of some of the most fiendish golfing country imaginable. After the early holes over relatively level ground, the course climbs and plunges through forests of pine and birch, presenting some extraordinarily tight holes. Most memorable are the 9th, only 186 yards but a good 200 feet straight down the mountainside; and the 14th, a 656-yard par-five running sharply downhill through the woods and reachable with two accurate long shots. Although under several feet of snow for almost half the year, the playing conditions in summer are excellent, the result of Herculean efforts by the club. Their endeavours have preserved a tight course where the emphasis is on percentage golf, particularly when approaching the elevated greens.

Greece/Italy/Spain

39 Glyfada GC, Athens

Set between gently rolling mountain slopes and the sparkling Saronic Gulf, Glyfada is Greece's premier course. The eighteen holes, constructed in 1967, were designed by Donald Harradine, who cleverly lined each hole with umbrella pines to create the chief hazards. Athens airport, a mere 500 yards from the practice tee, is a source of constant noise and can become an almost intolerable distraction. Nevertheless, the course's narrow dog-legs, fast greens and pine-dominated rough provide excellent surroundings for Mediterranean-type golf. From the back tees there is enough length to test the best, making the course very tight and favouring players with powerful drives. The toughest hole is the 9th, a 438-yard par-four, gently bending to the left with a deep hollow, often filled with water for tournament play, before the green.

40 Rome GC, Aquasanta

Golf has been played at Aquasanta, with its reputedly medicinal waters, for more than seventy years. Here the Rome Golf Club, set in low hills and crossed by meandering streams, offers luxuriant golf in historic surroundings, with views of old aqueducts and the legendary Appian Way. The course is short by championship standards but tight enough to be testing—the professional record is 68, only three under par. Strategically placed pines and other trees guard the fairways, and the network of streams form a hazard at several holes. The condition of this well-watered course is always superb, as might be expected of such an exclusive club. It is fairly level to play, with particularly featureless and deceptive greens.

41 Pevero GC, Sardinia

The terrain at Pevero is so imposing and unyielding that it forced the architect, Robert Trent Jones, to follow its contours. developing nature's own golf holes rather than reshaping and building them with machines. The 4th. at 385 yards. starts an exhilarating sequence, plunging into a valley with distant views of Corsica to a green set along one slope. It is followed by a downhill par-three with an enormous rock outcrop guarding the right and a lake to the left. The 6th is a par-four. along and across a lake. and it is succeeded by a 190-yard one-shotter back across the lake to a shallow green bunkered front and rear.

42 El Prat GC, Barcelona

A flat, sandy coastal stretch south of Barcelona has given rise to the most untypical of all Spanish courses at El Prat—and without doubt one of the finest. Created by the late Javier Arana in 1954, it is a masterpiece of understatement, making excellent but far from penal use of the abundant umbrella pines; the emphasis is on strategic positioning from the tee, with subtle moulding around the greens and minimal but significant bunkering. The course starts among pines close to the sea, but they are well spaced and the rough beneath is sparse. Then the holes move to more open country inland before turning along the shore to the clubhouse for the back nine. The second nine are slightly sterner, with the 14th epitomizing the whole course—it is a par-four needing a long iron second to a beautifully shaped green.

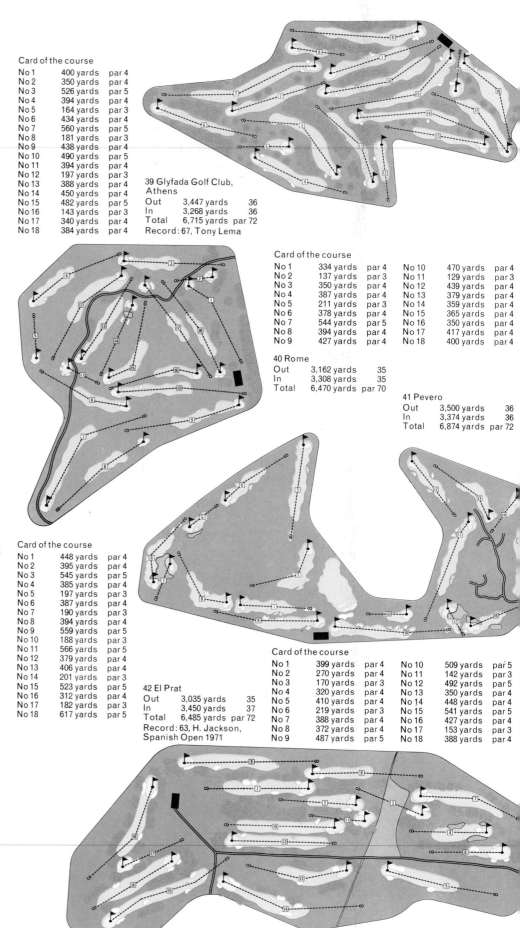

Card of the course

No 1	400 yards	par 4
No 2	350 yards	par 4
No 3	526 yards	par 5
No 4	394 yards	par 4
No 5	164 yards	par 3
No 6	434 yards	par 4
No 7	560 yards	par 5
No 8	181 yards	par 3
No 9	438 yards	par 4
No 10	490 yards	par 5
No 11	394 yards	par 4
No 12	197 yards	par 3
No 13	388 yards	par 4
No 14	450 yards	par 4
No 15	482 yards	par 5
No 16	143 yards	par 3
No 17	340 yards	par 4
No 18	384 yards	par 4

39 Glyfada Golf Club, Athens

Out	3,447 yards	36
In	3,268 yards	36
Total	6,715 yards	par 72

Record: 67, Tony Lema

Card of the course

No 1	334 yards	par 4	No 10	470 yards	par 4
No 2	137 yards	par 3	No 11	129 yards	par 3
No 3	350 yards	par 4	No 12	439 yards	par 4
No 4	387 yards	par 4	No 13	379 yards	par 4
No 5	211 yards	par 3	No 14	359 yards	par 4
No 6	378 yards	par 4	No 15	365 yards	par 4
No 7	544 yards	par 5	No 16	350 yards	par 4
No 8	394 yards	par 4	No 17	417 yards	par 4
No 9	427 yards	par 4	No 18	400 yards	par 4

40 Rome

Out	3,162 yards	35
In	3,308 yards	35
Total	6,470 yards	par 70

41 Pevero

Out	3,500 yards	36
In	3,374 yards	36
Total	6,874 yards	par 72

Card of the course

No 1	448 yards	par 4
No 2	395 yards	par 4
No 3	545 yards	par 5
No 4	385 yards	par 4
No 5	197 yards	par 3
No 6	387 yards	par 4
No 7	190 yards	par 3
No 8	394 yards	par 4
No 9	559 yards	par 5
No 10	188 yards	par 3
No 11	566 yards	par 5
No 12	379 yards	par 4
No 13	406 yards	par 4
No 14	201 yards	par 3
No 15	523 yards	par 5
No 16	312 yards	par 4
No 17	182 yards	par 3
No 18	617 yards	par 5

42 El Prat

Out	3,035 yards	35
In	3,450 yards	37
Total	6,485 yards	par 72

Record: 63, H. Jackson, Spanish Open 1971

Card of the course

No 1	399 yards	par 4	No 10	509 yards	par 5
No 2	270 yards	par 4	No 11	142 yards	par 3
No 3	170 yards	par 3	No 12	492 yards	par 5
No 4	320 yards	par 4	No 13	350 yards	par 4
No 5	410 yards	par 4	No 14	448 yards	par 4
No 6	219 yards	par 3	No 15	541 yards	par 5
No 7	388 yards	par 4	No 16	427 yards	par 4
No 8	372 yards	par 4	No 17	153 yards	par 3
No 9	487 yards	par 5	No 18	388 yards	par 4

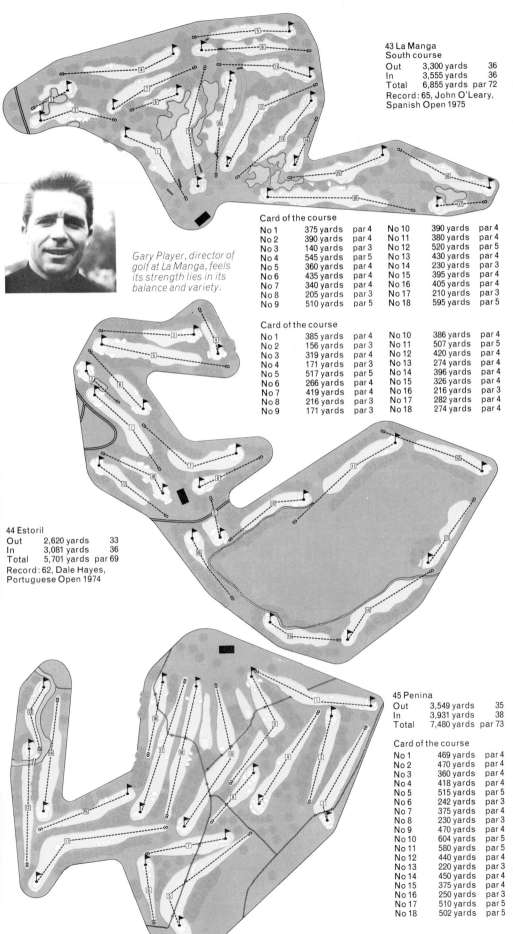

Gary Player, director of golf at La Manga, feels its strength lies in its balance and variety.

43 La Manga
South course

Out	3,300 yards	36
In	3,555 yards	36
Total	6,855 yards	par 72

Record: 65, John O'Leary, Spanish Open 1975

Card of the course

No 1	375 yards	par 4	No 10	390 yards	par 4
No 2	390 yards	par 4	No 11	380 yards	par 4
No 3	140 yards	par 3	No 12	520 yards	par 5
No 4	545 yards	par 5	No 13	430 yards	par 4
No 5	360 yards	par 4	No 14	230 yards	par 3
No 6	435 yards	par 4	No 15	395 yards	par 4
No 7	340 yards	par 4	No 16	405 yards	par 4
No 8	205 yards	par 3	No 17	210 yards	par 3
No 9	510 yards	par 5	No 18	595 yards	par 5

Card of the course

No 1	385 yards	par 4	No 10	386 yards	par 4
No 2	156 yards	par 3	No 11	507 yards	par 5
No 3	319 yards	par 4	No 12	420 yards	par 4
No 4	171 yards	par 3	No 13	274 yards	par 4
No 5	517 yards	par 5	No 14	396 yards	par 4
No 6	266 yards	par 4	No 15	326 yards	par 4
No 7	419 yards	par 4	No 16	216 yards	par 3
No 8	216 yards	par 3	No 17	282 yards	par 4
No 9	171 yards	par 3	No 18	274 yards	par 4

44 Estoril

Out	2,620 yards	33
In	3,081 yards	36
Total	5,701 yards	par 69

Record: 62, Dale Hayes, Portuguese Open 1974

45 Penina

Out	3,549 yards	35
In	3,931 yards	38
Total	7,480 yards	par 73

Card of the course

No 1	469 yards	par 4
No 2	470 yards	par 4
No 3	360 yards	par 4
No 4	418 yards	par 4
No 5	515 yards	par 5
No 6	242 yards	par 3
No 7	375 yards	par 4
No 8	230 yards	par 3
No 9	470 yards	par 4
No 10	604 yards	par 5
No 11	580 yards	par 5
No 12	440 yards	par 4
No 13	220 yards	par 3
No 14	450 yards	par 4
No 15	375 yards	par 4
No 16	250 yards	par 3
No 17	510 yards	par 5
No 18	502 yards	par 5

43 La Manga GC, Murcia

In the mild climate of the Costa Blanca, south of Alicante, the thirty-six holes that form the North and South courses of La Manga gaze out over the bay of Mar Menor. Set amongst more than 3,000 date palms, the courses—designed by American Robert Dean Putnam in 1971—are backed by a range of low, undulating mountains and distinguished by large bunkers, lakes and "barancas", deep ravines that swallow any mishit ball. The tees and fairways are of the highest quality, with plenty of room to manoeuvre, and the greens are spacious. The South course is the championship layout and here the short 3rd creates some interesting problems. At 140 yards, with a lake lying prominently to the right, it would normally present little difficulty. Because it was so easy, Gary Player suggested that a shallow bunker be placed in the middle of the green. This effectively reduces its size by half and forces the golfer to go for whichever side the flag is located.

44 Estoril GC, Lisbon

Set on high ground behind the Lisbon resort of Estoril, with excellent views out to sea, this short but highly challenging course has been a regular venue for the Portuguese Open and Amateur championships. Mackenzie Ross, who designed it in 1945, has made clever use of the pine and eucalyptus trees which, with the steeply sloping land, means that accuracy is more important than length. Placement off the tee, bold, well-struck approach shots and the regular quest of birdie-putts mark a round of golf here. At the 9th, with its 150-foot elevated tee, a deceptive mid iron shot must be played on to the contoured green 171 yards away. Not only must the stroke be to the heart of the severely bunkered green but it also has to contend with a fluky wind which blows from left to right and threatens to carry the ball into the flanking trees.

45 Penina GC, Algarve

The brainchild of Henry Cotton, who was for many years its overlord, Penina has surmounted its major disadvantage of being absolutely flat. During its construction on an old ricefield in 1964, 360,000 trees and shrubs were planted to separate the holes and provide visual relief as well as playing interest. The holes are imaginatively protected by a series of strategically sited drainage canals, lakes and massive sandtraps. This calls for precise, nominated shots, and rewards the thoughtful approach rather than the heroic. The well-watered, elevated greens, which Doug Sanders rated the best he had ever putted on, are a major feature of this twenty-seven hole layout, designed as part of a resort complex in the south of Portugal near Portimao. A number of championships have been played here, including the 1976 World Amateur Team Championship. With tees up to one hundred yards long, the Penina course can be extended to prodigious lengths for tournament play.

United States of America

46 Doral CC, Miami, Fla.

Doral is the epitome of Florida resort golf. Ninety per cent of the golfers who play there are winter vacationers, yet none of its four courses is in any way easy, the Blue undeniably being of championship calibre. Nick-named the "Blue Monster" by professionals, largely because of the remarkable final hole, this Dick Wilson inspired layout also has a stunning 9th. The 437-yard par-four 18th is an absolute dream of design, where water, on the left, has to be carried twice on the run in to a green half encircled by the same lake. The short 9th needs a real all-or-nothing shot, as 180 yards of water separate the green from the tee. In all, Wilson built eight lakes during construction and the holes, interspersed by a few palm trees, were tailored around them. The chief annual event is the Doral Open, a major stop on the United States tournament circuit.

47 Jupiter Hills Club, Tequesta, Fla.

Jupiter Hills is an ultra-exclusive club, a joint financial venture between architect George Fazio and two old friends, comedian Bob Hope and motor industrialist William Ford. It has turned out to be Fazio's favourite course and one to which he is constantly making subtle improvements. It is nearly impossible to pick the best hole. Even Fazio cannot make up his mind, but sometimes cites the 11th, a delightful par-three with a positively Machiavellian twist to its design. It has six tees and can be played at virtually any length between 195 yards and 120 yards, but it is the two angles of approach that the two tees offer that make the hole. The green is long and narrow and on one line straightaway from the tees; on the other it is slightly angled and therefore easier to hit, though protected by water. But the outstanding characteristic of the course is that it is hilly—a full sixty feet from its lowest to its highest point, an unheard of amount of "drop" in the flatness of Florida's "golf coast" stretching from the Palm Beaches to Miami.

48 Sea Island GC, St Simons Is, Ga.

Sea Island's oceanside golf course was laid out in 1929 on the Retreat Plantation—an early nineteenth-century cotton farm—by the English architects H. S. Colt and Charles Alison. They designed two nine-holers which now form eighteen of the club's thirty-six holes. The Seaside is the front nine and rolls over the broad undulating fairways set amongst the dunes, edged by the ocean and surrounded by waterways and marshland. The Plantation course, which makes up the back nine, scythes through great forests of oak and pine, occasionally touching the marsh and often crossing or playing alongside the lagoons. The greens are well elevated and trapped on all sides. The 7th hole, White Heron, is a real equalizer, as the drive has to carry a broad marsh inlet where a stiff breeze can nudge the ball into the sea. The alternative is to play to a thin peninsula of fairway, which leaves the second shot blind over two large bunkers with the brackish marsh threatening on the right. Bobby Jones first focused national attention on the club and his record of 67 stood for many years.

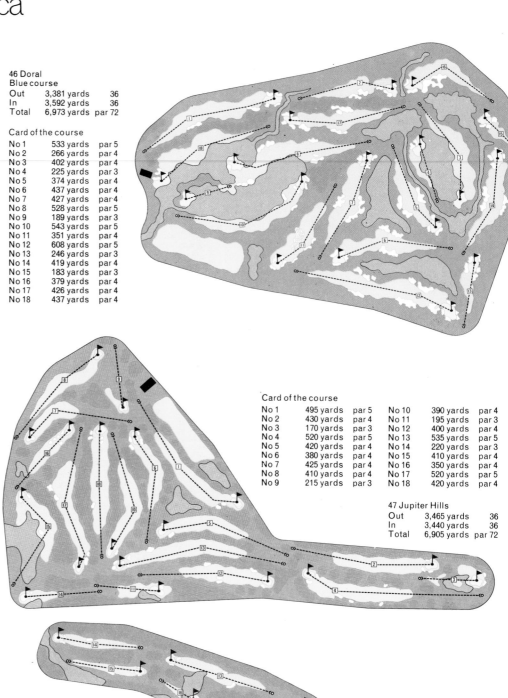

46 Doral
Blue course

Out	3,381 yards	36
In	3,592 yards	36
Total	6,973 yards	par 72

Card of the course

No 1	533 yards	par 5
No 2	266 yards	par 4
No 3	402 yards	par 4
No 4	225 yards	par 3
No 5	374 yards	par 4
No 6	437 yards	par 4
No 7	427 yards	par 4
No 8	528 yards	par 5
No 9	189 yards	par 3
No 10	543 yards	par 5
No 11	351 yards	par 4
No 12	608 yards	par 5
No 13	246 yards	par 3
No 14	419 yards	par 4
No 15	183 yards	par 3
No 16	379 yards	par 4
No 17	426 yards	par 4
No 18	437 yards	par 4

Card of the course

No 1	495 yards	par 5	No 10	390 yards	par 4
No 2	430 yards	par 4	No 11	195 yards	par 3
No 3	170 yards	par 3	No 12	400 yards	par 4
No 4	520 yards	par 5	No 13	535 yards	par 5
No 5	420 yards	par 4	No 14	220 yards	par 3
No 6	380 yards	par 4	No 15	410 yards	par 4
No 7	425 yards	par 4	No 16	350 yards	par 4
No 8	410 yards	par 4	No 17	520 yards	par 5
No 9	215 yards	par 3	No 18	420 yards	par 4

47 Jupiter Hills

Out	3,465 yards	36
In	3,440 yards	36
Total	6,905 yards	par 72

48 Sea Island

Out	3,371 yards	36
In	3,343 yards	36
Total	6,714 yards	par 72
Record: 63, Sam Snead, 1958		

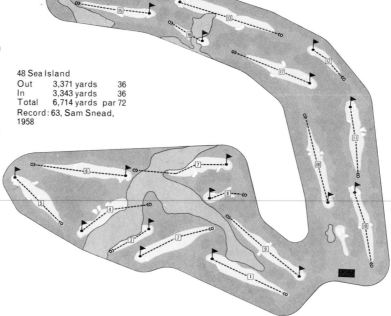

Card of the course

No 1	400 yards	par 4
No 2	431 yards	par 4
No 3	228 yards	par 3
No 4	382 yards	par 4
No 5	340 yards	par 4
No 6	480 yards	par 5
No 7	435 yards	par 4
No 8	197 yards	par 3
No 9	478 yards	par 5
No 10	375 yards	par 4
No 11	360 yards	par 4
No 12	225 yards	par 3
No 13	540 yards	par 5
No 14	409 yards	par 4
No 15	373 yards	par 4
No 16	161 yards	par 3
No 17	425 yards	par 4
No 18	475 yards	par 5

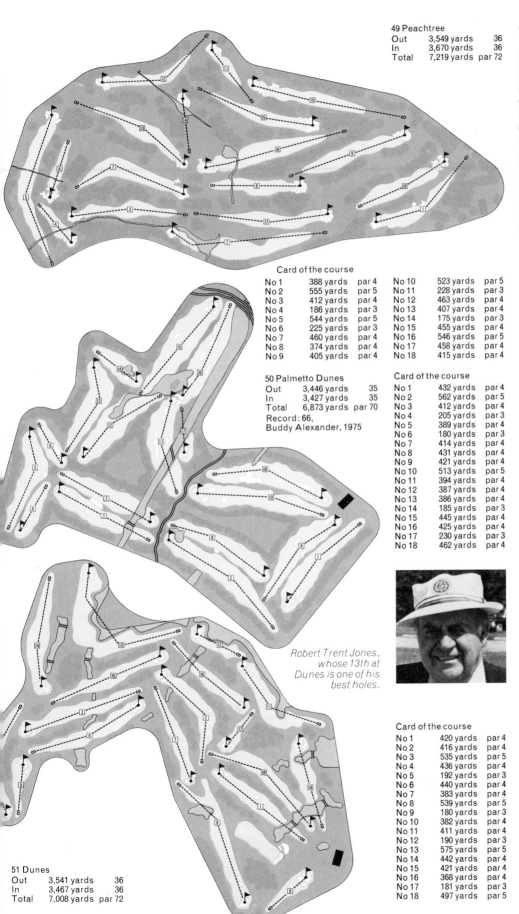

49 Peachtree		
Out	3,549 yards	36
In	3,670 yards	36
Total	7,219 yards	par 72

49 Peachtree GC, Atlanta, Ga.

To speak of Peachtree in Atlanta is to speak of Bobby Jones, for it was he who was the inspiration behind it. His ideas were followed by architect Robert Trent Jones, and Peachtree has ever since been one of the premier golf clubs of Atlanta and the place that Bobby Jones considered his golfing home in his later years. The course was built during the late 1940s amongst azaleas and dogwood in the typically hilly countryside around Atlanta. Marching up and down these hills in the hot summer months can make it purgatory to play, but the anguish is more than compensated for during the other seasons—particularly the spring. The start is awesome, with an initial 388-yard par-four, with two bunkers set in the dog-leg which force the drive out to the right of the fairway. The 2nd is simple but superb. A 555-yard par-five, it is bunkerless but has a green protected in front by a lake and stream.

Card of the course

No 1	388 yards	par 4	No 10	523 yards	par 5
No 2	555 yards	par 5	No 11	228 yards	par 3
No 3	412 yards	par 4	No 12	463 yards	par 4
No 4	186 yards	par 3	No 13	407 yards	par 4
No 5	544 yards	par 5	No 14	175 yards	par 3
No 6	225 yards	par 3	No 15	455 yards	par 4
No 7	460 yards	par 4	No 16	546 yards	par 5
No 8	374 yards	par 4	No 17	458 yards	par 4
No 9	405 yards	par 4	No 18	415 yards	par 4

50 Palmetto Dunes		
Out	3,446 yards	35
In	3,427 yards	35
Total	6,873 yards	par 70
Record: 66,		
Buddy Alexander, 1975		

Card of the course

No 1	432 yards	par 4
No 2	562 yards	par 5
No 3	412 yards	par 4
No 4	205 yards	par 3
No 5	389 yards	par 4
No 6	180 yards	par 3
No 7	414 yards	par 4
No 8	431 yards	par 4
No 9	421 yards	par 4
No 10	513 yards	par 5
No 11	394 yards	par 4
No 12	387 yards	par 4
No 13	386 yards	par 4
No 14	185 yards	par 3
No 15	445 yards	par 4
No 16	425 yards	par 4
No 17	230 yards	par 3
No 18	462 yards	par 4

50 Palmetto Dunes Resort, Hilton Head, SC

The George Fazio course at Palmetto Dunes, in the South Carolina golfing Mecca of Hilton Head Island, is one of the newest classic courses in America. Each fairway runs parallel to another on its right and, with the exception of the 3rd and 16th, there is out-of-bounds on the left of every hole. A mark of Fazio's work is his extravagant shaping of teeing areas. Not for him the square-cut tees so common in golf. At Palmetto they sweep in elegant curves around lakes, while others are circular and laid one after another like giant stepping stones. At the par-three 17th the terraced tees advance down a slope to the lagoon, leaving the rolling green 230 yards away and protected by a large sandtrap. At the 421-yard par-four 9th a massive oak tree blocks any approach to the green from the right side of the fairway, and the short 4th green is split into three distinct levels. Oak, magnolia and palmetto trees, together with the ever-present threat of water, add to the danger and beauty of this most unusual course. Bob Toski, one of the finest of all golf instructors, is Palmetto's Director of Golf.

Robert Trent Jones, whose 13th at Dunes is one of his best holes.

51 Dunes G & BC, Myrtle Beach, SC

Dunes is the hub of a resort complex on the northeastern shores of South Carolina that today contains no fewer than twenty-nine golf courses. Dunes was designed by Robert Trent Jones back in 1947, and is easily one of his best. He built the course on land with a colourful history; it was a deer and turkey hunting ground before becoming an Air Force target range during World War II—somewhat hazardous territory to plough up into a golf course. Jones incorporated in the layout his favourite design features: long tees, well-defined fairway traps to give the player a target off the tee, and huge, elevated, sometimes tiered greens. The 13th, a 575-yard par-five, is the most outstanding hole on the course. It dog-legs so severely around Singleton Lake that the golfer feels he is going back on his tracks. The hole bends a full 110 degrees through the line of play, and to add to the difficulty the approach to the green is between two flanking greenside traps supported by a single bunker on the far side. To make the green in two is a rare feat indeed.

Card of the course

No 1	420 yards	par 4
No 2	416 yards	par 4
No 3	535 yards	par 5
No 4	436 yards	par 4
No 5	192 yards	par 3
No 6	440 yards	par 4
No 7	383 yards	par 4
No 8	539 yards	par 5
No 9	180 yards	par 3
No 10	382 yards	par 4
No 11	411 yards	par 4
No 12	190 yards	par 3
No 13	575 yards	par 5
No 14	442 yards	par 4
No 15	421 yards	par 4
No 16	368 yards	par 4
No 17	181 yards	par 3
No 18	497 yards	par 5

51 Dunes		
Out	3,541 yards	36
In	3,467 yards	36
Total	7,008 yards	par 72

United States of America

52 CC of North Carolina, Pinehurst, NC

Standing apart and aloof on the Sandhills of Pinehurst, the exclusive private Country Club of North Carolina has three nine-hole courses, the creation of architects Ellis Maples and Willard Byrd and set amidst an expanse of trees and water. The championship course combines the Longleaf and the Dogwood nines; the third course, the Cardinal, is more colourful and scenic but is not used for competition. The back nine of the championship layout is strengthened by the abundant water hazards, which affect all but the 10th and 12th. At the 206-yard 16th, the carry is all water to a green guarded to the front and back by enormous sandtraps. For the timid, a piece of fairway on the right offers refuge from the endless water, but taking the safe route may mean dropping a shot. The lake runs alongside the two home holes from the 17th tee and encroaches on to the final fairway before drifting away to leave an unhindered approach to the last green.

53 Cascades GC, Hot Springs, Virginia

One of the world's most elegant and successful golf swings—that of Sam Snead—was created on this demanding course at The Homestead, Virginia. Built in 1923 by William Flynn, it is rated by Snead as the best training course for budding professionals because it demands every shot in the book from an infinite variety of hilly lies. The first nine holes are extremely tight through dense woodland, but then the course opens out with more emphasis on length from the tee. The 449-yard 4th is typical of the opening holes, needing a firm drive to the left to avoid trees, with the approach being played from a difficult sidehill lie. It was here that Snead began his professional career in 1934 and where, in 1967, French girl Catherine Lacoste became the first non-American, the first amateur and the youngest winner of the US Women's Open.

54 Congressional CC, Bethseda, Md.

President Calvin Coolidge opened Washington's Congressional Country Club in 1924, yet it was not until forty years of a chequered history had passed that the US Open came to the club in 1964. It resulted in an astonishing win for Ken Venturi in sweltering heat and high humidity. During World War II the club was taken over as a training ground for highly secret activities. Robert Trent Jones designed nine new holes in 1957 and revamped the original course in 1961. An amalgamation of the old and new forms the current championship layout. Situated in undulating, wooded country, the subtly contoured greens and large, well-placed bunkers are the course's main features. The opening 405-yard hole, played against the prevailing wind, sets the scene with a gentle left dog-leg to a heart-shaped green virtually surrounded by traps. Water appears for the first time at the 6th, cutting across the simple line to the green and surrounding the right side. The first par-five, the 9th, is just 599 yards, with trees narrowing the entrance to the green lying on the other side of a gully. The 18th, 465 yards to a green jutting into a lake below the vast clubhouse, is a fitting climax.

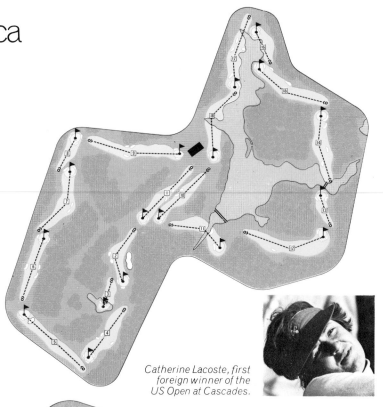

52 North Carolina		
Out	3,493 yards	36
In	3,480 yards	36
Total	6,973 yards	par 72

Card of the course

No 1	419 yards	par 4
No 2	409 yards	par 4
No 3	153 yards	par 3
No 4	371 yards	par 4
No 5	475 yards	par 5
No 6	440 yards	par 4
No 7	435 yards	par 4
No 8	221 yards	par 3
No 9	570 yards	par 5
No 10	374 yards	par 4
No 11	406 yards	par 4
No 12	547 yards	par 5
No 13	194 yards	par 3
No 14	448 yards	par 4
No 15	432 yards	par 4
No 16	206 yards	par 3
No 17	389 yards	par 4
No 18	484 yards	par 5

Catherine Lacoste, first foreign winner of the US Open at Cascades.

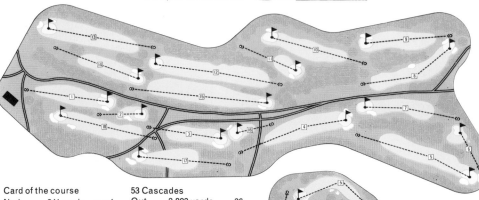

Card of the course		
No 1	341 yards	par 4
No 2	158 yards	par 3
No 3	297 yards	par 4
No 4	449 yards	par 5
No 5	445 yards	par 5
No 6	162 yards	par 3
No 7	396 yards	par 4
No 8	324 yards	par 4
No 9	311 yards	par 4
No 10	382 yards	par 4
No 11	188 yards	par 3
No 12	409 yards	par 4
No 13	434 yards	par 4
No 14	302 yards	par 4
No 15	496 yards	par 5
No 16	151 yards	par 3
No 17	307 yards	par 4
No 18	370 yards	par 4

53 Cascades		
Out	2,883 yards	36
In	3,039 yards	35
Total	5,922 yards	par 71

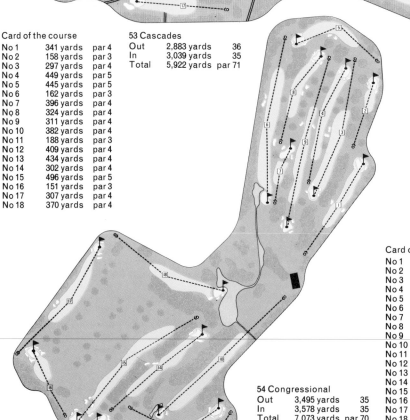

Card of the course		
No 1	405 yards	par 4
No 2	215 yards	par 3
No 3	459 yards	par 4
No 4	423 yards	par 4
No 5	408 yards	par 4
No 6	456 yards	par 4
No 7	168 yards	par 3
No 8	362 yards	par 4
No 9	599 yards	par 5
No 10	459 yards	par 4
No 11	399 yards	par 4
No 12	188 yards	par 3
No 13	448 yards	par 4
No 14	434 yards	par 4
No 15	564 yards	par 5
No 16	211 yards	par 3
No 17	410 yards	par 4
No 18	465 yards	par 5

54 Congressional		
Out	3,495 yards	35
In	3,578 yards	35
Total	7,073 yards	par 70

United States of America

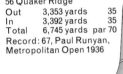
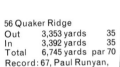

55 Baltimore

Out	3,304 yards	35
In	3,355 yards	35
Total	6,659 yards	par 70

Card of the course

No 1	424 yards	par 4
No 2	433 yards	par 4
No 3	387 yards	par 4
No 4	163 yards	par 3
No 5	425 yards	par 4
No 6	575 yards	par 5
No 7	349 yards	par 4
No 8	355 yards	par 4
No 9	193 yards	par 3
No 10	378 yards	par 4
No 11	424 yards	par 4
No 12	388 yards	par 4
No 13	158 yards	par 3
No 14	600 yards	par 5
No 15	425 yards	par 4
No 16	422 yards	par 4
No 17	175 yards	par 3
No 18	385 yards	par 4

56 Quaker Ridge

Out	3,353 yards	35
In	3,392 yards	35
Total	6,745 yards	par 70

Record: 67, Paul Runyan,
Metropolitan Open 1936

Card of the course

No 1	527 yards	par 5
No 2	425 yards	par 4
No 3	424 yards	par 4
No 4	408 yards	par 4
No 5	169 yards	par 3
No 6	446 yards	par 4
No 7	431 yards	par 4
No 8	359 yards	par 4
No 9	164 yards	par 3
No 10	201 yards	par 3
No 11	387 yards	par 4
No 12	422 yards	par 4
No 13	234 yards	par 3
No 14	525 yards	par 5
No 15	394 yards	par 4
No 16	427 yards	par 4
No 17	362 yards	par 4
No 18	440 yards	par 4

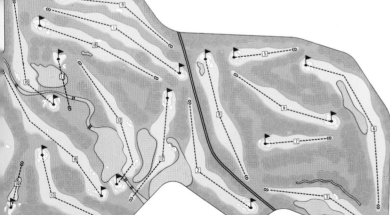

57 Concord

Out	3,666 yards	36
In	3,539 yards	36
Total	7,205 yards	par 72

Card of the course

No 1	530 yards	par 5	No 10	417 yards	par 4
No 2	443 yards	par 4	No 11	172 yards	par 3
No 3	415 yards	par 4	No 12	531 yards	par 5
No 4	586 yards	par 5	No 13	412 yards	par 4
No 5	211 yards	par 3	No 14	154 yards	par 3
No 6	382 yards	par 4	No 15	447 yards	par 4
No 7	224 yards	par 3	No 16	556 yards	par 5
No 8	443 yards	par 4	No 17	399 yards	par 4
No 9	432 yards	par 4	No 18	451 yards	par 4

Jess Sweetser, famous victor at Quaker Ridge.

55 Baltimore CC, Baltimore, Md.

Five Farms, which was once just the suburban course of the Baltimore Country Club, is now the hub of the club. It sits amid the rolling hills of Maryland's "hunt country", where horses have always been the major sport but from which golf is fast taking over. Designed by the late, great genius of architecture, A. W. Tillinghast, the course is not overly bunkered and neither is it tremendously long. But those hills present numerous sidehill lies after mishit drives and the greens can get fearsomely slick, although remaining awesomely true. Baltimore has been the scene of a number of major events, the last of which—and probably the most exciting—was the 1965 Walker Cup matches in which Britain and Ireland tied the US team at eleven points each, so breaking a string of losses dating back to 1938.

56 Quaker Ridge GC, Scarsdale, NY

Designed by A. W. Tillinghast in 1916, this exacting course in rolling, heavily wooded country a short distance from New York is relatively unknown compared with its illustrious neighbour, Winged Foot. Typical of the examination set at Quaker Ridge is the ninety degree dog-leg 7th, which needs a precise drive to the right side of the fairway to give a sight of the green more than 200 yards away uphill. The second shot must carry a brook and two fairway bunkers to a green with sand on three sides. The shorter, par-four 11th is distinguished by a stream which crosses in front of the tee, threatens the left side of the fairway and snakes back around the right side of the green. For good measure trees overhang the left side of the putting surface. Quaker Ridge has shunned the limelight of the big tournament circuit, but has set outstanding standards in its own amateur event with winners of the quality of Jess Sweetser and Willie Turnesa, winners of both the US and British Amateur championships, Paul Runyan, twice USPGA champion, and Masters winner Doug Ford.

57 Concord GC, Kiamesha Lake, NY

The Concord Hotel and its two eighteen-hole courses are set in the woods of the Catskill Mountains about two hours' drive north of New York City. Before 1963 the resort had an eighteen-hole layout, the International, and a small nine-holer, the Challenger. To these the Texan architect Joe Finger added the Monster. This course is incredibly long, measuring, from the back tee, a standard 7,205 yards—which can be stretched to 7,672 yards in exceptional circumstances. Finger wanted the longer distance to be played only when there was a strong following wind blowing off the mountains. The course borders on Kiamesha Lake and fine, though not extravagant, use of the water has been made on eight of the holes. The greens are grand, sprawling areas and the bunkering is subtle, in the true Finger style. At the 586-yard par-five 4th, a lateral water hazard runs for 220 yards down the left-hand side, gradually encroaching on to the fairway and making the 4th a hole that even the élite find hard to master.

United States of America

58 Oak Hill CC, Rochester, NY

Before play started in the 1965 US Open at Oak Hill, in New York State, Ben Hogan said that the East course was not tough enough to stage this premier event. He lost the championship to Cary Middlecoff by one shot with a two-over-par total of 282, and later revised his opinion to such an extent that he nominated the 445-yard 1st as the toughest opening hole he had ever faced. The first fairway appears generously wide, but accuracy from the tee is essential to afford any success with a second shot to a small green which is jealously guarded by encroaching trees, expertly positioned bunkers and a creek. This sets the tone for the entire course, with the 208-yard 3rd the most majestic of the par-threes and the vast 13th, 602 yards uphill, the king of the par-fives. During the second Open at Oak Hill in 1968, won by Lee Trevino, the 440-yard 6th, with a creek meandering along the right side of the fairway before swinging diagonally across the front of the green and down the left side, provided most torment for the players. The beauty and challenge of this fine course stand as testimony to the skill of Donald Ross.

59 Canterbury GC, Cleveland, Ohio

Only ten miles from Cleveland, the Canterbury course was designed by New Yorker Herbert Strong in 1922 and modified a few years later by the club's professional, Jack Way. It is not excessively long, but the problems caused by the fourteen dog-legs and the wind that blows off Lake Erie produce a course that favours the long hitter. From the 16th, the run-in is very tough and has sealed the fate of many a player. It is a 605-yard monster and the green, although unassailable in two, is just a 9-iron or a wedge away with the third. When played into the wind the short, 232-yard 17th can require a wood to reach the raised double-tiered green, flanked by bunkers and guarded by out-of-bounds on the right. Then comes Canterbury's last and most difficult hole, its fairway uphill for 438 yards and lined with trees, with out-of-bounds to the right and a viciously trapped green that is hidden from the tee. It is often said that if par is held on these three holes then victory is almost assured. The course has seen two US Opens, in 1940 and 1946.

60 Scioto CC, Columbus, Ohio

Scioto is the course where Jack Nicklaus developed from a pudgy junior to a world beater. Designed by Donald Ross in 1912, it carries all the hallmarks of his best works—greens nestling into the terrain, gentle slopes on the approaches, full use of the ground's natural contours and plenty of subtle problems which demand thought rather than power. The 436-yard 2nd is one of the great Ross holes. A stream crosses in front of the tee and runs up the left side of the fairway, which is bordered by trees and out-of-bounds on the right. Bunkers protect the tee shot landing area and the sloping green is guarded at the front. All four par-three holes on this magnificent course offer a stiff challenge. Toughest of all is the 235-yard 14th, a deceptive hole with a long carry over a rolling fairway. Scioto staged the 1926 US Open (won by Bobby Jones), the Ryder Cup matches of 1931 and both the American PGA and Amateur championships.

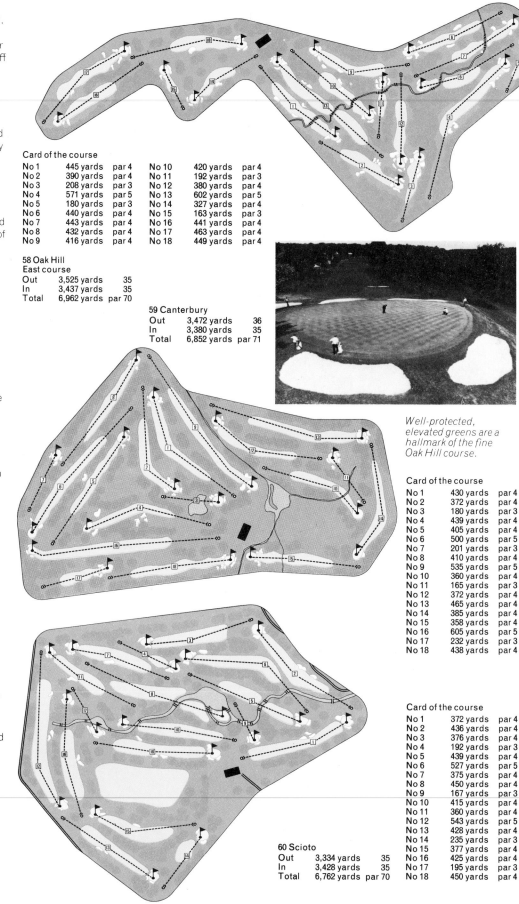

Card of the course

No 1	445 yards	par 4	No 10	420 yards	par 4
No 2	390 yards	par 4	No 11	192 yards	par 3
No 3	208 yards	par 3	No 12	380 yards	par 4
No 4	571 yards	par 5	No 13	602 yards	par 5
No 5	180 yards	par 3	No 14	327 yards	par 4
No 6	440 yards	par 4	No 15	163 yards	par 3
No 7	443 yards	par 4	No 16	441 yards	par 4
No 8	432 yards	par 4	No 17	463 yards	par 4
No 9	416 yards	par 4	No 18	449 yards	par 4

**58 Oak Hill
East course**

Out	3,525 yards	35
In	3,437 yards	35
Total	6,962 yards	par 70

59 Canterbury

Out	3,472 yards	36
In	3,380 yards	35
Total	6,852 yards	par 71

Well-protected, elevated greens are a hallmark of the fine Oak Hill course.

Card of the course

No 1	430 yards	par 4
No 2	372 yards	par 4
No 3	180 yards	par 3
No 4	439 yards	par 4
No 5	405 yards	par 4
No 6	500 yards	par 5
No 7	201 yards	par 3
No 8	410 yards	par 4
No 9	535 yards	par 5
No 10	360 yards	par 4
No 11	165 yards	par 3
No 12	372 yards	par 4
No 13	465 yards	par 4
No 14	385 yards	par 4
No 15	358 yards	par 4
No 16	605 yards	par 5
No 17	232 yards	par 3
No 18	438 yards	par 4

Card of the course

No 1	372 yards	par 4
No 2	436 yards	par 4
No 3	376 yards	par 4
No 4	192 yards	par 3
No 5	439 yards	par 4
No 6	527 yards	par 5
No 7	375 yards	par 4
No 8	450 yards	par 4
No 9	167 yards	par 3
No 10	415 yards	par 4
No 11	360 yards	par 4
No 12	543 yards	par 5
No 13	428 yards	par 4
No 14	235 yards	par 3
No 15	377 yards	par 4
No 16	425 yards	par 4
No 17	195 yards	par 3
No 18	450 yards	par 4

60 Scioto

Out	3,334 yards	35
In	3,428 yards	35
Total	6,762 yards	par 70

United States of America

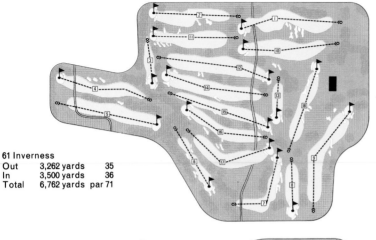

61 Inverness
Out	3,262 yards	35
In	3,500 yards	36
Total	6,762 yards	par 71

Card of the course
No 1	398 yards	par 4
No 2	385 yards	par 4
No 3	161 yards	par 3
No 4	466 yards	par 4
No 5	436 yards	par 4
No 6	372 yards	par 4
No 7	348 yards	par 4
No 8	210 yards	par 3
No 9	486 yards	par 5
No 10	363 yards	par 4
No 11	378 yards	par 4
No 12	523 yards	par 5
No 13	163 yards	par 3
No 14	448 yards	par 4
No 15	458 yards	par 4
No 16	409 yards	par 4
No 17	431 yards	par 4
No 18	327 yards	par 4

Ted Ray won the US Open at Inverness in 1920.

Card of the course (Chicago)
No 1	442 yards	par 4
No 2	443 yards	par 4
No 3	216 yards	par 3
No 4	540 yards	par 5
No 5	317 yards	par 4
No 6	397 yards	par 4
No 7	200 yards	par 3
No 8	410 yards	par 4
No 9	401 yards	par 4
No 10	133 yards	par 3
No 11	408 yards	par 4
No 12	415 yards	par 4
No 13	150 yards	par 3
No 14	356 yards	par 4
No 15	390 yards	par 4
No 16	527 yards	par 5
No 17	382 yards	par 4
No 18	421 yards	par 4

62 Chicago
Out	3,366 yards	35
In	3,182 yards	35
Total	6,548 yards	par 70

Record: 66, Bobby Jones, Walker Cup 1928

63 Butler National
Out	3,684 yards	36
In	3,607 yards	35
Total	7,291 yards	par 71

Card of the course
No 1	392 yards	par 4
No 2	552 yards	par 5
No 3	433 yards	par 4
No 4	400 yards	par 4
No 5	240 yards	par 3
No 6	442 yards	par 4
No 7	603 yards	par 5
No 8	195 yards	par 3
No 9	427 yards	par 4
No 10	433 yards	par 4
No 11	190 yards	par 3
No 12	469 yards	par 4
No 13	193 yards	par 3
No 14	435 yards	par 4
No 15	578 yards	par 5
No 16	385 yards	par 4
No 17	454 yards	par 4
No 18	470 yards	par 4

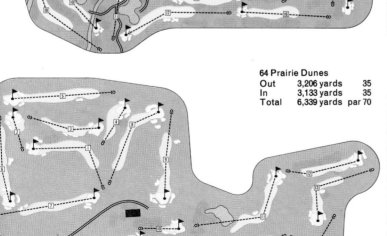

64 Prairie Dunes
Out	3,206 yards	35
In	3,133 yards	35
Total	6,339 yards	par 70

Card of the course
No 1	424 yards	par 4
No 2	150 yards	par 3
No 3	325 yards	par 4
No 4	160 yards	par 3
No 5	439 yards	par 4
No 6	382 yards	par 4
No 7	507 yards	par 5
No 8	420 yards	par 4
No 9	399 yards	par 4
No 10	169 yards	par 3
No 11	450 yards	par 4
No 12	327 yards	par 4
No 13	357 yards	par 4
No 14	337 yards	par 4
No 15	197 yards	par 3
No 16	420 yards	par 4
No 17	497 yards	par 5
No 18	379 yards	par 4

61 Inverness Club, Toledo, Ohio
The three US Open championships played at Inverness have all produced great drama—particularly in 1920, when big-hitting Ted Ray took the 275-yard shortcut over the trees at the dog-leg 7th to score birdies in each round on his way to victory. The addition of twenty yards and the subsequent growth of the trees do not encourage today's professionals to attempt this shot. The original Donald Ross layout of 1903 was updated by Dick Wilson in 1956. It allows ample room from the tee but requires second-shot accuracy to find the small, well-bunkered greens. At the 436-yard par-four 5th, for example, the correct approach is from the right side of the fairway, but this needs a carry of more than 200 yards over a creek. Aiming left off the tee leaves a tricky long iron second to a sloping bunkerless green.

62 Chicago GC, Wheaton, Ill.
Chicago was one of the five clubs which formed the US Golf Association in 1894—the same year that the club moved to its present site at Wheaton from Belmont, where it had been inaugurated two years earlier. The guiding light in those times was the famed Charles Blair Macdonald, who constructed the first course before it was completely redesigned and rebuilt during 1921 with the assistance of Seth Raynor. At 410 yards, the 8th is slightly double dog-legged and scarred by eight sandtraps, of which three abut a green that has a gently rolling surface and is set obliquely to the fairway. The club staged many early championships, including the Open three times and the Amateur four times.

63 Butler National GC, Chicago, Ill.
Located in the Oak Brook suburb of Chicago, Butler National, designed by George Fazio, is a new course which demands patience and precision from the tee. The greens have become renowned for their mysterious undulations, so tricky that they defeat even those most familiar with them. Water has been used imaginatively, coming into play at eleven holes. It creates a potent problem from the back tee at the par-three 5th, where a 240-yard carry is needed to hit a peninsula green which is also backed on the right side by water. At the 435-yard par-four 14th the same body of water has to be crossed twice on the route to the green, making it the most challenging hole on the course.

64 Prairie Dunes GC, Hutchinson, Kans.
Prairie Dunes could hardly be farther from the sea, yet the superb course is played across rolling sandhills characteristic of a true Scottish links—an impression heightened by the severe rough, so unusual on American golf courses. Originally a nine-hole course, designed in 1937 by Perry Maxwell, it was extended to 6,339 yards over a period of twenty years by his son, J. Press Maxwell. The 420-yard dog-legged 8th is a classic. Thick rough prevents any thought of a shortcut and a long iron second is necessary to reach a well-trapped, two-tier plateau green. The 169-yard 10th—played downwind, with a scrub-covered dune on the left, a cavernous bunker in front, a steep drop to deep rough on the right and more bushes beyond—is a hole Scotland would be proud to own.

United States of America

65 Colonial CC, Fort Worth, Tex.

It is often said that Ben Hogan's success was partly due to the fact that, having played his early golf at Colonial, every other course in the world was easy in comparison. There are not many pros who would disagree with that. Designed in 1935 by Perry Maxwell, it is 7.166 yards with a par of 70. Its trees, bunkers and river do not allow an all-out attack from the tee—placement rather than pure length being the key to success at every hole. This puts a premium on long, accurate second shots as at the 5th, a 466-yard par-four dog-leg to the right. A power fade from the tee may find the Trinity River under the trees, while a long straight tee shot could run across the bend in the fairway to thick trees on the left. Yet anything less than a drive to the centre of the fairway leaves an enormous shot to a green well protected by sand and more trees. The much shorter 9th still demands a perfect tee shot to allow a sight of the green buried deep in a grove of trees with water right across the front.

66 Cherry Hills CC, Denver, Colo.

Denver is the "mile-high" city and in its rarefied atmosphere the 6.955 yards of the Cherry Hills course play shorter than they read on the card. Designed by William Flynn in 1922 it was here, thirty-eight years later, that Arnold Palmer won his only US Open. Ben Hogan named the 470-yard 14th one of the most difficult par-fours in America. Its fairway rises from the tee with trees and out-of-bounds on the right; on the left, thick rough falls away to a creek. The hole then swings sharply to the left, offering a narrow opening to the green set between a deep bunker on the right and the ever-threatening creek which curls round and behind the left edge. The 14th starts a demanding finish which includes a 194-yard par-three to a very small green encircled by sand and trees. Then comes a short par-four 16th that demands supreme accuracy; an exacting 529-yard par-five to an island green; and finally the 489-yard 18th—named after President Eisenhower, a long-standing member—often described as one of golf's finest last holes.

67 Spyglass Hill GC, Pebble Beach, Calif.

Spyglass Hill is possibly the hardest of the three courses on the Monterey Peninsula. The hilly land tumbles down towards the sea, leaving fairways lined with windswept cypress trees and Californian pines liberally laced with areas of brilliant white sand. The course, designed by Robert Trent Jones and opened in 1966, makes heavy demands on both the mental and physical resources of those who play. On a windy day it can become almost impossible and in fact is rarely played at its full championship length of 6,810 yards. The opening holes are a fearsome introduction to the course's difficulties. The 1st is an enormous 600 yards that needs thunderous strokeplay even to approach a par. The next four holes are at the mercy of the wind, which often plays havoc with even the very best of shots. The course returns inland at the 6th, but trees now compound the problems set by the wind. The short 12th is played across a pond to a small, undulating green wedged between the water and a steep, bunkered rise. Over-clubbing can plug the ball in a trap or bounce it off the slope to roll back across the green and into the water.

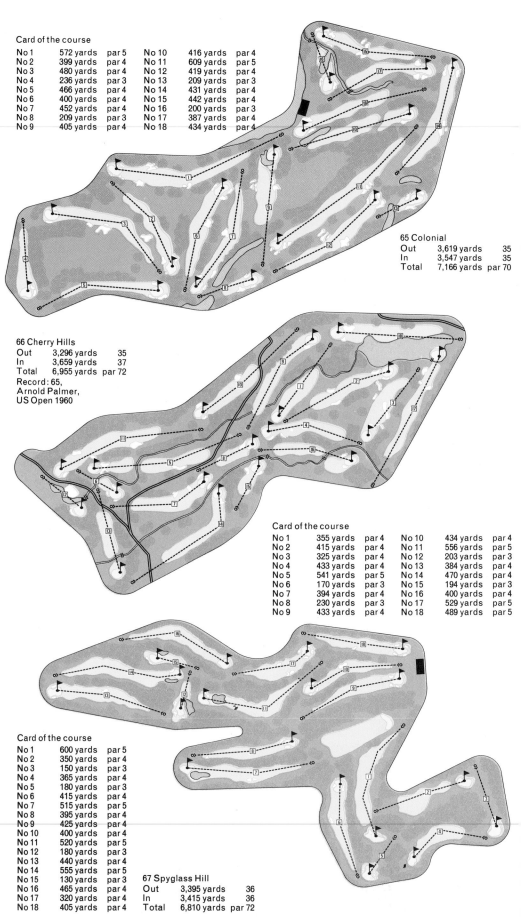

Card of the course

No 1	572 yards	par 5	No 10	416 yards	par 4
No 2	399 yards	par 4	No 11	609 yards	par 5
No 3	480 yards	par 4	No 12	419 yards	par 4
No 4	236 yards	par 3	No 13	209 yards	par 3
No 5	466 yards	par 4	No 14	431 yards	par 4
No 6	400 yards	par 4	No 15	442 yards	par 4
No 7	452 yards	par 4	No 16	200 yards	par 3
No 8	209 yards	par 3	No 17	387 yards	par 4
No 9	405 yards	par 4	No 18	434 yards	par 4

65 Colonial
Out	3,619 yards	35
In	3,547 yards	35
Total	7,166 yards	par 70

66 Cherry Hills
Out	3,296 yards	35
In	3,659 yards	37
Total	6,955 yards	par 72

Record: 65,
Arnold Palmer,
US Open 1960

Card of the course

No 1	355 yards	par 4	No 10	434 yards	par 4
No 2	415 yards	par 4	No 11	556 yards	par 5
No 3	325 yards	par 4	No 12	203 yards	par 3
No 4	433 yards	par 4	No 13	384 yards	par 4
No 5	541 yards	par 5	No 14	470 yards	par 4
No 6	170 yards	par 3	No 15	194 yards	par 3
No 7	394 yards	par 4	No 16	400 yards	par 4
No 8	230 yards	par 3	No 17	529 yards	par 5
No 9	433 yards	par 4	No 18	489 yards	par 4

Card of the course

No 1	600 yards	par 5
No 2	350 yards	par 4
No 3	150 yards	par 3
No 4	365 yards	par 4
No 5	180 yards	par 3
No 6	415 yards	par 4
No 7	515 yards	par 5
No 8	395 yards	par 4
No 9	425 yards	par 4
No 10	400 yards	par 4
No 11	520 yards	par 5
No 12	180 yards	par 3
No 13	440 yards	par 4
No 14	555 yards	par 4
No 15	130 yards	par 3
No 16	465 yards	par 4
No 17	320 yards	par 4
No 18	405 yards	par 4

67 Spyglass Hill
Out	3,395 yards	36
In	3,415 yards	36
Total	6,810 yards	par 72

United States of America

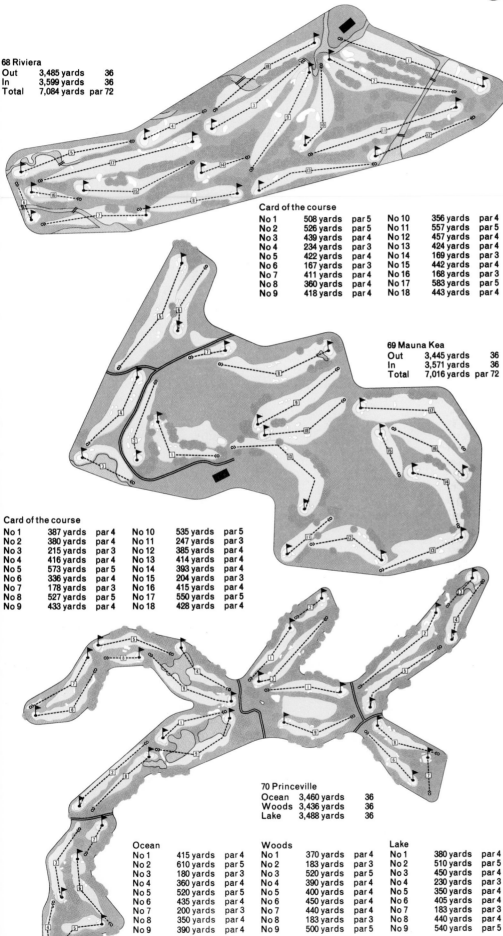

68 Riviera

Out	3,485 yards	36
In	3,599 yards	36
Total	7,084 yards	par 72

Card of the course

No 1	508 yards	par 5	No 10	356 yards	par 4
No 2	526 yards	par 5	No 11	557 yards	par 5
No 3	439 yards	par 4	No 12	457 yards	par 4
No 4	234 yards	par 3	No 13	424 yards	par 4
No 5	422 yards	par 4	No 14	169 yards	par 3
No 6	167 yards	par 3	No 15	442 yards	par 4
No 7	411 yards	par 4	No 16	168 yards	par 3
No 8	360 yards	par 4	No 17	583 yards	par 5
No 9	418 yards	par 4	No 18	443 yards	par 4

69 Mauna Kea

Out	3,445 yards	36
In	3,571 yards	36
Total	7,016 yards	par 72

Card of the course

No 1	387 yards	par 4	No 10	535 yards	par 5
No 2	380 yards	par 4	No 11	247 yards	par 3
No 3	215 yards	par 3	No 12	385 yards	par 4
No 4	416 yards	par 4	No 13	414 yards	par 4
No 5	573 yards	par 5	No 14	393 yards	par 4
No 6	336 yards	par 4	No 15	204 yards	par 3
No 7	178 yards	par 3	No 16	415 yards	par 4
No 8	527 yards	par 5	No 17	550 yards	par 5
No 9	433 yards	par 4	No 18	428 yards	par 4

70 Princeville

Ocean	3,460 yards	36
Woods	3,436 yards	36
Lake	3,488 yards	36

Ocean			Woods			Lake		
No 1	415 yards	par 4	No 1	370 yards	par 4	No 1	380 yards	par 4
No 2	610 yards	par 5	No 2	183 yards	par 3	No 2	510 yards	par 5
No 3	180 yards	par 3	No 3	520 yards	par 5	No 3	450 yards	par 4
No 4	360 yards	par 4	No 4	390 yards	par 4	No 4	230 yards	par 3
No 5	520 yards	par 5	No 5	400 yards	par 4	No 5	350 yards	par 4
No 6	435 yards	par 4	No 6	450 yards	par 4	No 6	405 yards	par 4
No 7	200 yards	par 3	No 7	440 yards	par 4	No 7	183 yards	par 3
No 8	350 yards	par 4	No 8	183 yards	par 3	No 8	440 yards	par 4
No 9	390 yards	par 4	No 9	500 yards	par 5	No 9	540 yards	par 5

68 Riviera CC, Pacific Palisades, Calif.

The golfing domain of show business stars since its opening in 1926, this great Californian course, designed by George Thomas, still numbers Gregory Peck and Dean Martin among its members and plays host each year to the Glen Campbell Los Angeles Open. It was here that Ben Hogan set his American Open record of 276, which stood for nineteen years, and, in 1950, made his historic comeback to golf after a near-fatal car crash. Massive reconstruction work was undertaken in 1974 to restore the small meandering stream which had become, over fifty years, a forty-foot-deep ravine; seventeen acres of land were reclaimed and the course was returned to its original glory. The spongy quality of the turf does not allow the ball to roll far and this makes the par-fives extremely difficult, particularly the massive, 583-yard 17th. Yet power is not the only requirement, for there are subtle problems set by the winding barranca and the arrangement of bunkers. At the 167-yard 6th, sandtraps proliferate. The first bunker lies in the dead centre of the fairway just short of the target; on the green itself there is a small shallow trap, and at the back a hillside bunker to swallow the over-clubbed stroke.

69 Mauna Kea GC, Kamuela, Hawaii

Robert Trent Jones's incredibly tough masterpiece at Mauna Kea on the Big Island of Hawaii has been refined by his son Robert from a course which only the élite among playing professionals could hope to master. The younger Jones adapted the layout so that it became acceptable for the average player—though even without some of its original savagery it still presents a number of formidable challenges. Carved out of desolate volcanic lava beds beside the ocean and over the foothills of vast mountains, it has developed the lush beauty to be expected on these scenic islands. The 3rd, with its view over the pounding Pacific to a green perched above volcanic rock 215 yards away, is not solved in one shot. The green carries the Trent Jones characteristic of sharp borrows and lightning speed, which rewards only the lightest of touches. But not every hole is as severe.

70 Princeville GC, Kauai, Hawaii

Built as three separate nines—aptly named Ocean, Lake and Woods—on a beautiful tract of land on Kauai, the most westerly of the large Hawaiian islands, this is undoubtedly one of the most outstanding examples of courses designed by Robert Trent Jones Jr. Vast tees and large greens allow many combinations, lengths and degrees of difficulty over a layout which features rolling fairways, strategic bunkers and generous use of lakes. The championship course is a combination of any two nines, depending on the strength and direction of the 15–20 mph trade winds—the effect of which can be judged by the professionals' choice of clubs at the 180-yard par-three 3rd on the Ocean course. Played downwind it requires no more than a 9-iron, or even a wedge. The sixty-foot elevated tee looks over the lake down on to the wide but shallow target, which is flanked at the back by two strategically placed sandtraps. On the 540-yard 9th of the Lake course, which takes two shots over water to reach the green, two eagle-threes were recorded during a four-ball in 1975.

Canada

71 Hamilton G & CC, Ancaster, Ont.

Ancaster, as Hamilton is commonly known, epitomizes the country club ambience. The turf is lush and springy, while the heavily wooded surroundings give the property an elegant seclusion. The championship layout takes its front nine from the West course and the remainder from the South. Both were designed as nine-hole courses by H. S. Colt in 1914, and in 1974 an extra nine-holer, the East, was added by Robbie Robinson. From a promontory, the opulent clubhouse overlooks the strong finishing hole, a 440-yard par-four, where the fairway winds around an S-shaped stream to a saucer-like green. Because of the water, the tee shot is normally played as a lay-up and the approach to the large green calls for a wood or a low iron for even the longest hitter. The Canadian Open has been played at Ancaster twice, in 1930 and 1948. In the first, Tommy Armour shot a six-under-par 64 to set a course record which still stands today.

71 Hamilton
Out	3,375 yards	35
In	3,375 yards	35
Total	6,750 yards	par 70

Record: 64,
Tommy Armour,
Canadian Open 1930

Card of the course
No 1	425 yards	par 4
No 2	457 yards	par 4
No 3	401 yards	par 4
No 4	543 yards	par 5
No 5	321 yards	par 4
No 6	216 yards	par 3
No 7	394 yards	par 4
No 8	195 yards	par 3
No 9	423 yards	par 4
No 10	343 yards	par 4
No 11	451 yards	par 4
No 12	385 yards	par 4
No 13	220 yards	par 3
No 14	424 yards	par 4
No 15	381 yards	par 4
No 16	181 yards	par 3
No 17	550 yards	par 5
No 18	440 yards	par 4

72 St George's GC, Islington, Ont.

St George's is distinguished by tight fairways, rolling terrain—and its estimated real estate value of $20 million. Situated in downtown Toronto, the course was designed by Stanley Thompson and opened for play in 1928. It was known as the Royal York and associated with the Canadian Pacific Railway until the company relinquished its interest after World War II. Not only the fairways twist and roll—even a putt over a flat surface is a rare treat on the well-trapped greens. At the 14th, a 446-yard par-four, the drive must avoid out-of-bounds on the left and carry a knoll, leaving a mid iron second shot down the hill to a green that is banked on the right and trapped on the left. The problems are intensified by a river which runs down the right side of the fairway and crosses just in front of the green. In the 1933 Canadian Open Joe Kirkwood, the eventual winner, was stymied behind a large oak at the 5th. He hit the ball out to the right and produced a total roundhouse hook to land the ball eight feet from the pin, and holed out for a birdie.

Card of the course
No 1	378 yards	par 4
No 2	420 yards	par 4
No 3	201 yards	par 3
No 4	480 yards	par 5
No 5	403 yards	par 4
No 6	146 yards	par 3
No 7	442 yards	par 4
No 8	217 yards	par 3
No 9	543 yards	par 5
No 10	377 yards	par 4
No 11	517 yards	par 5
No 12	383 yards	par 4
No 13	214 yards	par 3
No 14	446 yards	par 4
No 15	580 yards	par 5
No 16	203 yards	par 3
No 17	447 yards	par 4
No 18	400 yards	par 4

72 St George's
Out	3,230 yards	35
In	3,567 yards	36
Total	6,797 yards	par 71

Record: 64,
George Knudson,
Canadian Open 1968

73 Jasper Park GC, Alberta

Set in the rugged mountains of Alberta overlooking Lake Beauvert, Jasper Park has fairways that are invariably aligned with mountain peaks and roll through thick, rich woodland with breathtaking views over the valley, lake and river below. Originally designed in 1925 by Stanley Thompson, the course was rebuilt twenty years later and now follows an almost circular path, with the 9th at the farthest point in the traditional manner. Two short par-threes, the 12th (Tête Jaune) and 15th (The Bad Baby), are scintillating one-shotters to well-elevated greens. The 12th is played across two forward sandtraps and against a backdrop of trees; to the right of the triangular green is a large waste of sand. The 15th is no better—the green is set in splendid isolation, and presents itself as a true target where only a direct hit by a well-weighted short iron will bring results. The club has its own annual competition, suitably named the Totem Pole.

73 Jasper Park
Out	3,240 yards	34
In	3,350 yards	36
Total	6,590 yards	par 70

Card of the course
No 1	390 yards	par 4	No 10	485 yards	par 5
No 2	485 yards	par 5	No 11	395 yards	par 4
No 3	425 yards	par 4	No 12	185 yards	par 3
No 4	240 yards	par 3	No 13	595 yards	par 5
No 5	470 yards	par 4	No 14	370 yards	par 4
No 6	395 yards	par 4	No 15	150 yards	par 3
No 7	180 yards	par 3	No 16	375 yards	par 4
No 8	425 yards	par 4	No 17	360 yards	par 4
No 9	230 yards	par 3	No 18	435 yards	par 4

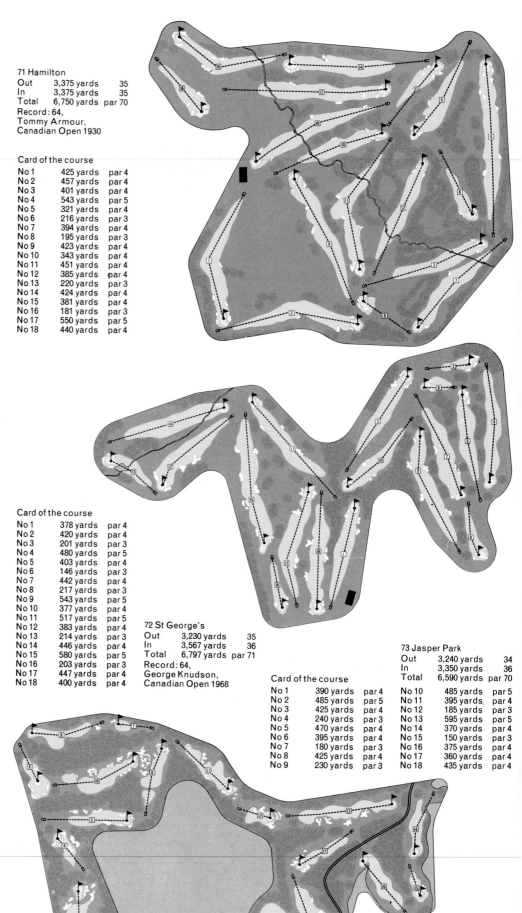

Canada/Mexico/Bermuda

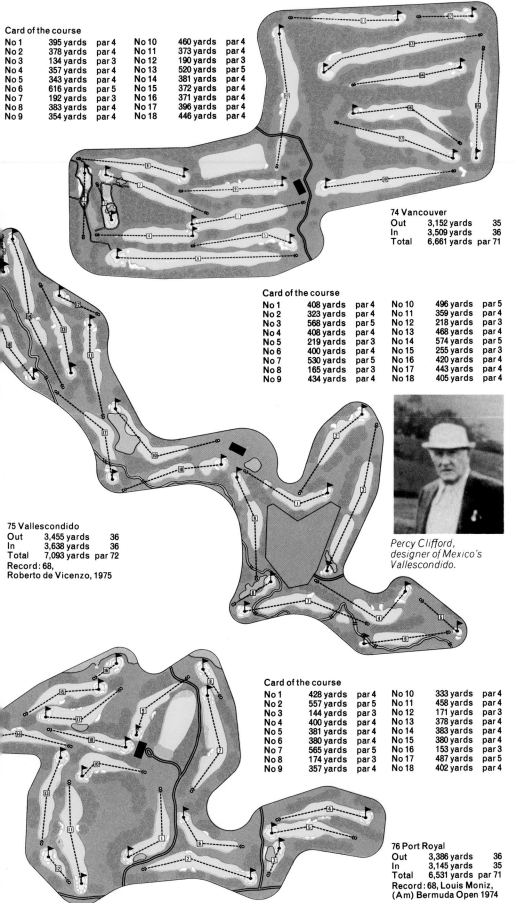

Card of the course

No 1	395 yards	par 4	No 10	460 yards	par 4
No 2	378 yards	par 4	No 11	373 yards	par 4
No 3	134 yards	par 3	No 12	190 yards	par 3
No 4	357 yards	par 4	No 13	520 yards	par 5
No 5	343 yards	par 4	No 14	381 yards	par 4
No 6	616 yards	par 5	No 15	372 yards	par 4
No 7	192 yards	par 3	No 16	371 yards	par 4
No 8	383 yards	par 4	No 17	396 yards	par 4
No 9	354 yards	par 4	No 18	446 yards	par 4

74 Vancouver

Out	3,152 yards	35
In	3,509 yards	36
Total	6,661 yards	par 71

Card of the course

No 1	408 yards	par 4	No 10	496 yards	par 5
No 2	323 yards	par 4	No 11	359 yards	par 4
No 3	568 yards	par 5	No 12	218 yards	par 3
No 4	408 yards	par 4	No 13	468 yards	par 4
No 5	219 yards	par 3	No 14	574 yards	par 5
No 6	400 yards	par 4	No 15	255 yards	par 3
No 7	530 yards	par 5	No 16	420 yards	par 4
No 8	165 yards	par 3	No 17	443 yards	par 4
No 9	434 yards	par 4	No 18	405 yards	par 4

Percy Clifford, designer of Mexico's Vallescondido.

75 Vallescondido

Out	3,455 yards	36
In	3,638 yards	36
Total	7,093 yards	par 72

Record: 68,
Roberto de Vicenzo, 1975

Card of the course

No 1	428 yards	par 4	No 10	333 yards	par 4
No 2	557 yards	par 5	No 11	458 yards	par 4
No 3	144 yards	par 3	No 12	171 yards	par 3
No 4	400 yards	par 4	No 13	378 yards	par 4
No 5	381 yards	par 4	No 14	383 yards	par 4
No 6	380 yards	par 4	No 15	380 yards	par 4
No 7	565 yards	par 5	No 16	153 yards	par 3
No 8	174 yards	par 3	No 17	487 yards	par 5
No 9	357 yards	par 4	No 18	402 yards	par 4

76 Port Royal

Out	3,386 yards	36
In	3,145 yards	35
Total	6,531 yards	par 71

Record: 68, Louis Moniz,
(Am) Bermuda Open 1974

74 Vancouver GC, Coquitlam, BC

Inspired by emigrant Scots, the Vancouver course was laid out in 1910 on a stretch of densely wooded, rolling coastal land. Giant pines and cedars line the narrow fairways, increasing the difficulty of the course and offering compensation for its lack of length. The front nine are considered the easier, although the 6th is more than 600 yards and needs a subtle approach shot to an irregularly shaped green, protected by a small pond that lies in front and just off to the left. On the back nine, the 16th—aptly called Graves—is a deceptive par-four of 371 yards. The hole dog-legs sharply left, leaving the green unsighted from the championship tee. The drive must reach the crook of the fairway, where the second shot needs a firm blast with a mid iron to make the small green, which sulks behind a single bunker and is encircled by trees. Before the urbanization of Vancouver, it took quite a trek through the British Columbian wilds to reach the club, which explains the old segregated dormitory accommodation in the original clubhouse.

75 Vallescondido GC, Mexico City

Vallescondido is a superior private course designed by Percy Clifford, with a membership that is restricted to 750. Situated just outside Mexico City, it sprawls over a beautiful valley; oak trees closely line the fairways and a meandering stream affects play on eight of the holes. The gently undulating ground means that sidehill lies often result from less than accurately positioned shots. This rolling nature of the layout means that good club selection can lead to the gaining of important yardage. On the front nine a small pond comes into play at the 165-yard par-three 8th, while on the back nine a solitary lake affects the 10th, a 496-yard par-five, and another small pond enters into the strategy of the short 15th. The 408-yard 4th ends with the green ninety degrees away from the initial line of play; the right of the fairway is flanked by sand and the green is effectively protected in front by a vast sandtrap.

76 Port Royal GC, Southampton

With six eighteen-hole courses and three nine-hole layouts in just twenty-one square miles of land, Bermuda is virtually one big golf club. Built in 1970, Port Royal was designed by Robert Trent Jones on high ground sweeping down to cliff edges overlooking the Atlantic, presenting a challenge considerably less lethal than many of his other designs. The greens are vast but gently contoured, and the surrounding bunkers do offer some leeway. From a tee on the cliff edge the spectacular short, 153-yard 16th is played across a yawning gap to a promontory which holds nothing more than the green, edged on three sides by sand. The course is over pleasantly undulating land where 200,000 new trees have been planted to blend in with the massive originals which survived the constructions. Three small lakes play their part—before the green at the 1st, on the left of the short 3rd and left again of the driving area at the sweeping dog-leg 17th.

Bahamas/Puerto Rico

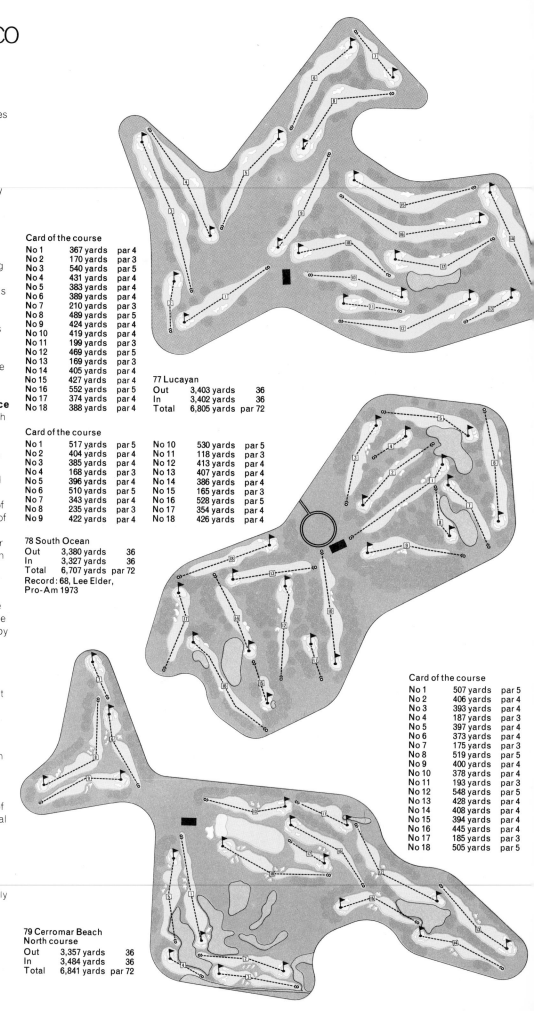

77 Lucayan CC, Freeport

The towns of Lucayan and Freeport are the centres of the gambling enterprises that lure so many people to the Bahamas. However, the Lucayan Country Club is far from being a gambler's paradise: it is a conservative club with a membership largely composed of American and Canadian businessmen. The course, designed by Dick Wilson and opened in 1964, sits on a natural hilly area overlooking the Bell Channel. One of its most interesting features is the extraordinary natural hazard of white coral rock that lies off the fairway beyond the normal rough and acts as a soul-destroying trap. If the ball lands here, finding it is a minor problem compared to the difficulties of playing out—if, indeed, that is possible. There is only one lake on the course and this runs the final 200 yards down the left-hand side of the 17th to haunt any hook-prone right-hander. Lucayan was the last golf club which the late, vastly admired American professional Craig Wood represented. It was here that he shot a 66 a matter of days before his sixty-sixth birthday.

78 South Ocean GC, Nassau, New Providence

Designed by Joe Lee and completed in 1971, South Ocean is one of the youngest—and probably the best—of Bahamian courses. Situated on New Providence Island near Nassau, the capital, it has eighteen holes of completely separate and identifiable character, cut through dense tropical jungle. Water comes into play at seven holes and the vast greens are matched by enormous areas of sand, some with trees in the middle, a trademark of Lee's work. He has also resisted the modern temptation to make every par-three a test of power rather than accuracy, and the 118-yard 11th—to an elongated green whose entrance is flanked by bunkers—is a welcome change, if no less demanding. Of the par-fives, the 528-yard 16th is virtually a double dog-leg, first round a lake on the right, then skirting a second stretch of water on the left before pitching to a green that is protected by four bunkers.

79 Cerromar Beach Hotel GC, Dorado

When Robert Trent Jones was invited to design a North and a South course at Cerromar, just a short walk from his famous thirty-six-hole complex at Dorado Beach, the challenge to produce equally good-looking golf of a totally different style was irresistible. He has achieved this by the more discreet use of the abundant water, particularly on the par-three and par-five holes, and by varying the greens from the large, contoured, sparsely bunkered type to the smaller, flatter, sand-surrounded designs. Although the combination of trees and water makes skilful shotmaking essential on many holes, these hazards are pulled back from the line of play at others to offer scenically exciting and less demanding golf. The North course is used for championship play and its outstanding par-threes call for the best stroke-making. At the 187-yard 4th the green is particularly narrow, well protected by inviting sandtraps and flanked by water on the right. The 11th is played from a raised tee 193 yards away and into the prevailing wind, with a lateral water hazard threatening on the left of the green and a large bunker protecting the right side.

Card of the course

No 1	367 yards	par 4
No 2	170 yards	par 3
No 3	540 yards	par 5
No 4	431 yards	par 4
No 5	383 yards	par 4
No 6	389 yards	par 4
No 7	210 yards	par 3
No 8	489 yards	par 5
No 9	424 yards	par 4
No 10	419 yards	par 4
No 11	199 yards	par 3
No 12	469 yards	par 5
No 13	169 yards	par 3
No 14	405 yards	par 4
No 15	427 yards	par 4
No 16	552 yards	par 5
No 17	374 yards	par 4
No 18	388 yards	par 4

77 Lucayan

Out	3,403 yards	36
In	3,402 yards	36
Total	6,805 yards	par 72

Card of the course

No 1	517 yards	par 5	No 10	530 yards	par 5
No 2	404 yards	par 4	No 11	118 yards	par 3
No 3	385 yards	par 4	No 12	413 yards	par 4
No 4	168 yards	par 3	No 13	407 yards	par 4
No 5	396 yards	par 4	No 14	386 yards	par 4
No 6	510 yards	par 5	No 15	165 yards	par 3
No 7	343 yards	par 4	No 16	528 yards	par 5
No 8	235 yards	par 3	No 17	354 yards	par 4
No 9	422 yards	par 4	No 18	426 yards	par 4

78 South Ocean

Out	3,380 yards	36
In	3,327 yards	36
Total	6,707 yards	par 72
Record: 68, Lee Elder, Pro-Am 1973		

Card of the course

No 1	507 yards	par 5
No 2	406 yards	par 4
No 3	393 yards	par 4
No 4	187 yards	par 3
No 5	397 yards	par 4
No 6	373 yards	par 4
No 7	175 yards	par 3
No 8	519 yards	par 5
No 9	400 yards	par 4
No 10	378 yards	par 4
No 11	193 yards	par 3
No 12	548 yards	par 5
No 13	428 yards	par 4
No 14	408 yards	par 4
No 15	394 yards	par 4
No 16	445 yards	par 4
No 17	185 yards	par 3
No 18	505 yards	par 5

79 Cerromar Beach
North course

Out	3,357 yards	36
In	3,484 yards	36
Total	6,841 yards	par 72

Virgin Islands/West Indies

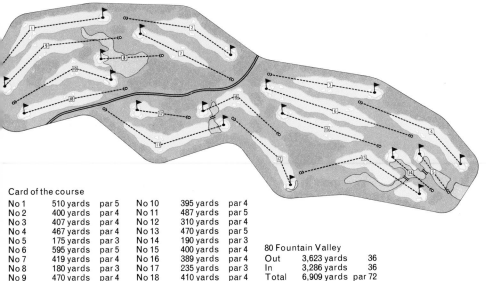

Card of the course

No 1	510 yards	par 5	No 10	395 yards	par 4
No 2	400 yards	par 4	No 11	487 yards	par 5
No 3	407 yards	par 4	No 12	310 yards	par 4
No 4	467 yards	par 4	No 13	470 yards	par 5
No 5	175 yards	par 3	No 14	190 yards	par 3
No 6	595 yards	par 5	No 15	400 yards	par 4
No 7	419 yards	par 4	No 16	389 yards	par 4
No 8	180 yards	par 3	No 17	235 yards	par 3
No 9	470 yards	par 4	No 18	410 yards	par 4

80 Fountain Valley

Out	3,623 yards	36
In	3,286 yards	36
Total	6,909 yards	par 72

80 Fountain Valley GC, St Croix

At St Croix on the Virgin Islands, an American protectorate, Robert Trent Jones has built a course of outstanding beauty and charm. Fountain Valley, the only eighteen-hole layout in the islands, is on the floor of a valley that is filled with trees, water and ravines, offering an awe-inspiring collection of views. Subtle teeing grounds are the key feature of the design, especially on the four short holes, three of which must be carried from the back tees, although alternative tees reduce the problem for the less accomplished. The first short hole is the 175-yard 5th, where the tees jut farther and farther out into the lake. From the championship teeing ground the shot requires a clear carry over the water, whereas from the ladies' tee the lake runs adjacent to the fairway, threatening any shot that is slightly hooked. The large green is trapped to the rear, penalizing those who over-club to ensure clearing the lake. Trade winds in the horseshoe-shaped valley both cool the course and add to its problems.

81 Tryall

Out	3,309 yards	36
In	3,089 yards	35
Total	6,398 yards	par 71

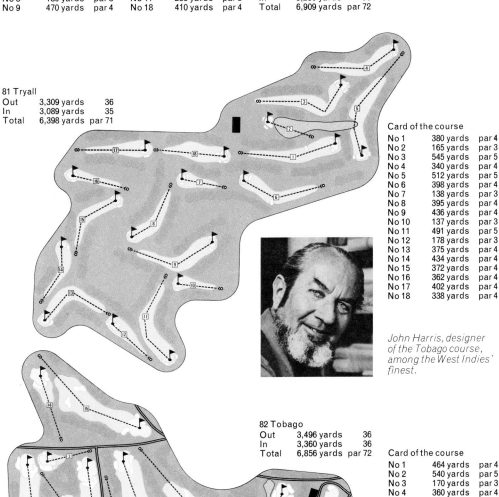

Card of the course

No 1	380 yards	par 4
No 2	165 yards	par 3
No 3	545 yards	par 5
No 4	340 yards	par 4
No 5	512 yards	par 5
No 6	398 yards	par 4
No 7	138 yards	par 3
No 8	395 yards	par 4
No 9	436 yards	par 4
No 10	137 yards	par 3
No 11	491 yards	par 5
No 12	178 yards	par 3
No 13	375 yards	par 4
No 14	434 yards	par 4
No 15	372 yards	par 4
No 16	362 yards	par 4
No 17	402 yards	par 4
No 18	338 yards	par 4

John Harris, designer of the Tobago course, among the West Indies' finest.

81 Tryall G & BC, Hanover, Jamaica

Sandy Bay lies on the western tip of Jamaica on near-mountainous land that has superb views over the ocean. Here, in the breach of the trade winds, is the Tryall course, a fine layout that was conceived by Ralph Plummer. The ground was so hilly that it seemed unlikely that anybody could build a course of such outstanding merit, but somehow Plummer managed to do so. It seems that the drive is always either straight up a steep hill or disappearing down one, but in this lies the secret of success on this switchback course. If the ball is kept in the sort of play that Plummer envisaged then there are surprisingly few sidehill lies and—once the apparently inherent difficulty is seen to have evaporated—the golf becomes straightforward and steady. On the back nine, the eloquent 137-yard 10th needs only a smooth, relaxed short iron to make the green. With the course's height there is generally a refreshing breeze blowing into the kitchen-hot valleys. Then, too, it is always pleasant to play through the palms and other tropical foliage.

82 Tobago

Out	3,496 yards	36
In	3,360 yards	36
Total	6,856 yards	par 72

Card of the course

No 1	464 yards	par 4
No 2	540 yards	par 5
No 3	170 yards	par 3
No 4	360 yards	par 4
No 5	405 yards	par 4
No 6	535 yards	par 5
No 7	215 yards	par 3
No 8	335 yards	par 4
No 9	472 yards	par 4
No 10	485 yards	par 5
No 11	445 yards	par 4
No 12	215 yards	par 3
No 13	510 yards	par 5
No 14	225 yards	par 3
No 15	445 yards	par 4
No 16	445 yards	par 5
No 17	195 yards	par 3
No 18	395 yards	par 4

82 Tobago GC, Tobago

Commander John D. Harris has a string of designs in more than thirty countries to his credit, and the Tobago course at Mount Irvine Bay is one of his classics. Set in gently rising country along the coast, there are sea views from every hole, fine water features and an abundance of massive palm trees. The sharply dog-legged 472-yard 9th is played from an elevated tee so that those who attempt the shortcut can clearly see the lake, trees and sand which stand in their way. This is a feature of Harris's designs—he believes that every hazard should be visible, acting as lighthouses to guide the player along the correct path. The five par-three holes are particularly challenging; only two are less than 200 yards. The 215-yard 7th is considered the best. The shot is to a long, narrow green with sand on the right and a drop to a lake on the left. The lush tees, fairways and greens, all grassed in tifton, are amply watered by the course's subterranean irrigation network.

Colombia

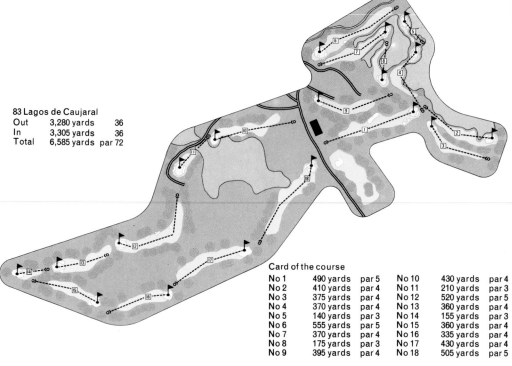

83 Lagos de Caujaral GC, Barranquilla

Designer Joe Lee built many problems into this
beautiful course: nine holes feature water—
several of them threatened on both sides—while
three par-fives have double dog-legs, and three
other holes have a seventy-five-foot drop from tee
to fairway. Mercifully, at 6,585 yards, the length is
not too demanding. Yet the strong trade winds can
make even the most modest par-four a drive and
long iron for the majority of golfers. The view from
the elevated 1st tee is of a narrow fairway between
dense trees to a well-trapped green—and this is the
widest fairway on the course. The double water
hazard is first featured at the 370-yard 4th, where
the tee shot must carry 200 yards to an island
fairway and counteract the prevailing wind
pushing the ball towards the water on the right. It is
then necessary to cross the water again to reach a
green which is also virtually surrounded by two
lakes, with bunkers to the left rear and right front.

83 Lagos de Caujaral

Out	3,280 yards	36
In	3,305 yards	36
Total	6,585 yards	par 72

Card of the course

No 1	490 yards	par 5	No 10	430 yards	par 4
No 2	410 yards	par 4	No 11	210 yards	par 3
No 3	375 yards	par 4	No 12	520 yards	par 5
No 4	370 yards	par 4	No 13	360 yards	par 4
No 5	140 yards	par 3	No 14	155 yards	par 3
No 6	555 yards	par 5	No 15	360 yards	par 4
No 7	370 yards	par 4	No 16	335 yards	par 4
No 8	175 yards	par 3	No 17	430 yards	par 4
No 9	395 yards	par 4	No 18	505 yards	par 5

84 El Rincon GC, Bogotá

"El Maestro" is the phrase that comes to the lips of
El Rincon members when they express their
feelings for the American architect Robert Trent
Jones and the course he built for them. He finished
his project on the outskirts of Bogotá in 1953 and
since then the only major change has been the
redirecting of the two nines; the opening half was
originally the back nine and vice versa. He planted
numerous trees on the flat plain and sank a
number of ponds that now come into play on eleven
of the holes as subdued and controlled hazards.
The fairways were planted with kikuyo grass and
are lined by very strong rough, while the greens
are swift, with a preponderance of typical Trent
Jones breaks. All the qualities of the course are
found in the 594-yard par-five 15th. A pronounced
dog-leg to the left means that a carry of at least 250
yards is needed to ensure a good line for the
second. The green is tucked behind a large water
hazard and bunkered in front.

84 El Rincon

Out	3,792 yards	36
In	3,724 yards	36
Total	7,516 yards	par 72

Record: 67,
Dennis Watson, 1975

Card of the course

No 1	415 yards	par 4
No 2	216 yards	par 3
No 3	423 yards	par 4
No 4	434 yards	par 4
No 5	626 yards	par 5
No 6	207 yards	par 3
No 7	553 yards	par 5
No 8	454 yards	par 4
No 9	464 yards	par 4
No 10	430 yards	par 4
No 11	438 yards	par 4
No 12	555 yards	par 5
No 13	390 yards	par 4
No 14	202 yards	par 3
No 15	594 yards	par 5
No 16	179 yards	par 3
No 17	465 yards	par 4
No 18	471 yards	par 4

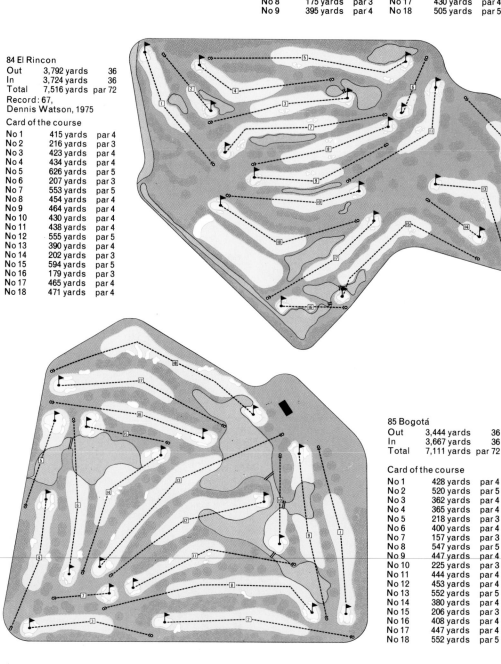

85 CC of Bogotá, Bogotá

The Country Club of Bogotá has two fine courses
set against the splendid backdrop of the Andes.
The championship layout, Los Fundadores, was
designed in 1950 by Dr Van Kleek, but eleven years
later Robert Janis elongated the teeing grounds,
reshaped the greens and added several new
bunkers. The generally humid climate leaves the
course moist for most of the year and keeps the
fairways and greens in superb condition. The
course offers a formidable challenge, its tight
fairways hemmed in by two large lakes and an
abundance of trees. The lush greens are well
watered and true. Good driving is the key to
success, particularly at the 447-yard 9th. The lake
lies below the tee and the drive must reach an
island fairway; the second, invariably a wood, must
then be hit across water to a thin, narrow green.
The uphill 18th is a daunting problem, 552 yards
long and dog-legging left around well-sited
bunkers. The second, bedevilled by more fairway
traps, is usually laid up short of water that cuts off
the green. The agony is ended with a simple pitch.

85 Bogotá

Out	3,444 yards	36
In	3,667 yards	36
Total	7,111 yards	par 72

Card of the course

No 1	428 yards	par 4
No 2	520 yards	par 5
No 3	362 yards	par 4
No 4	365 yards	par 4
No 5	218 yards	par 3
No 6	400 yards	par 4
No 7	157 yards	par 3
No 8	547 yards	par 5
No 9	447 yards	par 4
No 10	225 yards	par 3
No 11	444 yards	par 4
No 12	453 yards	par 4
No 13	552 yards	par 5
No 14	380 yards	par 4
No 15	206 yards	par 3
No 16	408 yards	par 4
No 17	447 yards	par 4
No 18	552 yards	par 5

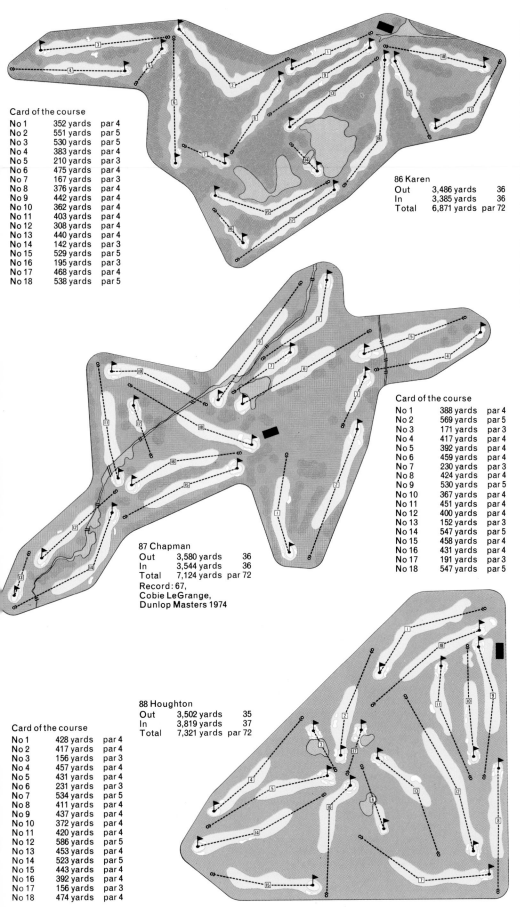

Card of the course

No 1	352 yards	par 4
No 2	551 yards	par 5
No 3	530 yards	par 5
No 4	383 yards	par 4
No 5	210 yards	par 3
No 6	475 yards	par 4
No 7	167 yards	par 3
No 8	376 yards	par 4
No 9	442 yards	par 4
No 10	362 yards	par 4
No 11	403 yards	par 4
No 12	308 yards	par 4
No 13	440 yards	par 4
No 14	142 yards	par 3
No 15	529 yards	par 5
No 16	195 yards	par 3
No 17	468 yards	par 4
No 18	538 yards	par 5

86 Karen

Out	3,486 yards	36
In	3,385 yards	36
Total	6,871 yards	par 72

87 Chapman

Out	3,580 yards	36
In	3,544 yards	36
Total	7,124 yards	par 72
Record: 67,
Cobie LeGrange,
Dunlop Masters 1974

Card of the course

No 1	388 yards	par 4
No 2	569 yards	par 5
No 3	171 yards	par 3
No 4	417 yards	par 4
No 5	392 yards	par 4
No 6	459 yards	par 4
No 7	230 yards	par 3
No 8	424 yards	par 4
No 9	530 yards	par 5
No 10	367 yards	par 4
No 11	451 yards	par 4
No 12	400 yards	par 4
No 13	152 yards	par 3
No 14	547 yards	par 5
No 15	458 yards	par 4
No 16	431 yards	par 4
No 17	191 yards	par 3
No 18	547 yards	par 5

88 Houghton

Out	3,502 yards	35
In	3,819 yards	37
Total	7,321 yards	par 72

Card of the course

No 1	428 yards	par 4
No 2	417 yards	par 4
No 3	156 yards	par 3
No 4	457 yards	par 4
No 5	431 yards	par 4
No 6	231 yards	par 3
No 7	534 yards	par 5
No 8	411 yards	par 4
No 9	437 yards	par 4
No 10	372 yards	par 4
No 11	420 yards	par 4
No 12	586 yards	par 5
No 13	453 yards	par 4
No 14	523 yards	par 5
No 15	443 yards	par 4
No 16	392 yards	par 4
No 17	156 yards	par 3
No 18	474 yards	par 4

86 Karen CC, Nairobi

Karen Country Club is situated on 216 acres of undulating woodland twelve miles west of Nairobi. The course was laid out in 1931 on farmland formerly owned by Baroness Karen von Blixen, after whom the district takes its name and where she wrote her classic novel *Out of Africa*. Red murrum clay soil renders the course hard underfoot during the long drought, but for most of the year the well-irrigated fairways are cool, green ribbons of turf winding through avenues of eucalyptus, acacias and thorn bushes. The greens are mostly an experimental blend of native Bermuda with some South African bent, giving a surface that putts fairly. The 2nd, a 551-yard par-five, is the longest hole on the course and demands both strength and skill. A dog-leg of almost ninety degrees appears at the length of an excellent drive, and the second shot has to avoid a sandtrap in the middle of the fairway about sixty yards short of the green—so either over- or underclubbing can cause trouble of one kind or another and make for an elusive goal.

87 Chapman GC, Salisbury

In 1928 Salisbury Rayton Athletic Club laid out a nine-hole course with sand greens over a very rough patch of African bush country, and two years later a second nine was playable. After World War II substantial improvements were made with the financial help of Sir Henry Chapman, and the club was renamed in his honour. Many hardwood cedars and conifers were planted to line the fairways, and the greens were properly grassed; in 1961 the association with Rayton was severed, twenty-eight new bunkers were positioned and the Nyamaranga River was deepened and dammed to create yet more hazards. The river widens to a lake at the 6th, a long par-four, and the average golfer may find that playing a safe lay-up second is more rewarding than going for the green with a long iron or a fairway wood. The 451-yard 11th has a hideous approach to the green: the second shot is a mid iron and the target lies on the other side of a fairway divided by a stretch of water, surrounded by a cluster of bunkers and interspersed with a few trees and shrubs.

88 Houghton GC, Johannesburg

As with so many of the early South African courses, Houghton—first played in 1926—was designed by the club professional, A. M. Copland. It was built on 155 acres of prime residential land which is now only three miles from Johannesburg City Hall. There are only three par-threes, and in the rarefied atmosphere of the Transvaal highveld (almost 6,000 feet above sea-level) even the mediocre golfer finds himself suddenly two clubs longer: many of the par-fours require a drive and a wedge or an 8-iron. The entire strategy of the course lies in the tight bunkering of the greens. The traps are cut into the putting surface and so positioned as to make accurate placement of the tee shot essential if there is to be any easy way to the pin. Particularly outstanding holes are the 4th, 5th and 18th, all par-fours that reward only the finest shot-makers. The course has changed since the Dunlop Masters in the early 1960s—it is now played in a different direction, with several new tees and traps.

Japan

89 Kasugai CC, Nagoya

Kasugai's East and West courses were designed
by the architect Seichi Inoue in the hills to the
west of Nagoya. Giant earth-moving machines
were used in cutting off the tops of hills and filling
the valleys to make the fairways—a common
method of construction in Japan. What is left is still
undulating and decidedly steep in places, which is
much to the Japanese liking. The clubhouse,
perched on the highest point, overlooks both
layouts, which are well defined by many young
conifers and small decorative ponds. These
obstacles also serve to provide some challenge.
For the 1975 Japan Open, played on the East
course, additional fairway sandtraps and
temporary trees were arranged to provide extra
difficulty. Korai grass is used for the putting
surfaces, giving the greens much variation in
both texture and colour from season to season. The
East course is 6,900 yards of rambling holes over
many hills, some of which are quite steep by world
championship standards. This provides a problem
of distance—an advantage to the long hitters but
frustrating for those who have less power.

90 Nasu International CC, Tochigi

Situated on Japan's northernmost island, Nasu
International Country Club is distinguished by its
year-round, one-green putting system, which is
contrary to the usual Japanese practice of
providing winter and summer greens. The course
has been carved through steep, hilly woodland
which eventually makes the 6,825 yards play longer
than the card reads, an effect exaggerated by the
almost constant cross-winds and numerous
sidehill lies. On the 6th and 7th, both par-fours,
the drive is blind, the fairways rising to a crest
before dipping to well-trapped greens. The long,
uphill 13th dog-legs to the right around a bunker
strategically placed to catch the sliced or the
over-ambitious drive. The lay-up second then has to
contend with the severe gusting winds to leave an
untroubled short iron to the target.

91 Yomiuri CC, Tokyo

The Yomiuri Country Club, to the west of Tokyo, is
part of a huge sporting complex built by the
Yomiuri Newspaper Group. The course, which is of
the highest class, was designed in 1964 by Seichi
Inoue, Japan's leading architect. He used his
considerable experience to create holes that are
adventurous without being unreasonable,
avoiding a drawback that mars many courses in
this mountainous country. At 6,962 yards it is well
set for distance, particularly in the lushness that
follows the mid-year wet season. It has a two-green
system which slightly interferes with the greenside
trapping, but generally sand areas are punishing
and fearsome. There are a number of blind shots
from the teeing areas and many shots have to carry
deep valleys, which are grassed as rough and
where the wind can play strange tricks with the
ball. Yomiuri has a high reputation amongst the
professionals and top-class amateurs—a sentiment
reflected by the decision of the Japan Golf
Association to stage the World Cup there in 1966.
It was won by the USA and the individual victor
was the Canadian George Knudson.

Card of the course

No 1	415 yards	par 4
No 2	390 yards	par 4
No 3	495 yards	par 5
No 4	160 yards	par 3
No 5	420 yards	par 4
No 6	460 yards	par 4
No 7	180 yards	par 3
No 8	495 yards	par 5
No 9	430 yards	par 4
No 10	400 yards	par 4
No 11	360 yards	par 4
No 12	195 yards	par 3
No 13	505 yards	par 5
No 14	435 yards	par 4
No 15	225 yards	par 3
No 16	420 yards	par 4
No 17	510 yards	par 5
No 18	405 yards	par 4

89 Kasugai East

Out	3,445 yards	36
In	3,455 yards	36
Total	6,900 yards	par 72

Card of the course

No 1	505 yards	par 5	No 10	490 yards	par 5
No 2	175 yards	par 3	No 11	360 yards	par 4
No 3	400 yards	par 4	No 12	200 yards	par 3
No 4	525 yards	par 5	No 13	500 yards	par 5
No 5	423 yards	par 4	No 14	412 yards	par 4
No 6	430 yards	par 4	No 15	460 yards	par 4
No 7	385 yards	par 4	No 16	410 yards	par 4
No 8	200 yards	par 3	No 17	150 yards	par 3
No 9	380 yards	par 4	No 18	420 yards	par 4

90 Nasu

Out	3,423 yards	36
In	3,402 yards	36
Total	6,825 yards	par 72

*George Knudson of
Canada opened with a 64
when he won individual
honours in the 1966
World Cup at Tokyo's
Yomiuri club.*

Card of the course

No 1	396 yards	par 4	No 10	425 yards	par 4
No 2	180 yards	par 3	No 11	507 yards	par 5
No 3	403 yards	par 4	No 12	432 yards	par 4
No 4	508 yards	par 5	No 13	450 yards	par 4
No 5	384 yards	par 4	No 14	364 yards	par 4
No 6	541 yards	par 5	No 15	194 yards	par 3
No 7	389 yards	par 4	No 16	410 yards	par 4
No 8	197 yards	par 3	No 17	510 yards	par 5
No 9	448 yards	par 4	No 18	224 yards	par 3

91 Yomiuri

Out	3,446 yards	36
In	3,516 yards	36
Total	6,962 yards	par 72

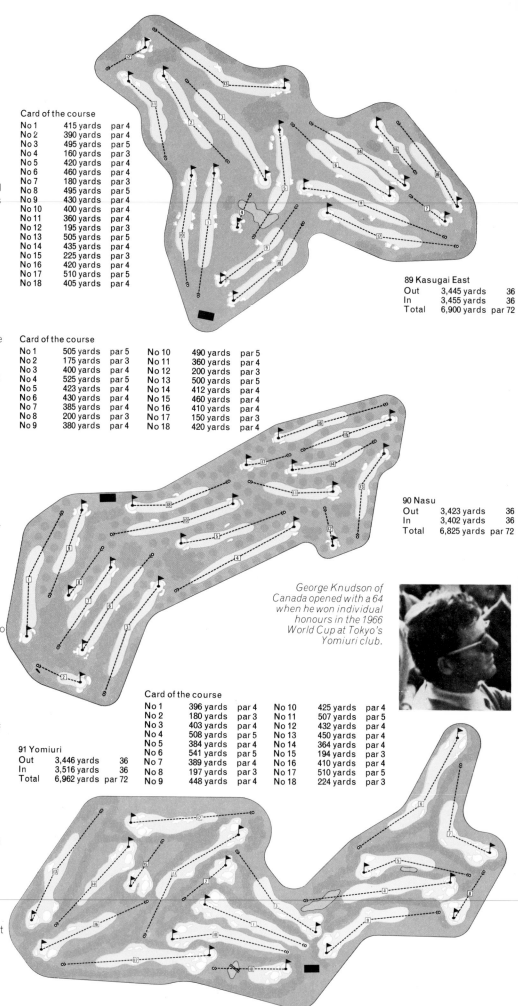

Philippines/Thailand/India

Card of the course

No 1	427 yards	par 4
No 2	323 yards	par 4
No 3	376 yards	par 4
No 4	345 yards	par 4
No 5	582 yards	par 5
No 6	434 yards	par 4
No 7	345 yards	par 4
No 8	167 yards	par 3
No 9	453 yards	par 4
No 10	383 yards	par 4
No 11	384 yards	par 4
No 12	439 yards	par 4
No 13	523 yards	par 5
No 14	435 yards	par 4
No 15	379 yards	par 4
No 16	206 yards	par 3
No 17	428 yards	par 4
No 18	449 yards	par 4

92 Wack Wack

Out	3,452 yards	36
In	3,626 yards	36
Total	7,078 yards	par 72

Lu Liang Huan, 1974 Philippine Open winner at Wack Wack.

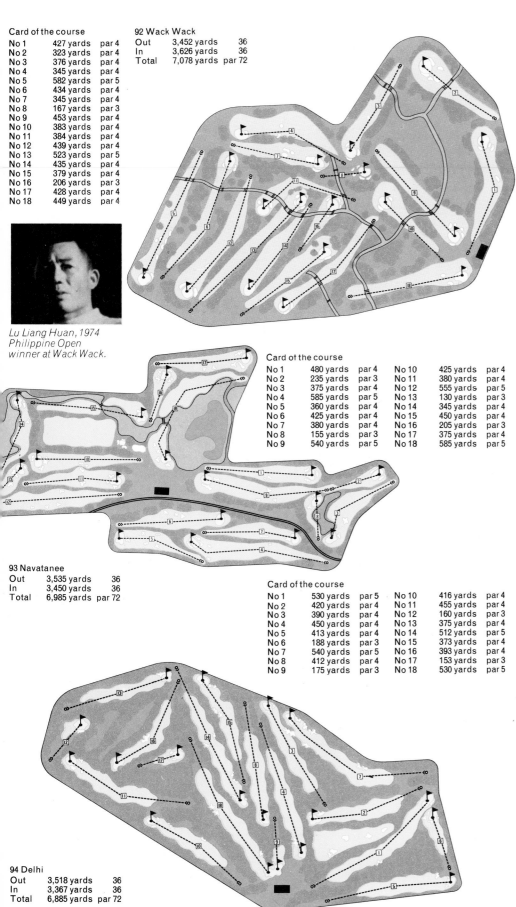

Card of the course

No 1	480 yards	par 4	No 10	425 yards	par 4
No 2	235 yards	par 3	No 11	380 yards	par 4
No 3	375 yards	par 4	No 12	555 yards	par 5
No 4	585 yards	par 5	No 13	130 yards	par 3
No 5	360 yards	par 4	No 14	345 yards	par 4
No 6	425 yards	par 4	No 15	450 yards	par 4
No 7	380 yards	par 4	No 16	205 yards	par 3
No 8	155 yards	par 3	No 17	375 yards	par 4
No 9	540 yards	par 5	No 18	585 yards	par 5

93 Navatanee

Out	3,535 yards	36
In	3,450 yards	36
Total	6,985 yards	par 72

Card of the course

No 1	530 yards	par 5	No 10	416 yards	par 4
No 2	420 yards	par 4	No 11	455 yards	par 4
No 3	390 yards	par 4	No 12	160 yards	par 3
No 4	450 yards	par 4	No 13	375 yards	par 4
No 5	413 yards	par 4	No 14	512 yards	par 5
No 6	188 yards	par 3	No 15	373 yards	par 4
No 7	540 yards	par 5	No 16	393 yards	par 4
No 8	412 yards	par 4	No 17	153 yards	par 3
No 9	175 yards	par 3	No 18	530 yards	par 5

94 Delhi

Out	3,518 yards	36
In	3,367 yards	36
Total	6,885 yards	par 72

92 Wack Wack G & CC, Manila

In 1933 a group of expatriate American businessmen in Manila bought a track of land at Mandaluyong and developed it into the Wack Wack course. Its name was inspired by the noise made by the innumerable flights of crows that were a pest to the players in the early days. The beautiful lake was created by damming a creek and has become an interesting hazard on several holes. During the 1960s the primitive table-top greens of the original construction were rebuilt along modern lines and several of the holes extended to bring the course up to 7,000 yards. The layout now leads the player over the gently undulating terrain, occasionally across streams and into the extremely well-trapped greens. At the end of the 1930s Wack Wack staged the first international Asian event, the Philippine Open. After World War II the club had a new lease of life and resumed the championship on a large scale, attracting players like Mangrum, Oliver, Burke, Harrison and Furgol from the USA together with a large contingent of Australian and Taiwanese.

93 Navatanee CC, Bangkok

Navatanee Golf Club possesses by far the best course in Thailand. Designed by Robert Trent Jones for its owner, Sukhum Navapan, this 6,985-yard par-72 layout entertained the 1975 World Cup, from which all players departed with high praise for its championship qualities. The course construction converted a large swamp of rice paddies and wasteland into a vista of green fairways, white sandtraps and plenty of water, the familiar Trent Jones trademark. It is grassed in tifton from tee to cup, providing a lush carpet of superb lies for fairway play and—for such a hot climate—smooth putting surfaces. Jones has placed a variety of teeing grounds for most holes, so adapting the layout to suit every golfer's needs. The last four holes represent a thrilling finish for a round, with disaster lying in wait for any false step —even at the final hole, a torrid par-five of 585 yards where a double water carry is particularly fearsome in any kind of wind.

94 Delhi GC, New Delhi

Built on the rubble of the old Mogul metropolis, the Delhi course, set amidst the grandeur of such ancient architectural monuments, has a fascination and beauty all of its own. The fairways— of pure couch grass—and the natural jungle rough have a verdant greenness after the monsoon rains which suggests coolness in an otherwise torrid climate. The layout has undergone several changes. At one time it ranged over wider territory, but the club now confines twenty-seven holes within a tight boundary, the main eighteen forming a championship course of high merit. It combines a need for length with a demand for extreme directness. Drives that curl into the wild bush rough are invariably unplayable, so necessitating the almost mandatory employment of an "agi-wallah", who performs the function of a fore-caddie while understudying the more responsible job of caddie. The club is a delightful meeting place for many of Delhi's sporting citizens and diplomats. Every two years it hosts the annual Indian Open championship, which is a part of the Asian tournament circuit.

Australia

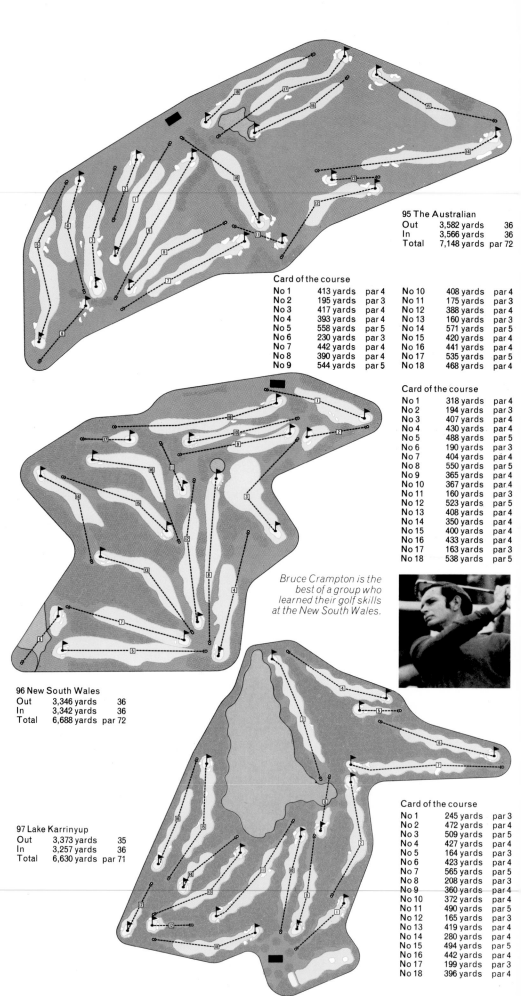

95 The Australian GC, Sydney

The Australian Golf Club, formed in 1882 and set in the heart of Sydney's busiest industrial area, is the oldest club in the continent. It moved to its present site in 1903 and twenty-three years later Alister Mackenzie laid the foundations of what is now the championship layout; modifications and renovations were completed under the guidance of Sloan Marpeth in 1967. Its twenty-seven holes lie in a large, often windswept, sandy basin, the rim of which is surrounded by many fine houses and an imposing array of club buildings. There are few trees, which gives the layout an open appearance in the classic Scottish style. The greens are often elevated and the primary hazards are the numerous yawning sandtraps and the lake, which affects the 16th and 17th. The first Australian Open was played here in 1904; the victor was the Honourable Michael Scott, who twenty-nine years later became the oldest player to win the British Amateur. Such is its suitability for championship golf that the Australian Open has been held here on many occasions since—and is likely to return for many years to come.

96 New South Wales GC, Matraville

Laid out by Alister Mackenzie in 1928, the New South Wales course at Sydney offers magnificent, panoramic views over the Pacific Ocean to the east and Botany Bay to the south; the spot where Captain Cook landed in 1770 is less than a par-four from the clubhouse. The land presents an unrivalled site for a course and the wind, ever-changing in both direction and strength, produces a stern challenge to golfers of all categories. The punishing undulations, bunkering and rough combine with the wind to make the chance of a low score for the average handicap player a question of fine control over shots that must always travel in shallow trajectories. The 190-yard par-three 6th, down among the rocks on the tip of the headland, is played over the water in the now immortal style of the 16th at Cypress Point. It is, perhaps, an early indicator of the influence Mackenzie was to have on golf course design.

97 Lake Karrinyup GC, Western Australia

As its name suggests, Lake Karrinyup is constructed around a lake set in a natural basin surrounded by sandhills. The lake is the home of many forms of wildlife and from any angle mirrors the beauty of the course. Created by Alex Russell in 1927, it bears a marked similarity to his home course of Royal Melbourne in the arrangement of the generously wide, couch grass fairways, the grand sandtraps and the large, flowing greens. Eucalyptus and many species of native wild flowers flourish in the sandy soil, forming an indigenous and attractive setting for each hole. A wind from the Indian Ocean can affect the scores by adding to the problems already set by the water and the bush. The 8th, a 208-yard par-three, is the only hole that is played directly over the lake and a strong low iron tee shot is often required when playing into the wind. The course is a popular venue for the Australian Open and Amateur championships, with winners such as Norman Von Nida in 1952 and Bruce Devlin in 1960.

95 The Australian

Out	3,582 yards	36
In	3,566 yards	36
Total	7,148 yards	par 72

Card of the course

No 1	413 yards	par 4	No 10	408 yards	par 4
No 2	195 yards	par 3	No 11	175 yards	par 3
No 3	417 yards	par 4	No 12	388 yards	par 4
No 4	393 yards	par 4	No 13	160 yards	par 3
No 5	558 yards	par 5	No 14	571 yards	par 5
No 6	230 yards	par 3	No 15	420 yards	par 4
No 7	442 yards	par 4	No 16	441 yards	par 4
No 8	390 yards	par 4	No 17	535 yards	par 5
No 9	544 yards	par 5	No 18	468 yards	par 4

Card of the course

No 1	318 yards	par 4
No 2	194 yards	par 4
No 3	407 yards	par 4
No 4	430 yards	par 4
No 5	488 yards	par 5
No 6	190 yards	par 3
No 7	404 yards	par 4
No 8	550 yards	par 5
No 9	365 yards	par 4
No 10	367 yards	par 4
No 11	160 yards	par 3
No 12	523 yards	par 5
No 13	408 yards	par 4
No 14	350 yards	par 4
No 15	400 yards	par 4
No 16	433 yards	par 4
No 17	163 yards	par 3
No 18	538 yards	par 5

Bruce Crampton is the best of a group who learned their golf skills at the New South Wales.

96 New South Wales

Out	3,346 yards	36
In	3,342 yards	36
Total	6,688 yards	par 72

97 Lake Karrinyup

Out	3,373 yards	35
In	3,257 yards	36
Total	6,630 yards	par 71

Card of the course

No 1	245 yards	par 3
No 2	472 yards	par 4
No 3	509 yards	par 5
No 4	427 yards	par 4
No 5	164 yards	par 3
No 6	423 yards	par 4
No 7	565 yards	par 5
No 8	208 yards	par 3
No 9	360 yards	par 4
No 10	372 yards	par 4
No 11	490 yards	par 5
No 12	165 yards	par 3
No 13	419 yards	par 4
No 14	280 yards	par 4
No 15	494 yards	par 5
No 16	442 yards	par 4
No 17	199 yards	par 3
No 18	396 yards	par 4

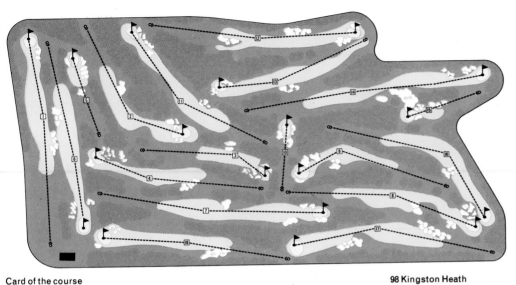

Card of the course

No 1	458 yards	par 4	No 10	143 yards	par 3
No 2	365 yards	par 4	No 11	402 yards	par 4
No 3	297 yards	par 4	No 12	478 yards	par 5
No 4	384 yards	par 4	No 13	353 yards	par 4
No 5	189 yards	par 3	No 14	542 yards	par 5
No 6	434 yards	par 4	No 15	155 yards	par 3
No 7	505 yards	par 5	No 16	422 yards	par 4
No 8	431 yards	par 4	No 17	457 yards	par 4
No 9	354 yards	par 4	No 18	428 yards	par 4

98 Kingston Heath

Out	3,417 yards	36
In	3,380 yards	36
Total	6,797 yards	par 72

Card of the course

No 1	364 yards	par 4
No 2	387 yards	par 4
No 3	412 yards	par 4
No 4	516 yards	par 5
No 5	394 yards	par 4
No 6	394 yards	par 4
No 7	170 yards	par 3
No 8	370 yards	par 4
No 9	591 yards	par 5
No 10	120 yards	par 3
No 11	287 yards	par 4
No 12	359 yards	par 4
No 13	222 yards	par 3
No 14	348 yards	par 4
No 15	428 yards	par 4
No 16	401 yards	par 4
No 17	480 yards	par 5
No 18	372 yards	par 4

99 Auckland

Out	3,598 yards	37
In	3,017 yards	35
Total	6,615 yards	par 72

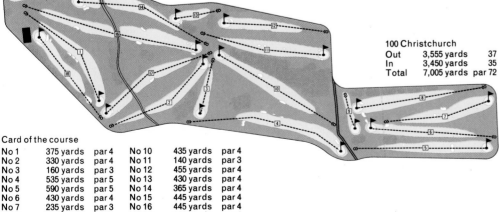

100 Christchurch

Out	3,555 yards	37
In	3,450 yards	35
Total	7,005 yards	par 72

Card of the course

No 1	375 yards	par 4	No 10	435 yards	par 4
No 2	330 yards	par 4	No 11	140 yards	par 3
No 3	160 yards	par 3	No 12	455 yards	par 4
No 4	535 yards	par 5	No 13	430 yards	par 4
No 5	590 yards	par 5	No 14	365 yards	par 4
No 6	430 yards	par 4	No 15	445 yards	par 4
No 7	235 yards	par 3	No 16	445 yards	par 4
No 8	420 yards	par 4	No 17	375 yards	par 4
No 9	480 yards	par 5	No 18	360 yards	par 4

98 Kingston Heath GC, Melbourne

Like many old clubs, Kingston Heath was born of necessity: an established club was forced off its course on municipal land near Melbourne city edge and so, faced with extinction, its members sought land farther out where the price was right and the soil conducive. They chose a site for Kingston Heath on the same sandy tract of land as Royal Melbourne, and the eventual result looks like its half-brother. The design, in 1925, was by Sydney professional Dan Souter, but three years later Alister Mackenzie undertook the bunkering. It is now a delightful mixture of flat and rising land, making easy walking and interesting golf. The holes vary in theme and, played for the first time, may even surprise. The fairways, lined by eucalyptus and tea-trees, are almost pure couch grass and lead on to greens that have fine surfaces of seaside bent, browntop and fescue mixed. The three par-threes are classic in conception and offer a fine challenge for perceptive strokemaking. The course is on the regular championship roster and has accommodated the Open three times.

99 Auckland GC, Middlemore

Middlemore, as the Auckland Golf Club is known, after the district in which it thrives, has an atmosphere that is both special and unique, even for New Zealand. Its homely wooden clubhouse looks out on a parkland setting of exemplary tidiness and passivity. Tall rows of fifty-year-old pines divide some fairways, while others are open to the sky. Built on clay soil, it has periods of discomfort when it is either wet and sticky or bone dry. But these periods are fleeting, and between-times Middlemore is a soft and gently undulating, interesting course of championship dimensions containing a wide variety of obstacles and challenges. The club was opened in 1910 and within two years a full eighteen holes, designed by the professional F. G. Hood, were ready for play. It has hosted the New Zealand Open five times and the Amateur seven times. The members tend to be elderly, and they prefer the course cleanly cut with little rough. But it is easily and quickly converted into quite a daunting monster.

100 Christchurch GC, Shirley

Christchurch Golf Club has a golfing tradition stretching back to 1873 when, like many a similar club in distant British colonies, it began on another site sparked by the enthusiasm of a handful of Scots. Popularly known as Shirley, after the garden suburb in which it dwells, the course follows a route which takes it away to the 9th in the old Scottish tradition. The holes tumble over small bumps and hollows, follow boundary fences—much to the frustration of right-handed slicers—and leap, towards the end, over a tiny burn. Pines, broom and gorse lend colour and age to the backdrop. The best and most daunting hole is the 4th, a 535-yard par-five which runs along the boundary fence, describing a gentle curve to the right. The green is made on the final step and is surrounded on three sides by the most punishing of indignities in golf, out-of-bounds. Here, the score for the unwitting, who opt to hit the green in two, often enters double figures. This feat needs either superb technique or an iron nerve. Playing short with an iron and pitching dead is best.

ACKNOWLEDGEMENTS
In a publication as comprehensive as this the editors inevitably draw upon the specialist knowledge of a great many experts, and special thanks are due to the following people whose assistance was particularly valuable: Pete and Alice Dye; George Fazio; Ronald Fream of Thomson Wolveridge Fream and Ass, USA; Ken Gordon; Bob Haines of Dunlop International Sports Co; Frank Hannigan and Frank Tatum of the United States Golf Ass; James Paterson Izatt; Robert Trent Jones and Arthur K. Hoffman of Robert Trent Jones Inc; Keith Mackenzie, secretary of The Royal and Ancient Golf Club of St Andrews; Cabell Robinson of International Planners Ltd; Chris Wilkinson of The Acushnet Co; and Michael Wolveridge of Thomson Wolveridge Ass, Australia.

The publishers also wish to thank all those golf clubs which are represented in this book, and whose assistance was invaluable, as well as the following individuals and organizations: Dale Antram, Firestone Tire & Rubber Co; Bahamas Tourist Office; Bermuda Tourist Board; British Transport Hotels Ltd; Duncan C. Campbell; Fred Corcoran of International Golf Ass; Danish Tourist Board; Tom Gardo of Sea Pines Co; Donald Grant Snr.; John D. Harris; Fred W. Hawtree; Steven J.H. van Hengel of Kennemer G & CC; Anders Jansen, editor of Svensk Golf; Colin Kidd; Gerald Micklem; Bill Menton, secretary, Golfing Union of Ireland; Bob Murphy, manager, Muirfield Village Golf Club; Ted Ostermann, editor of Golf (Germany); David Pearson Ass; David Physick; Jerry Pittman of Seminole GC; Rockresorts Ltd; Roger Rulewich; De la Rue Ltd; John Samuels, sports editor of *The Guardian*; Virginia Scott-Eliott; Janet Seagle of the USPGA; Arthur Jack Snyder, secretary American Society of Golf Course Architects; Peter Woollings, secretary Royal Antwerp GC; Vincent Yong, secretary Royal Selangor GC.

Index prepared by Brenda Hall MA, registered indexer of the Society of Indexers.

PHOTOGRAPHIC CREDITS
Photographs are listed from left to right in descending order. Abbreviations used are: RWF—Ronald W. Fream; A/DM—Allsport/Don Morley; AAR—Anthony Adams Roberts;

RTHPL—Radio Times Hulton Picture Library; USGA—Courtesy United States Golf Ass.

Half-title page: 16th green at Seminole, Florida, Woodfin Camp/Marvin E. Newman; Title page: 8th hole at Cajuiles, Paul Barton; Contents page: 7th green at Pebble Beach, Julian Graham; Pages 6/7: Courtesy John A. Mulcahy Ltd; 8: USGA; 9: RTHPL, USGA, AAR; 12: Michael Gedye, Michael Kay/Portland Studios; 13: Courtesy Aer Lingus, Michael Wolveridge, RWF, Michael Kay/Portland Studios; 14: Peter Dazeley, RWF, RWF, Peter Dazeley; 15: John L. Alexandrowicz, Leonard Kamsler, Bettmann Archive Inc; 16: Paul Barton, RWF, AAR, RWF; 17: RWF, RWF, Paul Barton, RWF; 18: David Pearson Associates/Paul Barton, Courtesy Firestone Tire & Rubber Co, RWF; 19: RWF, RWF, RWF, Colorsport; 20: RWF, RWF, Courtesy Eyre Methuen, RWF; 21: RWF, remainder Courtesy Robert Trent Jones Inc; 22: John L. Alexandrowicz, AAR, Richard A. Prendergast; 23: Bruce Coleman Ltd/Chris Bonington, RWF, RWF, RWF; 24: Woodfin Camp/Marvin E. Newman; 25: Woodfin Camp/Marvin E. Newman; 26: Barry von Below; 27: Michael Wolveridge; 28: Paul Barton; 29: RWF; 30: Courtesy Sea Pines/Tom Gardo; 31: AAR; 32: RWF; 34: RWF; 36/7: Woodfin Camp/John Marmaras; 38: G.M. Cowie; 39: Popperfoto, Gerry Cranham; 40: Michael Gedye; 41: Colorsport, E.D. Lacey; 42: Sportapics, Colorsport; 43: Michael Gedye; 46: Ian Joy, Bert Neale/Action Photos; 47: E.D. Lacey, Gerry Cranham, Frank Gardner, Gerry Cranham; 48: W.E. Skinner, Michael Gedye; 49: W.E. Skinner; 51: Eyre Methuen/Jack Crombie; 52: RTHPL, AAR; 53: A/DM, Gerry Cranham; 54: Eyre Methuen/Jack Crombie, remainder Syndication International; 55: Syndication International; 56: Michael Gedye; 58: A/DM, Eyre Methuen; 59: Bob Bird, E.D. Lacey; 60: Both RTHPL; 62: Bert Neale/Action Photos; 63: Michael Kay/Portland Studios; 64: Michael Kay/Portland Studios, Bettmann Archive Inc, Ray Green, Picturepoint, Frank Gardner; 65: E.D. Lacey, Gerry Cranham; 66: Colorsport; 67: Peter Dazeley; 69: RTHPL, Bert Neale/Action Photos; 71: A/DM; 72: A/DM, Colorsport, Gerry Cranham; 73: Popperfoto; 75: E.D. Lacey; 76: Bettmann Archive Inc, Bettmann Archive Inc, Associated Press; 77: Both Peter Dazeley; 78: RTHPL, Michael Gedye; 79: RTHPL, Michael Gedye,

Golf World USA; 80: Mel Petersen; 81: Mel Petersen, E.D. Lacey; 82: Bert Neale/Action Photos; 83: E.D. Lacey; 84: James Murray; 87: Tony O'Neill; 88: Both A/DM; 89: Courtesy Irish Tourist Board; 91: Courtesy Irish Tourist Board; 93: Reproduced by permission of The Trustees, The National Gallery, London; 97: Arne Schmitz; 98: Lars Lohrisch; 100: Mario Camicia; 101: Gerry Cranham; 103: A/DM; 104: Courtesy Robert Trent Jones Anstalt; 105: Michael Gedye; 106: Courtesy Robert Trent Jones Anstalt; 107: Courtesy Robert Trent Jones Anstalt; 108: Courtesy Robert Trent Jones Anstalt; 109: Both Michael Gedye; 110: RWF; 111: Bert Neale/Action Photos, Michael Gedye; 113: AAR; 114: USGA; 115: AAR; 116: RTHPL; 117: Woodfin Camp/Marvin E. Newman; 118: Paul Barton; 121: F.P.G.; 123: AAR; 124: Leonard Kamsler; 126: John L. Alexandrowicz; 127: Bert Neale/Action Photos, USGA, J. Edwin Carter, John L. Alexandrowicz; 128: James Brooks; 129: Photri, James Brooks; 130: Both James Brooks; 131: USGA; 132: Eyre Methuen; 133: Sports Illustrated photo by Robert Huntzinger Time Inc, USGA; 134: USGA; 135: Woodfin Camp/Marvin E. Newman; 136: RWF; 137: AAR; 138: AAR; 139: Colorsport, RWF, Sports Illustrated photo by Walter Iooss Jr Time Inc; 140: Courtesy Sea Pines/Bill Struhs; 141: AAR; 142: Both AAR; 143: Michael Gedye, Courtesy Winged Foot Golf Club; 145: USGA; 147: AAR; 148: AAR, USGA, AAR; 149: AAR, Bert Neale/Action Photos; 150: RTHPL; 151: USGA, Ray Green; 152: Courtesy Merion Golf Club; 153: USGA; 154: Bert Neale/Action Photos; 155: Woodfin Camp/Marvin E. Newman, RWF; 156: RWF; 157: RWF; 159: RWF; 160: Both RWF; 161: Both RWF; 162: Courtesy Firestone Tire & Rubber Co; 164: A/DM; 166: Courtesy Palmetto Dunes Resort Inc; 167: Leonard Kamsler; 168: Both USGA; 169: Bert Neale/Action Photos; 170: Colorsport; 171: Eyre Methuen; 173: Eyre Methuen; 174: RWF, Popperfoto; 175: AAR, USGA; 176: AAR; 177: AAR; 178: A/DM; 180/181: All Paul Barton; 183: Eyre Methuen; 184: Stanley Wong; 185: Stanley Wong; 186: Richard A. Prendergast; 188: Peter Dazeley, Courtesy Royal Montreal Golf Club/Graetz Bros; 189: Both Courtesy Bermuda News Bureau, Hamilton; 190: USGA; 191: Courtesy Bermuda News Bureau, Hamilton; 192: RWF; 193: Eyre Methuen; 195: Both Peter Thomson; 196:

Peter Thomson; 197: Peter Thomson; 199: Orion Press/Fumio Yamada, AAR; 200: RWF; 201: Both Orion Press/Fumio Yamada; 203: Eyre Methuen; 204: Eyre Methuen; 206: Colorsport; 208: Peter Thomson; 210: RWF; 211: RWF; 213: Michael Wolveridge; 214: RWF; 216: Eyre Methuen; 217: Michael Wolveridge; 219: Both Michael Wolveridge; 221: Both Michael Wolveridge; 223: Both Leonard Cobb; 225: Ray Pigney; 227–9: All Barry von Below; 230: A/DM, Basil Keartland; 231: A/DM; 232: Courtesy Robert Trent Jones Anstalt; 233: Michael Gedye; 235: Jerry Cooke; 236: Peter Dazeley; 237: Peter Dazeley, Ray Green; 238: Bildarchiv Kh. Schuster, Shostal Associates; 239: Shostal Associates; 240: All A/DM; 241: Michael Kay/Portland Studios; 244: RTHPL; 245: Bert Neale/Action Photos; 250: RTHPL; 253: Bert Neale/Action Photos; 257: A/DM; 259: Courtesy Robert Trent Jones; 260: E.D. Lacey; 261: RTHPL; 262: Leonard Kamsler; 263: RTHPL; 267: Courtesy Percy Clifford; 269: Courtesy John D. Harris; 272: Bert Neale/Action Photos; 273: A/DM; 274: A/DM; Back Jacket: RWF, E.D. Lacey.

ILLUSTRATORS
Feature courses—Harry Clow: Pages 38/39, 44/45, 48/49, 50/51, 56/57, 60/61, 62/63, 70/71, 74/75, 76/77, 80/81, 82/83, 84/85, 86/87, 90/91, 92/93, 94/95, 96/97, 98/99, 100/101, 102/103, 104/105, 106/107, 110/111, 114/115, 116/117, 124/125, 128/129, 134/135, 144/145, 156/157, 158/159, 162/163, 164/165, 178/179, 182/183, 190/191, 196/197, 198/199, 202/203, 204/205, 208/209, 214/215, 218/219, 220/221, 222/223, 228/229, 230/231; Allard: 132/133, 134/135, 140/141, 150/151, 184/185, 206/207; Chris Forsey: 122/123, 200/201, 210/211, 232/233, 238/239; Brian Delf: 68/69, 172/173, 180/181, 236/237; Charles Pickard: 146/147, 168/169, 192/193; Peter Morter: 136/137, 166/167, 186/187.
Classic course—Harry Clow: Holes 1, 2, 3, 6, 8, 9, 10, 12, 13, 14, 15, 16, 17, 18; Allard: 4, 5, 7, 11. Location maps, gazetteer diagrams—Arka.
Clubs and balls page 10/11—Peter Morter (except modern ball—Chris Forsey).
Studio Services—Arka; Roy Flooks; Mitchell Beazley Studio; PSG.
Research for contour map of Winged Foot's 11th green on page 22 by students of Manhattan College's School of Engineering. Map reproduced by kind permission of Winged Foot Golf Club.